Ethical Issues in Prison Psychiatry

INTERNATIONAL LIBRARY OF ETHICS, LAW, AND THE NEW MEDICINE

VOLUME 46

For further volumes:
http://www.springer.com/series/6224

Norbert Konrad • Birgit Völlm
David N. Weisstub

Editors

Ethical Issues in Prison Psychiatry

 Springer

Editors
Norbert Konrad
Institute of Forensic Psychiatry, Charité
University Medicine Berlin
Berlin, Germany

David N. Weisstub
The International Academy of Law
   and Mental Health
Faculty of Medicine, University of Montreal
Montreal, QC, Canada

Birgit Völlm
Section of Forensic Psychiatry
Division of Psychiatry
University of Nottingham
Nottingham, UK

Rampton Hospital, Nottinghamshire
   Healthcare NHS Trust
Woodbeck

ISSN 1567-8008
ISBN 978-94-007-0085-7   ISBN 978-94-007-0086-4 (eBook)
DOI 10.1007/978-94-007-0086-4
Springer Dordrecht Heidelberg New York London

Library of Congress Control Number: 2013944680

Preface

A high and possibly increasing prevalence of mental disorders in prisoners has been demonstrated in recent surveys. In comparison to the general population, prisoners have an increased risk of suffering from a mental disorder. It is a risk not restricted to any particular country/region. Mental disorders increase the risk of suicide, which is considerably higher in prisoners than in the general population. Suicide is the leading cause of death in penal institutions, especially during the early stage of confinement. For mentally disordered prisoners, there is often an increased risk of being victimized, as well as the potential for high rates of decompensation and deterioration. Risk assessment for legal-prognostic purposes has many methodological similarities to that dealing with risk of suicide of prisoners. The increased consultation of forensic psychiatry in this area reflects the interest of the relevant agencies in reducing the high suicide rate in prisons and jails. Some authors have suggested that the suicide rate among prisoners is a marker of the inadequate or even inhumane treatment in prisons.

A number of guidance documents by the United Nations International Resolutions (esp. Standard minimum rules for the treatment of prisoners), the Council of Europe (esp. Recommendation No R (98) 7 on the Ethical and organizational aspects of health care in prison), the World Medical Association (esp. Declaration of Tokyo 1975), the World Psychiatric Association (esp. Declaration of Hawaii 1977) as well as the Oath of Athens (International Council of Prison Medical Services 1979) touch upon prison psychiatry but lack more detailed guidelines for dealing with mentally disordered prisoners.

The 'principle of equivalence' states that prisoners should have access to the same standard of treatment as patients in the community. The objective of this notion is justice for the vulnerable who should not be subjected to additional punishment through deprivation from healthcare. However, this principle is rarely achieved, partly due to limited resources for the delivery of care to a particularly complex and multi-morbid population. Opponents of equivalent healthcare have argued that prisoners do not deserve the same (or even better healthcare) as they have often declined appropriate interventions in the community.

Ethical dilemmas in prison psychiatry do not only arise from resource allocation but also include issues of patient choice and autonomy in an inherently coercive environment. Furthermore, ethical conflicts may arise from the dual role of forensic psychiatrists giving raise to tension between patient care and protection of the public. This book will describe models of psychiatric healthcare in prison in several countries and discuss the ethical issues arising in this field. Relevant issues to be dealt with are the professional medical role of a psychiatrist and/or psychotherapist working in prison; the involvement of psychiatrists in disciplinary or coercive measures; and consent to treatment, especially the right to refuse treatment, the use of coercion, hunger strike and confidentiality amongst others. Perspectives from different countries will be presented. The book will end with conclusions and some considerations on good practice in prison psychiatry.

Berlin, Germany   Norbert Konrad
Nottingham, UK   Birgit Völlm
Montreal, QC, Canada   David N. Weisstub

References

Council of Europe Recommendation No R (98) 7 on the Ethical and organizational aspects of health care in prison. 1999. Strasbourg: Council of Europe.
International Council of Prison Medical Services. 1979. Oath of Athens. Adopted by the World Medical assembly, Athens, 1979.
The World Medical Association. 1975. Declaration of Tokyo. http://wma.net/e/policy/cl8.htm.
The World Psychiatric Association. 1977. http://wpanet.org.
United Nations. 1987. Standard minimum rules for the treatment of prisoners. http://unispal.un.org/UNISPALNSF/0/70D535E1E3DCA2B885256F010074C34D. Accessed 18 June 2013.

Contents

Part III Conclusion

Contributors

Julio Arboleda-Flórez Professor Emeritus, Departments of Psychiatry and of Community Health Sciences, Queen's University, Kingston ON, USA

Jocelyn Aubut Psychiatrist, Director General, Institut Philippe-Pinel de Montréal, and Clinical Associate Professor, Université de Montréal, Montreal, QC, Canada

Luis Fernando Barrios-Flores Department of Administrative Law, University of Alicante, Alicante, Spain

Helena Dias de Castro Bins State of Rio Grande do Sul Supreme Court, Porto Alegre, RS, Brazil

Moshe Birger Head, Division of Forensic Psychiatry, Israel Prison Service, Beer-Yaacov Mental Health Center, Ministry of Health, and Sackler Faculty of Medicine, Tel-Aviv University, Ramla, Israel

B.H. (Erik) Bulten Forensic Psychiatric Centre, Pompe Foundation, Nijmegen, The Netherlands

The Netherlands Radboud University of Nijmegen, Nijmegen, The Netherlands

Paul Cosyns University Forensic Centre, Antwerp University Hospital, Edegem, Belgium

Henry A. Dlugacz Beldock Levine and Hoffman LLP, New York, NY, USA

Jean-Luc Dubreucq Psychiatrist, Institut Philippe-Pinel de Montréal, and Clinical Associate Professor, Université de Montréal, Montreal, QC, Canada

Julie Duchaine Pharmacist, Institut Philippe-Pinel de Montréal, Montreal, QC, Canada

Alan R. Felthous Department of Neurology and Psychiatry, Forensic Psychiatry Division, Saint Louis University School of Medicine, St. Louis, MO, USA

Kris Goethals Collaborative Antwerp Psychiatric Research Institute (CAPRI), University of Antwerp, Wilrijk, Belgium

Marc Graf Forensic Psychiatric Hospital, Psychiatric Hospital of the University of Basel, Basel, Switzerland

Orsolya Hoffmann Swedish Prison and Probation Service, Stockholm, Sweden

Adarsh Kaul Offender Health, Nottinghamshire Healthcare NHS Trust, Nottingham

Lisa Knox Van Der Hout, Brigagliano and Nightingale LLP, San Francisco, CA, USA

Norbert Konrad Institute of Forensic Psychiatry, Charité, University Medicine Berlin, Berlin, Germany

Osamu Kuroda Department of Psychiatry, Tokyo Metropolitan Matsuzawa Hospital, Setagaya-ku, Tokyo, Japan

Julie Y. Low New York University Medical School, New York, NY, USA

Tanja Madjar Zavod Za Prestajanje Kazni Zapora Maribor/Maribor Prison, Maribor, Slovenia

Jacob Margolin Formerly Secretary of the Israel Society for Forensic Psychiatry, Tel-Aviv Area District Psychiatrist, and Medical Director of the Jerusalem Mental Health Center, Jerusalem, and the Jaffa Community Mental Health Center, Har Adar, Tel-Aviv, Israel

E.D.M. Masthoff Forensic Care and Treatment, Penitentiaire Inrichting Vught, Vught, The Netherlands

Muthoni Mathai Department of Psychiatry, College of Health Sciences, University of Nairobi, Nairobi, Kenya

Lennart Mossberg Probation Service, Norrköping Region, Sweden

Yoji Nakatani Kubota Clinic, Tokyo, Japan

Siva Nambi Department of Psychiatry, Sree Balaji Medical College and Hospital, Chennai, India

David M. Ndetai University of Nairobi, Nairobi, Kenya

Africa Mental Health Foundation (AMHF), Nairobi, Kenya

George B. Palermo Clinical Professor of Psychiatry, University of Nevada School of Medicine and Medical College of Wisconsin, Henderson, NV, USA

Helmut Pollähne Institute of Criminal Policy, University of Law, Bremen, Germany

Joester and Partner, Bremen, Germany

Vita Poštuvan Slovene Center for Suicide Research, Andrej Marušič Institute, University of Primorska, Koper, Slovenia

Marie-Hélène Régnier Assistant to the Director General, Institut Philippe-Pinel de Montréal, Montreal, QC, Canada

Jagannathan Srinivasaraghavan Southern Illinois University, School of Medicine, Marion, IL, USA

V.A. Medical Center, Marion, IL, USA

Danny Sullivan School of Psychology and Psychiatry, Monash University, Melbourne, VIC, Australia

Jose G.V. Taborda Department of Clinical Medicine, Federal University of Health Sciences of Porto Alegre, Porto Alegre, RS, Brazil

Nicoleta Tătaru Senior Consultant Psychiatrist, Psychiatry Ambulatory Clinic, Oradea, Romania

Māris Taube Department of Psychiatry and Addiction Disorders, Rīga Stradiņš University, Saulkrasti, Latvia

Lisieux Elaine de Borba Telles Mauricio Cardoso Forensic Psychiatric Institute, Porto Alegre, RS, Brazil

Francisco Torres-González Centro de Investigacion Biomedica en Red de Salud Mental (CIBERSAM), Granada University (Spain), Granada, Spain

Birgit Völlm Section of Forensic Psychiatry, Division of Psychiatry, University of Nottingham, Nottingham, UK

Rampton Hospital, Nottinghamshire Healthcare NHS Trust, Woodbeck

David N. Weisstub Philippe Pinel Professor of Legal Psychiatry and Biomedical Ethics, International Academy of Law and Mental Health (IALMH), Montreal, QC, Canada

Faculty of Medicine, University of Montreal, Montreal, QC, Canada

Christopher Wimmer Taylor and Company Law Offices, LLP, San Francisco, CA, USA

Eliezer Witztum Professor of Psychiatry, Faculty of Health Sciences, Ben-Gurion University of the Negev, Beer-Sheva, and Senior Psychiatrist, Beer-Sheva Mental Health Center, Beer-Sheva and "Ezrath-Nashim" Community Mental Health Center, Jerusalem, Israel

Part I
Introduction

Chapter 1
Prison Psychiatry

Norbert Konrad

1.1 Prison Conditions and Mental Health

Despite countless promises for a better life in prisons by national commissions, governments and the international community, there is a vicious cycle of neglect, abandonment, indignity, inhuman treatment, and punishment of persons with mental illness. From an American view, some authors have argued that the de-institutionalisation movement has resulted in new places of confinement for this population, such as jails, prisons and homeless shelters (Gostin 2008). Recently homelessness has become far more common among US state and federal prison inmates than the general population (Greenberg and Rosenheck 2008). On the other hand, at least in Norway, the rise in incarceration rates can only be attributed to de-institutionalisation to a very limited extent (Hartvig and Kjelsberg 2009). From a European view current national and international data bases are insufficient to firmly conclude or otherwise on a link between general psychiatry, forensic psychiatry, and penitentiaries and to identify inappropriate patient shifting (Salize et al. 2008).

People with mental illness who are diverted from jail to community-based services may experience fewer arrests and jail days (Case et al. 2009). On the other hand, poor illness management can result in more severe symptoms and more frequent relapses, which can in turn lead to illegal behaviour e.g. due to problems such as cognitive disorganization (e.g. theft, forgery, or extorsion occurring in the context of manic symptoms such as increased goal-directed behaviour), a distorted sense of reality (e.g. aggression in response to delusions or hallucinations), or increased substance abuse (e.g. driving while intoxicated, possession or sale of illegal substances).

N. Konrad (✉)
Institute of Forensic Psychiatry, Charité, University Medicine Berlin,
Berlin, Germany
e-mail: norbert.konrad@charite.de

N. Konrad et al. (eds.), *Ethical Issues in Prison Psychiatry*, International Library
of Ethics, Law, and the New Medicine 46, DOI 10.1007/978-94-007-0086-4_1,
© Springer Science+Business Media Dordrecht 2013

As a further result of poor illness management, and subsequent consequences such as frequent hospitalizations, inability to work or fulfil other social roles (e.g. as a parent), poverty, and stigma, clients often become demoralized and socially marginalized (MacCain and Mueser 2009).

Internationally, there is great variation in the conditions under which prisoners are kept (e.g. Gharaibeh and El-Khoury 2009). Factors which can influence psychological states include nutritional deficits (which in the case of niacin or vitamin B12 deficiency may even produce dementia), appalling hygienic conditions or maltreatment by prison staff (who may sometimes be acting out sadistic impulses) (Konrad 2001). These factors should play no role in those countries which adhere to the Standard Minimum Rules for the Treatment of Prisoners of the United Nations or the Council of Europe's (2006) guidelines, which to a large extent concur with those of the United Nations (1987).

A question of significance not only for legal outcome concerns the extent of prisoners' integration into the subculture, for example the extent to which they have relationships with fellow prisoners which are oppressive and the role they play in the environment in which they live. The mentally ill are at increased risk of being subject to harassment (verbal threats, discrimination, physical violence) and exploitation by their fellow prisoners. This may include sexual abuse, including rape.

Acutely mentally ill inmates are not infrequently dealt with under conditions which seem inappropriate when compared with psychiatric treatment in the health system. Inmates with a mental illness are more likely to have behavioral problems, to be victimized by higher functioning inmates, experience greater difficulties understanding and following rules and are more likely to have disciplinary problems (MacCain and Mueser 2009). Thus there are instances of mentally ill individuals being dealt with through disciplinary procedures and placed in isolation, even when they are incapable of understanding the functioning of the institutions or of following their rules (e.g. when they refuse to leave the cell when ordered to do so or violate rules about hygiene, for instance by showering fully dressed). Other typical behaviours of psychiatrically disturbed prisoners include acts of self harm, fire-setting and the neglect of personal hygiene (Konrad 2001).

1.2   Prevalence of Mental Disorders

The risks of serious psychiatric disorders are substantially higher in prisoners than in the general population: In a systematic review of 62 surveys from 12 different western countries including 22,790 prisoners (mean age 29 years, 81 % men), 3.7 % of the men had a psychotic illness, 10 % major depression, and 65 % a personality disorder, while 4 % of women had a psychotic illness, 12 % major depression, and 42 % a personality disorder (Fazel and Danesh 2002). Limitations of such research arise above all from the generally limited willingness of prisoners to cooperate, from the reliability of the survey instruments used (e.g. in detecting personality disorders), and from inter-rater reliability, which is not always adequately examined.

1.2.1 Recent Studies with Large Sample Size

A number of recent studies have confirmed the high prevalence of mental disorders in prisons. In a study by Brinded et al. (2001), all women and all remanded male inmates in New Zealand prisons and a randomly selected cohort of 18 % of sentenced male inmates were interviewed: Point prevalence rates (within the last month) were reported for schizophrenia and related disorders (4.2 % for women, 3.4 % for men on remand, 2.2 % for male sentenced prisoners), bipolar affective disorder (1.2 %; 1.0 %; 1.1 %) and major depression (11.1 %; 10.7 %; 5.9 %).

In New South Wales (Australia), 953 reception inmates (777 men and 176 women), representing over 30 % of all male receptions and 56 % of all female receptions during the study period, as well as 579 sentenced inmates, were screened. Twelve months prevalence of International Classification of Diseases (ICD)-10 diagnoses were reported for psychoses (10.7 % male receptions; 15.2 % female receptions; 4.2 % sentenced men; 5.7 % sentenced women), affective disorders (21.1 %; 33.9 %; 12.4 %; 20.4 %) and any disorder (42.0 %; 61.8 %; 33.0 %; 59.2 %) (Butler et al. 2005).

In a recent study from Europe, 57 % of a sample of adult Dutch prisoners on regular wards suffered from one or more Axis I disorders including substance abuse (Bulten et al. 2009).

Of a cohort of 7,046 men who were released from the Pennsylvania State prison system between 1999 and 2002, 25.9 % received mental health services while incarcerated (Metraux 2008). In a cohort of persons with schizophrenia and other psychotic disorders who experienced their first hospital admission, 9 % were incarcerated over a four-year follow-up period (Prince et al. 2007).

However, even among those detained on remand for relatively long periods, psychiatric illnesses may not always be recognised. The prisoner who is quietly psychotic is prone to being overlooked or ignored. The more behaviourally disturbed, on the other hand, are often viewed as a discipline problem, rather than as individuals with mental health needs (Birmingham 2004). Whilst staff responsible for admitting prisoners to custodial facilities generally only detect illnesses characterised by massively conspicuous behavioural abnormalities, the admission medical examination. which is obligatory in some countries, is also not a fully reliable filter for detection of psychiatric illnesses, particularly depressive disorders.

Variations in prevalence found in different studies may arise from the particular characteristics of the population examined – there is a higher prevalence of mental disorders in remand prisoner populations than in sentenced prisoners due to the possibility of diversion (Konrad 2001) as well as from the specific survey method. Thus generalisations across countries should be avoided.

To the extent to which comparisons have been undertaken with the general population, a greatly raised prevalence of psychiatric illness amongst prisoners has been found across countries and across diagnostic groups. Considering diagnoses individually, this is particularly marked for the dependence syndromes disorders (Konrad 2001).

Despite the variations which result from particular local characteristics and from differing research methods, a generalisation which may be made is that once the diagnosis of antisocial personality disorder, for which frequency estimates vary greatly because of limited inter-rater reliability, is excluded, drug and alcohol dependence generally constitute the most important diagnostic group (Konrad 2001).

1.2.2 Co-Morbidity

A number of studies have described co-morbidity in prisoners. Among youths processed in adult criminal court, 68 % had at least one psychiatric disorder and 43 % had two or more types of disorders (Washburn et al. 2008).

Dependence syndromes are amongst the most commonly recorded co-morbid disorders (Anderson et al. 1996; Brooke et al. 1996). Co-morbidity has been described particularly for the diagnoses of antisocial personality disturbance, alcoholism, drug dependence and major depression (Abram 1990).

The most prevalent Axis II disorders in a one-in five sub-sample of participants in a survey of psychiatric morbidity among prisoners in England and Wales (Coid et al. 2009) were anti-social (50 %), paranoid (23 %) and borderline (18 %) personality disorders. Antisocial and borderline personality disorders demonstrated high levels of co-morbidity with both Axis I and Axis II disorders. Over half of male prison detainees among newly imprisoned males in Italy (54 %) had a psychiatric disorder. One of every five detainees (21 %) had co-morbid substance use and psychiatric disorders (Piselli et al. 2009).

The use of illegal substances together with behavioural abnormalities and lack of treatment can create the route into prison. Co-morbidity presents particular challenges for treatment as it requires specific treatment programmes which differ from models of treatment used for single disorders (Teplin et al. 1996).

1.2.3 Prevalence of Special Disorders

Although there is some discrepancy on prevalence, it seems clear that high numbers of people with learning disabilities and difficulties are caught up in the criminal justice system. From the point of arrest through to release from prison, the criminal justice system routinely fails to recognize, let alone meet, the particular needs of these prisoners (Talbot 2009).

In German male imprisoned subjects from a juvenile prison (mean age 19.5 years), an Attention Deficit Hyperactivity Disorder(ADHD) prevalence of 45 % was detected, while in female prison inmates the lifetime prevalence of ADHD was 24.5 and 10 % for persisting ADHD according to Diagnostic and Statistical Manual (DSM-IV) criteria (Rösler et al. 2009).

1.2.4 Female Prisoners

Higher rates of psychiatric morbidity are found among female than among male prisoners (Anderson et al. 1996; Maden et al. 1994), suggesting that the filters in the selection processes outlined above may operate differently. Thus one would expect a greater level of need for treatment in the female penal system (Maden et al. 1994). Female prisoners also tend to be more willing to accept offers of treatment which may also be related to a better therapeutic atmosphere in female prisons. Furthermore, women's experiences of stigma are less severe when they enter (psycho)therapeutic treatment (Konrad 2001).

1.3 Adjustment to Prison

With the reduction in the range of external stimuli, the prisoner may sink into a state empty of thoughts and feelings, sometimes extending to complete apathy, or else may experience an intensification of the emotions associated with perceptions and an increase in imaginative activity including day dreaming. For those with narcissistic personality traits and disorders, fantasies can include the reversal of the previous failure and the anticipation of future successes in crime (Konrad 2001).

Individuals cope differently with feelings of profound desolation and emotional deprivation. Fears of maltreatment are of considerable significance for those prisoners who have maltreated or abused children, have been informers to prison or judicial staff, or who cannot pay debts (from drug purchase or gambling). Tendencies to regress may be expressed through an increasingly dilapidated physical state or in weight gain.

Among the many forms of experience provoked by the prison situation are sometimes fluid transitions to symptomatic pictures which meet ICD 10 criteria for adjustment disorders. The critical diagnostic feature of this disorder is that it would not have arisen without a critical life event as a psychosocial stressor, here imprisonment. Symptoms observed vary greatly both between individuals and over time for a single individual, and they include despondency, withdrawal into isolated ruminations in the cell, anxiety, stupor, agitation, and hostility. It has been suggested that adjustment reactions vary according to form of imprisonment (single or shared cells), but as yet there is no scientific evidence to support the propositions which have been made about the various factors which may be significant (variations in level of isolation including solitary confinement, differing sizes of rooms allowing retreat to different degrees, variations in daily routine and in characteristics of fellow prisoners, etc.).

Attempts to explain these prison reactions emphasise the triggering effects of particular stresses, such as the issuing of an arrest warrant, interviews by the police, being confronted with the statements of accomplices or witnesses, being denied visits, episodes of isolation, appointments for review of remand in custody, delivery of the indictment, end of trial, and the announcement of the judgement. General factors associated with imprisonment should also be taken into account: loss of social status, limitation of freedom of movement, living space and sphere of action, isolation through removal from the usual social networks, change in patterns of communication and profound alteration in previous living habits. It is difficult to gauge precisely the effects of these factors on a particular individual and the reduction in coping resources which they bring about. Stresses can also result from the uncertainty about how severe a punishment to expect, contemplation of the criminal act, and the experience of lack of understanding or contemptuous treatment from the prison staff (Konrad 2001).

Ways of reacting to these stresses and the development of adjustment disorders are widely regarded as being related to personality in that personality influences the significance of imprisonment for the individual, vulnerability to stress, and a tendency to get involved in stress producing situations such as arguments with fellow prisoners (Hurley and Dunne 1991).

Adjustment disorders are observed less frequently among sentenced prisoners (1.9 %) than among those on remand (7.6–18.5 %) (Gunn et al. 1991; Hurley 1989; Brooke et al. 1996). As length of imprisonment increases, symptoms diminish to a degree, with adaptation to life in prison becoming greater and new roles within the subculture which stabilise self-esteem adopted (Backett 1987).

1.3.1 Differential Diagnoses

If a prisoner has symptoms that meet criteria for a Major Depressive Episode in response to the imprisonment, the diagnosis of Adjustment Disorder is not applicable. Depressive illnesses are sometimes missed in prison medical practice. When a prisoner presents with physical complaints without organic correlates, in clinical practice in the criminal justice system a diagnosis is too often made of simulation or of a psychosomatic disorder without due consideration being given to the possibility of an affective illness. A depressive illness may also underlie apparently disruptive conduct in prison, e.g. when prisoners vandalise their cells (Maden et al. 1994).

Reactive psychoses, such as those manifested by foreigners in environments where they do not speak the language, can be classified as acute and transient psychotic disorders (ICD-10F23). In terms of differential diagnosis, strong consideration should be given to disorders related to psychotropic substances (above all delirium or psychotic symptoms) as well as to schizophrenia or delusional disorders.

The rarely observed Ganser syndrome is located on the continuum between adjustment disorder and true psychosis, in which the typical symptomatic picture involves talking past the point together with a qualitatively altered state of consciousness. This state, however, appears more frequently in situations where examinations are taking place than in everyday prison life. In this condition, the symptomatic picture is reported to be relatively stable during the generally short period for which it is manifest. The syndrome is more commonly observed among people with lower than average intelligence and with histrionic personality traits (Bellino 1973).

Many German psychiatrists maintain the distinction which originated in the last century between true psychoses and prison psychoses. The disorders regarded as true psychoses generally fit into the category of schizophrenic illnesses although psychopathology may be coloured by prison conditions in aspects such as the contents of delusions, whereas prison psychoses are specific reactions to imprisonment. However, prison psychoses have not been included in the international classification systems as a (clinical) disorder entity (ICD-10, DSM-IV). This lack of acceptance of a separate category is supported by a study comparing 91 patients with the diagnosis of 'prison psychosis' with 91 patients with a diagnosis of 'schizophrenia' (Gößling and Konrad 2004). In this study no differences were found between the two groups regarding psychopathological and forensic characteristics. One can thus put forth the hypothesis that 'prison psychoses' represents a construct originating from the distrust of the psychiatrist rooted in the transference/counter-transference processes of patients with double diagnoses (co-morbidity) like psychosis/antisocial personality (disorder). However, because there is actually no empirical evidence for the validity of 'prison psychosis', this diagnosis should no longer be used.

In comparison with other prisoners, prisoners with schizophrenic illnesses have a greater tendency to develop difficulties in obeying prison rules and in sustaining work roles within the institution. Because they more often behave in aggressive and violent ways, they are more often subject to disciplinary procedures (Morgan et al. 1993). Occasionally beliefs about being poisoned may be the basis for a refusal to eat which may be misinterpreted as a hunger strike. Even in countries where routine medical examinations are required, the presence of schizophrenic illnesses is not infrequently overlooked, especially when negative symptoms dominate the clinical picture (Anderson et al. 1996).

Simulation of psychiatric disorder, e.g. through feigning of psychotic symptoms, is infrequent, and can constitute a coping strategy, aimed at improving conditions of imprisonment or getting prescribed medications (Konrad 2001). Preserving professional perspective can become more difficult when an inmate tries to exploit the therapeutic relationship to obtain a desired, but often unstated, goal. By interpreting an inmate's behaviour as an attempt to meet identifiable needs, the psychiatrist can better understand those needs while depersonalizing and disengaging, as much as possible, from the struggle for power and control.

1.4 Suicide

In many places suicide is the leading cause of death in prison. Based on the results of international suicide research, there is a consensus that the suicide rate in penal institutions is several times higher than for the general population (Konrad et al. 2007). In this context it is important to take into account the fact that the prison population is not a representative sample of the general population.

People who break the law inherently have many risk factors for suicidal behaviour (they "import" risk), e.g. substance misuse, and the suicide rate is higher within offender groups even after their release from prison (Pratt et al. 2006). More precise comparative studies, taking account these selection factors, have not yet been published. The fact that inmates import risk does not mean that correctional services have no responsibility for the suicide of offenders; on the contrary, these vulnerable offenders should be treated while they can be reached inside the prison. In addition, imprisonment is another stressful event even for healthy inmates (as it deprives the person of important resources).

Another explanation advanced for the high rates of suicide within prisons is that the most commonly used method, hanging, used in 85 % of suicides (e.g. Rieger 1971; Thole 1976) in prison, is associated with a more limited chance of being saved compared to methods frequently used in suicide attempts outside prison. Suicides tend to occur by hanging when the victims are being held in isolation or segregation cells, and during times when staffing is the lowest, such as nights or weekends. There are also a number of suicides when prisoners are alone in their cell even if they are technically sharing a cell (Hayes 2006).

There is also a strong association between inmate suicide and housing assignments. Specifically, an inmate placed in and unable to cope with administrative segregation or other similar specialized housing assignments (especially if in a single cell) may be at increased risk of suicide. Such housing arrangements usually involve an inmate being locked in a cell for 23 h per day for significant periods of time (Metzner and Hayes 2006).

Apart from occupation of a single cell, the most important factors found to be associated with suicide in prisoners are recent suicidal ideation, a history of attempted suicide, and having a psychiatric diagnosis or a history of alcohol or drug abuse problems (Fazel et al. 2008). Poor social and family support, prior suicidal behaviour (especially within the last 1 or 2 years), and a history of psychiatric illness and emotional problems are common among inmate suicides. Prisoners identified as at risk of suicide/self harm have significantly higher rates of clinically significant symptoms of mental illness compared to the general prison population (Senior et al. 2007).

There is a greater suicide risk during remand custody than among sentenced prisoners, especially at the beginning of imprisonment. For example, the proportion of all suicides in prison which are recorded as having occurred during the first month of imprisonment has been reported as 42 % (Thole 1976), 46 % (Bogue and Power 1995) and even 73 % (DuRand et al. 1995); variations found in different studies may arise from the particular characteristics of the prison populations as well as from specific prison conditions. The high number of suicides in the first part of imprisonment may be explained by a condition described as 'imprisonment shock', which sees imprisonment as a stress factor (Harding and Zimmermann 1989) but which impacts variablydepending on the individual. Among those with dependence disorders, withdrawal symptoms have also been identified as important stressors (Bogue and Power 1995).

Another important factor in prison suicide is the current prison situation, e.g. difficulties with fellow prisoners, lack of work or persisting sleep disturbances (Liebling 1995). Moreover, suicidal inmates often experience bullying (Blaauw et al. 2001), recent inmate-to-inmate conflicts, disciplinary infractions or adverse information (Way et al. 2005). Whatever individual stressors and vulnerabilities may be operating, a final common pathway leading an inmate to suicide seems to be feelings of hopelessness, a narrowing of future prospects and a loss of options for coping. Suicide comes to be viewed as the only way out of a desperate and hopeless situation. Therefore, individuals who voice feelings of hopelessness or admit to suicidal intent or suicidal plans should be considered at high risk of suicide.

A clear and reliable differentiation between serious and weak suicide attempts cannot be made either from observation of manipulative behaviour or extent of planning and preparation or from the potential lethality of the methods used (Haycock 1989). However, in a study from California, about 60 % of the suicides were judged to have been foreseeable (Patterson and Hughes 2008).

Clinicians can use screening instruments, e.g. the Viennese Instrument for Suicidality in Correctional Institutions-VISCI (Frottier et al. 2008) or the Suicide Probability Scale (SPS, Naud and Daigle 2009). However, a clinical interview for the purpose of collecting complementary information is then recommended in order to arrive at a more accurate assessment of the actual suicide risk. Notwithstanding the importance of screening procedures, they play only a very small part in the prevention of prison suicides. In a prospective study the SPS score was found to be significantly higher in at least one of three types of suicidal behaviour: suicide, non-lethal self-harm and serious suicidal intentions; however, the SPS did not discriminate between inmates who went on to commit suicide and those who did not (Naud and Daigle 2009). All screening instruments can achieve is to inform staff that a particular prisoner has an elevated risk of attempting suicide at some stage in his or her period of incarceration; they do not predict when an attempt will occur or what the specific precipitants will be in a given case. Because many jail and prison suicides occur after the initial period of incarceration (some after many years), it is not sufficient to only screen inmates at the time of intake, but at regular intervals.

Staff culture and cooperation seem to be critical to the successful implementation of prison suicide prevention programmes. Best practices for preventing suicides in jail and prison settings are based on the development and documentation of a comprehensive suicide prevention plan with the following elements (Konrad et al. 2007), which are also listed in the guide on preventing suicide in jails and prisons published by the World Health Organization (2007):

- A training programme (including refreshers) for correctional staff and care givers to help them recognize suicidal inmates and appropriately respond to inmates in suicidal crises.
- Attention needs to be paid to the general prison environment (levels of activity, safety, culture and staff-prisoner relationships). In particular, the quality of the social climate of prisons is critical in minimising suicidal behaviours. While prisons can never be stress-free environments, prison administrators must enact

effective strategies for minimising bullying and other violence in their institutions, and for maximising supportive relationships among prisoners and staff. The quality of staff-prisoner relationships is critical in reducing prisoners' stress levels and maximising the likelihood that prisoners will trust staff sufficiently to disclose to them when their coping resources are becoming overwhelmed, feelings of hopelessness, and suicidal ideation.

- Procedures to systematically screen inmates upon their arrival at the facility and throughout their stay in order to identify those who may be at high risk.
- A mechanism to maintain communication between staff members regarding high-risk inmates.
- Written procedures which outline minimum requirements for housing high-risk inmates; provision of social support; routine visual checks and constant observation for acutely suicidal inmates; and appropriate use of restraints as a last resort for controlling self-injurious inmates.
- Elimination or minimizing ligature points and unsupervised access to potentially lethal materials in case of need of a suicide-safe environment.
- Mentally ill inmates who need psychopharmacological medication should receive them following strict procedures.
- Development of sufficient internal resources or links to external community-based mental health services to ensure access to mental health personnel when required for further evaluation and treatment.
- A strategy for debriefing when a suicide occurs to identify ways of improving suicide detection, monitoring, and management in correctional settings.

It has been shown that training significantly improved attitudes, knowledge, and confidence of prison officers, and that these improvements were maintained at follow-up (Hayes et al. 2008).

1.5   Suicide Attempts

In some situations, inmates who make suicidal gestures or attempts will be viewed as manipulative. These inmates are thought to use their suicidal behaviours to gain some control over the environment, such as being transferred to a hospital or moved to a less restrictive setting (Fulwiler et al. 1997). The possibility of a staged suicide attempt to instigate an escape, or for some other nefarious motive, must be an ever-present worry for security officers, particularly those working in maximum and super maximum security areas. Incarcerated men with antisocial or sociopathic personalities may be more prone to manipulative attempts as they are likely to have difficulty adapting to the over-controlled regimentation of prison life (Lohner and Konrad 2006).

Moreover, for some prisoners self-harming behaviour may be a possibility of reducing tension (Snow 2002). For incarcerated women, repeated self-mutilation (such as slashing or burning) may be a response to the stress brought on by confinement and the prison culture. As a matter of fact, self-mutilation and suicide attempts are not easily differentiated, even when inmates are asked about intent (Daigle and Côté 2006). There is evidence that many incidents involve both a high degree of suicidal intent and so-called manipulative motives such as wanting to draw attention to one's emotional distress or wanting to influence one's management, such as avoiding a transfer to another facility where family visits will be less frequent (Dear et al. 2000).

When correctional staff believe that certain inmates will attempt to control or manipulate their environment through self-destructive behaviours, they tend to not take the suicidal gesture seriously - not to give in to the manipulation. This is particularly true if an inmate has a history of past rule violations or infractions (Brown et al. 2004). However, suicide attempts, whatever their motivation, can result in death, even if this was not the original intent. Because of the limited number of methods available, inmates may choose very lethal methods (e.g. hanging) even in absence of a true wish to die, or because they do not know how dangerous the method is (Brown et al. 2004). Attempts with less suicidal intent should rather be seen as expressive than purposive, i.e. as a dysfunctional way of communicating a problem. The correct response would be to ask for the inmate's problems and not to punish him/her. Inattention to the self-destructive behaviours or punishment of self-destructive inmates through e.g. segregation may worsen the problem by requiring the inmate to take more dramatic risks. Thus, for acting-out and potentially self-injurious inmates programmes that foster close supervision, social support, and access to psychosocial resources are crucial.

1.6   Deliberate Self Harm

Deliberate self harm can be defined as a self-inflicted, direct physical injury, which is not intended to be life-threatening (Herpertz and Saß 1994). Although diagnostically heterogenous, self-injurers typically exhibit two prominent characteristics: negative emotionality and self-derogation. Self-injury is most often performed to temporarily alleviate intense negative emotions, but may also serve to express self-directed anger or disgust, influence or seek help from others, end periods of dissociation or depersonalization, and help resist suicidal thoughts (Klonsky and Muehlenkamp 2007). The major self-harming behaviours reported in prison are injuries by cutting, self-poisoning and inflicting burns (Konrad 2001).

Self-injurious behaviour is rarely a manifestation of a psychotic illness. In a study of US prisoners, half of the self-harmers gave a goal-directed motivation for their behaviour (Franklin 1988). Similar to the general population, within female self-harming prisoners, there is a trend for women of a younger age (mean 30 years, range 18–68) with index offenses involving violence or arson as risk-factors; higher rates of psychiatric symptomatology and previous psychiatric contacts are found in women with a history of self-harming behaviour compared with those without such history (Völlm and Dolan 2009).

Swallowing foreign bodies such as razor blades, batteries or cutlery can be perceived as a special form of deliberate self-harm. The motivational spectrum extends from responses to command hallucinations experienced by people with schizophrenia to suicidal tendencies or goal-directed action aimed at achieving a transfer to a hospital situated outside the penal institution. Multiple episodes of swallowing foreign bodies are not uncommon (Karp et al. 1991). Compared with a control group, metal swallowers had a raised prevalence of schizophrenic illnesses, personality disorders and dependence disorders (Tacke et al. 1975).

1.7 Special Situations in Custody

Solitary confinement in custodial institutions is in most countries a legally regulated exception to normal practice, which may, for example, be implemented in response to certain requirements regarding security. Those who reported being placed in solitary confinement in prisons were more likely to have an extensive history of previous psychiatric treatment and a diagnosis of schizophrenia and depression (Birmingham 2004).

Whilst isolation under experimental conditions over a 4 day period did not provoke any substantial psychopathological changes in healthy individuals (Walters et al. 1969), it seems that with substantially longer periods (at least 4 days), free floating anxieties, increased reactivity to external stimuli and distortions of perception, disruption of concentration, derealisation, pseudo-hallucinations and hallucinations in various sensory modalities (Grassian 1983) may manifest themselves. The picture will be shaped by a complex interaction between variables related to the individual (such as for example the presence of a personality disorder, or the extent of positive symptoms among people with schizophrenia) and type of isolation (e.g. degree of sensory deprivation, size of room). States of agitation and acts of self-harm may be observed as a result of isolation, and it can be assumed that suicide risk is raised (Bernheim 1994). The development of an acute confusional state followed by partial amnesia and delusions of persecution, often accompanied by hallucinations of an anxious character, has also been described. The symptoms generally fade a few hours after the ending of isolation (Grassian 1983). On the other hand, among schizophrenic patients who are susceptible to acute symptoms, a relapse of positive symptoms is possible (Grassian and Friedman 1986).

Indicators of behavioural decline include restlessness and agitation, concentration and memory impairment, irritability, anger, frustration intolerance, apathy, social withdrawal, dysphoria, mood and affective lability, generalized anxiety, panic attacks, irrational suspicion, and paranoia (Beven 2005).

The situation is made worse by the fact that some prisoners turn to the use of illicit substances to help them deal with long periods of isolation (Birmingham 2004). People with pre-existing psychiatric disorders may deteriorate, and others who are vulnerable to mental disorder may become mentally unwell during isolation.

Less clear and more controversial is the psychological impact of long-term confinement on inmates who do not have pre-existing mental illness. Despite claims to the contrary, it is currently not clear whether, how often, and under what circumstances such confinement causes persons to develop serious mental illness (e.g. psychotic symptoms and disabling depressive or anxiety disorders) (Metzner and Dvoskin 2006).

Depression in long term prisoners is common and may be related to the burden of imported chronic ill health as opposed to specific effects of imprisonment (Murdoch et al. 2008). The themes evoked in interviews with severely mentally ill long term prisoners suggest that their reactions to the prison environment arise in part from aspects of their psychiatric symptoms: they speak in more hostile and persecutory terms about their experience in prison, attributing suffering to external circumstances, while subjects with no psychiatric disorder evoked similar themes, but with a more introspective attitude (Yang et al. 2009).

1.8 Organisation of Therapeutic Services

In accordance with the principle of equivalence (e.g. Council of Europe 2006), every prisoner suffering from a serious mental disturbance should receive appropriate medical treatment as an outpatient and/or in hospital. Prisoners with psychotic illness often require hospital treatment because of life-threatening self-harm, risk of violence, victimization by other prisoners and difficulties in providing treatment within the prison.

As far as hospital treatment is concerned, two options may be envisaged according to health policy trends. On the one hand, it is often argued that from an ethical standpoint, mentally ill prisoners should be hospitalised outside the prison system, i.e. in a medical establishment that is part of the health system for the general public, in order to promote access to appropriate hospital psychiatric treatment. On the other hand, the existence of a hospital psychiatric unit within prisons makes it possible to administer treatment in optimum security conditions and to intensify the activities of the medical and social services within the prison system.

On the one hand, the role of prison psychiatry can be seen as offering psychiatric treatment with a pure therapeutic attitude without relation to any goal of imprisonment. According to this view, treatment standards developed in general psychiatry should be respected. On the other hand, the function of the psychiatric and psychotherapeutic treatment provided is expected to a certain extent to contribute to the rehabilitation of the offender, especially to prevent recidivism, and thus contribute topublic safety. Prison psychiatrists find themselves in ethically questionable territory if they carry out psychopharmacological or other medical interventions for which there is no primary medical indication, in order to allow judicial proceedings and the penal system to run smoothly (Konrad and Völlm 2010).

There is little evidence regarding the effectiveness of psychiatric interventions to prevent reoffending. Nevertheless there have been some studies on the management of mentally disordered prisoners with psychopharmacological and psychotherapeutic approaches and these will be discussed in the next paragraphs.

1.8.1 Psychopharmacological Approaches

A number of studies have investigated the effects of pharmacological interventions on aggression. A Cochrane review concluded that four antiepileptic drugs (valproate/divalproex, carbamazepine, oxcarbazepine and phenytoin) had been shown to reduce aggression in at least one study. However, for three of these drugs (valproate, carbamazepine and phenytoin) the authors found at least one other study where there was no significant improvement. The authors concluded that further research was needed to clarify which antiepileptic drugs are effective for which patients.

Patients identified as treatment-resistant who are prescribed clozapine are more complex in their pattern of illness and subsequent needs. Clozapine is effective in the treatment of psychoses in forensic psychiatric settings. Its benefits need to be balanced against the potential for adverse effects and problems ensuring adherence (Martin et al. 2008).

Training in illness self-management programs across institutional and community correctional environments had been found to be useful in some studies (MacCain and Mueser 2009). Adherence to prescribed antipsychotic medication among prisoners is similar to – perhaps slightly better than – that seen in community samples of people with psychoses. Adherence interventions may benefit from focusing on increasing personal relevance/benefit from medication and on enhancing motivation to maintain treatment (Gray et al. 2008).

Offering jail-based methadone maintenance therapy does not increase recidivism risks by eliminating the deterrent effect of imposed withdrawal, nor does it reduce recidivism in this population. Aside from the personal benefits that the patient can expect from reducing the use of illicit opiates, effective therapy outreach presents an important public health benefit by reducing the burden of diseases spread by injecting drug use, such as HIV (McMillan et al. 2008).

1.8.2 Psychotherapeutic Approaches

There is a broad array of group therapies offered in correctional settings focusing on providing information to prisoners as well as skill building (e.g. anger management, social skills, relaxation), peer support/insight development (e.g. empathy training) and recreational activities (e.g. art, music). Non-verbal therapeutic strategies may have a better effect than outside prison as many prisoners are not used to use verbal strategies in problem solving.

Regarding the management of aggressive behaviors in prison settings, improved affect, reduced aggression, and improved coping, particularly for adult males, were found after the implementation of twice-weekly Dialectical Behavioral Therapy-Corrections Modified (DBT-CM) groups held over 16 weeks (Shelton et al. 2009). Group interpersonal psychotherapy addressing depressive symptoms was found to be feasible for women in a prison substance use treatment program (Johnson and Zlotnick 2008). Therapeutic community treatment programs could also be an effective model for women with varied diagnoses and diagnostic complexities (Sacks et al. 2008). Interventions for prisoners with developmental disabilities should be adapted to meet their specific needs and include skills development, educational opportunities/ vocational training and cognitive-behavioral interventions (Talbot 2009).

References

Abram, K.M. 1990. The problem of Co©Occurring disorders among jail detainees. *Law and Human Behavior* 14: 333–345.

Anderson, H.S., D. Sestoft, T. Lillebaek, G. Gabrielsen, and P. Kramp. 1996. Prevalence of ICD-10 psychiatric morbidity in random samples of prisoners on remand. *International Journal of Law and Psychiatry* 19: 61–74.

Backett, S.A. 1987. Suicide in Scottish prisons. *The British Journal of Psychiatry* 151: 218–221.

Bellino, T.T. 1973. The Ganser syndrome: A contemporary forensic problem. *International Journal of Offender Therapy and Comparative Criminology* 17: 136–137.

Bernheim, J.C. 1994. Suicides and prison conditions. In *Deaths in custody: International perspectives*, ed. A. Liebling and T. Ward. Bournemouth: Bourne Press.

Beven, G.E. 2005. Offenders with mental illnesses in maximum- and supermaximum-security settings. In *Handbook of correctional mental health*, ed. C.L. Scott and J.B. Gerbasi. Arlington: American Psychiatric Publishing.

Birmingham, L. 2004. Mental disorder and prisons. *Psychiatric Bulletin* 28: 393–397.

Blaauw, E., F.W. Winkel, and A.J.F.M. Kerkhof. 2001. Bullying and suicidal behaviour in jails. *Criminal Justice and Behaviour* 28: 279–299.

Bogue, J., and K. Power. 1995. Suicide in Scottish prisons, 1976–93. *Journal of Forensic Psychiatry* 6: 527–540.

Brinded, P.M.J., A.I.F. Simpson, T.M. Laidlaw, N. Fairley, and F. Malcom. 2001. Prevalence of psychiatric disorders in New Zealand prisons: A national study. *The Australian and New Zealand Journal of Psychiatry* 35: 166–173.

Brooke, D., C. Taylor, J. Gunn, and A. Maden. 1996. Point prevalence of mental disorder in unconvicted male prisoners in England and Wales. *BMJ* 313: 1524–1527.

Brown, G.K., G.R. Henriques, D. Sosdjan, and A.T. Beck. 2004. Suicide intent and accurate expectations of lethality: Predictors of medical lethality of suicide attempts. *Journal of Consulting and Clinical Psychology* 72: 1170–1174.

Bulten, E., H. Nijman, and C. van der Staak. 2009. Psychiatric disorders and personality characteristics of prisoners at regular prison wards. *International Journal of Law and Psychiatry* 32: 115–119.

Butler, T., S. Allnutt, D. Cain, D. Owens, and C. Muller. 2005. Mental disorder in New South Wales prisoner population. *The Australian and New Zealand Journal of Psychiatry* 39: 407–413.

Case, B., H.J. Steadman, S.A. Dupuis, and L.S. Morris. 2009. Who succeeds in jail diversion programs for persons with mental illness? A multi-site study. *Behavioral Sciences & the Law* 27: 661–674.

Coid, J., P. Moran, P. Bebbington, T. Brugha, R. Jenkins, M. Farrell, N. Singleton, and S. Ullrich. 2009. The co-morbidity of personality disorder and clinical syndromes in prisoners. *Criminal Behaviour and Mental Health* 19: 321–333.

Council of Europe. 2006. Recommendation Rec (2006)2 on the European Prison Rules. https://wcd.coe.int/ViewDoc.jsp?id=955747

Daigle, M.S., and G. Côté. 2006. Non-fatal suicide-related behavior among inmates: Testing for gender and type differences. *Suicide & Life-Threatening Behavior* 36: 670–681.

Dear, G., D. Thomson, and A. Hills. 2000. Self-harm in prison: Manipulators can also be suicide attempters. *Criminal Justice and Behavior* 27: 160–175.

DuRand, C.J., G.J. Burtka, E.J. Federman, J.A. Haycox, and J.W. Smith. 1995. A quarter century of suicide in a major urban jail: Implications for community psychiatry. *The American Journal of Psychiatry* 152: 1077–1080.

Fazel, S., and J. Danesh. 2002. Serious mental disorder in 23,000 prisoners: A systematic review of 62 surveys. *Lancet* 349: 545–550.

Fazel, S., J. Cartwright, A. Norman-Nott, and K. Hawton. 2008. Suicide in prisoners: A systematic review of risk factors. *The Journal of Clinical Psychiatry* 69: 1721–1731.

Franklin, R. 1988. Deliberate self-harm: Self-injurious behavior within a correctional mental health population. *Criminal Justice and Behavior* 15: 210–218.

Frottier, P., F. König, T. Matschnig, M. Seyringer, and S. Frühwald. 2008. Das Wiener Instrument für Suizidgefahr in Haft. *Psychiatrische Praxis* 35: 21–27.

Fulwiler, C., C. Forbes, S.L. Santagelo, and M. Folstein. 1997. Self-mutilation and suicide attempt: Distinguishing features in prisoners. *The Journal of the American Academy of Psychiatry and the Law* 25: 69–77.

Gharaibeh, N., and J. El-Khoury. 2009. The state of health care provision and extent of mental health in the prisons of the Arab world: A literature review and commentary. *International Journal of Prisoners Health* 5: 241–250.

Gößling, J., and N. Konrad. 2004. Zur Entität der so genannten Haftpsychose. *R&P* 22: 123–129.

Gostin, L.O. 2008. 'Old' and 'new' institutions for persons with mental illness: Treatment, punishment or preventive confinement? *Public Health* 122: 906–913.

Grassian, S. 1983. Psychopathological effects of solitary confinement. *The American Journal of Psychiatry* 140: 1450–1454.

Grassian, S., and N. Friedman. 1986. Effects of sensory deprivation in psychiatric seclusion and solitary confinement. *International Journal of Law and Psychiatry* 8: 49–65.

Gray, R., D. Bressington, J. Lathlean, and A. Mills. 2008. Relationship between adherence, symptoms, treatment attitudes, satisfaction, and side effects in prisoners taking antipsychotic medication. *The Journal of Forensic Psychiatry & Psychology* 19: 335–351.

Greenberg, G.A., and R.A. Rosenheck. 2008. Homelessness in the state and federal prison population. *Criminal Behaviour and Mental Health* 18: 88–103.

Gunn, J., A. Maden, and M. Swinton. 1991. Treatment needs of prisoners with psychiatric disorders. *BMJ* 303: 338–341.

Harding, T., and E. Zimmermann. 1989. Psychiatric symptoms, cognitive stress and vulnerability factors. A study in a remand prison. *British Journal of Psychiatry* 155: 36–43.

Hartvig, P., and E. Kjelsberg. 2009. Penrose's Law revisited: The relationship between mental institution beds, prison population and crime rate. *Nordic Journal of Psychiatry* 63: 51–56.

Haycock, J. 1989. Manipulation and suicide attempts in jails and prisons. *Psychiatric Quaterly* 60: 85–98.

Hayes, L. 2006. Suicide prevention on correctional facilities: An overview. In *Clinical practice in correctional medicine*, ed. M. Puisis, 317–328. Philadelphia: Mosby/Elsevier.

Hayes, A.J., J.J. Shaw, G. Lever-Green, D. Parker, and L. Gask. 2008. Improvements to suicide prevention training for prison staff in England and Wales. *Suicide & Life-Threatening Behavior* 38: 708–713.

Herpertz, S., and H. Saß. 1994. Offene Selbstbeschädigung. *Nervenarzt* 65: 296–306.

Hurley, W. 1989. Suicides by prisoners. *Medical Journal of Australia* 151: 188–190.

Hurley, W., and M.P. Dunne. 1991. Psychological distress and psychiatric morbidity in women prisoners. *The Australian and New Zealand Journal of psychiatry* 25: 461–470.

Johnson, J.E., and C. Zlotnick. 2008. A pilot study of group interpersonal psychotherapy for depression in substance-abusing female prisoners. *Journal of Substance Abuse Treatment* 34: 371–377.

Karp, J.G., L. Whitman, and A. Convit. 1991. Intentional ingestion of foreign objects by MalePrison inmates. *Hospital & Community Psychiatry* 42: 533–535.

Klonsky, E.D., and J.J. Muehlenkamp. 2007. Self-injury: A research review for the practitioner. *Journal of Clinical Psychology* 63: 1045–1056, In Session.

Konrad, N. 2001. Psychiatry in custody and prisons. In *Contempory psychiatry*, Psychiatry in special situations, vol. 2, ed. F. Henn, N. Sartorius, H. Helmchen, and H. Lauter. Heidelberg: Springer.

Konrad, N., and B. Völlm. 2010. Forensic psychiatry. In *Ethics in psychiatry*, ed. H. Helmchen and N. Sartorius. Heidelberg: Springer.

Konrad, N., M.S. Daigle, A.E. Daniel, G. Dear, P. Frottier, L.M. Hayes, A. Kerkhof, A. Liebling, and M. Sarchiapone. 2007. Preventing suicide in prisons. Part I. Recommendations from the International Association for Suicide Prevention Task Force on Suicide in Prisons. *Crisis* 28(3): 113–121.

Liebling, A. 1995. Vulnerability and prison suicide. *British Journal of Criminology* 35: 173–187.

Lohner, J., and N. Konrad. 2006. Deliberate self-harm and suicide attempt in custody: Distinguishing features in male inmates' self-injurious behavior. *International Journal of Law and Psychiatry* 29: 370–385.

MacCain, S.J., and K.T. Mueser. 2009. Training in illness self-management for people with mental illness in the criminsal justice system. *American Journal of Psychiatric Rehabilitation* 12: 31–56.

Maden, A., M. Swinton, and J. Gunn. 1994. Psychiatric disorder in women serving a prisonsentence. *The British Journal of Psychiatry* 164: 44–54.

Martin, A., C. O'Driscoll, and A. Samuels. 2008. Clozapine use in a forensic population in a New South Wales prison hospital. *The Australian and New Zealand Journal of Psychiatry* 42: 141–146.

McMillan, G.P., S. Lapham, and M. Lackey. 2008. The effect of a jail methadone maintenance therapy (MMT) program on inmate recidivism. *Addiction* 103: 2017–2023.

Metraux, S. 2008. Examining relationships between receiving mental health services in the Pennsylvania prison system and time served. *Psychiatric Services* 59: 800–802.

Metzner, J., and J. Dvoskin. 2006. An overview of correctional psychiatry. *Psychiatric Clinics of North America* 29: 761–772.

Metzner, J., and L. Hayes. 2006. Suicide prevention in jails and prisons. In *Textbook of suicide assessment and management*, ed. R. Simon and R. Hales, 139–155. Washington, DC: American Psychiatric Publishing.

Morgan, D.W., A.C. Edwards, and L.R. Faulkner. 1993. The adaptation to prison by individuals with schizophrenia. *The Bulletin of the American Academy of Psychiatry and the Law* 21: 427–433.

Murdoch, N., P. Morrisd, and C. Holmes. 2008. Depression in elderly life sentence prisoners. *International Journal of Geriatric Psychiatry* 23: 957–962.

Naud, H., and M.S. Daigle. 2009. Predictive validity of the suicide probability scale in a male inmate population. *Journal of Psychopathology and Behavioral Assessment* 32: 333–342.

Patterson, R.F., and K. Hughes. 2008. Review of completed suicides in the California Department of Corrections and Rehabilitation, 1999 to 2004. *Psychiatric Services* 59: 676–682.

Piselli, M., S. Elisei, N. Murgia, R. Quartesan, and K.M. Abram. 2009. Co-occurring psychiatric and substance use disorders among male detainees in Italy. *International Journal of Law and Psychiatry* 32: 101–107.

Pratt, D., M. Piper, L. Appleby, R. Webb, and J. Shaw. 2006. Suicide in recently released prisoners: A population-based cohort study. *Lancet* 368: 119–123.

Prince, J.D., A. Akincigil, and E. Bromet. 2007. Incarceration rates of persons with first-admission psychosis. *Psychiatric Services* 58: 1173–1180.

Rieger, W. 1971. Suicide attempts in a federal prison. *Archives of General Psychiatry* 24: 532–535.

Rösler, M., W. Retz, K. Yaqoobi, E. Burg, and P. Retz-Junginger. 2009. Attention deficit/hyperactivity disorder in female offenders: Prevalence, psychiatric comorbidity and psychosocial implications. *European Archives of Psychiatry and Clinical Neuroscience* 259: 98–105.

Sacks, J.Y., K. McKendrick, Z. Hamilton, C.M. Cleland, F.S. Pearson, and S. Banks. 2008. Treatment outcomes for female offenders: Relationship to number of axis I diagnoses. *Behavioral Sciences & the Law* 26: 413–434.

Salize, H.J., H. Schanda, and H. Dressing. 2008. From the hospital into the community and back again – a trend towards re-institutionalisation in mental health care? *International Review of Psychiatry* 20: 527–534.

Senior, J., A.J. Hayes, D. Pratt, S.D. Thomas, T. Fahy, M. Leese, A. Bowen, G. Taylor, G. Lever-Green, T. Graham, A. Pearson, M. Ahmed, and J.J. Shaw. 2007. The identification and management of suicide risk in local prisons. *The Journal of Forensic Psychiatry & Psychology* 18: 368–380.

Shelton, D., S. Sampl, K.L. Kesten, W. Zhang, and R.L. Trestman. 2009. Treatment of impulsive aggression in correctional settings. *Behavioral Sciences & the Law* 27: 787–800.

Snow, L. 2002. Prisoners' motives for self-injury and attempted suicide. *The British Journal of Forensic Practice* 4: 18–29.

Tacke, B., Hanisch, A., Knaack, M., and Rode, I. 1975. Untersuchung psychiatrischer und psychologischer Faktoren, welche für Selbstbeschädigungen (das sog. Metallschlucken) von Häftlingen in Strafanstalten bestimmend sind. Opladen: Westdeutscher Verlag.

Talbot, J. 2009. No one knows: Offenders with learning disabilities and learning difficulties. *International Journal of Prisoner Health* 5: 141–152.

Teplin, L.A., K.M. Abram, and G.M. McClelland. 1996. Prevalence of psychiatric disorders among incarcerated women. I. Pretrial jail detainees. *Archives of General Psychiatry* 53: 505–512.

Thole, E. 1976. Suizid im Gefängnis. *ZfStrVo* 25: 110–114.

United Nations. 1987. Standard minimum rules for the treatment of prisoners. http://www.unchr.ch/html/menu3/b/h_comp34.htm. Accessed June 2010.

Völlm, B., and M.C. Dolan. 2009. Self-harm among UK female prisoners: A cross-sectional study. *The Journal of Forensic Psychiatry & Psychology* 20: 741–751.

Walters, R.H., J.E. Callagan, and A.F. Newman. 1969. Effect of solitary confinement on prisoners. *The American Journal of Psychiatry* 119: 771–773.

Washburn, J.J., L.A. Teplin, L.S. Voss, C.D. Simon, K.M. Abram, and G.M. McClelland. 2008. Psychiatric disorders among detained youths: A comparison of youths processed in juvenile court and adult criminal court. *Psychiatric Services* 59: 965–973.

Way, B.B., R. Miraglia, D.A. Sawyer, R. Beer, and J. Eddy. 2005. Factors related to suicide in New York state prisons. *International Journal of Law and Psychiatry* 28: 207–221.

World Health Organization. 2007. Preventing suicide in jails and prisons. Geneva. www.who.int/mental_health/prevention/suicide/resource_jails_prisons.pdf. Accessed June 2010.

Yang, S., A. Kadouri, A. Revah-levy, E.P. Mulvey, and B. Falisard. 2009. Doin g time: A qualitative study of long-term incarceration and the impact of mental illness. *International Journal of Law and Psychiatry* 32: 294–303.

Chapter 2
Ethics Within the Prison System

Helmut Pollähne

Addressing ethical issues in prison psychiatry – on a global scale as well as in national perspectives and concerning special problems (see Part II) – goes along with a more general discussion of ethics in psychiatry and in the prison system. Focusing on psychiatric problems in prisons and with prisoners (rather than criminal law problems in psychiatry and with patients), ethical issues in the prison system are of major interest. Confronted with extreme ethical and professional conflicts there may be no way out than the way out of the system: Resigning rather than resignation, opposition rather than pragmatism. However, this chapter aims to highlight areas of good practice in prison psychiatry rather than further cultivate frontlines.

Beyond the question of ethics within the prison system the ethics of the prison (and its system) and of punishment in general arises: Although both perspectives cannot be separated without losing important insights, especially concerning the interactions between the structures of the penal justice system within the actual criminal policy framework and prison reality, this chapter will focus on immanent issues facing existing prisons throughout the world, rather than questioning their right to exist. On an academic scale, topics of the legitimacy of criminal law, punishment and incarceration may seem more 'exciting', not least from an ethical perspective (cf. Boonin 2008), but neither the prisoners nor professionals would benefit from this (see Sect. 2.1). At any rate, the Chap. 4 covers some of these issues. One of the main ethical dilemmas, not only in academic discussions, is – not in prison psychiatry alone, but in the whole prison system – the limit of scientific research: this issue will be mentioned, but the reader is also referred to the chapter "Ethics of research in prison psychiatry" in this volume. One of the 'solutions' to some

H. Pollähne (✉)
Institute of Crimal Policy, University of Law, Bremen, Germany

Joester and Partner, Bremen, Germany
e-mail: pollaehne@strafverteidiger-bremen.de

N. Konrad et al. (eds.), *Ethical Issues in Prison Psychiatry*, International Library of Ethics, Law, and the New Medicine 46, DOI 10.1007/978-94-007-0086-4_2,
© Springer Science+Business Media Dordrecht 2013

of the ethical problems encountered in prison psychiatry might be the integration of prison health services into the general health service system, thus hoping those problems would not arise. Certainly ethical dilemmas should rather be avoided than setting up guidelines to handle them, but either way unavoidable ethical issues have to be solved.

The treatment of prison inmates is associated with a number of situations and conflicts raising ethical concern: "Excessive use of solitary confinement, lockdowns, unnecessary and humiliating strip, body cavity, and pat searches (sometimes exacerbated by being cross-gendered), long delays in processing calls for medical assistance, multiple celling, allowing prison conditions to become squalid, turning a blind eye to prisoner-on-prisoner abuse, chain-gang practices, and even institutional boredom, sometimes individually and often collectively violate ethical – even if not legal – demands that imprisonment not be cruel, inhuman, or degrading" (Kleinig 2008). Some of these problems will become more severe in the treatment of prisoners with mental disorders. Additional problems include: resource allocation, issues of patient choice and autonomy in an inherently coercive environment, the dual role of forensic psychiatrists giving raise to tension between patient care and protection of the public, the professional medical role of a psychiatrist and/or psychotherapist working in prison, the involvement of psychiatrists in disciplinary or coercive measures, consent to treatment, especially the right to refuse treatment or the use of coercion in forcing a prisoner to undergo treatment, hunger strike, confidentiality as well as the potential for high rates of decompensation and deterioration (Keppler et al. 2010). The high suicide rates among prisoners may be a marker of the inadequate or even inhumane treatment in prisons rather than an indication for the extent of mental disorders – or to put it differently: pathologizing these problems might become subject of ethical challenges.

Of course professionals within prison psychiatry (and in a certain sense even more so in prison psychology, see *Decaire* and *American Association for Correctional Psychology* 2010) not only face special ethical issues and challenges centered around mentally disordered prisoners but are also confronted with 'normal' prisoners and with the question of which prisoner is to be regarded mentally disordered (or not): This may be of advantage for the affected prisoner in terms of receiving adequate help on one hand; on the other hand, however, this may lead to further 'trouble' for him in terms of a psychiatric regime adding to the custody and correctional regime.

This chapter will discuss ethics within the prison system starting with short remarks on principles of the prison and its system (Sect. 2.1) followed by considerations on ethics in general (Sect. 2.2) and within the prison system in particular (Sect. 2.3). The main part will be formed by considerations of guidelines and recommendations devised as international (minimum) standards for the ethical treatment of prisoners in general (Sect. 2.4) and especially for the medical and psychiatric treatment (Sect. 2.5).

2.1 The Prison System

There is no uniform prison system. This is partly due to the variety of institutions that may be considered "prisons" in a broader sense, partly due to the classification of prisoners and the diversity within the prison as a system (see below).

The European "Prison Rules" (EPR), for example, "apply to persons who have been remanded in custody by a judicial authority or who have been deprived of their liberty following conviction. In principle, persons who have been remanded in custody by a judicial authority and persons who are deprived of their liberty following conviction should only be detained in prisons, that is, in institutions reserved for detainees of these two categories." But the Rules also apply to persons "who may be detained for any other reason in a prison; or who have been remanded in custody by a judicial authority or deprived of their liberty following conviction and who may, for any reason, be detained elsewhere" (10.1–3). Addressing "persons deprived of their liberty", the EPR speak of "prisons" as well as of "detention" and "custody". The standards of the European Committee for the Prevention of Torture (CPT-Standards 2009) refer to any place "where persons are deprived of their liberty by a public authority"; the CPT's mandate thus "extends beyond prisons and police stations to encompass, for example, psychiatric institutions, detention areas at military barracks, holding centres for asylum seekers or other categories of foreigners, and places in which young persons may be deprived of their liberty by judicial or administrative order". Furthermore, Art. 10 of the International Covenant on Civil and Political Rights (CCPR) applies "to anyone deprived of liberty under the laws and authority of the State who is held in prisons, hospitals - particularly psychiatric hospitals - detention camps or correctional institutions or elsewhere. States parties should ensure that the principle stipulated therein is observed in all institutions and establishments within their jurisdiction where persons are being held" (United Nations Human Rights Committee: General Comment [GC] 21, par. 2). As for this article "prison" is understood in the sense of the EPR.

Referring to the prison "system" draws attention to its place in the criminal justice system on the one hand and to the construction and organization of the prison as a system on the other hand (Zedner 2004). Within the criminal justice system the prison plays different roles: providing custody for pre-trial detention, incarceration for post-trial punishment, detention for post-punishment incapacitation or confinement for 'alternative' corrections. What they all have in common is the fact of imprisonment, being locked up involuntarily in a closed institution for an often extended period of time (as opposed to short term arrests in police stations, for example). This is true for other forms of detention, confinement, custody, etc. outside the criminal justice system as well, such as secure psychiatric hospitals, some homes for senior citizens or homes for juveniles. These institutions are therefore partly confronted with similar ethical challenges and the focus of committees for the prevention of torture, but nevertheless not the focus of this chapter. The prison as a system refers to differences in size, distinction, types of detention, treatment and security, to questions of staffing, organization, bureaucracy or management as well as state vs. private facilities and authorities.

According to international rules, prisons shall be restricted to certain objectives: The penitentiary system shall comprise "treatment of prisoners the essential aim of which shall be their reformation and social rehabilitation" (CCPR Art. 10 par. 3), which also means that "no penitentiary system should be only retributory; it should essentially seek the reformation and social rehabilitation of the prisoner" (GC 21 par. 10). In addition to the EPR that apply to all prisoners, the regime for sentenced prisoners shall be designed to enable them to lead a responsible and crime-free life: "Imprisonment is by the deprivation of liberty a punishment in itself and therefore the regime for sentenced prisoners shall not aggravate the suffering inherent in imprisonment" (EPR). Beyond the questions about why we legally punish people and for how long, however, there are many complex questions concerning how we should punish them: "We should structure prisons so that they afford inmates meaningful opportunities to live and act as responsible citizens, albeit citizens some of whose basic moral rights are legitimately and severely curtailed" (Lippke 2007).

We have to realize – in spite of all the well argued debates and even campaigns on abolition – that throughout most of the world the prison still is, and presumably will be for quite another while, not only the concrete symbol for at least the 'ultimate ratio' of criminal policies, but rather its 'backbone' (van Zyl-Smit and Dünkel 2001; Stern 2006). In societies where freedom is said to be the fundamental civil right, it is not surprising that detention is the fundamental punishment, not necessarily in terms of quantity but rather in terms of quality. Recently we have observed an overall increase in the rates of prisoners-per-population and a decrease in the rate of expenses-per-prisoner. At the same time expenses have been growing overall while budgets have been shrinking due to the described trends of relative mass imprisonment (van Zyl-Smit and Dünkel 2001; Downes 2001).

The traditional function of the prison, discipline and punishment through incarceration (Foucault 1995), was rationalized with ideas of correction and incapacitation (Zedner 2004; cf. Boonin 2008), but on a larger scale this does not make a difference: The role of the prison in the system of criminal policies seems to be more secure than ever – not anymore, however, only in terms of quality but more and more also in terms of quantity. Garland summed up what he called "the originating causes of mass imprisonment" as a result of the history of the closing decades of the 20th century: "anxieties about crime and violence; the demand for public protection; the notion that concern for victims excludes concern for offenders; political populism married to a distrust of the criminal justice system; the discrediting of social solutions to the problem of order; a stern disregard for the plight of the undeserving poor" (Garland 2001). However, the "perpetuating causes of mass imprisonment may be quite different", he continues – and in reference to Max Weber's work on "The protestant ethic and the spirit of capitalism" (from 1930) as well as his ideas on the "self-reproduction of institutions" identifies the outlines of a "new iron cage: It is quite possible that, given time, and the absence of concerted opposition, mass imprisonment will become a new 'iron cage' in Weber's sense of the term. ... The most striking example of this is the emergence of a penal-industrial complex, with newly vested interests in commercial prison contracts, and the jobs and profits they bring. ... As the market in private security expands, the delivery of penal legislation speeds up, and the crime control culture reproduces itself, we face the real possibility of being locked into this state of affairs. After all, the new arrangements spawn institutional investments and produce definite benefits, particularly for the social groups who are at the greatest distance from them. They entail a way of allocating the costs of crime – unjust, unequal, but feasible nonetheless" (Garland 2001; Downes 2001; Sudbury 2004; McMahon 1997).

But these arrangements – "new economies" in the prison system (detailed in Pollähne 2010) – also involve serious social costs that will become increasingly apparent. These costs include, according to Garland (2001), "the allocation of state spending to imprisonment rather than education or social policy budgets; the reinforcement of criminogenic processes and the destruction of social capital, not just for inmates but for their families and neighbourhoods (Mahmood 2004); the transfer of prison culture out into the community; the discrediting of law and legal authority among the groups most affected; the hardening of social and racial divisions". These are indeed at least five good reasons to argue against the perpetuating of the prison system in general and mass-imprisonment specifically, even if the arguments are not really new, the abolitionists would claim (Davis 2003). But how to achieve such goals seems to be more uncertain than ever. Nevertheless the discourse on the emergence of a security industrial complex in general and a "penal" (Beckett 1997) or rather "prison industrial complex" in particular, has become a main topic in scientific debate (Davis 2003; Sudbury 2004; Mehigan and Rowe 2007; Wacquant 2008). And still: "As the criminal justice system grows, the size, resources, and authority of the interest groups that benefit from its expansion are also augmented. These beneficiaries – including law enforcement, correctional workers, and a growing number of private firms – constitute what has become to be known as the 'penal-industrial complex' and are now mobilizing to ensure that the wars on crime and drugs continue" (Beckett 1997; Stern 2006; Sudbury 2004).

Prisons need to be understood as serving many functions, some of which are more obvious than others: "We need to describe the reality of the prison against the backcloth of contemporary sensibility. But these ideas about punishment and its purpose, and penal values, influence practice and constitute penal sensibility" (Liebling and Arnold 2004; Zedner 2004). In what way is the "carceral texture of society" related to the daily texture of the prison? Can prisons ever be anything other than places of punishment? (Zedner 2004, Christie 2000; on "punitivity" Kury and Ferdinand 2008; about "ethical dilemmas in the medical model", Sissons 1976).

It is hard to be optimistic about the future of prisons: "Given their infamous track records, it would be easier to call for their abolition than reform. Yet as a practical matter, it is exceedingly unlikely that prisons are going to disappear any time soon. Besides, there are theoretical reasons for believing that we should retain them. We would do better, it seems to me, to rethink what we want them to do and how. It seems clear that we cannot continue to structure them so that they are deeply hostile to the nurture and exercise of those skills and dispositions constitutive of responsible citizenship. Many who enter prisons from less than reasonably just societies have weak capacities for responsible citizenship to begin with. It is simply implausible to believe that subjecting such individuals to harsh and restrictive conditions will strengthen those capacities. Indeed, it is far more likely that such conditions will erode the relevant capacities and convince many offenders that they have little to gain from law-abiding conduct" (Lippke 2007).

2.2 Ethics

Ethics may be understood as "the moral principles governing or influencing conduct" (see the glossary in Kallert and Torres-Gonzáles 2006) – as if it was that simple to equalize ethics and morals. However, ethical guidelines for conduct are also not the same as lawful obedience: Obeying relevant laws – relevant especially in terms of the treatment of prisoners – should be regarded as one of the minimum ethical requirements; however, this does not mean that following lawful rules will fulfill these requirements and, even worse, might turn out unethical nonetheless. On the other hand, 'obeying' ethical guidelines may, in exceptional circumstances, lead to breaking the law, but will – in most cases – not serve as a legal justification.

Ethics is concerned with the study of "questions of right and wrong ... good or bad" in terms of "moral judgments we assign to actions and conduct" (Banks 2009). Addressing actions and conduct "within" the prison system we may skip over metaethics and focus on normative ethics on one hand, concerned with "ways of behaving and standards of conduct", and applied ethics on the other hand, solving "practical moral problems as they arise, particularly in the professions, such as medicine and law". Both perspectives provide us with "a way to make moral choices when we are uncertain about what to do in a situation involving moral issues. In the process of everyday life, moral rules are desirable, not because they express absolute truth, but because they are generally reliable guides for moral circumstances" (ibid). We need a system of rules and principles to help guide us in making difficult decisions when moral issues arise: "If we cannot draw upon an ethical framework, we have to rely on emotion, instinct, and personal values, and these cannot supply an adequate answer to moral dilemmas"; and only through studying ethics is it "possible to define unethical behavior. A full understanding of ethical behavior demonstrates that it includes not only 'bad' or 'evil', but also inaction that allows 'bad' or 'evil' to occur" (Banks 2009).

Ethical systems provide "guidelines or a framework to which one can refer to in the effort to make a moral decision" (Pollock and Becker 1995). A discussion of ethical systems also demonstrates "that often there is more than one 'correct' resolution to a dilemma and more than one way to arrive at the same resolution" (Pollock and Becker 1995); such systems can be identified as religious ethics (what is good conforms to a deity's will), natural law (what is good is what conforms to true human nature), ethical formalism (what is good is what is pure in motive), utilitarianism (what is good is what results in the greatest good for the greatest number) and the ethics of care (what is good is that which meets the needs of those involved and doesn't hurt relationships, etc.). What is needed is a set of principles to which we aspire in law and in contemporary moral and political philosophy, first virtues, the foundation of our social life, and also virtues that human beings need (Liebling and Arnold 2004).

Focusing on the prison system as part of the justice system and the professionals within these systems, ethics is inevitably high up on the agenda, for the criminal justice system "comprises professionals who exercise power and authority over others and who in some cases are authorized to use force and physical coercion against them" (Banks 2009). The laws as well as other accepted standards of behavior impose ethical rules and responsibilities on these professionals, who must be "aware of ethical standards in carrying out their functions. Ethics is crucial in decisions involving discretion, force, and due process, because criminal justice professionals can be tempted to abuse their powers" (Banks 2009) – in short: "Studying and applying ethics is a prerequisite for any competent criminal justice professional" (Banks 2009). And this is even more so true for professionals in the prison system, no matter if their profession is law or medicine, corrections or psychiatry, management or psychology. "Relations where strong power differences exist, where conflicts of interest are likely, or where decisions are made in uncertain situations are all areas where particular attention to ethics is needed" (Banks 2009).

Law enforcement ethics is particularly germane for a number of issues "relevant to police, the discretionary nature of policing, the authority of police, that fact that they are not 'habitually moral', the crisis situations, the temptations, and peer pressure" (Pollock and Becker 1995) such as "gratuities, corruption, bribery, 'shopping', whistle-blowing and loyalty, undercover tactics, use of deception, discretion, sleeping, sex on duty and other misfeasance, deadly force, and brutality" (Pollock and Becker 1995). Officers' codes of ethics know five common elements: "legality (enforcing and upholding the laws), service (protecting and serving the public), honesty and integrity, loyalty, and some version of the Golden Rule, or respect for other persons" (Pollock and Becker 1995). Good relationships between staff and prisoners may increase the chances of compliance with penal regimes, but they cannot guarantee it: "the sources of validity of value systems must be that they are 'good' and 'right' according to general conceptions of 'what humans should try to achieve or preserve in their lives as a whole'. Values and general principles need something other than instrumental justification or sources of authority. Consequentialism is not enough." (Liebling and Arnold 2004).

To return to the knotty relationship between ethics and law, we have to realize they are distinct. By law we generally mean "legislation, statutes, and regulations made by states and by the federal government on a host of subjects for the public good and public welfare" not intended to incorporate ethical principles or values, but sometimes – at least – "ethical standards will be reflected in laws" (Banks 2009). Legislation regulating the legal profession or other professions may give legal effect to certain professional codes of conduct, but ethical standards are not necessarily written down in form of laws or other rules. However, they should represent the collective experience of a society as they regulate the behavior of those who make up that society: "The fact that an ethical standard is not repeated or copied in a law does not affect the validity of that ethical standard" (Banks 2009) and sometimes, as mentioned earlier, laws can conflict with ethical standards, in a collective as well as in an individual perspective – civil disobedience may be one answer to this key ethical dilemma (Banks 2009). Somewhere in this triangle of morals, laws and ethics we will find the guidelines for conduct and the principles for the treatment of others – i.e.: prisoners. Discussing ethics within a social (sub-)system – i.e.: the prison – has to consider the practical philosophy of institutional philosophies as well as individual conduct.

2.3   Ethics Within the Prison System

"The degree of civilization in a society is revealed by entering its prisons" (Dostojewski 1860). Addressing ethics within the prison system we face ethical dilemmas and issues. The latter usually comprise issues of "public policy involving ethical questions" (see the summary in Banks 2009 and the material in Schmalleger and Smylka 2008), whereas an ethical dilemma is "the responsibility of an individual" and requires a decision to be made that involves "a conflict at the personal, interpersonal, institutional, or social level or raises issues of rights or moral character" (Banks 2009). Since there are many gray areas where there are no specific rules, laws, or guidelines laid out in advance, it is "not always easy to know which decision is the most ethical choice" (Banks 2009). To rely on or refer to "natural law" that represents "a search for moral absolutes that define what is 'normal' and 'natural'", may seem anachronistic, but nowadays, natural law arguments "have tended to gravitate towards arguments in favor of human rights" (Banks 2009).

From here on it does make sense to refer to international human rights standards, not merely in terms of "hard law" (conventions, covenants, treaties …), which should of course be obeyed, but especially in terms of the so called "soft law" (recommendations, standards, guidelines, etc.) issued by international renowned political (United Nations – UN; Council of Europe – CoE) and professional institutions (i.e. the World Medical Association – WMA). Returning to the categories of normative vs. applied ethics we should focus on standards for conduct on the one side and solutions for practical professional problems on the other. Addressing ethics within the prison system – and also "in correction" (Banks 2009) – means to outline standards for "guarding ethically" (Banks 2009). Arguing that "if offenders are to become responsible citizens, it was essential that they were treated in a civil manner by correctional authorities, whose task was to model good citizenship by protecting certain fundamental rights" (former commissioner of corrections in Massachusetts, Vose; Banks 2009), still holds true – unless we were not longer aiming for offenders and especially prisoners to become "responsible citizens". This would, however, constitute radical social exclusion, incompatible with international human rights standards: "Treatment that is intended to degrade or dehumanize inmates is not authorized by the sanctions society has imposed on them" (Kleinig 2001 and Banks 2009) or rather: may not be authorized by any society without following unethical paths. More recently, however, human rights activists "have shown how brutalizing and degrading practices continue to exist in the prison system";

similarly it has been claimed that "anything posing as a correctional ethics is a nonsense" and that the operation of a humane correctional system "is rendered almost impossible" (Banks 2009). Perhaps "far too much debate is centered on the humanity of what goes on in prisons as a substitute for thinking about why prisons as a social institution should continue to exist" (O'Connor 2006).

What is problematic about "cruel and unusual punishment" is that it is inhuman and degrading, because it displays "a failure of regard for one of the basic requirements for human interaction: A basic moral requirement for our interaction with others is a recognition of their oneness with ourselves as feeling, perceiving, and reasoning beings, and giving their feelings, perceptions, and reasons the same weight that we give our own" (Kleinig 2008). Human dignity has its foundations in our capacity to frame for ourselves the choices we make, the paths we tread, and the goals we pursue: "To 'carry oneself with dignity' is not simply to have a particular standing but also to assert control over the terms of one's self-presentation. The danger of imprisonment is that it will diminish both control and self-representation. It becomes an engine of degradation" (Kleinig 2008).

The notion that a guard's authority over inmates can become corrupted is well established in correctional studies and is frequently referred to as a category of ethical misconduct: "In essence, 'corruption of authority' refers to a practice by guards of deliberately refraining from enforcing prison rules and regulations" (Banks 2009); they operate as agents of social control with a role ambiguity as "a result of having to perform both treatment and custodial roles" (Banks 2009). The most obvious fact about the prison environment is that guards are vested with power and authority over the prisoners and exercise that power to control them in accordance with prison rules and regulations: "It is the exercise of this power that creates ethical issues and dilemmas" (Banks 2009; Goffman 1968; Zedner 2004).

When staff respect prisoners, "they unlock them on time, they respond to calls for assistance, and they try to solve problems. Staff are more likely to take this approach when they feel treated with respect themselves"; being treated disrespectfully or without dignity generates negative emotions (anger, tension, indignation, depression, and rage; Liebling and Arnold 2004). Although guards' discretionary powers have been curtailed over time, they nevertheless continue to exercise "significant discretion in carrying out their day-to-day tasks. Discretionary power can easily involve questions of ethical conduct, and some argue it is preferable to limit discretion even more by expanding the written rules and regulations of the prison" (Banks 2009). But discretion should be allowed "whenever there is an absence of policy or where the policy is vague or inconsistent, on the basis that full enforcement of prison rules, policies, and procedures is an impossibility. The discretionary power of guards is shaped less by formal rules than by 'an explicit understanding of the shared operational values and ethical principles that govern correctional practice'" (Banks 2009 referring to Pollock 2004).

Under what conditions should prisoners be kept? First off, Kleinig answers, "we need to remind ourselves that people are sent to prison as punishment and not for punishment. Conditions need not be easy, but neither should they be unduly harsh" (Kleinig 2008; Zedner 2004). The doctrine of 'penal austerity' gets what plausibility it has from the idea that punishment is to be seen as an imposition, not a benefit: "But the imposition is constituted by the confinement. More significantly, because the choice to imprison gives the state almost total control over the conditions of a person's life, the state also acquires the obligation to ensure that those conditions are acceptable and do not humiliate or degrade" (Zedner 2004; Goffman 1968). When the state incarcerates it assumes responsibility for the care of inmates: "First and foremost, that involves both a recognition of and a commitment to the preservation of their dignity", which should not be compromised during the period of incarceration, but should be reflected "in care for prisoners' physical and psychic well-being as well as concern for their better flourishing in future" (Goffman 1968). How material goods are delivered, how staff approach prisoners, how managers treat staff, and how life is lived, through conversation, encounter, or transaction, "constitute (above minimum threshold) key dimensions of prison life; these are the things that matter'" (Liebling and Arnold 2004). "We have used the term 'moral performance' in order to make our case that the prison is a moral place, and that prisons differ in their moral practices" (Liebling and Arnold 2004).

The ethical issue most commonly raised in relation to the provision of medical services to the inmate is "the question of interference with the prisoner's right to treatment, no matter what his offence" (Sissons 1976). The root cause of poor medical treatment in the prison is not solely a result of deliberate misuse or the withholding of adequate services, it is often the result of a difficult question of priorities: "The competitive situation of medical services within the prison system is rendered ambiguous, however, by the fundamental confusion which exists between the provision of medical care for an inmate who is suffering from a physical complaint and the function of medicine in relation to the criminal when crime is identified as individual pathology" (Sissons 1976). But "prison health is public health" (Keppler et al. 2010). The "principle of equivalence" demands: Prisoners should have access to the same standard of treatment as patients in the community in terms of justice for the vulnerable who should not be subjected to additional punishment through deprivation from healthcare (Pont in Keppler and Stöver 2010). The opposite would be "deliberate indifference" to a prisoner's health which may constitute "cruel and unusual punishment", prohibited by, e.g., the Eighth Amendment of the United States Constitution (see UTMB Institute for Medical Humanities 2007). There is a significant empirical link between aspects of "a prison's moral performance and (a) levels of psychological distress, anxiety, and depression found amongst prisoners; and (b) its suicide rate"; poor treatment leads to negative emotions - it is distressing and damaging for individuals (Liebling and Arnold 2004).

2.4   International Minimum Prison Standards

International covenants are binding upon the state parties due to the fundamental international principle of 'pacta sunt servanda', according to which treaties must be abided by: "Nevertheless, individual claims can usually not be made in reference to regulations contained in international treaties, since the individual is not normally a subject of public international law" (Conrady/Roeder in Kallert/Torres-Gonzáles 2006). Individuals are dependent on the implementation of the international rules by their national governments, i.e. the incorporation of international rules in national law: "This process of implementation and, more generally, the way state parties abide by the treaties they conclude, are being monitored by certain organs related to the respective treaty" (Kallert and Torres-Gonzáles 2006 and Pollähne 2007 about the Committee for the Prevention of Torture - CPT). Beyond the implementation of international "hard law" (i.e. human rights covenants) in state parties' practices (as a 'top down'-process), the "soft law" instruments (see below) are more likely to determine individual ethical-professional conduct (as a 'bottom up'-attempt and in search for "best practice").

2.4.1   Principles

Above all the Universal Declaration of Human Rights (1948), art. 2: "No one shall be subjected to torture or to cruel, inhuman or degrading treatment or punishment" (confirmed in the CCPR art. 7) has to be mentioned. All persons deprived of their liberty "shall be treated with humanity and with respect for the inherent dignity of the human person" (CCPR art. 10 par. 1). Although this right is not separately mentioned in the list of non-derogable rights in art. 4 par. 2 regarding "the peremptory nature of some fundamental rights", the UN-Human Rights Committee believes "that here the Covenant expresses a norm of general international law not subject to derogation" (GC 29 par. 13).

The EPR (2006) list the following Basic Principles:

1. All persons deprived of their liberty shall be treated with respect for their human rights.
2. Persons deprived of their liberty retain all rights that are not lawfully taken away by … sentencing them or remanding them in custody.
3. Restrictions placed on persons deprived of their liberty shall be the minimum necessary and proportionate to the legitimate objective for which they are imposed.
4. Prison conditions that infringe prisoners' human rights are not justified by lack of resources.
5. Life in prison shall approximate as closely as possible the positive aspects of life in the community.
6. All detention shall be managed so as to facilitate the reintegration into free society of persons who have been deprived of their liberty.
8. Prison staff carry out an important public service and their recruitment, training and conditions of work shall enable them to maintain high standards in their care of prisoners.
9. All prisons shall be subject to regular government inspection and independent monitoring.

2.4.2   Prohibition of Torture

The prohibition of torture (in the stricter sense) should not have to be mentioned when talking about the prison system for it may seem to be merely a question of criminal procedures and police interrogations. However "education and information regarding the prohibition against torture" should be "fully included in the training of law enforcement personnel (…), medical personnel, public officials and other persons who may be involved in the custody, interrogation or treatment of any individual subjected to any form of arrest, detention or imprisonment" (UN Convention Against Torture – CAT art. 10).

In their "Resolution on Prohibition of Physician Participation in Torture" the WMA-Council reaffirmed (Tel Aviv 2009) its Declaration of Tokyo "Guidelines for Physicians Concerning Torture and other Cruel, Inhuman or Degrading Treatment or Punishment" (2006) in relation to detention and imprisonment, which prohibits physicians from participating in, or even being present during, the practice of torture or other forms of cruel, inhuman or degrading procedures, and urges National Medical Associations to inform physicians and governments of the Declaration and its contents. The WMA also reaffirmed its Declaration of Hamburg (1997) "Support for Medical Doctors Refusing to Participate in or to Condone the use of Torture or other Forms of Cruel, Inhuman or Degrading Treatment" and also its resolution "Responsibility of Physicians in the Denunciation of Acts of Torture or Cruel or Inhuman or Degrading Treatment of which they are Aware" (2007), and urged national medical associations to speak out in support of this fundamental principle of medical ethics and to investigate any breach of these principles by association members of which they are aware. In the "Madrid Declaration on Ethical Standards for Psychiatric Practice" (2005) the WPA added that psychiatrists shall not take part "in any process of mental or physical torture, even when authorities attempt to force their involvement in such acts".

The Tokyo-Declaration emphasized that it is "the privilege of the physician to practise medicine in the service of humanity, to preserve and restore bodily and mental health without distinction as to persons, to comfort and to ease the suffering of his or her patients. The utmost respect for human life is to be maintained even under threat, and no use made of any medical knowledge contrary to the laws of humanity" (preamble). Physicians shall not "provide any premises, instruments, substances or knowledge to facilitate the practice of torture or other forms of cruel, inhuman or degrading treatment or to diminish the ability of the victim to resist such treatment"; shall not be present "during any procedure during which torture or any other forms of cruel, inhuman or degrading treatment is used or threatened", and must have "complete clinical independence in deciding upon the care of a person for whom he or she is medically responsible", for his/her "fundamental role is to alleviate the distress of his or her fellow human beings, and no motive, whether personal, collective or political, shall prevail against this higher purpose" (par. 2, 4 and 5; cf. *Morgan and Evans* 2003).

The WMA "Responsibility"-Resolution (2007) recognizes that "careful and consistent documentation and denunciation by physicians of cases of torture and of those responsible contributes to the protection of the physical and mental integrity of victims and in a general way to the struggle against a major affront to human dignity" (par. 16) and that "the absence of documenting and denouncing acts of torture may be considered as a form of tolerance thereof and of non-assistance to the victims" (par. 19). Recommended is the "ethical obligation on physicians to report or denounce acts of torture or cruel, inhuman or degrading treatment of which they are aware; depending on the circumstances, the report or denunciation would be addressed to medical, legal, national or international authorities, to non-governmental organizations or to the International Criminal Court", and an "ethical and legislative exception to professional confidentiality that allows the physician to report abuses, where possible with the subject's consent, but in certain circumstances where the victim is unable to express him/herself freely, without explicit consent" (rec. 9 par. 1 and 2, referring to par. 68 of the UN-Istanbul Protocol "Manual on the Effective Investigation and Documentation of Torture and Other Cruel, Inhuman or Degrading Treatment or Punishment", 1999; Frewer and Furtmayr 2007).

2.4.3   Inhuman or Degrading Treatment or Punishment

Inhuman or degrading treatment or punishment is mentioned in one breath with the prohibition of torture, and "does not include pain or suffering [however] arising only from, inherent in or incidental to lawful sanctions" (CAT art. 1 par. 1). At any rate the state parties have to prevent "other acts of cruel, inhuman or degrading treatment or punishment which do not amount to torture", when such acts are "committed by or at the instigation of or with the consent or acquiescence of a public official or other person acting in an official capacity" (CAT art. 16 par. 1).

CCPR art. 10 contains "a positive obligation towards persons who are particularly vulnerable because of their status as persons deprived of liberty"; they may not be "subjected to any hardship or constraint other than that resulting from the deprivation of liberty; respect for the dignity of such persons must be guaranteed under the same conditions as for that of free persons. Persons deprived of their liberty enjoy all the rights set forth in the Covenant, subject to the restrictions that are unavoidable in a closed environment" (GC 21 par. 3). This is a fundamental and universally applicable rule. Consequently, the application of this rule, as a minimum, cannot be "dependent on the material resources available in the State party. This rule must be applied without distinction of any kind, such as race, colour, sex, language, religion, political or other opinion, national or social origin, property, birth or other status" (GC 21 par. 4).

"Good order" in prison shall be maintained by taking into account "the requirements of security, safety and discipline, while also providing prisoners with living conditions which respect human dignity" (EPR 49). Disciplinary procedures should be mechanisms of last resort: "Whenever possible, prison authorities shall use mechanisms of restoration and mediation to resolve disputes with and among prisoners"; only conduct "likely to constitute a threat to good order, safety or security may be defined as a disciplinary offence" (EPR 56 and 57.1).

"Collective punishments and corporal punishment, punishment by placing in a dark cell, and all other forms of inhuman or degrading punishment" is prohibited; solitary confinement shall be imposed as a punishment "only in exceptional cases and for a specified period of time, which shall be as short as possible", and instruments of restraint shall never be applied as a punishment (EPR 60.3–6). Prison staff shall not use force against prisoners "except in self-defence or in cases of attempted escape or active or passive physical resistance to a lawful order and always as a last resort", whereas the amount of force used shall be "the minimum necessary and shall be imposed for the shortest necessary time"; staff who deal directly with prisoners shall be trained in "techniques that enable the minimal use of force in the restraint of prisoners who are aggressive" (EPR 64 and 66).

The CPT-Standards (2009) have so far and by far provided the most precise and detailed guidelines for the prevention of inhuman or degrading treatment or punishment (Pollähne 2007) in prisons as well as in psychiatric institutions. It would go far beyond the scope of this chapter to name but a few relevant standards: a thorough study is recommended!

2.4.4 Prisoner Status/Prisoners' Rights

The "recognition of the inherent dignity and of the equal and inalienable rights of all members of the human family is the foundation of freedom, justice and peace in the world" (CCPR preamble); each state has "to ensure to all individuals within its territory and subject to its jurisdiction the rights" recognized in the CCPR, without distinction of any kind, such as race, colour, sex, language, religion, political or other opinion, national or social origin, property, birth or other status (CCPR art. 2 par. 1; similar the European Convention for the Protection of Human Rights and Fundamental Freedoms – ECHR art. 1). "Everyone" has the right to respect for his private and family life, his home and his correspondence (ECHR art 8 par. 1), and there shall be no interference by a public authority with the exercise of this right "except such as is in accordance with the law and is necessary in a democratic society in the interests of national security, public safety or the economic well-being of the country, for the prevention of disorder or crime, for the protection of health or morals, or for the protection of the rights and freedoms of others" (ECHR art 8 par. 2). Addressing "all" members or individuals and the rights of "everyone" has to be understood as fully including prisoners as a rule with the necessity of justifying exclusions.

No public authorities and institutions, national or local, shall "engage in any practice of racial discrimination." (UN Convention on the Elimination of all Forms of Racial Discrimination – CERD-Committee, General Recommendation 13 par. 1). The fulfilment of this obligation very much depends upon "national law enforcement officials who exercise police powers, especially the powers of detention or arrest"; they should receive "intensive training to ensure that in the performance of their duties they respect as well as protect human dignity and maintain and uphold the human rights of all persons without distinction as to race, colour or national or ethnic origin" (UN Convention on the Elimination of all Forms of Racial Discrimination – CERD-Committee, General Recommendation 13 par. 2).

2.4.5 Staff and Management

Prisons shall be managed within an ethical context which recognises the obligation to treat all prisoners with humanity and with respect for the inherent dignity of a human person: "Staff shall manifest a clear sense of purpose of the prison system. Management shall provide leadership on how the purpose shall best be achieved. The duties of staff go beyond those required of mere guards and shall take account of the need to facilitate the reintegration of prisoners into society after their sentence has been completed through a programme of positive care and assistance"; at all times staff shall "conduct themselves and perform their duties in such a manner as to influence the prisoners by good example and to command their respect" (EPR 72 and 75). When selecting new staff the prison authorities shall place great emphasis on "the need for integrity, humanity, professional capacity and personal suitability for the complex work that they will be required to do" (EPR 77 and 78). The training of all staff shall include "instruction in the international and regional human rights instruments and standards" (EPR 81.4; cf. the CPT-standards 2009 chapter VIII and Pollähne 2010).

2.5 Ethical Standards for Prison Health and Psychiatry

Before addressing relevant ethical principles and human rights standards concerning prison health some general health recommendations and patients' rights should be recalled (cf. Alfredsson and Tomaševski 1998).

2.5.1 General Health Aspects

It is "the right of everyone to the enjoyment of the highest attainable standard of physical and mental health" (UN Covenant on Economic, Social and Cultural Rights – CESCR art. 12 par. 1). Health is "a fundamental human right indispensable for the exercise of other human rights"; everyone can claim health rights "conducive to living a life in dignity" (CESCR-Committee GC 14 par. 1). The right to health is closely related to and dependent upon the realization of other human rights, including "the rights to food, housing, work, education, human dignity, life, non-discrimination, equality, the prohibition against torture, privacy, access to information ..." which address integral components of the right to health (CESCR- Committee GC par. 3).

The right to health in all its forms and at all levels contains the following interrelated and essential elements: (a) *availability;* (b) *accessibility*: Health facilities, goods and services have to be accessible to everyone without discrimination [in] four overlapping dimensions: (i) non-discrimination: health facilities, goods and services must be accessible to all, especially the most vulnerable or marginalized sections of the population, in law and in fact, without discrimination on any of the prohibited grounds, (ii) physical accessibility, (iii) economic accessibility (affordability) and (iv) information accessibility; (c) *acceptability*: All health facilities, goods and services must be respectful of medical ethics and culturally appropriate, i.e. respectful of the culture of individuals, minorities, peoples and communities, sensitive to gender and life-cycle requirements, as well as being designed to respect confidentiality and improve the health status of those concerned; (d) *quality*" (GC 14 par. 12). In particular, CESCR States parties are under an obligation to respect the right to health by, inter alia, refraining from denying or limiting "equal access for all persons, including prisoners or detainees, minorities, asylum seekers and illegal immigrants, to preventive, curative and palliative health services"; furthermore to refrain from "marketing unsafe drugs and from applying coercive medical treatments, unless on an exceptional basis for the treatment of mental illness or the prevention and control of communicable diseases", which should be subject to specific and restrictive conditions, respecting best practices and applicable international standards (GC 14 par. 34).

The CoE-Convention "For the Protection of Human Rights and Dignity of the Human Being with regard to the Application of Biology and Medicine" (Oviedo-Convention on Human Rights and Biomedicine 1997) emphasizes "consent". An intervention in the health field may only be carried out after the person concerned has given "free and informed consent" to it on the basis of "appropriate information as to the purpose and nature of the intervention as well as on its consequences and risks"; the person concerned may freely withdraw consent at any time (art. 5). An intervention may also be carried out on a person who does not have the capacity to consent, "for his or her direct benefit": Where, according to law, an adult does not have the capacity to consent to an intervention because of a mental disability, a disease or for similar reasons, the intervention may only be carried out "with the authorisation of his or her representative or an authority or a person or body provided for by law", the individual concerned shall as far as possible "take part in the authorisation procedure" (ibid art. 6 par. 1 and 3).

The European Charter of Patients' Rights (2002) aims "to guarantee a high level of human health protection and to assure the high quality of services provided by national health services in Europe" and comprises the rights of every individual to (1) preventive measures, i.e. appropriate services to prevent illness; (2) access to the health services that his or her health needs require meaning "equal access to everyone, without discriminating on the basis of financial resources, place of residence, kind of illness or time of access to services"; (3) access to all kinds of information regarding their state of health, the health services and how to use them; (4) access to all information that might enable him or her to actively participate in the decisions regarding his or her health; this information is a prerequisite for any procedure and treatment, including the participation in scientific research; (5) freely choose from among different treatment procedures and providers on the basis of adequate information; (6) confidentiality of personal information, including information regarding his or her state of health and potential diagnostic or therapeutic procedures, as well as the protection of his or her privacy during the performance of diagnostic tests, specialist visits, and medical/surgical treatments in general; (7) swiftly receive necessary treatment within a predetermined period of time – this right applies at each phase of the treatment; (8) access to high quality health services on the basis of the specification and observance of standards; (9) to be free from harm caused by the poor functioning of health services, medical malpractice and errors, and the right of access to health services and treatments that meet high safety standards; (10) access to innovative procedures, including diagnostic procedures, according to international standards and independent of economic or financial considerations; (11) to avoid as much suffering and pain as possible, in each phase of his or her illness; (12) diagnostic or therapeutic programmes tailored as much as possible to his or her personal needs; (13) to complain whenever he or she has suffered a harm and the right to receive a response or other feedback; (14) to receive sufficient compensation within a reasonably short time whenever he or she has suffered physical, moral or psychological harm caused by a health service intervention.

The WMA set up an "International Code of Medical Ethics" (rev 2006) with the following general "duties of a Physician": to always "exercise his/her independent professional judgment and maintain the highest standards of professional conduct"; respect a competent patient's "right to accept or refuse treatment"; be dedicated to "providing competent medical service in full professional and moral independence, with compassion and respect for human dignity"; deal honestly with patients and colleagues, and report to the appropriate authorities those physicians "who practice unethically or incompetently or who engage in fraud or deception"; respect the rights and preferences of patients, colleagues, and other health professionals; certify only that which he/she has "personally verified"; strive to use health care resources "in the best way to benefit patients and their community" and – of course – "respect the local and national codes of ethics". Concerning his "duties to patients" a physician shall "always bear in mind the obligation to respect human life; act in the patient's best interest when providing medical care; owe his/her patients complete loyalty and all the scientific resources available to him/her"; respect a patient's "right to confidentiality"; in situations when he/she is acting for a third party, ensure "that the patient has full knowledge of that situation; not enter into a sexual relationship with his/her current patient or into any other abusive or exploitative relationship". From the "Declaration of Geneva" (2006) is to be mentioned the "pledge to consecrate my life to the service of humanity: I will practise my profession with conscience and dignity; the health of my patient will be my first consideration; I will respect the secrets that are confided in me, even after the patient has died; I will not permit considerations of age, disease or disability, creed, ethnic origin, gender, nationality, political affiliation, race, sexual orientation, social standing or any other factor to intervene between my duty and my patient; I will not use my medical knowledge to violate human rights and civil liberties, even under threat".

The WMA Declaration of Madrid (2009) also emphasizes the importance of professional autonomy calling for "the assurance that individual physicians have the freedom to exercise their professional judgement in the care and treatment of their patients" (art. 1), and reaffirming the importance of professional autonomy as an "essential component of high quality medical care and therefore a benefit to the patient that must be preserved" as an essential principle of medical ethics (art. 2).

It goes without saying that these principles also have to be applied to the health system within the prison system and to the role of physicians in this system.

2.5.2   Prison Health

Prison authorities shall safeguard the health of all prisoners in their care: "Medical services in prison shall be organised in close relation with the general health administration of the community or nation. Health policy in prisons shall be integrated into, and compatible with, national health policy. Prisoners shall have access to the health services available in the country without discrimination on the grounds of their legal situation. Medical services in prison shall seek to detect and treat physical or mental illnesses or defects from which prisoners may suffer. All necessary medical, surgical and psychiatric services including those available in the community shall be provided to the prisoner for that purpose" (EPR 39 and 40).

When examining a prisoner particular attention should be paid to: "a. observing the normal rules of medical confidentiality; b. diagnosing physical or mental illness and taking all measures necessary for its treatment and for the continuation of existing medical treatment; c. recording and reporting to the relevant authorities any sign or indication that prisoners may have been treated violently; d. dealing with withdrawal symptoms resulting from use of drugs, medication or alcohol; e. identifying any psychological or other stress brought on by the fact of deprivation of liberty; f. isolating prisoners suspected of infectious or contagious conditions for the period of infection and providing them with proper treatment; g. ensuring that prisoners carrying the HIV virus are not isolated for that reason alone; h. noting physical or mental defects that might impede resettlement after release; i. determining the fitness of each prisoner to work and to exercise; and j. making arrangements with community agencies for the continuation of any necessary medical and psychiatric treatment after release, if prisoners give their consent to such arrangements" (EPR 42.3).

Medical practitioners shall "have the care of the physical and mental health of the prisoners and shall see, under the conditions and with a frequency consistent with health care standards in the community, all sick prisoners, all who report illness or injury and any prisoner to whom attention is specially directed; (…) pay particular attention to the health of prisoners held under conditions of solitary confinement, shall visit such prisoners daily, and shall provide them with prompt medical assistance and treatment at the request of such prisoners or the prison staff and (…) report to the director whenever it is considered that a prisoner's physical or mental health is being put seriously at risk by continued imprisonment or by any condition of imprisonment, including conditions of solitary confinement" (EPR 43).

Of special importance the "WMA Declaration of Edinburgh on Prison Conditions and the Spread of Tuberculosis and Other Communicable Diseases" (2000) notes: Prisoners have the right to "humane treatment and appropriate medical care" referring to several UN-Standards for the treatment of prisoners (art. 1). The relationship between physician and prisoner is governed by "the same ethical principles as that between the physician and any other patient" (art. 2). Careful attention shall be paid to "protecting the rights of prisoners, regardless of their infected status, and according to the various UN instruments relating to conditions of imprisonment" (art. 7 par.1); the conditions in which detainees and prisoners are kept, whether they are held during the investigation of a crime, whilst awaiting trial, or after sentencing, shall "not contribute to the development, worsening or transmission of disease" and prisoners shall not be "isolated or placed in solitary confinement, without adequate access to health care and all appropriate responses to their infected status" (par. 2). Physicians working in prisons have "the duty to report to the health authorities and professional organisations of their country any deficiency in health care provided to the inmates and any situation involving high epidemiological risk for them" (art. 8).

In "Nurses' role in the care of detainees and prisoners" the International Council of Nurses (ICN, Position 2005) has noted that prisoners have "the right to health care and humane treatment: We condemn interrogation procedures and any act or behaviour harmful to mental and physical health". Prisoners also have the right "to clear and sufficient information; to refuse treatment or diagnostic procedures; and to die with dignity and in a peaceful manner". Nurses' primary responsibility is to those people who require nursing care: "In caring for detainees and prisoners nurses are expected to adhere to ethical principles and the following: Nurses who have knowledge of abuse and maltreatment of detainees and prisoners take appropriate action to safeguard their rights; do not assume functions of prison security personnel, such as body searches for the purpose of prison security; participate in clinical research on prisoners and detainees only with the prisoner or detainee's informed consent; collaborate with other health professionals and prison authorities to reduce the impact of crowded and unhealthy prison environments on transmission of infectious diseases such as HIV/AIDS and tuberculosis; abstain from using their nursing knowledge and skills in any manner, which violates the rights of detainees and prisoners; advocate for safe humane treatment of detainees and prisoners including clean water, adequate food and other basic necessities of life". This is because health professionals "have a moral duty to protect the physical and mental health of prisoners and detainees:" The ICN Code of Ethics for Nurses (Geneva 2005) affirms that "nurses have a fundamental responsibility to promote health, to prevent illness, to restore health and to alleviate suffering to all people, including detainees and prisoners. Nurses working in prison systems must observe the Standard Minimum Rules for the Treatment of Prisoners, which require that health services must be available to prisoners without discrimination."

2.5.3 General Psychiatry

The CoE-Assembly proposed the following rules concerning "problems and abuses in psychiatry" for a new recommendation: "a. the code of ethics must explicitly stipulate that it is forbidden for therapists to make sexual advances to patients; b. the use of isolation cells should be strictly limited and accommodation in large dormitories should also be avoided; c. no mechanical restraint should be used – the use of pharmaceutical means of restraint must be proportionate to the objective sought, and there must be no permanent infringement of individuals' rights to procreate; d. scientific research in the field of mental health must not be undertaken without the patient's knowledge, or against his or her will or the will of his or her representative, and must be conducted only in the patient's interest". Concerning the situation of detained persons it continues: "any person who is imprisoned should be examined by a doctor; a psychiatrist and specially trained staff should be attached to each penal institution; the rules set out above and the rules of ethics should be applied to detained persons and, in particular, medical confidentiality should be maintained in so far as this is compatible with the demands of detention; sociotherapy programmes should be set up in certain penal institutions for detained persons suffering from personality disorders" (CoE Rec 1235 [1998] par. 7 lit. a–d).

The recommendations "concerning the protection of the human rights and dignity of persons with mental disorder" aim to enhance the protection of the dignity, human rights and fundamental freedoms of persons with mental disorder, "in particular those who are subject to involuntary placement or involuntary treatment" (CoE Rec 2004(10) Guidelines art. 1) and "applies to persons with mental disorder defined in accordance with internationally accepted medical standards; lack of adaptation to the moral, social, political or other values of a society, of itself, should not be considered a mental disorder" (CoE Rec 2004(10) Guidelines art. 2). Any form of discrimination on grounds of mental disorder should be prohibited; persons with mental disorder should be entitled to exercise all their civil and political rights: "Any restrictions to the exercise of those rights should be in conformity with the provisions of the Convention for the Protection of Human Rights and Fundamental Freedoms and should not be based on the mere fact that a person has a mental disorder" (CoE Rec 2004(10) Guidelines art. 3 and 4).

Professional staff involved in mental health services should have appropriate qualifications and training to enable them to perform their role within the services according to professional obligations and standards: "In particular, staff should receive appropriate training on: protecting the dignity, human rights and fundamental freedoms of persons with mental disorder; understanding, prevention and control of violence; measures to avoid the use of restraint or seclusion; the limited circumstances in which different methods of restraint or seclusion may be justified, taking into account the benefits and risks entailed, and the correct application of such measures" (CoE Rec 2004(10) Guidelines art. 11).

In the "Madrid Declaration on Ethical Standards for Psychiatric Practice" (2005) the World Psychiatric Association (WPA) noted that medicine is both a healing art and a science: "The dynamics of this combination are best reflected in psychiatry, the branch of medicine that specializes in the care and protection of those who are ill or infirm, because of a mental disorder or impairment. Although there may be cultural, social and national differences, the need for ethical conduct and continual review of ethical standards is universal" (preamble par. 1). As practitioners of medicine, psychiatrists must be aware of the ethical implications of being a physician, and of "the specific ethical demands of the specialty of psychiatry: As members of society, psychiatrists must advocate for fair and equal treatment of the mentally ill, for social justice and equity for all" (par. 2). Ethical practice should be based on "the psychiatrist's individual sense of responsibility to the patient and judgment in determining what is correct and appropriate conduct", because "external standards and influences such as professional codes of conduct, the study of ethics, or the rule of law by themselves will not guarantee the ethical practice of medicine" (par. 3). They should keep in mind at all times "the boundaries of the psychiatrist-patient relationship, and be guided primarily by the respect for patients and concern for their welfare and integrity" (par. 4).

Psychiatrists serve patients by providing "the best therapy available consistent with accepted scientific knowledge and ethical principles" (ibid art.1). The patient should be accepted as a partner in the therapeutic process: "The psychiatrist-patient relationship must be based on mutual trust and respect to allow the patient to make free and informed decisions" (art. 3). When psychiatrists are requested to assess a person, it is their duty "first to inform and advise the person being assessed about the purpose of the intervention, the use of the findings, and the possible repercussions of the assessment", which is particularly important when psychiatrists are involved in "third party situations" (art. 5). There are aspects in the history of psychiatry and in present working expectations in some totalitarian political regimes and profit driven economical systems, that increase "psychiatrists' vulnerabilities to be abused in the sense of having to acquiesce to inappropriate demands to provide inaccurate psychiatric reports that help the system, but damage the interests of the person being assessed" (art. 13 par. 3). It is the duty of a psychiatrist confronted with "dual obligations and responsibilities at assessment time to disclose to the person being assessed the nature of the triangular relationship and the absence of a therapeutic doctor-patient relationship, besides the obligation to report to a third party even if the findings are negative and potentially damaging to the interests of the person under assessment" (art. 15).

Following the "Declaration of Hawaii" (WPA 1983) the psychiatrist "must never use his professional possibilities to violate the dignity or human rights of any individual or group and should never let inappropriate personal desires, feelings, prejudices or beliefs interfere with the treatment and on no account utilize the tools of his profession, once the absence of psychiatric illness has been established; if a patient or some third party demands actions contrary to scientific knowledge or ethical principles the psychiatrist must refuse to cooperate" (art. 7). Whatever the psychiatrist has been told by the patient, or has noted during examination or treatment, must be kept "confidential unless the patient relieves the psychiatrist from this obligation, or to prevent serious harm to self or others makes disclosure necessary" (ibid art. 8).

The WPA "statement and viewpoints on the rights and legal safeguards of the mentally ill" (Athens 1989) was meant as "a charter on the rights of mental patients", in a way extending and complementing the Hawaii Declaration. Persons suffering from mental illness shall enjoy "the same human rights and fundamental freedoms as all other citizens" and not be "the subject of discrimination on grounds of mental illness"; they have the right to "professional, human and dignified treatment" and shall be protected "from exploitation, abuse and degradation". Clinical trials and experimental treatments shall never be carried out on patients involuntarily hospitalized. Patients who are deprived of their liberty shall have the right to a qualified guardian or counsel to protect their interests, and to free communication, limited only as strictly necessary in the interests of the health or safety of themselves or others.

2.5.4   Prison Psychiatry

Persons with mental disorder should not be subject "to discrimination in penal institutions"; in particular, the "principle of equivalence of care with that outside penal institutions should be respected with regard to their health care. They should be transferred between penal institution and hospital if their health needs so require. Appropriate therapeutic options should be available for persons with mental disorder detained in penal institutions." Involuntary treatment for mental disorder "should not take place in penal institutions except in hospital units or medical units suitable for the treatment of mental disorder"; an independent system should monitor the treatment and care of persons with mental disorder in penal institutions (CoE Rec 2004[10] art. 35; a review of "minimum standards and best practices concerning mental health and substance use services in correctional settings" can be found in: Livingston 2009).

Persons who are suffering from mental illness and whose state of mental health is incompatible with detention in a prison "should be detained in an establishment specially designed for the purpose" (EPR 12). If such persons are nevertheless exceptionally held in prison there shall be special regulations that take account of their status and needs: "Specialised prisons or sections under medical control shall be available for the observation and treatment of prisoners suffering from mental disorder or abnormality who do not necessarily fall under the provisions of Rule 12. The prison medical service shall provide for the psychiatric treatment of all prisoners who are in need of such treatment and pay special attention to suicide prevention" (EPR and Pollähne 2007).

If a person whose behaviour is strongly suggestive of mental disorder is arrested, the person "should have the right to assistance from a representative or an appropriate personal advocate during the procedure and an appropriate medical examination should be conducted promptly at a suitable location to establish: the person's need for medical care, including psychiatric care, the person's capacity to respond to interrogation and whether the person can be safely detained in non-health care facilities" (CoE Rec 2004[10] art. 33).

In the "Resolution on the Abuse of Psychiatry" (2002) the WMA notes with concern "evidence from a number of countries that political dissidents and social activists have been detained in psychiatric institutions, and subjected to unnecessary psychiatric treatment as a punishment, declares that such detention and treatment is abusive and unacceptable and calls on physicians and psychiatrists to resist involvement in these abusive practices."

The "Statement on Ethical Issues Concerning Patients with Mental Illness" (WMA 2006) included the following "ethical principles": The discrimination associated with psychiatry and the mentally ill should be eliminated; this stigma often discourages people in need from seeking psychiatric help, thereby aggravating their situation and placing them at risk of emotional or physical harm (par. 7). Every physician should offer the patient the best available therapy to his/her knowledge, and should treat the patient with the solicitude and respect due to all human beings. The physician practising in a prison "can be faced with a conflict between his/her responsibilities to society and the responsibilities to the patient", his primary loyalty and duty must be to the patient's best interest; he should ensure that the patient is made "aware of the conflict in order to minimize feelings of betrayal, and should offer the patient the opportunity to understand measures mandated by legal authority" (par. 11).

A number of mentally ill prisoners may have to be regarded as persons with disabilities in the context of the UN Convention on the Rights of Persons with Disabilities (CRPD 2006), a fact that might be forgotten or not admitted: The CRPD is to be adopted in prisons as well, naturally, whenever and wherever "persons with disabilities" are affected (art. 1 par. 1, cf. art. 13 par. 2 concerning the training of prison staff "to help to ensure effective access to justice for persons with disabilities").

2.5.5   Special Challenges for Physicians and Psychiatrists

What is there to be said about capital punishment other than the human rights obligation to abolition? "Under no circumstances should psychiatrists participate in legally authorized executions nor participate in assessments of competency to be executed" (Madrid Declaration on Ethical Standards for Psychiatric Practice, WPA 2005 art. 3), which is equally true for other physicians and nurses (cf. the WMA Resolution on Physician Participation in Capital Punishment, 2008, and the ICN Position on torture, death penalty and participation by nurses in executions, 2006 and Beck 2009).

No one shall be subjected "without his free consent to medical or scientific experimentation" (CCPR art. 7 par. 2), which is valid even more so for prisoners: "Experiments involving prisoners that may result in physical injury, mental distress or other damage to health shall be prohibited" (EPR 48; cf. the WMA Declaration of Helsinki on Ethical Principles for Medical Research Involving Human Subjects, 2008; for details see Chap. 5).

The prison systems in many countries mandate body cavity searches of prisoners. Such searches, which include rectal and pelvic examination, may be performed when an individual enters the prison population and thereafter whenever the individual is permitted to have personal contact with someone outside the prison population, or when there is a reason to believe a breach of security or of prison regulations has occurred. "These searches are performed for security reasons and not for medical reasons. Nevertheless, they should not be done by anyone other than a person with appropriate medical training" (WMA-Statement on Body Searches of Prisoners 2005). If the search is conducted by a physician, it should not be done by the physician who will also subsequently provide medical care to the prisoner: "The physician's obligation to provide medical care to the prisoner should not be compromised by an obligation to participate in the prison's security system." The WMA urges all governments and public officials with responsibility for public safety to recognize that such invasive search procedures are serious assaults on a person's privacy and dignity, and that they also carry some risk of physical and psychological injury. To the extent feasible without compromising public security, the WMA exhorts "alternate methods be used for routine screening of prisoners, and body cavity searches be used only as a last resort; if a body cavity search must be conducted, the responsible public official must ensure that the search is con- ducted by personnel with sufficient medical knowledge and skills to safely perform the search; the same responsible authority ensures that the individual's privacy and dignity be guaranteed".

Hunger strikes occur in various contexts but they mainly give rise to dilemmas in settings where people are detained (detailed Pont and Riekenbrauck in Keppler and Stöver 2010); they are often a form of protest by people who lack other ways of making their demands known. "Genuine and prolonged fasting risks death or permanent damage for hunger strikers and can create a conflict of values for physi- cians" (WMA Declaration of Malta on Hunger Strikers 2006 preamble). Hunger strikers usually do not wish to die but some may be prepared to do so to achieve their aims. Physicians need to ascertain the individual's true intention, especially in collective strikes or situations where peer pressure may be a factor. "An ethical dilemma arises when hunger strikers who have apparently issued clear instructions not to be resuscitated reach a stage of cognitive impairment", because the principle of beneficence urges physicians to resuscitate them "but respect for individual autonomy restrains physicians from intervening when a valid and informed refusal has been made". An added difficulty arises in custodial settings, "because it is not always clear whether the hunger striker's advance instructions were made volun- tarily and with appropriate information about the consequences" (WMA Declaration of Malta on Hunger Strikers 2006 preamble).

In this context the WMA set up principles, that reach beyond the topic: "All phy- sicians are bound by medical ethics in their professional contact with vulnerable people, even when not providing therapy: Whatever their role, physicians must try to prevent coercion or maltreatment of detainees and must protest if it occurs; hunger strikers should not be forcibly given treatment they refuse: Forced feeding contrary to an informed and voluntary refusal is unjustifiable - artificial feeding with the hunger striker's explicit or implied consent is ethically acceptable; physicians must exercise their skills and knowledge to benefit those they treat: This is the concept of 'beneficence', which is complemented by that of 'non-maleficence' or primum non nocere. These two concepts need to be in balance. 'Benefit' includes respecting individuals' wishes as well as promoting their welfare. Avoiding 'harm' means not only minimising damage to health but also not forcing treatment upon competent people nor coercing them to stop fasting; physicians attending hunger strikers can experience a conflict between their loyalty to the employing authority (such as prison management) and their loyalty to patients: Physicians with dual loyalties are bound by the same ethical principles as other physicians, that is to say that their primary obligation is to the individual patient; physicians must remain objective in their assessments and not allow third parties to influence their medical judgement: They must not allow themselves to be pressured to breach ethical principles, such as intervening medically for non-clinical reasons" (The WMA-Tokyo-Declaration 2006, art. 6).

References

Alfredsson, G., and K. Tomaševski (eds.). 1998. *A thematic guide to documents on health and human rights*. The Hague: Nijhoff.

American Association for Correctional Psychology (ed.). 2010. *Standards for psychology in jails, prisons, correctional facilities, and agencies*. Alexandria: ACA. http://www.eurekalert.org/pub_releases/2010-07/sp-rsf070810.php. Accessed 17 Aug 2010.

Banks, C. 2009. *Criminal justice ethics: Theory and practice*, 2nd ed. Thousand Oaks: Sage.

Beck, W. 2009. Beteiligung von Ärzten an Folter und Todesstrafe. Menschenrechte, Berufsethik und Rollenkonflikte. In *Folter und ärztliche Verantwortung*, ed. H. Furtmayr, K. Krása, and A. Frewer. Göttingen: Unipress.

Beckett, K. 1997. *Making crime pay. Law and order in contemporary American politics*. New York: Oxford University Press.

Boonin, D. 2008. *The problem of punishment*. Cambridge: Cambridge University Press.

Christie, N. 2000. *Crime control as industry. Towards gulags, western style*, 3rd ed. London/New York: Routledge.

Council of Europe (CoE) Convention for the Protection of Human Rights and Dignity of the Human Being with regard to the Application of Biology and Medicine (Oviedo-Convention on Human Rights and Biomedicine). 1997. http://www.coe.int/t/dg3/healthbioethic/Activities/01_Oviedo%20Convention/

CoE-Assembly-Recommendation concerning Problems and Abuses in Psychiatry. 1998. http://assembly.coe.int/Main.asp?link=/Documents/AdoptedText/ta94/EREC1235.htm

CoE-Recommendation concerning the Protection of the Human Rights and Dignity of Persons with Mental Disorder. 2004. http://www.coe.int/t/dg3/healthbioethic/texts_and_documents/Rec(2004)10_e.pdf

Davis, A.Y. 2003. *Are prisons obsolete?* New York: Seven Stories Press.

Decaire, M. (undated). *Ethical concerns in correctional psychology*. http://www.uplink.com.au/lawlibrary/Documents/Docs/Doc93.html. Accessed 17 Aug 2010.

Dostojewski, F. 1860. *The house of the dead*. London: Penguin.

Downes, D. 2001. The *macho* penal economy. In *Mass imprisonment*, ed. D. Garland. London: Sage.

European Charter of Patients' Rights. 2002. http://www.activecitizenship.net/content/blogcategory/32/77/

European Committee for the Prevention of Torture (CPT) Standards. 2002, rev. 2009. http://www.cpt.coe.int/en/documents/eng-standards-scr.pdf

European Convention for the Protection of Human Rights and Fundamental Freedoms (ECHR). 1950. http://conventions.coe.int/treaty/Commun/QueVoulezVous.asp?NT=005&CL=ENG

European Prison Rules (EPR). 2006. https://wcd.coe.int/ViewDoc.jsp?id=955747

Foucault, M. 1995. *Discipline and punish*. New York: Vintage.

Frewer, A., and H. Furtmayr. 2007. *Istanbul-Protokoll: Untersuchung und Dokumentation von Folter und Menschenrechtsverletzungen*. Göttingen: V&R Unipress.

Garland, D. 2001. *The culture of control. Crime and social order in contemporary society*. Oxford: Oxford Universrity Press.

Goffman, E. 1968. *Asylums*. Harmondsworth: Penguin.

International Council of Nurses (ICN) Position on Nurses' Role in the Care of Detainees and Prisoners. 2005. http://www.icn.ch/images/stories/documents/publications/position_statements/A13_Nurses_Role_Detainees_Prisoners.pdf

ICN-Code of Ethics for Nurses (Geneva). 2005. http://www.icn.ch/about-icn/code-of-ethics-for-nurses/

ICN-Position on Torture, Death Penalty and Participation by Nurses in Executions. 2006. http://www.icn.ch/images/stories/documents/publications/position_statements/E13_Torture_Death_Penalty_Executions.pdf

Kallert, T.W., and F. Torres-Gonzáles (eds.). 2006. *Legislation on coercive mental health care in Europe*. Frankfurt: Peter Lang.

Keppler, K., and H. Stöver (eds.). 2010. *Gefängnismedizin*. Stuttgart: Thieme.

Keppler, K., H. Stöver, B. Schulte, and J. Reimer. 2010. Prison health is public health. *Bundesgesundheitsblatt* 53: 233–244.

Kleinig, J. 2008. *Ethics and criminal justice: An introduction*. Cambridge: Cambridge University Press.

Kury, H., and T.N. Ferdinand (eds.). 2008. *International perspectives on punitivity*. Bochum: Brockmeyer.

Liebling, A., and H. Arnold. 2004. *Prisons and their moral performance: A study of values, quality, and prison life*. Oxford: Oxford University Press.

Lippke, R.L. 2007. *Rethinking imprisonment*. Oxford: Oxford University Press.

Livingston, J.D. 2009. *Mental health and substance use services in correctional settings. A review on minimum standards and best practices*. Vancouver: International Centre for Criminal Law – Reform and Criminal Justice Policy. www.icclr.law.ubc.ca. Accessed 16 Aug 2010.

Mahmood, M. 2004. Collateral consequences of the prison industrial complex. *Social Justice* 31: 31–34.

McMahon, M. 1997. Kontrolle als Unternehmen. *Widersprüche* 17: 25–36.

Mehigan, J., and A. Rowe. 2007. Problematizing prison privatization: An overview of the debate. In *Handbook on prisons*, ed. Y. Jewkes. Portland: Willan.

Morgan, R., and M. Evans. 2003. *Bekämpfung der Folter in Europa*. Berlin: Springer.

O'Connor, T. 2006. *Correctional ethics*. www.apsu.edu/oconnort/3300/3300lect06.htm. Accessed 17 Aug 2010.

Pollähne, H. 2007. Der CPT-Bericht über den Deutschland-Besuch 2005. *Recht und Psychiatrie* 25: 120–131.

Pollähne, H. 2010. New economies in the prison system. In *Komplemente in Sachen: Kriminologie, Drogenhilfe, Psychotherapie, Kriminalpolitik*, ed. H. Pollähne and H. Stöver. Berlin: Lit.

Pollock, J.M. 2004. *Ethics in crime and justice*, 4th ed. Belmont: Wadsworth.

Pollock, J.M., and R.F. Becker. 1995. Law enforcement ethics: Using officers' dilemmas as a teaching tool. *Journal of Criminal Justice Education* 6: 1–20.

Schmalleger, F., and Smylka, J.O. 2008. *Corrections in the 21st Century – Ethical Dilemmas*. www.justicestudies.com/ethics04. Accessed 17 Aug 2010.

Sissons, P.L. 1976. The place of medicine in the American prison: Ethical issues in the treatment of offenders. *Journal of Medical Ethics* 2: 173–179.

Stern, V. 2006. *Creating criminals. Prisons and people in a market society.* London/New York: Zed Books.

Sudbury, J. 2004. A world without prisons: Resisting militarism, globalized punishment, and empire. *Social Justice* 31: 9–30.

UN: International Covenant on Civil and Political Rights (CCPR). 1966. http://www2.ohchr.org/english/law/ccpr.htm

UN-Convention Against Torture (CAT). 1984. http://www.un.org/documents/ga/res/39/a39r046.htm

UN-Convention on the Elimination of all Forms of Racial Discrimination (CERD). 1965. http://www2.ohchr.org/english/law/cerd.htm

UN-Convention on the Rights of Persons with Disabilities (CRPD). 2006. http://www.un.org/disabilities/convention/conventionfull.shtml

UN-Covenant on Economic, Social and Cultural Rights (CESCR). 1966. http://www2.ohchr.org/english/law/cescr.htm

UN-Istanbul Protocol: Manual on the Effective Investigation and Documentation of Torture and Other Cruel, Inhuman or Degrading Treatment or Punishment. 1999. http://www.ohchr.org/Documents/Publications/training8Rev1en.pdf

Universal Declaration of Human Rights. 1948. http://www.un.org/en/documents/udhr/

UTMB Institute for Medical Humanities. 2007. *Program on legal and ethical issues in correctional health.* www.utmb.edu/imh/CorrectionalHealth/law.asp. Accessed 17 Aug 2010.

van Zyl-Smit, D., and F. Dünkel (eds.). 2001. *Imprisonment today and tomorrow. International perspectives on prisoners' rights and prison conditions.* The Hague: Kluwer Law.

Wacquant, L. 2008. The place of the prison in the new government of poverty (prisons of poverty). In *After the war on crime: Race, democracy, and a reconstruction,* ed. M.L. Frampton et al. New York: New York University Press.

Weber, M. 1930. *The protestant ethic and the spirit of capitalism.* New York: Scribner's.

World Medical Association (WMA) International Code of Medical Ethics. (rev. 2006). http://www.wma.net/en/30publications/10policies/c8/index.html

WMA-Declaration on Ethical Principles for Medical Research Involving Human Subjects (Helsinki). 2008. http://www.wma.net/en/30publications/10policies/b3/index.html

WMA-Declaration of Geneva. 2006. http://www.wma.net/en/30publications/10policies/g1/

WMA-Declaration on Guidelines for Physicians Concerning Torture and other Cruel, Inhuman or Degrading Treatment or Punishment (Tokyo). 2006. http://www.wma.net/en/30publications/10policies/c18/index.html

WMA-Declaration on Hunger Strikers (Malta). 2006. http://www.wma.net/en/30publications/10policies/h31/index.html

WMA-Declaration on Prison Conditions and the Spread of Tuberculosis and Other Communicable Diseases (Edinburgh). 2000. http://www.wma.net/en/30publications/10policies/p28/index.html

WMA-Declaration on Professional Autonomy and Self-Regulation (Madrid). 2009. http://www.wma.net/en/30publications/10policies/20archives/a21/index.html

WMA-Declaration on Support for Medical Doctors Refusing to Participate in or to Condone the use of Torture or other Forms of Cruel, Inhuman or Degrading Treatment (Hamburg). 1997. http://www.wma.net/en/30publications/10policies/c19/index.html

WMA-Resolution on Physician Participation in Capital Punishment. 2008. http://www.wma.net/en/30publications/10policies/c1/index.html

WMA-Resolution on Prohibition of Physician Participation in Torture (Tel Aviv). 2009. http://www.wma.net/en/30publications/10policies/30council/cr_8/index.html

WMA-Resolution on Responsibility of Physicians in the Denunciation of Acts of Torture or Cruel or Inhuman or Degrading Treatment of which they are Aware. 2007. http://www.wma.net/en/30publications/10policies/t1/index.html

WMA-Resolution on the Abuse of Psychiatry. 2002. http://www.wma.net/en/30publications/10policies/a3/index.html

WMA-Statement on Body Searches of Prisoners. 2005. http://www.wma.net/en/30publications/10policies/b5/index.html

48 H. Pollähne

WMA-Statement on Ethical Issues Concerning Patients with Mental Illness. 2006. http://www.
    wma.net/en/30publications/10policies/e11/index.html
World Psychiatric Association (WPA) Declaration on Ethical Standards for Psychiatric Practice
    (Madrid). 2005. http://www.wpanet.org/detail.php?section_id=5&content_id=48
WPA-Declaration of Hawaii. 1983. http://www.wpanet.org/detail.php?section_id=5&
    content_id=27
WPA-Statement and Viewpoints on the Rights and Legal Safeguards of the Mentally Ill (Athens).
    1989. http://www.wpanet.org/detail.php?section_id=5&content_id=29
Zedner, L. 2004. *Criminal justice*. Oxford: Oxford University Press.

Chapter 3
Ethical Issues in Correctional Psychiatry in the United States

Henry A. Dlugacz, Julie Y. Low, Christopher Wimmer, and Lisa Knox

3.1   Introduction

By their nature, prisons distort human interactions. They may be chaotic and violent places, but even well-run, orderly prisons are created to isolate, control, and stigmatize their inhabitants; at the same time, they are governed by legal and ethical obligations to provide humane conditions of confinement and care for serious medical needs of inmates who are completely dependent upon the institution for the basics of survival. The names of some governmental agencies charged with imprisonment include the words "corrections" or "rehabilitation," signifying at least an aspiration for a mission beyond custody and control. A tension, sometimes destructive and sometimes creative, results when the competing normative values associated with these missions collide. Some individuals handle this situation with remarkable professionalism and compassion; some surrender to less admirable influences. This reflects more than variation in individual temperament; individual reactions to employment in corrections is strongly influenced by the expectations and examples created by those charged with system oversight as well as the characteristics of the setting itself (See, e.g., Haney et al. 1973). The same practice or

H.A. Dlugacz (✉)
Beldock Levine and Hoffman LLP, 99 Park Avenue 16th Floor,
New York, NY 10016, USA
e-mail: hdlugacz@blhny.com

J.Y. Low
New York University Medical School, 1 Fifth Avenue, Suite 1BB,
New York, NY 10003, USA

C. Wimmer
Taylor and Company Law Offices, LLP, One Ferry Building,
Suite 355, San Francisco, CA 94111, USA

L. Knox
Van Der Hout, Brigagliano and Nightingale LLP, 180 Sutter St., 5th Floor,
San Francisco, CA 94104, USA
e-mail: lisa.knox@gmail.com

N. Konrad et al. (eds.), *Ethical Issues in Prison Psychiatry*, International Library
of Ethics, Law, and the New Medicine 46, DOI 10.1007/978-94-007-0086-4_3,
© Springer Science+Business Media Dordrecht 2013

behavior which shocks the conscience when seen for the first time or from afar can come to appear chillingly pedestrian with long-term exposure. The objective perspective which accompanies outside oversight of correctional practice, whether via court-imposed monitoring, regulatory oversight, or well-developed systems of quality improvement which utilize the resources of professionals providing direct care across disciplines but also rely on analysis of aggregate data, is an important ethical counterweight to this natural tendency toward desensitization. Professional and visible frontline supervision which provides a clear sense of organizational mission and vision is critical for maintaining standards of conduct consistent with ethical guidelines.

When viewed structurally, no group of people — correctional officers, treatment staff, or the inmates themselves — is innately immune from the deforming effects of the environment. Inmates, with far too little constructive activity to occupy their minds, may become overly focused on their dissatisfactions or maladies. They may alternatively fabricate or mask symptoms of mental illness in an effort to obtain safer and more desirable housing assignments or access to needed programming. They may engage in behavior which, within the prison context, is viewed pejoratively as "manipulative" but, when seen objectively, is the functional equivalent of behavior which, if engaged in within other social contexts, might be considered more acceptable.

Staff, likewise, is not freed from the necessity of harmonizing — whether consciously or otherwise — the conflicts created by this situation. As a bridge between inmates and correctional staff on one hand, and mental health and medical staff on the other, no one is potentially more caught in the middle of these issues than the correctional psychiatrist.

Successful day-to-day functioning depends on making good choices in dozens of discrete situations: Do I prescribe medication to an inmate-patient who appears to be in distress but has a history of substance abuse and drug-seeking behavior? Do I support an inmate-patient's efforts to obtain a change in housing unit? Much in the same way that a therapist monitors for counter-transference in clinical situations, the correctional psychiatrist must become self-aware of maladaptive coping mechanisms, as long-term success depends upon it: Is there a tendency to over-identify with the punitive and dehumanizing aspects of prison life? Conversely, does the practitioner find him- or herself viewing all inmates as symbols of society's oppression of disenfranchised groups? While one or the other may be more consonant with an individual's worldview, either type of objectification places the psychiatrist at risk of making non-individualized and potentially unethical decisions.

The psychiatrist working within a jail or prison encounters similar ethical dilemmas as do his or her colleagues in community settings, but, additionally, must confront ethical considerations unique to or exacerbated by the confinement environment. Perhaps the most fundamental one is: Do I view the person sitting across the desk from me primarily as "my patient" or "an inmate" – an individual person, or a representative of a group?

While these issues disproportionally involve marginalized groups, large numbers of people are affected. The United States places an extraordinary number of people under the control of the criminal justice system. The trend toward incarcerating so many people, many of whom have serious mental disabilities as well as multiple medical and social difficulties, for longer periods of time followed by increased post-incarceration community supervision, has continued mostly unabated since the 1970s. Until recently, society paid scant attention to the fiscal and social costs associated with this decision. Yet, there are important ramifications of this policy direction related to public health and public safety concerns, the ability of the psychiatrist to meet legal and professional mandates, as well as attention to the sound stewardship of public dollars in a time of economic uncertainty (Dlugacz et al. 2007). None of these can be neatly isolated from ethical considerations for a psychiatrist practicing medicine within a correctional setting. Some of the ethical dilemmas discussed in this chapter, such as dual agency, are inherent to clinical practice in a confined, controlled environment, while others derive from the moral imperative to question the larger context in which treatment occurs and the ethical requirement to provide care meeting professional standards.

One critical aspect of that context is the diminishing access to public hospitals which further amplifies the importance of the medical care provided in jails and prisons. Specifically, the interim report of President Bush's Freedom Commission on Mental Health found that the US community-based "mental health delivery system is fragmented and in disarray" (The President's New Freedom Commission on Mental Health 2003). Seen in this way, correctional healthcare in the United States forms an essential part of the social safety net providing care to an often indigent population (King 2005). Ethical as well as public health mandates may increasingly elevate the healthcare (including mental health) role of correctional institutions; it may no longer be sufficient to accept what has long been taken for granted — that healthcare is necessarily and properly subjugated to the confinement mission of jails and prisons (King 2005; Dlugacz and Roskes 2009). Seen in this larger context, an important ethical issue is raised: Does seeking incremental improvements in substandard correctional mental healthcare merely ease the way of misguided public policy by facilitating large scale incarceration of people with severe mental disabilities? If so, is there a responsible alternative for the individual psychiatrist other than opting out of providing care within the system? If there is, what is the obligation of the individual psychiatrist to engage in advocacy for system change which permits adequate care?

It is also important to understand the more immediate context in which clinicians practice, and struggle to practice ethically. One highly regarded model for the assessment of healthcare quality is referred to as the Donabedian Triad (Glickman et al. 2008), which recognizes the necessity of assessing the organizational attributes or structure in which care is delivered as well as the process by which it is delivered and the outcomes which it obtains. The structure includes the physical characteristics, management, culture, organizational design, information management, and incentives that are present. All aspects of this triad may be dictated by forces beyond the direct control of the correctional psychiatrist:

- Are examination rooms confidential?
- Is there access to the information technology so essential to the modern practice of medicine?
- Do staffing patterns permit caseload sizes that allow individualized treatment?
- Is there sufficient custody staffing so that they may facilitate participation in treatment?
- Is there reasonable access to various levels of care including inpatient hospitalization when clinically indicated?

- Is the physician responsible to a healthcare or custody authority?
- What formulary and diagnostic tests are available?
- Does evaluation of inmates housed in extreme conditions of confinement legitimate a practice which many believe harms people with serious mental illness?

One example of structural concerns unique to the correctional setting is that most inmate-patients with mental illness will be released before their condition is fully resolved, and will not have access to the correctional system's mental healthcare after release. The American Medical Association's (AMA 2010) Ethical Standard 10.01, Fundamental Elements of Patient-Physician Relationship, provides that the patient has the right to continuity of healthcare, the physician has an obligation to cooperate in coordination with other providers treating the patient, and the physician may not discontinue treatment of a patient as long as further treatment is medically indicated, pointing to an ethical duty to facilitate reentry planning for some discharged inmates. The above are just some issues that implicate the need for the "system" as a whole to provide the correctional psychiatrist with the tools and autonomy to act ethically. This understanding also raises the related question of what ethical responsibility inures to a psychiatrist to advocate for a system that permits and facilitates ethical practice. Seen this way, professional organizations have a concomitant ethical duty to require and support needed change (Metzner and Fellner 2010).

After providing background data concerning levels of confinement and characteristics of the incarcerated population, this chapter will review the standards that govern the ethical practice of psychiatry in correctional institutions and explore specific ethical problems facing the American correctional psychiatrist.

3.2   Incarceration of Persons with Mental Illness in the United States

It is now well known that the United States incarcerates an astonishing number of people compared to Western European countries. At year-end 2011, American prisons and jails held almost 2.25 million inmates – 1 out every 107 adult American residents (United States Department of Justice, Bureau of Justice Statistics 2012). This is roughly equivalent to the entire population of Latvia (Central Intelligence Agency (CIA) 2009). It is estimated that between 8 and 19 % of prisoners are persons with serious mental illness, and another 15–20 % require some form of psychiatric care during their incarceration (United States Department of Justice, Bureau of Justice Statistics 1999; Metzner 2002; Magaletta et al. 2009). Offenders with mental disabilities are more likely to recidivate, more likely to recidivate for violent crimes, and receive longer sentences than offenders who do not have mental disabilities (United States Department of Justice, Bureau of Justice Statistics 1999). They are also more likely to be punished for disciplinary infractions while in prison (United States Department of Justice, Bureau of Justice Statistics 1999). Data from US studies indicate that two-thirds of all inmates with serious mental illness are rearrested and one-half are hospitalized within the first 18 months of release (Feder

1991; Hartwell 2008). One US study found that in the first two weeks following release inmates as a group were close to 13 times more likely to die as compared with other people with similar demographics (Binswanger et al. 2007).

Persons with mental disabilities may also suffer grievously from incarceration. The social isolation, sensory deprivation alternating with unpredictable stimuli, loss of autonomy, lack of continuity of care, and frequent, severe punishment for aberrant behavior that characterize some American prisons all may exacerbate mental illness and result in decompensation (Fellner 2008, 2009. But see O'Keefe et al. 2010, questioning this hypothesis). This, in turn, may produce inmates less capable of establishing productive, lawful lives upon discharge (Lovell et al. 2007).

3.3   Standards

There are a host of formal standards that inform the practice of psychiatry in American correctional institutions. As in other areas of the American legal system, actors are subject to a web of federal, state, and local legal requirements. These requirements can further be divided into constitutional standards and statutory and regulatory standards. This chapter focuses on federal constitutional standards. International legal standards, which tend to be more stringent (Fellner 2010), also merit consideration for the views and experiences of other nations they embody. Finally, professional psychiatric organizations have established ethical guidelines for practice.

It is worth considering how these standards inform ethical obligations. The applicability of the guidelines established by professional organizations seems self-evident: The members of the profession have, through experience and consultation, developed a set of guidelines representing best practices and standards of care. Upon becoming a member of that profession, one takes a vow to adhere to these standards.

Domestic legal standards are somewhat different. American legal standards arise from three sources: (1) the elected legislative bodies, which pass statutes; (2) the executive branches (which include elected actors and their appointees), which promulgate regulations and set policies for executive action; and (3) the judiciary (which is appointed in the federal system, and either elected or appointed in the states), which is responsible for ensuring that executive action conforms with legislative and constitutional requirements, and that legislative action conforms with the nation's and states' fundamental commitments expressed in their constitutions. As any practitioner knows, straying from these requirements exposes one to significant, potentially career-ending, liability. Familiarity with them can thus be justified by self-interest. However, awareness of these standards is also necessary in order to carry out ethical duties to one's patients. Legal standards, be they constitutional, statutory, or regulatory, represent the polity's collective determination of what must, and what must not, be done. They set an absolute minimum for conduct; that is why liability attaches to violations of them. In the context of psychiatry or other medical fields, they represent the nation's, states', and municipalities' expression of the basic standard of care. Further, when assuming membership in the profession, psychiatrists pledge to adhere to applicable law (American Psychiatric Association (APA) 2009). Domestic legal standards thus provide a key set of sources of ethical guidelines for mental health practitioners in American correctional institutions.

International standards are another matter. International treaties that the nation has not ratified do not become American law, though signing a treaty commits the nation to acting in accordance with the principles of that treaty (VCLT 1969). Even ratified treaties bind only governmental actors – individual, private actors will be legally bound only by statutes or regulations passed to implement those treaties. Absent conduct of breathtaking scope, no American psychiatrist will be prosecuted for violations of international law taken within the United States. Further, any judgment by the international courts against an individual would be unenforceable within the United States. The oath taken by psychiatrists on accession to the profession is silent on adherence to non-binding international standards. So how are they relevant? As professionals, psychiatrists owe an ethical duty to their patients to continually seek to improve their knowledge and their standards of practice. International legal standards, like domestic legal standards, represent the collective determination of the polities of appropriate standards of care. Unless one takes the view that the practice of psychiatry in other nations is somehow fundamentally different from practice in the United States, the experiences of psychiatrists in other nations – as embodied in standards of care developed in consultation with them – are worth consideration, if not outright adherence. This is the approach that the United States Supreme Court has developed with respect to international law in its jurisprudence concerning the federal Eighth Amendment's ban on cruel and unusual punishments: International law is not binding, but is an important source of information about whether a challenged punishment is out of step with the evolving standards of decency that inform the Court's decision whether a punishment is "cruel and unusual." Further, the US Supreme Court in three criminal procedure and criminal law cases, over vigorous dissent, has endorsed an expansive reading of international law principles in a domestic constitutional law context (Perlin and Dlugacz 2009). The possible US ratification of the UN Convention on the Rights of Persons with Disabilities could bolster efforts to use international human rights conventions to support claims seeking improved treatment for confined individuals; at present, it may be that international standards are most accurately viewed as forming a best practice approach warranting consideration by US psychiatrists and courts (Perlin and Dlugacz 2009; see, also *In the Matter of SCPA Article 17-A Guardianship Proceeding for Mark C.H.* (2010)). At a minimum, then, American practitioners owe an ethical duty to consider international standards – and the evolving best practices of the international community that they represent – when assessing their own conduct.

3.3.1 Domestic Professional Standards

American professional associations have issued both general codes of ethics that are applicable to all psychiatrists, including those practicing in correctional institutions, and more particular guidelines aimed at the specific concerns of correctional psychiatrists.

The American Psychiatric Association's *Principles of Medical Ethics With Annotations Especially Applicable to Psychiatry* (APA 2009), which builds on the AMA's ethics code, apply to all psychiatrists, regardless of their environment. It enunciates several principles pertinent to practice in correctional institutions, including the obligations to act "with compassion and respect for human dignity and rights," to "seek changes in those [legal] requirements which are contrary to the best interests of the patient," to "support access to medical care for all people," and to "regard responsibility to the patient as paramount."

The American Public Health Association's (APHA) *Standards for Health Services in Correctional Institutions* (APHA 2003) and the National Commission on Correctional Health Care's (NCCHC) *Standards for Mental Health Services in Correctional Facilities* (NCCHC 2008) address a host of structural and patient-specific concerns, including clinical independence, participation in forensic gathering for disciplinary proceedings, forced medication, and executions. Applications of these principles are considered below.

3.3.2 Federal Constitutional Requirements

As noted, there are federal constitutional, state constitutional, and federal, state, and local statutory and regulatory standards designed to ensure inmate' access to a minimum quality of psychiatric services while incarcerated. The predominant source of law, and the one most interesting for consideration of a correctional psychiatrist's ethical duties, is the Eighth Amendment to the United States Constitution.

The United States Supreme Court has interpreted the Eighth Amendment's ban on "cruel and unusual punishments" to establish minimum standards of medical care for prisoners. Courts have applied these standards to the provision of mental healthcare. In brief, "deliberate indifference . . . to serious medical needs of prisoners" amounts to "unnecessary and wanton infliction of pain" in violation of the Eighth Amendment's prohibition on cruel and unusual punishment (*Estelle* v. *Gamble* 1976). Because the Supreme Court has established that the Eighth Amendment's requirements are determined by an "evolving standard of decency," developments in a significant number of state policies can raise the standards of care that all states and the federal government must meet (*Graham* v. *Florida* 2010).

This standard includes both systemic and individual components. Systemically, courts have typically required that correctional institutions provide the following basic services: Screening and evaluation by which inmates with serious mental health disorders can be identified; a sufficient quantity of trained staff to provide individualized treatment to inmates with treatable, serious disorders; mechanisms for proper administration of psychotropic medication; adequate record-keeping; and a system to prevent suicides and respond to suicide attempts and other mental health emergencies (*Ruiz* v. *Estelle* 1980; *Madrid* v. *Gomez* 1995; *Coleman* v. *Schwarzenegger* 2009). An emerging consensus among some states and major cities that post-release planning is a necessary component of mental healthcare in the prison setting presents the possibility that this may become enshrined by the courts as another necessary element (Dlugacz and Low 2007; Mellow and Greifinger 2008; Dlugacz and Roskes 2009). Individually, the Eighth Amendment requires that the methods used to maintain control over or discipline an inmate with mental illness must have a valid penological purpose, and must take into account the individual's potential inability to conform his conduct to the rules of the institution or understand the reason for the punishment inflicted upon him (*Thomas* v. *Bryant* 2010).

Supreme Court precedent establishes that courts will defer to the proper exercise of judgment by a qualified professional (*Youngberg* v. *Romeo* 1982; Perlin 2005). However, the presumptive validity of a treatment decision made by qualified profes- sionals using professional judgment exists only to the extent that professional judgment was in fact brought to bear in making the determination in question. In the correctional system there are many factors militating against the genuine exercise of a psychiatrist's professional judgment, including financial, administrative, and disciplinary influences. Courts have not allowed these factors to excuse the failure to exercise professional judgment. For example, professionals have been found to have departed from this standard when: (1) no judgment was exercised at all; (2) judgments were made by non-professionals or unqualified professionals; or (3) judgments were made for inappropriate reasons such as budgetary limitations or staff convenience (Stefan 1993). As will be discussed below, this obligation to exercise professional judgment frequently runs up against the custodial demands of the correctional institution. These concepts reinforce that at times ethical behavior must be exercised by the system as a whole, and that individual conduct alone is insufficient to meet expectations.

3.3.3   International Standards

3.3.3.1   Partial Incorporation into American Law

The United States is party to three international treaties that concern ethical obliga- tions of mental health professionals in the correctional context. The prohibitions on torture and cruel, inhumane, or degrading treatment contained in the Convention Against Torture (CAT 1984) have been binding on the US since it ratified the treaty in 1994. The Universal Declaration of Human Rights (UDHR 1948), though not legally binding, also prohibits torture and cruel, inhumane, or degrading treatment. Article 8 of the International Covenant on Civil and Political Rights (ICCPR 1966), ratified by the US in 1992, contains similar prohibitions. Article 10 of the ICCPR further requires that "all persons deprived of their liberty shall be treated with humanity and with respect for the inherent dignity of the human person", which has been interpreted to protect the right to confidentiality and informed consent in healthcare (UN Human Rights Committee 1992). The United States has also signed, but not yet ratified, the Convention on the Rights of Persons with Disabilities (CRPD

2006), which affirms the right of persons with mental illness to equal protection under the law, and is a potential new source of law for those seeking to enhance the outcomes of inmates with mental illness through litigation or policy (CRPD 2006; Perlin and Dlugacz 2009).

The UN Standard Minimum Rules for the Treatment of Prisoners (SMRTP 1955), while not a binding treaty, provides some ethical guidance for correctional mental health practice. Rule 25.2 requires medical professionals to notify prison officials whenever continued confinement or conditions of confinement are negatively impacting a prisoner's mental health. Rule 83 recommends that medical staff provide for continuity of psychiatric treatment post-release (UN 1955).

Domestic professional associations have incorporated these and other relevant international instruments. The American Correctional Association (ACA) has referenced the SMRTPs as "the prototype" for prison standards (ACA 2004). The APA's standards for health services intend to ensure compliance with relevant international treaties and standards, including the Standard Minimum Rules, the ICCPR, and CAT (APHA 2003).

States have also incorporated the SMRTPs in correctional standards. In 1971, the Pennsylvania Department of Corrections became the first state correctional department to adopt the SMRTPs through an Administrative Directive. Five other states subsequently adopted them through Department of Corrections directives, while three states adopted them by executive order (Skoler 1975). Though the majority place some limitations on their application (most frequently, directing implementation only insofar as the SMRTPs do not conflict with federal, state, or local law), these limitations do not significantly alter the spirit or impact of the mental health provisions. While the SMRTPs may set a higher standard than that required by the Eighth Amendment, it is commonplace to American constitutional law that states may set standards more protective of individual liberties than that contained in the federal constitution (*PruneYard Shopping Center* v. *Robins* 1980).

A few US courts have considered international standards in cases involving inadequate prison healthcare. In *Estelle* v. *Gamble* (1976), the Supreme Court, while basing its finding that unnecessary suffering caused by lack of healthcare "is inconsistent with contemporary standards of decency" on domestic legislation and standards, noted that the SMRTPs are also in accord. The Oregon Supreme Court (*Sterling* v. *Cupp* 1981), Utah Supreme Court (*Bott* v. *DeLand* 1996), and United States District Court for the District of Connecticut (*Lareau* v. *Manson* 1980) have also relied in part on the ICCPR, UDHR, and SMRTPs in cases regarding prisoner treatment and living conditions. Though not concerned with prisoners' rights per se, a very recent lower New York State court decision considered the CRPD when setting the terms of a guardianship for a man with a mental disability (*In the Matter of SCPA Article 17-A Guardianship Proceeding for Mark C.H.* 2010).

Taken together, the incorporation of international ethical standards into domestic ethics codes and case law has to some extent integrated these principles into the standard of care for correctional mental health services. Per *Gamble*, mental healthcare violates the Eighth Amendment prohibition on cruel and unusual punishment only if it constitutes "deliberate indifference to serious medical needs".

However, the *Sterling*, *Bott* and *Lareau* courts imply that extreme deviation from the standard of care embodied in international treaties and protocols can rise to the level of deliberate indifference and violate prisoners' constitutional rights.

3.3.3.2 Differences in Standards of Care

International ethical standards, while cognizant of the need for psychiatrists to balance public obligations with duties to patients, accord much greater weight to patient obligations than domestic standards. Beyond principles of beneficence and non-malfeasance, international professional standards impose an affirmative duty on psychiatrists to protect the health of patients. While domestic standards often subordinate patient rights to applicable domestic law, under international standards human rights obligations are absolute.

The higher weight accorded to patient obligations is particularly clear in standards regarding informed consent. The World Health Organization (WHO 2005) has noted that patients in prison mental health facilities have the same rights to confidentiality and informed consent as any other involuntary confined patients. According to the World Medical Association ethics code (WMA 2009), this strong imperative to obtain informed consent in international standards prohibits forced medication to restore competency for trial or execution, and counsels against forced medication even where it may be in the patient's best medical interest. While domestic standards similarly limit forced medication to situations where an inmate is dangerous to himself or others, they place a much greater emphasis on compliance with state law, which may allow for forced medication for trial or execution.

This strong pro-patient stance is also reflected in international ethical standards regarding torture and interrogation. Unlike domestic standards, where the prohibition on torture is absolute but indirect participation in interrogation is allowed, international standards prohibit all participation in interrogation or torture. The World Medical Association's Declaration of Tokyo (WMA 1975) states that medical professionals should not participate in, condone, provide instruments or knowledge for, or even be present where torture or cruel, inhumane, or degrading treatment are used, or even threatened. The UN Principles for Medical Ethics (1982) also broadly prohibit physicians from applying their "knowledge and skills" to aid in any interrogation that may adversely affect the health of detainees. Physicians for Human Right's Guidelines for Prison, Detention and Other Custodial Settings (PHR 2002) go further, prohibiting even passive participation in torture or any form of punishment as a breach of loyalty to the patient.

International standards on torture also go beyond prohibition on participation, and impose an affirmative obligation to protect prisoners from harm. The PHR Guidelines (2002) for Health Professional Practice require physicians to "report to the custodial authorities and, where appropriate, to an independent medical authority" any situation where prisoners are possibly being subjected to torture or cruel, inhuman, or degrading treatment, unless reporting would cause further harm to the prisoner. PHR's Proposed General Guidelines for Health Professional Practice

(2006) extend this duty to any potential rights violations, requiring physicians to affirmatively resist "demands or requests by the state or third party interests to subordinate patient human rights to state or third party interests."

Many domestic standards contain no such obligation. Neither the APHA (2003) nor NCCHC (2008) standards mention an affirmative duty on the part of psychiatrists to report harm. While the AMA and APA require psychiatrists to report any "coercive" interrogations or violations of patients' rights to authorities, they also counsel that psychiatrists follow applicable national, state, and local laws (APA 2009). Where the two conflict (for instance, where local regulations require psychiatrists to prescribe involuntary medication for punitive purposes), the AMA and APA offer no solution.

3.4 Problems and Dilemmas

We discuss below a series of problems and dilemmas facing the psychiatrist practicing in the American correctional setting. These various dilemmas can be traced to a single underlying question: Does a psychiatrist's participation in the current American correctional system, which increasingly intends to punish and incapacitate inmates, rather than rehabilitate them, benefit the inmate patients, or simply legitimize a destructive public policy approach that incarcerates so many people with mental disabilities? This chapter proceeds from the assumption that it is ethical for the psychiatrist to participate but only when he or she undertakes legitimate efforts to improve conditions. This often cannot be accomplished by acting alone, but that reality does not absolve the psychiatrist, supported by professional organizations and meaningful internal quality improvement efforts when required, from making good faith efforts at reform (Metzner and Fellner 2010).

3.4.1 Realities of the Corrections Setting

The American correctional system has undergone dramatic changes in the past 50 years. For much of US history, the primary focus of the system, and the declared philosophical rationale for criminal sentencing, was to rehabilitate offenders so that they could be returned to productive participation in the community. Around the 1970s, the belief in the possibility of rehabilitation waned, and a punitive mindset driven by fear of crime and manipulated by public officials resulted in a system built conceptually around incapacitation of the offender and retribution for his offenses. These tendencies resulted not only in longer prison sentences, but also in the elimination of many programs designed to prepare prisoners for reentry – education, vocational training, and the like (Weinstein and Wimmer 2010). The term "corrections" now sounds like a euphemism, rather than the statement of purpose it once was.

Ironically, at the same time, conditions of confinement and resources to provide treatment improved within some systems, generally where required by court order or terms of consent decrees entered into by parties to litigation.

Over the same period, there has occurred a sea change in the American approach to mental illness. Institutionalization of persons with mental illness fell out of favor, and American states reduced their role in providing institutional care. However, little provision was made by the states for mental healthcare in the community, and private healthcare providers were not prepared for the sudden release of massive numbers of adults with mental illness. Again, over the same period, funding for social programs has been drained, leaving many individuals with mental disabilities without occupation, healthcare, or resources. The number of homeless or near-homeless persons with mental illness increased dramatically. Again, over the same period, and subject to some of the same conditions, drug addiction has increased dramatically, with similar outcomes. The result has been an over-burdened prison system which in some cases is without the capacity, resources, or political will to respond to the serious medical needs of its many inmates with mental illness or addiction (Abramsky and Fellner 2003).

Before the advent of managed care, correctional institutions represented one of the most different environments in which to practice psychiatry, and medicine in general, as the correctional institution represents a microcosm of unique financial and logistical pressures. Managed care organizations transformed the practice of medicine by creating their own unique microcosms as well, with new logistical and economic requirements for doctors. The challenge for physicians in the managed care era is to incorporate the best clinical care standards of medicine into the economic models established by different insurance companies. In effect, managed care physicians now must safeguard optimal clinical care against the continuous pressure to limit cost expenditures exacted by managed care agencies. Although the legal standards between tort and constitutional law may differ, for the physician, there is an ethical as well as legal mandate to provide good care to his or her patients, care that should meet the accepted clinical standards of the profession, as laid out by the relevant medical associations and the most recent clinical research. While some of the specific obstacles are unique to the correctional setting, this precept is no less applicable to the psychiatrist practicing in a jail or prison than it is to one providing care in a community setting.

In much the same way, physicians working in the correctional setting also work amidst sometimes conflicting duties. "[I]f professional ethics requires that treatment providers protect the well-being of those with whom they work, in what manner and under what circumstances can they work in a correctional institution consistent with the functions of that institution, one of which is to inflict punishment on convicted offenders?" (Schopp 2009).

This tension can be the reality for many psychiatrists working in the correctional system. A psychiatrist working in accordance with the ethical standards of his or her profession should have therapeutic care as the ultimate goal, but he or she is enclosed within a system that may contain rehabilitative aspects, but is punitive at its core. For example, in cases where psychiatric treatment may restore competency, the courts have determined that there is a "protected liberty interest in being free from involuntarily imposed treatment," but they balance this interest against the "important state interests" in preventing harm in the prison context and in bringing serious criminal charges to trial (*Sell* v. *United States* 2003; *Riggins v. Nevada* 1992; *United States* v. *Weston* 2001). Just as in a managed care entity, there are also economic pressures in a correctional institution. Correctional medicine may be administered by a for-profit company, an academic center, or the city or state. Regardless of the nature of the administration, there are always fiscal and formulary concerns.

Psychiatry practiced in the correctional setting may, in some instances, differ in quality and scope from psychiatry practiced in the community. This discrepancy in practice should not exist; yet the difference persists in some correctional settings for complex and varied reasons. Some of these reasons are considered in the sections that follow.

3.4.2 Dual Agency

There are numerous ethical conflicts that may arise from the uneasy relationship between the correctional psychiatrist's role as employee of the correctional institution and caregiver to the inmate – patient. The most fundamental conflict is the "dual agency" of the psychiatrist, being a participatory agent both to the patient and to the correctional institution. Situations that have clearly illustrated this inherent conflict of roles include correctional physicians participating in disciplinary proceedings, research, interrogation, or torture of prisoners. The ethical question underlying these issues is how the physician chooses between the possible benefit to the many (e.g. knowledge stemming from research discoveries) and the benefit to the incarcerated individual.

Dual agency means that there is an inherent conflict of interest: The physician has a responsibility to serve two masters, whose agendas may be quite different, thereby complicating the process of collecting data and formulating a report or implementing an intervention. The dilemma of double agency can involve schools, correctional institutions, or lawyers. Forensic psychiatrists can be influenced due to "the instinctual process of identifying with the goals of the people with whom one is working" (Applebaum 2008). In that vein, the fact that correctional psychiatrists are usually employed and remunerated by the correctional institution may also present an unavoidable conflict of interest. Psychiatrists whose "personal views distort the objectivity of their evaluations . . . [are not] competent forensic psychiatrists" (Dike 2008).

This fundamental problem plays out in various contexts – confidentiality, participation in disciplinary proceedings, forced medication, and interrogations and torture.

3.4.2.1 Confidentiality Requirements and Exceptions

Professional standards dictate that, with few exceptions, inmates are entitled to the same confidentiality protections afforded to all other patients. The APHA standards prohibit disclosing patient information without consent, except where necessary to respond to a "clear and present danger of grave injury to the prisoner or others or if the prisoner plans to escape" (APHA 2003). The NCCHC's 2008 standards include confidentiality of patient medical information as an essential element, subject only to the "duty to warn" exceptions discussed below (NCCHC 2008).

There are two generally recognized exceptions to confidentiality of inmate mental health information, both of which relate to safety and security concerns. First, most statutes and professional standards recognize an exception where there is an imminent risk of escape or rioting. The second exception is where an inmate poses an imminent risk of harm to himself or others. The second, commonly known as the "duty to warn," was established by the California Supreme Court in *Tarasoff* v. *Regents of the University of California* (1976). There, the court determined that a psychotherapist could be held legally liable for his failure to warn a third party that had been threatened by his patient, holding that "the confidential character of patient-psychotherapist communications must yield to the extent that disclosure is essential to avert danger to others. The protective privilege ends where the public peril begins." Most states have adopted *Tarasoff*'s duty to warn exception, though a few have narrowed the duty or declined to recognize it altogether (*People* v. *Bierenbaum* 2002).

Federal statutes, such as the Health Information Portability and Accountability Act of 1996, also impose a legal obligation to safeguard medical information, though their application in the prison context is limited. In June 2010 the Ninth Circuit became the eighth federal circuit to find that "prisoners do not have a constitutionally protected expectation of privacy in prison treatment records when the state has a legitimate penological interest in access to them" (*Seaton* v. *Mayberg* 2010). The majority of cases have dealt with disclosure of HIV status, which courts have found permissible in light of the state's strong interest in controlling the spread of a communicable, fatal disease. The Ninth Circuit found this "legitimate penological interest" extends beyond HIV control, to include the broader need to protect prisoners and staff from any communicable disease and/or violence.

However, while such disclosures may be permissible under the Constitution and federal privacy statutes, it is important to note that practitioners are still bound by the applicable state medical privacy acts, and professional standards.

Additional complications arise from the varied nature of the services provided by correctional psychiatrists. Depending on the institution, psychiatrists may provide direct services for the benefit of the patient such as crisis interventions, adjustment counseling, psychiatric medication and treatment, individual and group therapy, substance abuse treatment, and specialized lifestyle and skill-building programs (Bonner and Vandecreek 2006). They may also perform services for custodial purposes to benefit the institution, such as intakes, segregation reviews, special evaluations, parole board evaluations, suicide risk assessments, and violence risk assessments (*id.*). Aside from the risk of direct disclosure of direct services records to custodial personnel, there is also the risk of indirect and unintentional disclosure when the psychiatrist's knowledge of the patient gathered from direct services work influences her evaluation for custodial purposes. For example, a physician evaluating a patient for parole who is aware that the patient has expressed antisocial inclinations during psychiatric treatment will almost certainly bring that knowledge into her parole board evaluation, even if the patient's responses during the parole evaluation are appropriate. While that carryover may potentially benefit public safety, it is a violation of patient confidentiality in the absence of facts justifying application of the *Tarasoff* rule. Some have recommended that inmates be given detailed explanations of the varying functions undertaken by mental health staff, and the different rules regarding confidentiality that apply to them (*id.*), but many inmates with mental illness may not be able to appreciate and understand these distinctions.

3.4.2.2 Disciplinary Proceedings

Disciplinary proceedings to punish inmate violations of prison rules exist in every American correctional institution. They can result in a reduction of privileges, placement in segregation, or loss of good-time credits (and an accompanying extension of the time left to be served). Prisoners with mental illness are more likely than others to be charged with disciplinary infractions (United States Department of Justice, Bureau of Justice Statistics 1999).

As a result of litigation brought on behalf of prisoners, the Supreme Court has established that inmates are entitled to a fair hearing before they may be found guilty of a disciplinary charge. The hearing must include timely notice of the charges, the opportunity to call witnesses (which might include psychiatrists working in the prison), and the opportunity to present documentary evidence (which might include medical records) (*Wolff* v. *McDonnell* 1974). In the past 15 years, mental health practitioners have increasingly been called on to participate, in differing capacities, in prison disciplinary proceedings (Krelstein 2002). This increased involvement has arisen in part out of a concern – brought to the fore by litigation brought on behalf of prisoners – that prison officials were overlooking the role of mental illness in prisoners' rule violations (*id.*). Nonetheless, psychiatric involvement in disciplinary proceedings creates ethical dilemmas for the practitioner.

As elsewhere in American correctional psychiatry, the basic dilemma is whether the psychiatrist's participation in a punitive system will, on the whole, benefit the patient. The psychiatrist called upon to participate in disciplinary proceedings may be asked to determine whether the inmate is competent to proceed, whether mental illness may have contributed to the disciplinary infraction, whether the patient bears psychological responsibility for the infraction, and what types of punishment can be safely imposed (Krelstein 2002).

The first question for the psychiatrist receiving an inmate referral on these questions is one of the psychiatrist's competency to comment on the questions presented. The correctional population offers unique clinical challenges that may not have been covered in the psychiatrist's graduate studies (Bonner and Vandecreek 2006), and determining whether a patient is competent and whether mental illness contributed to a rule infraction demands a set of forensic skills not possessed by every practitioner. Self-policing is critical in this area. Courts and attorneys may be ill-equipped to determine whether the practitioner possesses the necessary expertise, and may also be especially reliant on the practitioner for competency determinations (Redding and Murrie 2010).

The second question is one of confidentiality. If the psychiatrist is called to testify or provide documents by prison officials, rather than by the patient, how can she do so without violating patient confidentiality? As noted above, can she separate the knowledge she has gained from evaluations undertaken for custodial purposes from those undertaken for the patient's benefit? Relatedly, can she testify or provide documents without fatally undermining the inmate patient's trust in her, which is key to successful outcomes?

The third question is one of harm. Participation in disciplinary proceedings on behalf of the institution makes the psychiatrist an active part, or at least complicit, in the punitive workings of the prison. Her testimony and records may be used to extend an inmate's sentence, deprive him of recreational or educational activities, or place him in solitary confinement – all potentially injurious of mental health. At the same time, favorable testimony (for example, in those facilities that consider it, evidence that an infraction was the product of mental illness, or that particular punishments are contraindicated), even if elicited by the institution, may spare the prisoner unnecessary harm, or, ideally, lead to a change in treatment plan aimed at addressing maladaptive behavior resulting from an exacerbation of symptoms. In reaching these conclusions, then, it is critical that the psychiatrist understand how her testimony will factor into the disciplinary proceeding.

3.4.2.3 Forced Medication

Courts have addressed the issue of correctional psychiatrists' dual loyalties primarily in the context of forced medication. While they have employed a balancing test to weigh prisoner rights against state interests, courts have generally supported restrictions that purport to protect public health and safety even where they place significant limitations on prisoner's rights. As a result, forced medication has been deemed legally permissible by courts in situations where they are prohibited by professional ethical standards and where due process protections are significantly curtailed as compared to analogous proceedings in civil hospital settings.

The APHA's correctional standards restrict the use of "restraints," which are defined to include "drugs to control behavior" to "emergency situations if needed to prevent prisoners from harming themselves or others," and for "the shortest time possible and with the least restriction possible" (APHA 2003). It prohibits the use of medication "as a means of coercion, discipline, convenience, or retaliation" by medical staff. Similarly, the NCCHC limits the use of forced medication to "emergency situations" in order "to prevent harm" and prohibits its use "simply to control behavior or as a disciplinary measure" (NCCHC 2008).

The ethical issues raised by the three situations – forced medication to stand trial, forced medication while incarcerated, and forced medication for execution – all turn on the same fundamental question: Does the treatment benefit the patient? Forced medication to render a criminal defendant competent to stand trial potentially exposes the defendant to criminal punishment: If he remains incompetent, he cannot be made to stand trial, and so will not be imprisoned. However, those adjudged to be incompetent to stand trial may be civilly committed for periods as long as or longer than the criminal sentence they would have received if convicted, and are entitled to far fewer procedural protections. Further, a criminal defendant who is rendered competent may be able to assist his attorney in mounting a defense.

Forced medication during incarceration, like forced medication outside the prison, violates patient autonomy – a fundamental decision about care is being made against the patient's will. However, there is a possibility of long-run benefits to the incarcerated patient that may justify that encroachment. As noted above, prison rules are many and strict and the consequences for violating them can be harsh. An inmate found guilty of disciplinary charges may, for example, lose exercise privileges, lose good-time credits that would have shortened his prison sentence, be transferred to another facility, or be placed in solitary confinement, with potentially devastating mental health consequences (Metzner and Fellner 2010). Placement in any sort of heightened detention will make it even more difficult for a psychiatrist to provide less intrusive methods of care such as counseling or monitoring of the inmate patient's condition. A transfer disrupts the continuity of care.

Forced medication for execution would seem to present the easiest case. Under current American constitutional law, one so mentally ill as to be unable to appreciate the reason for his execution cannot be executed. Medicating for the express purpose of permitting an individual's execution would not seem to serve the patient's interest in any manner. The austere vision of Kantian retributivism, which holds that the only way to honor an individual as a moral actor is to punish him in the same measure as his wrongful acts, fits poorly with the principles of beneficence and non-malfeasance underpinning professional ethical guidelines.

In *Washington* v. *Harper* (1990), the Supreme Court first sanctioned the use of forced medication in the prison context. The court weighed the state's "legitimate penological interest" in prison safety and security against a prisoner's liberty interest in remaining free from unwanted medication under the Due Process Clause of the Fourteenth Amendment. It found that the state may "treat a prison inmate who has a serious mental illness with antipsychotic drugs against his will, if the inmate is dangerous to himself or others and the treatment is in the inmate's medical interest." In doing so, the Court relied in part on medical ethics as a safeguard: Psychiatrists will not prescribe medication not in the medical interest of a prisoner because it would be contrary to medical ethics.

Two years later, in *Riggins* v. *Nevada* (1992), the Court suggested that forced medication to render an inmate competent for trial might be appropriate even if the inmate were not a danger to himself or others. It then definitively held in *Sell* v. *United States* (2003) that forced medication could be used to restore competency for trial where (1) individual factors do not lessen the importance of governmental interest in prosecution; (2) forced medication is "substantially likely" to render the defendant competent to stand trial without rendering the trial unfair; and (3) "alternative, less intrusive treatments are unlikely to achieve substantially the same results." The Court also left intact the *Harper* requirement that medication be in a prisoner's medical interest. Rather than address the ethical dilemma this type of forced medication poses, the Court focused on the narrow application of its ruling: Because courts will first examine forced medication on alternative, *Harper* grounds, in most cases "the need to consider authorization on trial competence grounds will likely disappear."

Though the Supreme Court has found that the Eighth Amendment prohibits states from executing prisoners who are insane (*Ford* v. *Wainwright* 1986), it has declined to address the issue of whether states may use forced medication to overcome the *Ford* prohibition. It has also declined to set a single standard that would govern all competency determinations under *Ford*, though it has held that a defendant who makes a "substantial threshold showing" of incompetency must have the opportunity to submit expert psychiatric evidence in support of his claim of incompetency (*Panetti* v. *Quarterman* 2007).

Courts that have weighed medical ethics have found that forced medication in this context is unconstitutional, because it is against the patient's medical interests. In *State* v. *Perry* (1992), the Louisiana Supreme Court found that forced medication for execution constitutes unconstitutional inhumane treatment. In doing so, it cited medical ethics standards as "further objective evidence" that the practice violated contemporary standards of decency. The South Carolina Supreme Court reached a similar conclusion in *Singleton* v. *State* (1993). It too looked to medical ethics, concluding that the "medical ethical position reinforces the mandates of our constitutional law" and prohibits forced medication for execution.

The only court that has interpreted the *Harper* standard to allow forcible medication for the purposes of restoring competency for execution did not consider medical ethics in its analysis. In *Singleton* v. *Norris* (2003), the Eighth Circuit ignored the obvious long-term medical harm of forced medication for execution, and found that the short-term medical benefit of involuntary medication satisfied the "medical interest" requirement of *Harper*. Unlike the courts in *Perry* and *Singleton*, the Eighth Circuit made no mention of the ethical dilemma posed by forced medication for execution.

3.4.2.4   Interrogation and Torture

In an attempt to balance the psychiatrist's dual loyalties to the patient and public, domestic ethical standards prohibit psychiatrist involvement in torture but allow for limited participation in interrogation. The AMA (2006) and APA (2006) both prohibit direct involvement in any form of torture. But the two associations took different positions with respect to participation in interrogation.

AMA policy permits indirect physician participation in interrogation "to develop general interrogation strategies that are not coercive, but are humane and respect the rights of individuals" (AMA 2006). The APA's policy is less strictly drawn, and permits: (1) aiding in general interrogation strategies that do not involve torture or cruel, inhumane or degrading treatment; and (2) evaluating detainees' need for medical and mental health services pre- or post-interrogation (APA 2006).

The two associations both take a strong position against direct participation, though this position is not universal among mental health professional organizations. Since 2006, the AMA has prohibited physician monitoring of an interrogation with intent to intervene: "Physicians must not conduct, directly participate in, or monitor an interrogation with an intent to intervene, because this undermines the physician's role as healer" (AMA 2006). By contrast, in 2005, the APA adopted a policy that allowed consultation and monitoring of individual interrogations with the intent of intervening (APA 2005). This position elicited a firestorm of controversy, with the APA issuing a number of qualifying statements and defending its position against public attacks in the medical journals.

The debate has not been merely theoretical. The United States' conduct of interrogation at detention facilities in the past decade has depended upon the active involvement of mental health professionals. Mental health practitioners participated in the development and implementation of a Behavioral Management Plan at the United States detention facility at Guantanamo Bay "to enhance and exploit the disorientation and disorganization felt by a newly arrived detainee in the interrogation process" (Joint Task Force – Guantanamo 2003). They also "have been part of a strategy that employs extreme stress, combined with behavior-shaping rewards, to extract actionable intelligence from resistant captives," and have shared medical records with interrogators (Bloche and Marks 2005).

The ethical considerations for a psychiatrist considering participation in interrogation are akin to those in disciplinary proceedings. Unlike forced medication for execution or to render a patient competent to stand trial, interrogation will occur with or without psychiatric involvement. There are multiple points at which the psychiatrist might become involved, each with different ethical implications – e.g., preparatory evaluation, emergency intervention, rehabilitation, or post hoc documentation (Taborda and Arboleda-Flórez 1999). It is conceivable that the presence of an impartial psychiatrist, with both the respect of the interrogators and the will to prevent abusive techniques, could reduce the risk of harm to the individual interrogated. However, it is unclear whether the psychiatrists involved in interrogations have had such will or wherewithal. Further, psychiatric involvement in the development of programs that capitalize on knowledge of mental functioning and the exploitation of human needs and fears is difficult to square with the principles of beneficence and non-malfeasance.

3.4.3 The Obligation to Systematically Examine and Improve Treatment

Correctional psychiatrists, like psychiatrists practicing elsewhere, have an ethical obligation to attempt to improve and monitor the quality of care that they provide. This should take the form of involvement in quality improvement, peer review and continuing medical education activities. This obligation can be particularly difficult to fulfill in the correctional setting.

For logistical and cultural reasons, correctional psychiatry practice can be isolating for the practitioner. Security measures in prisons often prevent correctional psychiatrists from communicating with one another frequently for peer supervision or continuing education meetings. Correctional psychiatrists need to be aware of this aspect of their practice and organize peer supervision and continuing medical education meetings to counteract the inherent isolation of their clinical settings.

Robust, interdisciplinary, quality improvement programs with the ability to bring needed changes to fruition are likewise critical. Correctional psychiatrists do not practice in a vacuum; turning their assessments and orders for care into actual patient care generally involves engagement with other healthcare disciplines and custody staff. The role of custody must be carefully considered in these undertakings. While considerations such as confidentiality must be given due weight, the reality is that meaningful remedies to many barriers to sufficient treatment often cannot be achieved without custody "buy-in". Areas of study should generally focus on high volume or high risk tasks and should include both process and outcome oriented measures.

Doctors of any specialty should be familiar with the principal organizations that formulate the standards for correctional healthcare. Three primary organizations are involved in setting the minimal healthcare standards in the correctional environment – the American Public Health Association (APHA), the National Commission on Correctional Health Care (NCCHC), and the American Correctional Association (ACA). However, since there are no data reflecting the adoption of these minimal standards to improve patients' overall health and safety, other organizations have stepped forward to further delineate improved standards. For the correctional physician, keeping abreast of all the standards issued by different organizations can be inordinately time-consuming, if it is possible at all, given typical workloads in the correctional setting. This, again, points towards the need for the healthcare delivery system and professional organizations to offer support and also underscores the need for continued training and peer review.

Patient quality control standards in the community may not be easily translated to a correctional setting, and there may be specific correctional quality control challenges that are rarely found in community healthcare settings. This dissonance between the two environments may lead to inappropriate and unintended differences in overall patient care quality. In 2010, a group of correctional care experts was convened in order to recommend correctional safety standards, adapted from the literature in quality improvement in community settings. In formulating correctional-specific standards, the participants agreed that "standards may derive from the general medical care literature but should be tailored to corrections" (Stern et al. 2010). They also decided that their recommendations should focus on patient safety as a primary quality goal. The participants arrived at a consensus of 60 proposed standards for patient safety in prisons, ranging from patient access to prenatal care to up-to-date medication lists. The principal goal of this expert consensus was to modify existing community standards into workable models for the correctional population.

In order to generate results from the issuance of a new set of standards, the standards must be introduced systematically to all correctional healthcare providers, and should be uniformly utilized across different regions, promoting consistent usage among doctors. The regional differences in funding and community standards of care complicate the application of this principle and have implications for ethical decision-making. Nonetheless, the bureaucracy inherent in many individual correctional systems should not be a barrier to the implementation of one clear set of standards that a task force can periodically update and modify, based on the current literature. One way to make these standards as widespread as possible is to have the different correctional organizations and expert panels jointly contribute to one set of standards, which would streamline the delivery of clear and concise information to doctors.

Significant obstacles notwithstanding, there is an ethical imperative to systematically and objectively assess the quality of care provided and institute remedial measures when the results of these studies indicate they are required. This is another example of the way in which the psychiatrist must act as part of the correctional and mental health service delivery systems to effectuate needed change. Individual action may frequently be insufficient, but that fact does not obviate the ethical duty. The healthcare authority and professional organizations should provide support for these endeavors.

3.4.4 The Psychiatrist as Leader

The application of ethics to psychiatry has resulted in a more thoughtful approach to the fundamental questions of human autonomy and beneficence that should underlay the practice of correctional psychiatry. An overview of medical ethics must include four ethical principles underlying all clinical decision-making. These four ethical pillars are autonomy (the obligation to respect the decision-making capacity of autonomous persons), beneficence (the obligation to provide benefits and to balance benefits against risk), non-malfeasance (the obligation to avoid causing harm), and justice (the obligation of fairness in the distribution of benefits and risks) (Beauchamp and Childress 2001).

No correctional patient is alike, given the complexity and variety of life dynamics, social and cultural factors, and individual clinical disorders. Correctional patients are also in the prison environment for a variety of different offenses, some of which may be particularly heinous. Nevertheless, a psychiatrist who knows and respects the four core elements of medical ethics will be guided towards the ethical resolution of these very complex cases. However, how these standards are implemented in day-to-day clinical correctional practice is affected by the structural organization of each correctional entity.

The principles of autonomy, beneficence, non-malfeasance, and justice together form the foundation of ethical decision-making in medicine, and they therefore have applicability to the practice of correctional psychiatry as well. Through a process of identifying the salient moral concern at issue in a particular case and methodically analyzing the underlying ethical principles, the range of appropriate clinical interventions should become evident.

Firstly, respect for the patient's autonomy is demonstrated by preserving clinical confidentiality. This deference to the patient's confidentiality is reflected in our legal system, which emphasizes liberty interests and patient rights. Secondly, the physician must consider beneficence and ensure that the patient is the ultimate beneficiary of clinical decisions made in a utilitarian, outcome-oriented mental health practice within the correctional system. Thirdly, to adhere to the principle of non-malfeasance, the physician must determine how to ensure his necessary logistical relationship with the correctional institution does not impinge on his clinical decision-making. Finally, the physician must ask if the clinical plan respects the ethical duty for justice, in so far as the proposed treatment is fair and equitable for as many of the involved parties as possible. Meeting this goal usually will require intensive education about mental illness for the correctional and security staff. This training should not only include basic information about the manifestations of psychiatric disorders, but how decompensation in patients can be prevented.

Correctional psychiatry encompasses situations in which numerous ethical questions are precariously arrayed. However, when undertaking psychiatric work as a correctional psychiatrist, utilizing the four ethical principles as guiding points increases the likelihood of a satisfactory clinical outcome for the patient as well as an ethical outcome for the physician.

3.4.5 Ethical Implications of Different Models of Care

Models for providing psychiatric care in prisons vary widely in the United States. The intervention and identification models themselves vary as do methods of finance and oversight.

In some systems, mental health treatment is provided by department of corrections employees; in others, private for-profit vendors may provide treatment in a government-run facility; some correctional facilities are operated entirely by private corporations under contract with governmental entities. In some systems, care is provided by academic medical centers operating within government-run institutions. This patchwork approach results at times in peculiar mixes wherein, for example, psychiatrists and other medical staff are employed by university-based medical centers, while non-psychiatric mental health staff are state employees.

Each model brings its own issues vis-à-vis funding levels, staffing competence and professional satisfaction, and availability of treatment resources and raises its own unique ethical issues specifically with regard to access to adequate care. One national survey of US jails found that 84 % reported that less than 10 % of inmates got mental health services of any type (Steadman and Veysey 1997). That same study found that only 43 % of jails had crisis intervention programs and 42 % provided psychiatric medications. The picture in prisons was not considerably better. One study of inmates with mental illness due to be released from state prisons within the 12 months revealed that only 57 % had received treatment (Beck 2000).

Attaining and sustaining ethical standards of practice within correctional settings, while always an area of individual concern, cannot properly be addressed apart from the model of service delivery and funding. The degree of independence afforded a practitioner is influenced by a variety of factors, including the reporting structure of the organization, the way in which care is compensated, and the incentives or disincentives which are built into compensation formulae.

Sometimes the question is as simple as "who is my boss?" Lines of authority outside of the custody "chain of command" can be helpful in fostering much-needed autonomy for physicians to make proper clinical decisions. Some advocate that care provided by academic medical centers provides the clearest path to independent clinical decision-making. In any case, fiscal factors such as access to expensive diagnostic procedures, specialty clinics, acute hospitalization as well as formularies reflecting evidence-based practices, are all important variables. It is not only the total dollar amount available, but the economic incentives which can affect the care provided. One example is a managed care capitated rate model of reimbursement in which a provider is allocated a fixed dollar amount per inmate-patient cared for regardless of the treatment provided. In such a case, there is an economic disincentive to providing access to more expensive treatment. By contrast, cost-plus models, where an entity is reimbursed for actual cost plus an enumerated amount for over-head, may lead to overutilization of expenses, tests, and medications. Each approach produces its own set of ethical issues related to the balancing of economic incentives with optimal practice as well as implications for the degree of autonomy afforded the clinician to act in accordance with standards of ethical practice.

3.5 Conclusion

The United States incarcerates a large number of people with serious mental illness, almost all of whom return to live in communities throughout the country. Many do not receive adequate treatment while they are incarcerated, and most do not receive adequate reentry planning prior to release. Many suffer from comorbid medical and social conditions, and some are only first identified during the incarceration screening process. Taken together, this makes psychiatry within jails and prisons perhaps the most important forum for the practice of public psychiatry in the US. While opportunities abound, the nature of the correctional institutions and limitations and conflicting normative values encountered by the physician practicing within them, makes ethical practice challenging. The psychiatrist should be aware of legal and ethical standards, and should make efforts to effectively advocate for systemic change which facilitates the ability of the individual clinician to act ethically. Autonomy and oversight are critical aspects of making this work.

References

Abramsky, S., and M. Fellner. 2003. *Ill-equipped: US prisons and offenders with mental illness.* New York: Human Rights Watch.

American Correctional Association. 2004. Resolution on the Prison Rape Elimination Act of 2003. Available at: http://www.aca.org/Government/reso.asp#8. Accessed 4 Aug 2004.

American Psychological Association. 2005. Report of the American Psychological Association Presidential Task Force on Psychological Ethics and National Security. http://www.apa.org/pubs/info/reports/pens.pdf

AMA. 2010. Code of medical ethics. http://www.ama-assn.org/ama/pub/physician-resources/medical-ethics/code-medical-ethics.page

American Medical Association Council on Ethical and Judicial Affairs. 2006. Physician participation in interrogation. (E-2.068, adopted 2006). http://www.ama-assn.org/ama/pub/physician-resources/medical-ethics/code-medical-ethics/opinion2068.shtml. Accessed 7 Dec 2010.

American Psychiatric Association. 2006. Psychiatric participation in interrogation of detainees: Position statement. http://www.psych.org/Departments/EDU/Library/APAOfficialDocuments andRelated/PositionStatements/200601.aspx. Accessed 7 Dec 2010.

American Psychiatric Association. 2009. *The principles of medical ethics with annotations especially applicable to psychiatry.*

American Psychological Association. 2005. *Report of the American Psychological Association Presidential Task Force on Psychological Ethics and National Security.* http://www.apa.org/pubs/info/reports/pens.pdf.

APHA. 2003. Standards for health services in correctional institutions. http://books.google.com/books/about/Standards_for_health_services_in_correct.html?id=Ey4n0b0rMpEC

Appelbaum, P.S. 2008. Ethics and forensic psychiatry: Translating principles into practice. *The Journal of the American Academy of Psychiatry and the Law* 36(2): 195–199.

Beauchamp, T.L., and J. Childress. 2001. *Principles of biomedical ethics.* New York: Oxford University Press.

Beck, A.J. 2000. State and federal prisoners returning to the community: Findings from the Bureau of Justice Statistics. Presented at the First Reentry Courts Initiative Cluster Meeting, Washington, DC, April 13, 2000.

Binswanger, I.A., M.F. Stern, R.A. Deyo, et al. 2007. Release from prison: A high risk of death for former inmates. *The New England Journal of Medicine* 356: 157–165.

Bloche, M.G., and J.H. Marks. 2005. Doctors and interrogators at Guantanamo Bay. *The New England Journal of Medicine* 353: 6–8.

Bonner, R., and L.D. Vandecreek. 2006. Ethical decision making for correctional mental health providers. *Criminal Justice and Behavior* 33(4): 542–564.

Bott v. DeLand. 1996. 922 P.2d 732 (Utah).

Central Intelligence Agency. 2009. *The world fact book 2009.* Washington, DC: Central Intelligence Agency.

Coleman v. Schwarzenegger. 2009. No. CIV S-90-0520 LKK JFM P, 2009 WL 2430820 (E.D. Cal.).

Convention on the Rights of Persons with Disabilities. 2006. http://www2.ohchr.org/english/law/disabilities-convention.htm.

Dike, C.C. 2008. Commentary: Is ethical forensic psychiatry an oxymoron? *The Journal of the American Academy of Psychiatry and the Law* 36(2): 181–184.

Dlugacz, H.A., and J.Y. Low. 2007. Key considerations in liability management and the correctional psychiatrist. In *Correctional psychiatry: Practice guidelines and strategies*, ed. O.J. Thienhaus and M. Piasecki. Kingston: Civic Research Institute.

Dlugacz, H.A., and E. Roskes. 2009. Clinically oriented reentry planning. In *Handbook of correctional mental health*, ed. C.L. Scott. Arlington: American Psychiatric Publishing, Inc.

Dlugacz, H.A., N. Broner, and S. Lamon. 2007. Implementing reentry – establishing a continuum of care of adult jail and prison releases with mental illness. In *Correctional psychiatry: Practice guidelines and strategies*, ed. O.J. Thienhaus and M. Piasecki. Kingston: Civic Research Institute.

Estelle v. Gamble. 1976. 429 U.S. 97.

Feder, L. 1991. A comparison of the community adjustment of mentally ill offenders with those from the general population. *Journal of Law and Human Behavior* 15(5): 477–493.

Fellner, J. 2008. Afterwords. *Criminal Justice and Behavior* 35(8): 1079–1087.

Fellner, J. 2009. Special comment: A human rights perspective on segregating the mentally ill. *Correctional Mental Health Report*11(1): 11.

Fellner, J. 2010. What do human rights offer correctional mental health professionals? An essay. *Correctional Mental Health Report*11(6): 83–85.

Ford v. Wainwright. 1986. 477 U.S. 399.

Glickman, S.W., K.A. Baggett, C.G. Krubert, E.D. Peterson, and K.A. Schulman. 2008. Promoting quality: The health-care organization from a management perspective. *International Journal for Quality in Health Care* 19(6): 341–348.

Graham v. Florida. 2010. 560 U.S.

Haney, C., W.C. Banks, and P.G. Zimbardo. 1973. Interpersonal dynamics in a simulated prison. *International Journal of Criminology and Penology* 1: 69–97.

Hartwell, S. 2008. Community reintegration of person with SMI post-incarceration. Center for Mental Health Services, Research Brief 5, May 2008.

Joint Task Force – Guantanamo. 2003. Camp delta standard operating procedures. United States Department of Defense. Available at: http://www1.umn.edu/humanrts/OathBetrayed/SOP%20 1-238.pdf. Accessed 28 Mar 2003.

King, L. 2005. Correctional medicine and community re-entry: The meaning of it all. Paper presented at the National Conference on Correctional Health Care, Denver, CO, October 2005.

Krelstein, M.S. 2002. The role of mental health in the inmate disciplinary process: A national survey. *The Journal of the American Academy of Psychiatry and the Law* 30(4): 488–496.

Lareau v. Manson. 1980. 507 F. Supp. 1177 (D. Conn.).

Lovell, D., L.C. Johnson, and K.C. Cain. 2007. Recidivism of supermax prisoners in Washington State. *Crime & Delinquency* 53(4): 633–656.

Madrid v. Gomez. 1995. 889 F. Supp. 1146 (N.D. Cal.).

Magaletta, Philip R., Pamela M. Diamond, et al. 2009. Estimating the mental illness component of service need in corrections – results from the mental health prevalence project. *Criminal Justice and Behavior* 36(3): 229–244.

Matter of the SCPA Article 17-A Guardianship Proceeding for Mark C.H. 28 Misc3d 765; 2010 N.Y. Misc. LEXIS 918 (Sur. Ct., NY Cty.) (Surr. Glen).

Mellow, J., and R. Greifinger. 2008. The evolving standard of decency: Postrelease planning? *Journal of Correctional Health Care* 14(20): 21–30.

Metzner, J.L. 2002. Class action litigation in correctional psychology. *The Journal of American Psychology and the Law* 30: 19–29.

Metzner, J.L., and J. Fellner. 2010. Solitary confinement and mental illness in U.S. Prisons: A challenge for medical ethics. *The Journal of the American Academy of Psychiatry and the Law* 38: 104–108.

National Commission on Correctional Health Care. 2008. *Standards for mental health services in correctional facilities*. Chicago: National Commission on Correctional Health Care.

O'Keefe, M.L., K.J. Klebe, et al. 2010. *One year longitudinal study of the psychological effects of administrative segregation*.

Panetti v. Quarterman. 2007. 551 U.S. 930.

People v. Bierenbaum. 2002. 301 A.D.2d 119 (N.Y.A.D. 1 Dept.).

Perlin, M.L. 2005. "With faces hidden while the walls were tightening": Applying international human rights standards to forensic psychology. Paper presented at the 30th Congress of the Society of Interamerican Psychologists, Buenos Aries.

Perlin, M.L., and A.H. Dlugacz. 2009. "It's doom alone that counts": Can international human rights law be an effective source of rights in correctional conditions litigation? *Behavioral Sciences & the Law* 27(5): 675–694.

Physicians for Human Rights. 2002. Dual loyalty & human rights in health professional practice; proposed guidelines & institutional mechanisms (A Project of the International Dual Loyalty

Working Group, A Collaborative Initiative of Physicians for Human Rights and the School of Public Health and Primary Health Care). University of Cape Town, Health Sciences Faculty. https://s3.amazonaws.com/PHR_Reports/dualloyalties-2002-report.pdf. Accessed 7 Dec 2010.

PruneYard Shopping Center v. Robins. 1980. 447 U.S. 74.

Redding, Richard E., and Daniel C. Murrie. 2010. Judicial decision making about forensic mental health evidence. In *Special topics in forensic practice*, ed. A.M. Goldstein. Hoboken: Wiley.

Riggins v. Nevada. 1992. 504 U.S. 127.

Ruiz v. Estelle. 1980. 503 F. Supp. 1295 (S.D. Tex.).

Schopp, R.F. 2009. Treating criminal offenders in correctional contexts: Identifying interests and distributing responsibilities. *Behavioral Sciences & the Law* 27: 833–855.

Seaton v. Mayberg. 2010. 2010 U.S. App. LEXIS 13335 at *7 (9th Cir. 2010).

Sell v. United States. 2003. 539 U.S. 166.

Singleton v. Norris. 2003. 319 F.3d 1018 (8th Cir.).

Singleton v. State. 1993. 313 S.C. 75.

Skoler, D.L.P. 1975. World implementation of the United Nations Standard Minimum Rules for treatment of prisoners. *Journal of International Law and Economics* 10: 453–463.

State v. Perry. 1992. 610 So. 2d 746 (La.).

Steadman, H.L., and B.M. Veysey. 1997. *Providing services for jail inmates with mental disorders*, Research in brief. Washington, DC: National Institute of Justice.

Stefan, S. 1993. What constitutes departure from professional judgment 17? *Mental and Physical Disability Law Reporter* 17: 207.

Sterling v. Cupp. 1981. 290 Ore. 611.

Stern, M.F., et al. 2010. Patient safety: Moving the bar in prison health care standards. *American Journal of Public Health* 100(11): 2103–2110.

Taborda José, G.V., and J. Arboleda-Flórez. 1999. Forensic medicine in the next century: Some ethical challenges. *International Journal of Offender Therapy and Comparative Criminology* 43(2): 188–201.

Tarasoff v. Regents of the University of California. 1976. 17 Cal. 3d 425 (Cal.).

The President's New Freedom Commission on Mental Health. 2003. *Achieving the promise: Transforming mental health care in America.*

Thomas v. Bryant. 2010. 614 F.3d 1288 (11th Cir.).

United Nations. 1948. Universal Declaration of Human Rights, GA Res. 217A (III) (1948).

United Nations. 1955. Standard Minimum Rules for the Treatment of Prisoners, ESC Res. 663 C (XXIV) & 2076 (LXII).

United Nations. 1966. International Covenant on Civil and Political Rights, GA Res. 2200A (XXI).

United Nations. 1982. Principles of Medical Ethics, GA Res. 37/194.

United Nations. 1984. Convention Against Torture and Other Cruel, Inhuman or Degrading Treatment or Punishment, GA Res. 39/46.

United Nations Human Rights Committee. 1992. CCPR General Comment No. 21: Replaces general comment 9 concerning humane treatment of persons deprived of liberty (Art. 10).

United States Department of Justice, Bureau of Justice Statistics. 1999. *Mental health and treatment of inmates and probationers*. Washington, DC: United States Department of Justice, Bureau of Justice Statistics.

United States Department of Justice, Bureau of Justice Statistics 2012. *Correctional Populations in the United States, 2011*. Washington, DC: U.S. Department of Justice, Office of Justice Programs, Bureau of Justice Statistics.

United States v. Weston. 2001. 255 F.3d 873 (D.C. Cir.).

Vienna Convention on the Law of Treaties (VCLT). 1969. http://untreaty.un.org/ilc/texts/instruments/english/conventions/1_1_1969.pdf

Washington v. Harper. 1990. 494 U.S. 210.

Weinstein, J.B., and C. Wimmer. 2010. Sentencing in the United States. In *Reentry planning for offenders with mental disorders: Policy and practice*, ed. H. Dlugacz. Kingston: Civic Research Institute.

Wolff v. McDonnell. 1974. 418 U.S. 539.

World Health Organization. 2005. *WHO resource book on mental health*. Geneva: Human Rights and Legislation.

World Medical Association. 1975. Declaration of Tokyo – Guidelines for physicians concerning torture and other cruel, inhuman or degrading treatment or punishment in relation to detention and imprisonment. http://www.wma.net/en/30publications/10policies/c18/index.html. Accessed 7 Dec 2010.

World Medical Association. 2009. Medical ethics manual. http://www.wma.net/en/30publications/30 ethicsmanual/pdf/ethics_manual_en.pdf. Accessed 7 Dec 2010.

Youngberg v. Romeo. 1982. 457 U.S. 307.

Chapter 4
The Evolution of Punishment and Incarceration

George B. Palermo

4.1 Introduction

The birth of jails preceded that of prisons, both of which primarily served a socio-utilitarian purpose. Historically, they go back to ancient times, appearing around 3,000–4,000 years ago. Their evolution goes pari passu with social changes, such as population growth, the establishment of towns and cities, property ownership rights, the agrarian and industrial revolutions, and the urbanization movement. At the same time, legal systems evolved.

Prior to the advent of the prison, people lived in communities with minimal organization and with no codified rules of law. They reacted to offenses on the basis of their emotions and in an aggressive-defensive mode that ideally would assure survival and respect. Generally, they reacted on the basis of "hurt" suffered by themselves or their kin. It was a hasty reaction to rectify wrongs suffered. The reactions were spontaneous and emotional, but expected and seen as due, as in the Biblical dictum, "An eye for an eye, a tooth for a tooth."

Throughout the years, the concepts of right and wrong became more important. Communities further evolved and they elaborated systems that were considered more equitable, not individual-driven but based on a collective consensus of what was just. It is logical to think that as communities became towns and cities, more interested in the welfare of their members, they began to lay down rules of acceptable social behaviors and penalties for disregarding them. This transition into legally codified behaviors was helped by various religious systems that depended on the way that people related to unknown forces and feared powerful gods, first of nature

G.B. Palermo (✉)
Clinical Professor of Psychiatry, University of Nevada
School of Medicine and Medical College of Wisconsin,
2169 Silent Echoes Drive Henderson, NV 89044, USA
e-mail: palermogb@juno.com

N. Konrad et al. (eds.), *Ethical Issues in Prison Psychiatry*, International Library of Ethics, Law, and the New Medicine 46, DOI 10.1007/978-94-007-0086-4_4,
© Springer Science+Business Media Dordrecht 2013

and later anthropomorphic. Religious precepts attempted to contain aggression and blood feuds, which undermined the cohesiveness of groups and communities. Crimes against persons became part of a developing system of justice. As more people became property owners, property crimes came to be viewed as an extension of a crime against the self and the rightful fruit of a person's labor.

Punishment for these crimes was slowly integrated into the system. Personal retaliation soon gave way to various types of penalties, such as forced labor, exile, or banishment, which were aimed not only at punishing but at shaming the offender (Peters 1995). However, as the number of inhabitants in urban areas increased, the individual acquired a certain anonymity and methods of punishment that aimed at shaming offenders no longer had the same deterrent effect. They no longer had to bear the scrutinizing and reproachful eyes of those who knew them. Removing them from society came to be thought of as a better way to deal with criminal behaviors and incarceration was implemented.

Thus, as urbanization became more extensive, the dispensation of justice moved from physical punishment or shaming to various periods of incarceration, depending on the degree and type of offense committed, and to various types of confinement, and eventually to the development of jails and prisons. That these were places of confinement is clear from their etymological roots. Jail derives from the Latin noun caveola, the diminutive of cavea, meaning cage or court. It describes the underground cave or hollow ambiance in which prisoners were placed on apprehension. Prison, instead, derives from the Latin verb prehendere, and the noun prensionem, meaning the act of seizing.

4.2   Historical Notes

4.2.1   Ancient Period

During the Middle Kingdom of ancient Egypt (2050–1786 BCE) Pharaohs used public beating and imprisonment as punishment for those offenses which upset society. Prisoners were regarded as slaves and were placed in work houses and subjected to hard labor. Their confinement varied according to the type of offense and an official scribe kept a record of the inmates.

In Babylonia, the Hammurabi Code (1792–1750 BCE), one of the most ancient codes of law, reports the use of prisons. People were confined for minor crimes and sentenced to hard labor. This type of punishment was also used by the Assyrians (height of Empire: 746–539 BCE).

In Genesis (39:20–23) it is reported that Joseph was confined to a prison for several years. Samson, when captured by the Philistines, was also placed in a prison. The Hebrews are reported to have placed offenders in temporary custody, especially prior to execution (Leviticus 24:12–23 and Numbers 15:32–36). When they were thought to have violated the covenant with God, offenders were also sentenced to exile or death through lapidation, burning, decapitation and beating. It is reported that the prophet Micah was imprisoned for a period of time. Jeremiah was imprisoned in the upper gate of Benjamin (Jeremiah 20:12) because his behavior had irritated Pashur, the son of the high priest and King Zedekiah. The Acts of the Apostles (4:3) reports that both Peter and John were detained by the Sanhedrin, even though briefly. Saul imprisoned the Christians (Acts 8:3; 9:2), and St. Paul, in his Letter to the Hebrews (10:34) mentions imprisonment, in addition to confiscation of property, as a form of punishment (Peters 1995).

In ancient Greece, from the seventh century BCE to the fifth century BCE, the polis was responsible for the punishment of criminals and for the laws which applied to both minor and major crimes. During the period of Draco (620 BCE), strict laws were enacted and enforced in cases of homicide. Those laws led to the frequently-used term "Draconian laws". These laws were later revised by Solon, the great Athenian jurist (594 BCE). A commonly held opinion of Athenians was that persons found guilty of a crime had to be confined in a prison and that their lack of freedom and/or their punishment should serve as an example to other citizens. At times they were chained in the desmoterios (place of chains). Confinement was viewed not only as retribution but also as a deterrent to further crime and as a method of redemption for offensive behavior (Peters 1995).

While Plato believed that people who committed serious crimes must be subjected to severe punishment, viewed by him as retributive and deterrent, he held that an uneducated offender who did not have the capacity to appreciate the nature of his wrongdoing needed primarily corrective sentencing, what today could be termed behavioral modification (Mackenzie 1981). In Athens, punishment consisted of stoning, tossing an offender from a precipice, or tying them to a stake until death. In the last case, the offender suffered public abuse while dying. The recidivistic offender was hanged. At times offenders were denied burial. In Athens, punishment was three pronged: physical, moral, and patrimonial. Patrimonial punishment consisted in fines, the confiscation of property, or the destruction of the condemned person's home (Peters 1995).

The Greek phylake (prison) was used both as a place of temporary confinement prior to trial or prior to punishment, and for long-term confinement, especially for slaves. The former use is remindful of the present day function of city and county jails. In prison, offenders were at times subjected to torture and execution.

The Romans had specific courts for particular offenses, with statutory penalties. In ancient Rome, persons found guilty of physical assault, theft, or destruction of private property were punished either with a pecuniary payment or, when that was not possible, after a 60 day period passed by the offender in prison with a death sentence. Prior to trial for any offense, the individual was imprisoned and the types of confinement were various. There was confinement to the home (ergastolo); the carcer, or prison, where the individual was chained; and the quarry-prison (latumiae), which was initially within the city walls on the Capitoline hill, one of the Seven Hills of Rome. The prison often had a pit in which people were confined and occasionally killed. As the city developed, the Romans built prisons outside of the city walls. Those prisons were often underground dungeons—dark, noisy and overcrowded. The prisoners were chained, at times abused and tortured, poorly fed and without supervision. The supervision of the prisons was made mandatory under the code of Emperor Theodosius (fifth century CE) and judges were mandated to inspect the jails or prisons. Humanistic emperors of Rome such as Hadrian and Constantine made the jail/prison a less harsh place for the prisoners and punishment was less severe (Parente 2007).

After centuries of social, military and political splendor, Rome went through a decadent period and eventually came to an end in 476 CE. During its early history, Roman law, based on the 12 Tables, dating back to 451 BCE. They became part of the Justinian Code. The Justinian Code consisted of a complex of judicial norms protecting private and public rights in the administration of justice in the Roman Empire. It was based on jus civile and jus gentium, meaning the common good of the individual and the nation (Dizionario Enciclopedico Italiano-Treccani 1970). It survived beyond the fall of the empire and still continues to influence the jurisprudence of many European countries.

4.2.2 Medieval Period to Late Renaissance

After the fall of Rome, the Christian church, already present for some centuries under the last Roman emperors, became more powerful and enforced its own law—Canon Law—designed to maintain control over people's misconduct. In addition to State prisons, ecclesiastical prisons began to appear (Parente 2007). These ecclesiastical prisons were present in France until the seventeenth century. The church, which had already been an important agent of social control, albeit with regional variations, was empowered over secular matters by Charlemagne (r. 768–814). The bishops' tribunals date from that period, and were not only for people guilty of heresy, but also disposed of common criminal matters. People found guilty of serious crimes were confined in the bishop's prison, at times even for life. If the defendant was found to be incorrigible, he would be turned over to a higher religious court, which usually meant capital punishment.

4.2.2.1 England

In England, between 600 and 1000 CE, during the Anglo-Saxon period, punishment in towns or shires often consisted in branding the offender. This was the usual sentence for crimes of arson, robbery, murder and false coinage, crimes that were considered as being against the King's peace. This was codified in the Constitution of Clarendon by Henry II in 1166 CE. Later, punishment became more severe and included capital punishment for treason, heresy, swearing, adultery and witchcraft. In Anglo-Saxon England, people found guilty of theft and witchcraft were at times imprisoned but more often they were punished, as in other European countries, with penalties that ranged from compensation or exile to mutilation and death (Peters 1995).

In England at the time of King William I, prisons included the Tower of London, Fleet Prison, and the Bulk House at Winchester. During the reign of Henry II, each English county had jails for offenders charged with felonies while awaiting trial. From the twelfth to the sixteenth centuries, punishment moved from fines to physical punishment. Fines were often combined with imprisonment during the fourteenth and fifteenth centuries.

The use of prisons increased and by the sixteenth century offenders guilty of crimes ranging from vagrancy to moral offenses could be sent to prison. Prisons were frequently franchised by the king, and the townships had the responsibility not only for building the prison but also for its upkeep. Life in prison was obviously uncomfortable and the prisoners were subject to pay for their maintenance. There were communal rooms, single cells, and segregation rooms or "holes" when, at the jailers' discretion, severe punishment was delivered. At times prisoners sentenced to capital punishment were tortured prior to execution. England had used capital punishment extensively for 200 years and offenders were executed even for misdemeanors. One hundred and sixty capital crimes were reported in English legislation in 1760 and by 1819 there were about 233 although many of them were never enforced (Foucault 1979).

The Milbank penitentiary in England was built in 1816. Its design included the Panopticon proposed by Bentham (1995). A Panopticon type of prison was also constructed in 1840 in Pentonville. A Panopticon prison combined surveillance and security, isolation and transparency (Foucault 1979). In 1842, five progressive stages of prison custody were actuated, including a diminished sentence for good behavior and/or the possibility for conditional discharge from the prison. The prison system was essentially reserved for callous and incorrigible offenders. The Pentonville and Milbank prisons eventually housed first offenders who, after a period of observation, were utilized for public works and later at times profited from conditional discharge.

4.2.2.2 France

In thirteenth century France, the prison was used for offenders charged with debt, perjury, conspiracy, robbery, blasphemy and kidnapping, when they were not exiled. There were prisons for the lower classes and for the nobility; the latter were better maintained. Habitual criminals were separated from occasional offenders. There was some food available, at least bread and water and, if the prisoners desired, they were allowed to purchase other food through the jailers, or their relatives were allowed to bring it to them. There was also the possibility for prisoners to obtain brief furloughs.

While the Châtelet in Paris housed both upper and lower class prisoners, by the time of the French Revolution the Bastille, initially a royal prison, housed mostly members of the lower class. It contained dungeons and eight towers with cells for confinement; it was poorly kept and its conditions were unhealthy. It was used as a prison until the revolution when it was destroyed by the revolutionaries. During the eighteenth century work houses were instituted.

The guillotine was used for the first time in March 1792, replacing the gallows, first used in England in 1760. The French doctor Joseph Guillotin proposed that the decapitation of a person condemned to death would bring about a more rapid death. Public execution preceded by torture had almost entirely disappeared by 1840. Even though still in use in 1972, execution by guillotine had slowly moved from the city square to the interior of the prison, becoming inaccessible to the public.

4.2.2.3 Spain

In Spain during the eleventh and the twelfth centuries, people were imprisoned for failure to appear in court or to post bond, but basically the prisons housed offenders of a type similar to those found in other European countries. Mutilation, blinding and execution were common forms of punishment. In 1265 CE, Alfonse X of Castile issued the legislative work Las Siete Partidas which, among other things, forbade the branding or mutilation of prisoners, and upheld prison hygiene.

4.2.2.4 Italy

In Italy, Castel Sant'Angelo in Rome, which at times served as a walled and protected residence for aristocrats and popes, also served as a place of confinement for common criminals and for persons accused of political crimes. Pope Boniface VIII approved the poena carceris in 1298 CE, becoming "the first sovereign authority in the Western tradition to determine that imprisonment as punishment was a legitimate instrument of a universal legal system" (Peters 1995, pp. 2930). Later, prisons were used by the church inquisitors for people accused of heterodoxy.

In Florence, during the thirteenth century, Le Stinche prison replaced summary execution. In Le Stinche prisoners were separated by age, gender, seriousness of the offense, and by their mental status. Later, Siena, Pistoia and Venice adopted the same approach and by 1559 Venice had constructed large prisons.

4.2.2.5 Germany

Prisons were used under Germanic law during the domination of Europe by the Franks. In Germany and the northern countries, temporary confinement was used and alternated with forced labor until the sixteenth century. Before the fifteenth century the period of imprisonment was usually short, but later at times people were kept in underground prisons for years, were chained in the towers of castles, or kept in monasteries. Prisons were usually used in lieu of more serious punishment, which included mutilation and capital punishment.

4.2.3 The Beginnings of Reform

In the 1600s, while existing prisons were highly functional places, a social interest in the construction of workhouses appeared. In these workhouses, like St. Bridget's Well, also known as Bridewell, in London, minor offenders and beggars were detained. Similar workhouses were also used in the Netherlands and in America (dating to 1596) during the colonial period. They housed beggars, young malefactors and people who obtained a reduction of penalty for good behavior. Work was mandatory and was performed as part of a group. In these workhouses the prisoners slept two or three to a bed and each cell contained between 4 and 12 people. They received wages for their work as well as religious indoctrination. This type of workhouse can be thought to be a forerunner of the reformed prison of the eighteenth century.

Exile was a frequent form of punishment in many European countries. Until 1750, criminals from Russia were exiled to Siberia; those from Spain and Portugal were sent to Africa; France sent its prisoners to South America. Since 1650 England had sent many criminals to the North American colonies, except for those who were still housed in the so-called convicts' ships on the river Thames. Prisoners sent to the colonies were those convicted of murder or other serious crimes. They were usually white English citizens who reached the American territory in chains. By 1776 the number of these exiled prisoners was in the tens of thousands. With the American Revolution the convicts were no longer sent to the New World, but England continued the practice of exile, substituting Australia as a penal colony. This also contributed to the development of prisons in England (Soothill 2007).

In the eighteenth century, prisoners in the Maison de Force in Ghent, Belgium, were obliged to do work for which they were remunerated. Their supervision was strict and their discipline was based on a system of moral pedagogy. Idleness was thought to be the cause of most crimes. The time length of a sentence was an issue, since a brief sentence (less than 6 months) was thought not long enough to properly address the offender's bad habits while it was believed that a life sentence would create despair in them, leading to a desire to rebel and escape.

Already in 1764, Beccaria (1983 [1775]) had spoken against the practice of exhibiting chained prisoners in public. Chain gangs were abolished by the beginning of the nineteenth century. He expressed the idea that the punishment frequently exceeded the crime itself. The pillory was abolished in France in 1789 and in England in 1837. By 1810, detention had become the essential form of punishment in France except for those crimes requiring the death penalty. Cities and counties began to construct their own prisons, together with houses of correction where offenders were kept for sentences up to 1 year. Main prisons were generally used for prisoners whose penalty was longer than 1 year (Foucault 1979).

4.2.4   The American Prison Experiment

In the United States the first prison was constructed in New Haven, Connecticut, in 1773. By 1790 prisons had been built in several states, some of them underground. The conditions in those prisons were very harsh. Some were located near taverns, men and women were housed together, food was scarce, the sanitary conditions were very bad and there was no discipline. In 1787, an organization called The Society for Alleviating the Misery of the Public Prisons, headed by Benjamin Rush, had been created in an attempt to implement necessary reforms.

The Ghent prison, perhaps modelled on St. Michaels' Prison in Rome, was a precursor of the Walnut Street Prison model in Philadelphia, Pennsylvania, established in 1790 and operated by the Quakers as a humane alternative to the prevailing standards, which included hanging and torture. The Walnut Street Prison became one of the first in the world to implement radical reforms (Roth 2006). In the prison, the prisoners were isolated but worked while in isolation, going through a basic apprenticeship. It was believed that in so doing they would avoid the bad influences of other inmates, and, through personal introspection, would rediscover the morals they had lost or had never had. The prison was essentially viewed as a place of confinement, the purpose of which was to transform the propensity of the prisoners for antisocial acting out into good habits. The men and women were separated; drinking of alcohol was not allowed; there were cells for solitary confinement where inmates were to meditate while avoiding moral contamination from other prisoners. Inmates received religious instruction and read the Bible.

In 1815, the State of New York established Auburn Prison, a prison that came to be seen by many states as being more economical than the Walnut Street Prison and therefore thought to be more successful. The inmates were exposed to harsh discipline with strong security measures. They were allowed to work together during the day, even though they had to maintain silence; at night they were confined in individual cells. A certain competition developed between the two prison systems—the Walnut Street Prison and Auburn Prison: which would achieve better rehabilitation of the convicts?

At the time that the above changes were taking place in Philadelphia and New York the Puritans were active in prison reform in Boston. Doubtless, the above systems were more humane than the criminal court of England which enforced harsh penalties and showed "…no concern at all about the reformability of the criminal…" (Dumm 1987). Nevertheless, in many prisons harsh punishments, even capital punishment, continued to be used.

Benjamin Rush, who in 1787 had founded the Society for Alleviating the Miseries of the Public Prisons, opposed public execution as a barbarous expression of punishment, asserting that it was the product of "the feeble influence of reason and religion over the human mind" (Foucault 1979). By 1835, a New York law ordered that executions were to be carried out within the prison walls or the enclosure adjoining the prison in the county where the prisoner had been tried (Friedman 1993).

The prison experiments in America by the Quakers and Puritans in Philadelphia, New York and Boston were based on a philosophy of moral and social rehabilitation of the offender. At the same time, the offenders were thought to be deserving of confinement for their own benefit and that of society. Indeed, it was believed that prisons were intended by the law not to punish, but to secure the offenders (Foucault 1979). However, as previously mentioned, the philanthropic approach in dealing with criminals regarded solitary confinement as important because it was believed that it would bring about changes in the moral character of the offenders leading to modifications in their conduct. This was the approach of the Quakers in Philadelphia: "Central to the Quaker mission was a radical modification of the system of criminal punishment....to establish institutions which would redeem rather than torture" (Dumm 1987).

The Quakers believed that merely putting the offenders to work would not change their habits because, they asserted, the habit of a righteous life could only be achieved through inner moral changes and a return to God. They viewed crime as a sin and saw faith and the fear of God as the only means to happiness and rehabilitation. In the Quaker approach, friendly persuasion took the place of physical coercion and became another form of control imposed on offenders. The Quaker ideas were part of the historical reality of that moment in American society, but their application was, by necessity, limited to a small carceral community and could only be actuated when the larger community was cohesive in sharing humane goals.

At the same time, reforms were being implemented elsewhere. In Ireland, Lord Crofton, who became Chief of the Penitentiary Administration in 1854, instituted outdoor work for the inmates whom he subdivided into five different classes, which progressed towards a conditional release or total freedom for good behavior, good work or good educational achievement. The inmates were paid for their work and they received differential treatment on the basis of their behavior. Professional training was available, leading to occupational possibilities for the inmate upon discharge from prison. This Crofton system lasted for only a period of 30 years, during which time some of the Irish prisons were shut down because criminality had lessened. By 1880, however, the number of offenders had reached high levels and it was again necessary to reopen the prisons.

4.3   The Beginning of the Modern Era

By the eighteenth century crime had come to be seen in a secular, rational way, and people, more aware of the environmental influences on human behavior expressed by Locke, began to endorse sociogenic factors in crime and to consider more fully its social consequences. The new carceral philosophy stressed crime prevention as the basic rationale of any just law. Retribution and severe punishment were thought to be insufficient for its control.

By the beginning of the nineteenth century strides had been made towards a more humane approach in dealing with criminals throughout the world, but especially in the United States. The ideological basis for that approach had originated in Europe with Rousseau, Montesquieu, and Beccaria, but the Europeans derived organizational ideas from the new and more humane prison system of the new world.

As the urban population grew, so, too, did the number of offenders who were sent to poorly planned city jails/prisons, which actually functioned as a holding tank, keeping in custody those individuals considered to be the rabble of society. The prisons began to house not only criminals but also vagrants, the destitute and the mentally ill. By the end of the nineteenth century most cities and counties had established jails/prisons that served the purpose of controlling the deviant population in the community (Stojkovic and Lovell 1992).

In 1885, an international prison congress was held in Rome, Italy. Sixty countries participated and some exhibited the type of cell used in the prisons of their country. Germany, Switzerland, Sweden, Norway, Italy, England, France, Denmark, Belgium, Hungary, Russia, Austria, Spain and the United States were some of the most important nations participating in the congress. The exhibition of the United States included models of the Walnut Street prison and the House of Correction in Concord, Massachusetts. The topics of discussion were centered on the sentencing of offenders and the possibility of assignment to public works. The radical changes that had occurred after 1885 when the penitentiary system altered its philosophy, embraced an efficient scientific approach to the correction and rehabilitation of offenders. Incarceration was mandated primarily in serious cases while probation and pecuniary sanctions were more frequently employed (Ferracuti 1989).

In 1901 at the International Law Congress of Amsterdam, and in 1925 at a similar congress in London, attention shifted from the prison to the person imprisoned and to the importance of the offender's psychopathology. That again furthered better understanding and better treatment of inmates. The reduction of a penalty for good behavior, already present in the Italian, French and German prison systems, also become a part of the English correctional system. During the first part of the twentieth century, however, the German penal system advocated the new principle of Volksgewissen, the conscience of the people, which gave judges the power to annul any kind of sentence, even retroactively, if it were contrary to the interests of the German people (Ferracuti 1989).

Following World War II, alternative measures of detention, such as probation and parole were adopted throughout the world, and the judicial and the penitentiary systems became more interested in the social reintegration of the inmates than in their punishment or moral changes. The liberalization of the law and the penal system, with stress on rehabilitation and social reintegration of the offender, together with the application of various forms of diversion, was meant to reduce the rate of criminality and recidivism.

Until 1960, in the United States most prisoners were held in antiquated prisons. The security prisons, like SingSing and Alcatraz, offered primarily custody and at times harsh punishment, but few rehabilitative programs. A comparison can be made between the prisons of 1860 and those of 1960. In 1860, petty criminals were treated more harshly. They were required to do hard labor; they were given a small diet and forced to sleep on boards. They were not allowed visits or letters and the only reading material they were supplied with was the Bible. However, they were able to wear their own clothes and they were able to order food from the outside. They could even hire someone to clean their cells. Every one of these prisoners was kept in solitude. In 1960, instead, petty criminals generally were forced to do boring but easy labor. They were supplied with a good diet and had easy access to a variety of reading materials. They also had their choice of several forms of recreation and they had the possibility to buy things in the prison. However, they had to serve longer sentences than those in the 1860s. Felons in the 1960s were under constant surveillance and assigned tasks to do. However, if they worked themselves up in status they were allowed part or fulltime education. They were given supportive counseling and even the possibility of home leave. There was more possibility for them to have visitors and to receive correspondence (Palermo and White 1998).

4.4   Present Status

As the twentieth century progressed, crime was increasingly thought to be the product of a criminogenic society. A new breed of professional criminologists began educational and therapeutic programs for jail and prison inmates and attempted to make the prison routine more acceptable and the conditions more livable, with milder discipline and more opportunity for recreation and rehabilitation for the inmates.[1] International treaty requirements regulated, among other things, the environment in which prisoners reside. These conditions range from the very primitive to very modern and prison architecture has become a very important part of the prison experience. However, too often, the prison environment is still one that annihilates the very soul of the inmate (McConville 2003). The unchanging, monotonous routine of the prison deadens the spirit of those prisoners who could be rehabilitated and the often unpredictable behavior of other inmates is a source of continuous fear.

At the same time, the crime rate increased and the rapidly growing population in the jails and prisons during the past decades has contributed to overcrowding. Most of the overcrowded prisons are near big cities and have become places of deadening routine, often filled with fear and violence (Morris 1995). As the prisons became more populated, rehabilitative measures become less available, because more time is spent by the custodial officers in supervision and control of the often unruly behavior of the inmates. As a result, the prison system has again moved towards a more rigid treatment of the inmates.

---

[1] In the United States there are both jails and prisons. Jails are generally under the jurisdiction of local authorities (cities and counties) and prisons are under the jurisdiction of state or federal authorities (Palermo and White 1998). Jails house people awaiting trial and those sentenced for a short period of time, usually less than 1 year. Prisons house those convicted of major crimes and sentenced for longer periods. The federal prisons are run by the Federal Bureau of Prisons and hold persons who have committed federal crimes (e.g., mail fraud, kidnapping, tax evasion).

Maximum security prisons were built throughout the United States and the continuous construction of prisons is foreseen for the twenty-first century. Already in the 1960s, a high level of violence had been witnessed within these maximum security institutions, violence perpetrated by inmates on other inmates. As Stojkovic and Lovell wrote (1992): "The violence now may not be administered by prison officials as in the past, but the violence promulgated by inmates against each other is no less harmful, nor is it anything else but a deviant form of punishment for noncompliance to coercive rules, even if those rules are part of the inmate culture" (Stojkovic and Lovell 1992). Growth in violence is occurring because of (1) gangs, (2) illicit drugs and the (3) difficulty of disciplining difficult inmates (Wortley 2003).

After 1961, requests for release from prisoners incarcerated in Federal prisons permitted by the United States Supreme Court following the *Monroe v. Pape* (1961) decision became very frequent. (That Court decision found, among other things, that police had entered the home of the petitioner [Monroe] without a warrant and it allowed him to pursue redress though civil litigation). Habeas Corpus suits themselves were to become so popular that by 1995 about 10,000 of such petitions were being filed yearly (Hanson and Daley 1995). The *Crain v. Bordenkircher* case (1986) followed an action initiated in 1981 by a group of inmates at the Moundsville (Virginia) Penitentiary, and became a milestone in defining what should be an adequate correctional institution. The totality of the institutions under scrutiny included building structures, heating, ventilation systems, lighting, food, recreational facilities, and strict hygienic conditions. Spatial density, social density and mobility within a given cell were also considered (*Rhodes v. Chapman* 1981). Visitation, exercise, recreation activities, and access to education and rehabilitation and even the adequacy of the institution law library were addressed by the rulings of the court. Deprivation of such things as exercise and recreation may be regarded as cruel and unusual punishment, as they are assumed to be necessary for the maintenance of physical and mental health (Ball 1997).

During the 1980s, disgust with prison conditions in the United States led to a veritable revolution of judicial intervention. "In most popular and scholarly accounts, this development [was] attributed to the efforts of civil liberties groups, prisoners' rights lobbies, enhanced media scrutiny, and other societal pressures that ended the autocratic reign of iron-fisted wardens" (DiIulio 1990). One of the major developments in judicial intervention regarding the reform of prison conditions was the closing of the aforementioned state penitentiary in Moundsville on July 1, 1992. Until then, "prisons were almost entirely in the hands of prison administrators, and the courts had maintained the traditional hands off attitude" (Ball 1997) and the prisoners at times were considered to be slaves of the state having lost their rights after being sentenced (see *Ruffin v. Commonwealth* 1871). In the sentencing at time of appeal in *Coffin v. Reichard* (1994), however, the court ruled that undue deprivation of prisoner liberties while in prison could be beyond what the law would allow, and therefore unconstitutional.

The American prison-industrial complex is a self-perpetuating system. Presently, there are 2.4 million incarcerated offenders and the recidivism rate is high due to difficulties encountered by offenders reentering society. Rehabilitation appears to be less important in the treatment of offenders, and ambivalent judicial and carceral policies, together with a social climate which supports stricter sentencing and less diversion, are the expression of a cyclical return of the past. Even though many attempts have been made to reform the jails and prisons by humanistic advocates and by legislators interested in the humane treatment of offenders, the results have been minor, temporary and intermittent.

Organizationally, the American correctional system has multiple components, including jails and prisons, community based facilities, halfway houses, home confinement, electronic bracelets and monitoring. The structure of the prisons continues to evolve as they become larger and technologically avant garde. They are generally of a more functional direct/podular supervisory type. This type of confinement allows not only more interaction among prisoners but also better supervision of them by the custodial personnel. Although this recent evolution of the prison structure reflects a change in correctional philosophy towards a management oriented approach to incarceration and stresses the personal responsibility of the inmate, the picture varies from prison to prison (McConville 2003).

4.5 The Incarceration of the Mentally Ill

A correlation between mental illness and criminal behaviors has always been asserted and recent literature indicates that such a connection exists (e.g., Arrigo 2002, 2004; Rothman 2002; Scull 2005; Siegel 2010; Silver et al. 2008). In the second half of the twentieth century the deinstitutionalization of psychiatric patients began in the United States and spread throughout the world. Although its original motivations were humane and well intentioned, its consequences have been mostly harmful and problematic for the patients and communities (Appelbaum 1994). Indeed, a large number of socially marginal mentally disordered people were left free to roam the streets, often deprived of basic necessities, including food, shelter, and medical and psychiatric care (Isaac and Armat 2000; Torrey 1998). They slept in public facilities and on the sidewalks of major cities. They created problems for businesses and communities at large (Torrey 2008). This situation continues to exist, even though the lack of care for the mentally ill in the community is less of a problem in countries with a well developed health system for all citizens, such as most European countries.

As, with the decrease in psychiatric bed numbers, the security of the mental institutions was no longer available, dealing with social disturbance was left by default to criminal justice system and the city and county jails. In a short period of time, the process of deinstitutionalization reversed the recognition of the mentally ill as people in need of attention and help. The efforts of Pinel, which had liberated them from the chains, literal and figurative, of the asylums, and of other humanitarian scholars who had created the new mental health institutions, which offered the best-known care and a possibility for reintegration into society, slowly disappeared. Penrose's (1939) balloon theory became more than evident; that is, there is an inverse relationship between prison and mental health populations. Jails and prisons became the repositories of the mentally ill, creating overcrowding of the carceral system and an overworked court system (Palermo et al. 1991).

Offenders who were mentally ill or suffering from serious personality disorders and those addicted to various illicit drugs and alcohol became a serious problem for the carceral system, whose staff was inadequately skilled for this new job. The interaction between the mentally ill offenders and the general offender population was mutually deleterious. The personnel, especially, was caught in the middle of a chaotic, non-programmed situation, and jails/prisons progressively became more disorganized, dehumanizing and unhealthy. The mentally ill had assumed an inappropriate status: that of the offender. This status quo was further alimented by economic factors and civil rights law. The mentally ill found themselves incorporated in a criminal justice system not suited to treat their needs. In this process of transinstitutionalization, at times, the mentally ill themselves, fearing psychiatrization, denied their illness (Palermo et al. 1982). Attempts were made to modernize many correctional facilities and many have established a mental health unit, however, at times poorly staffed to care for the mentally ill offenders. Some mentally ill offenders, because of their irrational and destructive behavior, were transferred to higher security prisons and the most dangerous to maximum security prisons.

This problem is ongoing. These offenders obviously do not belong in carceral institutions, but in mental institutions. Mental illness is not due primarily to a criminogenic society but to a genetic, biological predisposition to various stresses. Social forces could intervene by ameliorating the social conditions in which these people live, minimizing their stresses and preventing their possible illegal acting out. The plight of the incarcerated mentally ill should be looked upon as an expression of the progressive disintegration of the moral fabric of society. Unless society has well organized, highly functional structures in which the mentally ill can be properly diagnosed and treated and where they can find a continuum of care the present situation could worsen.

The court system could further develop mental health courts, in so doing lessening the burden of the criminal courts and directing mentally disordered offenders to special units, which would provide them with proper care within a therapeutic ambience. These courts should become part of a morally dedicated health system for mentally ill offenders (e.g., Palermo 2010). This would decrease prisonization and recidivism.

Sex offender legislation should be reassessed on the basis of sensible and objective rules. The therapy and rehabilitation of these offenders, who often suffer from a more-or-less-serious personality disorder, should take place during their sentencing period and their risk and dangerousness should be assessed again at the end of their sentences, without resorting to a civil commitment that is basically preventive detention for an indefinite period of time. Without reverting to institutionalization, an impossibility from an evolutionary point of view, society must face the cogent problem of the incarcerated mentally ill with honesty and humane interest. Support for these changes can be found in a deep sense of social justice and social ethics (Palermo and Farkas 2013).

4.6 Other Countries

It is impossible to present a history of the prisons in every country, each of which would require a chapter or book of its own. The brief sections that follow are representative of conditions existing in various parts of the world not considered previously.

Many European countries are going through a penal crisis, exceptions being Finland and other Nordic countries, the Netherlands, and Germany, which have done quite well in the prevention of overcrowding in their prison systems. The communitarian type of society of these societies has contributed to the reduction of their prison populations. In 2008, Finland, for example, had a prison population of slightly less than three and one-half thousand (3,370) that is, a rate of imprisonment of 64/100,000 population (Walmsley 2008). The approach in these countries is remindful of the "classical school of Cesare Beccaria (1963), whose theories were based on enlightenment social contract theories" (Cavadino and Dignan 2006). Germany's prison population ranges from 57 to 170/100,000 population, varying from Bundesland to Bundesland (Cavadino and Dignan 2006). Prison conditions are "relatively good by international standards" (Cavadino and Dignan 2006) and there is no crisis of resources. Prisoners' rights are guaranteed by the 1976 Prison Act. Basically, Germany has done well in crime control following the East–west unification.

4.6.1 Africa

While most Western developed countries have made progressive changes in their various justice systems and prison conditions by addressing human rights and improving their detention and penitentiary structures, only recently are the nations comprising the African continent beginning to make changes in the physical and psychological approach to their prisons and prisoners. The basic reasons for this delay lay in their economic and social philosophy, a philosophy of punishment that is a remnant of the colonial period and is still present in many countries (Dissel 2008). The rationale for imprisonment in colonial Africa was often to obtain compensation for victims. Prisons often were used to control political opponents, even employing the use of torture at times. In addition, they were used to isolate, control and punish the indigenous population. The indigenous peoples were frequently thought of as inferior and uncivilized, to be subjugated and punished. However, it has been argued that at present, with the possible exception of South Africa, such racially-tinged practices are no longer prevalent (Vetten 2008). Thus, a lack of good governance, a still-present colonial view of the purpose of prisons, and an increasing crime rate, together with a lack of the finances necessary for the betterment of conditions, have made it difficult to address the problems of the prisoners and raise them to a Western standard level.

Prisoners have been co-housed regardless of gender and age. The judicial system, when present and organized, acts very slowly. In many instances, offenders are detained for long periods because trials are delayed, at times for several years, and they often receive longer sentences than offenders in Western nations. For example, in Uganda and South Africa delays in trials and long prison confinement are very common (Wines 2005). This contributes to prison overcrowding, resentment on the part of the prisoners and correctional officers, physical abuse and other maltreatment, and sexual abuse, especially of, but not limited to, female prisoners. Among the most overcrowded prisons in the sub-Saharan African nations are those of Cameroon, Zambia, Burundi, Kenya and Rwanda (Walmsley 2005). Overcrowding brings about a proneness to communicable disease, because of the poor sanitation present in the old prisons and the inadequate hygiene among the prisoners. As in other prisons throughout the world, cases of HIV are prevalent in African prisons, often spread by tattooing, injected drug use or rape (United Nations Office on Drugs and Crime 2007). Even in the twenty-first century, many prisoners are reported to die of malnutrition, including in Kenya, Nigeria, Ethiopia, and Ghana.

The prison situation in Nigeria was so bad that in 2002 the government, upholding human rights, released 25,000 prisoners who were still awaiting trial after 10 years of detention (Integrated Regional Information Networks: IRIN 2006). Since the Ouagadougou Declaration on accelerating penal and prison reforms in Africa (rehabilitation and reintegration), Egypt has been experimenting with diversion programs and taking into consideration the possible use of restorative justice (Sambo 2000). South Africa and Uganda also have taken steps to improve the rehabilitation of prisoners (Legggett et al. 2005). The majority of African states having committed themselves to such steps, in 2002 the African Commission on Human and Peoples' Rights created the Office of the Rapporteur (Special Rapporteur Prison-S.R.P.), appointed for the purpose of checking on the humane conditions in prisons and, in so doing, protecting prisoners' rights (Viljoen 2005). In 2006, the Conference of Eastern Southern and Central African Heads of Correctional Services (CESCA) again upheld the necessity for the humane treatment of prisoners. CESCA was replaced by The African Correctional Association whose aim also is to transform the prison systems in Africa (ACSA 2008). The Kampala Declaration on Prison Conditions (1996) and the Council of Europe (2006) both emphasized the importance of improving prison conditions, not only the structures but the conditions in which prisoners live.

Although difficult to ascertain with precision, the rates of incarceration seem to vary widely in sub-Saharan Africa. United Nations statistics show a prison population of 688,000 in 2007 (United Nations Office on Drugs and Crime 2007). In 2003, the median rate for western and central African countries was reported as 50 and for countries in southern Africa it was 362/100,000 inhabitants (Walmsley 2003). Later sources point out that the median incarceration rate for southern African countries is more than seven times that for Central and West Africa (Walmsley 2008).

Improvements in incarceration structures in Africa often go undone because of a lack of financial resources or because of political upheaval. Nevertheless, African countries are striving to improve the conditions of the prisoners, to offer alternative forms of punishment (including the use of restorative justice), and to educate not only correctional staff but the judiciary in current correctional practices and, above all, in the importance of the human rights of the prisoners.

4.6.2   China

The most influential source of Chinese legal tradition was Confucianism (Liu and Palermo 2009). Indeed, prisons in China were first mentioned by Confucius and it is believed that Buddhist temples built in their proximity may have had the function of aiding in offender rehabilitation (Roth 2006). Conditions in early prisons were dismal and it was not until the beginning of the twentieth century that some prison reforms had begun in China. Following the Revolution of 1911, which had temporarily halted newer prison construction, more prisons were built throughout the country and this continued through the time of the Communist Revolution.

The number of prisoners in China is rather low relative to its population of more than one billion people (1,333,460,000 in 2009). Statistics vary, however. In 2007, the prison population was reported to be two and half million (189/100,000 population) (King's College Statistics, London) divided between those who committed a serious crime (e.g., political, property or violent crimes) and those who are addicted to drugs and alcohol, which are not considered serious crimes in themselves, and prostitution, or those guilty of causing minor social problems. These groups are directed to two different types of prison (laogai camps). The first are sent to Reform through Labor prisons or camps. In 2005, the United States Department on Human Rights reported approximately 500,000 detainees in such camps or prisons, where they are detained from 1 to 3 years, often without trial. Those in the second group, who have not committed a serious crime, are interned in Re-Education through Labor camps or prisons. In 2004, there were reportedly 350,000 detainees in these camps. Political dissidents are often sent to remote-region labor camps, such as in Tibet. Shourang stations house vagrants, runaways and those without identification papers. Also, Black Jails, illegal detention centers run for profit by private individuals, hold mostly ordinary people with grievances and petitions against the state. In addition, there is a large number of pre-trial detention centers (BBC News 2009).

Prison conditions are generally poor, food is often scarce, leading to malnutrition among the prisoners. Maltreatment and bullying by gang inmates is frequent. Oversight by guards is lacking. Even though China has legal provisions against torture, occasional use to obtain confessions from prisoners has been reported (Asia News 2011).

As in many other countries, both male and female prisoners are employed throughout the system in various roles, ranging from menial labor to more sophisticated occupations. This labor, which helps prison functioning, is also considered to have a rehabilitative purpose. Such rehabilitative efforts extend to political and educational ones, with many prisoners sentenced to spend their prison terms in the work camps, where they work long hours under harsh conditions and where corporal punishment is sometimes used (Lu and Miethe 2001). After having served one-half of a sentence or 10 years of a life sentence a prisoner may become eligible for early release, dependent on his repentance for the crimes committed or, at times, for some type of worthy service to the country (Roth 2006).

Confucianism has contributed to social control even in contemporary China. However, "[i]nstead of the power of li [filial piety or the duty of children to their parents in Confucianism], the legalists [called] for the state to make, publicize and indoctrinate law" (Zhong 2009). At the same time, community crime prevention is becoming ever more important (Zhong and Broadhurst 2007). Recently introduced Western legal principles of criminal law and punishment encourage the use of restorative justice methods that prefer non-criminal punishments. Such methods facilitate the restoration of relationships, the reparation of harm and the reintegration of offenders into the community. These restorative justice movements have primarily developed independent of movements outside China, indicating different motivations, influenced by the traditional legal system (Liu and Palermo 2009). The use of such methods will undoubtedly reduce the prison population in the future.

4.6.3 India

India, with a population of more than one billion people (1,150,000,000) had a prison population of approximately 370,000 in 2006 (Walmsley 2008), one of the lowest incarceration rates in the world relative to population. This low rate is thought to be due to strong family ties and widespread religious participation that blocks the propensity to criminal acting-out behavior. Prisoners are segregated by social class (caste), and juvenile offenders are detained in rehabilitative facilities. The penal facilities are under the jurisdiction of the State Government and Union Territories. There are 1,119 facilities, which are subdivided into central, district, sub- and open prisons.

In spite of the low incarceration rate, the facilities are overcrowded and 70 % of detainees await trial for long periods. Long detention periods and paucity of staff also contribute to the overcrowding. The poor conditions of the carceral system contribute to the custodial abuse of prisoners and disease. The quality of some Indian prisons was recently reported to be deplorable and not meeting international standards (Asian Center for Human Rights: ACHR 2010). Prison conditions had improved somewhat after the investigations of the Indian Committee on Jail Reforms of 1980, but these improvements were minimal because of a lack of financial resources (Roth 2006). Indian prison conditions are still reported to be harsh and intimidating, with inadequate medical care and frequent cases of malnutrition.

4.6.4 Singapore

Singapore is an important exception in Asia. Singapore, with a population of almost 5,000,000 (as of July 2010 estimates), had a prison population reported to be slightly under 12,000 (11,768) in 2007, a number that does not include those in rehabilitation centers (Walmsley 2008). In Singapore, there are extensive crime prevention programs and strong police-community relations. For instance, there is close collaboration between small police stations—Neighborhood Police Posts—and Residents Committees, groups of citizens within housing blocks (Austin 2005). The philosophical approach of working together to address neighborhood dysfunctions at the source aids in crime deterrence.

The Singapore prison service includes 14 prisons and drug rehabilitation centers (National Computer Systems: NCS 2011). Singapore, although having a very low crime and recidivism rate, has the highest incarceration rate in Asia (267/100,000 population in 2007). A wide range of penalties for criminal behavior is used—as Beccaria wrote, a penalty to fit the crime. The prisons are considered to be strict, yet humane. The cells are small and the prisoners reportedly sleep on cement beds, even though the prison complexes themselves are highly modern, with the use of the latest technology, including closed-circuit cameras for monitoring the activity of the inmates, computerized door closing, and intercom systems within the cells to facilitate contact between prisoners and the prison staff, especially in case of emergency. A zero tolerance policy requires that prisoners give up any gang affiliation. Better selection of correctional officers and a better inmate classification system contribute to the smooth running of the prisons (Roth 2006; Singapore Prisons Department 2002). The inmates are allowed to work within the premises and they are remunerated for it. The Spartan life in the prisons is suggestive of a military style, and the inmates are reminded that respect, duties and repentance are conducive to rehabilitation. The philosophy of rehabilitation in the prison takes into consideration the character of the offenders, who attend various rehabilitation programs prior to reintegration within society. The sophisticated computer system is employed by prison staff to retrieve up-to-date information regarding the prisoners and this rapid availability of information aids in the counseling given to them. At the same time, the inmates become more responsible and interested in getting through their prison experience in the most positive way possible. The correctional philosophy of Singapore is to protect society through safe custodial care and the rehabilitation of offenders. "Televisits" with family members are sometimes allowed because it is thought that contact with the family is very important in rehabilitative treatment (Singapore Prisons Department 2002). In order to help achieve this, if their conduct within the prison is good, some offenders are allowed to spend the last 6 months of their prison term in day-release-center supervision, with the possibility of home visits.

As stated, recidivism rates are low in Singapore and the country does not witness large numbers of violent crimes. This may be attributable to the strictness of its laws but also to its prison reforms. It has been said that Singapore offers incarceration with a human touch, a softer approach. Nevertheless, caning is sometimes employed as punishment (Roth 2006), and drug traffickers may receive the same penalty— capital punishment—as those convicted of homicide. However, criminal records for minor offenses may be expunged, the belief being that that will help offenders to secure a job following release from incarceration. Further, on release, the correctional system assists the individual in obtaining job training through the Singapore Corporation of Rehabilitative Enterprises. Ex-prisoners may also obtain counseling for drug abuse through the Singapore Anti-Narcotics Associates.

4.6.5 South America

A very brief mention should be made of the prison situation in South America. The prisons throughout the continent are generally overcrowded and there is wide disregard for the prisoners' human rights. In particular, Brazil, Argentina and Chile suffer from overcrowding, especially in the many prisons that are antiquated. The prison population has grown exponentially in these countries since 1992. In Brazil, for example, the prison population was 422,590 in 2007, but the prison capacity is only 233,907. Crime control in the community is poor and, as a result, the populations at times resort to lynching, vigilantism and death squads by gunmen hired by small shopkeepers or businesses (Dellasoppa 2000). In 2006, Argentina's carceral system included 218 prisons with a population of 60,621, having tripled in size since 1992 and exceeding 30 % of the actual prison housing capacity. In 2008, Chile had 167 prisons with a prison population of 48,855, more than double its 1992 census.

In general, prison cells are in poor condition, the food supply is inadequate and the nutrition of many prisoners is below average. There are very few health services or educational activities available to them and little vocational guidance is provided. Riots are frequent as prisoners demand that more attention be given to their civil and human rights. Such riots often end in the victimization of other prisoners, even to the point of death. The situation in these prisons is largely due to a lack of financial support from the various governments, but also to a recurrence of a political/carceral dictatorial prison philosophy. On a positive note, the countries are slowly moving towards a more democratic system (Salla and Ballesteros 2008).

4.7 Conclusion

During the latter part of the twentieth century correctional institutions throughout the world, with few exceptions, increasingly became the repository of persons who have been arrested for minor offenses. At times offenders are overcharged for their criminal offenses in order to secure a conviction. Frequently, trials and sentencing are delayed because of an overcrowded court calendar. Offenders may spend their sentences in houses of correction or they are returned to the community on probation. Most of them do not go through that period of reflection about their antisocial behavior and their carceral experience necessary for reaching a better understanding of their acts, which would help them avoid further misconduct. Indeed, offenders frequently become recidivists.

Prisons are meant to confine offenders and deprive them of their freedom—not to further punish them by exposing them to unhealthy surroundings, which would take us back 200 years to the pre-reform period of correctional institutions. Theories that advocate the abolition of the prison, such as those espoused by Griffith (1993) and his application of Biblical perspectives to the problem of prison, are utopian. Prisons, serving a basic function in the penal system, are here to stay. Nevertheless, the prison should be used with utmost discretion for particular cases and not for cases of offenders who could benefit from the assistance of social agencies whose basic purpose is to reeducate offenders. Such agencies can also contribute to the decrease in the number of first offenses, many brought about by the current social and economic situation.

As Cavadino and Dignan (2006) aptly wrote, "The march of globalization, free market forces and other rapid changes in technology, economics and culture –not least the fragmentation and destruction of traditional communities and traditional life-long jobs—has led to both an increase in crime and to deep-seated feelings of insecurity in the psyche of the late modern individual" (Cavadino and Dignan 2006). This has also brought about fear and hate of the "new stranger", the "other" of Garland (2001). People find it difficult to adapt to new realities and resign themselves to the continuous wave of migration of the poor from underdeveloped countries to more developed ones. There is widespread concern about job competition and personal security since the other, the outsider, has been increasingly demonized and often is regarded as dangerous. This pervasive and progressive social insecurity breeds criminal acting out. Also, an excessive criminalization of certain types of human behaviors has contributed to the imprisonment of many persons who could be handled in other types of facilities.

Arrigo and Milovanovic (2009) examined several philosophies of punishment and argued that "rather than [justifying] the use of prison as punishment, they add additional harm to society and in the process conceal their own contribution to facilitating crime" (Arrigo and Milovanovic 2009). A new approach to penology seems to be necessary, one that will enhance the offenders' awareness of their wrongdoing and help them to extricate themselves from the robotizing process of incarceration-release-incarceration. Such an approach should not only be limited to the offenders but to the environment in which they reside.

In many nations prisons are reported to have squalid cells. The prisoners are often malnourished and subjected to demeaning, abusive control. Too often they are subjected to abuses, their basic human rights are not upheld, even in the best prison facilities. A sense of demoralization affects not only the prisoners but the correctional officers and other persons involved in the prison management. Prison overpopulation contributes to the structural deterioration of often already-old prison facilities, as well as to their poor organization. It leads to intra-prison disturbances that delegitimize the penal system itself. Since there is no strict correlation between crime and incarceration (e.g., recently in the United States the crime rate diminished while the incarceration rate increased) prison overcrowding should be viewed more as the result of stricter sentencing guidelines and the criminalization of behaviors, too often the consequences of emotionally unfulfilled needs and misguided remedies (e.g., drug and alcohol addiction).

The penal culture is a culture of control, at times "preventive control," even "political control" in some countries. However, for the general population, restorative justice and mediation, already used throughout the world with satisfactory results, should be enhanced, especially in cases of misdemeanor or even in some minor felonious offenses. Both should be viewed as cathartic methods which allay fears and anger and give the offender the possibility to express guilt and remorse directly to his victim. Empowered neighborhood movements might help communities, law enforcement and the courts in dealing with the problem of deviance. Some problems could be addressed by social workers or others trained for such situations, without recurring to the police. Domestic violence calls for help should include a socio-psychological assessment of both spouses and/or cohabitants before any arrest is carried out.

Many scholars view crime as a call for help, viewing social misfits who commit crimes as people who, helped by treatment and rehabilitation, can eventually be successfully reintegrated into society. This approach does not apply to every person who commits a crime. However, we should not forget that many of the incarcerated, even though aware that their actions were wrong, were driven by negative socio-psychological and, in some cases, neurological factors. Basically, the origins of criminal behavior are within the individual and their relationships with others. Too often, laws, punishment and incarceration fall short of addressing the real issues.

References

ACHR. 2010. Asian Center for Human Rights. India. http://www.achrweb.org/countries/india.htm. Accessed 17 Jan 2011.

ACSA. 2008. African Correctional Services Association. http://www.dcs.gov.za/acsa/Home/History/aspx. Accessed 21 Jan 2011.

Appelbaum, P.S. 1994. *Almost a revolution: Mental health law and the limits of change*. New York: Oxford University Press.

Arrigo, B.A. 2002. *Punishing the mentally ill: A critical analysis of law and psychiatry*. New York: SUNY Press.

Arrigo, B.A. (ed.). 2004. *Psychological jurisprudence: Critical explorations in law, crime, and society*. New York: SUNY Press.

Arrigo, B.A., and D. Milovanovic. 2009. *Revolution in penology: Rethinking the society of captives*. Lanham: Rowman & Littlefield.

Asia News. 2011. Torture in China continues. http://www.asianews.it/news-en/Torture-in-China-continues-19488.html. Accessed 23 Jan 2011.

Austin, T. 2005. Life on the Atoll: Singapore ecology as a neglected dimension of social order. *International Journal of Offender Therapy and Comparative Criminology* 49: 478–490.

Ball, R.A. 1997. Prison conditions at the extreme. *Journal of Contemporary Criminal Justice* 13(1): 55–72.

BBC News. 2009. China 'running illegal prisons.' http://news.bbc.co.uk/2/hi/8356095.stm. Accessed 23 Jan 2011.

Beccaria, C. 1983 [1775]. In *An essay on crimes and punishments*, 4th ed, ed. A. Caso. Boston: International Pocket Library.

Bentham, J. 1995. Panopticon. In *The panopticon writings*, ed. M. Bozovic, 29–95. London: Verso.

Cavadino, M., and J. Dignan. 2006. *Penal systems: A comparative approach*. Thousand Oaks: Sage.

Coffin v Reichard. 1994. 143F.2nd 443.

Council of Europe Committe of Ministers. 2006. Recommendation Rec(2006)2 of the Committee of Ministers to member states on the European prison Rules. https://wcd.coe.int/ViewDoc. jsp?id-955747. Accessed 21 Jan 2011.

Crain v. Bordenkircher. 1986. 342S.E.2d 422 (W.Va.1986).

Dellasoppa, A.E. 2000. Brazil: Developing nation state. In *Crime and crime control: A global view*, ed. G. Barak, 1–12. Westport: Greenwood Press.

DiIulio, J.J. 1990. *Courts, corrections, and the constitution*. New York: Oxford University Press.

Dissel, A. 2008. Rehabilitaion and reintegration in African prisons. In *Human rights in African prisons (Ohio RIS Global Series)*, ed. J. Sarkin, 155–177. Athens: Ohio University Press.

Dizionario Enciclopedico Italiano-Treccani (Italian Encyclopedic Dictionary). 1970. s.v. Justinian Code. Rome: Istituto Poligrafico dello Stato, vol. V, 452–453.

Dumm, T.L. 1987. *Democracy and punishment*. Madison: University of Wisconsin Press.

Ferracuti, F. (ed.). 1989. *Carcere e Trattamento (Prisons and Treatment). Trattato di Criminologia, Medicina Criminologica e Psichiatria Forense (Treatise on Criminology, Criminological Medicine and Forensic Psychiatry)*, vol. 11. Milan: Giuffrè.

Foucault, M. 1979. *Discipline and punish: The birth of the prison* (trans: Sheridan, A.). New York: Vintage.

Friedman, L.M. 1993. *Crime and punishment in American history*. New York: Basic Books.

Garland, D. 2001. *The culture of control: Crime and social order in contemporary society*. Oxford: Oxford University Press.

Griffith, L. 1993. *The fall of the prison. Biblical perspectives on prison abolition*. Grand Rapids: William B. Eerdmans.

Hanson, R.A., and H. W. K. Daley. (1995). Federal Habeas corpus review: Challenging state court criminal convictions. *Bureau of Justice Statistics*, NCJ- 155504. Washington, DC: U.S. Department of Justice. http://bjs.gov/content/pub/pdf/FHCRCSCC.PDF. Accessed 12 Dec 2010.

Irin. 2006. Nigeria: Thousands of prisoners awaiting trial to be freed. http://irinnews.org/report. asp?ReportID=53167. Accessed 14 Jan 2011.

Isaac, R.J., and V.C. Armat. 2000. *Madness in the streets: How psychiatry and the law abandoned the mentally ill*. Washington, DC: Treatment Advocacy Center.

Kampala Declaration on prison conditions in Africa and plan of action. 1996. *Penal Reform International*. http://www.penalreform.org/publications/kampala-declaration-prison-conditions-africa. Accessed 21 Jan 2011.

Legggett, T., A. Del Frate, T. Peitschmann, and S. Kunnen. 2005. *Why fighting crime can assist development in Africa: Rule of law and protection of the most vulnerable. Summary*. New York: United Nations Office on Drugs and Crime.

Liu, J., and G.B. Palermo. 2009. Restorative justice and Chinese traditional legal culture. *Asia Pacific Journal of Police & Criminal Justice* 7(1): 49–68.

Lu, H., and T.D. Miethe. 2001. Community integration and the effectiveness of social control. In *Crime and social control in a changing China*, eds. Jianhong Liu, Lening Zhang, and Steven F. Messner, 105–122. Westport: Greenwood Press.

Mackenzie, M.M. 1981. *Plato on punishment*. Berkley: University of California Press.

McConville, S. 2003. The architectural realization of penal ideas. In *Prison architecture: policy, design, and experience*, eds. L. Fairweather and S. McConville, 1–15. Burlington: Architectural Press.

Monroe v. Pape. 365 U.S. 167 (1961).

Morris, N. 1995. The contemporary prison. In *The Oxford history of the prison. The practice of punishment in western society*, eds. N. Morris and D.J. Rothman, 227–259. New York: Oxford University Press.

NCS. 2011. NCS Success Stories. Prison Management System. http://www.ncs.com.sg/c/document_library/get_file?uuid=f8eb4862-5262-4cad-9f8f-114d214bbe67&groupId=10113. Accessed 21 Jan 2011.

Palermo, G.B. 2010. The Nevada mental health courts. *International Journal of Law and Psychiatry* 33: 214–219.

Palermo, G.B., and M.A. Farkas. 2013, 2nd ed. *The dilemma of the sexual offender*. Springfield: Charles C Thomas.

Palermo, G.B., and M.A. White. 1998. *Letters from prison: a cry for justice*. Springfield: Charles C Thomas.

Palermo, G.B., M. Smith, and F.J. Liska. 1991. Jails versus mental hospitals: A social dilemma. *International Journal of Offender Therapy and Comparative Criminology* 35(2): 97–106.

Palermo, G.B., E.J. Gumz, M.B. Smith, and F.J. Liska. 1992. Escape from psychiatrization: A statistical analysis of referrals to a forensic unit. *International Journal of Offender Therapy and Comparative Criminology* 36: 89–102.

Parente, A. 2007. *La Chiesa in Carcere [The church in prison]*. Rome: Ministry of Justice.

Penrose, L. 1939. Mental disease and crime: Outline of a comparative study of European statistics. *The British Journal of Medical Psychology* 18: 1–15.

Peters, E.M. 1995. Prison before the prison: The ancient and medieval worlds. In *The Oxford history of the prison. The practice of punishment in Western society*, eds. N. Morris and D.J. Rothman, 3–47. New York: Oxford University Press.

Rhodes v. Chapman, 452 U.S. 337 (1981).

Roth, M.P. 2006. *Prisons and prison systems: A global encyclopedia*. Westport: Greenwood Press.

Rothman, D. 2002. *The discovery of the asylum*. New York: Aldine Transactions.

Ruffin v. Commonwealth (62, Va. 790, 1871).

Salla, F., and P.R. Ballesteros. 2008. *Democracy, human rights and prison conditions in South America*. São Paulo: Núcleo de Estudos de Violência (Center for the Study of Violence).

Sambo, L.G. 2000. Editorial: The Ouagadougou Declaration and the challenges of strengthening health systems in the African region. *The African Health Monitor*. http://ahm.afro.who.int/issue12/pdf/AHM12Pages4to5.pdf. Accessed 21 Jan 2011.

Scull, A. 2005. *Most solitary of afflictions: Madness and society in Britain, 1700–1900*. New Haven: Yale University Press.

Siegel, L.D. 2010. *Criminology: Theories, patterns, and typologies*, 10th ed. Belmont: Wadsworth – Sengage Learning.

Silver, E., R.B. Felson, and M. Vaneseltine. 2008. The relationship between mental health problems and violence among criminal behavior. *Criminal Justice and Behavior* 2008(35): 405–426.

Singapore Prisons Department. 2002. National report on contemporary issues in corrections. http://www.apcca.org/News&Events/Discussion%20Papers%20-20agenda%201/Singapore. htm. Accessed 21 Jan 2011.

Soothill, K. 2007. Prison histories and competing audiences, 1776–1966. In *Handbook on prisons*, ed. Y. Jewkes, 27–48. Portland: Willan Publishing.

Stojkovic, S., and R. Lovell. 1992. *Corrections. An introduction*. Cincinnati: Anderson Publishing.

Torrey, E.F. 1998. *Out of the shadows: Confronting America's mental illness crisis*. New York: Wiley.

Torrey, E.F. 2008. *The insanity offense: How America's failure to treat the seriously mentally ill endangers its citizens*. New York: W.W. Norton & Co.

United Nations Office on Drugs and Crime. 2007. HIV and Prisons in Sub-Saharan Africa: Opportunities for Action. http://www.unodc.org/documents/hiv-aids/Africa%20HIV_Prison_Paper_Oct-23-07-en.pdf. Accessed 15 Jan 2011.

Vetten, L. 2008. The imprisonment of women in Africa. In *Human rights in African prisons (Ohio RIS Global Series)*, ed. J. Sarkin, 134–154. Athens: Ohio University Press.

Viljoen, F. 2005. The special rapporteur on prisons and conditions of detention in Africa: Achievements and possibilities. *Human Rights Quarterly* 27: 125–171.

Walmsley, R. 2005. Prison health care and the extent of prison overcrowding. *International Journal of Prisoner Health* 1: 9–12.

Walmsley, R. 2008. *World prison population list.* 8th ed. King's College London: International Centre for Prison Studies. http://www.kcl.ac.uk/depsta/law/research/icps/downloads/wppl-8th_41.pdf. Accessed 18 Jan 2011.

Wines, M. 2005. The forgotten of Africa, wasting away in jails without trial. *New York Times*, November 6, p11.

Wlamsley, R. 2003. *World prison population list.* 4th ed. King's College London: International Centre for Prison Studies. http://www.apcca.org/stats/4th%20Edition%20(2003).pdf. Accessed 22 Jan 2011.

Wortley, R. 2003. *Situational prison control: Crime prevention in correctional institutions.* New York: Cambridge University Press.

Zhong, L. 2009. *Communities, crime and social capital in contemporary China.* Portland: Willian Publishing.

Zhong, L., and R.G. Broadhurst. 2007. Building little safe and civilized communities: Community crime prevention with Chinese characteristics? *International Journal of Offender Therapy and Comparative Criminology* 51: 52–67.

Chapter 5
Forensic Research with the Mentally Disordered Offender

Julio Arboleda-Flórez and David N. Weisstub

5.1 Introduction

Mentally ill persons stand at the intersection of several social systems, particularly health and justice, but are equally the concern of the correctional and welfare systems. Health care systems claim control of the mentally disordered person on the premise that they suffer from an illness, indeed a disease for those mental health professionals bent on a biological understanding of mental conditions, and that such illness deprives them of the ability to make proper decisions and entitles them to specialized care, treatment and protection. The Justice system states that the mentally disordered are in need of protection from themselves and, more importantly, protection of others so that the mentally ill do not cause them harm. Correctional systems also lay claim to the mentally ill by virtue of the fact that a large number of them end up in prison and that prisons are veritable mental health institutions. Finally, the Welfare system 'claims' the mentally ill based on the fact that they are incapacitated to work and are in need of financial and housing support, and even aid-in-living supports for those most severely ill, such as persons suffering from dementia. Even when the mentally disordered commit offences, the Justice system considers that they should not be punished with the full force of the law.

J. Arboleda-Flórez (✉)
Professor Emeritus, Departments of Psychiatry and of Community Health Sciences,
Queen's University, Kingston ON, USA

483 River Ridge Drive, Glenburnie ON, K0H 1S0 USA
e-mail: julio.arboleda-florez@queensu.ca

D.N. Weisstub
Philippe Pinel Professor of Legal Psychiatry and Biomedical Ethics,
International Academy of Law and Mental Health (IALMH), Montreal, QC, Canada

Faculty of Medicine, University of Montreal, Montreal, QC, Canada
e-mail: admin@ialmh.org

N. Konrad et al. (eds.), *Ethical Issues in Prison Psychiatry*, International Library
of Ethics, Law, and the New Medicine 46, DOI 10.1007/978-94-007-0086-4_5,
© Springer Science+Business Media Dordrecht 2013

Health and Justice are both geared to protect the mentally disordered; their aims are the same. Their methods, however, differ; whereas health care can be understood as trying to protect the mentally disordered at the expense of their rights, justice can be seen as protecting their rights at the expense of their autonomy (Arboleda-Flórez 1999; Weisstub 1997). In its quest to develop protections for mentally disordered persons, the legal system has introduced a variety of structures, including guardianship laws, regulation and liability of caregivers, and exemptions from criminal liability. However, these regimes are designed to protect not only the mentally ill, but equally society. Unfortunately, as might be expected, these two antithetical objectives can lead to extremely difficult decisions, which not infrequently mean institutionalization. Yet it is a consequence of institutionalization, whether for short or long periods, that the mentally disordered become highly vulnerable to exploitation and abuse. Both their dependence upon others and their general lack of freedom to use independent judgment raises doubts about the voluntariness of their decisions. Furthermore, owing to the inherent nature of mental disorders, the cognitive capacity of affected individuals is frequently compromised, which affects their competence to make decisions in their best interest. These two factors place the mentally disordered among the special vulnerable populations who present specific problems in the context of human experimentation and consequently demand special attention for their protection when they become subjects of research.

The authors explore what makes mentally ill persons vulnerable, the issue of coercion, regulations and overseeing of the research enterprise, and the epidemiological burden of the mentally ill in prison. Following a reflection on psychiatric ethics as a way of understanding the theory and practice of ethical guidelines pertaining to mentally disordered offenders, recommendations are provided as reference points for maximizing protections while preserving the possibilities of socially beneficial research.

Abuse, stigmatization, and discrimination of mental patients have taken place since antiquity in every society and culture (Stuart et al. 2012). This chapter, however, will deal only with the potential for abuse when using vulnerable populations in biomedical research, the mentally ill constituting one of those populations, and when they are also part of another vulnerable population, prisoners. In these conditions the mentally ill are prone to be subjected to a double form of stigmatization and discrimination, being classified as both criminal and mentally ill. This double characterization could give rise to injustices where "offender patients are actively treated with less justice, in terms of claims to liberty and personal autonomy, as well as access to care" so that the ethical claims of forensic patients are repeatedly "trumped" by the claims of others (Sen et al. 2007).

5.2   Vulnerability

Vulnerability has been defined as 'a substantial incapacity to protect one's own interests owing to such impediments as lack of capability to give informed consent, lack of alternative means of obtaining medical care or other expensive necessities, or being a junior or subordinate member of a hierarchical group'. A person is vulnerable if 'by reason of old age, infirmity or disability (including mental disorder) he is unable to take care of personal needs or to protect himself from others' (The Law Commission of the United Kingdom 1993). In the context of research, 'vulnerability' would suggest 'an inability to protect oneself from exposure to an unreasonable risk of harm'.

The presence of several specific characteristics relating to group status, severity, permanency, fluctuation, and legal status alone or together would confer to a person or group a status of being vulnerable.

5.2.1 Group Status

People with intellectual disabilities, children, the elderly, people with mental illness, and prisoners are traditionally considered vulnerable, either because they are of an age when, legally, they cannot consent to any procedures (children) or have lost their decision-making capacity (elderly). People with intellectual disabilities will always be vulnerable at any age, but those who are mentally ill or in prison may become vulnerable only for periods of time. Among prisoners their vulnerability is a factor of their dependency and subordinate state, and the effects of long periods of institutionalization. In addition prisoners, while competent otherwise, may see their decision-making capacity compromised by inducements and coercion that affect the voluntariness of their decision.

Other groups of persons could be added as being vulnerable (minorities, politically alienated or discriminated populations, etc.), but these groups become more frequently the subjects of social research, although egregious exceptions in medical research are also well known for their targeting of disenfranchised populations (Reich 1985; Weisstub 1985).

Belonging to a particular 'vulnerable' population does not automatically confer a status of incompetence to make research decisions to any one of its members, although there is a proclivity of research committees to approach vulnerable populations from this perspective. In many instances this position is unfair, unrealistic, and discriminatory. Participation to enrol in a research project should not be denied solely on the basis that the potential research participant belongs to a vulnerable group or to several groups simultaneously. Such a situation should simply signal to researchers and research committees that the expectations for increased ethical awareness in the particular case, or group, should be raised.

5.2.2 Severity

Severity of a medical or mental condition is not a permanent feature of the 'condition', but a factor of the natural history of the disease, which could lead to full recovery, stabilization, or gradual deterioration and death. However, it is expected that on recovery there will be a gradual return to functionality at all levels, including competence to make research decisions. For example a surgical patient may be completely incapacitated, incompetent and, hence, vulnerable while under the effects of anaesthetics, and yet will recover all functions afterwards.

The degree of severity past which a person will be incompetent to consent is a matter for the clinicians and researchers to determine at the moment informed consent is sought. Medical or surgical conditions may not provide a status of research vulnerability, but severity of the condition will cause the patient to become incompetent and vulnerable from time to time. Apart from specific directions about the possibility of accepting advanced directives for participation in research, a blank cheque indicating future availability to become a subject of research is unethical under any circumstances, as nobody can determine with any certainty future capacity and competence to participate.

5.2.3 Permanency

Group status may confer a characteristic of vulnerability and potential incompetence at different periods and stages in life or permanently, as in the case of developmentally disabled persons who, having been born with the disability and being incompetent as a result of both age and disability, will remain incompetent despite entering maturity. Usually they will be vulnerable all their lives. On the contrary, children move from a state of complete dependency, vulnerability, and incompetence to one of increased independence, lesser vulnerability, and complete competence. Unfortunately the opposite occurs with the elderly. They will move from a state of complete independence and competence from the time they reached adulthood to a state of possible complete dependence and vulnerability during their senescence. Seldom would a mentally disordered person be incompetent permanently. Moreover, prisoners may only be incompetent during the period of their incarceration.

5.2.4 Fluctuation

A patient's capacity to make considered decisions, such as agreeing to participate in a research project, could deteriorate unexpectedly. This fact should be a matter of concern and vigilance for medical researchers. In addition, research subjects should have the right to withdraw from a study at any time without compromising a treatment regime or a therapeutic relationship. The interest of the patient must never be secondary to the interest of the researcher; however, even a fully competent person may find it difficult to object to continuing in a project because of dependency on the medical relationship, and the vulnerability inherent in such dependency; it then would be incumbent on the researcher to be aware of and to discuss at intervals the nature of the consent to remain in any research study (Arboleda-Flórez 2009). In addition, individuals who may experience fluctuating periods of incompetence may not have the capacity during those periods to object to their continuation in the project, or to retire their consent. This situation is common among people with mental illness who could also be prisoners. Arrangements for this eventuality should be made in advance, while the person is competent. The researcher should be keenly aware of changing medical conditions so as to be able to decide whether to withdraw the patient from the project, or even to override a research code provision when the patient is incapacitated and if the condition so demands. The vulnerability of the patient should always be recognized.

5.2.5   *Legal Status*

Legal status may change at any time in the life of a particular individual. With the rise of criminality and popular demands to be tough on crime, and the reverberations that these sentiments have had on public policy rhetoric, an anticipated consequence has been that prisons are now being filled with a large number of persons who are disenfranchised, mentally ill, or otherwise incapable of making decisions. The profile of detainees has been dramatically altered. It is understandable that persons in the prison environment will be prone to deteriorate through a conditioning process of dependency and subordination. Many prisoners break down and develop mental conditions, usually severe anxiety and depression, which at times are accompanied by suicidal ideation. Needless to say a prisoner in these conditions will not be competent to provide informed consent and, hence, will not be able to participate in a research project.

5.3   Voluntariness

Voluntariness is a sine qua non to participation in any research project. It is a requisite that applies to all research subjects, but it is of the utmost importance in regard to prisoners when they become subjects of research. Consent has to be given by an autonomous person, freely and voluntarily. Unfortunately, there may be many sound doubts about whether a prisoner is an autonomous person and whether informed consent can actually be obtained in a prison environment. Situations in which a hierarchical or subordinate relationship exist usually leave one person, or group of persons, in a position of dependency and vulnerability where inducements or manipulations could be used to make the vulnerable person agree to a particular act. Goffman's pioneer work described "total institutions" (1961) and explained how such environments strip people of privacy, dignity and identity, and eradicate the ethical attribute of voluntariness.

Within closed institutions, inmates are susceptible to persuasion though overt or subtle threats and/or undue inducements. More broadly students, for example, who are recruited by their professor to participate in the professor's research project when the same professor is in charge of evaluating their performance, or patients who are inducted into their researcher-physician's own research projects, may be particularly vulnerable and indeed feel "coerced" to participate. In these situations, the person may feel trapped between positive feelings of loyalty towards the superior or the person in charge of his clinical needs and negative feelings or fear of losing the dependent status and being left without support or even physical protection.

5.4   Coercion

In regard to the specific issue of "coercion," this term has been defined as the act of exercising power, usually by an agent who is intent on influencing the behaviour of others. The agent could do this by persuasion, but if this fails, the agent can make the other person do it against his will, by threats, force, or extortion. Thus, coercion may involve infliction of physical or psychological pain in order to enhance the credibility of the threat. The aim of the "coercing agent" is to seek cooperation or obedience in the coerced as well as to send a message to those who support him. As such, coercion is an overt manipulation of behaviour whose main characteristic is the simultaneous presentation of an offer and a threat. Coercion then works via a bi-conditional proposition composed of the simultaneous making of a threat and an offer, or 'thropher' (Steiner 1975), in which motivation and intentionality to coerce is a sine qua non in the coercer. While the coerced has freedom to choose a course of action between the threat and the offer, either way he chooses, he will come out the loser (Gorr 1989). The simple proposition "you can go and play after you do your homework" carries the offer of permission to play, but also the implied threat that this will be denied if homework is not done. If he goes to play without doing the homework, there will be repercussions and he will be the loser; if he does the home-work first, he is denying himself the enjoyment of his preferred choice, so he again is the loser. The field of action for the coerced is indeed very limited; he is caught in a triadic relationship between himself as agent, the object of his choice, and other agents, many of whom may be intent on exercising power through threats to prevent him from making his choice of objects.

Coercion is an intrinsic element in human relations. Persons at a certain level of authority seek to explain their commands and to seek the support of the others, but there is no doubt among the 'others' that if orders are not followed or requests are not acquiesced, or obeyed, there will be consequences. Thus, coercion works on a spectrum stretching from persuasion through to imposition; it is in contraposition to freedom, however defined. When freedom is defined in positive terms such as 'con-sisting of being one's master', then by following orders freedom is coerced. If, however, freedom is defined in negative terms such as 'not being prevented from choosing as others do' (Berlin 1969), then orders not to do something are coercive. More specifically in the field of psychiatry, when the patient enters into treatment voluntarily, there is always the open or veiled threat that imposition of coercive measures is a possibility and, sometimes even likely. Coercion is an ever-present characteristic of psychiatry and is highly prevalent in forensic psychiatry and in the field of correctional research. In general the stakes are very high for a prisoner who refuses to participate in a research project, not only because by so doing he denies himself the possibility of entering into a project that could potentially benefit him, but also because despite assurances to the contrary, the prisoner can never be sure that there will not be repercussions.

On a different level, ethical grounds become much more slippery and the boundaries more diffused if the researcher is also motivated by financial or other rewards, and therefore has an incentive to increase the recruitment or to keep the research subject in the study. Personal needs, conscious or unconscious, a wish to succeed and to be recognized, a need to keep the variables in the experiment under close control, a desire for advancement, or plain monetary greed, are powerful motivational tools for the researcher in these situations to turn a blind eye to the ethical realities of having to act if untoward effects start to materialize that may impact negatively on a research subject. These should be enough reasons to request that researchers do not involve their own students or patients in their research projects.

Specifically in clinical medical research, because of double or triple vulnerabilities of the patients and the motivational imperatives on the researchers, there is much to commend that the treating physician not be the same as the physician-researcher. It has been argued that, in this way, 'responsibility for the welfare of the patient is located unequivocally in one identifiable member of the research team, and if necessary, that person should defend the patient's good against the good of science'. In fact, it may also be that the patient has to be protected against less lofty interests of the researcher including fraud, sex bias, nepotism, and plain abuse of patients or prisoners, as exemplified by egregious cases that have been identified in some mental hospitals and prison research projects.

An outstanding example of unethical research was the Ewen Cameron case in Canada (Cooper and Cameron 1986), where a reputed professor of psychiatry mixed therapy with research, administering a bizarre number of electroconvulsive therapy treatments in order to demonstrate the importance of his theory on "depatterning" the brain from old memories and consequently improving major mental conditions (Weisstub 1998).

The Cameron case is still significant because it raises a number of questions about the necessity of peer review: the vetting of funding; the requirements of informed consent; the rights of patients to withdraw in the course of research; the distinction between therapy, innovative therapy and therapeutic experimentation relevant to disclosure requirements; the role of family members in protecting their next of kin; the place of lay advocates and concerned parties to represent their case for protection before a neutral overseeing body; the burden of Statutes of Limitations on plaintiffs who have suffered in research contexts about which they gain familiarity many years after the fact; and the obligations that should be placed on disciplinary professional boards to police situations of abuse.

The Cameron case posed hard and searching questions about the nature of the conflict of interests that arise in research, not only in university settings but also in prisons where captive populations live under the surveillance of medical practitioners who have given oaths of allegiance to the state as much as to their subjects.

The government of Canada commissioned an opinion by George Cooper QC in 1986 to review the transgressions that occurred at McGill University under the auspices of Prof. Cameron. It is intriguing to note that in his response George Cooper treated Cameron's practices as a matter of experimentation to show there was no established law and as therapeutic interventions to demonstrate that there was no violation of professional standards. In this Cooper received the wide support of professional experts. The lesson to be learned from the Cameron case is that governing moral principles without proper structures in place for surveillance will be time and time again shown to be inadequate to defend vulnerable populations.

Although "depatterning" was not done on prisoners, but on mental patients in a leading academic psychiatric institution, the elements of careless disregard for the well-being of others whose care was entrusted to psychiatric-researchers were the same. Other pertinent cases have emerged in Canada. Dorothy Parker (Tyler 1999), an ex-prisoner, sued the Government of Canada because of damages suffered; along with 22 other inmates, she was inducted into a research program testing LSD, which transpired in several federal penitentiaries in Ontario between 1960 and 1973. In Canada cases have also been documented about serious transgressions in bypassing consent requirements, including the effects of medication and the ingestion of pesticides (Regehr et al. 2000).

5.5   Ideological and Ethical Conundrums

In psychiatry, research roles are frequently blurred, which makes for an important subject of ethical scrutiny. The trajectory of practices can range from mild transgressions to situations where psychiatry has participated in torture and grievous violations of human rights. Psychiatry, more than any other profession within medicine, has found it difficult to escape the heavy hands of political authority. Interestingly, we can underline the fact that during liberal periods, psychiatry has been identified with extreme liberalism (Weisstub 1980). However, during periods of totalitarianism, equally psychiatry has been identified with the extremities of punitive practices, thereby giving rise to its isolation as the leading perpetrator of unethical practices within medicine (Van Voren 2009; Munro 2006; Reich 1985).

What then are the philosophical/ethical options available to psychiatry? Is there an 'internal' or 'aspirational' morality that can be located to subdue and resist the compromises demanded of it? Whatever the solutions that have been attempted within psychiatry at large, which have resulted in versions of virtue ethics, the identification of core principles, or psychoanalytically-oriented endeavours towards the creation of various interpretations of humanism, it is best to acknowledge that the debate within forensic psychiatry and its relationship to research have given rise to distinct issues.

It has been argued by Appelbaum (Appelbaum 1997, 2008b) that there is a definitive ethics which lies at the base of all forensically-related practices. He has asserted that the ethical conundrums that have questioned the ethical integrity of forensic projects can be resolved by identifying two core principles: truth telling and respect for persons. In Appelbaum's view, if forensic psychiatrists reveal their shortcomings with respect to scientific knowledge, then prima facie their ethical mandate will have been properly fulfilled. On meeting the threshold requirement of respect for persons, Appelbaum believes that in all forensic contexts, once psychiatrists have properly exposed their justice mandate to subjects as ethical actors, they should be relieved of any further ethical obligations. It appears to be the case that Appelbaum would apply this model to forensic research.

A group of Scandinavian researchers recently summarized and commented on the Appelbaum model as applied to the research context: "As long as the researcher does her best to find the truth according to scientific standards, the fact that her findings may be harmful for the research subjects is of no ethical concern, at least not as long as the subjects have been respected as persons, according to standard research ethical regulation about informed consent... We hold this analysis to be far too simplified to square with either coherent ethical theory or standard research ethical practice." (Munthe et al. 2012)

In our view, dissecting forensic work from issues of private morality, professional morality, institutional morality, and even political sensibilities, does not comport with the realities facing forensic research given the range of role-conflicts that are part of the forensic enterprise (McNeill 1993). It is probably a safe assertion that most mental health professionals doing forensic research feel the pressure to work on multiple tracks and have not yet found, and are unlikely to find, easy resolutions to their moral dilemmas. We should also note that even in epidemiological research unpacking ideological presuppositions is worthy of our attention (Tancredi and Weisstub 1991).

Clearing away the brush of confused moral identities, articulating the proper standard at which one must operate in different professional contexts and submitting a course of action for how to train professionals to be morally capable to know the standards and to apply them with appropriate resiliency is a major challenge. Put simply, how do we assure ourselves that professionals are morally capable in conducting, for example, forensic research on mentally disordered offenders? The issue of whether the discipline of forensic psychiatry should or can remain neutral, we believe, will remain part of an unending debate. In the forensic world, we are frequently left with dilemmas of how to cope with a morally confusing set of values, interests, or prejudices. The problem persists in how to exercise proper professional judgment in situations that appear to have a morally charged issue at stake.

By differentiating forensic research work in conceptual terms from inner morality, 'professional morality', institutional morality, and political and humanistic sensibilities, Prof. Appelbaum in effect sterilizes the forensic project. Concretely we might ask how should forensic researchers deal with respect for persons in circumstances where they have to cope with economic interests, prejudice, and nuanced role conflicts? Appelbaum seems to have attempted to solve the problem through a positivistic dissection, drawing boundaries in the interest of dissipating any confusion of roles that might arise.

Despite this conceptual move, in our view Appelbaum's position is best placed into the category of what is now conventionally understood in the bioethics literature as 'principlism'. This is philosophically related to the idea that a body of knowledge as a discreet category can be governed by a set of principles from which we can derive conduct and good action. This deductivist model has long-standing credentials in our Western philosophical tradition. Virtue theory, coming out of the Aristotelian tradition, has close affinities with principlism. Of similar stature are the classical formulations of Kant on the question of universalizability. He can be thanked for having illuminated the Enlightenment with the role of reason in arriving at core values such as autonomy and respect for persons. However, unlike the derivational logics of closed or complete metaphysical systems with a carefully honed ontology and epistemology, contemporary bioethics has frequently obscured the term.

In Appelbaum's defense it is correct to say that he insists on there being foundational or governing principles in forensic ethics. Nevertheless it is unclear how he is using the term principle. Our suggestion is that he is assessing the 'rules of the game', something which already exists, and then brings to the level of consciousness guidelines on how to do the job properly. Although this advice is better than an empty shell, critics would contend that it does not have the ammunition to fire properly under dire moral threat. They would insist that what is needed to constitute a 'moral professional persona' for a project such as forensic research is more complex than Appelbaum has allowed for.

For example, critiques can be mustered against Appelbaum from teleological sources by 'aspirationalists', whose concepts of morality convey the moral ground upon which all professional conduct done by psychiatrists, including forensic work, should be governed. This point of view, held by such philosophers as Pellegrino (1993) and Foot (1990), identifies a core morality to which a psychiatrist should turn when faced with any issue of conflicted loyalty. This morality refers to the intrinsic purpose of the vocation of being a mental health professional. To exempt a psychiatrist from the mandates of the professional undertakings of a doctor is regarded by them as an anathema, a direct contradiction of the notion of 'professional personhood' (Weisstub and Thomasma 2001). Any understanding of respect for persons separated from this mandate would appear to them as illogical and self-contradictory (Weisstub and Thomasma 2004).

To be fair in critiquing Appelbaum's position, it should be admitted that entering into a more elaborate map of values and conflictual situations might inevitably result in the politicizing of psychiatry, where ideology and subjectivity are destined to distort rationality and objective professionalism. It is our view that although psychiatric researchers should be inspired by broader social and ethical mandates than provided by Appelbaum, it is only true that through carefully constructed procedural mechanisms that baseline protections can be sustained. Nevertheless it is suggested here that enlightened interpretations of existing rules can be illuminated by a broadly conceived professional morality.

There have been various attempts to explore this avenue. In effect this is another way of stating that professional roles and functions should be understood in context. Numerous frameworks have been employed, such as systems theory (Ciccone and Clements 1984), in attempts to locate the clearest expression of the voices that are party to any given process; women, minorities, and victims, in addition to officialdom and authority figures.

In their work entitled "Forensic Ethics and the Expert Witness" (Candilis et al. 2007), the authors describe their position as 'narrative analysis'. Their framework, as is the case with Appelbaum's position, can be employed in the context of forensic research. They embrace the idea that cultural analysis is relevant in the forensic sector and that it is essential that forensic experts find vehicles to explore and articulate their own personal values, identifications, and life histories in order to do justice in a particular instance. Even though there are pitfalls linked to this process it is their belief that it is worth the risk to proceed this way in order to avoid doing injustice. Their position posits that failure to pursue this route increases the likelihood of unethical outcomes when, for example, there could be moral dissonance between certain species of forensic research and one's own ethical life history attached to a specified set of values.

Appelbaum's point of view, in contrast to a contextualist approach, is both more logical and clean. Notwithstanding this, from the lens of narrative ethics such a 'professional' could be regarded as a hollow scarecrow. It appears to be a premise of narrative ethics that once we take away the context of any given forensic project, the parameters are then abstracted and thereby reduced to rules of conduct which do not do justice to the relevant parties.

Narrative analysis requires that in each case we reposition each of the actors directed towards a moral conversation. The dramatization of the forensic encounter in these terms is attuned to a tradition within modern ethics associated with philosophers Buber (1937) and Levinas (1972). Curiously enough, it is problematic to apply their vocabularies to forensic populations where the subjects in question, almost by definition, have serious defects with regard to moral recognition. We are forced to consider whether narrative analysis leads to an ego-driven solipsism, to a soliloquy rather than a real human encounter.

In the search for a humanistically placed ethic for forensic research do we find that the alternative of narrative analysis takes us in a direction which is unrealistic and altogether too discretionary? After all, the forensic researcher is destined to always remain in a power position, even when searching for a thoroughgoing narrative analysis. Where does the forensic actor locate the ground for moral/professional discretion? If the answer is to be found only on an ad hoc basis, is the forensic researcher lured into a subjectivist trap? If a narrative ethic is to succeed it must be able to visualize the components of a case as part of a larger context. Such an introspective analysis is fraught with uncertainty as, by definition, it must allow for a meditation on the multiple layers of one's moral histories relating to family, prejudices, and a myriad of individual life-transformations. It requires a commitment that every effort be made to hear the voices or indeed to articulate them on behalf of parties in conflict, actually or potentially. To do otherwise, contextualists would submit, would be to abandon the in-depth role of being a professional. In this universe of discourse it becomes the responsibility of every forensic researcher to participate in a morally relevant exploration of the research enterprise.

Narrative ethics has been recently expanded into the domain of relational ethics, a position fashioned by nursing oriented ethicists who believe that forensic projects cannot be effectively and meaningfully realized without a process whereby the treaters or researchers enter into a morally/psychologically sensitive dialogue, however challenging and difficult (Austin et al. 2009).

The majority of professionals are well advised to be generally defensive insofar as removal from established protocols through excessive personal exposure can easily give rise to professional reprimands, or even litigation. Therefore, the ideal of 'narrative ethics' may in fact be a willow wisp rather than a practical vehicle for any real dialogue to occur. Perhaps the best we can expect in prison-type environments is for protocols to be carefully attended to and for oversight mechanisms to be as thorough and comprehensive as possible in the given circumstances. Bear in mind also, that the exigencies that are part of constricting economies have, for very practical reasons, frustrated the realization of best practices as revealed through current provisions.

It is probably the case that these aforementioned explorative modes can bring helpful insights and moral integrity to many problematic cases that arise both in treatment and research. It would seem erroneous therefore to banish this method if it does not contradict the rules of protection that have been instantiated within progressive legal frameworks designed specifically for vulnerable populations such as mentally disordered offenders. In any event, more research is needed and practical case studies reflected upon to properly assess these challenging approaches.

We know very little about how moral judgment takes place in professional contexts, both of psychiatric practice and research. The most rudimentary questions of how psychiatrists define a moral question have yet to be exposed. Commitments to qualitatively satisfying modalities of communication with patients and research subjects have still not been sufficiently resolved in hierarchical environments, such as prisons. The reconfiguration of the doctor-patient relationship has lead to some insights about the role of autonomy, but with strong caveats. Psychiatric practice and research capability have both shown increasing affinities with pharmacology, genetics, and neurology. Are we justified in observing that we now are faced with increased ethical risks for the reason that where the sciences have waxed, morality has often waned?

5.6 Rules and Regulations

The way out of relativism is to seek the grounding of a moral enterprise that has epistemological and ontological integrity, demonstrating a metaphysical philosophy spanning cultures and times. The prescribed resolution for forensic psychiatry and its research endeavours would be to identify a professional morality that could systematically override questionable ideologies and prejudices. Asserting the necessity of such an offering, alas, is easier than furnishing it. No such safe metaphysical refuge is in evidence. Frequently the consideration is whether the psychiatrist/researcher has developed a personal moral stature capable of resisting the 'mainstream' when called upon to provide arguments to brace the suspension of normative ethical behaviour specified within the moral culture in question.

It is not surprising that psychiatric researchers throughout mental health systems have desired that ethical professional training be put into place. However, to date, no satisfactory model has evolved short of generalized forms of pastoral-type training. We might ask: is there a process short of a solution which can be proposed?

Because of the elaborate antecedents of prisoner abuse, notably during WWII, and surprisingly due to the exposés of the extensive use of prisoners in the US from the 1950s until the 1970s non-therapeutic experimentation effectively drew to a close by the 1980s in North America and elsewhere. With the evolution of consent criteria and the introduction of various kinds of review procedures, most North American prison institutions respect a functional ban on such research except for special situations involving negligible risks. This state of affairs is exemplified and mirrored in the recent study undertaken by Gostin and others in 2006. In fact biomedical research within prisons is essentially not permitted in most of the industrialized world.

The American history is exemplary in this respect. Whereas in the late 1960s, 85 % of new drugs were prisoner-tested, by the 1980s the figure had dropped to approximately 15 %. It is worth observing furthermore that even where there are not explicit bans, occurrences are extremely rare because of the introduction of overseeing bodies and the existence of internal regulations. Finally the role of the media cannot be underemphasized.

At the present time we are justified in generalizing that protective guidelines, both in North America and Europe, as well as in international professional organizations and U.N.-type bodies have similar wording, earmarking the standards that have been globalized in codes and regulations. The consistent application of such standards, or a shared clarity with respect to interpretation, is another matter. Depending upon the jurisdiction, regulations come under the purview also of a series of constitutional rights, whether they be domestic, regional, or arrived at through intergovernmental covenants. At a practical level it is worth referring to the Council for International Organizations of Medical Sciences (CIOMS) Guidelines (1993) which point out that no internationally agreed-upon recommendation was achieved on the use of prisoners in biomedical research, despite a consensus about independent monitoring.

It has been our stated opinion since 1998 (Verdun-Jones et al. 1998) that either an explicit or indirect ban should be disallowed for prisoner non-therapeutic research. Rather we have emphasized the central issue of voluntariness and the insistence that related issues be carefully monitored through procedural safeguards. It was our focus that inmate inputs and participation within research ethics committees be introduced. Recent reports and critiques of existing guidelines have supported these earlier recommendations (Gostin et al. 2007; Onyemelukwe and Downie 2011). Additionally it is timely to continue to insist that prisoner participation be properly advanced through accessible and understandable consent forms. This requirement is paramount given the literacy profile of prison populations. The mentally disordered prison population represents an exaggerated version of this profile. We recommend that tests requiring adequate answers re critical components of the proposed research be reviewed by the relevant overseeing body.

While opposing an outright ban on non-therapeutic research with mentally disordered offenders, in the main to avoid excluding them from the potential benefits of research, we are cautious about the efficacy of surveillance. This is so due to the fact that the quality of ethically based surveillance is intrinsically tied to the level of integrity of the overseers. Having codes and instruments in place will not in itself be a reliable guarantee of adequate protection. We should not be naïve about the capacity of codes or legislation to bring unanimity or predictability for protecting research subjects. It is a lesson of history that the ethical guidelines proclaimed in Weimar Germany were helpless in protecting vulnerable populations despite the fact that they were stricter and more detailed than the celebrated Nuremburg Code of 1947 and the Helsinki Declaration of 1964 (Sass 1988).

It is now a truism that biomedical research is only considered permissible where the objective of the research is proportionate to the subjects' risk. In the category of mentally disordered offenders, this has resulted in tightly woven restrictions where if any risk at all could be introduced it would be of only a negligible proportion. Researchers are contemporaneously seen to have a positive duty to minimize risks and are obligated to take precautions at various stages of a research intervention. It is difficult to imagine a jurisdiction where such protections are not already in place by law, legislation, or custom. Before beginning an experiment researchers must carefully assess potential risks and avoid unnecessary ones, and make preparations to protect individuals against even remote possibilities of injury. During an experiment researchers are obligated to alert the overseeing body responsible for approving the protocols in question in the eventuality of new risks. Researchers are expected to provide ongoing support to monitor complications as they might arise and assure that consent or assent, as the case might be, are not compromised. Termination of an experiment when changed circumstances arise, altering the risk profile, is without question. Following an experiment researchers are obligated to offer follow-up support in order to avoid untoward consequences.

Risk assessments must be performed with respect to the risk profile of any experiment or research endeavour. With regard to the notion of negligible risk, it amounts to assessing that the probability and the magnitude of harm or discomfort anticipated in the research will not be greater than those ordinarily encountered in daily life or during the performance of routine physical or psychological examinations or tests. Within the risk assessment the determination must be made about the experiment or research project as an aggregate, since individual components of a protocol might be negligible in themselves but through repetition or prolongation might morph into something more substantial. At root there must be a positive interpretation in the final analysis that potential benefits must outweigh the potential risks or harms.

In 2006, the Committee on Ethical Considerations for Revisions to the Department of Health and Human Services Regulations for Protection of Prisoners Involved in Research set up by the Institute of Medicine in the US to review practices in the management of 'all persons whose liberty has been restricted by decisions of the criminal justice system' concluded that the key ethical considerations in the earlier National Commission Report (1979), respect for persons, beneficence and justice, should be retained as the basis for determining the conduct of research with prisoners, but recognized that these principles had evolved since they were enunciated in 1978 to another principle relating to collaborative responsibility in an effort to bring attention to 'the needs and responsibilities of all parties who will be involved with or affected by a research endeavor.' We concur that the concept of justice in research, which emphasized protection of vulnerable subjects from exploitation, has moved on towards a notion seeking to balance the need for protection of vulnerable subjects with the need for improved access to the benefits of research. Thus, a concept of "balancing justice" has been installed in replacement of the old concept of 'justice of protection.'

In the delicate arena where society deems it allowable to conduct research with mentally disordered offenders, and given the strictures that have been deployed to minimize risks and burdens, it is not surprising that ambiguities and ambivalences have arisen. Such a tension is revealed in the European Convention on Human Rights and Biomedicine (Convention 1997). It is not always clear that the results of research have the potential to produce real and direct benefits to a prisoner's health. Such a requirement, for example, is part of the European Convention. The condition that it is not possible to conduct research of comparable effectiveness with individuals capable of giving consent may equally not be clearly the case. The European Convention allows that in certain exceptional conditions research that cannot be connected to offering a direct benefit to the research subject, unable to consent to research, may be authorized. It is prescribed by the Convention that such research must be minimal, both with respect to risk and burden. Felicity Callard (2010) points out the discrepancy between the EU directives and the Convention. Where there are no potential benefits there is greater flexibility with the Directives. There is the requirement that there be minimization of pain, discomfort, foreseeable risk, etc. and that risk and distress be defined and monitored. But, as she puts it: "the differences between the Convention and the Directive bear witness to the intractable difficulty of adequately protecting research participants at the same time as not stopping biomedical research in its tracks." Depending upon one's interpretation of what constitutes negligible risk and minimum inconvenience, it is conceivable that certain overseers would choose to, practically speaking, ban research with mentally disordered offenders.

Norbert Konrad points out that there is a lesser known and relatively unacknowledged parallel system of control located in the specific European prison rules (Konrad and Völlm 2010; Committee 2006). In similar states outside of the EU there are Directives and Regulations that function in the same manner. Whatever the lack of widely shared awareness, the shortcoming has limited impact because the circumference of permissibility is so tight with respect to mentally disordered offenders even where a ban is not officially in effect, that one can safely rely in most instances on the responsiveness of research ethics committees. For the 50 % of the European countries that allow limited research there is insufficient information on the extent to which non-therapeutic research could ever go beyond negligible risk related to mentally disordered offenders, given the emphasis on obtaining informed consent (Salize et al. 2007).

5.7   Epidemiology and the Future of Forensic Research

Studies of the relationship between mental illness and violence have usually found that although there is an association between the two, the relationship typically flows through covariates such as history of violence, age, sex, alcohol and substance abuse, or personality disorders, not directly stemming from mental illness per se. That is, a definite causality mechanism has not been established even when some studies have reported an elevated relative risk. At the point of population risk, the attributable risk has been found to be negligible compared to other risks of violence in the population. In other words, mental illness is an insignificant source of violence in the community, but the type of violence purportedly committed by the mentally disordered garners disproportionate media coverage, rightfully because of the gruesomeness of some of the cases, and it engenders an exaggerated sense of personal risk.

Lessons can be drawn from cases of sudden criminal homicidal violence. The first lesson is that there are some common denominators to many violent incidents: the perpetrators are typically young males and mental instability or untreated or poorly treated mental illness have not been uncommon factors. Alcohol and/or drug abuse are usually associated factors. Studies of the association indicate that there is a relationship between mental illness and violence (Angermeyer et al. 1998) and a high prevalence of mental conditions has been a regular finding in most studies (Allodi et al. 1977; Bland and Dyck 1990; Hodgins and Coté 1990), but other authors who have adopted a public health perspective in comparing rates of crime in the general population disagree (Stuart and Arboleda-Flórez 2001). Violent offences committed by the mentally ill, however, underscore the need to rethink and to study more the nature of the association between mental illness and violence, and to consider whether we are asking the right questions when we study this putative association. Finally if mental illness is truly a factor in cases of violence, where should we ascribe the responsibility? To an extent possible mental patients should know of their condition and be responsible for its management, but responsibility must also be ascribed to mental health systems, to policies of deinstitutionalization and to lax legal systems that recycle mental patients back into the community when they have already been found not criminally responsible because of a mental condition. This last point is more salient when it is recognized that in many countries mentally disordered offenders are often released into the community bereft of clinical follow-up.

5.8   Conclusion

Short of complete philosophical resolutions, the global line of retreat has been at least to provide objective standards for research with mentally disordered offenders that can be embodied in common law rules, international treaties, or human rights declarations. Such provisions can be seen as adequate for a baseline preservation of human rights and ethical protections for the subjects of forensic research. They are not perfect or complete, but ample at this point in the history of liberal democracies. We should even be prepared to submit that we have arrived at a working consensus of how forensic research subjects should be treated to avoid miscarriages of their interests. We have abandoned the notion that research with such subjects should be banned. We have, on the other hand, seen the need to curtail abuse by drawing the line very carefully beyond instances of the most minimal level of risk. There is little disagreement to be found here.

It is surely an attractive ideal to have the aforementioned issues resolved through codification, tightly defined rules, or elaborate directives. However, it should be admitted that the inherent rigidity of such efforts has not borne fruit where contestable issues have confronted decision-makers in forensic research. The situation indeed has been aggravated by a lack of consensus about a core set of governing values, coupled by a perceived break-down in the moral integrity of the psychiatric professional in our predominantly relativistic industrially and technologically advanced cultures. There have been attempts to list general principles, even to isolate a pyramidal principle or organizing concept, such as human dignity (Ward and Willis 2010). Nevertheless, such attempts can be seen to be overly abstracted and of limited utility in the gray zones where psychiatric researchers claim that direction is needed (Mishara and Weisstub 2005; Weisstub 2002).

Much needed epidemiological research is warranted, even without consent, where identities cannot be linked to any apparent risk or harm to the subjects. Beyond that, we must provide protections for mentally disordered prisoners through the tight leash of carefully articulated risk-benefit balancing which has already been established, either by law or custom, throughout the industrialized world. Having said that, no set of rules or regulations will meet the range of challenges that present themselves. Although uncertain of its effectiveness, efforts should be continued to sensitize researchers to the need to respect research subjects through in-depth reflection on actual cases that occur in their respective working environments. Without such an emphasis on the need for ongoing reflection and/or dialogue, not only with professionals but also with research subjects, we will be working against the expressed interest of our given set of rules and regulations that are now in place. Because of the vulnerability of mentally disordered prisoners, it is clear that vigilance is required. Without all manner of communications and sharing of information at every stage in the process, committees of review will not achieve their goals. There should be a real commitment shown in the extended research environment for respecting the spirit as much as the letter of the law in the area of forensic research. In assuming the competence of many potential research subjects in prisons, we may be able to look forward to examples of respectful cooperation that will bring productive results to improve the life of mentally disordered offenders (Appelbaum 2008a). Such research advances in optimum conditions will ultimately contribute to societal protection while preserving dignity and respect for research subjects to the maximum possible.

References

Allodi, F., H. Kedward, and M. Robertson. 1977. Insane but guilty: Psychiatric patients in jail. *Canada's Mental Health* 25: 3–7.

Angermeyer, M., B. Cooper, and B. Link. 1998. Mental disorder and violence: Results of epidemiological studies in the ero of de-institutionalization. *Social Psychiatry and Psychiatric Epidemiology* 33: S1–S6.

Appelbaum, P.S. 1997. A theory of ethics for forensic psychiatry. *Journal of the Academy of Psychiatry and the Law* 25(3): 233–247.

Appelbaum, K.L. 2008a. Correctional mental health research: Opportunities and barriers. *Journal of Correctional Health Care* 14(4): 269–277. doi:10.1177/1078345808322607.

Appelbaum, P.S. 2008b. Ethics and the forensic psychiatrist: translating principles into practices. *The Journal of the American Academy of Psychiatry and the Law* 36: 195–200.

Arboleda-Flórez, J. 1999. Mental illness in jails and prisons. *Current Opinion in Psychiatry* 12: 677–682.

Arboleda-Flórez, J. 2009. Mental illness and violence. *Current Opinion in Psychiatry* 22(5): 475–476.

Austin, W., E. Goble, and J. Kelecevic. 2009. The ethics of forensic psychiatry: Moving beyond principles to a relational ethics approach. *The Journal of Forensic Psychiatry & Psychology* 20(6): 835–850.

Berlin, I. 1969. *Four essays on liberty*. London: Oxford University Press.

Bland, R., and R. Dyck. 1990. Prevalence of psychiatric disorders and suicide attempts in a prison population. *Canadian Journal of Psychiatry* 35: 407–413.

Buber, M. 1937. *I and thou*. New York: Scribner.

Callard, F. 2010. Between legislation and bioethics: The European convention on human rights and biomedicine. In *Ethics and psychiatry*, ed. H. Helmchen and N. Sartorius, 73–96. Dordrecht: Springer.

Candilis, P., R. Weinstock, and R. Martinez. 2007. *Forensic ethics and the expert witness*. New York: Springer.

Ciccone J.R., Clements C. 1984. Forensic psychiatry and applied clinical ethics: theory and practice. *American Journal of Psychiatry* 141(3): 395–399.

Committee of Ministers. 2006. Recommendation Rec(2006)2 of the committee of minsters to member states on the European prison rules. Council of Europe. https://wcd.coe.int/ViewDoc.jsp?id=955747.

Convention for the Protection of Human Rights and Dignity of the Human Being with regard to the Application of Biology and Medicine: Convention on Human Rights and Biomedicine (1997), Oviedo, 4.IV. 1997. European Treaty Series – No. 164, Council of Europe, Strasbourg.

Cooper, G., and E. Cameron. 1986. *Opinion of George Cooper Q.C. regarding Canadian government funding of the Allan Memorial Institute in the 1950's and 1960's*. Ottawa: Communications and Public Affairs, Dept. of Justice.

Council for International Organizations of Medical Sciences. 1993. *International ethical guidelines for biomedical research involving human subjects*. Geneva: CIOMS.

Foot, P. 1990. Ethics and the death penalty. In *Ethical practice in psychiatry and the law*, ed. R. Rosner and R. Weinstock, 207–217. New York: Plenum Press.

Goffman, E. 1961. *Asylums: Essays on the social situation of mental patients and other inmates*, 1st ed. Garden City: Anchor Books.

Gorr, M.J. 1989. *Coercion, freedom and exploitation*. Minnesota: Peter Lang Publishing.

Gostin, L.O., C. Vanchieri, and A.M. Pope. 2007. *Ethical considerations for research involving prisoners*. Washington, DC: National Academies Press.

Hodgins, S., and G. Coté. 1990. Prevalence of mental disorders among penitentiary inmates in Quebec. *Canada's Mental Health* 38: 1–4.

Institute of Medicine. 2006. *Ethical considerations for research involving prisoners*. Washington, DC: National Academies Press.

Konrad, N., and B. Völlm. 2010. Ethical issues in forensic and prison psychiatry. In *Ethics and psychiatry*, ed. H. Helmchen and N. Sartorius, 73–96. Dordrecht: Springer.

Levinas, E. 1972. *Humanisme de l'autre homme*. Paris: LGF.

McNeill, P.M. 1993. *The ethics and politics of human experimentation*. Cambridge: Cambridge University Press.

Mishara, B., and D. Weisstub. 2005. Ethical and legal issues in suicide research. *International Journal of Law and Psychiatry* 28(1): 23–41.

Munro, R. 2006. *China's psychiatric inquisition*. London: Simmonds and Hill.

Munthe, C., S. Radovic, and H. Anckarsäter. 2012. Ethical issues in forensic psychiatric research on mentally disordered offenders. *Bioethics* 24(1): 35–44.

National Commission for the Protection of Research Subjects of Biomedical and Behavioural Research. 1979. *The Belmont report: Ethical principles and guidelines for the protection of human subjects of research*. U.S. Department of Health, Education, and Welfare: Washington. http://www.hhs.gov/ohrp/humansubjects/guidance/belmont.html.

Onyemelukwe, C., and J. Downie. 2011. The tunnel at the end of the light? A critical analysis of the development of the Tri-Council Policy Statement. *Canadian Journal of Law and Society* 26(1): 159–176. University of Toronto Press. doi:10.1353/jls.2011.0006.

Pellegrino, E.D. 1993. Societal duty and moral complicity. *International Journal of Law and Psychiatry* 16(3): 371–391.

Regehr, C., M. Edwardh, and J. Bradford. 2000. Research ethics and forensic patients. *Canadian Journal of Psychiatry* 45: 892–898.

Reich, W. 1985. The world of Soviet psychiatry. In *The breaking of bodies and minds: Torture, psychiatric abuse, and the health professions*, ed. E. Stover and O. Nightingale, 206–222. New York: W. H. Freeman.

Salize, H.J., H. Dreßing, and C. Kief. 2007. *Mentally disordered persons in European prison systems – needs, programmes and outcomes (EUPRIS). Final report*. Mannheim: Central Institute of Mental Health.

Sass, H.M. 1988. Comparative models and goals for the regulation of human research. In *The use of human beings in research*, ed. S.F. Spicker, 47–89. Boston: Kluwer Academic Publishers.

Sen, P., H. Gordon, and G. Adshead. 2007. Ethical dilemmas in forensic psychiatry: Two illustrative cases. *Journal of Medical Ethics* 33: 337–341.

Steiner, H. 1975. Individual liberty. *Proceedings of the Aristotelian Society* 75: 33–50.

Stuart, H., and J. Arboleda-Flórez. 2001. A public health perspective on violent offences among persons with mental illness. *Psychiatric Services* 52(5): 654–659.

Stuart, H., J. Arboleda-Flórez, and N. Sartorios. 2012. *Paradigms lost: Fighting stigma and the lessons learned*. Oxford: Oxford University Press.

Tancredi, L.R., and D.N. Weisstub. 1991. Ideology and power: Epidemiology and interpretation in law and psychiatry. In *The anthropology of medicine, from culture to method*, ed. L. Rosemanucci-Ross, D.E. Moorman, and L.R. Tancredi, 301ff-. New York: Bergin & Garvey.

The Law Commission of the United Kingdom. 1993. *Mentally incapacitated and other vulnerable adults: Public law protection*, Consultation Paper No. 130. London: HMSO. At para 2.9.

Tyler, T. 1999. I was just a biological unit: Case of inmate use in LSD tests raises questions about the ethics of scientific experiments in Canada's jails. *The Toronto Star*, December 18.

Van Voren, R. 2009. *On dissidents and madness: from the Soviet Union of Leonid Brezhnev to the "Soviet Union" of Vladimir Putin*. Amsterdam: Editions Rodopi B.V.

Verdun-Jones, S., D.N. Weisstub, and J. Arboleda-Flórez. 1998. Prisoners as subjects of biomedical experimentation: Examining the arguments for and against a total ban. In *Research on human subjects*, ed. D.N. Weisstub, 503–530. Oxford: Pergamon.

Ward, T., and G. Willis. 2010. Ethical issues in forensic and correctional research. *Aggression and Violent Behavior* 15: 399–409.

Weisstub, D.N. 1980. Psychiatry and the political question. *International Journal of Law and Psychiatry* 30(3): 219–233.

Weisstub, D.N. 1985. Le droit et la psychiatrie dans leur problématique commune. *McGill Law Journal* 30: 221–232.

Weisstub, D.N. 1997. La recherche médicale en milieu carceral. *International Journal of Bioethics* 6: 87–93.

Weisstub, D.N. 1998. The ethical parameters of experimentation. In *Research on human subjects*, ed. D.N. Weisstub, 1–35. Oxford: Elsevier Science.

Weisstub, D.N. 2002. Honour, dignity, and the framing of multiculturalist values. In *The concept of human dignity in human rights discourse*, ed. D. Kretzmer and E. Klein, 263–294. The Hague: Kluwer Law International.

Weisstub, D.N., and D. Thomasma. 2001. Human dignity, vulnerability, personhood. In *Personhood and Healthcare*, ed. D.N. Weisstub, D. Thomasma, and C. Hervé, 333–370. Dordrecht: Kluwer.

Weisstub, D.N., and D. Thomasma. 2004. Moral capacity: The tension between professional nurture and universal nature. In *The variables of moral capacity*, ed. D.N. Weisstub and D. Thomasma, 139–149. Dordrecht: Kluwer.

Part II
Special Problems in Different Countries

Chapter 6
Ethical Issues in Australian Prison Psychiatry

Danny Sullivan

6.1 Introduction

Australia is a functioning democracy that has inherited many of its governmental practices from the United Kingdom, despite its location on the Pacific Rim. It is a commonwealth of six states and two territories, as well as some offshore dependencies. The latter are relevant as Australia has chosen to locate some immigration detention facilities on these islands.

An urban, developed country, Australia boasted a population of 22 million in 2010. Health care is provided by a range of private, state and commonwealth agencies and a commensurate mixture of funding streams. This is currently in a state of flux, although correctional systems are essentially determined by states or territories and there is no discrete commonwealth correctional system. The model of state-based service delivery results in disparate rates and systems of incarceration and mental health service provision, with limited national oversight.

The history of Australian immigration is also relevant in the current state of prison psychiatry. Australia was originally inhabited by its indigenous population, who are thought to have been continuously present for over 40,000 years before the arrival of colonising 'Westerners'. Indigenous Australians include both Aboriginal people and Torres Strait Islanders (from the islands off northern Queensland south of Papua New Guinea) and currently together constitute almost 3 % of Australia's population (Australian Bureau of Statistics [ABS] 2009).

Australia was claimed by England in 1770 and the first colony commenced in 1788. Early colonial history is marked by two recurring themes: the eradication of Aboriginals and the transportation of prisoners from England.

D. Sullivan (✉)
School of Psychology and Psychiatry, Monash University,
Melbourne, VIC, Australia
e-mail: Danny.Sullivan@forensicare.vic.gov.au

N. Konrad et al. (eds.), *Ethical Issues in Prison Psychiatry*, International Library of Ethics, Law, and the New Medicine 46, DOI 10.1007/978-94-007-0086-4_6,
© Springer Science+Business Media Dordrecht 2013

Aboriginals were treated poorly: their land was appropriated; they were paid less for the same work and in many places were not afforded the vote. They were in some places hunted and killed; and in others they were relocated, their children taken to be raised 'properly' and efforts were made to 'civilise' them. Such policies have continued until the 1970s (Dodson 2008).

This is relevant because some early prisons were developed to contain Aboriginal prisoners, and to Australia's disgrace a grossly disproportionate number of its few remaining indigenous people are or have been incarcerated. Currently over one in four prisoners in Australia is of indigenous background. In common with other indigenous people in colonised countries, Aboriginal and Torres Strait Islander people have excessive rates of mortality, morbidity, substance abuse and poor health. Life expectancy is markedly reduced compared to non-indigenous Australians.

The transportation of prisoners from England was associated with a strong moral element to the management of offending, with underclasses exiled for minor thefts and other petty offending. In addition many of those transported were of Irish background; some were political prisoners. In the nineteenth century there developed in Australia an egalitarian trend that permitted freed prisoners to make good. The stigma of descent from early convict transportees faded and a number of Anglo-Celtic Australians now proudly claim convict ancestry. Moreover, it is possible that transportation to Australia proved a splendid rehabilitation for many, despite the brutality of many of the penal colonies (Hughes 1987).

Such an egalitarian spirit and pride in descent from offenders has not carried forward into the twenty-first century. In recent years Australia has exhibited the same drastic increase in incarcerated population seen in the rest of the world. Incarceration of indigenous Australians is acknowledged but has not been addressed in any demonstrably effective manner.

6.2 Correctional Services

6.2.1 Prisons in Australia

Most prisons currently operational in Australia have been built in the last 50 years. There are prisons across all levels of security, and open prisons or periodic detention centres also exist in some jurisdictions. Australian prisons generally comply with international treaty requirements that differentiate between sentenced and remand prisoners (International Covenant on Civil and Political Rights 1976; Revised Standard Guidelines for Corrections in Australia 2004). However in some high profile cases, including so-called 'gangsters' and those accused of terrorism, much controversy has accompanied their detention in high security management units, typically in sentenced prisons (R v Benbrika and ors (Ruling No. 20) [2008] VSC 80).

Table 6.1 Populations, prisoner numbers and incarceration rates by state, gender and indigenous background

State	N prisons	Population[a]	Indigenous population[b]	N Male prisoners[c]	N Female prisoners[c]	Indigenous rate[d]	Non-indigenous rate[d]
New South Wales	31	7,238,800	152,685	10,130	817	2,064.4	158.7
Victoria	14	5,547,500	33,517	4,224	313	1,137.2	101.1
Queensland	10	4,516,400	144,885	5,168	447	1,442.5	120.8
Western Australia	14	2,296,400	70,966	4,367	405	3,343.4	174.5
South Australia	9	1,644,600	28,055	1,831	132	2,124.9	131.1
Tasmania	6	507,600	18,415	450	39	437.6	129.7
Australian Capital Territory	1	358,900	4,282	254	26	1,214.4	82.1
Northern Territory	2	229,700	64,005	1,048	49	1,728.9	164.4

[a]ABS (2010a)
[b]ABS (2009), projected figures to 2010
[c]Prisoner numbers reflect national prison census at midnight, 30 June 2010: ABS (2010b)
[d]Age standardised imprisonment rates/100,000 resident population, from ABS (2010b)

Although each state has its own criminal code or act, there are also commonwealth offences. However there are no commonwealth correctional facilities and those sentenced to imprisonment due to commonwealth offences are detained in facilities run by the states.

6.2.2 Current Prisoner Statistics

Statistics for prisoners in each state of Australia are summarised in Table 6.1.

The 2010 prisoner census sets out details of prisoners (ABS 2010a). The imprisonment rate nationally was 172.4 per 100,000. Among the most relevant statistics are: Just under one quarter of all prisoners are on remand; approximately half have been previously imprisoned; 7 % of prisoners are female; over one quarter of all prisoners are indigenous and as an age standardised imprisonment rate, indigenous people are 14 times more likely to be incarcerated than non-indigenous people. Rates of female prisoners and indigenous prisoners have been gradually increasing over the last decade. There are marked variations between states in incarceration rates.

States with a larger proportion of indigenous population are those with the larger rate of indigenous incarceration. This may reflect that remote local communities offer little infrastructure for community-based dispositions or may be indicative of increased tensions between indigenous people and authorities associated with increased incarceration.

6.2.3 Mental Health Services in Australian Prisons

In all states local service informants reported that they felt the degree of psychiatric input was insufficient to meet need. Additionally, services are provided by statewide forensic mental health services and there exist significant problems in linking those with mental disorders to general community mental health services upon release from prison.

In New South Wales, Justice Health provides all services to prisoners, including for mental health issues. Screening units located at urban prisons enable assessment of medical and psychiatric issues. Twenty-one out of 31 current prisons have visiting psychiatrist outpatient clinics. A recently developed secure hospital facility co-located with Long Bay Prison Complex includes a secure unit for adolescents. All eight justice centres and the only youth detention centre have visiting psychiatric staff. New South Wales is the only state that enables forensic community treatment orders: these provide for transfer to a mental health facility if the prisoner does not comply with treatment (Mental Health (Forensic Provisions) Regulation 2009).

Victorian prisons include male and female assessment units for mentally disordered prisoners. Involuntary treatment is provided by transfer to Thomas Embling Hospital, a 116-bed facility in urban Melbourne. Outpatient services are provided at almost all prisons by local nursing staff and visiting psychiatrists. Offence-specific programs are concentrated at Marngoneet Correctional Centre.

In Queensland forensic mental health services have been well-funded and have developed a range of innovative programs. Mentally disordered offenders can be transferred to The Park Centre for Mental Health, which contains 61 high secure beds. Unlike other Australian jurisdictions, Queensland enables transfer of mentally disordered prisoners to local mental health services. Forensic mental health services have developed transition programs to assist prisoners with mental disorder to be linked to general psychiatric services on release. A large scoping study on the needs of indigenous prisoners has recently been completed. Similar to other Australian states, the distance to some rural prisons renders it difficult for comprehensive services to be provided at all locations.

In Western Australia a single thirty-bed secure hospital provides inpatient assessment and treatment for acutely psychotic transferred prisoners. This includes court-ordered assessments. The forensic mental health service also provides outpatient clinics in some metropolitan prisons. However, given that the most distant prison is over 2,000 km from the capital city, Perth, some services are provided by videoconference (Sullivan et al. 2008). Western Australian prisons face significant problems due to location in distant regional areas, overcrowding, heat and a lack of Aboriginal interpreters (there are over fifty Aboriginal languages in Western Australia). To date there have been no systemic forensic mental health initiatives to address the differing mental health needs of indigenous prisoners.

South Australian prisons all have psychiatric outpatient clinics (referred to as in-reach services), including fly-in clinics at remote prisons. There exist infirmaries at two prisons which, although primarily for the purpose of providing medical assessment and minor treatments, are also used for psychiatric observation. Prisoners requiring transfer to hospital, usually detained under mental health legislation, are moved to the secure hospital, James Nash House. In the absence of an available bed, they are transferred to the Emergency Department of the Royal Adelaide Hospital and thence to a suitable closed general psychiatric bed where they are managed by non-forensically trained staff. Due to bed pressures these patients are sometimes prematurely returned to prison. Plans for a new secure hospital to replace James Nash House on the outskirts of Murray Bridge have been shelved indefinitely. It had been intended that this would be co-located with a new major prison. It is likely that James Nash House will continue to be located at its present site, although submissions have been made for an increase in bed capacity. Although special prison programs are run for indigenous prisoners, there is no specialist mental health input for indigenous prisoners.

Tasmanian prison services are concentrated at the Risdon Prison complex in eastern Hobart. A co-located and recently-built secure forensic hospital enables rapid assessment and transfer of mentally ill prisoners to a hospital facility. Mental health outpatient clinics run in most prisons and juvenile detention facilities.

The Australian Capital Territory has no dedicated forensic mental health beds. A new prison, the Alexander Maconochie Centre, can accommodate 300 prisoners and has mental health services provided by forensic mental health in-reach teams. However, those requiring treatment in a psychiatric facility are transferred to New South Wales facilities. In the future it is hoped that there will be provision for local secure beds.

The Northern Territory has only two prisons and very limited service provision through visiting sessional psychiatrists. Problems emerge when interpreters are in short supply, as some aboriginal prisoners speak limited English. There are profound difficulties in discharge planning as many communities are very remote.

Access to programs in prison is variable. Most Australian prison services provide basic cognitive skills programs and drug and alcohol programs. The availability of individual and offence-specific treatments differs significantly. Most states run specialised programs for sexual offending and there is an increasing availability of programs to address subpopulations with special needs: especially Aboriginal, youth and those with intellectual disability. However, most programs are separate from prison health and mental health services and there remain difficulties in access.

6.2.4 Prevalence of Mental Disorder

A number of studies have examined the prevalence of mental disorder in Australian prisons. It is notable that the results are consistent with other prevalence studies internationally. The burden of psychiatric morbidity is particularly borne by female prisoners and by indigenous prisoners.

The Australian Institute of Health and Welfare (AIHW) in 2010 published a comprehensive report detailing the health status of Australian prisoners (AIHW 2010).

Based on a 2009 census of 87 out of 93 prisons in Australia, including both public and private prisons, 37 % of all new prison entrants reported a mental health disorder at some time and 18 % were currently prescribed medication for a mental health related condition. Eighteen percent had a history of self harm and 43 % reported a head injury associated with loss of consciousness.

A similar 2005 prevalence study in New South Wales (NSW) (Butler et al. 2005) relied upon the Composite International Diagnostic Interview (CIDI) and used the National Survey of Mental Health and Wellbeing (McLennan 1998), a large study of the epidemiology of mental disorder in the Australian population as a comparator. The results indicated that female prisoners had more mental disorder than males, reception prisoners had more mental disorder than sentenced prisoners, and the most prevalent disorders were mood disorder, anxiety disorder, and post-traumatic stress disorder. Psychotic symptoms were evident in 9 % of prisoners in the last 12 months.

In the census, however (AIHW 2010), less indigenous prison entrants reported mental health conditions or the use of medication for mental health conditions. This might reflect that factors resulting in incarceration for indigenous offenders result in the remand of a less mentally disordered population; or that indigenous offenders are less able to access mental health services or are less likely to report symptoms or be diagnosed with mental disorders.

Indigenous mental health was surveyed in NSW in 2001 (Butler et al. 2007). Indigenous prisoners showed insignificant difference in rates of depression and psychological distress, although diagnoses were higher among women compared to non-indigenous prisoners. The study used a number of indigenous interviewers and was sensitive to cultural issues which might confound results.

Other indigenous prisoner surveys have reportedly found very high rates of mental disorder, particularly in women, and substance abuse (Heffernan et al. 2009).

The risk of suicide and particularly of drug overdose following release from custody has been clearly documented. Suicide risk was increased shortly after release, and was higher in those who had been admitted to the prison psychiatric hospital. Drug-related mortality was grossly increased in the two weeks after release from prison (Kariminia et al. 2007).

Earlier prevalence studies on mental disorder in Australian prisons were conducted in Victoria in the 1960s (Bartholomew et al. 1967) and late 1980s (Herrman et al. 1991). Sadly when the 1991 study suggested that "30–40 people with current psychotic disorders are serving sentences in the metropolitan prisons at any time," the authors could not have predicted that and the figure has probably since increased tenfold in Victorian prisons.

A study of mental disorder prevalence in female prisoners conducted in the last 10 years (Tye and Mullen 2006) relied upon operationalised diagnostic criteria and involved assessment by mental health professionals of the majority of female prisoners in Victoria, using a version of the Composite International Diagnostic Interview(CIDI) and the modified Personality Diagnostic Questionnaire (PDQ-4+). Rates of psychotic illness, personality disorder, post-traumatic stress disorder, depression and drug use disorders were all significantly increased compared to population norms. The researchers commented that the prisoners' disempowerment, abuse histories and mistrust made research difficult in prison. As they did not interview women in management cells, those with little English and those transferred to a secure mental health unit, their figures were likely an underestimate of prevalence of mental disorder.

A study in Queensland (White et al. 2006), using the Diagnostic Interview for Psychosis, suggested that about 10 % of remandees had a psychotic disorder. Most strikingly, 81 % were categorised as receiving no treatment at the time of their offence, and the same proportions had substance use disorders and were unemployed.

When compared with a community sample, Australian prison populations showed markedly increased rates of psychosis, substance use disorders and personality disorders (Butler et al. 2006). Rates of traumatic brain injury also appeared particularly high in a NSW prevalence study (Schofield et al. 2006).

Over-representation of intellectually disabled people was also noted among prisoners, resulting in the development of a brief screening test, the Hayes Ability Screening Index or HASI (Hayes 2002). Sadly this has not been implemented in any jurisdiction, although Queensland may in the near future begin screening for intellectual disability.

6.2.5   Practice Standards

The two main Australian standards relevant to prison psychiatry are the Revised Standard Guidelines for Corrections in Australia (2004), which were developed by all Australian state correctional services; and the National Statement of Principles for Forensic Mental Health (2002) which was developed as part of the Commonwealth Government's National Mental Health Strategy.

Revised Standard Guidelines for Corrections in Australia – excerpted

2.26 Every prisoner is to have access to evidence-based health services provided by a competent, registered health professional who will provide a standard of health services comparable to that of the general community. Notwithstanding the limitations of the local-community health service, prisoners are to have 24-hour access to health services. This service may be on an on-call or stand by basis.

2.27 Every prisoner is to have access to the services of specialist medical practitioners as well as psychiatric, dental, optical, and radiological diagnostic services. Referral to such services should take account of community standards of health care.

2.28 Every prisoner is to be medically examined by a suitably qualified health professional within 24 hours after being received into prison, and thereafter as necessary.

[…]

2.31 All prisoners who have a medical complaint shall be seen by a health professional at intervals appropriate to the diagnosis and prognosis in each case, according to good medical practice.

2.32 Health professionals should advise the officer in charge of the prison whenever it is considered that a prisoner's physical or mental health has been, or will be, injuriously affected by continued imprisonment or by any condition of imprisonment, including where a prisoner is being held in separate confinement. The officer in charge of the prison should immediately make a written report of such advice available to the appropriate senior officer with a view to effecting an immediate decision upon the advice that has been given. A copy of the health professional's report should be placed on the prisoner's medical file.

[…]

2.36 Prisoners who are suffering from a severe psychiatric illness should be managed by an appropriate tertiary or specialist health care facility.

2.37 Prisoners who are suffering from mental illness or an intellectual disability should be provided with appropriate management and support services.

2.38 Persons should not be remanded to prison custody solely for psychiatric or intellectual disability assessment.

2.39 Where a prisoner enters or is released from prison is under medical or psychiatric treatment, where appropriate, the prison health service should make arrangements

[…]

2.42 The confidentiality of medical information shall be maintained to preserve each prisoner's individual entitlement to privacy. However, medical information may be provided on a 'need to know' basis:

> with the consent of the prisoner, or
> in the interest of the prisoner's welfare, or
> where to maintain confidentiality may jeopardise the safety of others or the good order and security of the prison.

6.3   Ethical Issues in Australia

6.3.1   Indigenous Incarceration

Disproportionate rates of incarceration of indigenous people have already been noted in this chapter. The reasons behind these rates are complex and could reflect a number of possibilities which reflect upon the relationships between indigenous and non-indigenous people, and government and its agencies.

This may reflect underdiagnosis. The problem may relate to screening tools at reception which do not capture symptomatology in indigenous prisoners and are not validated in this population. It may show that in Australian prisons, mental health staff find it more difficult to diagnose mental disorder in indigenous prisoners. Or it may reflect that indigenous prisoners are sufficiently mistrustful that they minimise any representation of mental disorder.

In response to numerous Aboriginal deaths in custody, in 1987 the Royal Commission into Aboriginal Deaths in Custody was established, chaired by James Muirhead QC (Muirhead 1991). The Royal Commission systematically investigated nearly 100 deaths in custody from 1980 to 1989 and made a number of far-reaching

conclusions and subsequent recommendations. The full report is available electronically:
http://www.austlii.edu.au/au/other/IndigLRes/rciadic/

In part these recommendations focused upon shortcomings in the investigative
process for Aboriginal deaths in custody and methods of ensuring that processes for
investigation would in the future be robust and independent. Other recommendations focused on strategies to reduce indigenous incarceration rates and assist those
incarcerated; and to bolster procedures for monitoring those at risk of suicide and
reducing that risk. But the Royal Commission also focused upon socio-political
issues outside the circumstances of arrest and detention, including the need for
aboriginal "self-determination", health, education, housing, employment, land rights
and reconciliation.

This markedly progressive report located Aboriginal deaths in custody not
merely as a correctional failure but as symptom of a societal problem with remedies
which extended into many realms of the relationship between Aboriginal people,
government and the broader community. Unfortunately it appears that the main
outcomes have been the development of improved screening processes for at risk
prisoners, and observation cells for prisoners at high risk of suicide are now called
'Muirhead cells.'

Over 20 years later, a number of programs in the justice system have been developed to address restorative justice, diversion from custody, maintaining community
linkages and culture-sensitive issues. However, with the exception of Queensland,
there have been no systemic forensic mental health initiatives to address the differing
mental health needs of indigenous prisoners.

6.3.2   Equivalence

The National Statement of Principles for Forensic Mental Health (2002) upholds
the principle of equivalence as the benchmark for practice. The stated aim is that:

> Prisoners and detainees have the same rights to availability, access and quality of mental
> health care as the general population. Where health facilities are provided within a correc-
> tional facility, there should be appropriate equipment and trained staff, or arrangements
> made for such services to be available, at a standard comparable to regional and community
> standards. Services should ensure equality in service delivery regardless of an individual's
> age, gender, culture, sexual orientation, socio-economic status, religious beliefs, previous
> conditions, forensic status, and physical or other disability. This Principle of Equivalence
> applies to both primary and specialist mental health care.

In practice, the aspiration is not considered met in any jurisdiction. Service provision within correctional institutions is regarded as inadequate to meet need in
most states, and varies significantly by location, particularly in dispersal prisons.
Most states identify that workload and facilities are insufficient and at times these
compromise service provision. In one state there are few psychiatrists working in
the correctional system and most prison psychiatric care is provided by general
practitioners and not by psychiatrists. Few mental health services in prisons can
offer access to multidisciplinary teams.

All states identify insufficient secure mental health services accessible to prisoners in general. In a number of states very limited access of prisoners to appropriate mental health beds appears related to the stigma attached to prisoners, and lack of forensic mental health service control over admissions.

In general, confidentiality of the prisoner's health records is maintained. In all states the prisoner medical record is held by health care staff and is not accessible to correctional staff. In one state this is a recent development and prior to this correctional staff could access the medical record.

In some states there are moves to extend community treatment orders (CTOs) into prisons. The one state which does have provision for CTOs does not use them to enforce treatment within prison and non-compliance results in assessment for transfer to a psychiatric hospital. The notional concern that community treatment orders would be used to promote involuntary treatment in prison settings has prevented their use in other jurisdictions.

6.3.3   Organisation of Mental Health Care in Prisons

Marked disparities in incarceration rates and systems of mental health care exist between states and territories in Australia. This is a legacy of state government responsibility for correctional services and mental health, and the peculiar political environment which has influenced service development. In common with international trends, Australian jurisdictions have seen a trend to increasing incarceration over the last 20 years. All political parties while in power have sought to enhance their populist credentials by being seen to be 'tough on crime'.

Another prominent factor in service provision has been the growth of a 'purchaser/provider' ethos in correctional services. This has resulted in the outsourcing of some prisons to transnational corporations. However, in some states this business model has resulted in fragmented service provision and the seeming devolution of responsibility to contractors (Brouwer 2006).

In Victoria, for example, health care is overseen by a government department, but at a given prison different agencies are contracted to provide nursing, medical, psychiatric, pharmacy, substance abuse and psychological treatment. This results in poor communication between service providers. It has also compromised service providers, who are not permitted to provide advisory input or participate in scoping due to 'probity issues' or the perception that their contract interests might compromise their ability to provide sensible advice.

There are clear ethical issues implicit in outsourcing the management of prisons to profit-making agencies. Outsourced mental health service provision may be seen not simply as a core responsibility for a government, but as a way of outsourcing responsibility for adverse events to a mental health agency or contractor. This might include restrictions on public access to information about adverse events, preventing the public scrutiny which may serve to prevent abuse or neglect of vulnerable people in the ostensible care of the state.

In Australia the potential for abuse has been ostensibly managed by tight contract management, but if mental health services in private prisons are provided by sessional contractors without formal links to other forensic or public general services, the impact is to reduce the cohesion and systematic oversight of mental health service provision. When mental health services are provided by staff of one clinical service, that service can be tasked with oversight of competence, credentialing, professional ·development and clinical governance. However, when neither the contracting agency nor the contractor has any clinical governance role the professional standards of mental health care provision are a matter only for the clinicians concerned, and variability of practice may occur. In prisons this may include inappropriate prescribing of benzodiazepines and related sedatives, high rates of use of antipsychotic medication for reasons other than treatment of psychotic illness, and in some cases prescription of stimulants or other drugs prone to diversion and abuse. Furthermore, private organisations seeking to make a profit will generally do so by reducing labour costs, generally by employing less-qualified staff and reducing contact hours.

6.3.4   Special Populations

6.3.4.1   Aboriginals and Torres Strait Islanders

Aboriginal health has been the site of significant ideological struggle between those who argue that special programs and positive discrimination are necessary, and those who believe that Aboriginal health should be mainstreamed or subsumed into generic health provision. In practice, correctional agencies have recognised the need to address the needs of aboriginal prisoners and most services employ indigenous workers to address specific needs of Aboriginal and Torres Strait Islanders.

The same cannot be said for prison-based mental health services. Although psychiatric training in Australia requires some demonstrated competence in dealing with Aboriginal mental health issues, there is no systematic approach to dealing with culturally-specific issues relevant in assessment and treatment of mental health problems in Aboriginal and Torres Strait Islanders in prison. Mental health services are reliant on self-selection of staff interested in working with indigenous prisoners, and accumulation of experience if working in a service with a significant proportion of indigenous prisoners.

The prevalence of mental disorder diagnoses in indigenous prisoners differs from non-indigenous prisoners. Some of the studies mentioned in section 2.4 suggest that mental disorder is less prevalent than in other prisoners. A satisfying hypothesis would be that mentally ill indigenous people in contact with the correctional system are diverted from custody: however statistics clearly do not support this. This is likely to reflect under-diagnosis.

As noted above, the problem may relate to the validity of screening tools, difficulties of diagnosis mental disorder in indigenous prisoners or non-disclosure of symptoms due to mistrust.

Issues in the provision of mental health services to indigenous prisoners involve the frequent mistrust of government authorities and the complexities of helping people who have complex and transient associations with community groups, agencies and kinship groups, and whose personal histories are paradigm examples of alienation. Fragmented families, traumatic experiences in institutional care, long term unemployment, and multiple physical and mental comorbidities are all too often evident. Polysubstance abuse including a high prevalence of inhalant (petrol), cannabis and alcohol abuse complicate the picture.

In jurisdictions with a high proportion of indigenous prisoners there are innovations such as courts which involve tribal elders, or facility for elders to visit prisoners.

Prior to European settlement of Australia, indigenous people relied on customary law which provided for punitive sanctions against those who offended, or their relatives. Customary law has a complicated relationship with Australian law. In some cases Australian law has accepted that custom law punishments already exacted satisfy the needs of sentencing and further punishment would constitute double jeopardy. In other circumstances is appears that judicial consideration of custom law punishments does not meet the needs of the jurisdiction and further punishment is indicated.

This is recognised in the National Principles (2002) with the statement that:

> where appropriate, acknowledged as coming from indigenous communities that respect customary law; and recognition given to some aspects of that customary law where it affects the well-being or good management of the prisoner

6.3.4.2 International Prisoners

An increasing number of international prisoners are held in Australian prisons. These include Indonesian fishermen detained for illegally fishing in Australian waters, and international citizens charged with drug importation offences. In addition, an increasing number of international students who commit significant criminal offences may be detained for long periods of time.

These prisoners have foreseeable difficulties, requiring interpreters and having complicated legal arrangements. Furthermore their incarceration may involve significant social isolation and the absence of any external supports or sense of connectedness to other prisoners. Demoralisation is a real issue and has in some jurisdictions been dealt with through the provision of shared accommodation or through visiting welfare agencies. Mental health staff dealing with international prisoners may not be aware of the complexities of their incarceration and may have limited opportunity to develop a good understanding of their patients and the issues.

An observation of concern is that those organising drug importation may preferentially seek couriers or 'drug mules' with gambling problems, minors, the elderly or those with mental disorder, either through their vulnerability or because of the potential that they will be treated more leniently if convicted.

6.3.4.3   Immigration Detention

Immigration detainees are maintained in facilities separate from prisons. These are operated under the auspices of the (currently named) Department of Immigration and Citizenship but managed by contracted private agencies. Some facilities are in other countries, a situation which arose as part of the 'Pacific Solution' in which the Australian government provided funding to impoverished Pacific nations to locate the facilities in other jurisdictions and potentially to prevent access to further Australian legal appeal (Penovic and Dastyari 2007). A recent finding by the High Court of Australia made it clear that those detained offshore should have access to the same rights of appeal as those detained in Australian territory (Plaintiff M61/2010E v Commonwealth of Australia; Plaintiff M69 of 2010 v Commonwealth of Australia [2010] HCA 41).

These facilities, and earlier detention centres located in remote and isolated regions of Australia (Baxter Detention Centre in Woomera, 470 km from Adelaide; and Curtin Detention Centre, in Port Hedland 1,640 km from Perth), have been criticised because their locations greatly reduced access to legal, health and welfare services.

Currently secure facilities are located in four Australian capital cities and Christmas Island (northwest of the continent). Curtin Detention Centre was reopened in 2010, and new facilities have been opened in far north Queensland (Scherger) and South Australia (Inverbrackie). Approaches have been made to locate a detention facility in East Timor. Currently it appears that around 5,000 people are in immigration detention. There is much controversy about the detention of children and currently it appears that children are placed in "Alternative temporary detention in the community."

Mental health care is through contracted services; for those with more significant needs, transfer to local (state-run) mental health facilities remains an option. In the recent past, immigration detention centres were located in remote desert areas and transfer to state-run facilities was both logistically difficult and politically awkward. Those who have worked with populations in immigration detention will recognise that issues of mental disorder coexist with situational difficulties that are an artefact of detention and which confuse diagnosis and management (Harding-Pink 2004). At times the politics of the situation may intrude on the capacity to offer health care, such as when immigration staff insist on remaining present during clinical assessments or psychiatric interviews.

In particular there have been spectacular miscarriages of justice when mentally disordered people have been in immigration detention. Cornelia Rau was a psychotic woman who was detained in arduous conditions for 10 months before it was determined that she was an Australian permanent resident with psychosis (Palmer 2005). Vivian Alvarez Solon was a Filipina-born Australian national who had a mental illness and after sustaining a head injury, was wrongfully deported (Comrie 2005). The case had been expedited for deportation notwithstanding her medical and mental health conditions. Inquiries into these matters have been scathing about the failures of immigration detention and the limited mental health care available to those who subject to the immigration detention system.

In the Cornelia Rau inquiry, it was stated that:

> The detainee population requires a much higher level of mental health care than the Australian community. The infrequency of the consulting psychiatrist's visits to Baxter constitutes a serious shortcoming. Expert mental health opinion has it that more frequent, regular visits – together with a sufficient number and structure of mental health-trained nurses, psychologists and primary practitioners who could initially assess and triage for mental illness – would allow a more effective clinical system of care.

The review was highly critical of the contracted services provided by transnational corporations.

The mental health care of immigration detainees remains political dynamite and is of concern to many in Australia: the notion of multiculturalism and the background of most Australians as the children of immigrants is balanced against a longstanding xenophobia which has been exploited politically. Efforts by the federal government to locate immigration detainees in remote areas of Australia and in offshore dependencies suggest that the desire is either to deprive detainees of access to the legal process or remove the problem from the scrutiny of Australians. Protest action by detainees is inevitably framed as "criminal" and responses suggested are of imprisonment and deportation. There are clearly systemic barriers to the provision of mental health care to immigration detainees. Mental health services in immigration facilities remain ethically suspect: although needed, the political influences on service provision or contracted arrangements appear to prevent mental health staff from providing appropriate care.

6.3.4.4 Women

The number of women incarcerated has increased in all jurisdictions in Australia. The prevalence of mental disorder is higher than among male prisoners, with personality disorder and substance abuse problems the majority and psychotic illnesses and mood disorder grossly more prevalent than in the community (Tye and Mullen 2006).

In Victoria there is now a dedicated inpatient mental health unit, staffed by a full multidisciplinary team and offering therapeutic group programs as well as comprehensive mental health care. Interestingly this unit arose soon after criticism from judges aligned with sentence reductions and related to the paucity of mental health services available then (R v Rollo [2006] VSCA 154).

The relatively small number of female prisoners restricts the range of facilities and programs available. This is especially true for women with complex conditions such as eating disorders or with intellectual disability requiring behavioural management. Furthermore the small number of prisons means that sentences may be served distant from family and support services, particularly for indigenous women.

Fortunately most jurisdictions recognise that separating women from young children may be harmful to the children and that secure attachment may be best developed by having children stay in prison with their mothers. All jurisdictions offer facilities for children to reside in prison with their mothers following assessment. There is some variation in the upper age permitted, from 12 months to 5 years.

6.3.4.5   Intellectual Disability

People with intellectual disability are overrepresented in the correctional system and poorly served by it. In some states there exist specialist units designed to manage intellectual disabled prisoners, and staffed by prison officers who have chosen to work with this population, although in most states prisoners with intellectual disability are simply placed in generic protection or 'special needs' units.

The degree of need is almost certainly underestimated and under-resourced. In addition, the development of programs and treatment regimes geared to the needs of those with intellectual disability is almost non-existent. The other cognitively impaired population is those with acquired brain injury. This is considered under-recognised and there exist limited resources to address these issues (Baroff et al. 2008).

One of the primary problems is case-finding. Screening for intellectual disability is practicable but has not been resourced. Hayes (2002) developed and validated a reliable instrument to screen for intellectual disability. In Queensland a more recent test soon to be published may also have widespread acceptance (Heffernan E. 2009, personal communication). Difficulties remain for those of Aboriginal and Torres Strait Islander background, as usual neuropsychological assessments may not be valid (Dingwall and Cairney 2009). In addition screening of those requiring interpreters or translated tools is likely to be rendered more difficult and possibly not valid.

6.3.4.6   Sexual Offenders

In common with other western jurisdictions, a number of Australian states have enacted legislation providing for post-sentence detention of people who are considered at risk of further sexual offending. These controversial laws pose significant ethical problems for mental health professionals who may be involved in providing court reports, documenting issues which may subsequently be prejudicial to the prisoner in future court proceedings, and providing treatment (including anti-libidinal medication) for prisoners whose consent may be premised upon the threat of indefinite detention if they are not taking medication (McSherry and Keyzer 2009; Sullivan et al. 2005; Freckelton and Keyzer 2010). In particular, the focus on those who are preventively detained reduces resources available to the vast majority of sexual offenders who may benefit from treatment, without showing any impact upon offending rates (AIC 2010).

6.3.4.7   Terrorists

Australia has so far had few people convicted of terrorism. The problems noted in other countries – of prison engendering radicalism, and the difficulties of detaining multiple terrorism remandees or prisoners in conditions of high security – have not been such a problem in Australia. Nevertheless the conditions of detention have warranted rebukes from the judiciary (R v Benbrika and ors (Ruling No. 20) 2008 VSC 80), in part due to concerns about the effects of such regimes on mental health. Psychiatric staff have been involved in providing evidence about the mental health effects of such conditions, which have resulted in beneficial changes in conditions for terrorism detainees.

6.4   Conclusions

The provision of mental health services in Australian prisons is complex. In addition to the universal difficulties of providing psychiatric care to people in correctional institutions, Australia faces specific challenges related to the privatised or contracted services which may reduce effective communication between service providers. Every state has a separate prison service and most prison-based psychiatric services are estranged from the communities to which the prisoners will almost inevitably return. Consequently discharge planning and continuity of care is difficult to provide. In all jurisdictions the transfer of mentally disordered offenders to mental health facilities is delayed due to scarce resources, and, it can be argued, the stigmatisation of that population.

Vast distances in some states, and relatively small prison populations (in part due to state government responsibility for correctional services), has restricted the development of programs and necessary therapeutic interventions for numbers of subpopulations of prisoners.

Immigration detention facilities are essentially outside existing service systems and have been essentially maintained by contracted transnational corporations. The provision of mental health care in these facilities has been poor and has resulted in highly critical inquiries. Sadly, and despite strong censure, these reports, there is no indication that the Australian government has been able to address its egregious shortcomings in mental health care provision to immigration detainees.

Although Australian incarceration rates are generally low compared to world-wide statistics, there are substantial disparities which reflect local political and historical differences. However across all states, indigenous incarceration rates are appalling and are a matter of national shame. Earlier – prescient – efforts to determine the reasons for elevated rates of imprisonment considered that this is a symptom and the underlying pathology required multi-agency attention. This has not occurred and although death rates of Aboriginal and Torres Strait Islanders in custody have reduced a little, the continuing disparity in incarceration between indigenous and other populations reflects a fundamental failure of Australia to address this issue. Australian forensic mental health services have yet to address the issue of mental disorder among indigenous prisoners.

Overall, despite apparent compliance with international instruments, local guidelines which are salutary, and well-intentioned governmental mental health services, the provision of mental health services to prisoners remains constrained by a lack of resources. This affects both prison-based clinics and opportunities for transfer to hospital. Finally, immigration detention is a mental health disaster, but has been so political that there has been no opportunity for effective mental health service provision.

It remains astonishing that in an apparent functioning liberal democracy, mental health care should be privilege rather than a right for many of those detained, and a privilege essentially for the mainstream rather than minorities. The challenge for Australia is to extend quality mental health care to those in prison or detained, and to address the needs of vulnerable and voiceless populations. Equivalence, despite being the predominant principle indentified in national benchmarks, is a long way off.

Acknowledgments Thanks to the following psychiatrists who provided details of services in a range of states: Prof John Basson, Dr Michael Evenhuis, Dr Ed Heffernan, Dr Michael Jordan, Dr Len Lambeth, Dr Ken O'Brien, Dr Ed Petch.

References

Australian Bureau of Statistics. 2009. Experimental estimates and projections, Aboriginal and Torres Strait Islander Australians 1991 to 2021, cat no. 3238.0. http://www.abs.gov.au/AUSSTATS/abs@.nsf/allprimarymainfeatures/4EF9B192CB67360CCA256F1B0082C453. Viewed 3 Jan 2011.
Australian Bureau of Statistics. 2010a. Australian demographic statistics, Jun 2010. http://www.abs.gov.au/ausstats/abs@.nsf/mf/3101.0. Viewed 3 Jan 2011.
Australian Bureau of Statistics. 2010b. Prisoners in Australia, 2010, cat no.4517.0. http://www.abs.gov.au/ausstats/abs@.nsf/mf/4517.0. Viewed 3 Jan 2011.
Australian Institute of Criminology. 2010. Trend in sexual assault. http://www.aic.gov.au/statistics/violent%20crime/sexual%20assault.aspx. Viewed 3 Jan 2011.
Australian Institute of Health and Welfare. 2010. Health of Australia's prisoners 2009. http://www.aihw.gov.au/publications/index.cfm/title/11012. Viewed 3 Jan 2011.
Baroff, G.S., M. Gunn, and S. Hayes. 2008. *Offenders with developmental disabilities*. London: Wiley.
Bartholomew, A.A., L.A. Brain, A.S. Douglas, and W.S. Reynolds. 1967. A medico-psychiatric diagnostic review of remanded (without a request for a psychiatric report) male minor offenders. *The Medical Journal of Australia* 11(1): 267–269.
Brouwer, G.E. 2006. Conditions for persons in custody. Ombudsman Victoria. http://www.ombudsman.vic.gov.au/resources/documents/Conditions_for_persons_in_custody.pdf. Viewed 3 Jan 2011.
Butler, T., S. Allnutt, D. Cain, D. Owens, and C. Muller. 2005. Mental disorder in the New South Wales prisoner population. *The Australian and New Zealand Journal of Psychiatry* 39(5): 407–413.
Butler, T., G. Andrews, S. Allnutt, C. Sakashita, N.E. Smith, and J. Basson. 2006. Mental disorders in Australian prisoners: A comparison with a community sample. *The Australian and New Zealand Journal of Psychiatry* 40(3): 272–276.
Butler, T., S. Allnutt, A. Kariminia, and D. Cain. 2007. Mental health status of Aboriginal and non-Aboriginal Australian prisoners. *The Australian and New Zealand Journal of Psychiatry* 41(5): 429–435.

Comrie, N. 2005. Inquiry into the circumstances of the Vivian Alvarez matter. Department of Immigration and Citizenship, Canberra. http://www.immi.gov.au/media/publications/pdf/alvarez_report03.pdf. Viewed 3 Jan 2011.

Dingwall, K., and S. Cairney. 2009. The importance and challenges of assessing cognition in Indigenous Australians. *Australasian Psychiatry* 17(s1): S47–S50.

Dodson, M. 2008. Bringing them home: Report of the national inquiry into the separation of Aboriginal and Torres Strait Islander children from their families. Human Rights and Equal Opportunity Commission, Canberra. www.austlii.edu.au/au/journals/AUIndigLawRpr/1997/36.html. Viewed 3 Jan 2011.

Freckelton, I., and P. Keyzer. 2010. Indefinite Detention of Sex Offenders and Human Rights: The Intervention of the Human Rights Committee of the United Nations – Re Fardon, Communication No 1629/2007, Human Rights Committee of the United Nations, 18 March 2010; Re Tillman, Communication No 1635/2007, Human Rights Committee of the United Nations, 18 March 2010. *Psychiatry, Psychology and Law* 17(3): 345–354.

Harding-Pink, D. 2004. Humanitarian medicine: Up the garden path and down the slippery slope. *British Medical Journal* 329(7462): 398–399.

Hayes, S.C. 2002. Early intervention or early incarceration? Using a screening test for intellectual disability in the criminal justice system. *Journal of Applied Research in Intellectual Disabilities* 15(2): 120–128.

Heffernan, E., K. Andersen, and S. Kinner. 2009. The insidious problem inside: mental health problems of Aboriginal and Torres Strait Islander People in custody. *Australasian Psychiatry* 17(s1): S41–S46.

Herrman, H., P. McGorry, J. Mills, and B. Singh. 1991. Hidden severe psychiatric morbidity in sentenced prisoners: An Australian study. *The American Journal of Psychiatry* 148(2): 236–239.

Hughes, R. 1987. *The fatal shore*. London: Collins Harvell.

International Covenant on Civil and Political Rights. 1976. Vol. GA res. 2200A (XXI), 21 UN GAOR Supp. (No. 16) at 52, UN Doc. A/6316 (1966); 999 UNTS 171; 6 ILM 368 (1967).

Kariminia, A., M. Law, T. Butler, S. Corben, M. Levy, J. Kaldor, and L. Grant. 2007. Factors associated with mortality in a cohort of Australian prisoners. *European Journal of Epidemiology* 22(7): 417–428.

McLennan, W. 1998. Mental health and wellbeing: Profile of adults, Australia 1997. Australian Bureau of Statistics, cat no. 4326.0. http://www.abs.gov.au/ausstats/abs@.nsf/Productsby ReleaseDate/D5A0AC778746378FCA2574EA00122887. Viewed 3 Jan 2011.

McSherry, B., and P. Keyzer. 2009. *Sex offenders and preventive detention: Politics, policy and practice*. Sydney: The Federation Press.

Mental Health (Forensic Provisions) Regulation 2009 (NSW). http://www.austlii.org/au/legis/nsw/consol_reg/mhpr2009446. Viewed 17 Jan 2011.

Muirhead, J. 1991. Royal Commission into Aboriginal deaths in custody. Canberra: Australian Govt. Pub. Service. http://www.austlii.edu.au/au/other/IndigLRes/rciadic/. Viewed 3 Jan 2011.

National Statement of Principles for Forensic Mental Health. 2002. http://www.health.wa.gov.au/mhareview/resources/documents/FINAL_VERSION_OF_NATIONAL_PRINCIPLES_FOR_FMH-Aug_2002.pdf. Viewed 3 Jan 2011.

Palmer, M. 2005. Inquiry into the circumstances of the immigration detention matter of Cornelia Rau. Canberra: Department of Immigration and Citizenship. www.immi.gov.au/media/publications/pdf/palmer-report.pdf. Viewed 3 Jan 2011.

Penovic, T., and A. Dastyari. 2007. Boatloads of incongruity: The evolution of Australia's offshore processing regime. *Australian Journal of Human Rights* 13(1): 33–61.

R v Benbrika and ors (Ruling No. 20) [2008] VSC 80.

R v Rollo [2006] VSCA 154.

Revised Standard Guidelines for Corrections in Australia. 2004. http://www.aic.gov.au/criminal_justice_system/corrections/reform/~/media/aic/research/corrections/standards/aust-stand_2004.ashx. Viewed 3 Jan 2011.

Schofield, P.W., T.G. Butler, S.J. Hollis, N.E. Smith, S.J. Lee, and W.M. Kelso. 2006. Traumatic brain injury among Australian prisoners: Rates, recurrence and sequelae. *Brain Injury* 20(5): 499–506.

Sullivan, D.H., P.E. Mullen, and M.T. Pathé. 2005. Legislation in Victoria on sexual offenders: Issues for health professionals. *The Medical Journal of Australia* 183(6): 318–320.

Sullivan, D.H., M. Chapman, and P.E. Mullen. 2008. Videoconferencing and forensic mental health in Australia. *Behavioral Sciences & the Law* 26(3): 323–331.

Tye, C.S., and P.E. Mullen. 2006. Mental disorders in female prisoners. *The Australian and New Zealand Journal of Psychiatry* 40(3): 266–271.

White, P., D. Chant, and H. Whiteford. 2006. A comparison of Australian men with psychotic disorders remanded for criminal offences and a community group of psychotic men who have not offended. *The Australian and New Zealand Journal of Psychiatry* 40(3): 260–265.

Chapter 7
Penitentiary Mental Health Care in Belgium

Paul Cosyns and Kris Goethals

7.1 Introduction

The new century has ushered new innovations in mental health care in Belgian jails and prisons, following a century of inaction and neglect. Despite repeated pleas by several leading Belgian forensic psychiatrists, the political authorities did not see through the necessary reforms in order to bridge the severe gap between regular psychiatric care and penitentiary forensic psychiatric care. The primary reason for this situation is that, despite an extensive public health system, Belgium has not extended equitable care to prisoners. It remains the responsibility of the Justice Department to organize health care within jails and prisons but it never assumed this duty at an acceptable level; consequently, there is no quality control of the somatic or psychiatric care in jails and prisons.

A second reason for the comparatively low level of medical care in the Belgian penitentiaries is chronic overcrowding. Additionally, most prisons and jails were constructed in the nineteenth century. Modernization of the outdated infrastructure is too slow and insufficient. The European Committee for the Prevention of Torture and Inhumane or Degrading Treatment or Punishment (CPT) of the Council of Europe has repeatedly condemned Belgium for the confinement conditions of prisoners and the lack of quality of medical care inside jails and

P. Cosyns (✉)
University Forensic Centre, Antwerp University Hospital,
Wilrijkstraat 10, 2650 Edegem, Belgium
e-mail: paul.cosyns@skynet.be

K. Goethals
Collaborative Antwerp Psychiatric Research Institute (CAPRI),
University of Antwerp, Campus Drie Eiken, R3.27,
Universiteitsplein 1, 2610 Wilrijk, Belgium

N. Konrad et al. (eds.), *Ethical Issues in Prison Psychiatry*, International Library
of Ethics, Law, and the New Medicine 46, DOI 10.1007/978-94-007-0086-4_7,
© Springer Science+Business Media Dordrecht 2013

prisons (CPT-report on Belgium 2010). The Belgian government decided in 2009 to build several new prisons and a brand new penitentiary medical facility but it will take at least a decade to complete.

Following the arrest in the mid-nineties of a highly publicized case of a serial murderer and rapist, the Belgian public was shocked. This rather exceptional criminal case (Marc Dutroux) did initiate several new laws and developments in the organization of Belgian forensic care. The aims were: harsher punishment of sexual offenders, better protection of victims, and – last but not least – to develop a forensic pathway to control and treat sexual as well as mentally disturbed offenders. Concrete examples of the new trend are: the creation of specialized community treatment units for the treatment of released sex offenders (Agreement of cooperation between the federal state and the regional communities regarding the treatment of sexual abusers was approved by the federal laws of May 4, 1999, and March 12, 2000) and the building of two high security forensic hospitals in Belgium (Ghent and Antwerp). However, another important law of January 2005 is of note confirming the legal right of detainees to health care of the same quality as health care in the community (*Belgisch Staatsblad* 2005). This Law on Prisons and Prisoners' Rights (LPPR) is widely recognized as a milestone in Belgian penitentiary history (Verbruggen et al. 2008).

7.2   The Prevalence of Mental Disorders Among Prisoners in Belgium

Belgium (10.4 million inhabitants) has more than 30 prisons scattered throughout the country, even one in Tilburg, the Netherlands. The reason for this latter location is overcrowding in Belgian prisons. Indeed, the daily population is more than 10,000 prisoners for 9,000 places of whom 5,500 are convicted, 3,500 on remand, 1,000 are 'interned' (meaning not guilty because of insanity or severe mental disorder) and 50 are juvenile incarcerated delinquents. The incarceration rate is 100 per 100,000, considerably lower than the US with 753, and England and Wales with 154, but somewhat higher than France with 96 and Sweden with 74 (all per 100,000 people). During the last 10 years the penitentiary population increased by 21 %; 44 % of the prisoners are foreigners. Deficient language skills of therapist or prisoner is a major problem for psychiatric treatment. Moreover, there is an annual yearly turnover of 15.000.

Belgium has no official records of the prevalence of somatic or psychiatric disorders in this population, but the Prison Health Care Service (PHCS) notes an excess of the following pathologies as compared with the general society: tuberculosis (×16), HIV (×5), hepatitis C (×7), psychosis (×5), suicide (×6), alcohol and substance abuse (×7) (van Mol 2009). Prison doctors report an increase of psychiatric pathology among prisoners and this is a source of concern because the prison context is not suited for their treatment at all.

7.3   Organization and Supervision of Penitentiary Mental Health Care

Belgium is a complex federal state with three regions (Flanders with 6 million inhabitants; Wallonia, 3.4 million; Brussels, 1 million) and three communities (Dutch, French- and German-speaking): Belgians are Dutch-speaking in Flanders, French-speaking in Wallonia and bilingual in Brussels. The small German-speaking community (71,000 inhabitants) is located in Wallonia. The Justice Department is an exclusive federal matter and all the prisons are governed by the federal state. On the other hand, community treatment after release from a penal institution is mainly a matter of the local regions.

Somatic as well as psychiatric health care is offered free of charge to prisoners by the federal Prison Health Care Service. In each prison, basic medical and mental health care is provided by a small medical unit through general practitioners, psychiatrists and psychologists. Ten prisons deliver more specialized mental health care in psychiatric units for mentally ill prisoners with a total of nearly 350 beds. In addition Belgium has 'Institutes of social protection' for 'internees' ($\pm$ 500 beds). A person who has committed a criminal act and who is 'either in a state of insanity, or in a state of severe mental imbalance, or in a state of severe mental deficiency rendering him/her incapable of controlling his/her actions' will be interned (Belgian penal law). Internment is not a punishment but a measure of social protection for an undetermined period of time. Currently, the financial means at disposal for the treatment of mentally ill offenders are insufficient to provide an equitable level of quality of care. Internees may also be hospitalized in regular psychiatric hospitals but they are often reluctant to admit them. Treatment of offenders in general psychiatric hospitals is mostly paid for and controlled by the general Belgian social security system.

Two recently formed bodies play an important role in the supervision of penitentiary health care: the Central Supervisory Board of the Prisons and the Penitentiary Health Council. The 'Central Supervisory Board of the Prisons' and each 'Supervisory Commission' within each prison have the duty to supervise the general treatment of prisoners according to the applicable directives. Each prisoner has unlimited access to this body of independent members and each complaint is considered. Prison health care professionals are represented in the Penitentiary Health Council which has the duty to advise the minister of justice in order to improve the quality of care in the best interest of the detainee. The main points of their recommendations are:

- Progressive but full integration of the penitentiary health care system into regular health care,
- Complete professional independence of care providers,
- Access of all detainees to free health insurance, and
- Foundation of a Penitentiary Health Care Institute.

Apart from the last recommendation these recommendations are all in the process of being implemented. But, as quoted by Verbruggen et al. (2008), we must remain vigilant, "Belgian prison history is paved with good policy intentions which were subsequently 'reduced to administrable proportions'…The difference is that now prisoners are able to turn to judges to have their rights enforced."

7.4 Special Ethical Problems

7.4.1 Patient Rights and Coerced Treatment

The Law on Prisons and Prisoner's rights (LPPR) states that "The prisoner is entitled to health care that is on a par with health care in free society and which is adapted to his or her specific needs" (LPPR, Art. 88). This means that the Belgian Law on the Rights of the Patient (LRP 2002) is applicable to detainees. In summary, this law provides the following rights: access to a quality service, free choice of care giver, comprehensive information, informed consent, a medical file, possibility of inspection, possibility to copy medical files, protection of privacy, and complaints mediation. However, two rights are not applicable to Belgian detainees: there is no free choice of the doctor, and prisoners do not have the right to obtain copies of their medical files. However, the detainee can request the visit of a doctor of his choice at his own expense, but this freely chosen doctor can only advise the detainee. After examination of the detainee, this doctor communicates his advice about diagnosis, investigations, and treatment to the prison doctor (LPPR, Art. 91). Regarding copies of medical files: While they will not be given to the prisoner, copies can be sent to their agent. This agent can be a doctor from outside the prison, a lawyer, or a representative of his religion, appointed or accepted by the prison (LPPR, Art. 92).

Caregivers retain professional independence and their evaluations and decisions in relation to the health of the detainee are based solely on medical criteria. They cannot be forced to take actions that endanger their relationship of trust with the detainee. The role of care giver is irreconcilable with the role as an expert in prisons (LPPR, Art. 96).

Penitentiary mental health care professionals must comply with the LRP as well as with the standards of the medical profession. A detainee can, as any other citizen, complain to the provincial medical council about the treatment provided by a physician.

Duly informed prisoners must agree with treatment proposals and they have the right to refuse treatment within the same limits and rules as any other patients. The physician in charge must comply with the refusal of the duly informed patient. If the prisoner lacks the capacity to make an informed decision, the decision will be taken by the representative of the patient. If the psychiatrist in charge plans to overrule a serious life or health endangering refusal from the representative of the patient he can gain the advice of a forensic psychiatrist not involved in the case. In emergency cases the psychiatrist must take the decisions in the best interest of the patient as he would do for other patients. These rules of good medical practice are all provided by law (Law on the Rights of the Patient, August 22, 2002, Art. 8, §5 and Art. 15, §2).

7.4.2 Emergency Psychiatric Care

Emergency psychiatric inpatient care for prison inmates is presently discharged by the poorly staffed and under-equipped psychiatric prison wards. Acute psychotic patients require care in services with experienced and trained staff and such services do not exist within the prison system. Agreements have been made between general hospitals and the prison medical service to hospitalize emergency somatic cases from prison to general hospitals for treatment. This works successfully and the principle is accepted that it should also be possible for psychiatric indications. Until now, however, local circumstances determine the treatment practice due to the lack of a clear and accepted management plan.

7.4.3 Chemical Castration of Sex Offenders

In the recent guidelines of The World Federation of Societies of Biological Psychiatry (WFSBP), Thibaut et al. stated that the major ethical issues regarding sex offenders, including paraphilias, may reflect the need for public safety balanced against the public and even professional orientation towards punishment rather than treatment even where treatment is appropriate and effective (Thibaut et al. 2010). From an ethical point of view, the sex offender can be subjected to hormonal castration only if all of the following conditions are met (Belgian Advisory Committee on Bioethics 2006; Council of Europe 2004).

First of all, there are clear inclusion criteria:

- the patient has a paraphilia
- his condition represents a significant risk of serious harm to his health or to other persons
- no less intrusive means of providing appropriate care are available, and
- he consents to treatment.

Secondly, this hormonal (coerced) treatment must:

- address specific clinical signs, symptoms and behaviours
- be adapted to the patient's state of health
- take place in an appropriate medical environment under the responsibility of a psychiatrist and consulting endocrinologist
- be reviewed at appropriate intervals, and if necessary, revised, and
- be part of a written treatment plan

Although there is a requirement for the patient to consent to the proposed treatment, there is often some form of informal coercion, e.g., if the prisoners wants a conditional release from prison, he has to agree with the treatment proposal. Some ethical justifications can be cited regarding the use this type of coercion: treatment redresses competence, reduction in risk of violence, and is benefits for the rehabilitation of patients. Indeed, one can consider a new balance between conflicting values: first of all, the best interest of the patient and 'paternalism'; secondly, patient autonomy and 'coercion'; and finally, the best interest of the society and control of the patient for the sake of public safety. The latter is a primary duty of the probation officer. Moreover these conflicting values overlap with each other; relapse is obviously bad for the safety of society but also not in the best interest of the patient. Several actors interact with each other: patient, doctor; judicial coercer, and victim(s).

Surgical castration has never been performed in Belgium because of medical rules that consider prisoners insufficiently able to give a valid free consent for such an irreversible operation.

Hormonal castration may indeed include a restriction of individual rights and freedom, and while hormonal treatment diminishes significantly the risk of recidivism, the risk is not totally removed.

We are in agreement with the WFSBP professional guidelines of 'good psychiatric practice', which also address important ethical issues. The guidelines state, e.g., the duty of confidentiality and hence the splitting of treatment and expert teams. As mentioned above, the role of psychiatric care giver is irreconcilable with the role of psychiatric expert in prisons (LPPR, Art. 96). The process of splitting expert and treatment teams in each prison started in 2007 and is still ongoing. Psychiatrists of penitentiary expert teams produce reports within the framework of prisoners' individual detention plans, their placement and transfer, and answer questions from the penitentiary or judicial authorities. The medical confidentiality rule is not applicable for the psychiatric expert at least as far as material is concerned that is the topic of the opinion. By contrast, the psychiatrist of a treatment team is bound by the confidentially rule as is the case outside prison. Treatment teams have the duty to focus on the treatment of incarcerated mentally ill offenders (internees). However, some disadvantages of this splitting have been noted, such as difficulties in the exchange of information about a patient.

7.4.4 Substance Abuse

As in other countries, substance abuse is common in Belgian prisons and deaths due to overdose have been reported. Previously we noted some severe somatic complications of this abuse, such as hepatitis C and HIV. It is worth mentioning here initiatives of some prisons to install so-called 'drug free' wings. However, these experiments have not been successful. In order to control substance abuse in prison, we have to emphasize the importance of a multidisciplinary approach to which the medical service as well as the prison staff must contribute. The right balance must be found between care, repression and control of inmates, penitentiary personnel, and visitors. Controlled substitution programs with methadone are implemented in prison and with the help of specialized external care providers the prison mental health staff encourages addicts to engage in treatment programs for alcohol and drug abuse.

7.5   Future Prospects

It may be clear that penitentiary forensic mental health care in Belgium is at a turning point. The recent law of 2005 confirms the legal right of detainees to health care of the same quality as health care in the community. Belgium has a well developed and democratic mental health care system and we can only hope that in the future mentally ill prisoners will finally also benefit from it. The implementation of this law is an ongoing process with the following basic principles as accepted guidelines for the current developments of mental health care in Belgian prisons: the equivalence of mental health care, the continuity of care and the professional independence of care providers.

Another key issue concerns education and training of professionals in forensic psychiatry. While all agree that forensic psychiatry is an integral part of medicine and psychiatry, no Belgian medical school has a chair in forensic psychiatry. As a consequence Belgium lacks a centre of reference for education and research in this discipline. For example, in the Netherlands there are several chairs in forensic psychiatry, but only one of them is based in the faculty of medicine. All others are based in a faculty of law (Goethals and van Lier 2009). Although education is not the focus of this chapter, the ultimate success of the ongoing developments depends on it. Without adequate education and research a medical discipline has no real future.

References

Advice no. 39 (December 18, 2006) concerning hormonal treatment of sex offences. Belgian Advisory Committee on Bioethics. In *De adviezen van het Belgisch Raadgevend Comité voor Bio-ethiek 2005–2009*, LannooCampus, pp. 181–185.
Basic Law of January 12, 2005, Law on Prisoners and Prisoner's Rights (LPPR). *Belgisch Staatsblad.* February 1, 2005, 2815–2850.
Council of Europe. Recommendation no. rec(2004)10 of the Committee of Ministers to member States concerning the protection of the human rights and dignity of persons with mental disorder and its Explanatory Memorandum.
CPT report on Belgium. July 23, 2010: ref CPT/inf(2010)24. www.cpt.coe.int
Goethals, K., and E. van Lier. 2009. Editorial: Dutch training and research in forensic psychiatry. *Criminal Behaviour and Mental Health* 19: 286–290.
Thibaut, F., F. de la Barra, H. Gordon, P. Cosyns, and J.M.W. Bradford. 2010. The WFSBP task force on sexual disorders. The world federation of societies of biological psychiatry (WFSBP) guidelines for the biological treatment of paraphilias. *The World Journal of Biological Psychiatry* 11: 604–655.
van Mol, F. 2009. *Health care in prisons 2009, internal document of the prison health care service.* Belgium: Ministry of Justice.
Verbruggen F, Dierickx A, Vandesteene A, Van Mol F. 2008. Blood, sweat and…hope. In *Intramurale Medizin im internationalen Vergleich, Gesundheitsfürsorge zwischen Heilauftrag und Strafvollzug im Schweizerischen und internationalen Diskurs*, eds. B. Tag and T. Hillenkamp, 271–306. Berlin/Heidelberg: Springer.

Chapter 8
Ethical Issues in Prison Psychiatry: Forensic Mental Health Care in Brazil

Jose G.V. Taborda, Lisieux Elaine de Borba Telles,
and Helena Dias de Castro Bins

8.1 Introduction to Brazilian Law

Brazil follows the European continental law tradition based on Roman Law, which, together with English common law, constitutes the predominant legal system in the Western world (Taborda 2004).

Penal responsibility, in Latin countries, is based on penal capacity (imputability) and on culpability. Thus, only legally sane people can be found guilty. The concept of criminal insanity, in turn, requires the accused to present, at the time of the crime, some mental disorder and that on account of this pathology he would not be able to understand that what he did was wrong or he was incapable of behaving according to this understanding (this is, in general lines, very similar to the insanity test of the American Law Institute) (ALI 1962). The concept of "semi-imputability" is applied to individuals who understand the nature of the acts they have committed but may not be able to act accordingly. Insanity is always assessed retrospectively and consists of two strands, the cognitive and the volitive. Once declared insane, the defendant will be considered not guilty by reason of insanity (NGRI) and receive a criminal commitment (CC) – designated "Medida de Segurança", a safety measure,

J.G.V. Taborda (✉)
Department of Clinical Medicine, Federal University of Health Sciences
of Porto Alegre, Porto Alegre, RS 91900-540, Brazil
e-mail: jose@taborda.med.br

L.E. de Borba Telles
Mauricio Cardoso Forensic Psychiatric Institute, João Obino 383/602,
Porto Alegre, RS 90470-150, Brazil
e-mail: lisieux@telles.med.br

H.D. de Castro Bins
State of Rio Grande do Sul Supreme Court Carlos Huber 800,
Porto Alegre, RS 91330-150, Brazil
e-mail: helenabins@gmail.com

N. Konrad et al. (eds.), *Ethical Issues in Prison Psychiatry*, International Library
of Ethics, Law, and the New Medicine 46, DOI 10.1007/978-94-007-0086-4_8,
© Springer Science+Business Media Dordrecht 2013

according to Article 96 of Brazilian Penal Code – which will consist mostly of in-patient psychiatric treatment in a forensic psychiatric hospital (FPH) (Taborda 2001). When the sentence of CC is given to a mentally ill criminal its minimum duration (1–3 years of treatment) and the setting (in-patient or out-patient treatment) are determined by the judge according to legal criteria (severity of the offence), independent of what would be the most adequate medical indication (Brasil 1984). Besides, the maximum time for a CC is not established and its termination will only occur when the psychiatric expert declares that the patient is not dangerous (anymore). As the Brazilian law asks for a dichotomic and not speci-fied assessment (dangerous or not) instead of a prognostic and specified one (high, medium or low probability of committing an offence), cases of individuals with mental illness for whom CC represents lifelong imprisonment are common. This is one of the causes of overcrowding in FPHs in Brazil (Taborda et al. 2007).

In additions to the legally insane psychiatric patients, there are cases of prisoners who present psychiatric symptoms while on remand or while serving their sentence. This is what the Brazilian Penal Code, Article 41, calls "Superveniência de Doença Mental", supervening of mental illness. This is recognized as a high prevalence phenomenon and possibly growing in view of the progressive deterioration of the prison systems in the region. Nevertheless, a large number of these patients, due to prison overcrowding, are not detected and remain ill until a more dramatic manifes-tation of their illness occurs (overt psychosis or suicide). Others, however, are removed to the regional FPH, and this may lead to a serious problem, the double stigma of being a prisoner and mentally ill, as few will receive proper psychiatric treatment inside the penal institution (Taborda et al. 1999, 2000).

Thus, regarding the presence of mental illness, our prison population could be divided into two groups. The first is composed of the mentally ill who committed crimes and are submitted, by sentence, to psychiatric treatment for having been considered NGRI. These patients should remain interned in FPH during their treat-ment and while they are considered dangerous. The second group is composed of patients who committed offences, are sent to prison and during the serving of their term present with a mental disorder. Among criminals with a mental disorder detected prior to imprisonment but not considered insane, there may be many cases of substance related disorders and mild mental retardation (Taborda et al. 2007).

Brazil does not have sufficient FPHs to cope with the demand, which makes these hospitals more like asylums. Therefore it is fairly usual to find mentally ill individuals who were declared insane kept in prisons or sent to ordinary psychiatric hospitals if they do not present high levels of aggressiveness (Taborda et al. 2007).

8.2   Brazilian Prison System

Brazil is a Federal State formed by 26 states and a Federal District. Its territory occupies an area of 8,500,000 km^2, with a population of approximately 193 million inhabitants (Brasil 2010). The Brazilian Ministry of Justice, through the National Penitentiary Department, estimated the Brazilian prison population, in December

2009, at 473,626 prisoners. In the State of São Paulo, the most populated area in the country, the number of prisoners was 163,915. In the State of Rio Grande do Sul, where the authors work, the prison population reached 28,750 (Brasil 2009). It is estimated that, in Brazil, there are about 4,000 prisoners under CC, 538 of them being women (13.5 %), receiving inpatient treatment at FPHs (Brasil 2009).

In Brazil, attention given to the mental health of prisoners is very inconsistent with huge regional differences. One of the reasons is that both the Federal Union and the states are permitted to legislate on penitentiary and public health matters, resulting in 26 different legal norms. In addition there are economic differences between the various regions. A good example differences in provision is the variation of number of FPHs. There are 31 FPHs in total in the country. However, while key states such as São Paulo, Rio de Janeiro and Minas Gerais can count on many FPHs each, there are many states that do not have any (Brasil 2008). In these states, mentally ill offenders are sent to CC in general psychiatric hospitals presenting difficulties to non-forensic clinical staff and to the other patients, or they are unfortunately kept in penitentiaries in close contact with offenders who are not mentally ill receiving very minimal psychiatric care (Taborda et al. 2007).

The penal and public health systems are not linked. The public health system is governed by the Unified Health System – Sistema Único de Saúde (SUS) – which holds the universality and equality of care, which means that every Brazilian citizen has the right to have his health needs met (Pustai 2004). Even so, healthcare in prisons, involving medical or mental disorders, is not covered by the SUS. This means that the small budget of the penitentiary system provides for this. The exclusion of the prisoners from the SUS hence constitutes unconstitutional discrimination (Taborda et al. 2007).

In the State of Rio Grande do Sul the Dr. Maurício Cardoso Forensic Psychiatric Institute (FPH-MC) is the hub of psychiatric services for prisoners in the state. It is located in Porto Alegre, the state's capital city. It's a large old hospital, founded in 1925, with some asylum characteristics, in spite of the ongoing effort of staff to keep the quality of its service high. 728 mentally disordered patients are resident in the FPH-MC, receiving treatment under CC57; 7.8 % are female (Brasil 2008). Apart from its role established by Brazilian legislation (in-patient and out-patient treatment for prisoners under CC and in-patient treatment for prisoners who present with severe SMI), the hospital is also tasked with carrying out of psychiatric examinations in a criminal justice context, mainly the Penal Imputability Exam (PIE), and the Dangerousness Exam (DE). The first exam refers to the evaluation of insanity; the latter is a risk assessment.

Defendants submitted to PIE are mainly male, white and single, originating from small towns and presenting with low literacy and low professional qualifications. The most prevalent diagnoses are substance related disorders (alcohol or drugs) (Telles and Folino 2006; Telles 2007).

8.3   Prevalence of Mental Disorders in the Prison Population

The lack of comprehensive and carefully carried out epidemiologic studies, establishing the prevalence of mental disorders in prisons and even in the FPHs, is problematic. This omission reflects the disregard of those responsible for public policies in the last decades when dealing with the penitentiary system, reflected in the lack of investment, lack of improvement of material conditions and under-qualified staff. As the magnitude of the prevalence of psychiatric morbidity is unknown, there are no regular programs in most places to treat mental disorders in prison, or to prevent and treat substance-related disorders or suicide (Taborda et al. 2000).

In order to address this lack of evidence, a group of researchers from the School of Medicine of the Federal University of São Paulo, in which one of the present authors took part (Taborda), recently studied the prevalence of mental disorders in the prisons of that state. The study included structured interviews (Composite International Diagnostic Interview (CIDI), version 2.1) and assessed a random sample of 1,837 subjects, both males and females, representative of that prison population. Preliminary results showed an annual prevalence of 12.2 % of serious mental disorders in prison (psychosis and mood disorders) (Ribeiro WS, Quintana MIS, Higashi MK, Taborda JGV, Mari JJ, Andreoli SB, Mental disorders in the prison population of State of São Paulo: an epidemiological approach, unpublished). These data, if extrapolated to the Brazilian prison population as a whole, suggest that there may be about 60,000 seriously mentally ill inmates in Brazilian prisons, a figure well above the 32,000 psychiatric beds of the Brazilian public network maintained by the SUS.

8.4 Situation of Prisoners and Mentally Ill Patients in the Prison System

The Brazilian prison system doesn't have the capacity for the number of prisoners it keeps resulting in overcrowding of penitentiaries and police stations (Anistia Internacional 1999). It is estimated that 12 % of the prisoners remain in police stations for excessive amounts of time, while they should stay there for only 30 days (Souza and Versignassi 2008; Ermel 2009). In various places the sanitary facilities are insufficient and inadequate, resulting in risks to health. Besides, overcrowding in prisons promotes the spread of diseases such as AIDS and tuberculosis.

There is also insufficient nursing, dental and medical assistance in criminal justice institutions. Many prisoners are called upon to participate in taking care of sick inmates or of those with special needs such as paraplegics. Medical assistance in the community for this population is also restricted and there are very few hospitals that would receive them. Until a bed is found prisoners are kept handcuffed to their bed due to a lack of staff for observations (Rio Grande do Sul 2003). Consultation with medical specialists in the community does not always occur because there are not enough escorts.

Another shortcoming, identified also by Amnesty International, is the small number of police officers (Anistia Internacional 1999). This may result in the loss of control of the institution by the authorities, exposing inmates to violence and intimidation by other prisoners. In some states this has resulted in the formation of criminal gangs organized inside major penitentiaries. An example is the First Capital Command (FCC) which controls 80 % of prisons in the State of São Paulo (Souza and Versignassi 2008).

In Brazil, research on prison suicide and other forensic topics is just beginning. Coelho (2006) identified 20 suicides in the FPH-MC from 1985 to 2004, representing 10 % of the total deaths occurring in this period in the institution. Of these, 70 % were in the hospital under CC and the remaining 30 % were hospitalized for SMI. The average age of the first group was 42.7 years, and they had been hospitalized for an average of 9.9 years; in the second group the average age was 27.8 years and the length of hospitalization was 1 month. In both groups the dominant profile was male, white, single, childless, from the interior of the state, low professional qualification and low literacy. The most prevalent diagnosis was schizophrenia (55 %) and paranoid personality disorder (15 %). In 50 % of the cases there was comorbidity with abuse of alcohol and/or other psychoactive substances. The most common method of suicide was hanging at dawn and most prisoners had a history of prior suicide attempts.

Currently the federal government is seeking to reduce prison overcrowding and improve conditions of detention through the building of new penal institutions in collaboration with state governments. As this will not be sufficient to eradicate the current overcrowding, the federal government also aims to only imprison those convicted of serious crimes. A law introduced in November 1998 expanded the range of sentences available to judges as alternatives to custodial sentences for non-violent offenders who would otherwise be sentenced to imprisonment. The recruitment and training of teams of prison officers and health professionals are also planned in order to provide a more efficient service for this population (Anistia Internacional 1999). Recently, technical assistance has improved in prisons and FPHs through collaboration with national and international universities (Sampaio 2006). The establishment of a Medical Residency Program in Forensic Psychiatry in the State of Rio Grande do Sul also worked to better serve the population of inmates and patients there.

8.5 Services for the Mentally Ill

The number of mentally ill prisoners has been growing due to the stressors and poor prison conditions and due to changes in psychiatric service models resulting in the reduction of psychiatric beds in the community (Taborda and Arboleda-Flórez 2006). Although Brazilian law determines that every prisoner should be examined when he enters prison this does not always occur and only those who present gross symptoms will be attended to. This means, for example, that mental patients with mild symptoms may be considered by the penitentiary administration as simulators, causing a delay in the initiation of care for these patients and hence making it less effective with potential higher resources needed at a later stage, including transfer to an FPH.

According to Taborda et al. (2000), there is no program for prevention of suicide or use of psychoactive substances in this population, so that it is not surprising that suicides do occur in large numbers. The assistance in the PFHs, however, varies from state to state and the implementation of Progressive Discharge Programs, where adopted, has been contributing to greater social and family reintegration and recovery, thus leading to the termination of the CC and the discharge of patients (Cia 2006).

8.6 Ethical Challenges

In exercising their professional duties, physicians should be guided by the laws in force and by the principles that direct the practice of medicine. In the case of prison medicine, due to its peculiarities, the possibilities of ethical and legal conflicts increase, for, in spite of physician and prisoner establishing an essentially therapeutic relationship, this is of a triangular nature, since both are linked to a third subject, the penitentiary authority (Taborda and Bins 2008).

In the practice of forensic psychiatry in Brazil, some ethical topics are of particular importance, especially those relating to confidentiality, compulsory treatment, autonomy, the principle of equivalence and financial restrictions.

The confidentiality of the information provided by patients acquires special characteristics in prison environments. One potential source of conflict is the twofold role of the forensic psychiatrist – the clinical and the forensic one – which is a concrete example of a classical ethical dilemma in forensic psychiatry (Strasburger et al. 1997; Taborda et al. 2000), since the doctor treating the patient must be loyal both to his patient and to the prison administration which he serves. Even though their first duty is towards their patients, there are limits to medical confidentiality, e.g. the information patients provide will be included in their medical records and will be accessible to professionals performing future risk assessments. Except for this aspect, the prisoner has the same rights as an ordinary patient has to confidentiality (Taborda and Bins 2008). In some states, however, there is a serious confidentiality problem, as the in-patient treatment and the risk assessment are performed by the FPH staff where the patient receives his CC. The way to prevent this is to divide psychiatric staff into two groups: one that carries out the expert examination including risk assessment, the other one being in charge of patient treatment. This provision, however, on account of the scarce human resources, resulted in more difficulties with regards to the provision of good mental health care for forensic in-patients.

In relation to autonomy it must be borne in mind that most of the prisoners are competent to either refuse or to consent to treatment, thus they should only receive involuntary treatment if they do not have the capacity to consent or if there is an imminent danger to life. The situation of patients who are in FPHs under CC, however, is different, as the involuntary nature of their treatment has already been determined by a court (Taborda and Bins 2009).

In research with prisoners, the most important point to note is the respect for the autonomy of research subjects. Thus, one must be very careful to avoid undue inducements. One should not forget that the prisoner is deprived of freedom, so seemingly small rewards for free citizens may acquire disproportionate importance for him/her. Moreover, explicit advantages, such as reduction of sentence, cannot and should not be offered in exchange for participation in the research project (Taborda and Arboleda-Flórez 1999). In Brazil, given the precarious conditions of many prison facilities, one should take special care to not "purchase" prisoners' consent.

Regarding the distribution of resources for health care the Principle of Equivalence should be observed. According to this principle, the penitentiary services should provide the prisoners with health care services equivalent to those provided to the population in general (Niveau 2007). In this sense, the Principle of Equivalence is an application of the Principle of Justice in the correctional context and aims at preventing prisoners from being subjected to additional punishment by deprivation of health care. Unfortunately the Principle of Equivalence has not been observed in Brazilian prisons, as seen by the health conditions in prison facilities and by the public policies developed for this sector (Taborda and Bins 2008).

As noted above, In Brazil, under the aegis of the Federal Constitution of 1988, the SUS – the Unified Health System – was established. According to federal regulation and the laws that govern it, SUS should cover the entire Brazilian population. It is governed by the principles enshrined in Articles 196 and 198 of the Federal Constitution of 1988: universality, equity, regionalization, hierarchy, decentralization, comprehensiveness and public participation (Brasil 1988). Several criticisms can be made of the SUS – the most important one perhaps relates to the heterogeneity of the services provided; some places provide excellent care while others do not offer similar care. Furthermore, despite the explicit recommendation of the constitution and of the laws, Brazilian prisoners are totally outside this care system since prison hospitals and health services do not have their expenses reimbursed by the SUS and must seek financing within the already scarce penitentiary funding system. This discrimination results in damage to these health facilities and promotes the process of dilapidation of these institutions, thus violating the Principle of Equivalence (Taborda and Bins 2008).

Finally one must consider the role that the constant financial restrictions have played in the deterioration of Brazilian prison reality. There is a shortage of material and human resources, which makes the health care of prisoners truly dismal: the appalling prison conditions (overcrowding and lack of sanitation), new sources of physical and mental illnesses, add to the shortcomings of clinical staff. Thus, health needs not adequately met become sources of new diseases, creating a vicious circle of suffering (Taborda and Bins 2008).

8.7   Conclusion

The authors provided an overview of Brazilian prisons and of the situation of mentally ill offenders. The relationship between the Forensic Health System and the Public Health System and relevant ethical issues were discussed, mainly those related to the Principles of Universality and of Integrality stipulating that every Brazilian citizen has the right to have his/her health needs thoroughly attended to free of charge.

Despite these principles, the penitentiary conditions in Brazil are precarious and need to be improved. Imprisonment currently often results in a violation against the human rights of the prisoners, who have their basic needs unmet, including mental health needs. In order to properly plan the care for this population, the first step would be a comprehensive epidemiologic study, establishing the prevalence of mental disorders in prisons and in forensic psychiatric hospitals.

The proximity of prison centers and forensic psychiatric hospitals to various university centers has made it possible to carry out important research in the field of forensic psychiatry and related areas and this has also contributed to the better qualification of staff. However, more work is needed in education and training to ensure an appropriately qualified workforce for this challenging population.

References

American Law Institute. 1962. *Model penal code: Proposed official draft*. Philadelphia: ALI.

Anistia Internacional. 1999. *Brasil "Aqui Ninguém Dorme Sossegado": Violação dos Direitos Humanos Contra Detentos*. Porto Alegre/São Paulo: Anistia Internacional.

Brasil. Constituição da República Federativa do Brasil. 1988. *Diário Oficial da União*, 5/out/1988.

Brasil. Lei Nº 7.209/84 (Código Penal). 1984. *Diário Oficial da União*, 13 Jul 1984.

Brasil. Ministério da Justiça. Departamento Penitenciário Nacional (DEPEN). 2008. *Sistema Penitenciário no Brasil: Dados Consolidados*. Brasília: Ministério da Justiça. www.mj.gov.br/depen. Accessed 20 Apr 2010.

Brasil. Ministério da Justiça. Departamento Penitenciário Nacional (DEPEN). 2009. *Sistema Penitenciário no Brasil: Dados Consolidados*. Brasília: Ministério da Justiça. www.mj.gov.br/depen. Accessed 20 Apr 2010.

Brasil. Ministério do Planejamento, Orçamento e Gestão. Instituto Brasileiro de Geografia e Estatística (IBGE). 2010. *PopClock*. Brasília: IBGE. www.ibge.gov.br/home. Accessed 20 Apr 2010.

Cia, M. 2006. A Alta e a Desinternação Progressiva Como Forma de Efetivação dos Direitos Fundamentais dos Inimputáveis no Sistema Penal Brasileiro. *Revista do Conselho Nacional de Política Criminal e Penitenciária* 1(19): 183–197.

Coelho, E.R. (2006). Suicídios de Internos em um Hospital de Custódia eTratamento [Máster Dissertation]. Porto Alegre: PUCRS – PPG em Ciências Criminais.

Ermel, M. 2009. Superlotação das Cadeias: 12 % dos Presos Estão em Delegacias do País. *Zero Hora*, 1 Mar 2009.

Niveau, G. 2007. Relevance and limits of the principle of "equivalence of care" in prison medicine. *Journal of Medical Ethics* 33(10): 610–613.

Pustai, O.J. 2004. O Sistema de Saúde no Brasil. In *Medicina Ambulatorial: Condutas de Atenção Primária Baseadas em Evidências*, 3rd ed, ed. B.B. Duncan, M.I. Schmidt, and E.R.J. Giugliani. Porto Alegre: Artmed.

Rio Grande do Sul. 2003. Assembléia Legislativa. Comissão de Cidadania e Direitos Humanos. *Relatório Azul 2002–2003: Garantias e Violações dos Direitos Humanos*. Porto Alegre: Corag.

Sampaio, R.G. 2006. Os Paradoxos Conceituais Entre Saúde Mental, Direitos Humanos e Sistema Prisional. *Revista do Conselho Nacional de Política Criminal e Penitenciária* 1(19): 161–182.

Souza, F., and A. Versignassi. 2008. A Cadeia Como Você Nunca Viu. *Super Interessante* 22(3): 54–65.

Strasburger, L.H., T.G. Gutheil, and A. Brodsky. 1997. On wearing two hats: Role conflict in serving as both psychotherapist and expert witness. *The American Journal of Psychiatry* 154(4): 448–456.

Taborda, J.G.V. 2001. Criminal justice system in Brazil: Functions of a forensic psychiatrist. *International Journal of Law and Psychiatry* 24(4–5): 371–386.

Taborda, J.G.V. 2004. Os Sistemas de Justiça Criminal Brasileiro e Anglo-saxão: Uma Comparação. In *Psiquiatria Forense*, ed. J.G.V. Taborda, M. Chalub, and E. Abdalla-Filho. Porto Alegre: Artmed Editora.

Taborda, J.G.V., and J. Arboleda-Flórez. 1999. Forensic medicine in the next century: Some ethical challenges. *International Journal of Offender Therapy and Comparative Criminology* 43: 188–201.

Taborda, J.G.V., and J. Arboleda-Flórez. 2006. Ética em Psiquiatria Forense: Atividades Pericial e Clínica e Pesquisa com Prisioneiros. *Revista Brasileira de Psiquiatria* 28(2): 86–92.

Taborda, J.G.V., and H.D.C. Bins. 2008. Assistência em Saúde Mental e o Sistema Prisional no Brasil. *Revista de Psiquiatria (Hospital Júlio de Matos, Portugal)* 21(3): 164–170.

Taborda, J.G.V., and H.D.C. Bins. 2009. Ética em Psiquiatria Forense: Antigos Dilemas, Novos Desafios. *Revista Bioética* 17(2): 191–201.

Taborda, J.G.V., J.M. Bertolote, R.G. Cardoso, and P. Blank. 1999. The impact of primary mental health care in a prison system in Brazil. *Canadian Journal of Psychiatry* 44: 180–182.

Taborda, J.G.V., R.G. Cardoso, and H.C.P. Morana. 2000. Forensic psychiatry in Brazil: An overview. *International Journal of Law and Psychiatry* 23(5–6): 579–588.

Taborda, J.G.V., J.O. Folino, and R. Salton. 2007. Forensic mental health care in South America: An overview of the Brazilian and argentinian cases. *International Journal of Prisoner Health* 3(2): 125–133.

Telles, L.E.B. 2007. Perícias de Responsabilidade Penal Realizadas no Instituto Psiquiátrico Forense. *Multijuris: Primeiro Grau em Ação* 2(3): 44–49.

Telles, L.E.B., and J.O. Folino. 2006. Perfil de Reos Sometidos a Examen de Responsabilidad Penal en Porto Alegre, Brasil. *Revista de Psiquiatria Forense y Ley* 2(1): 05–13.

Chapter 9
Psychiatric Treatment in the Detention Systems of Quebec: Trying to Merge Prison and Therapeutic Cultures

Marie-Hélène Régnier, Jean-Luc Dubreucq, Julie Duchaine,
and Jocelyn Aubut

9.1 Introduction

More than 9.8 million persons are held behind bars around the world. The situation is particularly impressive in the United States, where the rate of detention reaches 756 inhabitants per 100,000 (Home Office [UK] 2008). The rate of confinement in Canada is also higher than in most Western countries with a rate of 116 inhabitants per 100,000 according to the Correctional Service of Canada (Daigle 2007).

In Western countries, one prisoner in seven is affected by a psychotic disorder or by major depression. This rate is two to four times higher than that of the general population and reflects the need of psychiatric care in prison, especially since these conditions are treatable. Besides, a significant number of prisoners suffer from anxiety, organic disorders, concussion, suicidal behaviour, substance abuse, attention deficit disorder, and other developmental disorders (Fazel and Danesh 2002).

Authors wish to thank Dre Renée Fugère, Psychiatrist at the Institut Philippe-Pinel de Montréal and the International Academy of Law and Mental Health for their collaboration to this chapter.

M.-H. Régnier (✉)
Assistant to the Director General, Institut Philippe-Pinel de Montréal,
10 905 boul. Henri-Bourassa Est, Montreal (Qc) H1C 1H1, Canada
e-mail: mh.regnier.ippm@ssss.gouv.qc.ca

J.-L. Dubreucq
Psychiatrist, Institut Philippe-Pinel de Montréal,
and Clinical Associate Professor, Université de Montréal,
10 905 boul. Henri-Bourassa Est, Montreal (Qc) H1C 1H1, Canada

J. Duchaine
Pharmacist, Institut Philippe-Pinel de Montréal,
10 905 boul. Henri-Bourassa Est, Montreal (Qc) H1C 1H1, Canada

J. Aubut
Psychiatrist, Director General, Institut Philippe-Pinel de Montréal,
and Clinical Associate Professor, Université de Montréal,
10 905 boul. Henri-Bourassa Est, Montreal (Qc) H1C 1H1, Canada

N. Konrad et al. (eds.), *Ethical Issues in Prison Psychiatry*, International Library of Ethics, Law, and the New Medicine 46, DOI 10.1007/978-94-007-0086-4_9,
© Springer Science+Business Media Dordrecht 2013

9.1.1 Federal and Provincial Correctional Systems

The responsibility regarding correctional systems in Canada is divided between federal and provincial governments. The Correctional Service of Canada (CSC) deals with offenders having a 2 year or longer sentence including life sentences. Provincial detention centres receive remanded persons and those who serve a sentence of fewer than 2 years. Remanded persons are those awaiting their trial or judgment (Ministère de la Sécurité publique 2010).

Mental healthcare in federal settings is well structured in a continuum of care model. Beginning with voluntary screening of all offenders when they arrive at a regional reception centre, detainees can then access basic mental healthcare in each institution or intermediate healthcare units in some institutions, if they need more intense care than that offered by a regular institution. Ultimately, offenders with acute mental disorders can be referred to one of the Regional Treatment Centres, designed to provide intensive mental healthcare. Afterwards, good discharge planning along with a partnership with community services allows for better transition to the community (Anonymous 2007).

Even though the CSC has a well-structured mental healthcare system, they certainly face ethical issues surrounding mental healthcare in their facilities. Since provincial detention centeres have less funding, staff and resources than federal ones, we will focus on ethical issues raised by those weaknesses.

9.1.2 Healthcare Services in the Province of Quebec

In Quebec, healthcare services are offered through a public system, i.e., there is free access and standardized care for the entire population. Healthcare in detention should follow the same principle. The Canadian Charter of Rights and Freedoms guarantees in Art. 15(1) that 'Every individual is equal before and under the law and has the right to the equal protection and equal benefit of the law without discrimination and, in particular, without discrimination based on race, national or ethnic origin, colour, religion, sex, age or mental or physical disability.' The same principle is found in the *Quebec Charter of Human Rights and Freedoms:* "Every person has a right to full and equal recognition and exercise of his human rights and freedoms, without distinction, exclusion or preference based on race, colour, sex, pregnancy, sexual orientation, civil status, age except as provided by law, religion, political convictions, language, ethnic or national origin, social condition, a handicap or the use of any means to palliate a handicap. Discrimination exists where such a distinction, exclusion or preference has the effect of nullifying or impairing such right." In the Civil Code of Quebec, Art.1 states: "Every human being possesses juridical personality and has the full enjoyment of civil rights." These laws include the right for detainees to access healthcare as if they were in the community.

In addition, the Act Respecting Health Services and Social Services, states in Art.4, 'Every person is entitled to be informed of the existence of the health and social services and resources available in his community and of the conditions governing access to such services and resources' and, in Art.5, 'Every person is entitled to receive, with continuity and in a personalized and safe manner, health services and social services which are scientifically, humanly and socially appropriate.' An issue for the Institute Philippe-Pinel de Montréal (herein after, Institute), which will be discussed later, relates to Art. 7, 'Every person whose life or bodily integrity is endangered is entitled to receive the care required by his condition. Every institution shall, where requested, ensure that such care is provided'.

In Quebec, public healthcare includes any establishment under the authority of the Ministry of Health and Social Services, which takes care, via regional agencies, of granting operating budgets and oversees the management of establishments as well as the quality of the care and other services offered. However, healthcare in detention centres is under the auspices of the Ministry of Public Safety. Care providers are correctional officer nurses (more often, correctional officer registered nursing assistants who have a smaller scope of practice than a registered nurse) who are dressed as correctional officers, and working in a correctional environment principally based on stabilization, control, and surveillance – not primarily on support and therapy. This is one of the main challenges when providing mental healthcare in detention. For example, requests from psychiatrists are often modulated by correctional requirements; this is also the case for medication, bed and seclusion management issues.

At the provincial level, a blatant legal gap is evident since detention centres are not subject to the Act Respecting Health Services and Social Services. The Act Respecting the Québec Correctional System mentions healthcare only in Art. 42, where the reasons for temporary absence for medical purposes are given. Mental health is only mentioned very briefly in the Regulation under the Act Respecting the Quebec Correctional System:

11. An inmate whose state of health so requires must be transferred to a hospital centre.

...

13. A health professional at the facility must submit a report to the facility director each time the health professional believes that the physical or mental health of an inmate has been or will be affected by the conditions of detention or by their extension.

9.1.3 The Role of the Institute Philippe-Pinel de Montréal

The Institute is engaged in a partnership with both federal and provincial systems. Inpatient services to Correctional Service of Canada include an adult sex offender program admitting male perpetrators of sexual assault who generally come from penitentiaries, and a psychiatric care unit for women with a federal sentence from all regions across Canada. Services are offered on a contractual basis and issues related to psychiatric care under this partnership are of a scope beyond the purpose of this paper. The Institute also offers psychiatric services (treatment and assessment) on a consultation basis in some detention centres in the province of Quebec and an inpatient assessment service for provincial detention centres. It has worked closely with the Quebec Ministry of Public Safety (Direction des services professionnels correctionnels – liaison, support et développement) to improve psychiatric services in detention.

The Institute in its functions relating to the clientele of forensic psychiatry or those presenting a high risk of violent behaviour, inevitably interacts closely with detention centres. The psychiatrists of the Institute working in detention centres situated in Montreal face a number of issues in their practice. Whether it is staff competence, lack of structure, safety, the decrepitude of premises, or the compliance with medical orders, their practice is plagued by uncertainty and by apprehension regarding the follow-up for the prisoners not only during detention, but also later when they are in the community.

The core of this paper will be a discussion around a number of clinical and ethical issues faced by provincial institutions under the responsibility of the Quebec correctional services. Canada is subdivided into ten provinces and three territories, and each province has its own correctional system. However, they all face similar issues regarding mental health care in detention. The views presented in this chapter represent those of the Institute on the subject.

9.2   Mental Illness and Detention

A research study performed in two of the 18 detention centres under the jurisdiction of the Quebec Ministry of Public Safety estimated that 14.1 % of the prisoners had, during the last month, presented a grave psychiatric disorder such as a psychotic disorder, major depression, or bipolar disorder (Daigle and Côté 2001). Furthermore, according to a review of several epidemiological studies in Canadian prisons, the lifetime prevalence of grave and persistent mental disorders in the detained population was estimated at more than 22 %. We can thus consider that approximately 6,000 Canadians battling with such a diagnosis are presently behind bars throughout the country (Côté and Hodgins 2003).

Between 45 and 90 % of the detainees presenting psychiatric disorders have previously been hospitalized with mental health issues (Pogrebin and Poole 1987; Schenllenberg et al. 1992). This raises question as to why prisoners having a mental health problem are nevertheless managed in the judicial system instead of the health care system. According to studies, the link between mental illness and being imprisoned is clear. This may be due to the presence of symptoms which are considered as deviations from the standard and which are difficult to tolerate by our society (Fujioka 2001). Furthermore, being affected by a grave psychiatric disorder quadruples the risk of aggression compared with the general population (Dubreucq et al. 2005).

Among the population of prisoners, those with mental disorders are more at risk of reoffending. A 6 year study showed that prisoners having a grave psychiatric disorder had a 2.4 increased risk of being imprisoned at least four times during this period, compared with other prisoners. In the United States, it was estimated that 15–24 % of the federal prison population needed a certain level of mental health care during detention. For those having received a diagnosis of a grave psychiatric disorder, 76 % received psychiatric care during their confinement (Baillargeon et al. 2009).

9.3 Prison or Hospital?

In the 1930's and 1970's, some hypotheses on the high prevalence of mental disorders in prison were formulated. Although formulated some time ago, these hypotheses are still relevant. Of particular note is the shift of the clientele, the criminalization of persons presenting with mental health problems and the clinical specificity of persons with mental disorders.

The theory of the shift of the clientele originates from Penrose, based on the concept of communicating vessels. According to the author, there is an inverse relation between the number of places available in prison and those available in psychiatric hospitals, the total number remaining, however, equal. This theory rests on two postulates: First, mental health problems predispose to criminal behaviour, therefore there is in any society a small number of persons presenting with socially unacceptable behaviour; second, those individuals are confined to detention in prison or hospitalization in psychiatric institutions which are possible avenues for the modern societies to isolate offenders (Penrose 1939); Therefore, if there is a decrease in the number of beds in psychiatric facilities, there will be an increase in the number of people in prisons.

The theory of criminalization of persons battling mental disorders goes back to the 1970s and brings to light certain social factors which could lead to the judicial system taking charge of these persons (Abramson 1972). According to Abramson, there is a limit to what society can tolerate as deviant behaviour. Societal pressure means that persons with mental disorders will be managed in the judicial system to ensure control of those deviant behaviours. Furthermore, if the health care system cannot keep the person who does not present a grave and immediate danger detained, there will be more pressure on the judicial system to incarcerate them.

According to Teplin, the presence of an additional psychiatric diagnosis, such as substance abuse, increases the likelihood of the offender being referred to the judicial system. Indeed, as mental health services rarely treat dependencies and detoxification services do not treat the main psychiatric disorders, these offenders are left within the judicial system. The judicial system thus becomes de facto the provider of services for the dual diagnosis clientele (Teplin 1984).

A more modern theory puts the emphasis on "crystallization". This means that depending on which system (judiciary or health) the person first passes through, subsequent decisions will replicate the first. In fact, police have discretionary power during an intervention to direct a person towards the "most suited" system according to *The* Act respecting the protection of persons whose mental state presents a danger to themselves or to others which came into force in 1998. This Act replaced the Mental Patients Protection Act and completes, as stated in Art. 1, the provisions of the Civil Code of Quebec "concerning the confinement in a health and social services institution of persons whose mental state presents a danger to themselves or to others, and the provisions concerning the psychiatric assessment carried out to determine the necessity for such confinement". A novelty was introduced by this act in Art. 8. It now allows a policeman to bring a person to an establishment of health without the authorization of the court and against the will of the individual concerned. The essential condition is that "the mental state of the person presents a grave and immediate danger to himself or to others".

The choice of bringing someone to either jail or hospital is likely to be greatly influenced by previous contacts of the person with one system or the other (Dessureault et al. 2000; Lamb and Weinberger 2005). For example, a study in a Californian prison concluded that 95 % of the prisoners with a grave psychiatric disorder had been arrested in the past (Lamb et al. 2007).

The rising number of psychiatric patients in detention centres at all levels of jurisdiction is also considered by many researchers as a consequence of the reform of health care which took place during the last decades, encouraging psychiatric deinstitutionalization by the "ambulatory switch" and causing rationalization of resources in mental health and difficulties in accessing psychiatric care (Joncas 2004).

In Quebec, psychiatric deinstitutionalization began in the 1960s, in the era of the introduction of antipsychotics, but also during the emergence of the principle of the least restrictive conditions for patients. During the following 30 years, the number of hospitalized psychiatric patients fell by 80 % and services were only partially offered in the community (Crocker and Côté 2009).

In 1962, the Bédard, Lazure, and Robert report denounced the fate of psychiatric patients in the "mega-hospitals" of Montreal and Quebec, and recommended a moratorium on the construction of psychiatric hospitals. Aiming for a more humane philosophy of care, the creation of departments of psychiatry in the regional hospitals was suggested.

The criteria of hospitalization in psychiatric in-patient settings are now more restrictive. Consistently, the average length of stay is shorter than previously; In Quebec, e.g., there has been a decrease of the number of beds from 20,000 in 1965 to 3,440 in 2004 (Dubreucq 2008).

In 1992, the Criminal Code of Canada (1985), which is enforced in all provinces, was amended and a new plan to manage accused mentally disordered individuals was created. According to Pilon (1999):

"...the terminology of the former insanity defence was amended so as to exempt from criminal liability persons who commit the act complained of while suffering from 'a mental disorder' ... To reflect that amendment, the consequential verdict was also changed from not guilty on 'account of insanity' to 'not criminally responsible on account of mental disorder.' ...

... a new definition with criteria for determining whether an accused is 'unfit to stand trial', something not previously spelled out in the Criminal Code, was also introduced. Subject to limitations, the courts also have the power to order involuntary treatment of a mentally disordered accused, for the purpose of rendering him or her fit to stand trial.

Furthermore, the case of an unfit accused must be reviewed by a court every 2 years, in order to determine whether sufficient evidence exists to bring the individual to trial. If the evidence is not sufficient, the accused is entitled to an acquittal.

Upon finding an accused not criminally responsible on account of mental disorder, a court is no longer obliged to order him or her to be held in strict custody. Instead, the court has the option of choosing an appropriate disposition or deferring that decision to a Review Board. In either case, the permissible dispositions include detention in hospital, discharge subject to conditions, or absolute discharge." (Pilon 1999).

According to Crocker and Côté (2009), the changes brought to the Criminal Code in 1992 led to an increased number of individuals found not criminally responsible because of mental disorders (herein after, NCRMD). In 2006, there were twice as many NCRMDs compared to 1992 in the province of Quebec, and an average of 4.5 NCRMDs per 100,000 inhabitants. On the other hand, not all these patients stay in psychiatry institutions for two main reasons: the small number of forensic beds available and the pressure put on psychiatric beds by the general population (Crocker and Côté 2009).

In spite of the reform of the Criminal Code in 1992, several psychiatric patients have been detained in prison because of a lack of health services. The comments of Judge McLachlin in the Winko judgement are particularly interesting on this subject: 'The need for treatment rather than punishment is rendered even more acute by the fact that the mentally ill are often vulnerable and victimized in the prison setting, as well as by changes in the health system that many suggest result in greater numbers of the mentally ill being caught up in the criminal process' (Winko v. British Columbia 1999).

9.4   Issues Surrounding Mental Health Care During Detention in Quebec Provincial Detention Centres

9.4.1   Screening Issues

Some deviant behaviours are tolerated until they break prison regulations. Therefore, the silently psychotic prisoner will often be ignored, whereas the disturbing psychotic will often be considered as having a disciplinary problem rather than a mental illness (Birmingham 2004).

In this context, it is useful to refer to the admission process at a detention centre. Is the mental state of the remanded or the detained objectively evaluated by competent staff? In fact, only an evaluation of the suicidal risk is made during the admission process which does not necessarily correspond to the time of arrival of the person at the detention centre. It may be done upon arrival in the sector or shortly after. In Montreal's detention centres, this evaluation has been performed since 2008, while in other detention centres in Quebec it has been systematized since 2002. Before the implementation of this procedure, the screening and the care of the suicidal clientele or of those having a mental health problem was weak in the provincial detention centres (Daigle and Côté 2001).

The Suicidal Risk Assessment Scale (herein after SRAS) is completed by a correctional officer, called the "tracking officer", and contains 9 items. The collected information is passed on to the unit coordinator who, if the result of the evaluation requires it, asks the specialized intervention team to complete a further evaluation with the "Assessment grid of the suicidal risk in prison" (ERSMC) which contains 14 items. If needed, the remanded or detained person will be directed to the infirmary where he will have access to a medical consultation and, if necessary, to a consultation with a psychiatrist. If a change of legal or clinical status of the imprisoned person occurs, the SRAS will be administered again. Furthermore, the continuous screening of the suicidal risk allows the administration of the ERSMC at any time when indicated by the wing personnel. To complete the SRAS, designated correctional officers receive a 1- to 2-h training while the ERSM grid requires a 4 day training.[1]

Besides this procedure, detention centres offer free access at any time to the Suicide Action Montreal line and to the Quebec Ombudsman as part of an agreement between those organizations and detention centres. The implementation of systematic evaluation of suicidal risk has resulted in a 66 % decrease of the calls to Suicide Action Montreal.[1] However, according to a study of the Ministry of Public Safety, Quebec remains the province with the highest rate of suicide of prisoners. In 2004–2005, this rate was 15 suicides per 10,000 prisoners in the province of Quebec detention centres compared to 4 per 10,000 in the other provinces (Lalande and Giguère 2009).

Regarding the evaluation of the mental state at admission, it is the accused or the detained himself who has to declare possible pathologies and give information about prescriptions (Daigle and Côté 2001). No systematic assessment is carried out and staff are not trained to perform mental state examinations. This gap causes an important delay in the identification of persons in need of mental health care. Furthermore, the turnover of the accused or detained, which is estimated to be 50 % per month, is an important factor in the difficulties in the implementation of screening.

Arrangements between correctional and health systems for the delivery of mental health care are not without difficulties. Some authors have suggested such arrangements create expenses linked to numerous transfers to hospitals as well as issues regarding security in less adapted settings. Furthermore, conflicts of philosophy and communication problems between the diverse stakeholders are frequent. Finally, access to the personal information and medical files of the detained is also a significant challenge (Bretch et al. 1996; Anasseril 2007).

---

[1] Personal communication with Denis Bouchard, Detention Counsellor, Chief of the suicide prevention program, Établissement de détention de Montréal.

9.4.2 Surveillance vs. Care

It is important to underline that each province has its own unique way of functioning and each faces different problems. Some are confronted with the decrepitude of the premises and with high staff turnover rates, whereas others struggle with issues of access to seclusion rooms, lack of nursing resources, and the absence of clear criteria for admission to the health care wing. All institutions face problems with recruitment to all positions, but most strikingly for nursing staff. With a demanding clientele and environment, and a great demand for nurses, detention centres are rarely their first choice.

Every detention centre across the province has the mandate to ensure the safe detention and surveillance of prisoners. There are two types of organizational structures at the infirmary regarding the type of staff working with the patients. In some centres, there are correctional officers and health services officers, i.e. nurses who are also correctional officers but whose tasks are only related to nursing. Although these health services officers are trained in nursing, the role of therapy in their position is limited. Indeed, after a period of stabilization, the continuation of the patient's stay in the infirmary is uncertain. Even in the detention centre where the nurses are not also correctional officers, but are employed by the local community service centre (LCSC), the problem of care in detention exists due to difficulties in defining the roles and responsibilities of the different professions, while at the same time facilitating collaboration between professionals.

For health service officers, issues arise regarding duality between the correctional and the caring role, e.g. in relation to confidentiality: information may have been disclosed during an episode of care but may then become relevant for correctional purposes.

It is important to note that there is no multidisciplinary team coordinating the treatment and rehabilitation of patients from a mental health perspective. Several years ago, such a structure was in place but due to budgetary constraints it was abolished.

In everyday life, nurses, employed by a LCSC or by the Ministry of Public Safety, are mainly appointed for physical healthcare. Nurses appointed to fulfil psychiatric nursing roles would allow closer follow-up of the patients' progress and facilitate the work of the psychiatrists by being able to consult with nursing staff and share their day-to-day observations of the patient.

Even if, in theory, healthcare professionals have autonomy, this is relative when taking into account constraints inherent to the prison system; the misunderstanding by the prison staff of the mission of mental health practitioners may go against practising medicine free from prejudices (Milly 2001).

The authors do not intend to make a judgment on the work of professionals in the criminal justice system. They manage a difficult clientele on a day-to-day basis within structural limits imposed by public safety concerns, but it has to be noted that a high standard of care is often mutually exclusive to the correctional environment. As attitudinal changes take time, we shall work in close collaboration with staff in a way that reconciles these two philosophies. One way to achieve this is to introduce the care of mentally ill offenders into general training schemes.

9.4.3   Living Conditions in Prison Infirmaries
and in Detention Wings

The living conditions in detention are challenging and not adequate in any detention centre. However, the physical arrangement of sectors and infirmaries are
different from one centre to the other and this is, in part, due to the years of
construction of the centres (1912, 1964, and 1996). Some centres have individual
cells for prisoners with mental health problems whereas others have shared areas,
i.e. shared cells or dormitories, each mixing prisoners with physical and mental
health problems.

Physically ill inmates have access to a physician and an infirmary. When specialized
care is requested, inmates are transferred to an appropriate hospital in order to
receive adequate health care. Mentally ill inmates who require medical assistance
will be referred to the physician who will evaluate the need to see a psychiatrist,
who serves as a consultant offering sessions in the detention centres on a regular
basis (1 or 2 days per week). The detainee with mental health problems will stay on
the wing or be transferred to the prison infirmary if he needs acute observation.
Seclusion rooms at the infirmary can be used for the mentally ill if needed.

The lack of privacy and the rigidity of the systems are factors increasing the
stress experienced by prisoners. Prisoners with mental health problems can be
detained in regular wings or transferred to the infirmary. If they are quiet and do not
present a risk for themselves or other prisoners, they will remain on the wings with
nursing staff (or correctional officers, depending on the centre) responsible for
distributing their medication. If they are too disturbed or if there are concerns about
their safety or that of other prisoners, they will be transferred to the infirmary
where they will be under constant observation by staff, but usually without entering
a therapeutic process. The turnover of prisoners is another important factor in the
difficulties encountered in offering therapeutic activities.

Without a doubt, detention can have a negative effect on the mental health of
prisoners. A research group studying the influence of environmental factors on
prisoners with a psychiatric disorder has reported that long periods of isolation in
the cells with limited intellectual stimulation contributed to the deterioration of the
prisoners' mental health and the emergence of feelings of anger, frustration and
anxiety. Some prisoners would spend an average of 8–9 h a day outside their cell.
However, it is not rare, in certain institutions, that prisoners spend close to 20 h a
day confined (Nurse et al. 2003). The stress experienced because of the confinement
and other psychosocial pressures, such as the estrangement of one's family or the
intimidation by peers also constitute risk factors for suicide in prison (Anasseril
2007). This problem was recognized by the World Health Organization in its guide
concerning the prevention of suicide in prison (World Health Organization 2007).

In most countries, correctional services are plagued by the lack of financing and
the disorganization of the mental health services (Association canadienne pour la
santé mentale 2009). One way to improve care and services in detention is to

transfer the responsibility of infirmaries to the Ministry of Health and Social Services. This would mean that every infirmary should implement the requirements of the Act Respecting Health Services and Social Services concerning the rights of users, the users' record, the organization of institutions, risk management and accreditation, to name but a few. A stricter follow-up of activities would bring an improvement of the services to the user and would allow the planning of clinical follow-up of the prisoners at the end of their sentence.

Action was recently taken in Quebec in that it was planned that health care dispensed in detention centres' infirmaries would be provided under the health and social services centres (HSSC), a multivocational institution operating a local community service centre, a residential and long-term care centre and, where applicable, a general and specialized hospital centre in a given geographical sector (Art.99.4 of the Act Respecting Health Services and Social Services). For each detention centre in the province, a HSSC would be designated to be responsible for all health services, including psychiatric services. These plans do not seem to have been taken any further by the government. It was left with the health and social services centres and with the detention centres of the concerned territories to establish agreements of services. However, from this, several challenges are anticipated regarding the status of the health services officers versus nurses from health and social services centres; for example, pension plans which are different between health and public safety, and, as expressed by health care officers in detention centres, the fear of a cultural clash.

This idea of reorganisation is not a new one. In 1989, a memorandum of understanding on responsibilities between the Ministry of Health and Social Services and the Ministry of Justice on the access to health services and social services for adult offenders was signed (Ministère de la santé et des services sociaux; Ministère de la sécurité publique 1989). The plan of this protocol is that adult offenders shall benefit from the complete range of the health and social services normally accessible to all citizens by law, according to the spirit of the Charter of Human Rights and Freedoms. Furthermore, several principles emanated from this agreement, among which are:

1. The adult offender is entitled to the same services of health and social services as any other citizen.
2. The adult offender whose health or psychosocial condition requires health and social services must be insured to receive adequate services beyond the judicial and correctional concerns.
3. The services to the adult offender have to be provided, as far as possible, by using the resources of the community in order to achieve continuity.

It was also planned that the Health and Social network would provide and assume the organization of health services to the detention clientele, if necessary, inside the detention centre; they would also assume the quality control of health services. Although this appeared to be a good concept at the time, and still is, for adequate services delivery, it was never fully implemented.

9.4.4 Treatment and Interventions Within the Prison System

The issue of prescriptions represents a major issue for psychiatrists working in detention centres. Even if the prescriptions of medications are well observed in terms of their composition, sometimes the mode of administration is slightly modified by the nursing staff, e.g. crushed medications is administered when this is not prescribed.

The use of seclusion rooms is another issue of concern. It is not rare that seclusion rooms are occupied by prisoners for administrative reasons such as lack of space in sectors or the need of increased protection for a particular prisoner. Patients who need seclusion can be transferred without the psychiatrist being notified because of administrative priorities. The cells at the infirmary, including seclusion rooms, are part of the prison capacity. Their use is therefore managed to answer the administrative needs of the centre. The overpopulation of detention centres does not help the resolution of this problem. Furthermore, according to a Director of Professional Services in one of the detention centers in Montreal, considering that the budgets granted to detention centres are related to prison capacity, removing these cells from the calculation means amputating budgets which are already limited.

According to the Canadian Mental Health Association, prisoners suffering from mental illness will frequently receive care below recognized standards or no treatment at all because of lack of personnel and the inadequacy of equipment (Association canadienne pour la santé mentale 2009).

The mental health care services received in detention are the main object of complaints forwarded by imprisoned persons to the Quebec Ombudsman and the Ministries of Health and Public Safety. Following a tour of all of the 18 detention centres in the province of Quebec, the Quebec Ombudsman, in association with the 'Groupe de défense des droits des détenus de Québec', denounced the lack of accessibility to healthcare professionals, the delays, the refusals to dispense prescribed medication, and errors during the distribution of medication, amongst other issues. All these problems seem to be even more important if they concern persons affected by mental disorders (Protecteur du citoyen 2005; Groupe de défense des droits des détenus de Québec 2004).

The Coroner's Office was involved in several cases related to deaths in detention centres as reported, for example, in coroner Dionne's report on a death in detention in 2007. The victim died from an acute cardiac arrhythmia in a seclusion room following an episode of psychomotor agitation. In his report, the coroner asserted that the disorganization of the care in forensic psychiatry in Quebec was of serious concern. He severely reprimanded the Ministry of Health and Social Services as well as the Ministry of Public Safety, who had not found any solution to the problem of overcrowding and therefore pushed psychiatric patients towards detention, where the care received is not always adequate. This report notes that aside from this death there were five other cases of psychiatric patients' deaths in the Montreal detention centres since 2000. Moreover, the coroner regreted that no measures were taken to improve the situation earlier (Dionne 2008) despite precise recommendations having been formulated by the coroner, Andrée Kronström, in her report on a similar event in 2000 (Kronström 2001) including regarding the capacity of hospitals to supply adequate care and the update of the 1989 protocol regarding health care in detention. However, no action to date has been taken to correct this situation.

In 2006, the federal report of the Honourable Michael J. L. Kirby, member of the Standing Senate Committee on Social Affairs, Science and Technology, underlined that '…the standard of care for mental health within correctional institutions (and in post-release settings) had to be raised to be equal with that available to 'non-offender' members of the general community. If the goal of incarceration is rehabilitation as well as public safety, this goal must be met' (Kirby and Keon 2006). In 2004, the Minister of Health and Social Services of the province of Quebec appointed a group of experts to work on the reorganization of the mental health services. A vast consultation arose and, finally, in 2005, the Minister released the 'Mental Health Action Plan 2005-2010' (Ministère de la Santé et des Services sociaux 2005). However, it is deplorable that there was no direct mention of treatment in correctional settings. As previously discussed, work is in progress to plan the hierarchical organization of forensic psychiatry, an important stage which constitutes the third phase of the implementation of the 'Mental Health Action Plan'. We do hope that the work by the Ministry of Health and Social Services and the forensic psychiatry group to complete the 'Mental Health Action Plan' yields fruit and has an impact on care in correctional settings.

This being said, some deaths that occurred in detention centres may have been avoided if the link with emergency services in psychiatry had been clearer. Hospitals generally have many reservations to admit patients coming from detention centres. If they do so, it will usually be for a very brief time only (for example, the amount of time for an injection).

9.4.5   Follow-Up

Follow-up occurs inside the detention centre, as well as after the end of a sentence. The prison philosophy involves a notion of time which repairs the misdeeds. It is not always that easy with psychiatric treatment. At the end of the detention, patients (or ex-detainees) will often return to the street. This does not break the cycle of criminality and detention for people with mental illness. The only way to achieve this and decrease the number of psychiatric prisoners in detention centres is to offer support at the end of the sentence. Utopian? Certainly. Essential? Absolutely.

As mentioned previously, the high turnover of prisoners does not allow for a valuable therapeutic process. Some will have access to a psychiatric consultation during their detention, some will have a prescription; but most will be released at the end of their sentence without any medical follow-up. This is particularly true for the homeless clientele. The total absence of liaison at the end of the sentence increases the phenomenon of revolving doors. Effectively, further to their release, approximately half of the prisoners battling against a problem of mental health return to prison during the next 3 years, because of lack of care in the community (Binswanger et al. 2007).

On the issue of organization of mental health services and the 'Mental Health Action Plan' of the Ministry of Health and Social Services, it is important to include, in the definition of the services offered in detention, the articulation of services available in the community which will be available upon release, including the guidance of the ex-prisoner through this process.

More and more structures are set up to avoid that persons having a mental health problem end up in detention and so that they receive appropriate health care. Mental health courts already exist in large cities of certain Canadian provinces such as British Columbia and Ontario. The same initiative has been in place in Montreal since 2008 at the municipal court level. A person considered fit to stand trial and criminally responsible can choose to participate in the 'Program of accompaniment Justice-Mental Health' (PAJ-SM). This is a joint pilot project of the city of Montreal, the Ministry of Justice, and the Ministry of Health and Social Services. The program was set up for a period of 3 years to ensure that judges and lawyers of the municipal Court are informed about dispositions in mental health, that the persons suffering from mental disorders, often deprived of resources, are offered solutions which correspond to their needs and to avoid judicial revolving doors (Douglas Mental Health University Institute 2010).

Other social initiatives to improve the interface between psychiatry and justice exist. 'Psychosocial emergency-Justice' (UPS-J), created in 1996, is a professional counselling service to assist the Court in determining the clinical and legal disposal of the accused. The program is coordinated by the health and social services centre Jeanne-Mance, the territory of which covers the downtown area of Montreal. The criminologists of the initiative are appointed by the Institute and intervene at the Court of Quebec (criminal and penal court) and at the municipal Court of Montreal within the PAJ-SM. The criminologists' interventions include a brief evaluation of the clinical state, the social situation and the therapeutic needs, as well as an estimation of the risks of re-offending and violence. The evaluation can also include an interview with the family or other significant person who can contribute to the evaluation and the connection with the professional services as well as the specialized housing services which are involved in the follow-up or which could help him. Objectives of this program include the avoidance of detention on remand for persons who require clinical help and to improve the quality of the link between the judicial system, health services, social services, community resources, and the natural environment.

9.5 Conclusion

It is the clash between these two cultures, correction vs. care, which underlies the majority of ethical issues surrounding care in detention. The work of psychiatrists stumbles on several constraints imposed by the imperatives of correction and the insufficiency of training of the correction officers on mental illness and the needs of the persons affected by mental disorders. Furthermore, the requests of psychiatrists regarding the reorganization of care are rarely prioritized by decision-makers of all levels given the lack of understanding of the particular needs of this clientele. This is also true for the healthcare network whose hesitation to admit the accused and detained contributes to their ostracism. In the absence of obligations for other hospitals to take care of the accused and the detainees in crisis, the stabilization and the return to detention will be the best that will be offered to this clientele. Besides, the short duration of the stays in the provincial detention centers and the absence of liaison do not allow to set up a structure which would break the cycle of revolving doors. The Institute is placed in a fragile balance between correction and care; correction which does not belong to us and care which is sub-optimal.

The Institute finds itself at the stage where the government is ready to reposition forensic psychiatry, considering the evolution of practice and the increase of demand. It is interesting to know that the Institute was built to offer services suited to the prisoners of the wing of the insane persons of the Bordeaux Jail, one of detention centres of Montreal. Over the years cases changed, programs developed, but the structure of forensic psychiatry remained more or less the same, clamped in multiple health care reforms. It is in the role of the Institute to intervene in detention. But now, what do we do as a hospital? Do we have to continue in sub-optimal conditions or do we have to continue hoping for a change? Must the clientele in detention centres be transferred to hospital centres, or must detention centres have multidisciplinary teams in mental health?

The Code of Ethics of Physicians states at Art. 32 that "A physician who has undertaken an examination, investigation or treatment of a patient must provide the medical follow-up required by the patient's condition, following his intervention, unless he has ensured that a colleague or other competent professional can do so in his place." Do we put our psychiatrists at risk of litigation considering the absence of liaison at the end of the sentence? Furthermore, when a psychiatrist asks for a hospitalization at the Institute and no bed is available or a court asks for the hospitalization of a prisoner and the admission must be postponed due to the lack of a bed, what shall we do? Do we expose ourselves to the risk of litigation?

Considering that the Act Respecting Health Services and Social Services states in Art. 101 that

"Every institution must, in particular,

(1) receive any person requiring services and assess his needs;
(2) dispense the required health or social services directly, or have them provided by an institution, body or person with which or with whom it has entered into a service agreement under section 108;
(3) ensure that its services are provided in continuity and complementarity with those provided by the other institutions and resources of the region, and that such services are organized in a way that reflects the needs of the population it serves;
(4) refer persons to whom it cannot provide certain services to another institution or body or to another person that provides them."

shall we, as an Institute, be the driving force which compensates for the provincial lack of organization in psychiatry?

The improvement of mental health care in detention can only be made concrete if there is an inter-ministerial will to do so. It will be important to get the most out of the development of an effective mode of collaboration between the various authorities, the empowerment of regions, the training, the technology, and the community resources in order to manage this population through meaningful co-responsibility.

We cannot leave untold the lack of interest of society for this clientele; nevertheless, we wish to underline that these persons must have access to care, which respects the standards recognized by the medical profession. In an era where punishment is fostered more than rehabilitation, it seems that it will be difficult to find the material and human resources to provide adequate care for inmates during and after their incarceration.

References

Abramson, M. 1972. The criminalization of mentally disordered behavior: Possible side effects of a new mental health law. *Hospital & Community Psychiatry* 23: 101–105.

Act Respecting Health Services and Social Services, R.S.Q., chapter S-4.2.

Act respecting the protection of persons whose mental state presents a danger to themselves or to others, R.S.Q., chapter P-38.001.

Act respecting the Québec correctional system, R.S.Q., chapter S-40.1.

Anasseril, D.E. 2007. Care of mentally ill in prisons: Challenges and solutions. *The Journal of the American Academy of Psychiatry and the Law* 35: 406–410.

Anonymous. 2007. A continuum of care – CSC launches a comprehensive mental health strategy. *Let's Talk* 32: 4–5.

Association canadienne pour la santé mentale. 2009, Mars 9. *L'Association canadienne pour la santé mentale exhorte le gouvernement à élaborer des solutions appropriées pour les détenus atteints de maladie mentale.* Retrieved 26 May 2010 from Législation psy: http://www.legislation-psy.com/spip.php?article2127

Baillargeon, J., I.A. Biswanger, J.V. Penn, B.A. Williams, and O.J. Murray. 2009. Psychiatric disorders and repeat incarcerations: The revolving prison door. *The American Journal of Psychiatry* 166: 103–109.

Bédard, D., D. Lazure, and C.A. Robert. 1962. Rapport de la Commission d'étude des hôpitaux psychiatriques. Québec: Commission d'étude des hôpitaux psychiatriques.

Binswanger, I.A., M.F. Stern, R.A. Deyo, P.J. Heagerty, A. Cheadle, J.G. Elmore, et al. 2007. Release from prison: A high risk of death for former inmates. *The New England Journal of Medicine* 356: 157–165.

Birmingham, L. 2004. Mental disorders in prisons. *Psychiatric Bulletin* 28: 393–397.

Bretch, R., C. Gray, C. Peterson, and B. Youngblood. 1996. The University of Texas Medical Branch – Texas Department of Criminal Justice Telemedicine Project: Findings from the first year of operation. *Telemedicine Journal* 2: 25–35.

Canadian Charter of Rights and Freedoms. 1982 s. 15, Part I of the Constitution Act, 1982, being Schedule B to the Canada Act 1982 (U.K.), c.11.

Charter of Human Rights and Freedoms, R.S.Q., chapter C-12.

Civil Code of Quebec, S.Q. 1991, c.64.

Code of Ethics of Physicians, R.Q. c. M-9, r.4.1.

Côté, G., and S. Hodgins. 2003. Les troubles mentaux et le comportement criminel. In *Traité de criminologie empirique*, ed. M. Le Blanc, M. Ouimet, and D. Szabo, 503–548. Montréal: Les Presses de l'Université de Montréal.

Criminal Code, R.S.C. 1985, c. C-46, s. 318(1).

Crocker, A.G., and G. Côté. 2009. Evolving systems of care: Individuals found not criminally responsible on account of mental disorder in custody of civil and forensic psychiatric services. *European Psychiatry* 24: 356–364.

Daigle, M. 2007. Mental health and suicide prevention services for Canadian prisoners. *International Journal of Prisoner Health* 3: 163–171.

Daigle, M., and G. Côté. 2001. Suicides et troubles mentaux chez les hommes incarcérés: Faut-il en appeler à une prise en charge communautaire? *Criminologie* 34: 103–122.

Dessureault, D., G. Côté, and A. Lesage. 2000. Impact of first contacts with the criminal justice or mental health systems on the subsequent orientation of mentally disordered persons toward either system. *International Journal of Law and Psychiatry* 23: 79–90.

Dionne, P.G. 2008. *Rapport d'investigation sur le décès de M. Justin Scott St-Aubin*. Québec: Bureau du Coroner.

Douglas Mental Health University Institute. 2010, Juillet 13. *The Programme d'accompagnement justice-santé mentale (PAJ-SM) in Montreal*. Retrieved from Douglas Mental Health University Institute: http://www.douglas.qc.ca/info/pajsm-montreal

Dubreucq, J.-L. 2008. Santé mentale des sans-abri: Faut-il intervenir davantage? *Psychiatrie et violence*, 8: http://id.erudit.org/iderudit/018663ar

Dubreucq, J.-L., C. Joyal, and F. Millaud. 2005. Risque de violence et troubles mentaux graves. *Annales Médico-Psychologiques* 163: 862–865.

Fazel, S., and J. Danesh. 2002. Serious mental health disorder in 23 000 prisoners: a systematic review of 62 surveys. *Lancet* 360: 545–550.

Fujioka, J. 2001. Helping mentally ill people break the cycle of jail and homelessness. *Psychiatric Services* 52.

Groupe de défense des droits des détenus de Québec. 2004, Décembre 15. *Soins de santé en milieu correctionnel: Le groupe de défense des droits des détenus de Québec demande une enquête*. Retrieved 26 May 2010 from Alter Justice: http://www.alterjustice.org/doc/communiques/com_081212.pdf

Home Office (UK). 2008. *World prison population list*, 8th ed. London: Research and Statistics Directorate of the UK Home Office.

Joncas, L. 2004. Les troubles mentaux en matière de droit criminel...pour ne pas y perdre la tête. In *Développements récents en droit criminel*, ed. S.d Barreau du Québec. Cowansville: Éditions Yvon Blais.

Kirby, M.J., and W.J. Keon. 2006. *Out of the shadows at last – Transforming Mental Health, Mental Illness and Addiction Services in Canada. Standing Senate Committee on Social Affairs, Science and Technology*. Ottawa: The Senate.

Kronström, A. 2001. *Rapport d'investigation sur le décès de M. Brian Bédard*. Québec: Bureau du Coroner.

Lalande, P., and G. Giguère. 2009. *La problématique du suicide en milieu carcérale et portrait de la situation dans les établissements de détention du Québec (du 1er janvier 2000 au 31 décembre 2006)*. Québec: Ministère de la Sécurité publique.

Lamb, R.H., and L.E. Weinberger. 2005. The shift of psychiatric inpatient care from hospital to jails and prisons. *The Journal of the American Academy of Psychiatry and the Law* 33: 529–534.

Lamb, R.H., L.E. Weinberger, J.S. Marsh, and B.H. Gross. 2007. Treatment prospects for persons with severe mental illness in an urban county jail. *Psychiatric Services* 58: 782–786.

Milly, B. 2001. *Soigner en prison*. Paris: PUF.

Ministère de la Santé et des Services sociaux. 2005. *Plan d'action en santé mentale 2005–2010*. Québec: La force des liens.

Ministère de la santé et des services sociaux, Ministère de la sécurité publique. 1989. *Protocole de partage des responsabilités entre le Ministère de la santé et des services sociaux et le Ministère de la sécurité publique concernant l'accès aux services de santé et aux services sociaux pour les personnes contrevenantes adultes.*

Ministère de la Sécurité publique. 2010, Janvier 20. Les services correctionnels au Québec. Retrieved from http://www.securitepublique.gouv.qc.ca/index.php?id=43. Accessed 26 June 2010.

Nurse, J., P. Woodcoock, and J. Ormsby. 2003. Influence of environmental factors on mental health within prisons: Focus group study. *British Medical Journal* 327: 480–485.

Penrose, L. 1939. Mental disease and crime: outline of a comparative study of European statistics. *The British Journal of Medical Psychology* 18: 1–15.

Pilon, M. 1999, October 5. Mental disorder and Canadian criminal law. Retrived from http://dsp-psd.pwgsc.gc.ca/Collection-R/LoPBdP/BP/prb9922-e.htm. Accessed 22 Oct 2010.

Pogrebin, M., and E. Poole. 1987. Deinstitutionalization and increase arrest rates among the mentally disordered. *Journal of Psychiatry and Law* 15: 117–127.

Protecteur du citoyen. 2005. Rapport annuel 2004–2005. Québec: Protecteur du citoyen.

Regulation under the Act respecting the Québec correctionnal system, R.S.Q., chapter S-40.1, r.1.

Schenllenberg, E., D. Wasilenki, C. Webster, and P. Goering. 1992. A review of arrests among psychiatric patients. *International Journal of Law and Psychiatry* 15: 251–264.

Teplin, L. 1984. Criminalizing mental disorder: The comparative arrest rate of the mentally ill. *The American Psychologist* 39: 794–803.

Winko v. British Columbia (Forensic Psychiatric Institute). 1999. 2 S.C.R. 625

World Health Organization. 2007. *Preventing suicide in jails and prisons.* Geneva: World Health Organization.

Chapter 10
Ethical Issues in German Prison Psychiatry

Norbert Konrad

10.1 Prison System Structure

In Germany, the federal penal law regulates the penal system. The practical organisation of the penal system is incumbent on each federal state and its own Ministry of Justice. Hence, penal institutions in Germany differ regionally: there are often separate institutions for remand prisoners, juveniles and women as well as low security prisons. Social-therapeutic institutions are usually facilities in (closed) regular prisons. Table 10.1 shows the development of the forensic clientele.

There was a total of 62,348 prisoners in German penal institutions as of March 31, 2008. As in other European countries, the number of prisoners has increased over the past decades. Including prisoners in pretrial detention, Germany has an imprisonment rate of about 100 per 100,000 inhabitants.

In Germany, mentally disordered offenders are subject to special legal regulations (Konrad 2001), which are based on the concept of criminal responsibility: Offenders who are not criminally responsible and not considered dangerous are hospitalized, if at all, in general clinical psychiatric institutions. If serious offenses are expected from offenders who are considered to have at least diminished criminal responsibility, they are admitted, regardless of therapeutic prospects, to special forensic psychiatric security hospitals (63 German Penal Code) under the authority of the Ministry of Health. The number of detainees housed there was 6,287 as of March 31, 2008 (www.destatis.de).

Offenders dependent on psychoactive substances with sufficiently good therapeutic prospects, independent of criminal responsibility, are admitted to special drug treatment facilities of forensic-psychiatric secure hospitals which are also

N. Konrad (✉)
Institute of Forensic Psychiatry, Charité, University Medicine Berlin,
Berlin, Germany
e-mail: norbert.konrad@charite.de

N. Konrad et al. (eds.), *Ethical Issues in Prison Psychiatry*, International Library
of Ethics, Law, and the New Medicine 46, DOI 10.1007/978-94-007-0086-4_10,
© Springer Science+Business Media Dordrecht 2013

Table 10.1 Forensic patients, prisoners and patients in general psychiatric hospitals (Old West-German states including West Berlin 1970–1990, as of 1995 unified Germany)

| Forensic psychiatry according to 63,64 German Penal Code | | | In comparison | |
Year	Psychiatric hospital (63)	Detoxification centre (64)	Prison	Gen. Psychiat. (available beds)
1970	4,222	179	35,209	117,596
1975	3,494	183	34,271	115,922
1980	2,593	632	42,027	108,904
1985	2,472	990	48,212	94,624
1990	2,489	1,160	39,178	70,570
1995	2,902	1,373	46,516	63,807
2000	4,098	1,774	60,798	54,802
2004	5,390	2,412	63,677	53,021
2005	5,640	2,473	63,533	53,021 (2004)
2006	5,917	2,619	64,512	52,923
2007	6,061	2,603	64,700	53,169
2008	6,287	2,656	62,348	53,061
2009	6,440	2,811	61,878	53,789
2010	6,569	3,021	60,693	54,035

Source: Federal Office of Statistics, Wiesbaden, Germany (2010)

under the authority of the Ministry OF health (64 German Penal Code). As of March 31, 2008, the number of detainees housed there was 2,656 (www.destatis.de).

All other mentally disordered offenders, including individuals with schizophrenia who are considered criminally responsible despite their illness, may be sentenced to prison, if no milder sanctions like a fine are ordered by the court. In individual cases, it may depend on coincidental constellations whether a mentally ill person is committed to a forensic psychiatric or penal institution.

10.2 Epidemiology of Mental Disorders

In Germany, there are only a few empirical studies on the prevalence of mental disorders in prison that examine a large, representative sample of a prison population with standardized diagnostic instruments and provide a diagnosis according to international classification systems. One study (Konrad 2004) examined the prevalence of mental disorders according to ICD-10 using a diagnostic expert system for mental disorders (DIA-X; Wittchen and Pfister 1997) within a sample of German male prisoners sentenced for not paying their fines (Table 10.2). The large percentage of persons (10 %) with a lifetime prevalence of psychotic symptoms is impressive. Another study (Missoni et al. 2003) examined the prevalence of mental disorders according to ICD-10 within a sample of German male remand prisoners (Table 10.2). Notable is the large percentage of persons (40 %) with lifetime prevalence of single or recurrent depressive episodes. Most of these depressive episodes, classified as adjustment

Table 10.2 DIA-X diagnoses in prisoners (Wittchen and Pfister 1997)

Prisoners not paying their fine	%	Remand prisoners	%
Alcohol use disorders	77	Alcohol use disorders	43
Nicotine dependence	64	Nicotine dependence	36
Substance use dependence (without alcohol)	20	Substance use dependence (without alcohol)	14
Specific phobia	39	Specific phobia	14
(Recurrent) depressive episode(s)	20	(Recurrent) depressive episode(s)	40
Dysthymic disorder	21	Dysthymic disorder	6
Psychotic disorders	10	Psychotic disorders	6

disorders, would not have arisen without imprisonment as a psychosocial stress factor or, to be more precise, a critical life event.

Due to the research deficit highlighted above, current data are not available to enable appropriate treatment planning with regard to the needs of mentally disturbed prisoners. Thus, no empirical basis exists for determining whether prisoners in Germany – as elsewhere (e.g. Lamb 2001) – have an increase in mental disorders attributable to inadequate dehospitalization programs.

10.3   Medical Services and Mental Health Care Provision in Prison

In-prison treatment has to address inmate-specific problems and circumstances, including post-release services. This includes both the functional impact and the severity of psychiatric symptoms (Harris and Lovell 2001). The high prevalence of mental disorders speaks in favor of the standardized application of diagnostic screening instruments as a component of the admission procedure in prison. German criminal law requires a medical examination, but no standardized psychiatric diagnostics, for every prisoner upon entering prison. "Out-patient" psychiatric treatment in prison is provided after the prisoner is referred by the staff physician to a psychiatrist.

The obligatory physical examination upon entering prison also includes an evaluation of a history of addiction in order to address possible dependency disorders or withdrawal symptoms. This is usually done according to a predetermined protocol (for example, the use of methadone and/or diazepam in decreasing doses for opiate withdrawal). The prison physician must assess suicidal risk, even if standardized instruments (e.g. Dahle et al. 2005) are not used.

Inpatient psychiatric care of prisoners is subject to wide regional variations in Germany. Some federal states (Baden-Württemberg, Bavaria, Berlin, Saxony, North-Rhine Westphalia) have psychiatric departments in penal institutions managed within the prison system. In the other federal states, in-patient and out-patient psychiatric care of prisoners is provided by external institutions and consulting specialists (Missoni and Rex 1997). External institutions for in-patient psychiatric care include forensic-psychiatric secure hospitals and general psychiatric facilities.

In-patient psychiatric care of prisoners in general psychiatric facilities frequently conflicts with the safety concerns of prison authorities. Their objections are reflected in the attitude of care-providing institutions, which - if they do not flatly refuse to treat prisoners, like 2/3 of the facilities in North-Rhine Westphalia and Rhineland-Palatinate do, question the treatment indication, willingness to be treated or responsiveness of the hospitalized patient and point out detrimental effects to the institution ranging from spoiling the therapeutic atmosphere to demotivating compliant patients and provoking recidivism (Konrad and Missoni 2001). It has been specifically stated that prison transferees disturb other patients, cause disciplinary difficulties and have a more demanding attitude. Based on the total number of hospitalized prisoners in North-Rhine Westphalia and Rhineland Palatinate in 1997, 0.1–2.3 % received in-patient psychiatric treatment in general psychiatric hospitals during their imprisonment (Konrad and Missoni 2001).

There are currently ten university institutes of forensic psychiatry and/or psychotherapy in Germany, which mainly provide expert opinions. Their involvement in psychiatric-psychotherapeutic care of prisoners as well as research projects and training of prison personnel is limited: only 2–7 prisoners are psychiatrically and 15 prisoners are psychotherapeutically treated by a university psychiatrist or psychologist on an out-patient basis. None of the university psychiatric institution in Germany offer in-patient psychiatric care for prisoners (Missoni and Konrad 1999).

There are no binding criteria in the German penal system for admission to a (n) (in-patient) psychiatric ward, especially no legal codes comparable to those governing hospitalization under civil law (so called PsychKG). In practice, prisoners who pose a danger to themselves, for example, after a suicide attempt or other self-destructive behavior, are frequently admitted. A special legal basis regulating hospitalization to psychiatric wards within the penal system does not exist; the penal detention code or criminal laws, which are federal law, neither stipulate nor prohibit psychiatric prison wards.

10.3.1 Special Ethical Challenges

Prison physicians have a responsibility to request from the appropriate authorities (e.g. courts) a forensic-psychiatric assessment in cases where they suspect a psychotic disorder, a severe personality disorder or markedly reduced intelligence that may affect the prisoner's criminal responsibility, ability to stand trial or fitness to undergo detention. In this context, forensic psychiatrists should:

- never, as a matter of principle, and in order to avoid a conflict of roles, assess their own patients; however, this principle is not respected everywhere in Germany.
- provide the legal client with their expert knowledge but also

- contribute to humanizing the criminal procedure by providing expert information and their special view on the development of delinquent behavior in order to be just to the accused,
- present their specialist knowledge in such a manner that it is readily understandable to the legal client, and thus provide a basis for independent decision-making.

Compulsory treatment of mentally disordered prisoners is regulated by the penal law, the pertinent provisions of which correspond to the standards for compulsory treatment within the framework of civil commitment laws (PsychKG). Compulsory treatment occurs within psychiatric facilities of prison hospitals. It is not necessary to send prisoners to general psychiatric facilities only for the purpose of compulsory measures as, e.g. in the UK or Sweden (Salize et al. 2007) as these measures can be applied within prison.

There are diverse problems in cases where an in-patient psychiatric ward exists in prison:

- The lack of mandatory legal criteria for admission to or release from a psychiatric prison ward can lead to the drive for acceptance, for example, by dissocial, disruptive or assaultative behavior. To avoid ethically questionable psychiatricization tendencies, a psychiatric prison ward should be reserved for the in-patient care of mentally ill prisoners, if and as long as those prisoners seriously endanger their lives, their health or especially important rights of others according to the PsychKG code.
- Prison subcultures and therapeutically counterproductive hierachization among patients is promoted if patients, instead of external personnel, are used to a certain extent as ward aides, e.g. for cleaning tasks, and the standard of hospital hygiene depends on their unlimited utilizability. This is not uncommon in Germany.
- Moreover, in relation to the professional code for nursing services in Berlin, nursing personnel in prison not only have to take part in gun training but also may have to carry a weapon, for example, during leaves of absence; this role impedes the formation of a trusting, empathetic relationship, leads to a confusion of roles and harms the therapeutic interaction with the patient.
- A typical conflict arises (see Case Report No 35 in Carmi et al. 2005) when prisoners suffering from anxiety, depression and/or suicidal ideas recover in a hospital setting, but relapse after return to prison. The concern of the treating team is the occurrence of an actual suicide of the patient if he returns to prison. In these circumstances it is of particular importance that the treating doctor provides some follow-up for the patient or at least organizes such ongoing treatment. Treatment continuity is better realised if the out-patient treatment is organised by the same institution as the in-patient treatment, as it is the case in Germany.
- Although inmates must receive the same quality of medical care as the general population according to the penal law, psychiatric care is subject to the ever-present risk of cost cuts, especially at times of tight budget constraints, and this may mean that psychiatric patients in prison do not experience equivalent treatment with regard to personnel, spatial and organizational aspects. The Psychiatric

Personnel Code is not legally binding for the penal system and may not be accepted as guiding criterion for the approximation of healthcare standards. Furthermore, lock-up times in closed prisons compete with treatment offers and the milieu-therapeutic structure of a hospital.

- When comparing general and prison psychiatric facilities in Germany, general psychiatry is usually better staffed with more highly trained personnel and offers more up-to-date therapy (Konrad and Missoni 2001). If one accepts that mentally ill prisoners should be treated in penal institutions (possibly even hospitalized), then the principle of "equivalence" should prevail in the care of incarcerated mentally ill persons. It is doubtful whether the majority of prisoners with psychiatric illnesses in Germany receive appropriate care such as that mandated by the European Convention on Human Rights and other international charters (Fazel and Danesh 2002).

10.3.2 Psychiatric Facilities in Berlin

Recent basic information or published data regarding mental health care of prisoners are not available for every state (Land) in Germany. This chapter focuses the situation in Berlin, because there there are more data available than for any other German state. In the State of Berlin, there were 9 penal institutions holding 5,090 prisoners as of February 10, 2010. 509 were remand prisoners, 386 juvenile prisoners, 37 were in preventive detention and 469 were incarcerated for not paying a fine.

The Department of Psychiatry and Psychotherapy in the hospital of the Berlin correctional facilities has over 36 inpatient beds in three units with various treatment options (Konrad 2005): a unit focusing on "psychoses" cares primarily for schizophrenic patients, who often concomitantly (Linaker 2000) suffer from a (mainly polysubstance) dependence, the unit therefore has a multidisciplinary orientation. The unit deals with patients in a supportive, encouraging, non-confrontational and low expressed emotion manner, which includes engaging patients who have thus far had either negative psychiatric experience or none at all. The other two units care for patients with primary diagnoses of personality disorder and adjustment disorder. The treatment concept of the latter concentrates on implementing activating measures or suppressing regressive tendencies and limiting hospitalization time.

The department is staffed with

- 2 psychiatrists, 5 doctors
- 1 occupational therapist
- 29 nurses
- In addition sessional contracts are in place for occupational therapy, art therapy, music therapy, sports therapy and several psychotherapeutic group therapies.

Germany has only one facility resembling complementary in-patient psychiatric care: The Berlin penal system offers a kind of semi-hospitalization in the form of a follow-up unit in closed prisons for those no longer requiring full in-patient care.

The unit is spatially integrated into a building of the normal prison, i.e. patients live under the same spatial conditions as the other inmates. The specially protected atmosphere is ensured by easier access to psychiatrists and nursing staff and to occupational and art therapy as in a day hospital (Konrad 2005).

Patients requiring out-of-hospital care should be treated in an out-patient department with a psychiatric-psychotherapeutic spectrum that ensures continuity and adequate length of treatment (Kallert 1996). Such an out-patient clinic exists in the Berlin penal system; it offers psychiatric out-patient (with more than 3,000 contacts per year) and psychotherapeutic outpatient treatment and is called the "Psychotherapeutic Counseling and Treatment Center" (PTB). The PTB is run by three part-time psychologists, each providing three half-day sessions, and is based on the model of an extramural out-patient psychotherapeutic treatment facility: Therapy is voluntary and basically open to all prisoners, and treatment is provided with the strictest confidentiality. The therapist is not involved in prognostic opinions, in the mitigation of prison conditions or prison planning procedures. In addition to counseling, the therapists offer individual behavioral therapy and psychodynamic psychology sessions, in 14-day intervals at the most. Even if the prisoners' mental disorders and individual suffering are the reasons for taking up contact and starting therapy, it was found in a quasi experimental design that treatment also led to an improved legal prognosis: After a mean of 4 years, the recidivism of offenders with at least 20 therapeutic sessions was recognizably lower with 35.9 % than that of an untreated control group in regular prison with 47.4 % (Dahle et al. 2003).

10.4   Quality Standards

There are no standardized psychiatric diagnostic tools for prisoners upon entering prison. Most mentally disordered prisoners in Germany are assessed and treated by prison physicians, who are usually specialists in general medicine and do not have any obligatory training in psychiatry. Standardized instruments for the assessment/treatment of mentally disordered prisoners are not generally applied.

The European Prison Rules (Council of Europe 2006) are widely unknown in Germany. However, it is of note that the German penal law is in accordance with these rules on many points.

There are a few lobby groups in Germany that only (Friends of Prison Psychiatry) or also (Federal Association of Prison Physicians and Psychologists 2010) address the needs of mentally disordered prisoners, but they have virtually no political influence.

10.4.1   Consent to Treatment

Consent to treatment should be sought from all patients, including offenders suffering from a mental disorder, provided they have capacity to consent. Furthermore, obtaining the patient's consent, especially in the case of psychiatric pathology, is essential if a "therapeutic alliance" is to be formed which is likely to make the patient more committed to the treatment offered.

A controversial issue in forensic psychiatry and a classical ethical dilemma is whether an incompetent prisoner has the right to refuse treatment or, framed differently, whether the right to refuse treatment supercedes his right to sanity. Some might argue that it is the duty of the treating psychiatrist to zealously persuade the patient, his guardian and, if need be, the courts, that a proposed treatment is indeed in the best interest of the individual, regardless of an expressed (and sometimes psychotic) wish against it. The question is if the courts recognize a patient's right to receive treatment to not remain psychotic (implicitly acknowledging the subjective torment and, at times, sheer terror of the psychotic individual). Abramowitz (2005) suggested that the courts will usually support treatment for an individual lacking capacity as long as it is consistent with professional standards of care, however, without asserting a specific, inalienable right of the individual to receive treatment.

If mentally ill prisoners refuse to accept medication, having made an informed decision not to consent, the problem arises as to whether it can be administered against their wishes. In line with principles of medical ethics a person cannot be forced to undergo treatment unless there is a risk to self or others. In such situations a multi-disciplinary discussion regarding the medical and ethical aspects of the individual case is necessary (Møller et al. 2007). The use of coercion, allowing the person to "choose" between the two evils of isolation or medication, should be avoided. Every effort should be made to persuade the person to cooperate.

In Germany compulsory treatment is possible in situations of imminent danger to self or others. In some cases a guardianship may be proposed to the courts. However, according to our experience the civil courts are reluctant to establish a guardianship, because they do not want to put further restrictions on an imprisoned person.

On occasion the decision to refuse treatment results from a conflict relating to non-medical issues; this is, for example, the case when a prisoner goes on hunger strike to protest against a judicial or administrative decision. In this situation the doctor should assess the state of health of the person concerned and subsequently make a detailed note in the patient's file to document that the individual has capacity to understand the treatment proposed but has refused treatment after being given detailed information if this is the case. Psychiatrists are regularly asked to assess the mental state of such prisoners, especially to answer the question if the refusal stems from paranoid ideas (e.g. to be poisoned).

The need for medical care of prisoners who persistently refuse food in order to make a protest is rare but challenging. Knowledge about the hunger strike quickly spreads and gets into the political arena. Governments want to resist the demands, which often have political overtones, but also do not want prisoners to die because of fear of a backlash of public opinion. Pressure is therefore brought on the prison health care staff, including psychiatrists, to keep the prisoners alive, if necessary, by force feeding. However, a doctor must obtain consent from the patient before applying his skills to assist him. The only exception is in an emergency when the patient is incapable of giving consent. Because the end stage of food refusal in coma, it follows that the patient is then not capable of giving or refusing consent and it is possible to argue that the doctor may then intervene by artificial feeding to save the patient's life. However, according to Pont and Wool (2006) this is not the case if the patient has made it clear beforehand that he refuses interventions to prevent death.

10.4.2   Confidentiality

Clarity of roles is crucial for forensic mental health practitioners. Cooperation between the different occupational groups in the penal system is certainly necessary and benefits the patients. If, however, confidentiality is not respected, the patient-physician relationship will be even more at risk in the therapy-hostile prison environment.

Medical confidentiality is regulated by law. In German practice, a separate "health file" is kept on each inmate, which contains medical documentation and advisory psychiatric findings and recommendations for the prison physician. This file is only available to medical personnel bound by professional confidentiality.

Confidentiality is central to the doctor-patient relationship. It enables the patient to develop trust, knowing information he discloses will be held in confidence. The doctor must not disclose information about the patient to third parties without the patient's consent except in a limited number of clearly specified circumstances, usually to prevent serious harm to the patient or others. If such a situation arises the patient should be informed about the disclosure and the reasons for disclosure clearly documented. Although this has traditionally received less attention, principles of confidentiality also apply to other professions, e.g. psychologists (Younggren and Harris 2008).

In forensic settings the principles of confidentiality may be threatened in a number of ways. For example, multidisciplinary working and liaison between agencies are the norm and are necessary and benefit the patient. However, the increased sharing of information about the patient makes it more difficult to maintain confidentiality and maybe contrary to the patient's expectations. Furthermore, due to the nature of the patient group, the prison psychiatrist may be under particular pressure to disclose information in pursuance of crime investigation or prevention. In addition to universally recognized exceptions of confidentiality some exceptions arise uniquely in correctional facilities. For example, psychiatrists may be expected to report to authorities serious inmate rule violations and plans for escapes or disturbances (Appelbaum 2005). They are also required to report to different agencies regarding the progress or otherwise of their patients with potentially far-reaching consequences. It is of utmost importance for the prison psychiatrist to not loose sight of the fundamental principles of confidentiality and to consider each request for disclosure of information on its merit and to weigh up each time whether such request is justified.

Psychiatrists in Germany may be expected to report to authorities serious inmate rule violations and plans for escapes or disturbances. There are different opinions among mental health professionals about where to draw the line for breaching confidentiality, e.g. what the exact definition of a security-threatening emergency is.

10.4.3 Disciplinary Measures

Mental health problems may be overlooked especially in prisoners who are quietly psychotic. The more behaviorally disturbed are often viewed as a disciplinary problem rather than as individuals with mental health needs (Birmingham 2004). Some of them are placed in disciplinary segregation instead of immediately receiving appropriate psychiatric care.

Of particular concern are disciplinary measures which are coercive by nature. Mentally disordered prisoners are more likely to become the subject of disciplinary measures due to misbehaviour that may be caused by the disorder. It is well known that specific coercive measures (e.g. solitary confinement) are likely to aggravate mental disorders. Thus, it is crucial to assess the mental state of a prisoner prior to implementing such measures in order to avoid any additional harm. There are European countries –like Germany- where all prisoners requiring punitive or disciplinary measures –or at least any prisoner known to suffer from a mental disorder- will be assessed for fitness to undergo disciplinary measures prior to their implementation. In other European countries, such an assessment is not stipulated (Salize et al. 2007).

This participation of medical personnel in the administration of punishment raises considerable ethical problems: Discipline and punishment are security and not health issues, and therefore the physician, who should be available to attend to the medical needs of prisoners under any form of punishment, has no role in deciding upon the administration of such punishment, e.g. in certifying that a person is mentally fit to withstand such a punishment, and should not be available for the purpose of (re-)establishing the prisoner's capacity to sustain a punishment (WHO 2009).

Somewhat surprisingly, in Germany, like in most European countries, disciplinary or coercive measures during imprisonment must be recorded though data are not published to allow scientific analyses. The data are an essential tool for assessing the appropriateness of such measures, particularly in the case of mentally disordered prisoners. In those cases where the use of close confinement of mentally disordered patients cannot be avoided, it should be reduced to an absolute minimum and be replaced with one-to-one continuous nursing care as soon as possible. In German practice, however, there is more isolation and observation by video than one-to-one continuous nursing. In such cases the prison psychiatrist is often confronted with ethical conflicts: Testifying acute suicidality in a mentally disordered prisoner without the possibility of adequate inpatient treatment may lead to a possibly traumatising situation, i.e. isolation with protective clothing and video observation.

10.5   Conclusion

Major deficits in German in-patient psychiatric care of prisoners are the lack of facilities for treating those with chronic mental illnesses and the inadequate management of acutely psychotic or delirious prisoners, which in many places leads to temporary "parking" in isolated cells (Missoni and Rex 1997). Moreover, there are too little data on the incidence of mental illnesses to even perform planning and quality assurance of medical services. The equivalence principle has failed as a fundamental guide in many places.

References

Abramowitz, M.Z. 2005. Prisons and the human rights of persons with mental disorders. *Current Opinion in Psychiatry* 18: 525–529.

Appelbaum, K.L. 2005. Practicing psychiatry in a correctional culture. In *Handbook of correctional mental health*, ed. C.L. Scott and J.B. Gerbasi. Washington: American Psychiatric Publishing.

Birmingham, L. 2004. Mental disorder and prisons. *Psychiatric Bulletin* 28: 393–397.

Carmi, A., D. Moussaoui, and J. Arboleda-Florez. 2005. *Teaching ethics in psychiatry: Case-vignettes*. Haifa: Unesco Chair in Bioethics.

Council of Europe. 2006. Recommendation Rec(2006)2 of the Committee of Ministers to member states on the European Prison Rules. Council of Europe.

Dahle, K.P., V. Schneider, and N. Konrad. 2003. Psychotherapie im Justizvollzug nach der Änderung des Strafvollzugsgesetzes. *Psychotherapy Psychology Medicine* 53: 178–184.

Dahle, K.P., J. Lohner, and N. Konrad. 2005. Suicide prevention in penal institutions: Validation and optimization of a screening tool for early identification of high-risk inmates in Pretrial detention. *International Journal of Forensic Mental Health* 4: 53–62.

Fazel, S., and J. Danesh. 2002. Serious mental disorder in 23000 prisoners: A systematic review of 62 surveys. *Lancet* 349: 545–550.

Federal Office of Statistics. 2010. Wiesbaden [Statistisches Bundesamt, Wiesbaden]. http://www.destatis.de/jetspeed/portal/cms/Sites/destatis/Internet/DE/Publikationen/Fachveroeffentlichungen/Rechtspflege/KrankenhausMassregelvollzug,property=file.pdf. Accessed 14 May 2010.

Harris, V.L., and D. Lovell. 2001. Measuring level of function in mentally ill prison inmates: a preliminary study. *The Journal of the American Academy of Psychiatry and the Law* 29: 68–74.

Kallert, T.W. 1996. Duties of a psychiatric-neurological consultation/liaison service in a prison setting. *Forensic Science International* 81: 103–116.

Konrad, N. 2001. Redevelopment of forensic-psychiatric institutions in former East Germany. *International Journal of Law and Psychiatry* 24: 509–526.

Konrad, N. 2004. Prävalenz psychischer Störungen bei Verbüßern einer Ersatzfreiheitsstrafe. *Recht & Psychiatrie* 22: 147–150.

Konrad, N. 2005. Managing the mentally ill in the prisons of Berlin. *International Journal of Prisoner Health* 1: 39–47.

Konrad, N., and L. Missoni. 2001. Psychiatrische Behandlung von Gefangenen in allgemeinpsychiatrischen Einrichtungen am Beispiel von Nordrhein-Westfalen und Rheinland-Pfalz. *Psychiatrische Praxis* 28: 35–42.

Lamb, H.R. 2001. Deinstitutionalization at the beginning of the new millennium. *New Directions for Mental Health Services* 90: 3–20.

Linaker, O.M. 2000. Dangerous female psychiatric patients: Prevalences and characteristics. *Acta Psychiatrica Scandinavica* 101: 67–72.

Missoni, L., and N. Konrad. 1999. Forensische Psychiatrie und Haftpsychiatrie. *MschrKrim* 82: 365–371.

Missoni, L., and R. Rex. 1997. Strukturen psychiatrischer Versorgung im deutschen Justizvollzug. *Zeitschrift für Strafvollzug und Straffälligenhilfe* 46: 335–339.

Missoni, L., M.F. Utting, and N. Konrad. 2003. Psychi(atri)sche Störungen bei Untersuchungsgefangenen. Ergebnisse und Probleme einer epidemiologischen Studie. *Zeitschrift für Strafvollzug und Straffälligenhilfe* 52: 323–332.

Møller, L., H. Stöver, R. Jürgens, A. Gatherer, and H. Nikogosian (eds.). 2007. *Health in prisons. A WHO guide to the essentials in prison health.* Geneva: WHO.

Salize, H.J., H. Dreßing, and C. Kief. 2007. *Mentally disordered persons in European prison systems – needs, programmes and outcomes (EUPRIS). Final report.* Mannheim: Central Institute of Mental Health.

WHO Europe. 2009. *Trenčín Statement on prisons and mental health.* Copenhagen: WHO Europe. http://www.euro.who.int./Document/E914202.pdf. Retrieved 10 Nov 2012.

Wittchen, H.U., and H. Pfister (eds.). 1997. *Instruktionsmanual zur Durchführung von DIA-X-Interviews.* Frankfurt: Swets & Zeitlinger B. V., Swets Test Services.

Wool, R., and J. Pont. 2006. *Prison health. A guide for health care practitioners in prisons.* London: Quay Books.

Younggren, J.N., and E.A. Harris. 2008. Can you keep a secret? Confidentiality in psychotherapy. *Journal of Clinical Psychology* 64: 589–600.

Chapter 11
Mentally Ill Prisoners: Indian Perspective

Siva Nambi and Jagannathan Srinivasaraghavan

11.1 Introduction

Mental health services in India as they exist today mostly follow the British model. Naturally, the early institutions for the mentally ill in the Indian subcontinent were greatly influenced by the ideas and concepts prevalent in England at that time. Mental asylums were built primarily to protect the community from the violent behavior of the insane and not necessarily for treatment. Accordingly, these asylums were constructed away from the towns with high fences, in buildings similar to military barracks. Their function was more custodial than curative.

The functioning of mental health care delivery in the early years of independence in India was based on the following parameters:

1. The then existing mental health care system was based on the British concept and no knowledge and understanding of cultural underpinnings of mental illness in the Indian context was taught or studied.
2. Significant shortage of trained personnel.
3. Non-pharmacological treatments of psychiatric disorders were limited.
4. The research literature focused mainly on the phenomenology of mental disorders and almost no valid epidemiological data was available.

Today, India with its population of nearly 1.2 billion faces a variety of health problems. The socio-demographic changes, epidemiological transition and media revolution consequent to urbanization, industrialization, migration, and changing

S. Nambi (✉)
Department of Psychiatry, Sree Balaji Medical College and Hospital, 600044 Chennai, India
e-mail: siva.nambi@gmail.com

J. Srinivasaraghavan
Southern Illinois University, School of Medicine, Marion, IL, USA

V.A. Medical Center, Marion, IL, USA

N. Konrad et al. (eds.), *Ethical Issues in Prison Psychiatry*, International Library of Ethics, Law, and the New Medicine 46, DOI 10.1007/978-94-007-0086-4_11, © Springer Science+Business Media Dordrecht 2013

lifestyles of people, have brought the severe burden of communicable and non-communicable diseases to the forefront.

Worldwide, on an average 32 % of all prisoners require psychological help. If one includes substance abuse, the figure goes beyond 60 %. Hence there is a need for focused attention on mental health. There is a need for early identification of mental illness among prisoners and for taking consequent steps. There is little documentation of the problems of psychiatrically ill prisoners, problem of referrals, discharge, follow-up and care while in custody. However, arrangements can be made for periodic visits by psychiatrists (Section 31 and 32 of the National Human Rights Commission recommendations on Mental Health Issues of Detentions 2008).

Mentally ill prisoners of India share a common plight with most of their counterparts in developing countries. There is no dignified or safe place for many of them. Mentally ill prisoners are unwanted and neglected everywhere; prisons try to move them elsewhere, but psychiatric hospitals are reluctant to admit them and relatives often refuse to let them stay in their home. These prisoners suffer double stigma being considered both "mad" and "bad" (Srinivasa Murthy 1997).

11.2   Mental Health in India

Mental health problems have long been recognized in every society. Communities had their own mechanisms of handling these problems, many of which are gradually being replaced by modern science. A greater understanding of mind and behavior from all dimensions has revolutionized the efforts of managing these problems in today's society.

A recent meta-analysis of 13 epidemiological studies in India comprising 33,572 individuals concluded that the prevalence estimate of mental disorders is 52.2 per 1,000 population. Among the various problems, organic psychoses (0.4 per 1,000), schizophrenia (2.7 per 1,000), affective disorders (12.3 per 1,000), mental retardation (6.9 per 1,000), neurotic disorders (20 per 1,000), and alcohol related disorders (6.9 per 1,000) are the major problems encountered in the country. Mental disorders were found to be more prevalent in urban areas, among women in the age group of 35–44 years, and in individuals of lower socioeconomic status. The study concluded that nearly 1.5 million persons suffer from severe mental disorders and 5.7 million persons suffer from various common mental disorders requiring immediate help.

11.2.1   General Characteristics of Mentally Ill Prisoners in India

- Mentally ill prisoners form less than 2 % of the total admissions in a state psychiatric hospital.
- The majority of them suffer from antisocial personality disorders and psychotic disorders, especially schizophrenia.

- Most of the mentally ill offender patients referred to psychiatric hospitals committed a major crime (mainly murder).
- A sizeable proportion of mentally ill prisoners are known to have abused alcohol and other drugs like cannabis.

11.3   Prisons in India

According to the National Crime Record Bureau 2008, there are total number of 1,140 jails in the country of which 107 are central jails, 208 are district jails and 678 are sub-jails (smaller jails situated in every taluk – county – head quarter where the remand prisoners are kept for a short term before they are sentenced and sent to the central jails), 14 are for women only; other jails number 73 (In India, "jail" is synonymous with prisons). Although, the total capacity of jails in India is only 233,543, the total number of prisoners is 326,519, thus overcrowding of jails is common in India. Men are 24 times as likely to be incarcerated as women. Sentenced prisoners account for 28.1 % of the prison population, remand prisoners for 66.7 %. Among the nature of crime, murder alone accounts for 58.6 %. There are 333 convicts, including women, awaiting execution in the country and there are 48,334 convicts serving life imprisonment.

11.3.1   Criminal Responsibility

Can a person commit a crime and plead "unsound mind" as a defense for escaping punishment? The answer is yes if the person can prove that he/she was of unsound mind at the time of committing the crime. A defense can be raised in several ways:

- Not guilty by reason of insanity.
- Diminished responsibility.
- Incapacity to form an intent because of automatism.

As per law, only this first category is applicable in Indian courts. The law for criminal responsibility in India is based on the McNaughton rules first established in England. Section 84 of the Indian Penal Code states "Nothing is an offence which is done by a person of unsound mind, incapable of knowing the nature of the act or that what he is doing is either wrong or contrary to law".

Indian Courts also differentiate legal insanity from medical insanity. Medical insanity covers abnormality of mind, delusions and other psychopathology. Legal insanity envisages that the unsoundness of mind of the subject must be such as to make the offender incapable of knowing the nature of the act, or knowing that what he is doing is wrong or contrary to the law. There are not many offenders in India claiming the insanity defense. These persons may be acquitted under Section 84 of Indian Penal Code. Even among those who make the claim, only a few have been considered to be not responsible for their crime because of unsoundness of mind (Somasundaram 2001).

In spite of the vigorous criticism from so many learned quarters, the McNaughton rules have found a secure place in the Indian law dating back to the time when Queen Victoria took over the control of the colonial Indian Empire.

11.4   Indian Law and Mentally Ill Prisoners

Within Indian law some regulations are of particular relevance for mentally disordered offenders.

I. The Code of Criminal Procedure, 1973 (Sections 328–333) has ample provisions to safeguard a mentally ill prisoner in India. Some of these provisions are

Section 328: Procedure in case of the accused being a lunatic.

Section 329: Procedure in case of a person of unsound mind tried before court.

Section 330:

  (a) Release of lunatic to relatives for treatment pending investigation or trial.

  (b) Transfer of a lunatic to a psychiatric hospital for treatment pending investigation or trial.

Section 331: Resumption of inquiry or trial.

Section 332: Procedure for an accused appearing before Magistrate or Court.

Section 333: Procedure if an accused appears to have been of unsound mind.

Section 334: Judgment of acquittal on ground of unsoundness of mind.

Section 335: Detention in safe custody of a person acquitted on grounds of unsoundness of mind

Section 336: Power of the State Government to empower an officer in charge to discharge.

Section 337: Procedure by which a lunatic prisoner is reported capable of making his defense.

Section 338: Procedure by which a lunatic detained is declared fit to be released.

Section 339: Delivery of lunatic to care of relative or friend.

Ii. Section 84 Of Indian Penal Code: Based on the McNaughton rules it is stated that "Nothing is an offence which is done by a person of unsound mind who is incapable of knowing the nature of the act or that what he is doing is either wrong or contrary to law".

Iii. Prisoners Act: The Indian Prisoners Act 1900 (Act III) has provision to transfer mental ill prisoners sentenced to a custodial sentence to a forensic ward of a psychiatric hospital for treatment.

11.4.1   Mentally Ill Prisoners in India

The admission and discharge of a mentally ill prisoner in India is governed by the Indian Mental Health Act 1987. There are three groups of mentally ill prisoners in forensic units of psychiatric hospitals and in secluded wards inside prisons in India.

1. Prisoners under trial (Section 330 of the Code of Criminal Procedures 1973): Mentally ill prisoners who were mentally ill at the time of committing a crime and are unfit to stand trial.

2. Sentenced prisoners (Section 30 of Act III of the Indian Prisoners Act 1900): Convicted prisoners who develop a mental illness during the course of imprisonment.
3. Guilty but insane (Section 335 of the Code of Criminal Procedures 1973): mentally ill prisoners who are acquitted at trial. Since no social support systems exist to provide for their care and treatment in the community, these prisoners continue to stay in the forensic units of psychiatric hospitals as per Section 27 of the Indian Mental Health Act 1987.

There has been a serious concern about the inadequate medical and psychiatric care for all the groups.

For many decades, many mentally ill, both those with criminal record and those without, have been admitted to jails, especially so in the Eastern part of India. Mental health professionals had for many decades been demanding the abolition of the practice of admitting mentally ill persons to jails. Following a public interest litigation, the Supreme Court of India on July 18, 1993, passed a landmark judgment ruling that "The admission of non-criminal mentally ill persons to jails is illegal and unconstitutional". As a result, the admission of mentally ill persons, in the absence of a crime, to prisons has almost ended all over the country.

Some of the (unpublished) studies of psychopathology of prisoners in Indian prisons reveal that there are nearly 60–80 % of prisoners who have one or more diagnosable psychiatric condition. The majority of male prisoners suffer from antisocial personality disorder and alcohol and drug addiction. Among women, most suffer from neurotic disorders. Nearly 95 % of mentally ill prisoners are men.

Among the mentally ill-prisoners in forensic units of psychiatric hospitals, the majority are under-trial prisoners (nearly 80 %); many of them suffer from psychotic disorders, especially schizophrenia, followed by antisocial personality disorder and substance use disorders. Most of the mentally ill in the forensic units of psychiatric hospitals have committed a major crime such as murder. Mentally ill prisoners constitute around 1–2 % of the patients in major psychiatric hospitals in India.

There are four options to develop the forensic psychiatric service in India:

1. Separate wards for mentally ill-prisoners inside the prison itself.
2. An exclusive forensic psychiatric hospital (special hospital).
3. A forensic psychiatric unit/ward inside a state psychiatric hospital with high security and constant care by mental health professionals.
4. Correctional settings for juveniles.

In the forensic ward of the psychiatric hospital, the emphasis should be on therapy and rehabilitation rather than control and containment.

As of now, mentally-ill prisoners are admitted to forensic units of psychiatric hospitals and are managed by psychiatrists. In some centers, the psychiatrists from the nearby hospitals visit the prisons periodically to treat the mentally-ill patients there. The juvenile delinquents are kept in safe correctional settings. As per the Care and Protection of Children Act of 2000 (Juvenile Justice Act 2000), children who commit crimes, irrespective of the presence or absence of a psychiatric diagnosis, are to be detained in special correctional settings. Children exhibiting severe abnormalities such as violence and unmanageable behaviors may be sent to psychiatric hospitals with agreement from the Juvenile Justice Board.

What is currently not available is an exclusive forensic psychiatric hospital (special hospital) despite the Indian Mental Health Act 1987 having made a provision for such an establishment. The most feasible model for forensic psychiatric services in a developing country like India is to have forensic units in psychiatric hospitals with high security and constant care by well-trained personnel. The concept of exclusive forensic psychiatric hospitals poses additional costs, additional trained personnel and increases the stigma of mental illness.

11.4.2 Forensic Psychiatric Services in India

The World Health Organization (WHO) Expert Committee on Mental Health, in its fourth report (1955), suggested that "Mental hospitals should not be asked to take custodial care of dangerous criminals. They should be cared for in special establishments for criminals, if detained in mental hospital premises, security by the police should be provided in a specially created ward for mentally ill prisoners."

However, forensic psychiatric services in India are poorly developed compared to the West. Persons suffering from mental illness, who are also offenders, are now considered as "mentally ill prisoners". Earlier, they were known as "criminal lunatics" but this terminology is not commonly used anymore. There are 37 state-run mental hospitals in India with a total bed number of around 20,000. The majority of these mental hospitals have a separate ward for mentally-ill prisoners.

11.5 Psychiatric Services in Prison – Indian Scenario

Psychiatric symptoms are common among many prisoners in the first 2 months of imprisonment but not all of them qualify for a diagnosis according to the International Classification of Diseases. Antisocial personality and substance abuse are usually the most common diagnoses. High rates of psychotic disorders exist in prisoners either under trial, remanded or convicted. The prevalence of psychotic disorders among prisoners is almost similar to that seen in the general population.

The most common reasons for transfer of mentally ill offenders from prison to a psychiatric hospital are the following:

- Violent and unmanageable behavior.
- Potential danger to self or others.
- Significant deterioration of a psychiatric illness.
- Treatment refusal in a highly disturbed patient.

In India, opinions are divided between the mental health professionals and the prisoners with regards to the question in which place to detain mentally ill prisoners.

Mental health professionals often prefer to keep these patients in prisons or if necessary in a forensic ward of a psychiatric hospital. Occasionally, they prefer to visit the prison periodically to give their opinion and take care of the mentally ill offenders. However, the majority of mentally ill prisoners in India prefer to stay in prison and are reluctant to go to a psychiatric hospital because they feel the comfort and facilities are much better in prisons than in the mental hospitals.

The plight of the mentally disordered offenders in India is pathetic. To quote Halleck (1986), "the insane criminals" have nowhere to go – no age or nation has provided a place for him. They are unwelcome and objectionable everywhere. The prisons thrust them out, the hospitals are unwilling to receive them. The law will not let them stay in their houses, the public will not let them go abroad and yet humanity and justice, the sense of common danger and a tender regard for those deeply degraded men, all agree that something should be done for him.

The discharge of the mentally ill prisoners from psychiatric hospitals in India is carried out in one of the following methods:

1. Under-trial prisoners who are admitted to a psychiatric hospital through a detention order under Section 330 of the Criminal Procedure Code 1973 are given active treatment in the psychiatric hospital. The visiting committee of the hospital – which meets every 3 months – monitors and assesses the mentally ill prisoners in psychiatric hospitals and recommends those fit for trial. At this point these under-trial mentally ill prisoners will be transferred to jail to await their respective court dates for trial. The fitness of mentally ill offenders for trial is mainly based on whether they are able to comprehend the questions put to them, whether they are oriented to person, time and place, whether they are in a position to understand the charges against them and the court proceedings, whether they are able to instruct their lawyer and whether they understand what type of punishment they may receive.
2. Prisoners who are admitted under the Criminal Procedure Code 335 (not guilty by reason of unsound mind) will also be given active treatment in hospital and once their mental state has improved and their relatives are willing to assume responsibility, they will be discharged and sent back to the community. If no relatives come forward to take care of the individual, they are transferred either to a non-forensic ward of a psychiatric hospital or to a rehabilitation center outside as per the direction of the hospital visitors.
3. Sentenced prisoners who develop a mental illness in prison following conviction are admitted as per the Indian Prisoners Act. Once their mental state has improved, they will be sent back to prisons and are advised to continue regular follow-up.

11.6   Mental Disorder and Crime

In a study of mentally ill offenders convicted of murder who were admitted to Government Rajaji Hospital, Madurai, 80 % were males and 20 % were females; 50 % of them were diagnosed with schizophrenia and 40 % of them were diagnosed as having a mood disorders; 10 % had personality disorders (Krishnaram 1988).

In a study of insanity related homicide, Rath et al. (1990) found that around 47 % of the mentally ill prisoners charged with murder were diagnosed with schizophrenia and around 20 % were noted to have alcohol and drug related disorders. The other disorders diagnosed included epilepsy, bipolar disorder, and mental retardation.

In a study of 182 mentally ill offenders of the forensic unit of the National Institute of Mental Health and Neurosciences (NIMHANS), Bangalore, by Pratima, it was found that the sample consisted predominately of males (92.8 %) with a mean age of 39. Around 13.3 % were facing a charge/had been convicted for murder or attempted murder. Assault was the next commonest offence. Schizophrenia was the commonest diagnosis (41.5 %) followed by mood disorders (23.2 %), organic mental disorders (16.7 %), and others.

However, an attempt to find an overall relationship between crime and mental disorders may be mistaken; the prevalence of serious psychiatric illness among the criminal population is low (Somasundaram 1980). There is an underrepresentation of personality disorders, alcohol, and drug abuse among mentally ill prisoners in the psychiatric hospital in contrast to the high prevalence of personality disorders, especially antisocial personality disorder, and alcohol and other substance use disorders in prison-based studies.

11.6.1 Prevalence of Mental Disorders Among Prisoners in India

A recent unpublished study assessing the prevalence of mental health problems among prisoners in the State of Karnataka, suggests that around 60 % of the total number of prisoners had some sort of mental health problems (according to the International Classification of Diseases, 10th edition [ICD-10]), including mental retardation. The majority had antisocial personality disorder and alcohol and other substance use disorders. Other psychotic disorders, especially schizophrenia and mood disorders, were much less prevalent. On the contrary, the majority of inmates of on forensic wards of psychiatric hospitals, suffer from schizophrenia (Somasundaram 1960, 1980; Nambi 2008). This is likely to be due to the non-referral of criminals with personality disorders to psychiatric hospital by the authorities. It is always a challenge to treat the mentally disordered with dangerous and severe personality disorders, whether it is in the prison or in mental hospitals. Some psychiatrists feel that severe antisocial personality disorders should not be considered as a clinical diagnosis amenable to treatment and that psychiatrists should not take responsibility for this group. The Indian Mental Health Act of 1987 defines a mental disorder as a treatable condition. It is viewed that management of individuals with dangerous and severe personality disorder should occur in a separate forensic psychiatric specialty hospital or in a separate block inside the prison itself.

11.6.2   Reasons of Transfer from Prison to Hospital

In a study conducted in Tihar central jail, Delhi, Chadda et al. (1998) reported that there were about 300 women prisoners of around 9,000 inmates (the actual capacity is only 2,000). Around 80 % of the prisoners were remand and under-trial prisoners, and 20 % of them were prisoners serving their sentence. Among the 9,000 inmates, only 72 male inmates were referred to the psychiatric clinic, i.e. less than 1 %. Most of them (80 %) were under trial. Diagnostic categories included schizophrenia, depression, bipolar disorder, anxiety disorders, and malingering. Stress of imprisonment contributed to the illness only in a small percentage of patients. Among admitted patients, the jail environment interfered with improvement. Frequent relapses were noted among the improved schizophrenic patients when transferred back to the jail.

In a 20 years retrospective study on the forensic ward in the Institute of Mental Health, Chennai, by Nambi (1992), the followings findings emerged:

Total number of admissions during 20 years	43,804
Number of civil (non-criminal) mentally ill persons	43,267
Number of mentally ill prisoners (Criminal Lunatics)	537
Percentage of mentally ill prisoners in the total inpatient population of the psychiatric hospital	1.22 %

11.7   Gender Differences

11.7.1   Mentally-Ill Women Prisoners

The majority of female offenders are being sent to prisons not because of the seriousness of their offences, but because of the persistence of their nuisance. In India, female criminality is infrequent compared with that of males. This may be due to lower recognition, identification and underreporting. The most common offences committed by women in India are stealing, shoplifting, prostitution, and drug peddling. Violent crimes are less common among Indian women. The most common psychiatric problems associated with offending in women include hysteria, premenstrual tension, drug abuse, and antisocial personality disorder. Rarely women suffering from severe mental illnesses like schizophrenia and bipolar disorder commit major crimes like assault and murder. Very often Indian women are forced to indulge in crime as a self defense especially against their alcoholic husband's indulgence in domestic violence. In a Chennai based study (Nambi 1992), it was found that out of 537 mentally ill prisoners admitted to a large state psychiatric hospital during a 20-year period, only 26 were females (4.84 %). The most common crime among mentally ill women prisoners admitted to the psychiatric hospitals through a detention order was murder and the commonest diagnosis was schizophrenia.

Table 11.1

Diagnosis	Percentage (%)
Schizophrenia	62.2
Depression	7.6
Mental retardation	7.6
Personality disorder	3.8
Other psychiatric disorders	18.8

11.7.2   Hospitalized Mentally Ill Female Prisoners – Diagnostic Profile

Diagnoses of women (as per ICD-10) on the forensic ward in the Institute of Mental Health, Chennai (Nambi 1992), are shown in the Table 11.1:

11.8   Juvenile Offences – Indian Scenario

In India, 15 % of children have serious emotional disturbances (World Health Report 2001). The facilities available to take care of them are inadequate. The high risk factors for developing juvenile delinquency (conduct disorder) in India are: Low socioeconomic status, parental pathology including death or separation of a parent, alcoholic father, unwed mother, antisocial personality in any one of the parents and birth trauma causing minimal brain damage and epilepsy.

The Indian Penal Code 1860 provides some immunity against punishment to children. For example, Section 82 states that nothing is an offence which is done by a child under 7 years of age. Section 83 states that nothing is an offence which is done by a child above 7 years of age and below 12 years, who has not attained sufficient maturity of understanding to judge the nature and consequences of his conduct on that occasion.

11.8.1   Care and Protection of Children Act 2000 (Juvenile Justice Act 2000)

This Act aims to regulate the provision of care, protection, treatment, development opportunities and rehabilitation of neglected or delinquent juveniles. (Juvenile in the context of this Act means a child under the age of 18).

The Juvenile Justice Act in India deals with three types of children

(a) Delinquent
(b) Neglected
(c) Uncontrollable

Juveniles should not be confined to jails. Special facilities for treatment of children and juveniles like observation and juvenile homes and after-care institutions should be established in all the States. The offences committed by juveniles should be tried in juvenile courts and this Act provides for the establishment of Juvenile Welfare Boards in all districts.

11.9 Drug Abuse and Crime – Indian Scenario

Unfortunately, there is an alarming increase in criminal activity associated with alcoholism and other substance use disorders in India, which has increased many times over during the last few decades. Apart from alcohol, the other common two drugs which are highly abused by many Indians, are opium and its products and cannabis. The amount of crime committed by addicts is vast. They include both major and minor crimes. In a study in Chennai (Nambi 2008) around 80 % of the "brown sugar" (heroin) addicts and multiple drug abusers were found to have a premorbid psychopathic personality based on the past history and criminal behavior. Around 70 % of them had indulged in criminality like stealing, assault, etc. Another study in the Institute of Mental Health, Chennai (Nambi 1998), regarding the prevalence of alcohol and drug abuse amongst mentally ill prisoners revealed that 50 % of the mentally ill prisoners had abused alcohol and around 17 % of the mentally ill prisoners had abused cannabis prior to their commission of crime. The consequences of the drug and related problems and the association with crime has emerged as one of the foremost medical, psychological and legal implications in many of the metropolitan areas in India. In India, The Narcotic Drugs and Psychotropic Substances Act 1985, as amended in 1996, deals with all crimes and punishment related to narcotic drugs in India. The punishment envisioned is very stringent, but the implementation has so far not been very effective.

11.10 Suicide Among Mentally Ill Prisoners

Approximately 14 suicides occur every hour in India. More than one hundred and twenty five thousand individuals lost their lives by suicide in 2008 (National Crime Record Bureau 2008). Underreporting of completed and attempted suicides is very common in all parts of the country and the reasons are multiple. What is recorded in the official records of the National Crime Record Bureau is therefore only the tip of the iceberg.

It has been observed that social and economic causes have led most of the males to commit suicide, whereas emotional and personal causes mainly drive females to end their lives. Suicides because of "family problems" and illness accounted for 48.7 % of total suicides. The commonest methods of committing suicide in India include self-poisoning (35 %), self-immolation or fire-setting (killing one self by setting fire after pouring kerosene or petrol over the body) (8.8 %), drowning (6.7 %) and hanging (32 %).

Overcrowding, sensory deprivation, isolation, and poor contact and communication with relatives are some of the important causes of suicide among prisoners. Apart from these social causes we found that psychological reasons add to increase the number of suicides among mentally ill prisoners inside jail. Suicide among mentally ill prisoners is not at all uncommon in Indian prisons, but they are often under-reported. Exact statistics about suicide among mentally ill prisoners in India are not available.

11.11   Ethical Issues of the Mentally Ill Prisoners in India

Ethical issues in the population of interest here in India primarily relate to service provision. For example, as noted above, there are no separate specialty hospitals for forensic psychiatric patients in India. Hence they are forced to stay within regular mental hospitals or, worse, inside the prison, thereby the already existing stigma becomes worse. The WHO expert committee on Mental Health in its report (1955) suggested that the dangerous mentally ill criminals shall be kept in special establishments. Even the Indian Mental Health Act (1987) has made provision for the establishment of a special forensic psychiatric hospital. However, so far, this has not been forthcoming.

There are only 37 state-run mental hospitals in India, where most of the mentally ill prisoners are kept and the problem of overcrowding is always present on the wards. Mental health is not provided with adequate budgets in many states and hence the facilities available are inadequate and the living conditions in these hospitals are not up to the standard.

In some of the mental hospitals in India, especially in West Bengal, many homeless mentally-ill (non-offenders) were detained inside prison. Only in the recent past, after a Supreme Court Judgment in response to a Public Interest Litigation, these patients were released from prisons and sent to hospitals for treatment.

Persons who have been acquitted because they have committed the crime under the influence of mental illness (as per Sec. 84 of Indian Penal Code) are difficult to discharge from mental hospitals to the community because either they do not have adequate social support or due to administrative procedural delay or due to the ongoing illness related risk of re-offending.

Prisons in India are still governed by the century old Prisons Act 1894 and the Prisoners Act 1900. The application of a century old law in the changed sociopolitical scenario is bizarre and it is out of tune with the entirely transformed picture of human society. During the past few decades, several organizations, intellectuals, and a committee set up for jail reforms have expressed their views on the importance of reviewing the laws.

The living conditions in many prisons continue to be poor, dehumanizing and in violation of basic human rights standards. There has been a plethora of recommendations for the improvement of these conditions both from the apex judiciary and by the National Human Rights Commission. However, large chunks of these recommendations have not seen the light of the day. Overcrowding is the greatest practical hindrance to efforts of reforming the Indian prison system. Some prisons house as much as three times more inmates than their capacity. If the situation is so pathetic for all the prisoners in general, we can only begin to understand how mentally ill prisoners, suffering the double stigma, are treated inadequately and inhumanly inside prisons. It is time to think of better networking, effective prison reforms and their true application, education, and overall society's contribution to the improvement of prison conditions. We must seek solutions both inside prisons and outside in society for better care and improved quality of life for mentally ill offenders.

Some of the basic principles for the treatment of prisoners (as adopted and proclaimed by the General Assembly of United Nations Resolution 45/111 of December 14, 1990) are:

1. All prisoners shall be treated with respect due to their inherent dignity and value as human beings.
2. Prisoners shall have access to the Health Services available in the country without discrimination on the grounds of their legal situation.

India is still far away from achieving these standards.

11.12 Conclusions

Prisons in India are overcrowded institutions and the majority of them provide poor living conditions, lack of meaningful activity, endemic substance abuse, recurrent violence and sexual exploitation. Loss of freedom, separation from family and friends, uncertainty about the future, and the traumas of prison life all contribute to making living in prison a stressful experience. Psychiatric symptoms are common during the first 2 months of imprisonment. Thus the majority of psychiatric problems among mentally ill prisoners occur in under trial and remand prisoners. Prisons that contain adequate mental health services are exceptional and inmates with mental health problems remain undetected because of the absence of trained prison staff. Mental health problems in India are more common in socially disadvantaged, minimally educated and unemployed persons. Personality disorder, alcoholism, and substance abuse are the most common diagnoses in studies conducted among prison inmates, whereas schizophrenia, alcohol-related disorders, mood disorders, organic mental disorders, and mental retardation are the common diagnoses in studies conducted in forensic wards of psychiatric hospitals. Although a complete range of mental disorders will be encountered by the prison doctors, suicide and self-injury, violence towards other inmates and paranoid syndromes are of special relevance in prison psychiatry in India.

Mental health facilities in Indian prisons are meager. Hence, arrangements should be made for visits of psychiatrists on a periodic basis, at least once a week. Prisoners with mental health problems should be kept separately or preferably shifted to psychiatric hospitals. However, due to overall shortage of trained manpower in mental health care, both in district hospitals and psychiatric hospitals, this may not become possible in the near future. Thus, there is a need to augment the mental health care system, both in terms of manpower and infrastructure. There is also a need to move from custodial care to a community mental health care approach (National Human Rights Commission recommendation on detention 2008).

The problems faced by the psychiatrist treating mentally ill prisoners in India include a near total lack of any follow-up of their behavior in the community and whether they are continuing their treatment or not. In the Indian penal system, wide discretionary powers are vested with the courts in enquiring into the mental condition of suspected mentally abnormal offenders (Nair 1992). This causes deterioration and relapse of already treated and improving mental disorder.

In summary, it is emphasized that there is an urgent need for improving the conditions in jails and developing separate forensic psychiatry specialty hospitals for better management and quality of care to the mentally ill prisoners in India.

References

Chadda, R.K., et al. 1998. Clinical profile of patients attending a prison psychiatric clinic. *Indian Journal of Psychiatry* 40(3): 260–265.
Halleck, S.L. 1986. *The mentally disordered offender*, 86–1471. Washington, DC: US Department of Health and Human Services, NIHM Publication. US Convent Printing Office.
Krishnaram – Mentally Abnormal Offenders. 1988. A study of 15 convicts of Murder. Proceedings of 21st annual conference of Indian Psychiatric Society, South Zone Conference, Tiruchirapalli, October, 1988.
Mental Health Act 1987, (Act No 14, 1987). 2007. Delhi: Commercial Law Publishers, India.
Nair. 1992. Judicial Activism in Giving The Mentally Insane Offender His Due, Cochin Law Review.
Nambi, S. 1992. A twenty years retrospective study of mentally Ill female prisoners in a Major State Mental Hospital in India. Paper presented at the Annual National Conference of Indian Psychiatric Society, New Delhi.
Nambi, S. 1998. Prevalence of alcohol and substance abuse among mentally Ill prisoners. Paper presented at the Annual National Conference of the Indian Psychiatric Society, Jaipur.
Nambi, S. 2008. *Legal aspects of psychiatry – Indian perspective*. Chennai: Manashanthi Mental Health Care Publications.
Narcotic Drugs and Psychotropic substances Act 1985. (with Amendments in 1996). Universal Law Publishing Company.
National Human Rights Commission – Recommendations on Detention. 2008. www.nhrc.nic.in.
Rath, N.M., et al. 1990. A study of insanity related homicide. *Indian Journal of Psychiatry* 32(1): 69–71.
Somasundaram, O. 1960. Guilty but insane. *Indian Journal of Psychiatry* 2(2): 80–85. April–June 1960.
Somasundaram, O. 1980. Murder in Tamil Nadu. *Indian Journal of Psychiatry* 22: 288–294.

Somasundaram, O. 2001. Criminal responsibility – an overview. *Indian Journal of Psychological Medicine* 24: 1, Indian Psychiatric Society, South Zone.

Srinivasa, Murthy. 1997. *Human rights of "mentally ill individuals-an Indian experience"*. Commemorative Brochure (16–18). Calcutta: 180 Year Celebration of Institute of Psychiatry.

The Indian penal code 1860. 1987. Eastern Book Company.

The Juvenile Justice (Care and Protection of Children) Act 2000. 2004. Professional Book Publishers.

Chapter 12
Ethical Issues in Prison Psychiatry in Israel

Jacob Margolin, Moshe Birger, and Eliezer Witztum

12.1 Introduction and Background

The State of Israel, established 64 years ago, in May 1948, is a country in Western Asia located on the eastern shore of the Mediterranean Sea. Geographically it contains diverse features within its relatively small area. Israel is the world's only predominantly Jewish state, with a population of 7.5 million people, of whom 5.7 million are Jewish. Arabs, Muslims, Christians and Druze form the country's additional ethnic groups, and other smaller groups include Bedouins, Circassians and Samaritans.

Israel is a developed country and a representative democracy with a parliamentary system and universal suffrage. The Prime Minister serves as head of government and the Knesset (the Israeli Parliament) serves as Israel's legislative body.

J. Margolin (✉)
Formerly Secretary of the Israel Society for Forensic Psychiatry,
Tel-Aviv Area District Psychiatrist, and Medical Director of the Jerusalem
Mental Health Center, Jerusalem, and the Jaffa Community Mental Health Center,
P.O. Box 262, Har Adar 9083600, Tel-Aviv, Israel
e-mail: Jacob.margolin@gmail.com

M. Birger
Head, Division of Forensic Psychiatry, Israel Prison Service, Beer-Yaacov Mental Health
Center, Ministry of Health, and Sackler Faculty of Medicine, Tel-Aviv University,
P.O. Box 2058, Ramla 7212001, Israel
e-mail: moshe.birger@beerness.health.gov.il

E. Witztum
Professor of Psychiatry, Faculty of Health Sciences, Ben-Gurion University of the Negev,
Beer-Sheva, and Senior Psychiatrist, Beer-Sheva Mental Health Center,
Beer-Sheva and "Ezrath-Nashim" Community Mental Health Center,
4 Revadim Street, Jerusalem 9339115, Israel
e-mail: elyiit@actcom.co.il

N. Konrad et al. (eds.), *Ethical Issues in Prison Psychiatry*, International Library
of Ethics, Law, and the New Medicine 46, DOI 10.1007/978-94-007-0086-4_12,
© Springer Science+Business Media Dordrecht 2013

The economy, based on the nominal gross domestic product, was the 41st-largest in the world in 2008. Israel ranks highest among Middle Eastern countries on the UN Human Development Index, and has one of the highest life expectancies in the world. Jerusalem is the country's capital, although it is not recognized internationally as such, while Israel's main financial center is Tel Aviv.

Israel is a multicultural state by its nature. Its population includes those of different origins, cultures and religions. Even among the Jews, who compose the majority of the population, one can find a significant variability in terms of origin, society, and cultural and religious background.

The quality of a society can be ascertained through the quality of its prisons. It seems that there is no better mirror of the Israeli society and the State of Israel than the Israeli Prison Service (IPS). This organization was developed in parallel to the Israeli State, and it reflects political, cultural and societal processes that shaped the State of Israel since its very beginning: violence, drugs, sexual offending, corruption and road accidents. In 2009, there were about 23,000 prisoners in 32 prisons (http://www.ips.gov.il/Shabas/tipul_prisoner/Prisoners+Info/prisoners_no.htm, last retrieved on August 8, 2010; in Hebrew).

The IPS is a security organization that has a clear social mission and is an integral part of Israel's system of law enforcement. Its chief roles include the holding of prisoners and detainees under secure and suitable conditions, while preserving their dignity, meeting their basic needs, and providing corrective tools to inmates for whom such tools are appropriate. The function of these corrective tools is to improve the prisoners' capacity for reintegrating into regular society after their release. The corrective tools are provided in coordination and cooperation with relevant national, regional and municipal authorities and organizations. To achieve that goal, the IPS makes every effort to continually enhance the professional skills of its prison guards and to develop suitable and humane incarceration facilities that meet the demands of the law and the security and corrective treatment needs of IPS prisoners and which express a thorough utilization of advanced technology.

Many ethical dilemmas were prevented as a result of the Israeli government's decision to distinguish between the functions and the responsibilities of the mental health services of prisoners and detainees, and the IPS. The mental health services are managed by the Ministry of Health, whereas security and logistics are run by the Ministry of Public Security (Silfen 1985). This division enables the psychiatric system to operate according to special Israeli laws that are designated for handling such issues as psychiatric commitment, forced treatment, and patient rights (Treatment of Mental Patients Act 1991; Patients' Rights Act 1996).

The mental health services of the IPS are supplied by the forensic psychiatric section of the Be'er Yaacov-Ness Ziona Governmental Mental Health Center. The section (also called IPS Mental Health Center) includes two active psychiatric wards (open and closed), located within the central prison of the IPS, and outpatient clinics within other prisons, supplying ambulatory services to the prisoners. The various mental health services of the IPS include ongoing, continuous psychiatric treatment as well as forensic examinations and assessments. The professional staff includes psychiatrists, psychologists, clinical criminologists, nurses, social workers, occupational therapists, and administrative staff. Apart from multi-professional individual and group treatments, the mental health professionals supply the following: ambulatory examinations and expert opinions to courts about mental health and treatment needs of prisoners; risk assessments of various prisoners; assessment of prisoners' competence for leave and parole; expert opinion about prisoners' appeals; professional advice to prison authorities regarding prisoners' treatment; participating in various local multi-professional tribunals and committees (e.g., incest, family violence); and professional connections and co-ordinations with other community agencies (e.g., families, social security, social workers, mental health clinics).

IPS's mental health center also serves as training and teaching center in multiple clinical areas: psychiatry, psychology, social work, nursing, clinical criminology, and occupational therapy. The center is affiliated with the Sackler School of Medicine of the Tel Aviv University, as well as other faculties at Hebrew University and Bar-Ilan University. Students of the above professions are practicing in IPS's mental health center in order to get their professional license. The teaching and training facilities are intertwined with the research activities of the center.

It is well known that being in prison causes a lot of stress for almost every prisoner, due to lack of personal freedom and autonomy, removal from support systems, diminished self-value, and sexual deprivation. Research surveys have shown high frequencies of psychiatric disorders among prisoners: the most comprehensive survey was published by Fazel and Danesh (2002). One can appreciate the extent of mental disturbances among Israeli prisoners by data of hospitalizations and ambulatory treatments. Thus, according to the Israeli Ministry of Health Annual Statistics for 2003–2004 (Ministry of Health 2004), 399 prisoners were hospitalized in the psychiatric wards of the IPS Mental Health Center between July 1st, 2003, and 31st July, 2004. 209 (52 %) were new admissions, and 190 (48 %) were recurrent ones. Psychotic disorders were diagnosed in 53.4 % of cases, personality disorders in 25.8 %, organic disorders in 5.3 %, alcohol and/or drug addiction or abuse in 4.8 %, neurotic disturbances in 3.8 %, mental retardation in 0.8 %, and other diagnoses were given in 6.1 % of cases. The data also suggested that about 3 % of all prisoners in Israel (in 2003–2004) needed psychiatric hospitalization.

In Israeli prisons, there are detailed rules regarding the treatment of prisoners who are at risk for committing suicide. Thus, prisoners who are at high suicidal risk are observed every 15 min, and in certain places a closed-system TV is used. It should be mentioned, however, that these measures are no substitute for direct communication with the attending professionals, who prevent suicide attempts by early recognition of signs of stress, and by personal and group treatment for prisoners who tried to commit suicide or are threatening in doing so.

In spite of the distinction mentioned above (between the IPS and the professional mental health services), some ethical issues cannot be avoided. Some of these issues are unique to the State of Israel, which is a multicultural state by nature. In their daily routine, mental health professionals working within the IPS have to be very sensitive to religious and ethnic diversity. They have to be well acquainted with different peculiarities, such as how to address a religious Jew who committed a sexual crime without offending him, and how to motivate him to participate in a sex offenders' treatment program. They also have to be familiar with the ways in which a distinctive ethnic origin reflects itself in psychopathology and also in criminology.

An important and large group of IPS's inmates consists of minorities (mostly Arabs, but also Ethiopian and Russian immigrants, and foreign workers from all around the globe and refugees from the Sudan, Eritrea, etc.). Although some of them speak Hebrew, the mental health professionals prefer to communicate with them through an interpreter, in their mother tongue. Another large group consists of security detainees, some of whom have been involved in serious terrorist assaults. With this group the mental health professionals have to maintain a humanitarian and professional approach, and be aware of counter-transference reactions, especially in periods following terrorist attacks.

In this chapter, using case vignettes, the following issues will briefly be discussed: solitary confinement, restrictions and prohibitions, incarceration of prisoners with severe deterioration in mental state, treatment of illegal immigrants, suicide prevention, and treatment of security detainees. Unfortunately, no statistics are publicly available about the scope of the problems. Special attention will then be paid to the issue of treating sexual offenders in Israeli prisons, as reflected in a detailed case vignette that includes clinical as well as legal aspects.

12.2 Solitary Confinement

Generally speaking, solitary confinement is advocated in cases where the inmate poses a severe and immediate danger to himself or others. In a few cases it is applied when there is an immediate threat to the inmate by other prisoners. Throughout the years, the IPS tried to engage psychiatrists in the process of decision making regarding the suitability or unsuitability of placing an inmate in solitary confinement. At the same time, civil rights organizations have tried to mobilize prison psychiatrists towards objecting to and protesting the mere notion of solitary confinement, whenever a case is raised.

According to the policy of the Israeli Ministry of Health and the Israel Medical Association, no physician should be involved in the decision-making process regarding solitary confinement. It also has stated that solitary confinement in itself can be hazardous to the mental health of any individual.

Currently, a physician and a guard conduct a daily review of solitary confinement wards. Upon detecting any mental health problem, the inmate is transferred for a psychiatric assessment that can result in a recommendation to remove the inmate from confinement. Such recommendations are generally followed by the IPS.

Case Vignette – 1

A short time after taking the position of the director of the IPS psychiatric services, one of the authors (Moshe Birger: MB) started examining solitary confinement inmates. It was noted that in most cases, no major psychopathology was found.

One particular inmate, however, who had received high publicity due to his involvement in serious state security crimes, was diagnosed as suffering from paranoid schizophrenia (according to the DSM-IV-TR criteria). Without any delay, a delicate process was initiated in order to enable him to be released from solitary confinement. Although the inmate refused any psychiatric treatment, he moved was back in the main prison system, and was in contact with other inmates. This led to a significant improvement in his mental condition.

A second inmate was diagnosed as suffering from chronic residual schizophrenia with prominent negative symptoms. This particular patient was quiet and harmless, and in the eyes of a non-professional he did not present any particular challenge. However, there was a reluctance to release him because he had committed serial homicides. He was transferred to a closed psychiatric ward within the prison system, where intensive treatment using atypical antipsychotics was started. A few months later his condition was much improved, enabling him to be released to a ward designated for the aftercare of mental patients, from which he could obtain leave outside the secure perimeter.

12.3 Restrictions and Prohibitions

A second and much more important issue concerns restrictions and prohibitions according to IPS rules, for inmates manifesting suicidal or offensive behavior, and for security detainees. In both populations, Israeli law enables IPS authorities to enforce regulatory measures such as solitary confinement, closed circuit TV monitoring, etc. In the case of security detainees, such as suicide-bombers, total segregation from criminal inmates is required. Suicidal or dangerous inmates are regularly assessed for the threat they pose towards others or to themselves, and precautionary measures are changed according to the risk level. Any inmate, including security detainees, can make an appeal to a court, demanding improvement of his conditions.

Case Vignette – 2

An aggressive inmate was hospitalized on the closed psychiatric ward due to a psychotic disorder. Shortly afterwards, his mental condition improved, but the IPS authorities who feared that he might still behave in a dangerous way, insisted that he be kept in his cell. However, in as much as the mental health professionals regard the freedom of movement, as well as the ability to participate in social activities, occupational therapy and group therapy, as mandatory activities in the process of rehabilitation, they insisted that the responsibility for his behavior should remain in the hands of the medical director of the ward and not be given over to IPS authorities. This led to the convening of a special forum of experts, in which it was clearly decided that the medical view should have priority over security issues.

This decision also enabled medical professionals to release detainees hospitalized for forensic evaluation from their prison cells, so that professionals would be able to monitor their behavior in a less restricted environment, as well as observe their interactions with other inmates. In many cases, substantial important information was obtained through this procedure. Detainees (including security ones) who were supposedly mute, started to communicate, and those who formerly spoke incoherently were found to communicate coherently when talking to their families and lawyers.

12.4 Incarceration of Prisoners with Deteriorated Mental Conditions

A third issue relates to the complex medical and forensic aspects of continued incarceration of inmates with extremely deteriorated mental conditions. From time to time, patients are brought for psychiatric assessment suffering from schizophrenia or dementia in such a deteriorated state that their mental condition prevents them from understanding where and why they are being held. In such cases, the whole notion and aim of punishment might be meaningless. In addition, their continued stay in a stressful environment might worsen their mental condition (Fazel et al. 2002).

In cases where psychiatric professionals conclude that no danger would be imposed on others or the prisoner upon release, the mental health professionals acting in concert with the IPS Chief of Medical Services enabled prisoners with such serious mental disorders to get parole or discharge and transfer to a civil institution, where they could be provided with adequate care in a more optimal environment.

Case Vignette – 3

A 72-year-old person serving a life sentence for the murder of his wife some 16 years ago, was diagnosed as suffering from a rapidly progressive multi-infarct dementia. A request for parole was initiated by the legal consultants, and after it was finally guaranteed by the President of the State of Israel, it was possible to discharge him from prison and admit him to a geriatric institution, where he was well taken care of until his death 3 years later.

12.5   Treatment of Illegal Immigrants

In recent years, an increasing number of refugees and foreigners seeking work are entering Israel illegally. Many are caught and detained by a special unit of the Israeli Ministry of Internal Affairs (Oz Unit). This group of inmates has been living under very stressful conditions. Some have endured a long and perilous journey, crossed borders, and have been subjected to abuse or attacks. Many of them have escaped from war zones, famine, or from persecution based on their racial and religious background. Many of them are caught shortly after arrival, but some of them have managed to live for some time in Israel, and have succeeded in obtaining jobs and accommodation. Their detention, incarceration and finally expulsion to their countries of origin or any other willing country only add to their accumulated sorrow. Some of these individuals were admitted to mental health units, generally due to psychotic or depressive states. They present not only with ethnic and language differences, but also with different culture-bound symptoms. Since they do not have any legal status, they are of less significance for aid agencies such as the Israeli Association for Prisoners' Right, which aims at improving prisoners' conditions, or the Israeli Physicians' Association for Human Rights, which aims at providing proper medical treatment, not to mention the International Committee of the Red Cross, which supervises the care of security and foreign detainees. Once stabilized, many of them are sent to remote countries, sometimes awaiting trial and punishment. Even in cases where the country and town of destination are known, difficult decisions have to be made as to whether to inform the medical authorities about the patient's mental condition, not knowing the use which will be made of such information. It is important to mention that the Israeli authorities act in accordance with the United Nations High Commissioner for Refugees (UNHCR). Thus, in many cases individuals are granted asylum in Israel.

This situation, which is typical not only to Israel but also to many other Western countries, creates a conflict between moral and professional ethics of mental health professionals and the prevailing laws of immigration.

Case Vignette – 4

A 28-year-old man from a Western African state was arrested shortly after illegally crossing the border of Israel. He was incarcerated in a prison in the central part of Israel, among fellow illegal immigrants. Shortly after his arrival, he developed a psychotic state and was admitted to a psychiatric ward in the prison. When his psychosis subsided, he was able to tell his tragic story. He described himself as an opposition member in his country who was persecuted by the current regime. He pleaded with his treatment team to enable him to stay and work in Israel. In spite of the compassion felt for him by all of his mental health professionals, he had to leave the ward and was subsequently sent to a neighboring African country. He was provided with a detailed medical report, emphasizing the humanitarian aspects of his condition, in the hope that he would be treated properly.

12.6 Suicide Prevention

Suicide is a serious health problem. The World Health Organization (WHO) estimates that a suicide attempt occurs approximately every three seconds, and one completed suicide occurs approximately every minute (WHO 2007). This means that more people die by suicide than by armed conflict. Preventing suicide has become an important international health goal. The causes of suicide are complex. Some individuals seem especially vulnerable to suicide when faced with a difficult life event or a combination of stressors. The challenge of suicide prevention is to identify people who are most vulnerable under particular circumstances, and then to effectively intervene. Researchers have identified a number of factors that interact to place an individual at a higher risk for suicide (WHO 2007). The ways in which these factors interact to produce suicide and suicidal behaviors are complex and not well understood. Various tools have been used to identify specific high-risk groups – populations of special concern – because they commit suicide at higher-than-average rates. Prisoners have higher suicide rates than their community counterparts (WHO 2007). For example, in pretrial facilities housing short-term inmates, the suicide rate is 10 times that of the community. In facilities housing sentenced prisoners, the suicide rate is 3 times higher than in the community (WHO 2007). For every death by suicide, there are many more suicide attempts. Any combination of the following factors may account for the higher rates of suicide in correctional settings: (1) Jails and prisons are repositories for vulnerable groups that are traditionally at a high risk for suicide, such as young males, the mentally ill, socially disenfranchised, socially isolated, substance abusers, or previous suicide attempters. (2) The psychological impact of arrest and incarceration and the day-to-day stress associated with prison life may exceed the coping skills of vulnerable individuals. (3) There may be no formal policies and procedures to identify and manage suicidal inmates. (4) Even if appropriate policies and procedures do exist, overworked or untrained correctional personnel may miss the early warning signs of suicidality. (5) Correctional settings may be isolated from community mental health programs so they have poor or no access to mental health professionals or treatments (WHO 2007).

Due to some recent events in Israel where several well-known prisoners committed suicide, the IPS has instituted rigorous suicide prevention measures. Upon admission to the prison, each inmate is assessed for suicidal risk by means of a specially designed questionnaire. In the case of potentially suicidal inmates, several measures can be taken such as constant supervision of inmates at risk, confinement to special wards, as well as the use of restraints. These measures, which were taken after carefully studying the existing policies in different western countries, raised debate between the psychiatric staff and the prison's authorities. One controversial issue regarded the double-edged quality of restraint, which on one hand can prevents self-harm but on the other hand may cause discomfort as well as the labeling of a suicidal inmate as dangerous, irresponsible, etc. Ethical issues that arise in the care of suicidal patients within the prison context are constantly discussed by the various mental health professionals working in the IPS. Bell's conclusion is pertinent in such situations: "The psychiatrist is bound to the suicidal patient in an 'I-Thou' relationship in which she views herself as heteronomously impelled to engage the despairing prisoner in a way which seeks to engender a sense of hope, trust and self worth as a valued member of human society. This may, on occasion, include a brief period of isolation in a wet cell to protect the patient from the consequences of his own despair" (Bell 1999).

Case Vignette – 5

A prisoner well known to the Israeli media, who was kept under constant surveillance, managed to commit suicide in spite of all the precautionary measures that were taken. Among the many points that were made in the review of the case, one pertained to the fact that the thorough surveillance he was under actually created a state of isolation due to which important communication channels were blocked. Communication is important for all prisoners but had particular significance to this prisoner who was known to derive self-esteem by entertaining the people around him. The conclusion drawn was that instead of a rigorous application of restrictive measures, a special plan should be tailored according to the individual's needs and personality.

12.7 Security Detainees

Due to Israel's particular situation, many prisoners are detained due to involvement in terrorist attacks. Most of them serve their sentences in prisons that were primarily designed for their incarceration. Not surprisingly, due to their ideological orientation, most of them are devoid of serious psychiatric problems, but there are some individuals committed to psychiatric wards for suffering from major psychiatric disorders. The professional staff is involved in the process of forensic evaluation, and is expected to render an opinion regarding the mental state of a prisoner accused of terrorist acts in order to assess his responsibility for his deeds and his capacity to stand trial. A major component of the expertise relies upon the observation of the detainee's behavior on the ward. It was therefore agreed after negotiations with the IPS that in spite of the possible danger posed by security detainees towards other inmates and staff, they would be allowed to roam relatively freely, so that their behavior can be monitored for the purpose of the forensic evaluation.

In cases in which the mental condition of a security detainee deteriorates in solitary confinement the psychiatrist intervenes, and requests transfer to a cell with other inmates. Needless to mention that any examination of a security prisoner, for whom even a psychiatrist is an enemy, is much more difficult due to significant counter-transferential issues, but nevertheless the psychiatric staff has been able to handle this situation successfully.

Case Vignette – 6

A 17-year-old Palestinian was arrested due to involvement in minor terrorist activities. Due to his peculiar behavior which was manifested by harassing his fellow prison inmates, he was sent for a psychiatric evaluation in an adolescent psychiatric ward. The clinical diagnosis was borderline IQ and behavioral problems. It was recommended that he should be followed up by a psychiatrist. The psychiatrist's recommendations were sent to the military court. The presiding judge, who was convinced that the prisoner's mental condition put him at risk of being attacked by fellow prison inmates, decided to discharge him to the Palestinian Authority.

12.8 Treatment of Sexual Offenders in Israeli Prisons

The treatment of sexual offenders, and more specifically the treatment of high-risk sexual offenders, is a subject of great importance for practitioners, professionals, policymakers and the public at large. Traditional treatment is thought to largely center upon cognitive-behavioral methods and other psychotherapeutic techniques (Marshall and Barbaree 1988; Rosler and Witztum 2000). In paraphilic sex offenders, the use of antiandrogenic pharmacotherapy is regarded as a most important factor with or without concomitant psychotherapy (Rosler and Witztum 2000). Such medication is used to lower testosterone levels, which may lead to a significant decrease of deviant and non-deviant sexual urges. Rather than using the irreversible and arguably 'barbaric' option of surgical castration, antiandrogenic pharmacotherapy achieves the same results, but through less invasive and non-permanent means. Such medication is often known under its more popular and emotive term of 'chemical castration' and this is how the media has imprecisely categorized the treatment. Antiandrogenic medication does not require surgical intervention and its effects can be reversed, often through the simple withdrawal of the drugs involved. It should also be mentioned that in Israel, for those men of the ultra-orthodox Jewish population who have sexual drives towards children, the offense is not only forbidden by the State Law, but also by the Halacha, the Jewish religious Code of Law. Such offenders usually hate themselves for their uncontrolled drives and even beg for pharmacotherapy as an efficient means of handling them (Rosler and Witztum 1998, 2000).

Pharmacotherapy in the treatment of sexual offenders has been in practice since the 1940s, although through time the drugs involved have changed. Such treatment raises legal and ethical issues, in particular issues such as whether the treatment should be voluntary or mandatory; whether it should even be classified as treatment or should instead be seen as punishment, and finally whether it should be used only with convicted offenders or made freely available to all (Harrison 2008).

In the State of Israel, beginning two decades ago, Rosler and Witztum initiated intensive research and then treatment of sexual offenders with the Gonadotrophin Releasing Hormone (GNRH) agonist Triptorelin in the form of a monthly injection, with very high efficacy. The GNRH agonist down regulates GNRH receptors at the level of hypothalamus, thus leading to a reduction in LH and subsequently testosterone levels. This treatment is voluntary and requires informed consent of all patients involved, as well as a thorough medical, psychiatric and psychological evaluation (Rosler and Witztum 1998, 2000). In March 2005 the Israeli Ministry of Health authorized the inclusion of Triptorelin Acetate (Decapeptyl®) in the 'Health Basket' (a term used in Israel to designate all the obligatory kinds of medical treatments to be included in health insurance and decided upon by the Israeli government) for the reduction of abnormal sexual desire and activity in individuals with pedophilia.

In Israel, the number of incarcerated sexual offenders has been steadily increasing from a total number of 350 offenders in 1997 to 1,300 in 2009. About 60 % of convicted sexual offenders in Israel have committed offenses against children under the age of 13. It is estimated that half of those are diagnosed with pedophilia, whereas the other half consists of child molesters or incest sex offenders (www.ips.gov.il, retrieved on May 24, 2009). The growing number of sexual offenses against children has become a major public concern, and during the last 10 years substantial legislative measures has been passed by the Israeli Knesset. A law safeguarding the community from sexual offenders has been operative since 2006 (Public Defense from Sexual Offenders Act 2006). This law stipulates that the risk posed by any sexual offender who is discharged to the community is assessed by mental health professionals who were assigned by the Israeli Ministries of Health and Social Welfare for the purpose of risk assessment. In the case of moderate to high levels of dangerousness, the state can apply for supervisory measures, with specifications that are adjusted according to the level of dangerousness and the nature of the offenses. The measures include prohibition of drugs or alcohol, monitoring the content of home computers, restricting work with minors, etc. A special unit of the IPS has been assigned to this task. It is hoped that during 2010 a supplement to this law, providing for the regulation of sexual treatment programs in both prisons and civil settings, will be approved by the Knesset.

Psychiatric treatment for sexual offenders in the IPS according to current professional knowledge has been provided for many years. Since there is no mandatory treatment for sexual offenders in Israel, such treatments have been provided after obtaining informed consent from the patient. Over the years, the treatment modalities have been thoroughly changed with traditional, dynamic psychotherapeutic approaches being replaced by group cognitive-behavioral therapy, coupled with broader use of pharmacotherapy when indicated (Birger et al. 2011).

Upon admission to prison, each sexual offender is clinically assessed for the assignment of suitable therapy. In some prisons various ongoing group therapy programs based on a psycho-educative approach are conducted for a period of 1.5 years. Sexual offenders who pose a greater risk of recidivism are assigned to groups that follow principles of relapse prevention. The target population consists of convicted sexual offenders, many of whom are assessed as highly dangerous offenders, who committed serious crimes. Pharmacological interventions are therefore essential for the control of their sexual drives.

The pharmacological interventions used are mainly indicated in the cases of paraphilias (when behavior is based upon deviant sexual fantasies or urges) or uncontrollable sexual drive (hyper-sexuality). First, the level of dangerousness according to the prevailing criteria is assessed. The patients will also be evaluated for underlying medical conditions and concomitant medication use. Subsequently, the patients are evaluated for additional comorbidities, and are then divided into three main groups: patients without any significant comorbidity; patients with DSM-IV axis-I comorbidity, such as psychotic illness; and patients with severe personality disorder.

Pharmacological treatment of sexual offenders in prison who have antisocial or severe borderline personality disorders is to be considered with caution due to problems regarding adherence, litigation and manipulation. Clinical experience suggests that such people do not usually continue these treatments upon release from prison.

Favorable results have been obtained by treating schizophrenic patients who have co-morbid paraphilic disorders with a combination of antipsychotic and anti-androgenic medication/GNRH agonists. In these special populations, a marked reduction in sexual drive and deviant and non-deviant sexual fantasies was observed (Birger et al. 2011).

It is worth mentioning that since inmates with severe personality disorders as well as schizophrenic patients make poor candidates for group therapy, providing them with an adequate pharmacotherapy is of crucial importance.

Treatment goals include suppression of deviant sexual fantasies and urges, thus reducing the risk of further victimization, while maintaining normophilic sexual drive. Since this is seldom achievable when using pharmacological agents, a difficult ethical dilemma arises regarding the deprivation of a vital bodily function – sexual activity. This may also explain the reason why many of the inmates who wish to participate in psychotherapeutic modalities are usually unwilling to receive medications reducing sexual drive. Other reasons for a lack of motivation, as assessed by the professional team of the mental health services of the IPS, are denial of the crime or of the underlying sexual pathology, and fear of side effects. It seems that in cases of short duration of incarceration, inmates are not motivated enough to obtain treatment.

In Israeli prisons, antiandrogenic medication is given in cases of paraphilias and hyper-sexuality. This treatment requires special attention when given in this unique setting. It is important to be very cautious regarding side effects since the prisoners do not have immediate, free access to a treating physician. Some of the prisoners might be litigious or pose a latent threat to the treatment staff. Non-adherence to treatment or false report of therapeutic effects are other problems presented by this population.

The prison environment is devoid of pedophilic sexual stimuli. In addition, the official policy strictly forbids any use of pornography. Since antiandrogenic treatment may involve prominent side effects such as osteoporosis and renal function impairment, some professionals suggest that drug treatment during imprisonment is unnecessary and should be considered only when the prisoner is about to be released. However, other professionals argue for initiation of treatment in the early stages of incarceration. They claim that the sooner treatment is started, the less the tendency that the sexual offender will psychologically minimize his offences, and the more likely that the sexual offender will assume responsibility for his actions (La Fond 2005).

The provision of treatment for sexual offenders requires knowledge in the fields of psychiatry, psychology, criminology, sociology, law, ethics, anthropology, policing and even theology. Pharmacological treatment requires the collaboration of a multidisciplinary team including a psychiatrist, an endocrinologist and a forensic psychologist or clinical criminologist. Forensic psychiatrists in prison need to have special training in the diagnosis of paraphilias, and in the understanding of the link between mental disorders and sexually abnormal behavior, the advantages and limitations of psycho physiological methods such as PPG (unfortunately still not in use in Israel) in assessment and treatment, the use of medication in addition to psychological methods in the treatment of sexual offenders and risk assessment of sexual offenders (Gordon and Grubin 2004). Good clinical practice also requires performing many lab tests, with well planned follow-up. These preconditions cannot be fulfilled in many countries, due to the lack of training facilities and budgetary constraints.

The pharmacological treatment of sexual offenders also requires extensive knowledge of the availability and underlying biological mechanisms of the existing compounds. Regarding pharmacological treatment, apart from sound theoretical knowledge, significant clinical experience is needed. Risk assessment and treatment of sexual offenders are taught in academic courses.

According to Israeli law, inmates are entitled to short passes (allowing leave into the community) once having completed a quarter of their prison term (http://www.hov.what2do.co.il/Page21977.asp, last retrieved on August 8, 2010; in Hebrew). In the case of sexual offenders, this privilege requires a preliminary risk assessment, and usually short passes are denied to these prisoners. Although administering antiandrogenic therapy significantly reduces sexual drive and thus can enable passes, the passes are not given since the association of therapy with secondary gain is unwanted. According to cognitive behavioral theories, treatment outcome is more successful when motivated by internal factors such as guilt, or a genuine wish to recover. It is noteworthy that in most sexual offenders, the initial motivation for therapy is based on secondary gain factors (Tierney and McCabe 2002). On the other hand, short leaves are regarded by some professionals as an important component, among other psychosocial interventions, enabling the reintegration of sexual offenders in their natural environment. This approach advocates that pharmacological treatment should be started as soon as possible, after the completion of all the assessment procedures.

One of the main obstacles in the administration of pharmacotherapy to a large group of inmates in Israel is that, unlike in other countries, the issue of follow-up and supervision is still not officially settled. No public treatment facilities exist, and released prisoners find it hard to finance treatment. Furthermore, supervision mainly relies upon subjective reports and the measurement of testosterone levels. Treatment facilities in the community should therefore be available and accessible, preferably with accompanying supervisory measures.

Pharmacological treatments that intervene with sexual function present an ethical dilemma due to the deprivation of a basic bodily function. Sexual activity is psychologically related to a sense of vitality, personal identity and gratification. Furthermore, when such medication is given to sexual offenders, it should be continued on a long term base. It is considered ethically challenging to conduct well designed clinical studies in prisons (Dignam 2003). Even in non-prison settings, well designed controlled studies for pharmacological interventions in patients with paraphilias and in sexual offenders are still lacking because of several significant methodological and financial obstacles (Guay 2009).

Administering pharmacological treatment also imposes an ethical dilemma regarding the issue of informed consent. The doctrine of informed consent states that the patient must be competent to make a decision, he should be fully informed of the side effects of the medical treatment offered to him, and the decision must be reached free of coercion (Grisso and Appelbaum 1998). This doctrine is deeply ingrained in Israeli law, specifically in the Patients' Rights Act of 1996. Can an incarcerated sex offender give meaningful informed consent? Should we as mental health professionals offer this treatment in this particular setting? There are no clear answers to these questions. While some argue that informed consent is unlikely to be achieved in conditions where an incarcerated sexual offender's refusal to accept therapy may have a negative impact on his release terms (which might implicate some form of mental coercion) (Scott and Holmberg 2003), others claim that denying these prisoners the opportunity of making such a decision serves to deprive them of the possibility of safe and free living in the community (Berlin 2003). This dilemma is further complicated by the additional and perhaps conflicting ethical obligation of the psychiatrist to society (Steinfels and Levine 1978). The psychiatrist treating the incarcerated offender must always maintain a sensitive balance between the needs and wishes of his individual patient and the potential threat to the public and society stemming from recidivism.

Case Vignette – 7

The following case, based on a legal article published by lawyers of the Public Defense Unit in the Israeli Ministry of Justice (Lernau and Pat 2009), illustrates some of the dilemmas mentioned above. The patient, Mr. A, is 56-year-old Jewish repentant male, married with two children, whose eldest son died at the age of 22. He was arrested and charged with sexual assault of a child, and during his detention he applied to one of the authors (Eliezer Witztum: EW) for pharmacotherapy in order to lessen his sexual drive. After comprehensive assessment and evaluation, including psychodiagnostic tests, he was diagnosed as a non-pedophilic child molester. He was found suitable for treatment, which was started at his expense while he was on remand. On the basis of the on-going treatment, and the probation officer's reports, the Israeli Supreme Court decided that Mr. A need not be detained during his legal procedures but would be able to stay at his home, in house detention. Mr. A continued his treatment (at his expense), receiving monthly injections for 30 months, before he was convicted and sentenced to four and a half years in prison. Upon entering prison, he was denied continuation of his treatment. The reason given for this denial was that treatment was unnecessary in prison due to a lack of sexual stimuli. It was promised that treatment would be reconsidered towards the end of Mr. A's prison term.

Mr. A appealed against the prison's medical authorities' decision to stop his treatment. He argued that treatment was stopped due to a general policy, without consulting his physicians. It was also argued that Mr. A had the right to continue medical treatment that had proven to be very efficient in reducing the level of his dangerousness, and had improved his well-being and quality of life. The court accepted his appeal and ordered to continue Mr. A's treatment in prison. However, the medical authorities of the prison continued denying treatment, arguing that their medical conscience did not allow them to give treatment that in their professional opinion was unnecessary in prison and that even may cause serious side-effects. An urgent court session was called for by Mr. A's lawyers (one of them wrote the legal article mentioned above), and the court heard the medical opinions of all of the various professionals (including EW and MB). At the end of the session it was agreed that in Mr. A's special circumstances, he should continue his treatment in prison, at the expense of the IPS.

In practice, sexual offenders who agree to accept medical treatment receive benefits beyond reduction of their problematic sexual drive. First, treatment

---

(continued)

Case Vignette – 7 (continued)

participation leads to decreased level of dangerousness, assisting them in requests for leave or parole (in Israel, the period of parole can be given after serving two thirds of the prison sentence). Second, in some cases it can be argued that receiving treatment in itself reduces the need for supervision, according to the 2006 Public Defense from Sexual Offenders Act. Third, understanding that sexual offending against children stems from a known psychiatric disorder (pedophilia), which in many cases can be treated by pharmacological and psychotherapeutic measures, is both important and meaningful. Such an understanding can open up the way for judicial tolerance and for implementation of a therapeutic jurisprudence in legal procedures, akin to those developed in drug addiction (Dorf and Fagan 2003; Winick and Wexler 2003).

12.9   Summary

Psychiatrists working in prisons and jails know very well that they engage in stressful and complicated work in the tough world behind bars. Ethical issues encountered while practicing psychiatry in correctional settings can be unique, and quite different from the ethical problems of those working in other facilities.

Prison psychiatrists in Israel are part of the Ministry of Health, and not of the Israeli Prison Service (IPS). This means that these physicians are subject to the same professional and administrative regulations as psychiatrists working in public practice. However, prison psychiatrists practice in a different climate than their colleagues, and they have to handle various daily dilemmas. Only the most important and frequent ones were mentioned in this chapter.

A special part of psychiatric practice in the IPS is the management and treatment of sexual offenders. Although thus far no consensus exists regarding the full indications for pharmacotherapy in this population, it seems that the mental health professional team in the IPS is currently more apt to take a broader, more positive view toward drug treatment for reducing sexual drive in carefully examined sexual offenders.

References

Bell, D. 1999. Ethical issues in the prevention of suicide in prison. *Australian and New Zealand Journal of Psychiatry* 33: 723–728.

Berlin, F.S. 2003. Sex offender treatment and legislation. *Australian and New Zealand Journal of Psychiatry* 31: 510–513.

Birger, M., T. Bergman-Levy, and O. Asman. 2011. Treatment of sex offenders in Israeli prison setting. *The Journal of the American Academy of Psychiatry and the Law* 39: 100–103.

Dignam, J.T. 2003. Correctional mental health ethics revisited. In *Correctional mental health handbook*, ed. T.J. Fagan and R.K. Ax, 39–56. Thousand Oaks: Sage Publications.

Dorf, M.C., and J.A. Fagan. 2003. Problem-solving courts: From innovation to institutionalization. *American Criminal Law Review* 40: 1501–1511.

Fazel, S., and J. Danesh. 2002. Serious mental disorder in 23,000 prisoners: A systematic review of 62 surveys. *The Lancet* 359: 545–550.

Fazel, S., J. McMillan, and I. O'Donnell. 2002. Dementia in prison: Ethical and legal implications. *Journal of Medical Ethics* 28: 156–159.

Gordon, H., and D. Grubin. 2004. Psychiatric aspects of the assessment and treatment of sex offenders. *Advances in Psychiatric Treatment* 10: 73–80.

Grisso, T., and P.S. Appelbaum. 1998. *Assessing competence to consent to treatment: A guide for physicians and other health professionals*. New York: Oxford University Press.

Guay, D.R.P. 2009. Drug treatment of paraphilic and nonparaphilic sexual disorders. *Clinical Therapeutics* 31: 1–31.

Harrison, K. 2008. Legal and ethical issues when using antiandrogenic pharmacotherapy with sex offenders. *Sexual Offender Treatment* 3(2). http://www.sexual-offender-treatment.org/70.html. Last retrieved on August 2, 2010.

La Fond, J.Q. 2005. *Preventing sexual violence: How society should cope with sex offenders (law and public policy: Psychology and the social sciences)*. Washington, DC: American Psychological Association.

Lernau, H., and N. Pat. 2009. Has a change occurred in the policy of the Israel Prison Service in regard to pharmacotherapy for sexual offenders who attacked children? *Hasanegor (The Defender)* 143: 4–9 (in Hebrew).

Marshall, W., and H. Barbaree. 1988. The long-term evaluation of a behavioural treatment programmed for child molesters. *Behaviour Research and Therapy* 26: 499–511.

Ministry of Health. 2004. Mental health in Israel. Statistical annual 2003. http://www.old.health.gov.il/download/forms/mentalReport2003.pdf. Last retrieved on August 8, 2010; in Hebrew.

Patients' Rights Act. 1996. *Israeli law book*. 1591: 327.

Public Defense from Sexual Offenders Act. 2006. *Israeli law book*. 2050: 234.

Rosler, A., and E. Witztum. 1998. Treatment of men with paraphilia with a long-acting analogue of gonadotropin-releasing hormone. *The New England Journal of Medicine* 338: 416–422.

Rosler, A., and E. Witztum. 2000. Pharmacotherapy of paraphilias in the next millennium. *Behavioral Sciences & the Law* 18: 43–56.

Scott, C.L., and T. Holmberg. 2003. Castration of sex offenders: Prisoners' rights versus public safety. *The Journal of the American Academy of Psychiatry and the Law* 31: 502–509.

Silfen, P. 1985. Prison-psychiatry: Medical or correctional discipline? *Medicine and Law* 4: 239–249.

Steinfels, M., and C. Levine. 1978. In the service of the state: The psychiatrist as double agent. *Hastings Center Report* 8(Special Suppl): 1–24.

Tierney, D.W., and M.P. McCabe. 2002. Motivation for behavior change among sex offenders: a review of the literature. *Clinical Psychology Review* 22: 113–129.

Treatment of Mental Patients Act. 1991. *Israeli law book*. 1339: 58.

WHO. 2007. *World Health Organization and International Association for suicide prevention: Preventing suicide in jails and prisons*. Geneva: WHO.

Winick, B.J., and D.B. Wexler (eds.). 2003. *Judging in a therapeutic key: Therapeutic jurisprudence and the courts*. Durham: Carolina Academic Press.

Chapter 13
Current Status of Prison Psychiatry and Its Relationship with General Psychiatry in Japan

Yoji Nakatani and Osamu Kuroda

13.1 Introduction

The treatment of offenders with mental disorders is generally addressed at the ambiguous intersection of the criminal justice and the mental health systems. This entanglement of systems presents prison psychiatry with intricate problems. Strict rules govern correctional institutions. Therefore, psychiatric practices are complicated by a variety of challenges.

For the past several decades, considerable efforts have been made to reform psychiatric treatment in Japan. However, the benefit to mentally ill prisoners from this progress remains unclear. In view of the relationship between prison psychiatry and general psychiatry, this article briefly describes the histories of penal administration and mental health legislation, the treatment system and recent trends regarding offenders with mental disorders, current issues of prison psychiatry and related ethical problems in Japan.

13.2 Development of Penal Administration

13.2.1 History

The criminal justice and penal administration systems in Japan have developed in parallel with the overall modernization of the country in the late nineteenth century. Along with various reforms in the legal system during the Meiji era (1868–1912),

Y. Nakatani (✉)
Kubota Clinic, 3-2-4 Yokokawa, Sumida-ku, Tokyo 130-0003, Japan
e-mail: yojinaka47@yahoo.co.jp

O. Kuroda
Department of Psychiatry, Tokyo Metropolitan Matsuzawa Hospital
2-1-1 Kamikitazawa, Setagaya-ku, Tokyo 156-0057, Japan
e-mail: osysrk5331@yahoo.co.jp

N. Konrad et al. (eds.), *Ethical Issues in Prison Psychiatry*, International Library
of Ethics, Law, and the New Medicine 46, DOI 10.1007/978-94-007-0086-4_13,
© Springer Science+Business Media Dordrecht 2013

improvements were made in the prison system, transforming the gloomy world of Kangoku (an archaic Japanese word for prison) into more humane institutions. Thus, the Prison Law — the first modern law dealing with incarcerated prisoners and detainees— was enacted in 1908 (Correction Bureau 2009b). Throughout the Taisho (1912–1926) and early Showa (1926–1989) eras, the prison system developed under reformist ideas, with the introduction of more specialized treatments. Additionally, an introduction of regulations for hygiene during the 1920s contributed to a decrease in the morbidity and mortality rates of prisoners (Ohashi 2006; Shikita and Tsuchiya 1992).

Toward the end of World War II, air raids led to the physical deterioration of numerous penal facilities. Moreover, a shortage of food led to a rapid increase in inmate mortality. During the post-war period, social unrest and a sharp rise in criminality resulted in the overpopulation of correctional institutions (Ohashi 2006). Accordingly, the Japanese government reconstituted the prison administration system to resemble the American approach to correction, e.g. respecting prisoners' human rights and providing rehabilitation under probationary supervision. Consequently, reformatories and detention homes were established for juvenile delinquents. Since the late 1950s, a progressive stage system for the treatment of prisoners has developed. For this purpose, the Rule for Classification of Prisoners was implemented in 1972 (Shikita and Tsuchiya 1992).

13.2.2 Current Law

Since its enactment in 1908, the Prison Law has been enforced without substantial revisions until recently. As its inconsistency with social changes and more contemporary ideas of correction were recognized, a movement toward a revision in the Prison Law was initiated. High-profile incidents that occurred in one particular prison also contributed to this movement for revision (Nakane 2005). From 2001 to 2002, prison officers from the Nagoya Prison used violence toward inmates, causing two deaths and one injury. Once disclosed, the scandal was featured in newspapers provoking harsh criticism of the prison administration for having overlooked human rights violations involving the illicit use of physical restraints. The Parliament actively discussed the problems of abuse and negligence of prisoners. Subsequently, the Ministry of Justice set up the Correctional Administration Reform Council composed of private experts who aimed for an overall reform of prison administration as well as a total revision of the Prison Law. The Council also discussed a range of problems related to medical treatment of prisoners including such issues as the insufficient delivery of medical services, the lack of independence of medical staff from security staff, and inadequate examination of cases of unnatural deaths in penal facilities.

Based on the recommendations of the Council, a new law came into effect in 2006, which was subsequently revised in 2007 designated as the Act on Penal and Detention Facilities and the Treatment of Inmates and Detainees (hereafter referred to as 'Inmates and Detainees Act') (Correction Bureau 2009b).

This Act specifically aims to assure the transparency of prison administration, clarifying the rights and duties of inmates and staff, as well as facilitating inmates' reintegration into the community. Regarding the medical treatment of inmates, Article 56 of the Inmates and Detainees Act stipulates that for the purpose of maintaining the health of inmates and hygiene in facilities, penal institutions must provide inmates with the same level of hygienic and medical measures available to the general public.

One recent innovation was the introduction of the Private Finance Initiative (PFI) as an effective method for utilizing private capital and expertise as well as gaining the understanding and support of the general public through a joint effort between the public and private sectors. As of October 2008, four PFI managed institutions became operational (Research and Training Institute 1990–2009).

13.3 Institutions and Medical Services

13.3.1 Institutions

As of April 2009, there were 69 prisons (including seven juvenile prisons) with 8 branches, and 8 detention houses with 104 branches across Japan (Research and Training Institute 1990–2009). Generally, prisons and juvenile facilities accommodate sentenced inmates, while detention houses are mainly for prisoners awaiting trial. Currently, these institutions fall under the jurisdiction of the Ministry of Justice. The Correction Bureau and the eight regional correction headquarters supervise the function of the penal institutions (Correction Bureau 2009b).

13.3.2 Medical Services

Medical services are provided in accordance with the type of penal institutions. In addition to general penal institutions where few doctors and medical specialists are assigned, there are four special medical centers, two psychiatric and two general, which accept inmates requiring special medical care. Three out of the four special medical centers are accredited as hospitals by the Medical Service Law (Correction Bureau 2009b).

The Inmates and Detainees Act stipulates that an inmate may be transferred to a hospital outside a penal institution when necessary. This procedure is usually employed for emergency cases, such as myocardial or cerebral infarction. In 2006, the number of emergency cases was 1,018. Although the transfer of prisoners to hospitals raises security issues, the Correctional Administration Reform Council advised that a transfer should not be avoided due to security reasons (Fukushima 2007).

The shortage of physicians in correctional facilities is a constant worry for correctional authorities. In 2007, the total number of full-time physicians was 208 falling short of the minimum number required which was 226 (Fukushima 2007).

Previous studies have demonstrated various reasons for physicians' unwillingness to work in prison settings (Sugita et al. 2010). For example, it is difficult to acquire professional skills in facilities with poor staffing levels and equipment. Furthermore, physicians are required to see all types of patients as a primary care doctor and building a good doctor-patient relationship may be difficult to achieve in this setting. Incarcerated individuals tend to be demanding and may make trivial complaints. Physicians may be at risk for unwarranted malpractice lawsuits. Later, we will discuss the serious issue personnel shortage for the proper treatment of psychiatric disorders.

13.4 Current Prison Population

13.4.1 Number of Prisoners

The highest number of prison inmates registered on record was in 1948. The number gradually decreased, reaching a record low in 1992. Since 1992, however, the number of prisoners has been increasing (Hamai 2006).

Nevertheless, only a minority of offenders are actually imprisoned. For example, the number of sentenced inmates who were newly admitted to prison in 2006 was approximately 33,000 which only accounts for 1.6 % of the cases handled by the public prosecutor's office. The average daily number of inmates in penal institutions was 80,335 (70,248 sentenced and 10,087 awaiting trial) in 2006, which was an increase of approximately 30,200 over the past decade (Correction Bureau 2009b). Since 2007, this number has slightly decreased. As of December 2008, there were 76,881 inmates (67,672 sentenced and 9,209 awaiting trial). Approximately 36.8 % of the penal institutions operate beyond capacity (Research and Training Institute 1990–2009).

Watanabe (2007) examined the relationship between criminality rates, sentencing policies, and the prison population between 1980 and 2005. He found that the average length of prison sentences among newly incarcerated inmates steadily increased during this period, which may be an important factor affecting the rapid growth of the prison population. This increase may be related to a recent trend in the courts for passing longer custodial sentences, particularly for robbery and other life-threatening offences (Research and Training Institute 1990–2009). The revision of the Criminal Law and the Criminal Procedure Law in 2004 raised the upper limits for prison terms for serious offences, which may also have had an impact on the prolongation of sentences. Although the number of personnel in penal institutions has considerably increased, the persistent overpopulation is still worrisome for authorities (Correction Bureau 2009b).

Compared to countries in Europe and North America, the size of the prison population in Japan is relatively small. International statistics (International Centre for Prison Studies 2010) regarding world prison populations, including pre-trial detainees, have revealed that prison population rates (per 100,000 of the national population) were 756 in the United States (in 2007), 116 in Canada (in 2007–2008), 153 in England and Wales (in 2008), 96 in France (in 2008) and 89 in Germany (in 2008). In contrast, the prison population rate was only 63 in Japan (in 2006).

13.4.2   Age and Gender

Since 1988, the percentage of newly admitted inmates aged 65 years or older has steadily increased both for males and females. The number of sentenced inmates aged 60 years or older increased by approximately 2.7 times from 3,158 at the end of 1996 to 8,671 at the end of 2006. As of 2008, the percentage of persons aged 65 years or older among the total of newly admitted inmates accounted for 7.0 for males and 9.3 for females (Correction Bureau 2009b; Research and Training Institute 1990–2009).

A recent survey demonstrated that elderly inmates tend to have numerous difficulties concerning health and living conditions after release. Although each institution focuses considerable attention on this disadvantaged group, additional collaborations between probation offices and medical and social welfare organizations are required to further improve rehabilitation efforts for the elderly (Research and Training Institute 1990–2009).

The aging prison population may be related to an overall trend in people arrested for criminal offenses. While the number of offenders under the age of 65 has recently declined, the number of those aged 65 or older continues to increase. The elderly are predominantly arrested for non-violent offenses, such as theft and embezzlement. Additionally, more than 80 % of elderly female offenders committed a shoplifting offense. It appears that this trend in the elderly criminal population reflects the rapid aging of Japanese society, in which over 22 % are currently older than 65 years (Research and Training Institute 1990–2009). The recent economic downturn may also be an additional reason: a growing number of elderly people who are in dire circumstances commit minor property offenses.

The number of female inmates sentenced increased by approximately 2.5 times from 1996 to 2006, accounting for 7.6 % of the total prison population in 2008 (Research and Training Institute 1990–2009). Currently, violation of the Stimulant Control Act is the most prevalent type of offense among female inmates, accounting for 35.2 % of the population.

13.5   Development of Mental Health Legislation

13.5.1   History

Before addressing the issues in prison psychiatry, we will present a review of mental health legislation in Japan. Similar to legislation regarding penal administration, mental health legislation developed as a part of a reform of the legal system in the late nineteenth century. The Act for the Custody for Insane Persons, the first law pertaining to the mentally ill, was passed in 1900. The main purpose of the law was to establish regulations regarding the custody of the insane. However, at that time, psychiatric institutions were so scarce that a large portion of the mentally disordered were confined to their own homes. After World War II, the Mental Hygiene Act was enacted (1950), which was more progressive than its predecessor.

During the late 1950s and throughout the 1960s, psychiatric practices in Japan underwent dramatic changes, including a sharp increase in the number of psychiatric beds. The government encouraged the investment of private mental hospitals. Although this policy was perceived to be innovative at the time, it brought about a range of problems due to institutionalism. Successive scandals in mental hospitals, such as the abuse and neglect of patients, were revealed during the 1970s, leading to severe criticism of psychiatric treatment. These circumstances encouraged the government to implement a radical reform of mental health legislation. After numerous debates, the Mental Health Act came into effect in 1988. This act was later replaced by the current law, the Mental Health and Welfare Act of 1995.

13.5.2 Current Law

The aim of the current law is to promote the well-being of the mentally disordered by providing them not only with medical care but also assistance for rehabilitation and social independence. Of its various provisions, the following are the most notable:

1. Designated physicians for mental health. A physician may be qualified by the Ministry of Health and Welfare to perform duties regarding restrictions of patients' rights.
2. Persons liable for the protection of patients. The guardian, spouse, or individuals who exercise parental power over a mentally disordered person shall be liable for the protection of that person.
3. Forms of hospital admission. The Act provides five forms of admission of which the following three are the most common:

   • Voluntary admission: Hospitals are obliged to admit patients upon their own request whenever possible.
   • Admission for medical care and protection: The decision regarding admission is made by a designated physician but requires the consent of the person liable for the protection of the patient. The patient's own consent is not required.
   • Involuntary admission on an order by the prefectural governor: This will be presented in the next chapter.

4. Psychiatric Review Boards. These Boards are established by the prefectural governor and are comprised of designated physicians, legal professionals, and other

expert professionals for the protection of patients' rights. The Boards, upon reviewing reports from hospitals and requests from patients, can order either a discharge or improvement in the treatment of a patient.
5. Measures for improving rehabilitation and community care. This Act provides various measures for patients living in the community, such as Mental Health and Welfare Centers and other facilities for providing outpatient medical treatment and financial support.

13.6 Management of Offenders with Mental Disorders

13.6.1 Traditional System

Managing offenders with mental disorders is a difficult task for both the mental health and criminal justice systems. Depending on the extent to which the person is held accountable for their illegal acts he or she is dealt with by either of the two systems. In terms of criminal responsibility, Article 39 of the current Criminal Law, enacted in 1907, rules that 'an incompetent person shall not be punished; a person with diminished competence shall be given a mitigation of punishment.' However, the law does not provide any procedures for the subsequent management of persons acquitted due to insanity.

Until recently, the only way to divert those persons from the criminal justice system and into the mental health system was through requests from public prosecutors for involuntary admission in accordance with the Mental Health and Welfare Act. For an offender with a mental disorder who is not indicted or acquitted by the court, the public prosecutor files a report with the prefectural governor. If, as a result of an examination by two or more independently designated physicians, the person is deemed to be unfit and liable to cause personal injury unless admitted, the prefectural governor shall order an involuntary admission to a public hospital or other designated hospital. Once introduced to the mental health system, the person is treated in the same manner as any other involuntarily admitted patient. Thus, the criminal court no longer intervenes in the management of the person.

If the court finds an offender with a mental disorder guilty and they are subsequently convicted and serve a prison sentence, they may be provided with psychiatric treatment within the correctional system.

Thus, Japan is unique in that, until recently, it did not have any specialized legal provisions for offenders with mental disorders. Those persons were managed either as involuntarily admitted hospital patients or as mentally ill prison inmates. The reform plan by the Ministry of Justice for managing offenders acquitted due to mental disorders dates back to the prewar era. The long history of disputes over this subject matter is described in further detail elsewhere (Nakatani 2000) and only certain issues will be discussed hereafter.

13.6.2   New System

A new law, the Act for the Medical Treatment and Supervision of Persons with Mental Disorders Who Caused Serious Harm (hereafter referred to "Medical Treatment and Supervision Act") was enacted in 2005 (Nakatani et al. 2010). This Act aims to provide intensive psychiatric treatment to offenders with mental disorders, attributing great importance to their reintegration into the community. Special facilities for the system are being set up in which multidisciplinary care will be provided.

Consequently, as shown in Fig. 13.1, the actual management of offenders with mental disorders involves three distinct procedures based on different laws. These procedures, which may appear complex, are concisely explained in the following paragraphs.

13.6.2.1   Procedures Based on the Mental Health and Welfare Act

In emergency cases, the police file a report with the prefectural governor on any offender who is suspected to be mentally disordered. In cases where the police do not perceive that emergency care is required, the person is sent to the public prosecutor's office. Next, based on the results of a psychiatric evaluation, the public prosecutor makes a decision on the person's criminal responsibility. If the person is deemed to be insane, the public prosecutor drops the case and files a report with the prefectural governor. However, if the person is deemed to have diminished responsibility, the charge can be dropped at the public prosecutor's discretion. Based on a report by the public prosecutor, the prefectural governor orders two or more designated physicians to conduct an examination of the individual. When the designated physicians have agreed that the person is mentally disordered and liable to cause personal injury unless admitted to hospital, the prefectural governor orders the involuntary admission of that person, which must be concluded when the person is no longer regarded as a danger to others or to oneself.

13.6.2.2   Procedures Based on the Medical Treatment
and Supervision Act

This procedure applies to an individual who commits a serious criminal offense in a state of insanity or diminished responsibility. "Serious offenses" are specifically defined under the law as follows: homicide, robbery, bodily injury, arson, and sexual crimes (rape and indecent assault). All categories, except for bodily injury, include an attempt to act. There are two channels of referral by the public prosecutor to the District Court. The first channel concerns a person for whom the public prosecutor withdraws a charge. The second channel concerns a person who is acquitted or given a mitigated sentence without imprisonment in a criminal trial. Following a

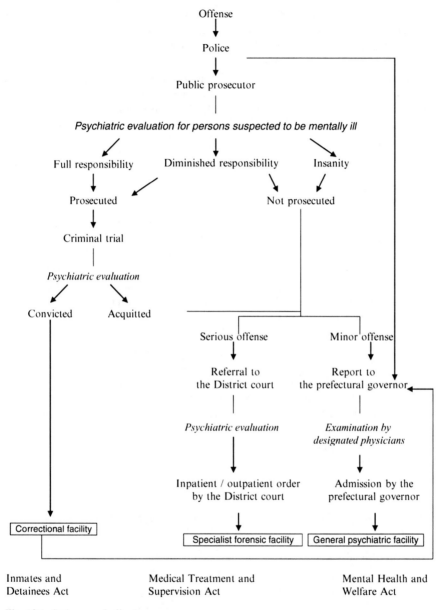

Fig. 13.1 Pathways of offenders

referral, the District Court orders a psychiatric evaluation and sets up a special panel which consists of a judge and a psychiatrist. Based on the results obtained from the psychiatric evaluation, the two panel members exchange opinions based on their respective legal and medical backgrounds and agree upon a verdict. Possible verdicts include an inpatient treatment order, an outpatient treatment order, or no treatment order. The Act stipulates that the Court shall order treatment "if it is deemed necessary to provide the person with treatment under the law in order to improve the person's mental conditions that existed at the time of the act and to promote his or her rehabilitation without recurrence of a similar act". Multi-disciplinary personnel in a "designated inpatient treatment facility" carry out the inpatient treatment. A person who is given an outpatient order or whose inpatient order is concluded is placed under "mental health supervision", according to which mental health facilities and probation services collaborate to help patients live in the community.

13.6.2.3 Procedures Based on Criminal Law

Following the prosecution of a person who is judged to have full or diminished responsibility, the Court may order an additional psychiatric evaluation. If the person is acquitted or given a mitigated sentence without imprisonment, he or she shall be placed under the Mental Health and Welfare Act (in case of minor offenses) or the Medical Treatment and Supervision Act (in case of serious offenses). Imprisoned offenders may be given psychiatric treatment in correctional institutions as discussed in the next part of this chapter.

To summarize, the Japanese legislation is unique in that offenders with mental disorders are treated within three distinct systems, namely, general psychiatry under the Mental Health and Welfare Act, specialist forensic psychiatry under the Medical Treatment and Supervision Act and prison psychiatry under the Inmates and Detainees Act. However, the links among these systems are very limited. The enforcement of the Medical Treatment and Supervision Act has certainly established a new era in the management of offenders. However, as discussed later, mentally ill inmates in correctional institutions are unlikely to benefit from this progress.

13.7   General Trends of Offenders with Mental Disorders

Based on official statistics, 2,859 offenders were mentally disordered or suspected of having a mental disorder in 2008, accounting for approximately 0.8 % of the total number of individuals arrested for penal code offenses (Research and Training Institute 1990–2009). However, since these figures are contingent upon police involvement, it is probable that the rate of mental disorders within the offending population was underestimated, particularly for those suffering from milder disorders, including mild mental retardation or certain types of personality disorders. Since the rate was reported to be 0.6 % in 1999, there has only been a slight increase over the past 10 years. The percentage rates were relatively high among individuals who committed arson (14.3 %) and homicide (10.2 %). Among those 2,859 mentally disordered offenders, 520 were not indicted by the public prosecutors and 11 were acquitted by the courts for reasons of insanity (Research and Training Institute 1990–2009).

In that same year, the public prosecutors referred 379 individuals who committed serious offenses to the District Court in accordance with the Medical Treatment and Supervision Act. The majority (88 %) of them were referred to the Court after their charges were dropped. Based on the court's decision, 257 cases were given an inpatient treatment order, while 62 were given outpatient treatment orders (Research and Training Institute 1990–2009). After the implementation of the Medical Treatment and Supervision Act in 2005, there have been no substantial changes to these figures and estimates.

According to the Mental Health and Welfare Act, persons who commit offenses that are not regarded as serious may be involuntarily admitted to a hospital based on an order from the prefectural governor. In 2008, the number of this form of admission was 2,066, accounting for 0.6 % of all admissions to psychiatric hospitals (Research Group on Mental Health and Welfare 2010). The number of these involuntary admissions has gradually decreased since the time of the Mental Hygiene Act, the predecessor of the Mental Health and Welfare Act. Since the provision for this category of admission applies not only to persons who are deemed dangerous to others, but also to those who are at risk to injure themselves, it is impossible to infer how many offenders may be included in this category.

Thus, according to the aforementioned figures and estimates there have been little increases in the number of offenders who have been treated within the provisions set forth by either general or specialist forensic psychiatry in recent years.

13.8   Prevalence of Mental Disorders Among Incarcerated Inmates

In contrast, the number of incarcerated inmates diagnosed with mental disorders is increasing in correctional institutions. Moreover, the number of inmates who were diagnosed as having any kind of mental disorder aside from personality disorders on admission has been gradually increasing. While the estimate of inmates was 876 (3.6 % of the total of newly admitted inmates) in 1999, it grew to 1,835 (6.3 % of the total of newly admitted inmates) in 2008. Among those recognized as mentally disordered in 2008, 237 had mental retardation; 253 had neurotic disorders, while 1,214 had other mental disorders, such as schizophrenia, substance use disorders, or mood disorders (Research and Training Institute 1990–2009).

Figure 13.2 illustrates the changes over the past decade based on results from a 1-day annual survey (Mochizuki et al. 2010).

The data represent two specific groups. The first group is comprised of inmates who had to leave work due to illness; while the second group was comprised of inmates who remained at work while receiving medical treatment. Presumably, the inmates from the first group suffered from more serious illnesses. In 2008, the

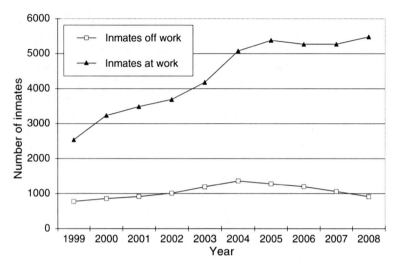

Fig. 13.2 Numbers of mentally ill inmates who are off work due to severity of illness and those who are at work while receiving treatment

number of inmates in the first group was 259 (0.3 % of the total number of inmates), while the number of inmates in the second group was 5,486 (7.1 % of the total number of inmates). Thus, the numbers had increased for both groups. In particular, the number of people in the second group had doubled over the past 10 years. As for the distribution of mental disorders according to ICD-10 (World Health Organization 1992), among the first group the diagnostic category of F2 (schizophrenia, schizotypal and delusional disorders) was most prominent, accounting for 39 % of the total. Among the second group, F1 (mental and behavioral disorders due to psychoactive substance use) was the most common diagnostic group accounting for 37 % of the total, followed by F3 (mood disorders) and F4 (neurotic, stress-related and somatoform disorders).

Although details of clinical profiles are not available, some conclusions can be drawn from the aforementioned prevalence figures. Symptoms of schizophrenia tend to be chronic and debilitating. Consequently, it appears that correctional institutions accommodate a considerable number of inmates who are unable to serve their term of "imprisonment with work" due to schizophrenia.

Additionally, the high prevalence of psychoactive substance use disorders is another important issue. It has been suggested that a large number of those inmates diagnosed with F1 disorders are addicted to methamphetamines, which is the most commonly abused drug in Japan (Research and Training Institute 1990–2009). Due to the fact that methamphetamine-induced mental disorders are often prolonged, even up to several years after cessation of substance use, some inmates with addictions may require continuous psychiatric treatment.

With regard to an increase in the number of patients with mood or neurotic disorders, the aging rate of the prison population may be relevant here; however, this cannot be confirmed due to the lack of available data.

It is interesting to compare the aforementioned figures with data and figures from international studies. For example, Fazel and Danesh (2002) examined serious mental disorders in 23,000 prisoners by reviewing 62 surveys from 12 Western countries and found that among male prisoners, 3.7 % had psychotic illnesses, and 10 % had major depression. Interestingly, among female prisoners, 4.0 % had psychotic illnesses, while 12 % had major depression. In contrast, in Japan, 1.1 % of prisoners (both male and female) were diagnosed with schizophrenia, schizotypal or delusional disorders, and 1.5 % were diagnosed with mood disorders. Therefore, the percentages of inmates with serious mental disorders in Japan appear to be substantially lower compared to Western countries. This discrepancy may be due in part to the differences observed in screening procedures for mental illnesses. In Japan, it is likely that some mentally ill inmates are overlooked due to the shortage of psychiatrists and other mental health care professionals (Kuroda 2008). However, various additional factors may contribute to this discrepancy, and further studies are needed to investigate these differences.

13.9   Ethical Issues in Prison Psychiatry

13.9.1   A Growing Burden and a Shortage in Personnel

In addition to the overcrowding and aging of the prison population, the growing number of inmates in need of psychiatric treatment is posing a heavy burden on correctional institutions. Inmates with schizophrenia requiring intensive care have steadily increased. Furthermore, the prevalence of dementia is expected to rise as a result of the rapid aging of the Japanese population. Eating disorders may pose an additional concern. According to a recent report (Satoh 2007), the medical staff in correctional institutions increasingly takes care of eating disordered females who require both physical and mental care due to a refusal of diet or self-mutilation habits.

Since most facilities are understaffed with regard to psychiatric personnel, staff experience difficulty in coping with this growing burden. As of April 2007, there were only a total of 26 full-time psychiatrists in Japanese penal institutions (Nakane 2007). Although four special medical centers are staffed with trained psychiatrists, most ordinary prisons depend on part-time psychiatrists (Kuroda 2008). As a rule, an inmate with severe mental illness is transferred to a special medical center within the prison if necessary, but transfers tend to be delayed, given the limited number of psychiatric beds (Satoh 2007).

13.9.2   Lack of Diversion Within the Systems

Realistically, it is unlikely that mentally ill inmates will be transferred from correctional institutions to general psychiatric hospitals, even if their illnesses are severe.

The rule for hospital transfers established by the Inmates and Detainees Act is generally employed for emergency cases involving only physical illnesses including myocardial or cerebral infarction. Although no exact figures are available to present, it is understood that hospital transfer of an inmate due to severe mental illness is done only for exceptional cases.

Regarding the Mental Health and Welfare Act, there are no provisions in place for prison to hospital transfers. The Medical Treatment and Supervision Act, which governs the management of offenders who are found not guilty, is also inapplicable to sentenced inmates.

Accordingly, in the Japanese system, offenders are almost exclusively treated within correctional facilities, once they are sentenced to imprisonment.

13.9.3 Discontinuity in Care

The lack of liaison between prison psychiatry and general psychiatry is most evident with regard to the subsequent psychiatric treatment of offenders released from prison. Upon release, the mentally ill may be confronted with significant obstacles in the community. Needless to say, continuity in mental health care and social support is a crucial aspect of preventing the relapse of illness and recidivism. The inconsistency within the systems, however, impedes the transition from life in prison to living in the community.

Even in cases where severely disturbed inmates require hospitalization, the only procedure for admission involves recourse to the form of involuntary admission established by the Mental Health and Welfare Act. Article 26 of the Act indicates that the head of the correctional institution must report to the prefectural governor when an inmate suspected to be mentally ill is released. If the person is deemed to be mentally disordered and liable to cause personal injury as a result of examination by two or more designated physicians, then he or she shall be admitted to a hospital based on an order from the prefectural governor.

According to nationwide statistics (Health Statistics Office 1999–2008) (see Fig. 13.3), there has been a sharp increase in the number of applications according to Article 26, from 325 applications in 1999 to 2,303 in 2008.

More prominently, this trend was also seen in a prefecture within a metropolitan area. Ashina et al. (2008) reported that, among all categories of applications for involuntary admission, those made by the head of a correctional institution have increased the most significantly. While they accounted for 1.7 % on average during a 5-year period between 1996 and 2000, this figure rose to 28 % in 2005. Ashina et al. drew attention to the fact that a large proportion of those applications concerned persons who suffered from substance use disorders or mental retardation and committed misdemeanors in poverty. Many of them had no stable home or relatives and were in need of social support.

However, as the graph in Fig. 13.3 illustrates, only a substantial minority of Article 26 cases are actually admitted to a hospital. This is presumably due to the

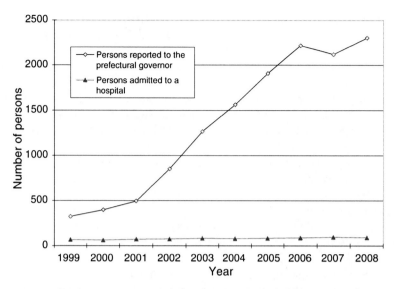

Fig. 13.3 Numbers of persons who are reported by the head of the correctional institution to the prefectural governor on release from prison and those who are actually admitted to a hospital

fact that most of those persons do not meet criteria for involuntary admission according to the Mental Health and Welfare Act, which stipulates that a person must be at risk for causing personal injury. Therefore, those who are not involuntarily admitted remain untreated, unless they seek help on their own. Additionally, it is impossible for them to enter the procedural system of the Medical Treatment and Supervision Act which does not cover admission following release from prison. Therefore, neither the Mental Health and Welfare Act nor the Medical Treatment and Supervision Act provide any effective measures for post-release care for inmates with mental disorders.

13.9.4 Insufficient Legal Safeguards

In general psychiatry, a series of legal reforms emphasizes the role of a patient's autonomy (Nakatani 2000). To prevent infringements to patients' rights, the Mental Health and Welfare Act of 1995 offers various rules including mandatory regular reports on patients' status by the superintendent of a psychiatric hospital, supervision of the Psychiatric Review Board, duties of designated physicians performing the necessary restriction of patients' actions, as well as other provisions. Chapter 5 of the Act is of particular relevance and contains rules concerning psychiatric inpatients, e.g. the assignment of a person responsible for the protection of the patient (who ensures medical treatment is delivered and represents the patient in medical decisions), voluntary and involuntary admissions, procedures necessary for seclusion and physical restraint, review of regular reports, and patients' right for requesting discharge.

It is important to note, however, that these rules (from the Mental Health and Welfare Act) do not apply to a person who is incarcerated in a correctional institution. The Psychiatric Review Boards do not intervene in the management at those facilities. In other words, the treatment of patients in correctional facilities, including special medical centers, is regulated by a different law, the Inmates and Detainee Act.

For the supervision of the treatment of inmates, the Inmates and Detainee Act established the Penal Institution Visiting Committee which is composed of a maximum of ten members who are appointed by the Ministry of Justice. The purpose of the Committee is to provide opinions regarding the treatment of prisoners to the governor of the institution through interviews with and assessments of the inmates (Correction Bureau 2009b). However, the Committee also occasionally deals with problems related to the medical treatment of patients. Thus, complaints regarding psychiatric patients may be handled by this Committee.

In 1996, the Ministry of Justice issued a notification which aimed to call attention to the early recognition of mental disorders, appropriate treatment, consultation of specialists, assistance at the time of release from prison, and so on (Kuroda 2008). Unfortunately, however, correctional institutions do not adopt the same standards of psychiatric ethics observed in general psychiatry.

13.9.5 Problems Related to Increased Severity of Punishment

Imprisonment can have a detrimental effect on mental health through confinement and isolation (Birmingham 2004). Furthermore, prisoners serving a life-sentence include a disproportionately high number of mentally ill people (Barry et al. 1993).

In Japan, criminal courts have handed out more severe punishments since the early 2000s. The increasing public concern regarding crime is one of the causes for this trend toward longer sentences (Hamai 2006). Notably, however, this increase in public concern has occurred irrespective of an actual rise in the crime rate. Evidently, this public awareness contributing to the myth of a worsening in public safety (Hamai 2006), reflects such contemporary social conditions as the high unemployment rates, changes in values and sensation-seeking media reports on atrocious crimes. The number of persons sentenced to life imprisonment with work has increased yearly. It peaked with 125 individuals in 2004, but then dropped to 63 in 2008 (Research and Training Institute 1990–2009).

Article 28 of the Criminal Law stipulates that a person sentenced to imprisonment with work shall be released on parole if the following requirements are fulfilled: clear signs of repentance, motivation to start a new life, no recidivistic behavior and the public's acceptance regarding the person's release. This provision applies to inmates serving life sentences who have already served 10 or more years of their prison term (Research and Training Institute 1990–2009).

Interestingly, the number of inmates released on parole has gradually decreased since 2004, accounting for 50.1 % of the total number of releases in 2008. For life sentenced prisoners, release on parole has become more difficult. The average number between 1981 and 1986 was 46.4; this gradually decreased to four in 2008. As for life sentenced prisoners who are released on parole before having served a maximum of 20 years, the number, which was 54 parolees in 1979, also significantly decreased. It has continued to be at the single-digit level since 1996, and there have been no parolee releases since 2003 (Correction Bureau 2009a, b).

Mentally ill inmates often serve the maximum length of their sentences, because they seldom qualify for a release on parole. Inmates in life imprisonment find themselves in bleak situations and are more likely to develop or experience an exacerbation of a mental disorder compared to their peers serving determinate sentences. Therefore, they are scarcely deemed eligible for release on parole, because it is difficult for them to display motivation to change.

In a recent study, Matsuno (2000) reported on 13 cases of life imprisonment where inmates were transferred to a special medical center for the treatment of their mental illnesses. The inmates' mental illness had become exacerbated during the course of their imprisonment. The patients were on average 67.4 years old, and 3 of the 13 had already served 45 years of their sentence. Seven had schizophrenia; the others were diagnosed with mental retardation or organic brain disease. As Matsuno demonstrated, the requirements for release on parole seem unfeasible for inmates suffering from a severe mental illness.

Capital punishment is still permitted in Japan and causes intricate problems in mental health. The number of death penalty cases rose to double-digit figures in 2000, before dropping back down to five cases in 2008 (Research and Training Institute 1990–2009). In most cases, the execution of the death penalty is carried out several years after sentencing. As a result, there has been an accumulation of inmates who are awaiting execution. As of December 31, 2008, the number of inmates to be executed was 100 (Research and Training Institute 1990–2009).

Death row inmates are prone to be mentally disturbed, and require psychiatric intervention. In certain cases, questions regarding their competency for execution are raised. In contrast to the United States where competency to stand trial or be executed is a controversial issue, in Japan it is rarely discussed. The Criminal Procedure Act stipulates that the Minister of Justice shall suspend the execution of an incompetent person. In 2005, the Japanese Society of Psychiatry and Neurology, the largest organization of mental health professionals, provided their opinion on the participation of psychiatrists in the execution of the death penalty, drawing attention to the deterioration of the mental states of death row inmates (Japanese Society of Psychiatry and Neurology 2005). The report did not clearly state that psychiatrists should not participate in this process. Rather, it emphasized the importance of investigating the actual process of how death

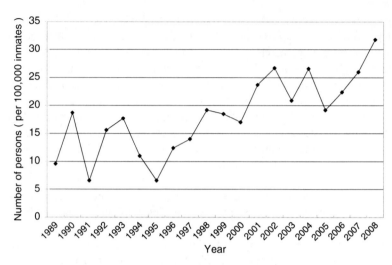

Fig. 13.4 Completed suicide per 100,000 inmates in penal institutions

row inmates are deemed to be competent, given that the process is not made public. Thus far, this matter has not been widely discussed in the psychiatric literature and warrants further attention.

13.9.6 Suicide

As illustrated in Fig. 13.4, suicide rates in penal institutions (the numbers of individuals per 100,000 inmates, including those awaiting trial) have risen, even though the increase has not been steady. In 2008, the number of completed suicides was 25, i.e. 32.2 per 100,000 inmates.

Previous research has demonstrated that the suicide rate in detention facilities in the United States was 36 in 2006 (U.S. Department of Justice 2010). In England and Wales, the average number of deaths due to suicide per 100,000 for the 3-year period ending in 2008 was 91 (BBC News 2009). Compared to these figures, the suicide rates in Japanese penal institutions are low. Nevertheless, they are not negligible given the current increasing trend. Compared to the abundance of literature on prison suicide in Western countries, professionals' concern regarding the suicide rate in Japan has thus far been limited. During the revision of the Prison Law, the problem of suicide was not discussed as an important matter (Nakane 2005). Information regarding the details of suicide cases, including demographic data, psychiatric and criminological profiles, method of suicide, as well as additional factors is not easily accessible to researchers. To the best of the authors' knowledge, there has been no systematic survey or scientific research focusing on prison suicides. However, in view of the overpopulation of facilities as well as the shortage in staff, further investigation of this critical matter is warranted.

13.10   Conclusions

Japanese correctional institutions appear to be managed well on the whole, with maintained order and relatively rare occurrences of incidents including suicide, prison escapes or riots. However, with regard to the treatment of mentally ill inmates, there are significant issues to still be resolved. Prison psychiatry is confronted with various problems including being understaffed while the number of patient is on the rise, insufficient legal safeguards, lack of a diversion system, discontinuity in psychiatric care upon release, to mention but the most notable problems.

Psychiatric treatment of offenders in Japan is based on three subspecialties, that is, general psychiatry, specialist forensic psychiatry and prison psychiatry. One concern is that prison psychiatry has been a "closed" subspecialty which has developed independent of general psychiatry, and is under the control of the criminal justice system rather than the mental health system. Accordingly, the Mental Health and Welfare Act, which controls general psychiatry, is not applicable in correctional settings.

It is possible that this situation is one of the main causes for most psychiatrists' reluctance to participate in prison psychiatry. Prisons are generally perceived as an inappropriate place for clinical practice. Therefore, the shortage of prison psychiatrists may be resolved by increasing incentives.

Thus, an important question remains. Does the recent implementation of specialist forensic psychiatry solve these problems? The new system implemented for insane persons who caused serious harm established by the Medical Treatment and Supervision Act is generally welcomed in psychiatric circles. Therefore, with huge investments, the new facilities are highly staffed, equipped and secured. Unfortunately, this high quality of treatment is inaccessible for offenders who are found guilty and imprisoned, because the Act only applies to offenders for whom the public prosecutor has withdrawn charges or those acquitted or given a mitigated sentence without imprisonment. In order to make use of the new facilities that provide proper care to imprisoned inmates, revisions of laws should be performed.

To address the problems outlined in this chapter, the diversion system at various levels of the criminal justice system established by the Mental Health Act and related laws and policies in the United Kingdom may serve as a model. According to this system, offenders, including sentenced prisoners, can be diverted to the mental health system if they need medical treatment. Barry et al. (1993) noted that a prison to hospital transfer provision is an important safeguard that ensures that severely disordered offenders are treated in the appropriate settings, though it may be underused.

To conclude, prison psychiatry should be regarded as an essential part of general psychiatry. Offender patients require more assistance than non-offender patients. From this perspective, it is essential to establish an integrated system to resolve the inconsistency between different systems for disadvantaged individuals who are both offenders and mentally ill.

References

Ashina, K., T. Ota, R. Mukai, et al. 2008. The tendency and the problems of the article 26 notification (the notification by heads of correctional institutions) in recent years——an analysis of the cases in Gunma prefecture from fiscal 2001 to fiscal 2006. *Shiho seishin igaku (Japanese Journal of Forensic Mental Health)* 3: 44–52 (in Japanese).

Barry, M., Gudjonsson, G., Gunn, J. et al. 1993. The mentally disordered offenders in non-medical settings. In *Forensic psychiatry. Clinical, legal and ethical issues*, ed. J. Gunn and P. J. Taylor, 732–793. Oxford: Butterworth-Heinemann.

BBC News .2009. Prison suicide rate cut in 2008. http://news.bbc.co.uk/2/hi/uk_news/7806840. stm. Accessed 13 Sept 2010.

Birmingham, L. 2004. Editorial: Mental disorder and prison. *The Psychiatrist* 28: 393–397.

Correction Bureau, Ministry of Justice. 2009a. Current status of correction. *Hoso jiho (Lawyers Association Journal)* 61: 1801–1878 (in Japanese).

Correction Bureau, Ministry of Justice. 2009b. *Penal institutions in Japan.* http://www.moj.go.jp/KYOUSEI/kyousei03-1.pdf. Accessed 28 Apr 2010.

Fazel, S., and J. Danesh. 2002. Serious mental disorder in 23,000 prisoners: A systematic review of 62 surveys. *Lancet* 359: 545–550.

Fukushima, Y. 2007. Current status and future issues of correctional medical treatment. *Keisei (Japanese Journal of Correction)* 118: 24–33 (in Japanese).

Hamai, K. 2006. *Hanzai tokei nyumon* (Introduction to criminal statistics). Tokyo: Nippon hyoronsha (in Japanese).

Health Statistics Office, Vital and Health Statistics Division, Ministry of Health, Labor and Welfare. *Eisei gyosei hokokurei* (Report on Public Health Administration and Services) 1999–2008. http://www.e-stat.go.jp/SGI/estat/NewList.do?tid=000001031469. Accessed 28 Apr 2010 (in Japanese).

International Centre for Prison Studies. 2010. *World prison population list*, 8th edn. http://www.kcl.ac.uk/depsta/law/research/icps/downloads/wppl-8th_41.pdf. Accessed 13 Sept 2010.

Japanese Society of Psychiatry and Neurology. 2005. The opinion of the Society on psychiatrists' participation to the execution of death penalty. Second report. *Seishin shinkeigaku zasshi (Psychiatria et Neurologia Japonica)* 107: 776–777 (in Japanese).

Kuroda, O. 2008. Current status and issues of psychiatric treatment in Japanese penal institutions. *OT Journal* 42: 1008–1013 (in Japanese).

Matsuno, T. 2000. A clinical psychiatric study on mentally disordered life-sentenced prisoners. *Kyousei igaku (Journal of Correctional Medicine)* 48: 1–12 (in Japanese).

Mochizuki, Y., M. Kato, K. Kitamura, et al. 2010. Ten-year trends in diseases of inmates in Japan 1998-2008: Target areas for strengthening correctional medical care. *Kyosei igaku (Journal of Correctional Medicine)* 58: 27–34 (in Japanese).

Nakane, K. 2005. Reform of penal administration: new development of treatment of inmates. *Reference* 657: 57–66 (in Japanese).

Nakane, K. 2007. Current status and issues of correctional medicine. *Reference* 680: 95–106 (in Japanese).

Nakatani, Y. 2000. Psychiatry and the law in Japan. History and current topics. *International Journal of Law and Psychiatry* 23: 589–604.

Nakatani, Y., M. Kojimoto, S. Matsubara, et al. 2010. New legislation for offenders with mental disorders in Japan. *International Journal of Law and Psychiatry* 33: 7–12.

Ohashi, H. 2006. History and present circumstances of correctional medicine. In *Shiho seishin igaku* (Forensic mental health), vol. 6, eds. M. Matsushita, T. Yamauchi and A. Yamagami et al. Tokyo: Nakayama shoten (in Japanese).

Research and Training Institute, Ministry of Justice. *Hanzai hakusho* (White paper on crime) 1990–2009 (in Japanese).

Research Group on Mental Health and Welfare. 2010. *Mental health and welfare in Japan 2010.* Tokyo: Taiyo Bijutsu (in Japanese).

Satoh, K. 2007. Current status and issues in Hachioji special medical center. *Keisei (Japanese Journal of Correction)* 118: 34–42 (in Japanese).

Shikita, M., and S. Tsuchiya. 1992. *Crime and criminal policy in Japan. Analysis and evolution of the Showa Era, 1926–1989.* New York: Springer.

Sugita, M., T. Honjo, H. T., et al. 2010. Symposium: Particularities and difficulties of correctional medicine. *Kyosei igaku (Journal of Correctional Medicine)* 58: 79–115 (in Japanese).

U.S. Department of Justice, National Institute of Correction.2010. *National study of jail suicide. 20 years later.* http://nicic.gov/Downloads/PDF/Library/024308.pdf. Accessed 13 Sept 2010.

Watanabe, J. 2007. The review of the impact of crime and criminal justice policy on prison population. *System Dynamics* 6: 17–28 (in Japanese).

World Health Organization. 1992. *The ICD-10 classification of mental and behavioural disorders: Clinical descriptions and diagnostic guidelines.* Geneva: World Health Organization.

Chapter 14
Overcrowded Prisons and Low Psychiatric Provision: The Situation of Mentally Ill Prisoners in Kenya

Muthoni Mathai and David M. Ndetai

14.1 Introduction

Kenya is situated in the eastern part of the African continent between 5° North and 5° South latitude and between 24° and 31° East longitude. It borders Tanzania to the South, Uganda to the West, Ethiopia and Sudan to the North, Somalia to the Northeast and the Indian Ocean to the Southeast.

The population of Kenya is estimated at 38.6 million (Kenya Bureau of Statistics (KBS) 2009). About 56 % of the Kenyan population live in poverty with over half of those living below the absolute poverty line (Kenya Demographic Health Survey 2003). Kenya has a human development index (HDI) of 0.47 ranking 128 out of a total of 169 countries in 2010 (UNDP 2010).

The number of practicing physicians has been estimated at less than 5,000 resulting in a ratio of doctors to population of 17 per 100,000 (WHO 2009). The availability of psychiatrists, however, lags far behind other medical specialties. There are an estimated 77 psychiatrists for a population of 40 million in Kenya. The majority are stationed at the teaching hospital in Nairobi or are in private practice in Nairobi. The ratio of psychiatrists to population has remained fairly stable in the last 10 years at 1: 514,200 in 1997; 1: 543,396 in 2004 and 1: 528,571 in 2006 (Ndetei et al. 2007).

Kenya shares the fate of many low income countries in having a high crime rate, a slow and inefficient judicial system and low medical coverage. The result is overcrowding of prisons and high morbidity among prisoners.

M. Mathai
Department of Psychiatry, College of Health Sciences, University of Nairobi, Nairobi, Kenya

D.M. Ndetai (✉)
University of Nairobi, Nairobi, Kenya

Africa Mental Health Foundation (AMHF), Nairobi, Kenya
e-mail: dmndetei@uonbi.ac.ke

N. Konrad et al. (eds.), *Ethical Issues in Prison Psychiatry*, International Library of Ethics, Law, and the New Medicine 46, DOI 10.1007/978-94-007-0086-4_14,
© Springer Science+Business Media Dordrecht 2013

14.2   Conditions in Kenyan Prisons

Kenya inherited the penal system from the British Colonial government on its independence in 1963. The current running of prisons is regulated by an act of parliament- The Prisons Act 1967, revised in 1977 (The Prisons Act 1967). The Penal Code and Kenya's old constitution, while having several shortcomings, contain fairy liberal laws with regards to treatment of prisoners. Kenya has also ratified a number of international instruments protecting the rights of prisoners and detainees, including the African Charter on Human and People's Rights. However, there is a big discrepancy between the legal provisions and the actual conditions in prison.

Media and other reports over the last decade have consistently pointed at prison populations three or more times larger than capacity. A 2001 report placed the population in Kenyan prisons at an average of between 36,000 and 40,000 in institutions the capacity of which is meant for approximately 14,000 (Government of Kenya and Penal Reform International 2001; Amanda, Dissel 2001).

Nearly all prisons in Kenya are characterised by overcrowding and poor living conditions. Although serious attempts have been made to improve the conditions of convicted prisoners in the last few years, the environment in remand prisons remains deplorable. Congestion, inadequate sanitary conditions and poor hygiene lead to quick spread of diseases. There is also inadequate food, clothing and bedding. There is frequent mixing of young offenders and adult offenders leading to abuse of minors. There have even been cases of suffocations and deaths due to overcrowding (Amanda, Dissel 2001; BBC News 2004; Lewis 2008). Medical and psychological/counselling services are highly compromised in these circumstances.

14.3   The Prevalence of Mental Disorders in Kenyan Prisons

Very few studies have been done on the mentally ill in Kenyan prisons. In fact there is no study looking at the prevalence and pattern of mental disorders in Kenyan prisons.

It is, however, clear that the prevalence of mental illness in Kenyan prisons should not be underestimated. A study done in Nairobi on non convicted prisoners in remand prisons is probably the best that we have to go by.

Conducted in 2006 and using the SCIDI (Structured Clinical Interview for DSM-IVAxis I disorders) and the Modified IPDE (International Personality Disorder Examination), the study found a very high level of undiagnosed psychiatric morbidity among females on remand at 84 %. Out of these, personality disorders accounted for 38 %, mood disorders for 25 %, and anxiety disorders for 29 % (panic disorders 10 %, Posttraumatic stress disorder (PTSD) 6 %, Generalized Anxiety Disorder (GAD) 7 %, social phobia 3 %). Adjustment disorders accounted for 13 %, while Obsessive Compulsive Disorder (OCD), schizophrenia, and somatization disorders constituted 3 % each. The prevalence of psychiatric disorders in males was 77 %.

Personality disorders accounted for 42 %, mood disorders 17 %, anxiety disorders 15 % (panic disorders 3 %, PTSD 9 %). OCD accounted for 3 % and somatization disorders for 3 %. No cases of GAD or social phobia were recorded among the males. Surprisingly high prevalence rates of schizophrenia at 12 % and adjustment disorder, also 12 %, were recorded. Although this study did not assess alcohol dependency, it reported 65 % substance use, particularly alcohol, among females and 67 % among males with a 12 % co-morbidity between substance use and other psychiatric disorders (Mucheru 2006).

While these figures may reflect the prevalence of psychiatric disorders among non convicted prisoners, there are certain factors which may contribute to lower figures in the convicted prison population. Among these are that being on remand is often associated with high levels of anxiety related to the uncertainty about the outcome of the court procedure – note the high levels of adjustment disorders (12 %). Secondly, it is not unusual for mentally ill persons to be temporary detained in remand institutions to be released later even without being charged once it becomes clear to the detaining authorities that they are mentally ill. In fact it is not uncommon for large numbers of homeless mentally ill persons to be collected in a kind of 'clean-up the city' action only to be released after some time – this may account for the high prevalence of schizophrenia (12 %), which is far above the prevalence of schizophrenia in the general population. Similarly, alcohol and other substance users may be arrested and detained on charges of being drunk and disorderly only to be released after a few days after paying a fine.

Another study of 2006 looked at psychiatric disorders among convicted male sex offenders at a maximum security prison. The prevalence of Axis I disorders in this study was found to be 35.5 % and the prevalence of Axis II conditions was 34.2 %. Among the Axis I disorders, 71 % were diagnoses of substance use with anxiety disorders making up for 15.8 % and mood disorders, mainly depressive, 13.1 % (Kanyanya 2006).

These two studies suggest a possible high prevalence of mental disorders in Kenyan prisons; they are, however, not a true reflection of the situation having been conducted among special groups of prisoners.

14.4 The Prisons Act with Reference to Mental Health

The welfare of sick prisoners is covered under the Prisons Act which emphasizes the prisoner's right to treatment (The Prisons Act 1967).

Section 39 reads: 'In the case of illness of a prisoner detained in a prison in which there is not suitable accommodation for such a prisoner, the officer in-charge, on the advice of the medical officer, may order his removal to a hospital and in the case of an emergency such a removal may be ordered by the officer in charge without the benefits of the medical officer.' (Prisons Act Cap 90 Section 39).

Furthermore, Section 38 specifies measures to be adopted for mentally ill prisoners: 'Whenever a medical officer is of the opinion that any prisoner is of unsound mind, he may … direct that such prisoner be removed to any mental hospital in Kenya and be there detained, and such order shall be the authority for the reception of the prisoner for his detention in such mental hospital until removed or discharged' (Prisons Act Cap 90 Section 38).

The Act stipulates that prisoners are then discharged back to prison on being found to be of sound mind or, if their imprisonment term has expired, back to the community. If, on the other hand, the imprisonment term expires before a patient is ready for discharge he can be further detained in the mental hospital as an involuntary patient under the Mental Health Act (The Prisons Act 1967; The Mental health Act 1991).

The law, therefore, does make provisions for the treatment of mentally ill patients. However, there are several hindrances to its implementation.

Under the Prisons Rules part III 25 the Act states that a medical officer should examine a prisoner on admission to prison and subsequently at least once a month (The Prisons Act 1967). Although these rules do not specify mental illness, a well qualified medical officer would be able to pick up a mental illness if he had the opportunity to spend time with each prisoner. However, with the low medical officer coverage and high turnover-rate, this ideal is rarely realised. Additionally, few of the prisons have a resident doctor; the health services in most prisons are run by less qualitfied health workers with minimal training in psychiatry.

14.5 The Organisation of Mental Health Care in Jails and Prisons

The prevailing practice in most prisons is that patients are sent to see the medical officer on request or if noticed by the warders to be sick. It is therefore often left to the judgment and will of prison warders, who have daily contact with prisoners, to recognize mentally ill prisoners and take action. Under these circumstances most mentally disordered patients remain unrecognized and untreated in prisons, sometimes with catastrophic results. In fact, patients with psychotic symptoms have been known to have been punished for what was seen as non-compliance with prisons regulations.

Even after a mental illness is recognized in a prisoner, there are barriers to entry into a treatment system. While nearly every province in Kenya has a psychiatric in-patient facility with a psychiatrist in attendance, very few district hospitals have such a facility and even more rarely a psychiatrist. Most mentally ill prisoners cannot be attended to in the prison where they are held but are referred to the provincial psychiatric hospital or the national referral hospital in Nairobi. It has been known for transfer of patients to a psychiatric hospital to be delayed for weeks or even months as arrangements are made back and forth to transfer them from one part of the country to another.

14.6   The Prevailing Conditions in Prisons

The conditions of prisons have a more negative impact on mentally ill persons compared to the mentally well prisoners. However, the wretched of the wretched are the non-convicted mentally ill persons held in remand prisons across the country awaiting trial.

If prisons are overcrowded the remand holding facilities are even worse. Sometimes they are so congested that there is barely sitting room, in small poorly ventilated dirty rooms with no sanitary facilities or water. Prisoners sleep or sit-sleep on the cement floor with barely a piece of tattered blanket. Because they have not been sentenced they are not entitled to full food rations or uniform, or any form of activity. Clothes get worn out to bare threads in remand prisons.

The hardest hit are mentally ill remanded prisoners, they are bullied and abused, their food is taken away and sometimes even the tattered clothes they have are stolen from them by other prisoners. Their level of hygiene deteriorates quickly and they are frequently inflicted by skin diseases and parasitic infestations. Due to delays in the judicial system, with frequent adjournments, they sometimes wait for a long time before getting a court hearing. There have been reports of prisoners languishing in remand for as long as 10 years waiting for their cases to be determined (Daily Nation 2010). Eventually when they get to court those who were sick have gotten worse and even those who may have been well controlled, prior to arrest, have relapsed. Confused, they are unable to plead, and at this point the magistrate may order that they be sent for psychiatric treatment until able to plead.

The sight and smell of confused mentally ill prisoners clothed with a small piece of torn blanket brought for psychiatric review at major health facilities is an experience most mental health workers in Kenya have experienced and are unlikely to forget.

The patient is lucky if his health facility has a psychiatric unit and available beds. However, before admission arrangements have to be made to have a guard released from prison duty to guard the patient. If a prison is experiencing staff shortages or has too many other patients admitted in other wards in hospital, the psychiatric patient is returned to the prison until a guard can be made available. If it is an open ward it is common practice to handcuff the patient to the bed.

Some psychiatric patients are treated as outpatients being brought for review at the hospital, a process that is often also limited by the availability of prison guards and/or transport.

14.7   The Fate of Mentally Ill Prisoners

While mentally ill patients who have committed minor crimes are often released by the courts when they eventually get there, patients who have committed serious offences or capital crimes have to be retained in psychiatric hospitals for long periods of time.

In Kenya there is only one forensic psychiatric unit – the maximum security unit of Mathari mental hospital in Nairobi. This is the facility where patients who have committed serious crimes, usually capital offences, are held for treatment. If they have not undergone trial they receive treatment until they are fit to plead. If, on the other hand, they have undergone trial and have been found guilty but insane, they are held at this facility indefinitely to await presidential pardon. Recommendation for release back into the community is based on the reports of a medical review board.

14.8   Ethical Issues Related to the Handling of Mentally Ill Prisoners

While there may be many ethical issues related to the management of mentally ill prisoners, the glaring ethical issues are related to violations of their human rights through denial of treatment, either because their being ill is unrecognised or denied, or because there are no facilities for treating them, and being held under extreme inhumane conditions in the remand prisons for long periods of time awaiting the wheels of a slow, inefficient judicial process to turn.

Verbal reports from patients seem to indicate that mentally ill persons in Kenyan prisons are often stigmatized and verbally and physically abused by the prison personnel.

These are the issues that have to be addressed as a matter of urgency – mentally ill persons should not be doubly punished for whatever misdemeanour or crime or supposed crime they have committed by being held in inhumane conditions. There is a need to address the issue of early recognition of mental illness in prisoners and removal to an environment where they can have the benefit of treatment in reasonable settings.

Forensic Psychiatry as a speciality in Kenya is poorly developed. All psychiatrists, in particularly those in public service, are called upon to act in the capacity of a forensic psychiatrist. The shortage of trained mental health workers in the country is not going to be solved soon as much depends on shifting the recognition of mental disorders to correction officers and the medical personnel in charge of prison facilities. Indeed where there are police officers or prisons officers who have had the benefit of increased awareness of mental illnesses, a large number of arrested patients find their way to psychiatric units because such officers are quick to recognise the problem and transfer the patient without holding them at the remand centres.

14.9   The Future

The future welfare of prisoners and mentally ill prisoners in Kenya is bound to change dramatically under the Bill of Rights of the new Kenyan constitution. Under paragraph 21 (2) – 'All state organs and all public officers have the duty to address the needs of vulnerable group within society...' (included in the list of these groups are persons with disabilities). Paragraph 21(4) goes on to emphasize the state's commitment to international obligations- 'The state shall enact and implement legislation to fulfill its international obligations in respect of human rights and fundamental freedoms.'

Paragraph 25 refers to rights and fundamental freedoms which shall not be limited – freedom from torture and cruel, inhuman or degrading treatment or punishment.

Paragraph 28 emphasizes the right to human dignity: 'Every person has inherent dignity and a right to have that dignity protected'.

Paragraph 29 – on freedom and security of the persons – prohibits deprivation of freedom arbitrarily or without just cause, detention without trial, violence from public or private sources, torture, physical or psychological, corporal punishment and treatment or punishment in a cruel, inhuman or degrading manner.

Furthermore paragraph 49 – Rights of arrested persons – covers what has long been seen as overdue, the holding of mentally ill persons on remand: It states that such persons are to be brought before a court and charged as soon as reasonably possible but not later than 24 h after being arrested (Constitution of Kenya (Amendment) Bill 2010).

The welfare and humane treatment of mentally ill prisoners is clearly covered under the Bill of Rights but the question remains: how soon and how thoroughly will it be implemented, and will the State set aside the necessary resources to make this possible?

References

Amanda, Dissel. 2001. Prison conditions in Africa. Research report written for the Centre for the study of Violence and Reconciliation. ppja.org/regional-information/africa/prison%20Africa. pdf. Sept 2001.

BBC NEWS/Africa/Kenya prison conditions slammed, September 29, 2004. http://news.bbc. co.uk/2/hi/3701398.stm.

Constitution of Kenya (Amendment) Bill. 2010. *Government of Kenya*. Nairobi: The Government Printer.

Daily Nation. February 14, 2010. Thousand languish in Kenyan Prisons. http://www.nation.co.ke/ News/-/1056/862008/-/vqj44i/-/index.html.

Kanyanya, I. M. 2006. Psychiatric morbidity among convicted male sex offenders at Kamiti maximum security prison. Unpublished dissertation of the department of Psychiatry, College of Health Sciences, University of Nairobi.

Kenya 2009 population and housing census highlights 2010. www.knbs.or.ke/Census%20Results/ KNBS%20Brochure.pdf.

Kenya Demographic Health Survey. 2003. National Council for Population and Development, Central Bureau of Statistics, Office of the vice president, Ministry of Planning and National development [Kenya], & Macro International Inc, Calverton Maryland (USA).

Lewis, R. 2008. Human Rights House Foundation (HRHF) Norway: Report based on coverage by the KHRC, Oscar Foundation, Free Legal Aid Clinic Kenya case study on the Thika prison, IRIN Africa, and Sunday Monitors Kampala newspaper. http://humanrightshouse.org/ Articles/5465.html.

Mucheru, M.E. 2006. Undiagonsed Psychitric morbidity among remanded prisoners in Nairobi, Kenya. Unpublished dissertation of the department of Psychiatry, College of Health Sciences University of Nairobi.

Ndetei, D.M., F.A. Ongecha, V. Mutiso, et al. 2007. The challenges of human resources in mental health in Kenya. *South African Psychiatry Review* 10: 33–36.

Penal Reform International. 2001. *Towards methods of improving prison policy in Kenya*. Penal Reform International. Details of the 2001 roundtable conference on Kenyan prison policy, organised by the government of Kenya and PRI, with the support of the Foreign and Commonwealth Office of the United Kingdom. www.penalreform.org/files/rep-2001-improving-kenyan-policy-en.pdf.

The Mental health Act. 1991. *Government of Kenya. Laws of Kenya. Chapter 248*. Rev. ed.. Nairobi: The Government Printer.

The Prisons Act. 1967. *Government of Kenya. Laws of Kenya. Chapter 90*. Rev. ed. 1977. Nairobi: The Government Printer.

UNDP. 2010. Human development report. http://hdrstats.undp.org/en/countries/profiles/KEN.html.

WHO. (2009). *Kenya country profile. WHO humanitarian appeal*. Country Kenya.

Chapter 15
Ethical Problems of Forensic and Prison Psychiatry in Latvia

Māris Taube

15.1 The Prevalence of Psychiatric Disorders in Latvian Prisons and Available Treatment

Latvia is one of the three Baltic States and is located on the Eastern shores of the Baltic Sea. It was a part of the Soviet Union until 1991 when it regained its independence. The area of Latvia is 65,589 km² and it has a population of approximately 2.26 million. The ethnic composition is 59.3 % ethnic Latvians, 27.8 % ethnic Russians, 3.6 % ethnic Belarusians, 2.5 % ethnic Ukrainians, 2.4 % ethnic Poles and 4.4 % other nationalities. Latvia is a democratic parliamentary republic. It joined the European Union in 2004 (Latvian Institute 2010).

15.1.1 The Structure of the Prison System in Latvia

Latvia had 11 high-security and one minimum-security prison in 2009 as well as one detention centre for juvenile offenders. There were 6,873 people in prison on 1 January 2009 (Puķīte 2009); 4,981 of them had already been sentenced while 1,892 were awaiting sentencing. The rate of people in prison per 100,000 of the population is more than 300; this is higher than most other European countries. The large number of prisoners who are currently in prison but who have not been sentenced gives cause for concern regarding the speed at which the courts operate and can create additional risks for the development of mental and behavioural disorders.

M. Taube (✉)
Department of Psychiatry and Addiction Disorders,
Rīga Stradiņš University, Rīga, Enkuru Street 2, Saulkrasti, LV 2161, Latvia
e-mail: taube@latnet.lv

N. Konrad et al. (eds.), *Ethical Issues in Prison Psychiatry*, International Library of Ethics, Law, and the New Medicine 46, DOI 10.1007/978-94-007-0086-4_15,
© Springer Science+Business Media Dordrecht 2013

15.1.2   The Health Care System in Prisons

The health care system in prisons in Latvia has been developed separately from the public health care system. The European Committee for the Prevention of Torture and Inhuman or Degrading Treatment or Punishment has expressed its concerns regarding this situation, based on its regular visits to Latvia since 1999 (CPT 2001). The health care system in prisons is regulated by the Regulations of the Cabinet of Ministers (Ministru kabinets 2007); these stipulate that prisoners can obtain primary medical care, except planned dental treatment, and secondary health care. All emergency care services are also available to prisoners. Out-patient care is provided in the Medical Department of the prison, and in-patient care is provided in the Prison Hospital. The regulations determine that a prisoner has to undergo a health check on entry into prison and an annual health check, including a physical and mental health review. The regulations also stipulate that prisoners receive the most effective and cheapest medicine which has to be administered in the presence of prison staff.

The European Commission has drawn attention to the unsatisfactory treatment of prisoners in the Prison Hospital mainly because of unsuitable facilities. Consequently, the state built a new Prison Hospital at the cost of 6.2 million lats (8.82 million Euros) in 2007. The new hospital has four units – a surgery unit with 25 beds, a general medical unit with 45 beds, a tuberculosis unit with 30 beds and a psychoneurological unit with 60 beds (Puķīte 2008). The Psychoneurological Unit is designated for patients with mental and behavioural disorders, particularly those prisoners who suffer from mental and behavioural disorders as a result of the use of psychoactive substances. Before the new hospital was built patients with mental and behavioural disorders were treated in the old hospital. It must be said that this hospital did not meet the requirements of a health care institution in Latvia. The European Commission applauded the opening of the new hospital (CPT 2009). A variety of specialists are employed in the hospital, including a cardiologist, a traumatologist, an ophthalmologist, an ear, nose and throat doctor, an endocrinologist, an endoscopist, a specialist in functional diagnostics and an addiction psychiatrist. It may be significant that the number of psychiatrists was increased from two in the old hospital to four in the new one.

15.1.3   Mental and Behavioural Disorders in Prisons

Unfortunately, there has been no scientific research regarding the prevalence of mental and behavioural disorders in prisons in Latvia. Consequently, data has to be obtained from official reports or statistical reviews of prisons. These reports are prepared annually by the Latvian Prison Administration, which is part of the Ministry of Justice. They are based on the documented information regarding the health problems of prisoners in all Latvian prisons and are publicly available. The Prison Hospital also prepares statistical reviews which provide information

Table 15.1 Prevalence of mental and behavioural disorders in prisons in Latvia between 2007 and 2009 (Puķīte 2008, 2009; CPT 2001)

	1 January 2007	1 January 2008	1 January 2009
Total number of prisoners	6,548	6,548	6,873
Prisoners with mental and behavioural disorders, except those who have mental and behavioural disorders as a result of psychoactive substance use	3,582	4,113	5,438
Prisoners with mental and behavioural disorders a result of psychoactive substance use	1,091	1,056	1,235

regarding the number of patients who have spent time in the Prison Hospital by diagnosis, number of hospital days, etc. The assessment of the state of health of new prisoners and the annual health checks also allow for the collection of information regarding the number of people with mental and behavioural disorders in prisons. Table 15.1 demonstrates that the number of people with mental and behavioural disorders in prisons is very high.

It is disturbing that on 1 January 2009, 79 % of all prisoners were diagnosed as having mental and behavioural disorders, excluding those with mental and behavioural disorders resulting from psychoactive substance use. The figure was 63 % in 2008.

Six people committed suicide in prisons in Latvia in 2006, compared with 7 in 2007 and 4 in 2008 (Puķīte 2007, 2008, 2009). The number of suicides in Latvia in 2008 was 5.8 per 10,000 prisoners. By comparison, the average rate in Europe was 9.9 per 10,000 in 2004. The highest rate was in Slovenia – 27.3 per 10,000 – while the rate in Lithuania was 14.1 and 6.3 per 10,000 in Estonia (Stöver et al. 2008).

15.1.4   In-Patient Care in the Prison Hospital

Practically all prisoners with mental and behavioural disorders are treated in the psychoneurological unit of the Prison Hospital when they need in-patient care. It is therefore useful to analyse the statistical information available on those patients. Analysis reveals that 122 prisoners with mental and behavioural disorders were placed in in-patient care in 2009. This means that only 1.8 % of all prisoners with mental and behavioural disorders received in-patient psychiatric treatment. It is possible that cases with neurotic, stress-related and somatoform disorders or disorders of adult personality did not require in-patient care. However, it is unlikely that this applies to all prisoners with disorders like this. Table 15.2 shows the distribution of in-patients admitted to the Prison Hospital in 2009 by diagnosis.

As can be seen from Table 15.2, patients suffering from organic, including symptomatic mental disorders and neurotic, stress-related and somatoform disorders, comprised the largest group. However, the longest term treatment based on average

Table 15.2 The distribution of in-patients admitted to the Prison Hospital in 2009 classified by diagnosis according to the ICD-10 Classification of Mental and Behavioural Disorders

Diagnosis	Number of in-patients
Organic, including symptomatic, mental disorders F00–F09	35
Mental and behavioural disorders due to psychoactive substance use F10–F19	9
Schizophrenia, schizotypal and delusional disorders F20–F29	19
Mood (affective) disorders F30–F39	4
Neurotic, stress-related and somatoform disorders F40–F49	25
Disorders of adult personality and behaviour F60–F69	19
Mental retardation F70–F79	11
Total	122

bed days per patient was found in the group suffering from schizophrenia, schizotypal and delusional disorders. The average length of treatment in hospital for patients with disorders of this kind was 62.4 days while the average length of treatment in hospital for patients of all mental and behavioural disorders (F00–F99) was 34.2 days. The comparatively small number of patients diagnosed as psychotic in the Prison Hospital compared to the number of patients diagnosed as neurotic could be explained by the fact that psychotic patients are more often defined as insane and undergo treatment in secure psychiatric units or psychiatric hospitals. If a person becomes mentally ill while he/she is in prison, then the length of custody is reviewed by the Criminal Court system so that the person can receive treatment outside prison as soon as possible.

15.1.5 Human Resources

Taking into account the high prevalence of mental and behavioural disorders in prisons, it is important to understand the resources of medical staff available for the treatment of patients. 15 social workers were employed in prisons in 2008, providing individual or group treatment; they carried out 2,455 individual consultations. There were 18 psychologists working in prisons in 2008. They provided consultations as requested by the prisoners, interventions in crises related to suicidal behaviour and psychological diagnostics. There were 1,762 individual consultations and 2,124 series of consultations provided. An individual consultation consists of one session with a psychologist. If the issue is not resolved in one session, then a series of consultations takes place. 800 psychological profiles of prisoners were written, as well as 2,257 psychodiagnostics and 187 interventions in cases of crisis were carried out in 2008 (Pukīte 2009). It is possible that these activities helped to reduce the prevalence of mental and behavioural disorders. It is also important to mention that a great deal of support is given to training and employment activities for prisoners. For example, 2,278 prisoners were involved in educational activities in 2008 and

1,379 prisoners took part in different types of employment activities. Spiritual support also plays an important role. This can take the form of services of different religions, individual support from chaplains, Christian educational activities, etc.

15.2   The System and Scope of Forensic Psychiatry

When evaluating the ethical aspects of forensic psychiatry, it is important to be aware of the system of forensic psychiatry in Latvia, its scope and specific features. The evidence of forensic psychiatric experts can often determine the future of an individual – e.g. he/she will receive psychiatric treatment in a hospital or will serve a sentence in prison.

Forensic psychiatry is a sub-discipline of psychiatry in Latvia. A forensic psychiatrist is a specialist psychiatrist. Consequently, they need to acquire additional knowledge and practical skills to obtain this status. The task of forensic psychiatrists is to study the clinical expressions of psychological disturbances, provide diagnoses, predict the potential development of the disorders and associated risk and to provide treatment along with rehabilitation. All these tasks have to be implemented within a particular legal framework (Taube et al. 2007).

If, during legal proceedings, suspicion arises that a person could have mental health problems which have influenced his/her behaviour during the process of committing a crime, a forensic psychiatrist becomes involved. Forensic psychiatry is regulated by a number of specific laws. The most significant of them are the Criminal Law (Saeima 1998b), the Law of Criminal Procedure (Saeima 2005), the Civil Law (Saeima 1937), the Law of Civil Procedures (Saeima 1998a) and the Law of Forensic Experts (Saeima 2006). The most important question that the court needs to answer is if the person, during the process of committing a crime, was of sound mind or not - which means that the person because of his/her mental disorder or mental illness could not understand or manage his/her behaviour (Saeima 2005). In Latvian legislation, apart from the concept of insanity, there is also a concept of diminished responsibility, which means that a person, during the process of committing a crime, was not fully able to understand his/her actions or to manage these actions as a result of his/her psychiatric disorder. In order to determine responsibility, the court appoints appropriate individuals to carry out psychiatric or psychological or complex examinations. Complex is taken to mean – a combination of psychiatric and psychological investigations. From an ethical point of view very sensitive issues are sometimes arbitrated in a civil court when assessing the ability of a person to manage a property or financial resources. The number of examinations undertaken in Latvia between 2006 and 2008 are shown below in Table 15.3.

Examinations of people who could have mental health problems which have influenced their behaviour during the process of committing a crime can be carried out in out-patient units at psychiatric hospitals or in psychiatric hospitals as an in-patient. The court experts can be invited to attend court sessions to give evidence during the trial; experts testified in 450 cases in 2008. If a person has committed a

Table 15.3 The number of examinations carried out in Latvia by types of examinations 2006–2008

Type of expertise	2006	2007	2008
Psychiatric examinations	903	1,006	1,077
Psychological examinations	29	32	75
Complex – psychiatric and psychological examinations	338	404	257
Total number of examinations	1,270	1,442	1,409

very serious crime and has been arrested and remanded in a high security prison, the examination is carried out in a specialised unit with similar security systems to those in prison. There is only one department authorised to carry out these specialised psychiatric examinations in Latvia. This is a psychiatric unit in Rīga that can guarantee an appropriate level of security. The unit is well-equipped and conforms to the requirements of a psychiatric hospital. It is quite common that prisoners who do not have any mental disorders simulate them to spend some time in a hospital which provides a higher level of comfort compared to a prison.

The results of an analysis of forensic examinations conducted in 2008 show that the minority of examinations concluded that the examinee was "insane". Of 817 examinations carried out in 2008, 117 concluded that the examinee was not mentally disordered; in a further 100 cases more investigations were deemed to be necessary (new examination in different settings, other methods, use of different experts, etc.). However, in 600 cases mental and behavioural disorders were established. Of these 600 people with mental and behavioural disorders only 177 could be described as "insane" and 62 as having diminished responsibility. Table 15.4 shows the relationship between the diagnosis in the examination and the recommendations for an individual to be declared insane or having diminished responsibility.

It can be seen that insanity or diminished responsibility are most often linked with organic – including symptomatic – mental disorders, schizophrenia, schizotypal and delusional disorders and mental retardation.

After taking expert opinion, the court determines the method of compulsory medical treatment for those patients judged to be insane or having diminished responsibility based on the evidence of the forensic expert. These compulsory medical treatment options are defined in the Law of Criminal Procedures (Saeima 2005). They are: out-patient treatment, inpatient treatment in a general psychiatric hospital or general hospital psychiatric unit or treatment in a secure psychiatric clinic or unit. The secure psychiatric unit is similar to the specialised unit for forensic examinations described in 2.5 in that it provides a security system equivalent to a prison. This unit was established based on high standards of psychiatric treatment and takes into account the fact that patients are treated in this unit for a prolonged time and also that their mental and behavioural disorders are serious. The unit is legally part of a psychiatric hospital although it is situated outside the premises. There is only one secure forensic unit of this type in Latvia which is located in Rīga. The unit was established with the support of the Psychiatric and Psychotherapy Clinic of Bayreuth, Germany (Prof. M. Wolfersdorf, Director). There are only 4 patients in

Table 15.4 The relationship between the diagnosis after examination and compulsory medical treatment in Latvia in 2008

Diagnosis	Number of examinations	Recommended to be recognised as having diminished responsibility	Recommended to be recognised as insane
Organic, including symptomatic, mental disorders F00–F09	174	14	34
Mental and behavioural disorders as a result of psychoactive substance use F10–F19	49	–	8
Schizophrenia, schizotypal and delusional disorders F20–F29	111	6	94
Mood (affective) disorders F30–F39	9	1	1
Neurotic, stress-related and somatoform disorders F40–F49	10	1	1
Behavioural syndromes associated with physiological disorders and somatic factors F50–F59	1	–	–
Disorders of adult personality and behaviour F60–F69	62	3	1
Mental retardation F70–F79	168	37	38
Behavioural and emotional disorders with onset usually occurring in childhood and adolescence F90–F98	16	–	–
Total	600	62	177

each room. Patients have access to a well-equipped sports hall and there are occupational therapy, cooking and gardening activities. All activities are highly structured; this is possible because of the relatively high staffing levels compared to other psychiatric units. The quality of treatment, rehabilitation and the premises themselves are also better than other psychiatric units. Patients who develop mental disorders while in prison receive treatment in the psychoneurological unit of the Prison Hospital.

When determining compulsory medical treatment, the court takes into account the recommendations of the forensic experts. Nevertheless, the court makes the final decision and may invite other experts, order more examinations or go against the recommendations of the experts. The adoption of the Law on Forensic Experts (Saeima 2006) has played an important role in the establishment of the forensic psychiatric and court medical systems in Latvia. The court medical systems are complex in their approach to carrying out all the necessary examinations – technical, medical, psychiatric, etc. This law has defined the status of the forensic expert, the institutions which can carry out the examinations, the procedures regarding the certification of experts, the necessity to establish a register of experts, the organisation of the Board of Forensic Experts and other issues (Saeima 2006).

There are several types of compulsory medical treatment in Latvia associated with different levels of restrictiveness. The least restrictive measure is out-patient treatment followed by in-patient care. The most restrictive measure is in-patient care in a secure psychiatric unit. Out-patient care is usually provided in the out-patient department of a psychiatric hospital close to where the patient lives. In-patient treatment is carried out in a psychiatric unit or a psychiatric hospital and also based on where the patient lives. However, secure forensic-psychiatric treatment is only provided in Rīga. If the condition of a patient improves during treatment and the risk of him/her committing a further crime is considered to be decreased, those involved in the treatment of the patient can advise the court to change the compulsory medical treatment from a more to a less restrictive measure or to discontinue the treatment. The court does not decide the length of treatment; the main reason to change or discontinue compulsory medical treatment is the state of health of the patient. The court reviews the necessity to change or discontinue compulsory medical treatment at 6-month intervals. The usual practice is that treatment in the secure forensic-psychiatric unit is changed to treatment in a general psychiatric hospital or unit and later to out-patient care when possible. The final step is the termination of compulsory medical treatment. In general, these patients are treated together with other patients in psychiatric hospitals or units. This is because there are no specialised units except one secure forensic-psychiatric unit where patients are treated for a prolonged time, including lifelong treatment. When patients are treated as out-patients they have to visit a psychiatrist regularly – at least once a month – and if necessary, take medication. All patients who receive compulsory medical treatment are registered because of the extent of risk.

15.3 Ethical Aspects in Forensic and Prison Psychiatry

Despite the recent positive developments in Latvian forensic and prison psychiatry mentioned, there are still a number of ethical problems which need to be resolved.

One of the problems is the separation of forensic psychiatry from the general state system of psychiatry. Prisoners should be able, if necessary, to receive the same psychiatric treatment as those people in mainstream society. However, there are several forms of treatment such as occupational therapy and psychosocial reha-bilitation which are only available to a limited extent to prisoners. The new Prison Hospital is under the supervision of the Ministry of Justice and therefore falls outside the general health care system. The Regulations of the Cabinet of Ministers Regarding the Organisation of the Health Care System and its Financing (Ministru kabinets 2006) stipulate that the costs of health care services for imprisoned people are part of the budget of the Ministry of Justice. In reality, this means that people in prison are allocated less financial resources for medical services compared to patients outside the prison system. This is directly linked with, for example, access to new generation medicine. As a result of limited financial resources the Prison Hospital could have problems providing its patients with new generation medicine.

The subsistence cost for one prisoner in hospital was 17 Euro/day in 2007 (Puķīte 2008); this makes it unlikely for patients to receive atypical neuroleptics, the daily cost of which can be approximately 10 Euro. Nevertheless, the Prison Hospital provides patients with the necessary medicine but chooses the cheapest. Occasionally a discussion arises regarding the equivalence of care. It is argued that any person who has paid his/her taxes should be entitled to adequate health care, including prisoners. This issue is not only financial but ethical. However, the health and psychiatric care of prisoners is not seen as an important issue in society, particularly in these difficult financial times.

The biggest problems occur for those patients with mental and behavioural disorders who have to return to prison following treatment in the Prison Hospital and to continue medical treatment. There is a difference between the way that the state finances the treatment and reimburses the use of pharmaceuticals for imprisoned patients. In general, patients with mental and behavioural disorders in mainstream society have unlimited access to out-patient visits to a psychiatrist. These visits would be state – financed and the costs for drugs would also be fully or partly state – financed. However, even in the general community, there are still differences in the financial support of medication for particular patient groups. For example, individuals diagnosed as clinically depressed receive medication at 50 % of the normal cost but those with schizophrenia receive them free of charge. This compensation method also includes newer generation pharmaceuticals. Unfortunately, the payment system described above does not apply to prisoners because their health care services are provided from the smaller budget of the Ministry of Justice. It is therefore possible that a patient who has received a specific kind of high quality medication before imprisonment will not receive the same medication in prison. As a comparison, the Regulations of the Cabinet of the Ministers regarding the Organisation of the Health Care System and its Financing (Ministru kabinets 2006) state that prisoners who have HIV/AIDS or tuberculosis can receive specific pharmaceuticals which are guaranteed from the budget of the Ministry of Health but prisoners who have mental and behavioural disorders can only receive the necessary medicine from the budget of the Ministry of Justice.

A similar problem arises regarding access to methadone substitution. Users of opiates can receive methadone substitution therapy in the community but when they are imprisoned this therapy is not available. The United Nations Office on Drugs and Crime (UN Office on Drugs and Crime 2009) actively supports the implementation of methadone substitution therapy as a right. It has recommended the introduction of changes to the legal system in Latvia to ensure that methadone substitution therapy for drug addicts is available in prisons. The attitude of prison governors was sceptical and negative at first; some say this is understandable given the problems linked to the illegal use of drugs in prisons in Latvia and concerns regarding the dishonest use of methadone substitution therapy.

Another ethical problem in forensic psychiatry is the timely access to medical examinations for those patients with mental and behavioural disorders when issues regarding criminal responsibility are raised. Those in remand have to spend lengthy periods of time in prison awaiting sentencing; this is not regarded as acceptable in some European countries. Latvia has already lost several cases in the European Court of Human Rights (European Court of Human Rights 2007) because of these delays.

Examinations of those people arrested and who have mental and behavioural disorders are carried out in the secure forensic-psychiatric examination unit in Rīga. The conditions there are good and opportunities for medical treatment are freely available. This creates another potential ethical problem; some prisoners who do not have mental and behavioural disorders pretend to have them in order to stay in this more comfortable and less restrictive environment. Some have used this unit as a mean of escape from prison. Staff are medically qualified but may not be highly experienced in matters of security. It is also possible that prisoners with mental and behavioural disorders are placed with those who do not have these disorders. This situation cannot guarantee a safe environment for patients but instead can create a situation where criminals can influence patients.

When a patient has been diagnosed as being of diminished responsibility or as insane he/she can receive the necessary treatment. However, there is still a concern because of the heavy work load of the courts and the length of the legal proceedings. This means that patients with mental and behaviour disorders can spend lengthy periods waiting for sentencing and cannot gain access to the necessary treatment.

Another ethical problem is linked to the fact that the experts in forensic psychiatry bear a significant ethical and legal responsibility because their opinion may directly affect the future of a patient or criminal. There is always a risk that somebody will simulate mental and behavioural disorders to avoid punishment and, after spending several years in a psychiatric hospital, can be released. According to the Law of Criminal Procedure (Saeima 2005), any medical institution can ask a court to change the compulsory medical treatment if a patient is considered to have recovered. The duration of compulsory medical treatment is not linked to the duration of sentence that would be given to this person for their crime if he/she would not have been recognised as having reduced responsibility.

The experts providing forensic-psychiatric opinions need high levels of professional skill and integrity to avoid being influenced in their work. Psychiatric experts in Latvia have a long tradition of high levels of psychiatric skills stretching back to the historical influences of Russian and German nosological psychiatry. Additional skills and competencies are necessary when determining if a prisoner has diminished responsibility or is insane. This practice, although quite common in Europe, is new in Latvia. When assessing the possibility of diminished responsibility, attention has to be paid to the specific characteristics of the defendant and also to the circumstances of the crime. Unfortunately, the idea and definition of diminished responsibility can be very tempting for criminals and can add to the ethical and legal pressure on experts.

There is also another aspect in dispute. This is the diagnosis of being "socially dangerous". The relevant legislation in Latvia stipulates that a person who has committed a crime and, as a result of medical examination, has been ordered to receive compulsory medical treatment has to be automatically registered as a socially dangerous person. This status does not depend on the seriousness of the crime – a person who has committed a similar crime but has not been ordered to receive compulsory medical treatment would not be defined as a socially dangerous person. At the same time the Law on the Criminal Process (Saeima 2005) outlines several options for compulsory medical treatment methods as described above. As an alternative to compulsory medical treatment the law stipulates that, if a patient is not regarded as socially dangerous, he/she can be trusted to the care of his/her relatives or other care-providers under the supervision of a health care institution and based on where the patient lives without extra restrictions. The definition of socially dangerous allows for individuals to be cared for by their relatives, but brings with it a number of consequences. For example, a person has to be registered and can be subject to visits by police, psychiatrists, etc. This issue of defining a person as socially dangerous has also been discussed in conjunction with the development of the Law on Psychiatric Assistance. Defining someone as a socially dangerous person and the register of socially dangerous people causes human rights concerns and the rights of individuals in society. Some think that the criteria for defining the status of a socially dangerous person have to be more precisely defined by the courts on a case by case basis.

It is a strange phenomenon – that general psychiatric units and hospitals in Latvia receive less money and therefore less staff and treatment options than the secure psychiatric unit in Rīga. As a result, when the medical conditions of patients improve and they receive permission from the court to continue their psychiatric treatment in a general psychiatric hospital or unit, they may be unhappy about this as they do not understand why they are not provided with the same level of rehabilitation, occupational therapy activities and sports activities or why they have to share a room with 5 or 6 other patients. At the moment, however, the overall situation of psychiatric hospitals and units is improving and patients can receive more appropriate levels of treatment in general psychiatric settings.

References

European Committee for the Prevention of Torture and Inhuman or Degrading Treatment or Punishment (CPT). 2001. Report to the Latvian Government on the visit to Latvia carried out by the European Committee for the Prevention of Torture and Inhumane or Degrading Treatment or Punishment (CPT). http://www.cpt.coe.int/documents/lva/2001-27-inf-eng.pdf. Accessed 18 Feb 2010.
European Committee for the Prevention of Torture and Inhuman or Degrading Treatment or Punishment (CPT). 2009. Report to the Latvian Government on the visit to Latvia carried out by the European Committee for the Prevention of Torture and Inhumane or Degrading Treatment or Punishment (CPT). http://www.cpt.coe.int/documents/lva/2009-35-inf-eng.pdf. Accessed 21 Feb 2010.
European Court of Human Rights. 2007. Affaire Nazarenko c. Lettonie, http://cmiskp.echr.coe.int/tkp197/portal.asp?sessior. Accessed 6 Mar 2010.
Latvian Institute. 2010. http://www.li.lv/index.php?option=com_content&task=view&id=12&Itemid=1060. Accessed 18 Feb 2010.
Ministru kabinets. 2006. Ministru kabineta noteikumi nr. 1064 Veselības aprūpes organizēšanas un finansēšanas kārtība. http://www.likumi.lv/doc.php?id=150766. Accessed 5 Mar 2010.

Ministru kabinets. 2007. Ministru kabineta noteikumi nr. 199 Noteikumi par apcietināto un
notiesāto personu veselības aprūpi izmeklēšanas cietumos un brīvības atņemšanas iestādēs.
http://www.likumi.lv/doc.php/doc.php?id=154964&from=off. Accessed 18 Feb 2010.

Puķīte, V. 2007. Latvijas Republikas Tieslietu ministrijas Ieslodzījuma vietu pārvaldes 2006. gada
publiskais pārskats. Latvijas Republikas Tieslietu ministrijas Ieslodzījuma vietu pārvalde.
http://www.ievp.gov.lv/?sadala=92. Accessed 21 Feb 2010.

Puķīte, V. 2008. Latvijas Republikas Tieslietu ministrijas Ieslodzījuma vietu pārvaldes 2007. gada
publiskais pārskats. Latvijas Republikas Tieslietu ministrijas Ieslodzījuma vietu pārvalde.
http://www.ievp.gov.lv/?sadala=92. Accessed 18 Feb 2010.

Puķīte, V. 2009. Latvijas Republikas Tieslietu ministrijas Ieslodzījuma vietu pārvaldes 2008. gada
publiskais pārskats. Latvijas Republikas Tieslietu ministrijas Ieslodzījumu vietu pārvalde.
http://www.ievp.gov.lv/?sadala=92. Accessed 18 Feb 2010.

Saeima. 1937. Civillikums. http://www.likumi.lv/doc.php?id=90223. Accessed 28 Feb 2010.

Saeima. 1998a. Civil Procedure Law. http://www.likumi.lv/doc.php?id=50500. Accessed 28 Feb
2010.

Saeima. 1998b. The Criminal Law. http://www.likumi.lv/doc.php?id=88966. Accessed 28 Feb
2010.

Saeima. 2005. Criminal Procedure Law. http://www.likumi.lv/doc.php?id=107820. Accessed
28 Feb 2010.

Saeima. 2006. Law On Forensic Experts. http://www.likumi.lv/doc.php?id=144788. Accessed
28 Feb 2010.

Stöver, H., C. Weilandt, H. Zurhold, C. Hartwig, and K. Thane. 2008. Final Report on Prevention,
Treatment, and Harm Reduction Services in Prison, on Reintegration Services on Release from
Prison and Methods to Monitor/Analyse Drug use among Prisoners. http://ec.europa.eu/health/
ph_determinants/life_style/drug/documents/drug_frep1.pdf. Accessed 24 Aug 2010.

Taube, M., R. Krievkalna, R. Klotiņa, A. Kišuro, V. Līce, and I. Šlosberga. 2007. *Psihiskās
veselības aprūpe Latvijā 2006*. Rīga: Public Health Agency.

United Nations Office on Drugs and Crime. 2009. Implementation of Methadone Maintenance
Programme in Olaine District. http://www.unodc.org/balticstates/en/grants/latvia/2010/Olaine_
proj.html. Accessed 5 Mar 2010.

Chapter 16
Ethical Issues in Prison Psychiatry in the Netherlands

E.D.M. Masthoff and B.H. (Erik) Bulten

16.1 Introduction

Studies have shown that the prevalence of psychiatric disorders in Dutch prison populations is high. Furthermore, it is suggested that the degree of psychopathology in such populations is substantial and growing. Currently, within the Dutch prison system, the provision of forensic psychiatric care is an important topic. Policy makers involved in this matter have defined their primary goals based on the following three notions. First, the offer of psychiatric care within the prison system should be equivalent to the treatment options in free society. Second, ex-detainees must be provided with aftercare of good quality which, in contrast to the usual outcome in these matters, is provided directly upon release from prison. Third, by means of the improvement of forensic psychiatric care, a substantial reduction of the rate of recidivism (of criminal behavior) is pursued. At this moment, the feasibility of these goals in daily practice is questionable.

First, this chapter will provide an overview of some relevant facts and figures regarding the Dutch prison system and the detained mentally ill. Subsequently, the renewed forensic mental healthcare system and the daily practise of forensic care within the prisons will be described. After that, several dilemmas and ethical issues

E.D.M. Masthoff (✉)
Forensic Care and Treatment, Penitentiaire Inrichting Vught, Vught, The Netherlands
e-mail: e.masthoff@dji.minjus.nl

B.H. (Erik) Bulten
Forensic Psychiatric Centre, Pompe Foundation, Nijmegen, The Netherlands

The Netherlands Radboud University of Nijmegen, Nijmegen, The Netherlands
e-mail: e.bulten@pompestichting.nl; e.bulten@acsw.ru.nl

N. Konrad et al. (eds.), *Ethical Issues in Prison Psychiatry*, International Library
of Ethics, Law, and the New Medicine 46, DOI 10.1007/978-94-007-0086-4_16,
© Springer Science+Business Media Dordrecht 2013

in Dutch prison psychiatry will be discussed. With that, the following topics will
be covered:

- To what extent should and can the principle of equivalence of care be met in
  Dutch prisons?
- Which factors determine whether a detainee is provided with or deprived of
  forensic psychiatric care and to what extent do detainees have an autonomous
  choice in this process?
- Which ethical conflicts may arise from the dual role that forensic healthcare
  professionals play in individual patient care on the one hand and public safety on
  the other hand?

16.2 Dutch Prison Statistics

From the 1970s on, the number of prisoners in the Netherlands has increased
substantially with a culmination point in 2005 (approximately 17,600 prisoners
within a total Dutch population of 16.3 million people). This resulted in a 'imprisonment rate' (number of prisoners per 100,000 inhabitants) of 108 in the Netherlands,
higher than that in nearby countries like Belgium, France and Germany. Between
1997 and 2004, Dutch prison capacity was raised by 50 %. However, after 2005 the
imprisonment figures have decreased progressively. A recent count (reference date
January 2010) revealed a total number of only 12,150 detainees within a population
of nearly 16.6 million people (imprisonment rate of 73) of which 11,260 (92.7 %)
detainees were imprisoned, 615 (5.0 %) stayed extramurally (e.g. electronic
detention) and 275 (2.3 %) were placed in forensic mental healthcare facilities[1].
This declining prison rate was unforeseen and is remarkable because in the same
period (and still currently) the Dutch government has strongly advocated rigorous
and repressive actions against criminality to improve public safety. Suggested
explanations for the declining imprisonment rate are not unambiguous. A politically
popular causal relationship to an assumed reduced crime rate is questioned by
experts, although severe crime types such as theft accompanied with violence, manslaughter and murder are indeed less prevalent than they were several years ago. The
dropping occupancy of prison capacity is contrasted with a higher risk of arrest and
quicker punishment for criminals (more convictions per year) and also with the
continuing high proportion of prisoners (more than half of them) detained again
within 2 years after their release. One probable reason for the emptying of prisons
is the rise of the community based sentences, which are increasingly used by
judges instead of short custodial sentences. What also plays a role is that first-time
offenders are given alternative punishments more often. An additional explanation
for the reduced prison rate is that more offenders with psychiatric disorders are
treated in psychiatric hospitals rather than being detained in prison. Apart from that,

---

[1]The presented figures were obtained form the Dutch Prison Service (Dienst Justitiële
Inrichtingen; DJI).

an increasing number of the most dangerous of those offenders (with predicted high risk of severe recidivism) are residing in so called 'longstay forensic psychiatric care units' of forensic psychiatric hospitals from which release is a rarity.

Seven out of ten prisoners in the Netherlands have Dutch nationality. Approximately 46.7 % of all prisoners are natives of the Netherlands, 8.7 % are Surinamese, 6.3 % are Aruban or Antillean (natives of the Kingdom of the Netherlands), 6.2 % are Moroccan and 4.0 % are Turkish. The remaining 28.1 % of prisoners are born elsewhere. Less than 7 % of all prisoners are female. The most common crimes are violent crimes (>40 %), drug offences and property crimes (both around 20 %). Approximately 40 % of detainees are awaiting trial (first instance, appeal or cassation at the Supreme Court), whereas the rest are serving a prison sentence, being held in foreigner custody (for the purpose of deportation) or staying in prison under any other legal arrangement.

Studies have shown that the prevalence of psychopathology in prison populations ranges up to 70 %, much higher than in the general population (Black et al. 2007; Butler et al. 2006; James and Glaze 2006; Brugha et al. 2005; Andersen 2004; Fazel and Danesh 2002; Brinded et al. 2001; Bulten et al. 2001; Bland et al. 1998; Singleton et al. 1998; Schoenmaker and Van Zessen 1997). Furthermore, it is suggested that the severity of psychopathology in such populations is growing (Zwemstra et al. 2003; Blaauw et al. 2000). Recently (in 2010), the required normative need for forensic psychiatric care ('provider-assessed': determined by the clinician or care provider) was investigated amongst Dutch prisoners (management information of the Dutch Prison Service). It was concluded that in up to 8 % of prisoners inpatient psychiatric care is indicated. Furthermore, 41 % of the prisoners with such a clinical indication were in need of highly intensive clinical forensic mental health-care because of their severe and/or complex psychopathology. Although all kinds of psychiatric diagnoses occur in the Dutch prison population, (combinations of) psychotic disorders, affective and anxiety disorders, (cluster B) personality disorders, substance-related disorders, pervasive developmental disorders, attention-deficit/hyperactivity disorders, sexual disorders (e.g. pedophilia), and mental retardation are the most prevalent. Prisoners requiring the most attention of forensic mental healthcare providers are the psychotic and/or personality-impaired patients with hetero-aggressive and/or self-destructive behavioural disturbances.

16.3   Innovation of Forensic Psychiatric Care in Dutch Prisons

During the past few years, the structure of forensic mental healthcare in the Dutch prison system has been substantially reorganised. This process of change was initiated as a result of several political recommendations. It was pointed out repeatedly that it was necessary to improve the quality and quantity of forensic psychiatric care (which is mental healthcare, including professional care for addicts and the mentally retarded, provided within a certain legal framework) because of the high prevalence of psychopathology amongst detainees. This need was not so much promoted out of care but rather due to the assumption that psychopathology can be considered a factor that promotes criminal behavior. Indeed, research into the deficiencies that lead to crime had – apart from working / career problems, friends and activities related to offending behavior and financial problems – established psychological problems, drug abuse and moderate to severe problems regarding thinking patterns as such criminogenic needs (Vogelvang et al. 2003). Philipse et al. (2010) describe mechanisms that are supposed to play a role in the way in which mental disorders contribute to or cause criminal behavior:

- impairment of moral judgement (lacunar conscience) and/or anti-social and procriminal moral attitudes (e.g. in psychopathic and/or antisocial personality disorders);
- impulse control problems;
- biased perception of reality (e.g. in paranoid delusions);
- loss of free will ('control override', e.g. in imperative hallucinations);
- lack of empathy, or impairment of 'theory of mind' (the cognitive inability to imagine how another experiences the situation; Barnes-Holmes et al. 2004).

Results of research into the correlations between specific mental disorders and delinquent behavior should be interpreted with some caution because of a possible (partial) overlap between both concepts and the risk of circular reasoning (Philipse et al. 2010). E.g., a suspect of a sexual offence with minors could be regarded as a pedophile too easily whereas this diagnostic conclusion in turn could (possibly unjustly) enhance the corroboration of the mentioned incrimination. Taken such limitations into account, it can be assumed that individuals with psychotic disorders are involved in violent (criminal) behavior more often than those without such diagnoses (Hodgins et al. 2007; Brennan et al. 2000; Taylor and Gunn 1999), that the same is true for those with substance use disorders who also commit significantly more property crimes (Bennett et al. 2008), that persons with psychopathic personality profiles have increased risks of all kinds of delinquent behavior (Hildebrand 2004; Hare 2003), and that persons with certain paraphilias have an increased risk of being involved in some types of sexual offences (Olver and Wong 2006; Hanson and Morton-Bourgon 2005; Kafka 2003).

Whereas in the early 1980s, the effectiveness of psychiatric treatments aimed at reducing recidivism was perceived rather pessimistically, nowadays such interventions are seen more optimistically. The 'What Works' perspective provided a conceptual and theoretical framework for reducing recidivism of criminal behavior (Bulten et al. 2008; Andrews and Bonta 2007; McGuire 1995). Initially, subsumed in the 'risk-need-responsivity model', a set of three principles was developed (1980s) and formalized (from the 1990s onwards) to assess and rehabilitate criminals. The risk principle implied that the level and intensity of care provided to (former) detainees should be dependent on the recidivism risk which, as was assumed, could be reliably predicted. The need principle focused on making criminogenic needs (those features of an offender's characteristics and circumstances that are predictive of future criminal conduct) targets of intervention. The responsivity principle referred to how the treatment should be provided. In addition to the general approach of interventions, it was recommended to consider specific staff and client characteristics and to match the style and mode of intervention accordingly (Andrews and Bonta 2007). Later, several principles were added to enhance and strengthen the design and implementation of effective interventions. For example, the principles of professional discretion and therapeutic integrity were described. Another important principle addressed correctional agencies and managers, providing policies and leadership that facilitate and enable effective interventions (Andrews and Dowden 2007; Andrews and Bonta 2006; Andrews 2001).

The latter brings us back to the actions of the policy makers in the Dutch prison system regarding forensic care. From January 2007 onwards, the financial budgets reserved for the promotion of forensic mental healthcare were transferred from the Ministry of Health, Welfare and Sport to the Ministry of Justice. Furthermore, within the Prison Service (Dienst Justitiële Inrichtingen; DJI), several projects ('Renewal of Forensic Care'; 'Modernizing the Prison System') were launched to improve forensic mental healthcare within the prison system. The goals that were formulated regarding this process of innovation were the following:

• Prisoners should have access to psychiatric treatment with the same standard as patients in the free society ('principle of equivalence' as included in the European Prison Rules from 1987 and in the revision of these rules by the Counsel of Europe in 2006 (Counsel of Europe 2006)).
• So called 'unnoticed psychiatric patients' should be detected and provided with appropriate care (a Dutch parliamentary investigation made it obvious that a substantial number of mentally ill prisoners had not been brought to the attention of forensic mental health caregivers because these prisoners did not seek care and were not noticed, mainly because they lacked deviant behavior that disrupted the prison environment).
• Ex-detainees must be provided with aftercare of good quality which, in contrast to the usual outcome in these matters, starts directly upon release from prison. Unless such is contraindicated, prisoners with an indication for clinical forensic care should be placed in forensic mental healthcare facilities in the community during the last part of their prison sentence.
• By means of the improvement of forensic psychiatric care, a substantial decrease of the crime recidivism percentage is pursued.

In order to achieve these goals, the prison service financed forensic capacity (N = 320) in several community mental healthcare facilities throughout the country in order to be able to place prisoners in these facilities during the last phase of their detention more easily than before. Furthermore, the capacity of forensic care units within the prison system was increased (N = 700 compared to N = 385 before) and concentrated into five regional Penitentiary Psychiatric Centres (PPC's). Apart from this change in daily practice, revisions of legislation are underway. The 'Forensic Care Act' (prevailing within the prison system) and the 'Obligatory Mental Care Act' (prevailing within the community) are passing through Dutch legislation. More than the current Penitentiary Principles Act and the Prison Regulations (De Groot 2009), the future 'Forensic Care Act' should provide a suitable framework for an adequate forensic mental healthcare system in the Netherlands.

16.4   Forensic Psychiatric Care in Dutch Prisons in General and in the PPCs

Forensic psychiatric care in Dutch prisons is coordinated and provided by the so-called psycho-medical consultation (in Dutch: Psycho-Medisch Overleg; PMO). This consultation structure is available in every Dutch prison. Core members of the PMO are a forensic psychologist (chairperson and coordinator of the forensic care pathways for individual detainees), a forensic psychiatrist (on a consultative basis), a general practitioner (responsible for the somatic care) and a nurse. Other health-care professionals may be present on invitation. The focus of the PMO is the process of individual assessment, needs assessment, counseling, (basic) treatment and after-care for individual detainees and the regular evaluation of this process. In daily practice, the first indication for the need for psycho-medical care is often given by staff (prison guards) or by the nurse who screens all new prisoners. Experience suggests that detainees who show care-seeking behavior and/or those with striking behavioral problems are more often under the care of the PMO, whereas care-avoiders and/or detainees with 'silent mental disturbances' are at high risk of being overlooked. Part of the 'Modernizing the Prison System' (in Dutch: Modernisering Gevangeniswezen; MGW) is an effort to develop and implement a screening instrument suitable for all detainees to detect psycho-medical (e.g., psychopathology, suicide risks) and social problems in order to provide appropriate care for all prisoners who need it. Another aspect of the MGW project is that all staff members will be trained in the techniques of so called 'motivational treatment'. This subproject involves enhancing the communication skills of all employees pursuing the goal of encouraging prisoners to develop self-motivation and taking responsibility for their own rehabilitation in order to achieve the aim of recidivism reduction. This requires that employees become aware of the important contribution they can make to a prison environment where people become receptive to behavioral change.

In regular prison wards, the availability of healthcare professionals is limited. If clinical psychiatric care is needed for a prisoner (based on the type and severity of their mental illness), the forensic psychologist and psychiatrist request such care. If such care is necessary and no contraindications exist (amongst other factors, contraindications can be the need for maximum security and/or a long remaining sentence), the detainee can (and should) be transferred to a mental healthcare facility in a non-correctional setting (within the legal framework of the Penitentiary Principles Act). A prerequisite for such a voluntary transfer is the commitment of the prisoner. In case the described placement is contraindicated or refused by the prisoner, a transfer to a PPC can be accomplished.

Within the five regional PPCs, the forensic mental healthcare is of a higher standard than the basic care available within the regular prison regimes. In the PPCs the staff-prisoner ratio is substantially higher and more different types of healthcare professions are available. Psychologists, psychotherapists, psychiatrists, general practitioners, (social) psychiatric nurses, social workers, psychomotor therapists, expressive therapists, drama therapists and music therapists cooperate to provide imprisoned patients with appropriate care. Furthermore, the staff in the PPCs are not regular prison guards but are so called 'care and treatment facility workers' (in Dutch: zorg en behandel inrichtingswerkers; ZBIW-ers), which are (mostly) former prison guards who are trained and skilled in taking care of psychiatric patients. The patients reside in relatively small wards of 12 beds or less (even individual programs are possible). Different social environments are provided within the PPCs. There are (highly) structured environments for inmates with (cluster B) personality disorders, protective environments for those with a diagnosis of psychoses and supportive environments for depressed and anxious patients. There is an intensive care unit for (extreme) psychiatric crises, and there are specific facilities for females and for those with sexual deviancies. There is also a clinical diagnostic ward with extensive (neuro) psychological testing and observation facilities. All kinds of treatments are offered within the PPCs, e.g. psychopharmacotherapy (including involuntary treatment), different types of psychotherapy, several nonverbal therapies and various skills based modules (e.g. anger management, social skills training, addiction focused group therapies). Although the PPCs try to provide equal treatment options to those available in the non-incarcerated population, diagnostic assessments and psychiatric interventions within the PPCs are limited by the restrictions posed by the coercive environment and by limited financial means. Overall the following tasks are assigned to the regional PPCs:

- assessment of the mental state of prisoners;
- stabilization of mental instability and improvement of maladjusted (e.g. aggressive, suicidal) behavior of prisoners;
- provision of appropriate medical care and treatment;
- enhancing motivation and treatment readiness in prisoners;
- referral to mental health care facilities in the community (continuity of forensic care);
- reduction of criminal behavior.

The renewed forensic care system in Dutch prisons described above is currently still in its infancy and will need further (mostly qualitative) improvement in the next few years. Nonetheless, it seems to have the potential to meet the required mental healthcare standards in the future. A good indication of this is that several of the interventions that Ruddell (2006) found to be partly or fully effective in American correctional facilities are currently provided within the Dutch prison system:

- screening of detainees for mental disorders at the beginning of their detention;
- screening of detainees for suicidal risk at the beginning of their detention;
- provision of suitable living environments on the wards;
- availability of a coordinator for psycho-medical care;
- training of staff in the detection and handling of psychiatric disorders among prisoners.

16.5   Ethical Issues and Dilemmas

16.5.1   The Principle of Equivalence

The right of all persons deprived of liberty to enjoy the highest attainable standard of health is guaranteed in a wide range of international instruments, including human rights treaties at international and regional levels, United Nations resolutions and agreed model standards and guidelines for the treatment of prisoners adopted by the UN General Assembly (Lines 2008). Although the principle of equivalence (Vlach and Daniel 2007; Birmingham et al. 2006; Wilson 2004) is one that enjoys broad consensus, it is far from obvious that it is achieved in daily forensic practise (Lines 2006).

Within the Dutch prison system, policymakers have tried to determine what the term 'equivalence of healthcare' should mean in correctional settings and subsequently they made this interpretation the main focus of the project 'Renewal of Forensic Care'. Initially, the equivalence principle was described quite generally as 'care equivalent to mental healthcare available in the free society, taking the detention situation into account'. Therefore, at first, regular mental healthcare programs were used as bases for forensic care programs for the PPCs. However, gradually it became evident that both the specific characteristics of the detention situation and the treatment goals in prison deviated greatly from those in non-correctional settings. An advisory group was installed, which provided the following guidance regarding the principle of equivalence.

It was argued that the detention setting is a complicating factor when it comes to providing medical and psychological care and treatment. This is reflected in (1) the impact of the criminal proceedings and imprisonment on the psyche and disorder, (2) the notion that the detention regime determines the treatment environment, (3) a mostly short or uncertain duration of the detention, (4) the heterogeneity of the target group with various mental disorders and different required security levels and (5) the prevailing penal frameworks and boundaries. According to the advisory group, equivalent disorder-targeted-treatment is aimed at reduction of suffering, learning to deal with constraints and improving the psychosocial condition and functioning. However, in providing forensic care within the prison setting, an additional important (and perhaps the most prominent) treatment goal should be the reduction of risk of recidivism, which is in fact the most distinguishing factor between forensic and regular psychiatric care. After all, besides punishment (reprisal) and example setting (general prevention), another target of imposing a custodial sentence is the return to society for detainees in more favorable circumstances. One of those circumstances is the mental status of the detainee which may be seen as a criminogenic factor (see above).

Recidivism reduction also plays an important role in the draft text of the upcoming Forensic Care Act. In Article 2.1 of this draft act (version April 2009) it is merely stated that the implementation of custodial sentences, with due regard for their character, as much as possible, should be used for the rehabilitation of the forensic patient and the reduction of the likelihood of recidivism so to derive benefits for the safety of society. Thus, in the provision of forensic care to prisoners, recidivism reduction is an important task and therefore efforts in the PPCs should focus on this.

However, this focusing on recidivism reduction also leads to dilemmas. The population of the PPCs partially consists of crime suspects awaiting trial. For these patients, the formulation of the crime scenario, structural risk assessment and/or relapse prevention are not obvious. Furthermore, in patients sentenced to imprisonment the strength of the relationship between the psychopathological factors and the committed crime (if present at all) will vary widely as will the recidivism risk. Finally, the generally relative short stay of individuals in a detention setting will substantially limit the possibilities for offering relapse-reducing treatment interventions (the risk-need-responsivity principles may conflict with reality). Therefore, especially for detainees with short sentences and for suspects not yet convicted, other treatment goals are important, namely, relief of psychopathological symptoms and realization of continuity of care following release from prison.

In our opinion, the discrepancies between regular care and care and treatment in detention settings can be elaborated further in terms of advantages and disadvantages. Generally, factors regarded as benefits of the detention setting consist of the regularity and external structure provided by the day program, stimulus poverty (little distractions and/or temptations), the forced context (the legal possibilities to impose sanctions and/or correctional measures in case of certain behavioral problems), the possibilities for interventions enhancing treatment motivation (consequences of participating or not in offered treatment), the physically healthy environment and the (relatively) alcohol and drug free social climate. Disadvantages can be the restrictive culture (which can be in contradiction with providing care), a break with the social circle, loss of employment and housing, decrease of individualization, loss of privacy and autonomy, limited possibilities to channel emotions and behavior, limited practise of alternative behaviors, negative influence by fellow prisoners and the short or uncertain duration of detention mentioned previously. Furthermore, it is important to notice that healthcare professionals need specific expertise in the treatment of psychiatrically disturbed prisoners, such as understanding of and dealing with aggressive behavior, psychotraumata, psychopathy and unreliability, risk assessment and management, the impact of the detention setting, prevailing legal frameworks, the available mental healthcare facilities outside the correctional setting and liaison psychiatry/psychology.

Following the above, the influence of the detention setting on treatment opportunities is substantial. Therefore, it is concluded that the therapeutic setting provided by PPCs is at most only partially comparable to that of a regular mental healthcare facility. Thus, the treatment programs, guidelines and protocols from the mainstream mental health services cannot be used in the PPCs unreservedly.

A more obvious comparison is that between the PPCs and forensic mental healthcare settings. A significant part of the complicating factors that the prison system entails in relation to treatment in detention (such as population heterogeneity, impact of criminal proceedings, legal framework) also applies to these specific settings. Furthermore, most of the above mentioned social drawbacks and personal constraints due to imprisonment are not exclusive to the detention setting. In addition, most forensic hospitals are also rather well secured and thus do, to some extent, resemble a correctional setting. Apart from these similarities, it is obvious that some of the disadvantages prevailing from the prison system apply less (or not at all) to forensic hospitals (e.g. restrictive culture, limited opportunities for individual programming). In our opinion, these dissimilarities are partly due to aspects of the prison culture and the resulting treatment of detainees. Investing in staff and management in order to enhance their skills with regard to the latter and a critical evaluation of care processes may lead to improvements. The introduction of external psychiatric treatment expertise in the prison system could have a positive influence as well.

Besides the above considerations on the principle of equivalence (related to the characteristics of the detention setting and the treatment goals), it is important to mention the financial framework in which forensic care is provided in Dutch prisons. As mentioned previously, the financial budgets reserved for the promotion of forensic mental healthcare were transferred from the Ministry of Health, Welfare and Sport to the Ministry of Justice. From this budget, the forensic care in prisons is funded. In addition, care is purchased from external providers with the dual purpose of introducing specialized care in prisons and creating opportunities to (conditionally) place detainees in non-correctional (care) settings during the last phase of their imprisonment (continuity of care).

The financial framework limits the availability of care in quantitative and qualitative terms and it hinders the achievement of the principle of equivalence. Currently the budget for forensic care in prisons is fixed, but at some time (at least within the PPCs) it will make place for a system of product registration, billing and financing. This system should give more insight into the actual costs of forensic mental healthcare making it possible to determine the extent to which achieving equivalent care in prisons is financially feasible. In our opinion, it is not to be expected that equivalent care in Dutch prisons will ever be (totally) financially accountable. The reason for this is obvious: it will always be a political dilemma to spent large quantities of taxpayer's money on care for criminal offenders.

16.5.2 Providing Forensic Care

The typical route through which detainees are provided with forensic mental healthcare in the Dutch prison system was described above. Potentially useful in this context is the theoretical framework for goal-directed care within the prison system as was proposed by Bulten et al. (2008). This framework differentiates between prisoners with emotional suffering and those without, between prisoners with and without care-seeking behavior and between the need for care from an objective and a subjective point of view. Based on these classification principles, the following six subgroups of detainees are formulated:

1. Detainees who don't experience emotional suffering, who don't seek help and who objectively don't have a psychiatric disorder. In these cases there is no subjective need for care, no care-seeking behavior and no objective need for care (these detainees rightly don't receive psycho-medical care).

2. Detainees who, although they don't experience psychiatric complaints, have a mental disorder (e.g. a psychosis). In these cases there is no subjective need for care and no care-seeking behavior, but there is an objective (normative) need for care.
3. Detainees who do experience a subjective need for care but who do not show care-seeking behavior and in whom no objective need for care is present.
4. Detainees who do experience a subjective need for care and who do show care-seeking behavior but in whom no objective need for care is present.
5. Detainees who do experience a subjective need for care but who do not show care-seeking behavior and in whom an objective need for care is present.
6. Detainees who do experience a subjective need for care and who do show care-seeking behavior and in whom an objective need for care is present.

When detainees actually receive forensic mental health care a further differentiation is proposed concerning the goal of the provided care: care in order to treat mental health problems versus care related to limiting criminal recidivism.

When this theoretical framework is set against the daily practice of screening detainees for mental problems and treatment need, several ethical issues emerge. Subgroup 2 contains care-avoiders, whose degree of awareness and understanding about being mentally ill is limited or even absent, but who are in need for normative mental healthcare. One ethical problem is that these detainees could be overlooked by healthcare professionals if their psychopathological symptoms are hardly noticeable and/or do not attract sufficient attention at first glance[2]. Another ethical issue arises when detainees belonging to subgroup 2 (or 5), identified as in normative need for mental healthcare, actually refuse psychiatric treatment. In such case, the laws and regulations of the Dutch prison system (De Groot 2009) allow compulsory admission of detainees to the above mentioned PPCs. The criteria for such an admission are the (suspicion of) the presence of a psychiatric disorder combined with an (estimated) objective (normative) need for mental healthcare only. These conditions are far from equivalent when compared with those required in compulsory psychiatric admissions in free society. Namely, in the latter case, the risk criterion should be additionally met, meaning that the patient exhibits behavior, dangerous to himself and/or to his environment. Furthermore, a written medical statement prepared by an independent psychiatrist is obligatory (within the prison system a simple referral by a healthcare professional is sufficient). Finally, in free society, the criteria for the compulsory admission to a psychiatric hospital are reviewed by a civil court whereas this procedure does not exist within the prison system. Although a detainee can formally object to this kind of admission, this objection has no delaying effect and such complaints are (strangely enough) in the first instance dealt with by the official (in Dutch: de selectiefunctionaris) who had decided upon the compulsory admission in the first place. And, even though it is possible for the detainee to appeal to an independent commission, such a procedure usually takes several months.

---

[2] As mentioned above, at the present moment, efforts are made to develop and implement a screening instrument within the Dutch prison system in an attempt to identify this group.

16.5.3 Compulsory Treatment

Another ethical issue arises when a detainee, once placed in a PPC, still refuses psychiatric treatment and if the responsible healthcare professional considers compulsory psychopharmacological intervention. In Dutch law, a warden has the authority to order forced administration of medication to a detainee when a physician (forensic general practitioner and/or psychiatrist) considers it a necessary action. The intervention is to be performed by a physician or his substitute (nurse supervised by a physician). When the need for compulsory medication is based on a mental disorder, a psychiatrist must be consulted. The forced administration of medication is only permissible if it is necessary to avert risks for the safety of the patient and/or his surroundings. This criterion refers to actions of self-harm, aggression against persons or property, arson, verbal violence, severe threats of violence, etc. Even if a serious threat has not yet occurred, there may be an indication for compulsory treatment. In such a case, past experience with the patient and his previous behavior can be used to predict the expected risk of dangerous behavior in the absence of treatment. Apart from the presence of dangerous behavior resulting from psychopathology, the formal criteria of proportionality, subsidiarity and efficiency should also be satisfied. The proportionality criterion refers to the requirement that the benefits of forced administration of medication, which is a serious violation of physical integrity, should outweigh the safety risks. Subsidiarity implies that less drastic means to avert the danger were considered but were not regarded as effective. The efficiency criterion refers to the notion that the intervention used should be a known effective remedy to reduce the risk. In addition, the forced intervention should only be used to avert a serious threat and not just to provide long-term therapeutic treatment. These considerations in the process of forced psychopharmacological interventions recurrently lead to the ethical dilemma whether or not the autonomy and integrity of the detainee should be violated in the interest of risk reduction.

16.5.4 Hunger Strike

Another ethical dilemma occurs in cases of hunger strikes, a regular phenomenon in Dutch prisons. A hunger strike can be a powerful tool for prisoners to obtain (media) attention. In general, a hunger strike is not interpreted as attempted suicide but as a form of protest. The hunger striker does not want to die, but tries to enforce a change in his living conditions while accepting death as the ultimate consequence of his actions (Jacobs 2009). Food refusal can be maintained during an extensive period (up to about 2 months), which does not apply to a refusal to take fluids. A strike involving refusal of fluids does not provide much negotiating time (fast somatic deterioration) and is therefore not often used as leverage (Van Es et al. 2000).

In Dutch law, the forced administration of fluids and nutrition to break the hunger strike is a regulated possible intervention in which the constitutionally guaranteed right to self-determination of the detainee is overruled. The ethical dilemma with hunger strikes is whether or not to intervene against the will of the hunger striker. The mental competence of the hunger striker is an important issue in this matter. If the hunger striker is not judged to have capacity, does not choose food/fluid refusal out of his/her own free will and/or does not or not sufficiently foresee the consequences of his/her actions (e.g. induced by psychopathology such as psychosis or major depression), forced administration of fluids and food is obviously indicated sooner than when the hunger striker is completely mentally competent. If the prisoner has full capacity, which is usually the case in daily practise, the will of the detainee and his right for self-determination are usually respected. In such cases, prison policy suggests to not forcefully break the hunger strike, but to provide care to minimize the physical and psychological damage to the hunger striker, when such damage is not an intended effect of the hunger strike.

Besides these common considerations, sometimes a rather dubious argument is inserted into the discussion. Indeed, preventing a defendant from both avoiding the judicial process and subsequently undergoing punishment for committed crimes is sometimes considered to be a sufficient argument for forcefully breaking a hunger strike. In the Netherlands, the opinions on this matter are divided. The hunger strike of a suspect of murder on a prominent Dutch politician (who was convicted for this crime later), stirred up the discussion on the subject. The Minister of Justice introduced 'public interest' (meaning the proceed of justice as referred to above) as a possible legitimate argument for a compulsory medical act in case of a deliberate hunger strike. However, both a human rights organization for doctors, nurses and paramedics, the Inspectorate for Health (In Dutch: IGZ) and various national medical associations disagreed with this view of the Minister. They judged force-feeding in cases of a hunger strike by a mentally competent person absolutely inadmissible (Jacobs 2009). At the European level, a similar duality is apparent between policy makers and the European Court of Justice case law on the one hand and healthcare professionals on the other hand. Therefore it is not evident that this ethical dilemma will be resolved soon.

16.5.5 Professional Confidentiality

Various healthcare professionals are employed within the Dutch prison system in general and within the PPC's in particular. It is up to these professionals to provide (equivalent) psycho-medical care to detainees when such care is necessary. In this regard, for healthcare professionals there is no difference in providing care in correctional and non-correctional settings. Indeed, both inside and outside the detention setting, largely the same 'laws on care' apply such as: the Act on Quality of Healthcare Institutions (in Dutch: Kwaliteitswet Zorginstellingen; KWZ), the Act on Medical Treatment Contracts (in Dutch: Wet op de Geneeskundige Behandelovereenkomst, WGBO) and the Medical Professions Act (in Dutch: Wet op de Beroepen in de Individuele Gezondheidszorg, BIG) (Sluijters et al. 2008). Apart from that, healthcare professionals working within the prison system are also expected, to some degree, to be involved in the judicial process itself. As a consequence, conflicting interests raise ethical dilemmas in daily practice. Some of these dilemmas will be discussed below.

First, it is important to understand the different roles that healthcare professionals play within the specific judicial process in which the prisoner is involved. It is not unusual that a healthcare professional provides care within the prison system and at the same time serves as an independent expert in criminal trials. In such cases, it is appropriate that the healthcare professional is not acting as an expert witness in matters in which he or she was previously involved as a care provider (the reverse can be complicated but is not necessarily unworkable). Furthermore, expert witnesses such as psychiatrists and psychologists, but also probation officers, can inquire about the psychological condition of detainees who they report about in court. In such cases care providers in prison only provide information if the detainee with whom a therapeutic working alliance exists explicitly gives consent, unless there are compelling reasons to breach professional confidentiality. If information is provided by the care givers, it is good practice to inform the detainee about the possible implications. An ethical dilemma might occur if a suspect of a crime authorizes healthcare professional to provide information about his psychological condition while not realizing that such information can sometimes have a negative impact on his legal position. The healthcare professional should act in a transparent way in these matters and should properly balance the different interests (within the therapeutic relationship the interest of the patient has the highest priority).

In addition to the complicated role of healthcare professionals within the judicial process, it is worth mentioning that these professionals can also be confronted (as victims or as witnesses) with new delinquent behavior of detainees during their detention period, which can be similar to the crimes for which they had been imprisoned in the first place. In such cases – as in free society – it is recommended to report this criminal behavior to the police and/or to the public prosecutor when the seriousness of the situation justifies breaking professional confidentiality. In these situations, the public interest (the safety of the society) should prevail over the individual interests of the detainee.

Another ethical dilemma arises from the framework of the project MGW (see above) relating to so-called 'boards for leave'. According to the MGW such boards will be installed in every Dutch prison. Such committees should consist of a warden and a head of detainee affairs. Depending on the length of a sentence imposed on a detainee, these boards will give advise or make decisions in relation to the liberty policy and / or sentence planning. The liberty policy refers to leaves and / or conditional releases from prison, whereas the sentence planning alludes to the proposed transfer of detainees to less secured settings. The committee advises or decides to grant or withhold leave and/or on the imposition of special conditions in addition to the standard conditions for early release from prison. The committee is advised by the so-called 'multidisciplinary consultative body' (in Dutch: multidisciplinair overleg; MDO), in which, among other contributors, health-care professionals are represented, including, most prominently, a psychologist or – within a PPC – a treatment coordinator. Thus, these healthcare professionals may find themselves in a difficult position. On the one hand, they provide care for the detained patient and in this position they are obliged to comply with the care laws mentioned above. On the other hand, they are required to provide advice on the liberty policy and / or sentence planning based on their professional knowledge of the detainee. In this situation, conflicting factors might be: the interest of the detainee, the interest of the community and the individual interest of the healthcare professional. For example, is it appropriate to provide information about a detainee without his or her consent, thus breaking professional confidentiality in the interest of the safety of society? Or, is it appropriate to break confidentiality concerning a psychotic patient because it seems in the best interest for this patient (confidentiality would interfere with provision of good care)? In general, it is recommended to respect and maintain professional confidentiality and to only report on matters arising from the therapeutic relationship if the detainee has authorized the healthcare professional to do so. However, it is conceivable that the objective interest of the individual patient or the public interest can provide substantial arguments to divert from this approach.

Furthermore, the advisory role of the healthcare professional regarding the imposition of sanctions and/or order and security measures on detainees, is worth mentioning. These sanctions and measures may involve placing the detainee in seclusion, using handcuffs and/or shackles, camera surveillance and restrictions in visiting rights, telephone and/or mail communications. Although in all these matters, according to the applicable laws and regulations, the decision lies with the warden of the prison facility, healthcare professionals are frequently (and in some cases this is required by law) involved in a consultative manner. Here too, care and security interests might conflict. In such situations, the healthcare professional is often well-aware of the fact that he or she is not only a therapist but also an employee of the Ministry of Justice and a contributor to the judiciary.

Finally, an ethical dilemma can result from the previously mentioned aim to renew forensic care in order to achieve continuity of mental health care for released detainees, hoping that this integrated care will result in a reduction of criminal recidivism. Again, the healthcare professional is confronted with the dilemma whether the interests of society or that of the individual detainee prevails and, if the latter would be the case, how this interest could best be served (does the prisoner actually know what is in his best interests?). Surely, it is possible that these different interests are compatible, but inconsistencies between them will often be evident.

16.6   Conclusion

According to the results of several epidemiological studies, it is obvious that the prevalence of mental disorders within the Dutch Prison system is substantial. Based on the principle of equivalence, there is an increasing need for high standard professional mental healthcare within correctional settings. Apart from that, reducing recidivism, also by means of psychiatric treatment, is becoming a more prominent and important objective. Because of these two trends, healthcare professionals are becoming more involved in the judicial process, procedures and daily correctional practice. Collateral effects of this positive development regarding prison mental healthcare are several fundamental ethical dilemmas that policymakers and care-givers face. In this chapter we discussed various ethical issues concerning the inter-pretation of the principle of equivalence, the feasibility of the implementation of this principle in terms of financial boundaries and basic limitations of the detention setting, the determinants of forensic care and the often ambivalent position of the healthcare professional in the complex prison system. It is unlikely that the ethical dilemmas discussed will be solved easily, if at all. In fact, they are inherent to providing care in a setting that is not primarily intended for such a purpose.

References

Andersen, H.S. 2004. Mental health in prison populations: A review with special emphasis on Danish prisoners on remand. *Acta Psychiatrica Scandinavica* 110: 5–55.

Andrews, D.A. 2001. Principles of effective correctional programs. In *Compendium 2000 on effective correctional programming*, ed. L.L. Motiuk and R.C. Serin, 9–17. Ottawa: Correctional Services of Canada.

Andrews, D.A., and J. Bonta. 2006. *The psychology of criminal conduct*, 4th ed. Newark: LexisNexis.

Andrews, D.A., and J. Bonta. 2007. Public Safety Canada Corrections Research: User Report 2007–06. www.publicsafety.gc.ca

Andrews, D.A., and C. Dowden. 2007. The risk-need-responsivity model of assessment and human service in prevention and corrections: Rehabilitative jurisprudence. *Canadian Journal of Criminology and Criminal Justice* 49: 439–464.

Barnes-Holmes, Y., L. McHugh, and D. Barnes-Holmes. 2004. Perspective-taking and theory of mind: A relational frame account. *The Behavior Analyst Today* 5: 15–25.

Bennett, T.H., K. Holloway, and D.P. Farrington. 2008. The statistical association between drug misuse and crime: A meta-analysis. *Aggression and Violent Behaviour* 13(2): 107–118.

Birmingham, L., S. Wilson, and G. Adshead. 2006. Prison medicine: Ethics and equivalence. *The British Journal of Psychiatry* 188: 4–6.

Blaauw, E., R. Roesch, and A. Kerkhof. 2000. Mental disorders in European prison systems. *International Journal of Law and Mental Health* 23: 649–663.

Black, D., T. Gunter, J. Allen, et al. 2007. Borderline personality disorder in male and female offenders newly committed to prison. *Comprehensive Psychiatry* 48(5): 400–405.

Bland, R.C., S.C. Newman, A.H. Thompson, and R.J. Dyck. 1998. Psychiatric disorders in the population and among prisoners. *International Journal of Law and Psychiatry* 21: 273–279.

Brennan, P.A., S.A. Mednick, and S. Hodgins. 2000. Major mental disorders and criminal violence in a Danish birth cohort. *Archives of General Psychiatry* 57: 494–500.

Brinded, P., A. Simpson, T. Laidlaw, et al. 2001. Prevalence of psychiatric disorders in New Zealand prisons: A national study. *The Australian and New Zealand Journal of Psychiatry* 35(2): 166–173.

Brugha, T., N. Singleton, H. Meltzer, et al. 2005. Psychosis in the community and in prisons: A report form the British national survey of psychiatric morbidity. *The American Journal of Psychiatry* 162(4): 774–780.

Bulten, E., A. Vissers, and K. Oei. 2008. A theoretical framework for goal-directed care within the prison system. *Mental Health Review Journal* 13(3): 40–50.

Bulten, B.H., J. Zwemstra, and M.J. Pulles. 2001. Behandeling in detentie ter vermindering van recidive. [Treatment in prison with the intention to diminish recidivism]. *Maandblad voor de Geestelijke Volksgezondheid*, [Monthly Magazine of Public Mental Health] 4:300–315.

Butler, T., G. Andrews, S. Allnut, et al. 2006. Mental disorders in Australian prisoners: A comparison with a community sample. *Australian and New Zealand Journal of Public Health* 40: 272–276.

Counsel of Europe. 2006. European Prison Rules, Recommendation 3, 11 Jan 2006.

De Groot, M.F.M. 2009. *Penitentiaire beginselenwet [Penitentiary Principles Act]*. Deventer: Kluwer.

Fazel, S., and J. Danesh. 2002. Serious mental disorder in 23000 prisoners: A systematic review of 62 surveys. *Lancet* 359: 545–550.

Hanson, K.R., and K.E. Morton-Bourgon. 2005. The characteristics of persistent sexual offenders: A meta-analysis of recidivism studies. *Journal of Consultative Clinical Psychology* 73: 1154–1163.

Hare, R.D. 2003. *Manual for the revised psychopathy checklist*, 2nd ed. Toronto: Multi-Health Systems.

Hildebrand, M. 2004. Psychopathy in the treatment of forensic psychiatric patients. Assessment, prevalence, predictive validity and clinical implications. PhD Thesis, Amsterdam: University of Amsterdam.

Hodgins, S., J. Alderton, A. Cree, A. Aboud, and T. Mak. 2007. Aggressive behaviour, victimisation and crime among severely mentally ill patients requiring hospitalisation. *The British Journal of Psychiatry* 191: 343–350.

Jacobs, P. 2009. Hongerstaking in detentie [Hunger strike in detention]. In *Detentie. Gevangen in Nederland [Detention. Captive in the Netherlands]*, ed. E.R. Muller and P.C. Vegter, 453–489. Alphen aan den Rijn: Kluwer.

James, D.J., and E. Glaze. 2006. *Mental health problems of prison and jail inmates*. Bureau of Justice Statistics Special Report. NCJ 213600, Washington, DC: U.S. Department of Justice, Bureau of Justice Statistics.

Kafka, M.P. 2003. Sex offending and sexual appetite: The clinical and theoretical relevance of hypersexual desire. *International Journal of Offender Therapy and Comparative Criminology* 47(4): 439–451.

Lines, R. 2006. From equivalence of standards to equivalence of objectives: The entitlement of prisoners to healthcare standards higher than those outside prisons. *International Journal of Prisoner Health* 2(4): 269–280.

Lines, R. 2008. The right to health of prisoners in international human rights law. *International Journal of Prisoner Health* 4(1): 3–53.

McGuire, J. (ed.). 1995. *What works: Reducing re-offending: Guidelines from research and practise*. Chichester: Wiley.

Olver, M.E., and S.C.P. Wong. 2006. Psychopathy, sexual deviance, and recidivism among sex offenders. *Sexual Abuse. Journal of Research and Treatment* 18: 65–82.

Philipse, M., E. Bulten, and H. Nijman. 2010. Psychische stoornissen en delictgedrag [Psychiatric disorders and criminal behavior]. In *Reizen met mijn rechter. Psychologie van het recht. [Tavelling with my judge. Psychology of law]*, ed. P.J. Van Koppen, H. Merckelbach, M. Jelicic, and J.W. De Keijser, 67–89. Deventer: Kluwer.

Ruddell, R. 2006. Jail interventions for inmates with mental illnesses. *Journal of Correctional Health Care* 12: 118–131.

Schoenmaker, C., and G. Van Zessen. 1997. *Psychische stoornissen bij gedetineerden [Mental disorders in prisoners]*. Houten: Bohn Stafleu Van Loghum.

Singleton, N., H. Meltzer, and R. Gatward. 1998. *Psychiatric morbidity among prisoners in England and Wales*. London: Stationery Office.

Sluijters, B., M.C.I.H. Biesaart, G.R.J. De Groot, and L.E. Kalkman-Bogerd (eds.). 2008. *Gezondheidsrecht. Tekst & Commentaar [Health law. Text & comments]*. Deventer: Kluwer.

Taylor, P.J., and J. Gunn. 1999. Homocides by people with mental illness: Myth and reality. *The British Journal of Psychiatry* 174: 9–14.

Van Es, A., C.C.J.M. Van Ojen, and A.M.C. Raat. 2000. *Honger naar recht, honger als wapen: handleiding voor de medische en verpleegkundige begeleiding van hongerstakingen [Hunger for justice, hunger as weapon: manual for the medical and nursing supervision of hunger strikes]*. Amersfoort: Johannes Wier Stichting.

Vlach, D.L., and A.E. Daniel. 2007. Commentary: Evolving toward equivalence in correctional mental health care – a view from the maximum security trenches. *The Journal of the American Academy of Psychiatry and the Law* 35(4): 436–438.

Vogelvang, B., A. Van Burik, L. Van der Knaap, and B. Wartna. 2003. *De prevalentie van criminogene factoren bij mannelijke gedetineerden in Nederland [The prevalence of criminogenic needs among male prisoners in the Netherlands]*. Adviesbureau van Montfoort: WODC.

Wilson, S. 2004. The principle of equivalence and the future of mental health care in prisons. *The British Journal of Psychiatry* 184: 5–7.

Zwemstra, J., P.J. Van Panhuis, and B.H. Bulten. 2003. Schizofrenie in de gevangenis: Over de prevalentie, achtergronden en kenmerken van gedetineerden met schizofrenie en over de mogelijkheden en de beperkingen van hun behandeling [Schizophrenia in prison: Prevalence, backgrounds and characteristics of prisoners with schizophrenia and the opportunities and the limitations of their treatment]. *Maandblad voor de Geestelijke Volksgezondheid [Monthly Magazine of Public Mental Health]* 1: 53–63.

Chapter 17
Ethical Issues in Prison Psychiatry in România

Nicoleta Tătaru

> ... *bad treatment and living conditions* – for prisoners with mental health problems - *almost invariably lead to human rights violations, and it is the duty of each government to do everything possible to prevent such violations from taking place*. Robert van Voren (2009a)

România, like other Eastern Europe countries, lies at the crossroads between the Western world, the Middle East and Asia. As a former communist country, it was behind the Iron Curtain until December 1989. România continues the process of transition from communism to democracy and an open market economy. It has a population of 20.254.866 (Census 2012) covering 237.500 km^2 with 42 districts.

17.1 Mental Health Services in România

România has approximately 900 psychiatrists for 20, 25 million people (4.16 per 100.000 population), most of them practicing in large cities. Of those, 260 are child psychiatrists (1.19 per 100.000 population). Most psychiatrists work in the Public Health Services and the remainder work in private practice. There are a relatively small number of clinical psychologists and social workers working in the mental health services. There is a shortage of trained mental health nursing and allied mental health staff working in the public and the private mental health services.

Most psychiatric services are provided by public mental health services (hospitals and out-patient services) run by the Ministry of Health; there are no private psychiatric hospitals. In România there are 16,700 beds for people with mental disorders (76/100.000 inhabitants), of which 4,600 beds are for the chronic mentally ill. There

N. Tătaru (✉)
Senior Consultant Psychiatrist, Psychiatric Ambulatory Clinic, Oradea, România
e-mail: nicol_tataru@yahoo.ca

N. Konrad et al. (eds.), *Ethical Issues in Prison Psychiatry*, International Library of Ethics, Law, and the New Medicine 46, DOI 10.1007/978-94-007-0086-4_17, © Springer Science+Business Media Dordrecht 2013

are 37 mental hospitals, 75 psychiatric units in general hospitals, four forensic low/medium security psychiatric hospitals and one high security forensic psychiatric unit in a prison. There are also 66 psychiatric outpatient clinics (community mental health services) (Tătaru 2005; Minister of Health 2006).

The special needs of mentally ill people have not always been recognized and respected. Stigma remains an obstacle in ensuring access to good care for mentally ill patients and affects the patients' quality of life and their social status. Stigma about mentally ill people leads to the development of negative attitudes (including those of health professionals), poor quality of treatment and services. The national budget for health care is low, and even lower for mental health services.

Despite anti-discrimination legislation, community tolerance for mentally ill people has decreased and unemployment has increased. The mentally ill feel rejected and marginalized in the community. For mentally ill people who have committed a crime, there is a double stigma: 'he/she is mad and bad' (van Voren 2009a).

The new Mental Health Law was implemented in Românía in August 2002. This was the first step towards the reform of the mental health services and the standard of care of mentally ill patients. Chapter 4 of the Mental Health Law lists the types of mental health services in Românía along with the standards of care for people with mental disorders.

In 2005 the Mental Health Law (2002) was reviewed and amended. The reviewed sections have included the criteria for involuntary admission to psychiatric hospitals, procedures of involuntary treatment for the mentally ill, restriction of patients' entitlements, rights to complain and confidentiality issues (Minister of Health 2006; Mental Health Law 2002).

17.2 Human Rights and Their Relevance in Forensic Psychiatry

Addressing the issues of the protection of human rights and the dignity of persons with mental disorders has only occurred relatively recently in the history of Românía. However, even as early as 1520 Neagoe Basarab, the Voivode of Wallachia (1512–1521), wrote in 'The teachings of Neagoe Basarab to his son Theodosie' about the absence of punishment for persons with mental disorders, and their living in the monasteries during their illness.

Society is equally interested in maintaining the autonomy and the well-being of its citizens as well as protecting them from risks and dangers caused by mental disorders. The protection of human rights and the dignity of persons with mental disorders should to be upheld throughout the community, including in the prison environment.

Forensic Psychiatry is a subspecialty of psychiatry, "in which scientific and clinical expertise is applied in legal contexts involving civil, criminal, correctional, regulatory or legislative matters, and in specialized clinical consultations in areas such as risk assessment or employment" (American Academy of Psychiatry and the Law 2005).

Forensic psychiatry, which is at the interface between mental health and the law, is focused on assessment and treatment of people with mental disorder who commit crimes and consequently enter the justice system.

Each country has its own laws, but legislation must respect the international mandates and principles concerning human rights and the protection of persons with mental disorders (Eaton et al. 1976). The forensic psychiatrist must understand these laws and principles, and apply that knowledge to the interface between the criminal justice system and mental health.

Forensic psychiatry is required to adhere to the same ethics, rules, and principles found in general medicine (Wettstein 2002). Overall, România's legislation respects the international mandates of the United Nations and the World Health Organization concerning the protection of the mentally ill. The legislation stipulates the framework for providing adequate treatment and care to the mentally ill persons and the need for respecting the human rights of any person and particularly the human rights of persons with mental disorders. The most important principles derived from these documents are: respecting human dignity, recognizing equal civil rights, access to medical care including medical treatment and social support, professional and family rehabilitation. The legal rights, financial rights and other personal interests of patients with mental disorders must also be protected.

In România, forensic psychiatry is not recognized as a subspecialty. General psychiatrists work as forensic psychiatrists but they do not participate as an expert witness in court; they work in general psychiatric hospitals or in forensic psychiatric hospitals. Issues such as the competency of a person with mental health issues to stand trial and criminal responsibility are assessed by a panel of psychiatrists who provide written psychiatric reports to the courts (Tătaru et al. 2010). Complex assessments may require both psychiatric and psychological evaluation and are provided by psychiatrists and clinical psychologists. Currently, Romanian legislation recognizes that all specialists in psychiatry are competent to prepare psychiatric reports for the courts. Determination of criminal responsibility is ultimately made by the court, after considering the input from the psychiatrist(s).

17.3 Romanian Mental Health Legislation

Involuntary psychiatric treatment is allowed by law if a person suffers from a mental disorder and is a risk to himself or others (Mental Health Law 2002). Involuntary commitment of incompetent patients takes into consideration the best interest of the patient, but also the well-being of the family and the potential risk to others and the community

The standards and practice of involuntary commitment to a psychiatric hospital have changed three times since World War II (1965, 1980, and 2002). The Mental Health Law (2002), which emphasises the protection of a patient's rights (4), has replaced a number of previous legislations: Decrees 12/1965 and 313/1980. Modalities of involuntary commitment to psychiatric hospitals and to forensic psychiatric hospitals are regulated by the Mental Health Law 2002 (amended in 2005) and also by Art 948 of Romanian Civil Code.

There are legal and ethical issues with respect to involuntary hospitalisation because it restricts a person's liberty. According to the Madrid Declaration of the World Psychiatric Association in 1996 (Declaration of Madrid 1996), treatment must always be in the best interest of the patient in respect of his dignity and the legal and human rights.

17.4   Involuntary Treatment and the Mentally-Impaired Prisoner: Ethical Issues

Psychiatrists are involved in the care of mentally ill prisoners, those found guilty and those found not guilty by reason of insanity. They must balance the need to ensure the safety of the patient and also the community, which often requires hospitalization in a psychiatric facility. In addition, the psychiatrist faces challenging professional, ethical and legal issues in regard to caring for the person with mental illness, including: the principles of individual freedom, civil liberties and autonomy; informed consent and the right to treatment (or the right to refuse treatment); involuntary hospitalization; confidentiality and the doctor patient relationship (Tătaru et al. 2010; Andreasen Nancy and Black 2006).

Nancy Andreasen (Andreasen Nancy and Black 2006) divides the legal issues pertaining to mental illness into: (a) civil (involuntary hospitalization, the right to treatment, the right to refuse treatment, child custody), (b) criminal (competency of the patient to stand trial and criminal responsibility) and (c) personal issues (doctor-patient relationship, confidentiality, informed consent, malpractice and decision-making that requires testimony). Forensic psychiatry has expanded to include new areas of interest and functions, such as civil competencies and other issues such as informed consent and the right of patients to refuse treatment (Gutheil 1999).

The fitness to stand trial of a person with mental illness is determined by the Court after the person has been evaluated by a psychiatrist or a psychiatric commission. If a patient is found unfit to stand trial for a minor offense, he/she is referred for voluntary or involuntary psychiatric treatment in a psychiatric hospital or to an out-patient mental health service.

In Român-a, both the concepts of insanity and diminished responsibility are recognized and decided upon by the court following an assessment provided by a medico-legal commission of three (or more) doctors, one medico-legal practitioner and two psychiatrists (Criminal Code, Chapter II, Art. 44–51 and the new Criminal Code, Chapter III, Art. 26–33 for evaluating the criminal responsibility, completed by the Criminal Procedural Code, Art. 116–127, and Civil Procedural Code, Art. 201–214) (Criminal Code 2006; Criminal Procedural Code 2006; Civil Procedural Code 2005).

If a person is found not guilty for reasons of insanity, there are three legal options for his/her care and involuntary treatment depending on the level of dangerousness: (1) hospitalization in a maximum security psychiatric hospital if the dangerousness is permanent and severe; (2) in less severe cases the person is placed in a low/medium security forensic psychiatric hospital and (3) if the risk to the community is considered low the person is admitted to a civil psychiatric hospital or referred for involuntary outpatient treatment. Patients on involuntary treatment orders are reassessed regularly, at least every 6 months, which is similar to the situation in other countries in this region (Marinov and Velinov 2009; van Voren 2009b).

The psychiatrists' clinical evaluations should be performed in the spirit of honesty and objectivity (American Academy of Psychiatry and the Law 2005; Gutheil 1999). There are differences in the ethical implications between forensic psychiatry and general psychiatry in regards to the relationship between the psychiatrist and the patient. For general psychiatry, the ethical approach is that of the traditional doctor-patient relationship, as in general medicine. However, in forensic psychiatry the relationship can be 'examiner-examinee' as well as the traditional relationship 'doctor-patient' when the psychiatrist is also the treating doctor of the patient (Gutheil 1999). That is, the forensic psychiatrist can have dual, and at times conflicting, responsibilities of caregiver and assessor for the patient. Psychiatrists have to obtain informed consent for evaluation, just as they do for treatment, but they have to make clear the ethical distinction between consent for evaluation and consent for treatment (American Academy of Psychiatry and the Law 2005).

Consent to treatment is linked to human dignity, personal liberty and the inviolability of the person. Patients need to have the right to refuse the treatment, e.g. when they believe that their quality of life would be compromised by treatment. Patients also have the right to know what their diagnosis is. The psychiatrist takes a considered approach when informing a patient of their diagnosis, taking into consideration the risk profile of the patient, and ensuring the patient understands the benefits, risks and available alternatives for treatment (Tătaru 2008; Kaplan and Sadock 1991). They should also include caregivers in this process.

The involuntary commitment of a mentally ill person to a psychiatric inpatient unit or to involuntary treatment in an out-patient clinic is based upon the mental state and the risk posed by the individual's behaviour. There are legal and ethical limits to involuntary hospitalisation. The new legislation (Mental Health Law 2002, amended in 2005) prevents the indefinite hospitalisation of mentally ill individuals which was possible before the 1965 revision. Termination of the involuntary treatment is decided by court after a new evaluation by a medical board. The courts decide if and when a patient has to be discharged from the involuntary treatment order (Criminal Code 113). The follow-up and supervision of the patient becomes the responsibility of the Department of Health and the Ministry of Justice.

The forensic psychiatrist has to deal with additional ethical dilemmas to those encountered by psychiatrists working in civil psychiatric mental health services. For example, the dual role of the psychiatrist as an objective assessor and as a doctor in the doctor-patient relationship, the issue of limited confidentiality, limited consent to treatment and the need to balance the patient's medical care and social well-being with public safety and expectations are some of the issues. Furthermore, the clinical process in forensic psychiatry may be in conflict with the judicial outcome for the patient. For example, the psychiatric assessment may find a person has a diagnosis of a personality disorder but does not suffer from a major mental illness while the court may rule that person is 'not guilty by reason of insanity'.

Other ethical/professional issues arise when the psychiatrist panel recommends the discharge of a patient from involuntary hospitalization or involuntary treatment and the court rules to continue the involuntary status of the patient. These differences between the medical opinion and the court's decision of managing the mentally ill offender may be in part explained by the fact that in România psychiatrists do not act as expert witnesses in the court process. This precludes psychiatrists the opportunity to present and discuss their medical opinions directly with the court.

The legal premise for specialized treatment of persons deemed dangerous to others is to ensure public safety while the treatment of suicidal or severely disabled persons (who are a danger to themselves) is to ensure their safety. However, in România there are a lack of specialized institutions for patients with comorbid mental disorders and highly dangerous behavior (Tătaru et al. 2010).

Legislation also safeguards the legal rights of the individuals who have committed a crime. Patients suffering from a serious mental illness who are considered a high risk to the community are usually treated in a medium-security forensic psychiatric hospital. There are four such forensic hospitals in România. Individuals considered to be a high risk to the community are hospitalised in Jilava Prison, the only high-security forensic psychiatric hospital in România.

17.5 Delivering Mental Health Services in Prison

> The prison system, including the criminal law, is usually a reflection of the attitude of governments, politicians and citizens towards crimes and criminals. (Raes and van Voren 2009)

A person charged with having committed an offense is considered not guilty until an independent court has assessed his/her guilt and a verdict has been made. This implies that such a person should be treated according to United Nations charter for human rights (Tătaru et al. 2010; van Voren 2009b; Raes and van Voren 2009; Konrad et al. 2007). Criminal law provides the criteria, procedures and measures for punishment of persons who commit, and are found guilty of, an offense.

The aims of sentencing are achieved through the Prison Services objectives, which are to contain prisoners securely, to provide humane and lawful treatment and, importantly, to reduce the risk of re-offending through rehabilitation, education and reintegration in the community (Marinov and Velinov 2009).

The imprisonment rate in România is 155 per 100.000 population (International Centre for Prison Studies 2008). This is similar to rate in other European countries: Bulgaria (148) Slovakia (155) Hungary (156) England and Wales (148) and Germany (93).

There is an increased prevalence of mental disorders in prisoners compared to the general population. Prison psychiatrists provide treatment for mental illness within the prison complex. The prisoner is referred by a general practitioner to a forensic psychiatrist under the criteria established by regulations in Romanian Prison Law. România's only a high-security forensic psychiatric in-patient unit (the Psychiatry Department, Penitentiary Hospital, Bucureşti) is part of the Jilava Prison. The Penitentiary Hospital is a 390 bed prison hospital, of which 85 beds are for persons suffering mental illness (almost 85 % are men). The majority of prisoners in the forensic unit are diagnosed with personality disorders.

The prevalence of severe mental disorders in the prison population in România is low, mainly because of the court diversion system which prevents mentally ill persons being imprisoned and recommends hospitalization in an external forensic psychiatric hospital or in a general psychiatric hospital.

Mentally disordered patients who commit a crime, offenders with first-episode psychosis or other severe mental disorders, and those who have established mental disorders when entering the criminal justice system can be hospitalized and treated in the forensic psychiatric unit. These mentally ill offenders are evaluated regularly by the forensic psychiatric commission that makes recommendations to the Court (Tătaru et al. 2010; Buda 2006).

The psychological effects of imprisonment are well known and include depression, self harm, suicide attempts and completed suicide. The rate of these problems is higher in the prison population compared to the general population. Suicide is the leading cause of death in custodial services and institutions, especially during the early stage of imprisonment. Factors which increase the suicide risk of offenders are the following: bullying by guards and other prisoners, aggression and sexual assault. For prisoners with a mental illness, there is also a high risk that their mental illness will relapse (Konrad et al. 2007).

The human rights of the prisoners, the right to treatment and the right to receive an acceptable quality of care are fundamental rights for all prisoners. For this reason, they also have the right to be re-evaluated by the forensic psychiatry commission for determining the need for involuntary treatment or hospitalization. The request for re-assessment is the obligation of the prosecutor. The information required for re-assessment is usually obtained from the files of prison psychiatrists or other prison physicians. In some cases the prison sentence can be temporarily suspended until a significant improvement in the prisoner's health status has occurred, which is determined by another forensic psychiatric assessment. Secure confinement can then be ordered in a forensic psychiatric institution, outside of the prison system, if it is necessary.

The criminal law and its procedures should ensure a high quality of pre-trial psychiatric assessments to assist the courts to distinguish between offenders who are not responsible, or have diminished responsibility, based on their mental state at the time of the offence (Tătaru et al. 2010; Raes and van Voren 2009).

Normally, psychiatrists and psychologists involved in such assessments should be independent expert witnesses to the court to ensure there is no conflict of interest.

In România, no ethical problem arises here as psychiatrists don't act as expert witnesses to the courts.

Unfortunately, in România and in almost all other countries, the legislation doesn't permit involuntary treatment of mentally ill prisoners while they are in prison. A mentally ill prisoner who refuses treatment therefore remains untreated until they are referred to a psychiatric hospital where they can be treated as an involuntary patient under the umbrella of the Mental Health Legislation. Of note, the current legislation allows involuntary treatment of mentally ill patients in the community under a Community Treatment Order but this cannot be applied in a prison setting. It could be argued that Community Treatment Orders should extend to prisons as the prisons are part of the community. Moreover, a mentally ill prisoner cannot be transferred involuntarily to a psychiatric hospital for treatment until they fulfill the criteria for an involuntary admission. Essentially, a mentally ill prisoner has to become significantly unwell before he becomes 'eligible' for involuntary transfer to a psychiatric facility. The legislation should be amended to permit the involuntary treatment for mentally ill offenders in prison, once the patient is assessed, and treatment is recommended, by a psychiatrist.

Discharging a patient from a secure treatment setting has significant challenges because of the negative public image of forensic psychiatric patients. At worst, the patient's discharge consists of nothing more than release back into society, where they depend upon their own social network, if they have one at all, and no psychiatric follow-up.

There is a high percentage of recidivism if patients return to an unstable social milieu and/or without adequate clinical follow-up arrangements. România, like Bulgaria and Serbia, has no after-care and resettlement organizations and there are few social workers who can assist patients to re-integrate into the community (Tătaru et al. 2010; Marinov and Velinov 2009; van Voren 2009b).

17.6   Conclusions

All forensic psychiatrists are expected to adhere to the general moral principles of society and to the ethics of the medical profession, such as the Oath of Hippocrates, Declaration of Geneva 1948, International Code of Medical Ethics 1949, Declaration of Helsinki 1964, Declaration of Hawaii 1977, Declaration of Madrid 1996, and the Declaration of Paris, 2005.

In addition, they must advocate for, and ensure the protection of human rights for prisoners with mental illness and remain vigilant in monitoring for the potential for abuse in psychiatry (Tătaru et al. 2010; Marinov and Velinov 2009; van Voren 2009b; Tătaru 2008). Unlike other psychiatrists, they may find themselves torn between what may be legally right and what may be ethically right for a forensic mental health patient.

Debate about various ethical issues in this specialized field of mental health continues, such as that of limited confidentiality and the patient's needs versus societal needs and expectations.

Historically, involuntary treatment of incompetent patients with mental illness (which can take place in a hospital or in the community) takes into consideration the best interest of the patient and also the best interests of those of the family/carer(s) and the wider community. The involuntary treatment of prisoners, however, is a contentious issue; currently there is no mechanism that permits the involuntary treatment of mentally ill prisoners, unless they deteriorate to such an extent that they require hospitalization. Legislation for the involuntary treatment of a patient under a Community Treatment Order should be extended to prisons as they are part of and belong to the community.

There have been some improvements in the quality of care delivered in the mental health services (including the forensic psychiatric hospitals) in România since the implementation of the Mental Health Law 2002. However, there are significant areas of unmet need and research is needed to evaluate whether prisoners with mental disorders receive appropriate care to the standard mandated by the European Convention on Human Rights (Konrad et al. 2007).

The most important problems facing forensic psychiatry and prison mental health in România and other Eastern European countries include insufficient care programs, the lack of multi-disciplinary treatment teams, a lack of psychosocial rehabilitation programs and programs for the re-integration of forensic psychiatric patients back into the community (Tătaru et al. 2010; Marinov and Velinov 2009).

It is important that we continue to advocate for improved standards of care for forensic patients whilst they are in custody, and upon release into the community, if we are committed to diverting the typical trajectory of such patients away from recidivism and poorer health outcomes in the future.

References

American Academy of Psychiatry and the Law. 2005. American Academy of Psychiatry and the Law Ethics Guidelines for the Practice of Forensic Psychiatry. Bloomfield: American Academy of Psychiatry and the Law, 1995.

Andreasen Nancy, C., and W.D. Black. 2006. Legal issues in psychiatry. In *Introductory textbook of psychiatry*, 3rd ed, ed. N.C. Andreasen and W.D. Black, 667–678. Washington, DC/London: American psychiatric Publishing, Inc.

Buda, O. 2006. *Iresponsabilitatea-Aspecte medico-legale psihiatrice cu aplicaţii în dreptul penal, civil şi al familiei, Editura Ştiinţelor Medicale*. Bucureşti: Editura Juridică.

Civil Procedural Code. 2005. Ed. Bucureşti: All Beck.

Criminal Code. 2006. Legea Nr.301/28 June 2004, Monitorul Oficial al Românei, Partea I, Nr.303/12 April 2005, with validity in 1 September 2006.

Criminal Procedural Code. 2006. Ed. Bucureşti: All Beck.

Declaration of Madrid. 1996. Approved by the General Assembly of the World Psychiatry Association on 25 August 1996 in Madrid, and amended by General Assembly in Yokohama, Japan in August 2002 and in Cairo in September 2005.

Eaton Jr., M.T., M.H. Peterson, and J.A. Davis. 1976. Psychiatry, 3rd ed, 419–444. New York: Medical Examination Publishing, Co., Inc.

Gutheil, T.G. 1999. Ethics and forensic psychiatry. In *Psychiatric Ethics*, 3rd ed, ed. S. Bloch, P. Chodoff, and S. Green, 346–361. Oxford: Oxford University Press.

International Centre for Prison Studies. 2008. http://www.prisonstudies.org/

Kaplan, H.I., and B.J. Sadock. 1991. Forensic Psychiatry. In *Synopsis of Psychiatry Behavioral Science. Clinical Psychiatry*, 6th ed, 820–835. Philadelphia: Lippincott Williams & Wilkins.

Konrad, N., J. Arboleda-Florez, A.D. Jager, K. Naudts, J. Taborda, and N. Tătaru. 2007. Prison psychiatry. *International Journal of Prisoner Health* 3(2): 111–113, 1744–9219.

Marinov, P., and V. Velinov. 2009. Bulgaria: A European Union Member Lagging Behind in Forensics. *Mental Health Reforms*, Special issue: Forensic Psychiatry and Prison mental Health 2:18–21.

Mental Health Law. 2002, amended in 2005. Monitorul oficial al României, XIV, Nr. 589/8-Aug 2002, Mental Health Law. Nr.487.

Minister of Health. 2006. *Government of România, recent developments in Mental Health Policy and Legislation in România.*

Raes, D., and R. van Voren. 2009. Developing prison mental health services in countries in transition: Challenges, constraints and opportunities. *Mental Health Reforms*, Special Issue: Forensic psychiatry and Prison mental Health, Global Initiative on Psychiatry (GIP) 2:4–10.

Tătaru, N. 2005. Country Profile-Psychiatry and Geriatric Psychiatry in România. *Bulletin of the Board of International Affairs of the Royal College of Psychiatrists* 7: 12–15.

Tătaru, N. 2008. Practice of competence assessment in dementia in Romania. In *Competence assessment in dementia*, ed. G. Stoppe and EDCON, 151–155. Vienna: Springer.

Tătaru, N., P. Marinov, A. Douzenis, A. Novotni, and B. Kecman. 2010. Forensic psychiatry in some Balkan countries. *Current Opinion in Psychiatry* 23: 472–480.

van Voren, R. 2009a. Editorial. *Mental Health Reforms*, Special Issue: Forensic psychiatry and Prison mental Health, Global Initiative on Psychiatry (GIP) 2:3.

van Voren, R. 2009b. Initiating reform in prison mental health and forensic psychiatry in Serbia. *Mental Health Reforms*, Special Issue: Forensic psychiatry and Prison mental Health, Global Initiative on Psychiatry (GIP) 2: 16–17.

Wettstein, R.M. 2002. Ethics and forensic psychiatry. *The Psychiatric Clinics of North America* 25(3): 623–633.

Chapter 18
Ethical Issues of Mental Health Care in the Slovene Prison System

Vita Poštuvan and Tanja Madjar

The average daily number of prisoners (both convicted and on remand) in Slovenia in 2009 was 1,415.8 (Annual Report 2009) and with an overall capacity for 1,098 prisoners the average occupancy rate for prisons was 128.94 %. The highest occupation rate (204.6 %) was found in Ljubljana prison, followed by Dob prison (187.1 %). Ljubljana prison is the biggest prison in the country with an average of 435.9 prisoners incarcerated in 2009 (and capacities for 233 people) (Annual Report 2009).

The number of inmates has grown in the last 10 years and overcrowding is a significant issue. Projects to provide better housing in the Slovene prison system are ongoing.

18.1 The Prevalence of Mental Disorder Among Prisoners in Slovenia

The Slovene prison system does not have exact data on the prevalence of mental disorders in prisons as there is no system to gather and report these data.

Nonetheless, a recent study (EUPRIS 2007; Uršič-Perhavc et al. 2007) showed that, according to ICD-10, F4 (Neurotic, stress-related and somatoform disorders) disorders were the most frequent in Slovene prisons. This was following (in descending order) by F1 (Mental and behavioural disorders due to psychoactive

V. Poštuvan (✉)
Slovene Center for Suicide Research, Andrej Marušič Institute,
University of Primorska, Muzejski trg 2, 6000 Koper, Slovenia
e-mail: vita.postuvan@upr.si

T. Madjar
Zavod Za Prestajanje Kazni Zapora Maribor/Maribor Prison,
Vošnjakova 16, 2000 Maribor, Slovenia
e-mail: tanjave@gmail.com

N. Konrad et al. (eds.), *Ethical Issues in Prison Psychiatry*, International Library
of Ethics, Law, and the New Medicine 46, DOI 10.1007/978-94-007-0086-4_18,
© Springer Science+Business Media Dordrecht 2013

Table 18.1 Statistics on deaths and suicides in prisons in Slovenia

Year	Total number of deaths	Number of suicides	Suicides as a percentage of total deaths (%)	Average number of inmates	Mortality rate per 100,000 prisoners	Suicide rate per 100,000 prisoners
1995	9	3	33.33	772	1,165.8	388.6
1996	7	5	71.43	682	1,026.4	733.1
1997	4	2	50.00	763	524.2	262.1
1998	10	4	40.00	810	1,234.6	493.8
1999	1	1	100.00	949	105.4	105.4
2000	7	4	57.14	1,131	618.9	353.7
2001	7	4	57.14	1,203	581.9	332.5
2002	7	4	57.14	1,148	609.8	348.4
2003	4	3	75.00	1,120	357.1	267.9
2004	1	0	0.00	1,132	88.3	0.0
2005	6	2	33.33	1,137	527.7	175.9
2006	4	1	25.00	1,268	315.5	78.9
2007	8	3	37.50	1,339	597.5	224.0
2008	7	3	42.86	1,364	513.2	219.9
2009	4	2	50.00	1,416	282.5	141.2
1995–2009	**86**	**41**	**47.67**	**16,234**	**529.8**	**252.6**

substance use), F6 (Disorders of adult personality and behaviour), F3 (Mood [affective] disorders), F5 (Behavioural syndromes associated with physiological disturbances, and physical factors), F2 (Schizophrenia, schizotypal and delusional disorders), F0 (Organic, including symptomatic, mental disorders) and F7 (Mental retardation).

Suicide is a significant indicator of mental ill health. Slovenia has one of the highest suicide rates in the world (about 20 per 100,000 inhabitants in 2008). There were 75 self-inflicted injuries reported in the year 2008 and 69 in the year 2009 in prison. In 2009, medical health care was provided to 40 % of inmates (28 persons) with self-inflicted injuries and there were six hospitalisations in psychiatric hospitals. The most frequent self-inflicted injuries were cuts, hanging, blows, swallowing of items and poisoning. In 2008, three prisoners and in 2009 two prisoners (all male) committed suicide; the suicide rate was about 12 times higher than in the general population (for 2008: 220; see Table 18.1). Suicide is the leading cause of death in prisons (more than half of deaths) and the most common suicide method is hanging (76.67 %), followed by overdose (16.67 %) and cuts (6.67 %) (Annual Report 2008, 2009 and internal databases of Prison Administration). The experience of prison staff highlights that prisoners often report feelings of hopelessness, powerlessness, and an inability to see solutions for their problems, feel distress because of imprisonment, worsening of their relationships with others, or have problems with substance abuse.

The government monitors the status of mental health of imprisoned persons on the basis of daily reports of extraordinary events in all prison facilities. Additional information on this subject is published annually as a report by the Prison Administration.

18.2   The Organisation of Mental Health Care
in Jails and Prisons

18.2.1   The Health Care System

The laws that regulate health care in prison in Slovenia are:

• Enforcement of Penal Sentences Act and the laws that follow this order
• Law on Health Care and Health Insurance (Zakon o izvrševanju kazenskih
  sankcij 2007)
• The rules on enforcement of security measures for compulsory psychiatric
  treatment and care in health care services, compulsory psychiatric treatment and
  compulsory treatment of alcohol and drug abuse (Zakon o zdravstvenem varstvu
  in zdravstvenem zavarovanju 2006)
• European prison rules
• Human rights in prisons, Council of Europe
• Mental Health Act
• Patients' Rights Act, which enables the right to appeal in cases of mistreatment
  in health care treatment (Zakon o pacientovih pravicah 2008)

Health care in the prison system is organised in collaboration by the Ministry of
Justice, Ministry of Health, Ministry of Finance and The Health Insurance Institute.
Since 2009, the prison health care system has been part of the public health care
system and it functions in line with the basic health care insurance. Before that date,
the health care of prisoners was solely organised by the Ministry of Justice (direct
contracts were made between prisons and individual doctors), which was more
problematic in terms of financing and providing the same quality of care and
insurance benefits than for the general population.

The situation has improved significantly since the new arrangements have been
put in place. Health insurance benefits are now available both for the inmates on
remand, who do not have any other medical insurance, and for convicted prisoners,
including juvenile prisoners, and for those in re-education facilities and in obligatory psychiatric or addiction treatments. Furthermore, imprisoned foreigners have
the same rights. The prison administration (Ministry of Justice) covers the costs of
basic health care insurance, and the Ministry of Health covers the potentially higher
costs of additional health care.

Inmates essentially have the same rights regarding health care as other citizens.
They are entitled to the health care according to the Health Care Law, with the
exceptions mentioned in the 58th article of the Law on Enforcement of Penal
Sentences. These are the rights that cannot be fulfilled during the time of imprisonment. E.g., inmates have limited options in choosing their personal GPs as the
prison GP becomes their personal GP. Prisoners also do not have the right of treatment
at home, treatment abroad, treatment at a health resort, sick-leave (even though they
work within the prison), health care for family members, funeral expenses or travel
reimbursements for medical treatment reasons.

The prison healthcare network includes 11 prison outpatient clinics, but does not have prison hospitals or wards. Local health care facilities are responsible for providing primary health care for prisons, as prison outpatient clinics are part of the public health care network. They have a team of GPs, a psychiatrist, dentist and gynaecologist responsible for the local prison facilities. The prison does not have any direct contracts with doctors, but still employs nurses. General practitioners work from one to three times per week in the prison setting (depending on the prison size). They are under the control of the Ministry of Health and members of a public network of outpatient clinics in Slovenia.

There were 45,139 examinations done in 2009 within the prison outpatient clinics. Usually there are no delays or waiting lists for GP visits. There were 5,584 examinations by psychiatrists, 3,810 by dentists, 1,162 lab tests, and 730 examinations by gynaecologists (in women's prison), dermatologists and others. There was a decrease of psychiatric and dental examinations in comparison to 2008 and there were also fewer treatments done outside the prison (Annual Report 2009).

In cases of intensive care needs, prisoners are referred with an official order to external services, such as specialist clinics or specialised hospitals, all part of the general health care system. Health care personnel in prison assess the urgency of the referrals and manage the appointments. Waiting times for the prisoners are usually of the same duration as for the general population. Emergency cases are immediately transferred to the nearest general hospital or an emergency ambulance is called.

According to the Annual Report 2009, there were 5,632 external examinations done in that year, which is a 10 % decrease compared to 2008. Male prisoners had 5,328 appointments, mostly in diagnostic labs for X-rays, computed tomography (CT), electroencephalography (EEG), ultrasound (1,179), as well as attending trauma clinics (839), internal medicine clinics (646), dentists (669), or others. Female prisoners had 194 specialised examinations outside the prison system, most of them in internal medicine clinics (56) followed by diagnostic labs to do X-rays, CT, EEG (20), optical clinics (14), trauma clinics (51), etc. Juvenile inmates had 110 examinations, most of them in trauma, psychiatric, otorhinolaryngology clinics, and optics.

In 2009 there was a 3 % decrease in inmate hospitalisations. One hundred and eighty three prisoners were hospitalised; 106 were escorted during that time and 77 were not. Most of the hospitalised persons were male (with escort 104, without escort 69) and the other eight were female (two escorted). Only two juvenile inmates were hospitalised, both without escort. The majority of hospitalisations was in general hospitals (66) and the rest in psychiatric facilities (35). Sixty-one hospitalisations occurred in the University Clinical Centre Ljubljana.

In 2009, there were 11,986 days of sick leave, a 24 % increase from 2008. Out of this number, 10,616 (males: 10,602, females: 0, juvenile: 14) were spent within the prisons and 1,370 (males: 1,320, females: 32, juvenile: 18) within the external hospitals.

18.2.2   The Mental Health Care System

For the purpose of providing mental health care, every prison in Slovenia, in addition to general nurses and doctors, also employs mental health professionals.

In total, there are 13 psychiatrists, who are part of the public health care system, as well as institutional staff such as psychologists, teachers/educators and social workers. All psychiatric inpatient care is provided by public psychiatric hospitals, as there are no forensic departments, hospitals or special medical settings for prisoners in Slovenia.

Mental health professionals are available from 8–12 h daily (from Monday to Friday), but their presence depends on job specifications. Psychiatrists are available from once weekly to once per month and psychologists, nurses or educators every day. In cases of psychiatric emergencies, if no mental health professionals are available, emergency services responsible for the general public are called.

18.2.3 Collaboration with Governmental and Non-governmental Organisations Outside the Prison System

Other institutions outside the prison system play an important part in the mental health care of prisoners. There are different ways of initiating this collaboration: prison GPs, psychiatrists or other prison staff might refer the prisoner to institutions outside. Alternately, the prisoner might express a wish to seek additional help in other institutions. For example, there is an established practice of good cooperation between the prison system and the Centre for Treatment of Drug Addiction (in Ljubljana), a governmental organisation. Other frequent options for treatment are psychiatric clinics, local outpatient clinics for alcohol addiction (AA), local AA groups, self-help alcoholic clubs and other centres for the treatment of substance abuse. The NGO network in this field is also quite developed and their counselling and support staff might deliver their service (e.g. individual therapy/treatment) even within prison wards. There are cases when prisoners continue these treatments even after serving their prison sentence.

As other citizens, prisoners are covered by basic health insurance and given a valid insurance card. With this card, a prisoner can visit any health care facility during periods of leave or holidays. They can also visit private health care providers if they pay privately, similar to the general population. Prisoners who are not permitted leave may visit health care providers with escorts.

18.2.4 Individual (Mental Health) Care for Prisoners

When entering the prison system, personnel perform an initial assessment of the inmate's needs. Usually, no psychiatric diagnosis is made in this phase, as time-limitations do not allow that. Prison personnel also assess background history, suicidality, social network contacts, current mental health and social status, and behaviour and criminal history. Within 24 h the prisoner has an appointment with a general practitioner, who makes the decision as to whether the inmate is fit to serve his/her punishment in the prison. Prisoners are not given access to mental health professionals automatically, but the option to receive psychiatric help is presented to them as appropriate.

Almost all prisoners see a psychologist during their imprisonment. The majority of psychologists' work in prison consists of counselling (40.56 %) or debriefing (25.54 %) as well as informative interviews (20.66 %). Other work demands, such as introductory interviews (10.89 %) and crisis interventions (2.34 %) are also carried out (Annual Report 2009). Crisis interventions are implemented in situations of acute personal distresses, suicidal ideations, self-inflicted injuries, depressive mood and acute emotional strain.

The form of help and its content depend on the inmates' problems, motivation and the professional background of the psychologist (e.g. CBT orientation). Psychologists mainly offer help to inmates with regards to violent behaviour, alcohol addiction, illegal drug addiction, self-harm behaviour, distress, etc. The work of the psychologists is carried out in individual and group settings.

In 2009, there were 4,186 sessions performed by prison psychologists in total. There were 256 continuing sessions, which lasted on average of 6.6 sessions. That number increased despite a 14 % annual decrease of persons receiving psychological help (in 2009 there were 1,009 persons involved). During the same time there were 5,584 psychiatric sessions carried out. Besides the work described above, psychologists and psychiatrists were involved in collaboration with other institutions. Treatment for drug addiction includes methadone therapy in collaboration with local drug addiction specialists.

18.2.5   Assessment at Entry and Release

New prisoners go (in addition to the entry assessment) through a further assessment by psychologists, social workers and pedagogues – the aim of which is a comprehensive individualised plan of work. The period during which these assessments are completed is defined by the law as the entrance phase and is performed within a month of entry for every new prisoner. Prison personnel thus get to know the prisoner and his problems while assessing his/her attitudes toward the crime committed, problems in his life, family and personal history, social network and support, education and work experiences, etc. According to the data collected, an individual plan of work is set for the newly accepted inmate, where the short- and long-term goals of professional sessions, activities and prison living are set. Individual plans of work can be changed during the imprisonment, as they are updated regularly.

Even during the sentence and especially before release, post-sentence problems are assessed. There is an individualized approach to this assessment, which is adjusted to the needs of the inmate (e.g. his/her accommodation, employment, motivation to undergo treatment, collaboration with other institutions, medical treatment). There is no actuarial or structured risk assessment tool in Slovenia that is applied before the prisoner is released from prison to help in predicting the risk of re-offending. Instead the risk of re-offending is assessed on the basis of professional judgement and the behaviour of the inmate throughout his prison term.

18.2.5.1   Costs

Prisoners' health care insurance and health care costs while incarcerated, which also include mental health care, are covered by a collaboration of Prison Administration, Ministry of Health and other partners. Some further issues regarding mental health care will be discussed below.

18.3   Special Ethical Problems Concerning Mental Health in the Slovene Prison System

Professional work with prisoners has its basis in the following principles:

- The principle of humane treatment
- The principle of active participation of prisoners in the treatment programme
- The principle of individualisation of interventions
- The principle of social rehabilitation (EUPRIS 2007)

These principles are applied in the prisoners' day-to-day care. The prisoners' individual work plans are based on their needs. The work plan is prepared in collaboration with the inmate. On the whole, treatment is humane and the methods for rehabilitation are good. Once both sides agree on the work plan, there is an expectation that the prisoner is motivated and active to fulfil his part of the plan, which includes his/her active participation. Professional staff is in charge of the implementation of the goals by providing activities in line with the needs of the inmate. Staff is committed to confidentiality of personal data and the individualisation of approaches and demands. During imprisonment there is a strong cooperation with the prison's social work service, which takes care of post-sentence problems. The social work service is also responsible for looking for better ways to improve the quality of life after punishment, which is another aspect of rehabilitation.

The overall organisation of mental health care in prisons in Slovenia raises several ethical questions. Some of these issues are similar to those discussed in other countries, others are specific to the Slovene environment. Some of these are also frequently on the agenda of two main organisations, which try to protect human rights (in mental health care) of the prisoners – the Human Rights Ombudsman and the Ombudsman for Patients' Rights.

18.3.1   The Principle of Equivalence

The Slovene prison system tries to provide equivalence of health care to the inmates with regard to the general population. The equivalence of mental health care is provided through access of prisoners to a GP, psychiatric care and psychological support within the prison, and the possibility of referrals outside the prison system.

18.3.1.1   Freedom to Choose

Prison mental health care does not provide the right to choose a personal GP, psychiatrist or psychologist. These are allocated by the prison administration or more accurately by each prison centre as these are the only logistically effective ways of treatment. One could argue that a prisoner does not have the freedom to choose his/her own treatment staff, in particular his personal GP and does therefore not have an equivalent care compared to the general population. But we have to take into account that every prisoner (as previously described) also has the possibility to seek other health care, which enables his/her freedom to choose.

Furthermore, imprisonment usually results in a change of prisoners' GP, which might sometimes be problematic in terms of the personal relationship built with their doctor. In Slovenia, GPs work as the primary gatekeepers of more specialised healthcare services, thus the patient-doctor relationship and knowledge of medical history is of great importance. The exchange of health care records will be easier once electronic health care records are introduced in Slovenia.

Despite these ethical considerations, at this moment the current status seems the only feasible solution for the prison system in Slovenia; namely, it is logistically not possible to make contracts with several GPs or to transfer inmates to different locations for their GP visits.

18.3.1.2   Waiting Times

Waiting times for people within the prison might be an important issue in considering equivalence of care. Delays are possible, but the prison administration claims they are no longer than those in the general population (EUPRIS 2007). The prison system in Slovenia might in fact sometimes provide quicker mental health care than in the general population. The prisoners rarely establish access to other health care providers by themselves: the prison medical staff usually arranges visit at specialised clinics, which may result in shorter waiting times.

18.3.1.3   Additional Mental Health Care Outside the Prison System

If a prisoner wishes to have access to psychiatric or psychotherapeutic help outside the prison system, there are different procedures to achieve this. If a GP agrees with the referral and this can be provided within the basic health care insurance, a referral is usually performed without problems. However, if a prisoner wishes to receive specific treatment (e.g. psychiatric treatment/psychotherapy in the private sector) not covered by state insurance, treatment is provided in accordance with the prisoner's financial situation. Prisoners who have sufficient funds, and appear motivated, and where prison staff feel the treatment is indicated, are able to access additional treatment. They can also get treatment without problems during periods of leave. Others, who do not have their own funding, cannot access additional treatment even if they are motivated to do so. This problem does not only apply to prison mental health though, but mental health in Slovenia in general. Nonetheless, such cases are rare, as the Slovenian health care system provides a whole range of treatment options. Also, prison centres always help in finding a solution for cases without funding and encourage any motivated prisoners to get additional treatment.

Networking Problems

The networking of the Slovene prison system with institutions outside the prison and the public health care system is needs based. Namely, the law defines the relationship with only a small number of institutions, while other collaborations rely on the actual needs of prisoners. It is an advantage for the prisoner if there is an already established relationship with the institution where he/she needs additional help from. This might in turn differ in different prisons throughout Slovenia.

The law regulates the collaboration of the prison system with the Social Work Centre (SWC). Based on that collaboration there is frequent communication about the ongoing sentence between both parties. The SWC delivers a report on their previous experience with the inmate and his family. The depth of the communication of both sides depends on the inmate's wishes.

Networking with other institutions also depends on the motivation of the inmate. In these cases institutions do not have any guidelines or specified ways of collaboration: there is no rule regarding what data is needed, needs to be communicated as well as time frames. This is the main reason that the problems in this field are solved individually, dependent both on the prison, the person in charge and the institution. This problem is the same for institutions in public health, NGOs or possible private mental health providers.

It would be helpful if the uncertain and formally unclear situation of networking would be unified and possibly more prescribed (but still flexible). This way there wouldn't be uncertainties in information exchange and shared responsibilities would be more easily implemented.

Table 18.2 reflects the extent of cooperation of prison staff with institutions from outside the prison system. No exclusively mental health care organisation (e.g. self-help AA groups) is specified in this list. In 2009, the prison system collaborated most frequently with Social Work Centres (56.7 %) and with NGOs and educational organisations (23.6 %).

18.3.1.4 Confidentiality

The prison protects all personal data according to the Personal Data Protection Act of Slovenia (Zakon o varstvu osebnih podatkov 2004). Diagnoses of mental disorders are documented in the health care record of the inmate and this information is not available to any non-medical prison staff. Only the psychiatrist and GP have access to this data and they do not share it with other personnel.

Table 18.2 Cooperation with institutions outside the prison system in 2009 (Annual Report 2009)

Institution	Number of contacts
Social Work Centre	1,516
Employment Service of Slovenia	146
Working organisations	146
Red Cross or Caritas	179
Health care providers	70
Education system	217
Housing organisations	69
ZPIZ (The Institute of Pension and Invalidity Insurance of Slovenia)	41
Elderly homes	15
Single people homes	0
Other	35
Total contacts	2,670

Prison psychologists perform their assessments of prisoners' mental health problems independently from the psychiatrist's work or sometimes with his/her (informal) recommendation. Sometimes prison psychologists may ask for a psychiatric assessment. Detailed information, dilemmas or problems occurring during the treatment are shared by psychologists with a limited number of professionals, who work in the prison's rehabilitation unit. The information may also be shared within the supervisory meetings (e.g. monthly professional supervision), where participants are obliged to protect personal data. Psychologists also protect the data according to the Psychologists' Ethical Code.

18.4 Specifics in Prisoners' Mental Health Treatment in Slovenia

18.4.1 Motivational Factors

18.4.1.1 Motivation for Treatment

Motivation to get involved in treatment is a key element in the treatment of mental health problems. The prison staff's experience shows that individuals in prison usually have little or no motivation for treatment and often misuse it as a means of manipulation. Prison personnel should therefore be trained to identify the genuineness of the motivation for change. There are standardised instruments, which measure such motivation, but they are not available in Slovenia at present. Prison staff therefore have to rely on their experience, professional knowledge and previous behaviour of the prisoner in their judgement.

The Slovene prison system offers a number of programmes and activities, which aim to increase the motivation of prisoners.

Examples of ongoing activities to increase motivation are (Annual Report 2009):

• Prison staff helps to increase the awareness of prisoners regarding personal hygiene, physical conditions, responsibilities for active leisure-time (hobbies) and helps in developing and maintaining social networks. Besides, they encourage prisoners to go to work to develop working habits, self-confidence, meaningful activities. etc. or to start education programmes. This increases the insight of prisoners and their motivation for change.
• Additionally, the choice of different mental health programmes also increases motivation. There are motivational workshops and (psycho-)education available for the prisoners, where individual motivation is addressed. All of these activities address the change of the life-style of prisoners and increase their mental health.

Each prisoner is able to participate or withdraw from these kind of programmes or treatment voluntarily. Thus we face an important dilemma, where society wishes to rehabilitate the inmate, but s/he is not motivated and is thus not involved in the treatment.

18.4.1.2   Motivation and Specific Mental Health Problems

As discussed, motivation plays a key role in treatment options available to prisoners. It is important to point out that low motivation might be caused by specific mental health problems, such as depression, anxiety and/or personality disorder. As less motivated prisoners get fewer opportunities to receive help, these individuals are caught in a vicious circle where the disorder itself reduces the level of motivation and at the same time leads to a lack of treatment offered which then leads to more severe levels of illness. These issues are (if possible) addressed in individual work of prison psychologists.

18.4.1.3   Standardised Treatment Guidelines

There are specific mental health programmes and guidelines (e.g. treatment of sexual abuse, substance abuse) developed within specific prison facilities. Rules about those involved in these programmes are clearly set. Every prison facility implements those programmes according to their possibilities and needs. It would be valuable in the future to evaluate these programmes, their reliability and validity across all prison centres in Slovenia, and to provide clear clinical treatment guidelines.

Substance abuse, which is one of the most prevalent problems of prison mental health care, might be treated outside the prison system where prisoners follow the treatment according to the national guidelines on substance abuse. Good communication with organisations in social and health care and in the NGO sector enables the prison system to include prisoners in the ongoing and highly needed programmes outside its system. The rules and criteria for enrolment of prisoners in these programmes are transparent, so the inmate has a good idea about what is expected from him/her. The time of enrolment is set according to each prisoner's needs.

18.4.2 Compulsory Treatment

Compulsory treatment is regulated within the Mental Health Act (Zakon o duševnem zdravju 2008) passed in 2008, currently in its first phases of implementation. A person can be treated involuntary if s/he is a threat to him/herself or a threat to other people. Involuntary treatment is restricted to emergency cases and can be implemented within prison wards or general (psychiatric) health care – depending on the risks.

Other compulsory treatments within the mental health care in the Slovene prison system are:

1. Compulsory psychiatric treatment in health care facility
2. Compulsory psychiatric treatment in outpatient clinics
3. Compulsory treatment of addiction

In 2009 there were 88 prisoners with such a measure in the Slovene prison system (annual decrease of 31 % compared to previous year). Among new prisoners there was one person with a measure of compulsory psychiatric treatment, nine for alcohol addiction and 18 for drug addiction.

18.4.3 Medical Treatment of Mental Disorders

The treatment of prisoners is the responsibility of health personnel, which is not part of the prison system and the prison administration has no influence on drug prescriptions for inmates. Reasons for prescribing may include mental health problems and effects of the imprisonment, which may produce more anxiety and (auto-)aggressive behaviour.

Benzodiazepines are the most commonly used drugs in prisons, followed by antipsychotics, antidepressants and mood stabilizers. It is estimated that between 30 and 50 % of inmates take regular (prescribed) psychotropic drugs. Atypical (second generation) antipsychotics are prescribed to prison inmates to a similar extent as in general psychiatry. General practitioners, psychiatrists or other physicians are authorised to prescribe psychotropic drugs to inmates. The intake of prescribed drugs is supervised (to ensure swallowing) in cases of severe mental disorder or suicidal inmates (EUPRIS 2007).

18.4.4 Hunger Strikes

Hunger strikes are a way to express distress and dissatisfaction with the prison system in all categories of inmates. There were 39 people (2.75 %) involved in hunger strikes in 2009. Hunger strikes are more common among inmates on remand (26 persons) compared to other sentenced prisoners. Reasons for hunger strikes include avoidance of detention, acceleration of legal proceedings or to express dissatisfaction with the prison's decisions. Everyone involved in hunger strikes was treated according to their human rights and there were no health consequences (Annual Report 2009).

18.4.5 Lack of Forensic Departments and Hospitals

As noted above, inmates use general health facilities (such as specialised outpatient clinics or psychiatric hospitals) when in need for more intensive care. The lack of forensic or specialised wards is associated with some problems:

- Public psychiatric health care organisations are not set and adjusted for the prison population.
- In cases of hospitalisation, full-time observation by prison guards is usually needed, requiring additional resources.
- The presence of a prisoner (and his/her guards) in a general psychiatric institution often causes difficulties in the work of medical personnel and disrupts other patients.
- In some cases (if not ordered by the courts) general psychiatric wards do not approve the admission of a prisoner to their organisation or are not happy about their presence.

Slovenia does not have specific prisons or prison wards for specific populations. Each prison includes inmates who committed different criminal acts and have varying problems. The prison location is chosen according to the inmate's permanent address and the length of the imprisonment (there is only one prison facility dedicated to those with the longest sentences). Most of the prisons therefore are not specialised in the treatment of specific problems, but need to cope with a vast variety of issues. Negotiations on the establishment of the forensic hospital, which would among others things, provide better mental health care, are ongoing.

18.4.6 Funding

The funding system of mental health care in prisons in Slovenia brings about some ethical considerations. The prison system provides insurance for all prisoners, either on remand or sentenced. This allows medical care for many who lack the basic existential requirements for health insurance (e.g. the unemployed not paying health-insurance). Thus, the prison administration provides the opportunity for medical care, also and in particular regarding mental health. We have previously discussed the funding considerations of basic insurance and the rights that go with it. The misuse of these rights might happen, but on very rare occasions.

18.4.7   Assessment of Mental Health and Suicidal Risk

18.4.7.1   Mental Health

There is currently no standardisation regarding the tools used for the assessment of the mental health or wellbeing of the prisoner in the Slovene prison system. We believe that our system would benefit from more standardised tools and procedures.

18.4.7.2   Suicide

The period of the highest suicide risk in the Slovene prison system is the first week of detention, as 30 % of suicides occur then. The category of inmates most at risk are remand prisoners. The prison administration adopted The Suicide Prevention Strategy at the end of year 2003. The main features of the strategy are staff training, systematic suicide screening on admission, handling the potentially suicidal inmates, interventions, follow-up review and debriefing, and evaluation. The 54-h staff training is focused on recognition, identification and support of inmates with suicidal ideation and real life case studies are used. The topic of suicide prevention is an obligatory part of staff training.

Every detainee is assessed with a suicide screening tool at reception. This assessment is an important part of the individual treatment plan. The items of screening tool are:

- Lack of close family or friends in the community
- History of drug or alcohol abuse
- Psychiatric history
- Position/respect in community. Community response to (shocking) crime
- Previous suicide attempts
- Suicidal ideation
- Signs of depression (crying, apathy, emotional flatness, etc.)
- Presenting as anxious, afraid or angry
- Strange, unusual behaviour, disorientation
- Influence of alcohol or drugs
- Signs of withdrawal
- First time in prison

The initial suicide assessment is usually performed by the prison guards (who are trained appropriately) by simply ticking YES or NO on the assessment form. Nevertheless, the suicide assessment is an important advance in the Slovene prison system. Since the adoption of The Suicide Prevention Strategy there has been an improvement in suicide rates and rates of self-injury decreased.

Every prison centre has a list of high-suicide-risk inmates. They are never placed in single cells unless they are a risk to other inmates. There are treatment plans and the level of supervision is specified. The level of risk is regularly reassessed in team meetings. Debriefing is provided for all staff that were involved in the care of a prisoner committing suicide. There were also cases of roommates debriefing.

The items described above only allow a basic estimation of those who have a risk of suicidal behaviour and are aimed to discriminate those who need special attention and facilities. If suicidal risk is present, the prison's psychologist provides the prisoner with psychological support and a more detailed assessement. Psychologists or other professionals usually do not use any standardised tools for the suicide assessment – rather, they rely on clinical interview data gathering.

18.5   Recommendations for the Future

To be able to provide better care for prisoners with mental health problems, we make the following recommendations.

18.5.1   Standardisation

18.5.1.1   Assessment of Suicidal Risk

Suicide risk is regularly assessed at entry into the Slovene prison system and this is a good practice. What we would recommend for the future is to improve the standardised procedures following the assessment. Specifically, psychologists should be encouraged to follow guidelines and to use reliable tools after suicide risk at intake has been established. There are developed tools for suicide assessment available in Slovenia (e.g. Paykel scale), but the system would need implementation, including education of staff, and the evaluation of gathered data. This would also allow the establishment a dataset on the frequency of suicidal ideation among prisoners.

18.5.1.2   Assessment of Mental Health

Mental health can be easily assessed with screening, diagnostic or other psycho-metric tools. Many of these tools are available in Slovene language, but they have not been implemented within the prison system. As described above, there is no time for psycho-diagnostics at the first interview at intake. It would be desirable if there were short standardised screening questionnaires for the assessment of general wellbeing, depression, anxiety, and possibly addictive disorders applied.

18.5.2   Epidemiological Statistics

We emphasise the need to provide more exact statistics of mental disorders in prisons. This epidemiological data would give us a more exact estimation of the population needs and thus might help planning improvements of health care provided.

18.5.3   Staff Education and Expert Associations

At the moment there is no special training needed to work as a psychologist or psychiatrist in prison. Psychologists in prisons are not qualified in clinical psychology. The only requirement for working in prison is to have a degree such as a BA in psychology (equivalent to second level of the Bologna Process in European Higher Education) without additional specialisations or training. The benefit of more specialised education of psychologists would be an improved ability to apply psychotherapy or other more specific forms of interventions.

For a more holistic approach to inmates, it would be valuable to have more interdisciplinary teams. Currently, psychiatrists are excluded from these teams and their treatment is completely independent from other measures in prison. Additionally, there would be value in the establishment of national teams (even informally) concerning specific prison mental health issues.

18.5.4   Decrease of Stigmatisation of Prisoners with Mental Disorders

Prisoners with mental disorders are being stigmatised twice: first for being imprisoned and secondly because of their mental condition. There should be more emphasis given to the de-stigmatisation of mental disorders within this population. This way, people would seek help in the earlier stages of mental disorder. As sometimes mental disorders are at the root of the criminal acts themselves, better treatment options and willingness to participate in turn may lead to a non-criminal life outside prison.

18.5.5   Forensic Hospitals and Networking

Currently there are issues regarding the safety of prisoner needs whose mental health conditions disturb the prison dynamics or lead to a risk to self or others. Forensic hospitals would be a significant advantage in Slovene penology for this reason; they would ensure a more normal prison life for non-disturbed inmates and would provide care for prisoners with mental health problems. Besides, a team of professionals in such a hospital would mean a step further in mental care of inmates. We hope the forensic hospital will be realised in the near future.

Better networking with institutions outside the prison system would be valuable. Clear rules should be set on how to collaborate between institutions. This would mean that there would be no doubt on how networking is implemented, e.g. responsibilities and data protection. This could eventually lead to the formation of teams of prison mental health professionals.

18.5.6   Aftercare

Throughout the sentence prisoners are encouraged (or even demanded by law) to get involved in some treatments, e.g. drug or substance addiction treatment. The cooperation of the prison system with the Social Work Centres and the Employment Service of Slovenia can has a positive effect on the future quality of life of prisoners, particularly at the time of release. However, despite their strong efforts problems persist as there is a lack of mental health facilities for people coming out of prisons in Slovenia. The systems that provide for the general population are usually over-stretched or even overcrowded.

18.5.7   Social Skills Training

More options of social-skills training might increase motivation for change in the Slovene prison system. Among these, we would recommend communication training, assertiveness, problem solving and anger management courses, which should be offered to prisoners in a similar way that they are offered outside the prison. These courses could take place at specific time-intervals (e.g. every 3 months) and would offer basic changes of behaviour. It is recommended that these programmes are implemented in a group setting.

Acknowledgments We wish to thank Mrs Olga Uršič-Perhavc and Mr. Aleksander Kotnik (both from Prison Administration of the Republic of Slovenia) for their fruitful contributions and professional comments on the chapter. Special thanks also to Ms Barbara Bernik Zupančič for her text review.

References

EUPRIS- Treatment of mentally ill or disordered persons in European Prison Systems – needs, programmes and outcomes. 2007. Mannheim: Central Institute of Mental Health. Available http://ec.europa.eu/health/ph_projects/2004/action1/docs/action1_2004_frep_17_en.pdf
The National Prison Administration. 2008. *Annual report*. Ljubljana: The National Prison Administration.
The National Prison Administration. 2009. *Annual report*. Ljubljana: The National Prison Administration.
Uršič-Perhavc, O., V. Poštuvan, J. Svetičič, and B. Bernik Župančič. 2007. Slovenia. In *Treatment of Mentally Ill or Disordered Persons in European Prison Systems – needs, programmes and outcomes (EUPRIS)*, eds. Marušič Slovenia A., J.H., Salize, H., Dressing and C. Kief. 270–274. Mannheim: Central Institute of Mental Health. Available http://ec.europa.eu/health/ph_projects/2004/action1/docs/action1_2004_frep_17_en.pdf
Zakon o duševnem zdravju. 2008. Uradni list Republike Slovenije, number 77, 11097–11110.
Zakon o varstvu osebnih podatkov. 2004. Uradni list Republike Slovenije, number 86, 10389–10405.

Zakon o izvrševanju kazenskih sankcij. 2007. Uradni list Republike Slovenije, number 110, 11305–11328. Enforcement of Penal Sentences Act and the laws that follow this order.

Zakon o zdravstvenem varstvu in zdravstvenem zavarovanju. 2006. Uradni list Republike Slovenije, number 72, 7637–7657. Law on Health Care and Health Insurance.

Zakon o pacientovih pravicah. 2008. Uradni list Republike Slovenije, number 15, 1045–1061. Patients' Rights Act.

Chapter 19
Quality and Ethical Problems of Mental Health Services in Prisons in Spain

Luis Fernando Barrios-Flores and Francisco Torres-González

19.1 The Penitentiary System in Spain

19.1.1 Relevant Laws and Regulations

19.1.1.1 International Regulations

There are a number of international regulations Spain has ratified that have relevance to the topic of mental health in prison as follows:

- Universal Declaration of Human Rights, December 10, 1948. Pursuant to S.10(2) of the Spanish Constitution, the rules concerning human rights and fundamental freedoms shall be construed in agreement with said constitution and the international conventions and agreements ratified by Spain.
- International Covenant on Civil and Political Rights, 19 December 1966, ratified by Spain on April 13, 1977.
- International Covenant on Economic, Social and Cultural Rights, 19 December 1966, ratified by Spain on April 13, 1977.
- Convention for the Protection of Human Rights and Fundamental Freedoms, November 4, 1950, ratified by Spain on September 26, 1979. Art. 5, dealing with the right to freedom and guarantees in cases of loss of freedom, is of special interest.
- European Convention for the prevention of torture and inhuman or degrading treatment or punishment, November 26, 1987, ratified by Spain on April 28, 1989.
- Convention for the protection of Human Rights and dignity of the human being with regard to the application of biology and medicine: Convention on Human Rights and Biomedicine (Oviedo Convention), April 4, 1997, ratified by Spain on October 20, 1999 (hereinafter CHRB).

L.F. Barrios-Flores (✉)
Departament of Administrative Law, University of Alicante, Alicante, Spain
e-mail: luisfbarrioss@ua.es

F. Torres-González
Centro de Investigacion Biomedica en Red de Salud Mental (CIBERSAM),
Granada University (Spain), Granada, Spain
e-mail: ftorres@ugr.es

N. Konrad et al. (eds.), *Ethical Issues in Prison Psychiatry*, International Library of Ethics, Law, and the New Medicine 46, DOI 10.1007/978-94-007-0086-4_19, © Springer Science+Business Media Dordrecht 2013

19.1.1.2   Spanish Constitution

There are a number of laws relevant to the issue of prison psychiatry in Spain.

The Spanish Constitution of December 27, 1978 (hereinafter SC) outlines the general conditions of imprisonment and human rights. It states that:

- Punishment entailing imprisonment and security measures shall be aimed at re-education and social rehabilitation and may not involve forced labour. The person sentenced to prison shall enjoy, during the imprisonment, the fundamental rights afforded by the Constitution except those expressedly restricted by the sentence, the purpose of the punishment or the penitentiary law (Art. 25).
- Everyone has the right to life and to physical and moral integrity, and under no circumstances may be subjected to torture or to inhuman or degrading punishment or treatment (Art. 15).
- Everyone has a right to protection of their health. It is incumbent upon the public authorities to organize and supervise public health measures by means of preventative measures and the necessary benefits and services (Art. 43).
- The public authorities shall develop and follow a policy of preventative care, treatment, rehabilitation and integration of the physically, sensorically and mentally handicapped by giving them the specialized care they require, and affording them special protection for the enjoyment of the rights granted to all citizens (Art. 49).

19.1.1.3   Penal and Penitentiary Rules

There are two penal laws in Spain:

- The Organic Act 10/1995 of November 23, 1995, Penal Code (hereinafter PC)[1]: The PC includes regulations about involuntary placement for mentally ill offenders. The Act has introduced the modernization of security measures for mentally disordered patients and for those with drug or alcoholic related problems. The fundamental changes are: 1) the introduction of a maximum duration of the measure, 2) judicial control of the execution of the measure and 3) a variety of powers that are attributed to the judicial authority in order to cease, substitute or suspend the execution of the measure.
- The Act of Criminal Prosecution, September 14, 1882 (hereinafter LCP): procedures for inmates that are diagnosed and declared mentally ill after sentencing (substitution of penalty of imprisonment by involuntary placement).

The Spanish penitentiary system is regulated by:

- The Organic Act 1/1979, September 26, 1979, General Penitentiary (hereinafter OLGP) provides basic norms for the penitentiary system. This Act was promulgated after the approval of the SC. This meant a radical change in penitentiary norms and standards within the Spanish context.
- Royal Decree 190/1996, February 9, 1996, Penitentiary Regulation (hereinafter PR): This gives detailed regulations for the regime and operation of the penitentiary establishments. It substitutes most of the previous regulations of the Royal Decree 1201/1981, May 8, 1981, and has introduced for the first time important regulations for forensic-psychiatric detention.

---

[1] In Spain there is a special class of laws called 'Organic Laws'. They relate to regulations concerning fundamental rights and freedoms recognized in the Constitution (life, freedom, safety, etc.) (Art. 82.1 SC).

Furthermore, it has improved regulations with regards to psychiatric placements: It envisages the existence of 'Psychiatric Units' in penitentiary centres in addition to the existing Psychiatric Penitentiary Hospitals. It also regulates the constitution of 'Multidisciplinary Teams', which have treatment responsibilities and prepare reports regarding the execution of the measures of penal psychiatric placement.

- The Royal Decree 1201/1981, May 8, 1981, Penitentiary Regulation (hereinafter PR 1981) regulates the functions and duties of psychologists and health care staff in penitentiaries.

- Decree 329/2006, September 5, 2006, Penitentiary Regulation (only for Catalonia): regional regulation equivalent to the national regulation.

19.1.1.4 Legislations Regarding Health

The two principle procedures regarding the rights of patients (including those in prison) are: Act 41/2002, November 14, 2002 (hereinafter APL) and Act 14/1986, April 25, 1986 (hereinafter GHL). Though regional procedures exist, these laws form their foundation.

The APL is the basic act governing patients' autonomy, as well as the rights and obligations relating to information governance and clinical documentation. Because of its importance the most relevant articles of this act are cited here:

Art. 1. Scope. The purpose of this Act is to regulate the rights and obligations of patients, service users and professionals, as well as of the health centres and services, both public and private, regarding the autonomy of patients and clinical documentation and information.

Art. 2. Basic principles. (1) Respect for a person's free will, dignity and privacy shall guide all activities involving obtaining, using, filing, keeping and transferring clinical documents and information.

(2) As a general principle, any intervention relating to health care requires the prior consent of the patient or service user. Consent, which should be obtained after providing the patient with the necessary information, shall be given in writing in the cases envisaged in the Act.

(3) A patient or service user has the right to freely choose, after receiving the necessary information, between the clinical options available.

(4) A patient or service user has the right to refuse treatment, except in the cases laid down in the Law, and such refusal shall be given in writing.

(6) A professional who provides healthcare and assistance is obliged not only to carry out the techniques correctly, but also to fulfil his duty in relation to clinical documents and information, and to respect the decisions freely adopted by the patient.

Art. 8. Informed consent. (1) Prior to any action being taken in relation to a patient's health-care, his consent must be freely given after having received the information envisaged in Section 4 and evaluated the options available. [.....]

(5) A patient is free to withdraw his consent in writing at any time.

Art. 9. Limits to informed consent and consent given by legal representatives. [.....]

(2) A doctor may perform clinical interventions that are indispensable for a patient's health without the latter's consent in the following cases:

...

b) When a patient's physical or mental well-being is in serious, immediate danger and it is not possible to obtain his consent, by consulting members of his family or those close to him when circumstances permit.

(3) Consent shall be given by a patient's representative in the following situations:

a) When, in the opinion of the patient's doctor, the patient is not capable of making a decision or when his mental or physical state prevents him from understanding the situation. When the patient has no legal representative, consent may be given by a member of his family or a person related to him *de facto*.

b) When the patient is legally incapacitated. [.....]

(5) When recourse is made to consent given by a representative, it shall be in keeping with the circumstances, in proportion to the patient's needs and in his favour, while respecting his personal dignity. The patient shall participate as much as possible in the decisions taken throughout the healthcare process.

The GHL affirms:

Art. 10. Everyone has the following rights in relation to the various public healthcare services:

(1) Respect for their personality, human dignity and privacy and the right not to be discriminated against on the grounds of race, gender, morals, ideology, political or trade union affiliation, financial status or social class. [.....]

(15) While respecting the specific financial system of each healthcare service, the rights enshrined in paragraphs (1), (3), (4), (5), (6), (7), (9) and (11) of this section shall also be exercised in relation to private health services.

19.1.2 Penitentiary Administration and Penitentiary Establishments

The Kingdom of Spain consists of 17 Autonomous Communities (AC) or regions with different levels of autonomy. Each AC consists of one or more provinces (departments). There are a total of 50 provinces and two cities with special statute: the autonomous cities of Ceuta and Melilla in North Africa.

Except for Catalonia, the penitentiary system is managed by the General Secretary of Penitentiary Institutions, attached to the Ministry of Interior.

In Catalonia the penitentiary system is managed by the Secretary of Penitentiary Services, Rehabilitation and Juvenile Justice, attached to the Department of Justice of the Generalitat of Catalonia (autonomous government of Catalonia).

The Spanish Prison System is a national system that consists of 64 penitentiaries (62 ordinary and 2 psychiatric establishments) dispersed throughout the ACs and managed by the central Government. Only Catalonia has independent control of the facilities located within its AC: currently 11 ordinary penitentiaries and one 'Psychiatric Penitentiary Pavilion'. There are also 24 'Social Integration Centres' or 'Open / Semi-Open Centres' and two 'Mothers' Units'.

Both, the General Penitentiary Administration and the Catalan authority, operate on two different levels: central and local. The central level includes various services and administrative units for direction, inspection and coordination. The administration of the penitentiary centres constitutes the local level.

Spain's prisoner population has shown a sharp increase in recent years, doubling in numbers in less than 20 years (Table 19.1):

Table 19.1 Number of prison inmates in Spain 1990–2010, National Statistics Institute

Year	1990	1991	1992	1993	1994	1995	1996	1997	1998	1999	
Inmates	33,058	37,857	41,894	46,076	47,144	44,956	41,903	42,756	44,370	44,197	
Year	2000	2001	2002	2003	2004	2005	2006	2007	2008	2009	2010
Inmates	45,104	47,571	51,882	56,096	59,375	61,054	64,021	67,100	73,558	76,079	76,951

19.2 Prevalence of Mental Disorders in Spanish Prisons

There have been no official statistics on the prevalence of mental disorders in Spanish prisons until recently. This lack of data was finally remedied in part by a study designed by Spain's Directorate General of Penitentiary Institutions in 2006 (DGIP 2006), based on information from medical records. The published outcomes were: 50.4 % of prisoners had no psychiatric diagnosis, 24 % prisoners were drug users, 12.1 % had a dual pathology, and 13.5 % had a psychiatric diagnosis but did not use drugs. Certainly this classification is rather general, but this is the only data available at present.

Another study, the PreCa (Prevalence of mental disorders in prison) (Vicens Pons 2009), is pending publication. This study is based on interviews of 708 prisoners in 5 prisons in different areas of Spain.

19.3 Psychiatric Care in Prison

19.3.1 Overview

The Prison Administrations are under the obligation to watch over the life, integrity and health of all prisoners (Art. 3.4 OLGP). Health care is comprehensive and includes prevention, treatment and rehabilitation (Art. 207.1 PR). The equivalent care principle (equity) is guaranteed by law (Art. 208.1 PR); it comprises medical and health care as well as pharmaceutical services (Art. 208.1 and 209.3 PR), both of which are free of charge for prisoners. In the Central Prison Administration (we have no data for Catalonia), the procurement of certain pharmaceutical products is made by the General Secretariat of Prison Institutions (centralized procurement), although other drugs are purchased directly by the prisons. The expenditure for atypical antipsychotics in 2007 came to 6,849,002.48 Euros. The total expenditure for all pharmaceutical products in 2007 was 32,145,463.46 Euros. 69.1 % of the total budget for pharmaceutical products was for HIV/AIDS drugs, 20.1 % for atypical antipsychotics, 10.2 % for chronic Hepatitis C treatments, and 0.6 % for vaccinations.

Unless there are security reasons to the contrary, the prisoners may also, at their own expense, request medical services from professionals in the wider community who are not appointed by the Prison Administration (Art. 36.3 OLGP and 212.3 PR).

The health care system is divided into two levels of care: primary and specialized (Art. 209 PR). At the primary care level, all prison establishments must be equipped with an infirmary and rooms for psychiatric observation, with a certain number of beds per population in each prison (Art. 37 OLGP and 213.1 PR). There is a Primary Care Health Team in each prison, comprising at least one general practitioner, one qualified nurse and one health care assistant although in practice there are several health professionals of each category in every prison. Moreover, there are doctors and nurses on 24-h duty, all year round. Family practitioners are in charge of caring for the physical and mental health of inmates and therefore they are required to have basic knowledge of psychiatry (Art. 36.1 OLGP) although they may request the assistance of specialised doctors. The regulations also provide for regular psychiatric consultations (Art. 207.1 PR). The specialist doctors are contracted via agreements with other health administrations, private institutions or even on an individual basis (Art. 212.2 PR).

Specialised care is ensured via Spain's National Health Service (the public health service that covers all of Spain) either through consultations or hospitalization. There are Prison Hospital Units for inmates in every province, equipped with the appropriate security measures. Art. 20.2 GHL provides that: Patients who require hospitalization to treat their conditions shall be admitted to the psychiatric units of general hospitals. These are general psychiatric units – not penitentiaries. Some hospitals provide 'Units of Restricted Access' which are secure units for medical or psychiatric patients with police presence for safety reasons, The 'Study on Mental Health in Prison Contexts' (DGIP 2007), which outlines a 'Global Mental Health Policy', was completed in December 2006. The most relevant policy outlined in this document was the approval of the 'Framework programme for comprehensive care for psychiatric patients in prison centres (PAIEM)', which is currently being implemented. According to this framework, the purpose of an intervention for prisoners with a serious or chronic illness is to: (1) Detect, diagnose and treat any inmates who suffer from a mental disorder and refer them to rehabilitation programmes; (2) Enhance patients' quality of life, increase their personal independence and their adaptation to the environment; (3) Optimize reintegration into society and adequate referral to community social and health resources. Interventions include detection, diagnosis, treatment, rehabilitation and reintegration into society.

Under the PAIEM, important principles in the healthcare for prisoners with mental disorders include independence; quality and continuity; referral to external resources; multidisciplinary work; cooperation of health-related institutions, organizations and social resources; inter-prison coordination and coordination between prisons and the wider community; and educational training and research. Three programmes have been set up to achieve this: (1) medical care (detection of mental disorders, implementation of medical treatment and referral to rehabilitation programmes), (2) rehabilitation, and (3) reintegration into society. The PAIEM is designed to be adapted to the characteristics of each prison.

The care model in place in Spain has been criticised by some specialists who consider that prison institutions are not the ideal place for the mentally ill who have committed crimes. Instead, they suggest treating such patients in general hospital psychiatric units and in a community setting (Hernández and Herrera 2003). Some authors are of the opinion that, although this would be the ultimate goal, the immediate aim should be to ensure that current inmates of penal institutions receive truly equivalent care (which may currently not always be achieved owing to the lack of specialists) and enjoy the same rights, and that mental health professionals have an enhanced role in decision-making. An institution's activities should reflect what is expected from its name; otherwise, a 'label fraud' might exist (Barrios 2007a).

19.3.2   Inmates

All inmates (pre-trial prisoners and sentenced prisoners) are examined by a general practitioner within 24 h of entering prison (Art. 214.1 PR). The purpose of this examination is to detect any physical disease or mental illness and to proceed accordingly (Art. 288.1 PR 1981). If there is a suspicion of mental disorder the inmate is examined by a psychiatrist. The prison's psychiatrist, if any, will examine the prisoner to detect potential mental disorders and prescribe adequate treatment (Art. 288.2 PR 1981).

If a mental disorder is detected at the time of admission or in the course of serving a sentence in prison, the patient is sent to the prison's infirmary if the disorder is mild or to an external general hospital, if the disorder is serious and is acute.

In cases of psychiatric diagnoses that affect an inmate's prison status (e.g. transfer to Psychiatric Penitentiary Hospital) a panel of experts is convened comprising a specialist in psychiatry, a forensic pathologist, and the prison's primary care physician; a report by the Observation and Treatment Team (comprising the head of the team, a lawyer, a psychologist, and a social worker and a member of education staff) is also received (Art. 39 OLGP).

If an inmate shows signs of having a mental disorder after being sentenced to imprisonment, the prison governor provides for observation of the inmate and sends notice to the sentencing court. The court may then issue an order for the prisoner to be sent to an appropriate institution (Art. 991-994 LCP). In such cases, the enforcement of the sentence is suspended and a security measure of deprivation of liberty is issued (psychiatric institutionalization in prison or, occasionally, in a general psychiatric institution) (Art. 60 PC) (Vizueta 2007; Gómez-Escolar 2007).

19.3.3   Mentally Disordered Offenders

If, in the course of legal proceedings, a court deems that when the criminal offence was committed, the accused was unable to understand that the act was unlawful or to act in consequence of such understanding owing to a psychiatric anomaly or disorder, the accused is declared to be immune from prosecution (Art. 20.1 PC) or the accused is declared of diminished responsibility, when not all the requirements are met for acquittal (Art. 21 PC). The court may then impose a custodial measure for medical treatment in a relevant establishment for the type of psychiatric anomaly or disorder concerned (Quintero 1996; García 1997; Santos 2001; Sanz 2003; Sierra 1997). This may be a prison (the most common option) or a different secure setting. The internment may not exceed the duration of the deprivation of liberty that would have been imposed if the accused had been declared mentally capable (Art. 101.1 PC). Security measures other than internment or deprivation of liberty may be imposed, e.g. deportation from Spain for foreign nationals, prohibition to reside in certain places, mandatory residence in a specific place, prohibition to go to certain places, events or establishments where alcoholic beverages are sold, family custody, withdrawal of a driving permit, withdrawal of a firearms licence, prohibition to approach a victim or a victim's family members, prohibition to speak to the victim or the victim's family members and treatment in the community.

Those who are admitted to Psychiatric Penitentiary Hospitals (forensic psychiatric hospitals) and Prison Psychiatric Units (the latter are pending implementation) are: (a) detainees and prisoners who have psychiatric disorder if the judge rules their admission for observation purposes and the issuing of a relevant report; (b) persons who are declared immune to prosecution by a court and who are sentenced to deprivation of liberty (psychiatric institutionalization) as a security measure, and (c) convicts whose mental illness is subsequent to their court case, when a Court decides they should be transferred to another institution (Art. 184 PR).

Care for inmates of Psychiatric Penitentiary Hospitals and Prison Psychiatric Units is entrusted to a multidisciplinary team comprising psychiatrists, psychologists, family practitioners, nurses and social workers. These health professionals and assistant staff are also required to implement rehabilitation programmes (Art. 185 PR). Hospitals and prisons are required to put in place a general programme of rehabilitation activities and individual rehabilitation programmes (Art. 189 PR).

Psychiatric institutionalization is always time limited. It may not exceed the sentence that would have been imposed if the accused had been liable to prosecution (Art. 101 PC). It can be for a briefer period. The Judge of Penitentiary Surveillance in charge of prison supervision is required to provide an annual report to the sentencing court in which he suggests whether to: (a) continue the deprivation of liberty, (b) rule that the deprivation shall cease, (c) suspend the measure for a period that does not exceed the time that remains to be served according to the sentence, (d) substitute the deprivation of liberty for a different measure (generally treatment in the community) (Art. 97 PC) (Fernández 2003; García 1997).

Before submitting recommendations, the judge in charge of prison supervision assesses the reports issued by the doctors and professionals involved in the care of the patient concerned (the multidisciplinary team).

Usually, if institutionalization ends before the sentence is served, it is replaced by a security measure called 'external medical treatment' (treatment in the community), which does not involve deprivation of liberty. After ratifying the measure, the Prison Administration requests the cooperation of the general Health Administration (Spain's National Health Service) to ensure that psychiatric treatment continues after the patient is released (Art. 185.2 PR). Thus, after leaving the secure setting or Prison Psychiatric Unit, the released patient is referred to a local Mental Health Unit in his or her place of residence. The Court can also rule that the relevant social services shall assist and care for the released patient (Art. 106 PC).

19.4 Consent to Treatment and Right to Refuse Treatment

As a general rule, medical and health care is always provided with the prisoner's informed consent (Art. 210 PR). In theory, therefore, the same rules on treatment that apply to anyone else in Spain also apply to prisoners: (a) informed consent is required (Art. 2.2 and 8 APL) and (b) the right to refuse treatment (Art. 2.4 APL).

Nonetheless, there are two important differences between general health legislation and prison regulations. Concerning treatment, the APL provides in Art. 9.2.b) that

> (2) A doctor may perform clinical interventions that are indispensable for a patient's health without the latter's consent in the following cases:
>   b) When a patient's physical or mental well-being is in serious, immediate danger and it is not possible to obtain his consent, nor to consult members of his family or those close to him when circumstances permit.

However, prison regulations are stricter. Art. 210.1 PR asserts:

> No clinical interventions may be performed on prisoners without their informed consent. A doctor may only give prisoners treatment without their consent if the latter's life is in immediate danger. The doctor may perform clinical interventions that are indispensable to save the patient's life, and shall request the relevant authorization from a court, when necessary. A report on these actions shall be sent to the Court.
>   Art. 210.2 PR admits involuntary treatment if there is a risk of harm to others.

The difference lies in the fact that whereas patients in the community may give their consent or refuse to receive treatment even when their life is at serious risk, inmates may not refuse treatment if their life is endangered. Therefore prisoners can be force fed in accordance with the law as explained below.

The second difference between prisoner patients and those in the wider community concerns hospitalization. Patients who have the required legal capacity to do so may decide whether they desire to be admitted to hospital, except for if there is a risk to public health (not including violence towards others) or a serious and immediate danger to their physical integrity. If the patient cannot give consent through absence of legal capacity (declared by the judge) or by lack of competence (assessed by the doctor) the consent is possible by proxy (relatives) (Art. 763 Spanish Civil Procedure Act). In a prison context, however, a doctor may be of the opinion that a patient should be admitted to hospital regardless of whether he is competent and consents to hospitalization, in which case the Prison Administration must request authorization from the court (Art. 210.3 PR).

In summary, therefore, mentally disordered patient inmates have less rights to make decisions regarding their medical treatment, including admission to hospital than patients in the wider community.

19.5   Coercive Measures

19.5.1   Compulsory Medical Treatment

It has been mentioned above that compulsory medical treatment is more widely applied in a prison context than in the wider community. To give an example: The Spanish Supreme Court, in a ruling dated 18 October 2005, recognised the entitlement to compensation of the parents of a prisoner who died of AIDS. The patient, who in this case was legally competent, had refused to continue taking the medication prescribed by the prison doctors. The Court established the Prison Administration's duty to "protect the life and health of the inmates" (Art. 3.4 OLGP), and therefore medical intervention being legitimate and even compulsory when a prisoner's life is at risk, regardless of the latter's refusal to be treated. The Court pointed out that the Prison Health Administration should have used coercive measures to administer treatment. To that effect, the Court cited Art. 45.1.b) OLGP, which provides that lawful coercive measures may be used with the authorisation of the prison's governor, who shall give notice of the decision to the judge in charge of prison supervision 'to prevent the inmates from causing harm to themselves, other people and property'.

19.5.2   Restraint

The PR provide for the use of coercive measures both in ordinary prisons and in prison hospitals and prison psychiatric units.

In ordinary prisons, coercive measures may only be used to: (a) prevent inmates from escaping and using violence; (b) prevent inmates from causing harm to themselves, other people or property; (c) overcome the inmates' active or passive resistance to orders given by prison staff in the course of their duties (Art. 45.1 OLGP). The coercive measures permitted in implementation of the above are: temporary isolation (seclusion), physical or mechanical restraint, rubber bullets, appropriate sprays and handcuffs (Art. 72.1 PR).

In Psychiatric Penitentiary Hospitals and prison psychiatric units indications for the use of coercive measures for therapeutic purposes are set out in Art. 188.3 PR, as follows:

> Coercive measures are employed in exceptional circumstances. They shall only be admissible when prescribed by a doctor and for the minimal time required for the pharmacological treatment concerned to have effect. The patient's dignity shall be respected at all times. In those cases where there is no medical alternative to coercive measures, a report on the relevant medical grounds and decision to employ them shall be immediately sent to the relevant judicial authority.

The regulations on ordinary prisons have given rise to three basic issues: (a) the absence of medical grounds for the employment of coercive measures in ordinary prisons, (b) the regulations only provide for the use of handcuffs and do not recognise the existence of safer and less damaging methods (standard restraint straps), and (c) the non-existence of a protocol with instructions, precautions, controls and guarantees for the employment of coercive measures for therapeutic purposes. In the past few years, several authors have described the situation and suggested a solution for the deficiencies (Barrios 2005; 2007b). In addition, it is worth mentioning that during a visit to Spain of the Council of Europe's Committee for the Prevention of Torture and Inhuman or Degrading Treatment or Punishment (CPT) from 19 September 2007 to 1 October 2007 [CPT/Inf (2011) 11, pars. 88–91], special attention was paid to the employment of coercive measures in prisons. Previously, the report to the Spanish Government on another visit from 22 July to 1 August 2003, the CPT recommended [CPT/Inf (2007) 29, pars. 125–127]: (a) that the practice of immobilising patients be reviewed at the Seville facility [Psychiatric Penitentiary Hospital of Sevilla], (b) that a clearly defined policy be drawn up for both establishments (Sevilla and Alicante) and (c) that appropriate steps be taken to ensure that patients are not held in seclusion for long periods and that a detailed policy on the use of seclusion is drawn up.

The first Prison Administration to regulate the use of coercive measures for psychiatric purposes was Catalonia in 2002. Subsequently, the Secretariat for Prison Services, Rehabilitation and Youth Justice issued Guideline No. 3/2004, dated 29 November 2004, which regulates the procedure to be followed in situations of unforeseen aggressive behaviour on the part of patients in Psychiatric Units (Instrucción 2004).

Subsequently, the Directorate General of Prisons Administration – currently the General Secretariat for Prison Institutions – issued Guideline No. 18/2007, dated 20 December 2007, on mechanical restraints (Instrucción 2007). It is implemented in all prison environments (ordinary and psychiatric).

Guideline No. 18/2007 states:

Mechanical restraint shall be used for medical and therapeutic purposes at the decision of a medical professional or, if none is available, by a licensed nurse. In such cases, mechanical restraint is a medical measure applied to patients.

Guidelines No. 3/2004 and No. 18/2007 set forth the fundamental principles for adopting such measures (respect for the patient's dignity, minimal restraint, need, and proportionality), when they are indicated and counter indicated, who can prescribe them (only a doctor), who supervises the restraint measures, where restraint takes place (an infirmary), the restraint mechanisms used (only standard straps, never handcuffs), and so on.

There are no regulations in place for coercive measures employed in psychiatric institutions in the wider community, although most of them have adopted clinical protocols for that purpose (Torres and Barrios 2006).

19.5.3   Seclusion

Art. 213.1 PR requires infirmaries to 'have special rooms for secluding patients for medical reasons, if necessary'. The precept construes that it applies to patients with infectious or contagious diseases, since Art. 37. c) OLGP provides that all establishments will be equipped with a "contagious patients unit" distinct from the "unit for psychiatric observation and the service for addicts" (Art. 37. b) OLGP).

There are no nation-wide regulations on the isolation of psychiatric patients in Spain. In Catalonia, however, the above-mentioned Guideline No. 3/2004 regulates the seclusion of psychiatric patients for therapeutic purposes. It states that:

> the purpose of confining an inmate admitted to a psychiatric unit to a cell specifically designed for confinement or in the patient's own cell, is to isolate the inmate from the rest of the prison population in order to prevent or put an end to behaviour that is a potential risk to the patient or third parties, and to restore the patient to his or her normal psychological, emotional, and behavioural state.

Only a psychiatrist or the doctor on duty may prescribe seclusion (the officers in charge of supervision may also do so temporarily). The Guidelines describe the situations in which the measure may be used (it may never be employed as punishment or a penalty), regular visits to the patient by the doctor and nursing staff (at least once every 8 h), monitoring by the officers in charge of supervision (at least once every 4 h), when the measure should end (according to the doctor's orders), the living regime (according to the doctor's orders), and so on.

19.6   Hunger Strike

The issue of hunger strikes in prison arose when the inmates belonging to a group of Spanish terrorists (GRAPO) carried out two hunger strikes in 1989. The Prison Administration sent a request to the judges in charge of prison supervision for an order to use force feeding. The case was taken to Spain's Constitutional Court, which issued three rulings (SSTC No. 120/1990, dated 27 June 1990; No. 137/1990, dated 19 July 1990; and No. 11/1991, dated 17 January 1991). All three rulings dismissed the appeals lodged by the GRAPO prisoners and authorised force feeding. The Constitutional Court based the rulings on the following grounds: (a) The special relationship between prisoners and the Administration, in which the former are subject to the latter; (b) the Prison Administration is compelled to safeguard the life and health of the inmates; (c) the special relevance of the asset 'life'; (d) the hunger strike was based on illegitimate demands (it was against the isolation and dispersal of prisoners), and (e) compulsory medical care is not a violation of a fundamental right. Two of the 12 Court magistrates issued dissenting votes, on the grounds that: (a) no additional right to a prisoner's fundamental rights exists, since such rights can only be restricted "by the content of the verdict, the intention of the sentence, and prison legislation" (Art. 25.2 SC); (b) the obligation to provide care does not authorise the Administration to use any available method; (c) the right to refuse care exists, and (d) force feeding cannot be based on the legitimacy or illegitimacy of the purpose pursued. One of the Magistrates concluded that: '…

addressing the issue from the latter perspective – that of a patient who is also a prisoner – instead of the approach adopted by the verdict – that of a prisoner who is also a patient – would have permitted the arrival at a more favourable solution to the granting of protection'.

After the above-mentioned rulings, PR provided in Art. 210.1 (cited above): 'Prisoners may only be given treatment without their consent if their life is in immediate danger…'.

Seventeen years later, the issue arose again when a well-known ETA terrorist went on a hunger strike. In a ruling issued on 21 January 2007, the Audiencia Nacional (National Hearing), Spain's central criminal court, applied the Constitutional Court's earlier decisions to authorise force feeding of the prisoner.

Therefore, in Spain, whereas force feeding cannot be applied when an ordinary citizen who has legal capacity goes on a hunger strike (pursuant to Art. 2.4 APL, right to refuse treatment), force feeding is authorised when a prisoner goes on a hunger and his or her life is in danger, regardless of the prisoner's legal capacity. Nonetheless, a number of experts have expressed a contrary position (Silva 1989; García 1992; Ruiz 1993; Cervelló 1996).

19.7   Suicide

In Spain, as in other countries, one major problem in prisons is suicide. The numbers of deaths owing to suicide over the past few years are shown in Table 19.2:

Spain is currently putting a Suicide Prevention Programme in place in all prisons. The programme establishes suicide risk profiles and provides for potentially suicidal inmates to be monitored by qualified professionals.

The most important factors of risk in Spanish prisons are considered to be:

(a) the psychological impact of the deprivation of freedom
(b) having committed certain crimes against the person, sexual crimes or crimes in the family environment
(c) news in the mass media on the committed crime
(d) living conditions in the prison
(e) separation from the family and lifestyle changes
(f) recent legal changes resulting in prolonged stay in prison and increasing number of prisoners (Instrucción 2005)

Table 19.2 Suicide rates in Spanish prisons 2003–2007

Year	Suicides	Rates ×/1,000 inmates
2003	28	0.60
2004	40	0.79
2005	33	0.63
2006	25	0.46
2007	27	0.47

The main problem, however, is overcrowding in Spanish prisons (the prison population in 1990 was 33,035; in 2009 it came close to 75,000) without proportionate increases in staffing. This prevents adequate monitoring of the inmates at risk.

19.8   Confidentiality

Spanish legislation in general guarantees that medical data is kept confidential. In general health services, Art. 2.1 APL provides that:

> the dignity owed to human beings and the protection of their individual wishes and privacy shall govern any activity that seeks to obtain, use, file, safeguard and transmit medical information, reports and records.

Art. 7.1 ads:

> Everyone is entitled to the protection of confidential data concerning their health, and no one should have access to such data without prior authorisation within the Law.

This issue concerns the right to information on individuals' health conditions and medical data. Thus, Art. 5.1 APL provides:

> The holders of the right to receive information are the patients. Close relatives, such as family members or an unmarried partner, may be informed with the patient's expressed or implied consent.

Prison regulations also provide the principle of the protection of confidentiality. Art. 215.1 PR asserts:

> The data in individual medical records shall be kept confidential and adequately filed and safeguarded, to be accessed only by authorised staff.

Two key issues pose a problem, however: (a) whether information on a prisoner's health should be given to his or her family, even without the prisoner's consent; and (b) who should be construed as 'authorized staff' with regard to access to medical records.

In the first case, Art. 52.1 OLGP provides that a prison's governor shall give information concerning a prisoner's death, accident or serious disease to the closest family member or to the person designated for that purpose by the prisoner. Prison regulations provide that even when a prisoner has legal capacity (despite a mental disorder) and does not want information on his or her state of health to be given to his close family or friends, the prison governor is obligated to give the information. This contradicts the above-mentioned Art. 5.1 APL, which guarantees that only the individuals authorised by the prisoner shall be informed.

With regard to the second issue, Art. 16.1 APL states: The prison's care professionals who are in charge of a patient's diagnosis and treatment shall have access to the patient's medical records as a key instrument for providing adequate care. Art. 16.4 APL provides: Health centre administration and management staff may only have access to medical history data that is relevant for their functions. The main problem lies in the fact that prison management staff does not have sufficient access to medical records.

19.9 Biomedical Research

Prison regulations set very strict standards for biological research in prisons. Art. 211 PR provides:

1. Prisoners may only participate in medical research when the said research is expected to have a direct and significant beneficial effect on their health and offers the same guarantees as for non-prisoners.
2. Research on humans shall adhere to strict ethical principles, particularly with regard to informed consent and confidentiality. Research conducted in prisons shall require authorization by an Ethics Committee and shall adhere to any other procedure that guarantees respect for ethical principles.
3. Inmates shall be informed of the existence of any epidemiological studies carried out in their prison that may affect them.

In general, and also in a prison environment, the basic regulations that govern such issues in Spain are the CHRB and Act No. 14/2007, dated July 3, 2007, on Biomedical Research (hereinafter BIL).

The CHRB is well known, while Art. 20 BIL provides that, in general: (a) prisoners who are legally incompetent may give their consent to research, providing they have legal capacity to give such consent (in Spain the absence of legal capacity is established by a civil Judge; individuals may lack legal capacity for some areas, such as managing their finances, but not for others, such as self-determination); and (b) in any other case, the following requirements shall apply: (1) the outcomes of the research are liable to have real or direct benefits for their health, (2) no equally effective research can be conducted on individuals who are legally capable of giving their consent; (3) the individuals who participate in the research received written information on their rights and of the limits of the research set forth in this Act and the regulations that govern it, which are designed to protect participants, providing the individual is in condition to receive such information; (4) the legal representatives of participants of the research have given written consent thereto, after being given full information as provided in Art. 15, and shall take into consideration any wishes or objections previously expressed by the individuals concerned. Moreover, information for people with disabilities shall be provided according to their special needs.

Notwithstanding this, under exceptional circumstances, research that is not liable to have a direct benefit for the health of the participating patients may be conducted if, in addition to the requirements of the previous paragraph, the following conditions are met: (a) The research seeks to significantly improve knowledge of the individual's disease or condition, thereby benefitting individuals of the same age or with the same disease or condition, within a reasonable period of time; (b) The research involves minimal risk and cost for the participant; (c) Notice is sent to the public prosecutor's office that the research has been authorised.

We have no records that biomedical research ethics have been violated in Spain as the Prisons Administration is particularly meticulous in that field.

19.10 Professional Role of Psychiatrists

There are very few psychiatric specialists working full time in prison environments in Spain. Their salaries are not very attractive and they are submitted to a strict regime of conflicts of interest (for example, they are not allowed to have a private practice in their profession). Part-time specialists are also lacking, and their consultation schedules are limited. There is much to be done, given the fact that mental disorders in Spanish prisons are widespread.

There are no psychiatrists in ordinary prisons to guide decision-making bodies (e.g. to submit proposals regarding release, relaxation of restrictions and so on), and very few in psychiatric prisons. This situation needs to be addressed by the Prison Prisoner Treatment Boards (ordinary prisons) and the Multi-disciplinary Teams (psychiatric prisons).

For many years, continuing education for mental health professionals has been neglected. Currently, a basic training is underway. Education on ethical-legal issues is practically non-existent, however.

There have been some improvements in the dual role of care and testimony as experts (some psychiatrists are recruited exclusively as experts), although much remains to be done. Psychiatrists (in many cases) and psychologists (in all cases) who treat patients are also required to give testimony as experts before a court, which implies a certain 'contamination' of their functions (Barrios 2000). It is worth pointing out that psychiatrists and psychologists face a serious dilemma. The Spanish Code of Ethics and Medical Ethics, dated 10 September 1999, for instance, provides that doctors who work for the government must perform in accordance to the provisions of the Code and that 'their testimony as experts or medical inspectors is incompatible with dispensing medical care to the same patient' (Art. 41). Nonetheless, mental health professionals working in prisons may receive orders from their superiors, and frequently from judicial bodies, to contravene the medical ethics mandate. The dual role of health care and expert testimony inside and outside of prison environments is not sufficiently guaranteed in Spain.

References

Barrios, L.F. 2000. Imparcialidad y objetividad del perito psiquiatra. *Revista de Estudios Penitenciarios* 248: 9–43.
Barrios, L.F. 2005. Coercitive methods in penitentiary practice. Therapeutic principles. *Revista Española de Sanidad Penitenciaria* 7(1): 1–10. edit. en.

Barrios, L.F. 2007a. Origen, evolución y crisis de la institución psiquiátrico-penitenciaria. *Revista de la Asociación Española de Neuropsiquiatría* 100: 473–500.

Barrios, L.F. 2007b. El empleo de medios coercitivos en prisión: Indicaciones regimentales y psiquiátricas. *Revista de Estudios Penitenciarios* 253: 61–100.

Cervelló, V. 1996. La huelga de hambre penitenciaria: Fundamento y límites de la alimentación forzosa. *Estudios Penales y Criminológicos* XIX: 51–164.

DGIP. 2007. Estrategia global de actuación en salud mental. Dirección general de Instituciones Penitenciarias. Madrid.

DGIP. 2006. Estudio sobre salud mental en el medio penitenciario. December 2006. Área de Salud Pública. (June 2007). Subdirección General de Sanidad Penitenciaria (Dirección General de Instituciones Penitenciarias).

Fernández, L. 2003. Ejecución de las medidas de seguridad. *Estudios Jurídicos. Ministerio Fiscal* 4: 43–130.

García, M. 1997. *Fundamentos y aplicación de penas y medidas de seguridad en el Código Penal de 1995*. Pamplona: Aranzadi.

García, R. 1992. *Las relaciones de especial sujeción en la Constitución Española*. Madrid: Tecnos.

Gómez-Escolar, P. (2007). Algunas cuestiones sobre la medida de seguridad de internamiento psiquiátrico. *Estudios de Derecho Judicial* (Ejemplar dedicado a "El Juez de Vigilancia Penitenciaria y las medidas de seguridad") 127:119–206.

Hernández, M., and R. Herrera. (Eds.it). 2003. *La atención a la salud mental de la población reclusa*. Madrid: Asociación Española de Neuropsiquiatría. Colección de Estudios: no 30. Madrid.

Instrucción. 2007. Instrucción 18/2007, December 20, on mechanical restraint. Dirección General de Instituciones Penitenciarias. Madrid. http://www.derechopenitenciario.com/comun/fichero.asp?id=1429

Instrucción. 2004. Instruction 3/2004, November 29, Regulation of procedures of action in situations of patients' unforeseen aggressiveness admitted into the Units of Penitentiary Psychiatry (Secretaría de Servicios Penitenciarios, Rehabilitación y Justicia Juvenil). Barcelona. http://www.derechopenitenciario.com/comun/fichero.asp?id=1480

Instrucción. 2005. Instruction 14/2005, August 10. Program on prevention of suicides. Dirección General de Instituciones Penitenciarias. Madrid. http://www.derechopenitenciario.com/comun/fichero.asp?id=573

National Statistics Institute. http://www.ine.es/

Quintero, G. 1996. *Comentarios al nuevo Código Penal*. Pamplona: Aranzadi.

Ruiz, A. 1993. Autonomía individual y derecho a la propia vida (Un análisis filosófico-jurídico). *Revista de Estudios Constitucionales* 14: 135–165.

Santos, A.A. 2001. *La imposición de medidas de seguridad en el proceso penal*. Granada: Comares.

Sanz, A.J. 2003. *Las medidas de corrección y seguridad en el proceso penal*. Valladolid: Lex Nova.

Sierra, M.V. 1997. *Las medidas de seguridad en el nuevo Código Penal*. Valencia: Tirant lo Blanch.

Silva, J.M. 1989. Aspectos de la comisión por omisión: fundamento y formas de intervención. El ejemplo del funcionario penitenciario. *Cuadernos de Política Criminal* 38: 367–404.

Torres, F., and L.F. Barrios. 2006. Chapter 12. Legal report – Spain. In *Legislation on coercive mental health care in Europe. Legal documents and comparative assessment of twelve European countries*, eds. T.W. Kallert and F. Torres-González, 293–323. Frankfurt am Main: Peter Lang Europäischer Verlag der Wissenschaften.

Vicens Pons, E. 2009. Aproximación a la metodología para el estudio de los trastornos mentales en población penitenciaria. El estudio Preca. *Revista Española de Sanidad Penitenciaria* 11(1): 17–25.

Vizueta, J. 2007. El trastorno mental grave apreciado después de dictarse sentencia firme: el art. 60 del Código Penal. *Revista Electrónica de Ciencia Penal y Criminología*. 4(9): 1–15. http://criminet.ugr.es/recpc/09/recpc09-04.pdf

Chapter 20
Ethical Issues in Prison Psychiatry in Sweden

Orsolya Hoffmann and Lennart Mossberg

20.1 Structure of the Prison System

20.1.1 General Information

The Swedish Prison and Probation Service is a part of the judicial system. The aims of Sweden's criminal justice policy are to reduce criminality and increase security in society and to help prisoners re-adapt to society. The Prison and Probation Service's main duties are to implement prison sentences and probation services, to be responsible for the supervision of conditionally released persons, to implement community sentences and to prepare pre-sentence reports in criminal cases.

The Prison and Probation Service is also responsible for remand prisons. In addition, it operates its own transport services and also transfers detained persons who are, for example, to be deported from Sweden. To achieve its goals and carry out its duties the Prison and Probation Service has a Head Office, six regional offices and a Transport Service. Each region has remand prisons, prisons and probation units which co-operate to help its clients adjust in the best possible way to a life without crime. In terms of administration, the Prison and Probation Service is also the senior authority for the National Parole Board and the 28 probation committees.

The head of the Prison and Probation Service is the Director General. The six regions are led by Regional Directors and all the prisons and remand prisons have a Governor. The Regional Director is also the head of the medical services. From 2006 onwards Regional Directors have had a coordinator (a nurse) for the medical services.

O. Hoffmann (✉)
Swedish Prison and Probation Service, Stockholm, Sweden
e-mail: hunor@stockholm.bostream.se

L. Mossberg
Probation Service, Norrköping Region, Sweden

N. Konrad et al. (eds.), *Ethical Issues in Prison Psychiatry*, International Library
of Ethics, Law, and the New Medicine 46, DOI 10.1007/978-94-007-0086-4_20,
© Springer Science+Business Media Dordrecht 2013

Table 20.1 Security level of prisons 2010

	A	B	C	D	E
Number of prisons	2	4	16	19	25

The Prison and Probation Service had an annual budget of 7,000 MSEK (900M US$ or 730M EUR) for 2010.

The Swedish Parliament abolished capital punishment in peace in 1921 and in war in 1972. However, no executions have been carried out since 1910.

20.1.2   Prisons

There are 55 (in 2010) prisons in Sweden. These prisons do not differ from region to region, with the exception of the maximum security facilities. The aim is to place all inmates depending on their needs. They are accommodated in rooms, 7–9 m² in size, furnished with a bed, a fixed table and a chair, a wash-basin with running water and a television set. In some prisons and remand prisons there are small units for inmates with psychiatric or somatic needs. The prisons are divided into six security levels, where A is the highest level and F the lowest. Some prisons can have two units with different security levels. (See Table 20.1).

There are 4,901 prison places available (95 % occupied on 2010 March). The maximum number of inmates per prison is 225. In 2009, the number of persons who began to serve a sentence in prison was 9,805 and 3,022 persons began to serve their sentence in the community under close supervision with electronic monitoring. The number of clients under probation was 14,424. The basic approach of Swedish criminal justice policy is that the sanctions involving deprivation of liberty should be avoided wherever possible, since such sanctions do not generally improve the individual's chances to re-adapt to a life in freedom. In Sweden there are 74 persons in prison per 100,000 inhabitants compared with, e. g., 756 per 100,000 inhabitants in the USA and 629 in Russia.

There are special units for the motivation and treatment of drug addicts. In 2009, 3,466 persons (3,087 men and 379 women) have successfully completed one of the 18 treatment programs in prison.

20.1.3   Remand Prisons

In Sweden there are 31 remand prisons with a total number of 1,893 places (March 2010). The largest remand prison has places for 301 inmates. Some inmates can have restrictions imposed for a long time while being detained in a remand prison. This means they may not be allowed to meet other inmates, make phone calls or have visitors. In some cases, even access to television and newspapers is denied.

In addition to housing inmates who are awaiting investigation by the police, trial or transport to prison, remand prisons are also used to detain individuals who are in custody in accordance with the following laws:

LVU	Lagen om Vård av Unga (The Care of Young Persons Act)
LVM	Lagen om Vård av Missbrukare (The Care of Alcohol and Drug Abusers Act)
LOB	Lagen om Omhändertagande av Berusade (The Care of Persons under the Influence of Drugs Act)
UTL	Utlänningslagen (The Aliens Act)

Detainees in accordance with LVU, LVM and LOB are few in number and are held on remand for only a short time (from a matter of hours to 1–2 days). There are more UTL detainees and they may be held for several months.

20.2   Medical Services and Mental Health Care in Prison

20.2.1   General Information

The medical services provided for inmates are regulated by law. There are medical care service units in all prisons and remand prisons in Sweden. This means that there is a nurse on duty during normal working hours and in some remand prisons there is a nurse on duty even on weekends and public holidays. Some of the nurses have psychiatric training, but this is not a job requirement. Doctors visit the prisons mostly on a weekly basis and the larger prisons and remand prisons also have psychiatrists who visit the prisons regularly. The nurses are employed by the prisons while the doctors are contracted as consultants and are paid by the prisons. The doctors are mostly remunerated at the same rates as private doctors in the community, which is higher than the salaries in the County Council Hospitals. All health care is at the level of an outpatient unit. If an inmate needs medical care as an inpatient, he or she will be transported to the local County Council Hospital. There are no prison hospitals in Sweden.

20.2.2   Committee for Prison Medicine

The Swedish Prison and Probation Service has had a Committee for Prison Medicine since 1981. The reason for the establishment of this committee was the unexplainable difference in the prescription of medications with a potential to be abused among the various prisons (benzodiazepines, opioides). The committee has been very active in following up the prescription of these medications. There is a unique documentation system concerning the prescriptions in different prisons and remand prisons and of the different groups of medicines, classified according to the ATC system (Anatomical Therapeutic Chemical classification system). The Committee publishes statistics every year and these provide very good feedback for every doctor. Since 1983, the Committee has published Basläkemedel inom kriminalvården (Basic Pharmacotherapy in the Prison and Probation Service), a booklet with recommendations for medication for the most common symptoms and diseases in the prison population. There is a new edition every second or third year.

20.2.3 Health Screening

There is a health screening program for inmates in remand prisons. This is carried out by nurses. This screening program is for both mental and somatic problems and consists of a non-structured questionnaire without screening for suicidal behaviour. The security staff in Swedish remand prisons are trained to recognize disturbed behaviour and contact the health services if necessary. Many of them are specially trained to recognize suicidal behaviour. The risk of parasuicide or suicide is highest in remand prisons. Screening for suicidal behaviour is carried out at the beginning of the detention by the security staff with the help of a standard form. If the suicide risk is high, medical staff gets involved in assessment and prevention.

All inmates with substance abuse problems are offered screening for HIV and hepatitis A, B and C, and those who have not had hepatitis B are vaccinated.

Inmates may be isolated from other prisoners, either at their own request or on a compulsory basis if necessary. A doctor must examine a prisoner if he or she has been continuously isolated for a period of 1 month.

Any prisoners who are kept isolated from other prisoners because they present a danger to their own life or health, or who are kept in mechanical restraints (bound by belt), must be examined by a doctor as soon as possible.

There are round-the-clock routines for handling emergency health cases at every prison. If there is medical staff at the prison, they make the first assessment, otherwise the inmate will be taken to the nearest hospital.

According to the Official Secrets Act there is restricted access to information about patients within the health care services. The medical staff do not share information with the security staff and the patients' medical files are kept separate, accessible only to the medical staff. Sometimes, mostly in cases of suicidal or self-destructive behaviour, the security staff form part of the treatment group; in this case they have access to the information about the patient they need.

20.2.4 Psychiatric Care

The quality of psychiatric care in a prison is likely to meet the public mental health standards. Most of the psychiatrists have been working for a long time with inmates and can handle their problems well. However, most of the psychiatrists are not trained in addiction medicine and there is a need for this training.

All inmates who want to meet a psychiatrist are allowed to do so. In Sweden there is a shortage of psychiatrists in public health care services. Collaboration with the public mental health care services varies from region to region. If there is a need for psychiatric hospital care, mostly as compulsory treatment, inmates have to be referred to a Public Psychiatric Hospital. The staff in those units are usually not trained to handle the special problems of inmates (substance abuse and aggressiveness) and this mostly results in an early return to the prison. In some cities there are special wards which treat patients mostly from prisons (for example in Stockholm) and there the cooperation between the public mental health care services and the prisons is better.

Compulsory psychiatric care of inmates in Sweden is regulated by the Forensic Psychiatric Care Act, which is different from the Compulsory Psychiatric Care Act. Compulsory psychiatric care is only allowed at a psychiatric clinic and never in prison. For security reasons, the wards that can accept inmates for compulsory treatment must be approved by the government.

There are psychologists employed in every region, but the number varies from region to region. These psychologists are involved in both psychotherapy and treatment programs. Some prisons have consulting psychologists as well. Most of the psychologists have had psychodynamic training, but some of them work with cognitive methods but there are a few cognitively trained psychologists. Accessibility to a psychologist varies from prison to prison; in some places the psychiatrist assesses the need for psychological treatment, in other places the selection of clients to meet the psychologist is not made on the basis of evidence but on the demand of the inmate.

There are three diagnostic groups that are clearly overrepresented in the prison population: substance abuse disorders, personality disorders (including psychopathy) and ADHD (Attention-Deficit/Hyperactivity Disorder). The treatment of withdrawal symptoms is very common in remand prisons and is similar to the treatment used in addiction clinics. There are special treatment programs for preventing relapses into substance abuse and for sex offenders. Both drug addicts and sex offenders are placed in special wings with treatment programs. These inmates are generally not allowed to meet other prisoners. The drug addicts are protected from contact with drugs and the sex offenders from harassment by the other prisoners. Concerning personality disorders, there are cognitive training programs to reduce criminality and aggression. There are projects in some prisons for the diagnosis and treatment of ADHD.

20.2.5   Substance Abuse

Tobacco smoking has not been permitted in prisons, except in open-air areas, since January 2008. Inmates are given help for smoking cessation. The result is a decreasing number of inmates who smoke but an increasing number of inmates who use snuff.

Since 1987 (with an interruption from June 1999 to February 2002) an HIV-epidemiological study has been carried out at the main remand prison in Stockholm. All persons arrested or detained who were identified by injection marks or otherwise as illicit drug users were invited to participate in a voluntary study consisting of an HIV and hepatitis test and an interview on risk behaviour. This study helped to spread information about HIV and about possibilities for testing and improved the early identification of new cases. The number of HIV-tested drug addicts in Sweden is high and seroprevalence is low. This study developed into a program for screening inmates with substance abuse for HIV and hepatitis in all remand prisons in Sweden.

To improve the treatment of substance abusers in prisons, the CDG (Central Drug Group) was started up in 2001. The CDG is a specialist group connected to the Head Office, which prepares action plans, provides support and ensures quality. As a result of their work there are outreach teams in remand prisons, special units for motivation and treatment and therapeutic communities with evidence-based treatment programs. All these programs are now incorporated in the routine activities and the CDG has been disbanded. For the assessment of substance abuse the ASI (Addiction Severity Index) and MAPS (Monitoring Area Phase System) are used. Treatment of heroin addicts with buprenorphine or methadone starts before their release from prison if necessary, but the treatment is usually not provided during the whole sentence.

The aim of the Swedish Prison and Probation Service is to offer a drug-free environment to all inmates. In the battle for this goal there are some improved security arrangements – for example, sniffer dogs are now used.

There are no needle-exchange programs in prisons in Sweden. Annual random screening of urine-samples in the Stockholm region shows declining numbers of drug-positive results during the last 6 years. Eighty-six percentage of inmates were clean from all analysed drugs (14 % were drug positive samples, refusers or diluted urine samples). The main drugs used in prison are benzodiazepines, cannabis, buprenorphine and androgen anabolic streoids.

20.2.6 *Economy*

The budget for mental health care is a part of the overall prison budget. The nurses' salaries are negotiated by their Trade Union, which is generally and traditionally very strong in Sweden. Up to now, the doctors have negotiated their appointment every second or third year with the Governor of the prison. These Governors are not medically trained, so they have a limited capacity to judge the doctors' ability to work with the inmates. This has resulted in big differences in the doctors' competence in prison medicine and addiction medicine. From 2006 onwards, negotiations concerning doctors' appointments have been the responsibility of the Regional Director. In addition, there has been a centrally-placed coordinator for medical services in every region to assist the Regional Director since 2006.

The number of nurses has decreased during the last few years. The goal is that one nurse will be responsible for 100 inmates in the prisons.

There is no limit to the cost of medicine and every inmate is offered all necessary medication, but there is a central discussion about costs and the medical units try to use the cheaper generic medicines. This is similar to the situation in the general public, where pharmacists are supposed to provide patients with the cheapest generics.

20.3   Epidemiology of Mental Disorders

20.3.1   General Information

The Forensic Psychiatric Act was passed in 1992. The purpose of this new act was to reduce the number of offenders sentenced to forensic psychiatric care and the number of forensic psychiatric assessments and to limit the number of forensic psychiatric assessments. This has also resulted in an increased number of prison inmates with psychiatric problems. There are no central statistics in Sweden about the number of inmates treated for mental disorders apart from suicide rates and substance abuse. However, the epidemiology of mental disorders has been investigated several times during the last 15 years.

20.3.2   Recent Studies

To assess the need for psychiatric care in the prison system, Westin (1992) carried out an investigation in all the prisons in Sweden. A questionnaire was sent to the various prisons to find out how many inmates they had with a psychiatric illness (psychosis) and with other psychiatric disturbances (all those with a need of psychiatric care but without psychosis) and how many of them had substance abuse problems.

This questionnaire was completed mostly by nurses, sometimes by psychiatrists or by one of the security staff. The highest numbers of inmates with a psychiatric illness and disturbance were reported by psychiatrists. Therefore the results of the investigation might underestimate the problem. Table 20.2 shows the findings of this study.

A study carried out by Levander et al. (1997) assessed a prison population in South Sweden using structured interviews. The dropout rate was more than 50 % due to difficulties in speaking Swedish or English or in getting transport to other prisons. 30 % of the inmates had a lifetime prevalence of an Axis I disorder and 28 % at the time of the assessment; 75 % had a personality disorder and 23 % had a PCL-R score ≥ 26; 41 % suffered from dyslexia. Substance abuse figures were also high with 17 % for alcohol and sedatives, 24 % for narcotics and 19 % for alcohol and narcotics.

Table 20.2 Psychiatric morbidity in prisons (Westin 1992)

	Prisons	Remand prisons
Number of inmates	3,538	1,163
Psychiatric disease	74 (2.1 %)	31 (2.7 %)
Psychiatric disturbance	588 (16.6 %)	105 (9 %)
Substance abuse	460 (13 %)	96 (8.3 %)

In another study, 50 inmates on Gotland (an island South-East of the mainland) were assessed. Personality disorders and/or substance abuse were diagnosed in 75 % of prisoners, psychopathy in 25 %, dyslexia in 50 %, and an Axis I diagnosis in 33 %. About 25 % had symptoms of ADHD.

During one year (September 1996–1997) Holmberg et al. (1999) investigated a total of 12,687 individuals who were detained at any time during the observation period. Of these, 294 inmates (2.3 %) received psychiatric treatment in hospital or in a psychiatric unit at least once. Inmates convicted of murder/manslaughter, arson, rape or unlawful threat were two to five times more likely to require psychiatric treatment than the general prison population. Furthermore, their average individual number of psychiatric inpatient days was approximately twice that of inpatients convicted of other types of crime.

While 10 % of the total study population underwent a pre-trial forensic psychiatric examination, 45 % of those who ended up receiving psychiatric treatment during their prison term had been investigated by a forensic psychiatric specialist before being tried in court.

There are central statistics of suicide rates within the prison system. The number of suicides has been stable at a low level throughout, see Table 20.3.

The Remand Prison Study is an ongoing study in Stockholm Remand Prison, it was later extended to the Gothenburg Remand Prison. The aim of the study is to assess drug abuse and provide screening for hepatitis A, B and C and HIV. Interviewing and taking blood samples are carried out by nurses; if a blood test is positive in any one of the analyses a doctor informs the individual about the result and invites the patient to follow up. Tables 20.4 and 20.5 show substance misuse, age of amphetamine and opiate users, number of intravenous drug users (IDU) who were HIV tested before the interview and the number of new HIV positive cases (Remand Prison Study, Non-published data).

20.4   Quality Standards

20.4.1   Quality System

The National Board of Health and Welfare, which is the ministry responsible for health care in Sweden, was made responsible for supervising health care within the Swedish Prison and Probation Service on 1 January 1997. The Director General has set up a quality system for health care in prisons which is described in a manual.

Table 20.3 Suicide rate in prisons and remand prisons in Sweden

	1995	1996	1997	1998	1999	2000	2001	2002	2003	2004	2005	2006	2007	2008	2009
Prison	2	3	1	3	1	1	2	3	1	2	3	1	1	1	0
Remand prison	2	3	4	7	1	4	2	5	7	5	4	5	12	5	2

Table 20.4 Substance abuse in Stockholm Remand Prison 2005

	Invited to participate	Accepted	Women (%)	IDU (%)	IDU women (%)	IDU amphet- amine (%)	IDU opiates (%)
Stockholm	718	612 (85 %)	11	66	14	64	36
Gothenburg	371	329 (89 %)	10	55	14	76	24

Table 20.5 Average age, HIV test rate and new HIV cases from the Remand Prison Study

	Average age, amphetamine	Average age, opiates IDU	HIV tested before (%)	New cases of HIV
Stockholm	38.3	33.0	90.5	5 (3 amphetamine, 2 opiates)
Gothenburg	35.0	30.3	91.8	0

This manual presents the principles of the quality system and the general performance of health care, including the special demands of the prison system and the laws concerning health care in prison. Following the directives in this manual, all the health care units have prepared local routines for ensuring quality. This quality system is a dynamic and flexible system that is updated regularly. It includes an incident reporting system, which means that all events that might involve a risk for the patient must be reported (the most common problem concerns the distribution of medication). These reports are sent to the Head of Health Care, who is also the Regional Director. There are meetings held in every region, called quality meetings, at which the health-care representatives (doctors and nurses), the governors of the prisons and remand prisons and the Regional Director participate. The frequency of these meetings varies from region to region, but the required occurrence is at least twice a year.

Apoteksbolaget (the national pharmaceuticals retailing firm, which until recently had a monopoly in Sweden) has the responsibility for the quality control of the storage and the administration of medication.

Lex Maria is a law in Sweden which states that all health care units are bound by law to report all incidents in which a patient, in connection with treatment or examination, suffers a serious injury or illness or runs the risk of a serious injury or illness and this also applies in prison.

This report must be sent to the National Board of Health and Welfare, which does not otherwise actively participate in the quality control of health care in prisons.

Those inmates who are dissatisfied with the health care in prison have the same options to complain as patients in general in Sweden. During the last few years, the board responsible for dealing with health-care complaints, HSAN (Hälso- och Sjukvårdens Ansvarsnämnd), received a decreasing number of complaints from prisons annually.

The assessment of mentally disordered inmates in prison is the responsibility of a psychiatrist. All the consulting psychiatrists are specialists, some of them with many years of experience of dealing with patients with personality disorders and substance abuse. Every year about 350 people undergo forensic psychiatric examinations before going to prison. Evaluation of mental health with the same depth is not possible in the prisons due to the lack of resources. There are no standardized instruments for screening or investigating mental disorders.

The staff dealing with the treatment of mentally ill inmates (nurses, security staff) have no psychiatric training. There are psychiatric units in some prisons, but neither the level of training of the staff nor the accessibility to mental-health professionals really differs from the other units.

20.4.2 Medical Confidentiality

Medical confidentiality is regulated by law and is taken seriously. The medical file of an inmate is never accessible to others than those who are involved in the health care of the inmate. To avoid problems, like knowledge of current abuse which cannot be shared with the security staff, the medical staff never check the urine samples for drug screening, but they have access to the results from the security staff. Sometimes there is a need to share information with the security staff in the inmate's own interest (for example, risk of suicide attempts, self-harm, acting-out behaviour, etc.). In such cases, the information is limited to emergency needs.

The Swedish prison doctors founded an association in 1994 called SKLF (Sveriges Kriminalvårdsläkares Förening, the Swedish Society for Prison Medicine). This society deals, among other things, with ethical questions. The discussions during the last few years included the following topics: whether it is ethical that prison nurses should take specimens by order of the prosecutor; how to handle the fact that doctors could be forced by law to perform an intimate body search by order of an authority and the fact that all doctors, including prison doctors, are forced by law to report to the police mentally ill patients who are not able to handle a licensed weapon.

20.5 Ethical Aspects

20.5.1 Introduction

Ethical and moral issues that fall outside the normal medical framework are constantly arising in prison medicine, and prison health care is a never-ending source of new experience and new knowledge. The duties of the doctor are based on our ethical principles: to do good, not to cause harm and to respect self-determination and justice. Ethical considerations are part of the everyday life of treatment and feelings of compassion for the prisoners must be balanced at the same time as a dignified distance must always be maintained in the consultation room in order to create a professional relationship. If one does not behave with charity towards the patient and does not take into consideration his or her vulnerability, the treatment will always be unethical, regardless of the aim.

A comprehensive view is one way of summing up the humanistic picture of mankind. Human beings are both individuals and members of a group, they are both subjects and objects, they have responsibility and the ability to choose, they are creative and they must relate to what is right and what is wrong. These central humanistic values form the basis of medical work, even in the special field of prison medicine where the patients represent the criminal subculture.

It should be fairly obvious that the view that a human being is a moral creature who continuously relates to what is right and wrong necessarily forces the acceptance of ethical principles. Swedish law states that the treatment of offenders in prisons should be designed to promote the readjustment of the prisoners to society and to counteract the harmful effects of imprisonment. Thus the care of offenders in Sweden has a double aim: to punish by means of imprisonment and to provide care that aims to promote readjustment to society.

An important Swedish ethical/legal paradigm, enshrined in the Swedish constitution, states that every citizen has to be protected from physical interference from the state. This basic protection is in agreement with a statement from the WMA (World Medical Association 1993) which makes it clear that body-searching of prisoners shall not be carried out by doctors except on strictly medical grounds, and that doctors providing treatment may not be used by authorities in, for example, security work.

20.5.2 International Guidelines

"Kalk's refusal" has become a symbol of the ethical conflicts that doctors in prison medicine are confronted with. Dr Kalk in South Africa had to accept prisoners for treatment in his hospital but refused to send them back to prison since he knew how badly they were treated there. The conflicts in Sweden are different, concerning, for example, body-searching of those under arrest, the treatment of prisoners on hunger strikes, certain medical treatments and urine testing.

At the end of 1946, 100 doctors gathered in London as representatives of medical associations in 32 countries and formed the first international medical organisation, the World Medical Association (WMA). The main aim of the WMA was to encourage and make it easier for doctors to meet and set up networks. A doctor's work in remand prisons and prisons involves considerable ethical risks. It has therefore been necessary to work out principles for medical ethics appropriate for the treatment of prisoners in order to support prisoners, prison doctors, nurses and authorities. Central documents and prison-medicine guidelines that are still in operation are the WMA's Nuremburg Codex (1949, requiring the patient's agreement in medical research), the Helsinki Declaration (1964, regulating biomedical research) and the

Tokyo Declaration (1975, stating that doctors shall not participate in torture, nor in forced feeding [if two independent doctors judge that the prisoners has a clear and rational understanding of the consequence of his/her hunger strike]).

The Hawaii Declaration of 1977 (World Psychiatric Association) states that no forced treatment may be given unless the patient, owing to mental illness, lacks the ability to express his/her will, cannot decide what is best for him/her or is a serious risk to others.

In 1982 the UN General Assembly adopted a resolution that:

- Doctors are obliged to provide prisoners with treatment of the same standard as is afforded to those who are not prisoners.
- Doctors must not, actively or passively, engage in torture or other cruel, inhuman or degrading treatment or punishment.
- Doctors must not be involved in any professional relationship with prisoners whose purpose is not solely to evaluate, protect or improve their physical and mental health.
- Doctors shall not use their knowledge and skills to assist in the interrogation of prisoners in any way that may have an adverse effect on their physical or mental health and that is not in accordance with accepted international norms. This applies in particular to the general minimum rules concerning the treatment of prisoners.
- Doctors must not certify or participate in the certification of prisoners or detainees that they are in a fit state to receive any form of treatment or punishment that may adversely affect their physical or mental health, nor shall they in any way participate in the infliction of any such treatment or punishment which is not in accordance with the relevant international instruments.
- Doctors shall not participate in any procedure of restraining a prisoner unless such a procedure is determined in accordance with purely medical criteria in order to protect the physical and mental health of the prisoner, other prisoners or the guards.

The European Committee for the Prevention of Torture and Inhuman or Degrading Treatment or Punishment (CPT 2011) gives clear directions concerning the quality of prison medicine. A detainee must have access to a doctor who in turn is able to make use of a fully equipped hospital. A detainee must have access to treatment that is of the same standard as is available in the community. A detainee must be guaranteed that the doctor utilises professional confidentiality and he must also have the possibility to consent to the forms of treatment that are planned. The inmates' demands must of course be in line with evidence-based treatment. Relevant measures to prevent ill health (violence, suicide, infections) must be provided.

The empirical ethics of prison medicine were set out in recommendations from the Council of Europe in 1998. The right to health care in prison is clarified by the principles of access to a doctor, normalisation, agreement, professional secrecy, prevention of illness and professional independence. The specific role of a prison doctor is linked to general requirements that clarify his/her obligations to represent the patient. A prison doctor must be well educated in both general medicine and psychiatry and must provide information about health care, prevention and training and pay special attention to the occurrence of violence. It is invaluable that in the Swedish prison services there is an awareness both that a prison doctor often faces difficult ethical dilemmas and that it is important to continuously develop his/her activities so that they are compatible with good health care.

All these rules are easily understandable in the light of the often cruel and inhuman ways in which various cultures treat offenders and political opponents. The rules are valuable because they define where the limits are and make it clear that the role of the prison doctor is not custodial but is to provide treatment.

20.5.3   Swedish Rules

Sweden conforms to The Ethical and Organisational Aspects of Health Care in Prison with one exception: remand prisoners are not entitled to ask for consultation with their own doctor. In view of the high number of inmates in remand prisons with substance abuse, following this recommendation could lead to ongoing drug abuse. However, the prison doctor may contact the inmate's own doctor, if the inmate allows it, in both remand prisons and prisons.

The Swedish normalisation principle of 1974 makes it clear that people in custody have the same right to treatment and care as any other citizen. The normalisation principle means that the regular organs of society – within the framework of their respective duties – must also take responsibility for prison inmates and that such inmates undoubtedly have the same right to social support and aid as other citizens. The law concerning correctional treatment in prisons also lays down that: "If an inmate requires health care, he must be treated in accordance with the directions given by the doctor." If a necessary examination and treatment cannot be provided within the prison, the public medical services should be utilised and – if necessary – the inmate should be transferred to a public hospital.

Thus Swedish legislation follows the guidelines of internationally accepted medical ethics that there must be an equivalence of care.

Attention must be paid to patients with special needs by providing, for example, adequate access to premised by those with disabilities. There has to be organised collaboration with psychiatric services for those who are mentally disturbed, and continuous assessment of the risk of suicide must be implemented within the prison service's own organisation.

20.5.4   Prison Medicine

As the medical treatment and health care of those in remand prisons or prisons is in many respects essentially different from ordinary treatment and care; prison medicine therefore has its own special profile (Bertrand and Harding 1993). The large percentage of patients who have personality disorders and are drug abusers, imprisonment itself and the environment of remand prisons and prisons are examples of factors that seriously affect the possibilities for providing professional diagnostic, therapeutic and nursing services.

Drugs are a central element in prison subculture and influence the life of the inmates in different ways. Protein-rich food, special diets and anabolic steroids are used to build up muscles; other drugs are used to provide highs and feelings of euphoria or to relieve anguish, anxiety and boredom. Prisoners in high-security prisons are the criminal elite while the more or less down-and-out inmates of local prisons live in 'criminal misery'.

The prison population is at present at a very high level. Confrontations, 'sucking-up', testing, incidents, complaints, lies, manipulative behaviour, simulation and dissimulation are typical features of prison life. A large number of detoxification treatments are carried out in the Stockholm remand prisons and during a 2 year period it is estimated that that most of the intravenous substance abusers in the Stockholm region have been in contact with the prison services.

20.5.5 Pharmacological Treatment

The ABC of pharmacological therapy according to Basic Pharmacotherapy in the prison and probation service is restrictive in prescribing analgesics (pain-killers), benzodiazepines and drugs that stimulate the nervous system. The basic mechanisms by which medicines can lead to addiction problems are the same as for illegal drugs, even though the effects are often less evident and the social context in many cases is different. Analgesics that affect the central nervous system run an obvious risk of creating addiction due to their ability to activate opioid receptors. Codeine is the classic example of this group, which in Sweden is not classified as a narcotic as the codeine content of single tablets is considered too low. Another substance, dextropropoxyphene, has a grave risk of toxicity in combination with alcohol. This will lead to it being removed from the register in the European Union in 2011. A third substance causing concern is tramadol, which is reported as having a lower risk of dependence. This drug was initially launched principally as an inhibitor of serotonin and noradrenalin re-uptake but has a considerable opioid activity, principally by active metabolism, and is therefore a clear addiction risk. Several benzodiazepines, principally those with a rapid effect and a short half-life, have a considerable addiction risk and are discussed in a separate section. The soporifics zopiclone (Imovane) and zolpidem (Stilnoct) were initially launched with the hope that they completely lacked a potential for addiction. However, their mechanisms are rather similar to those of the benzodiazepines and even though the risk of addiction is lower it is not negligible. The use of drugs in prison medicine demands clear routines. With the aim of increasing security in the use of drugs, the Swedish prison service has adopted a system called apo-dose whereby the prescribed medicine is prepared at a pharmacy and delivered in dose packets.

As early as the mid-1970s those responsible for medicines in the state of Utah, USA, realised that benzodiazepines and certain other tranquilizers are not suitable for use in prisons. Increased threatening behaviour and greater aggressiveness resulted from their prescription and prisoners who were treated with benzodiazepines often behaved extremely oddly with self-mutilation, the injection of saliva, knife attacks and the like. When the treatment strategy was changed, the picture improved quite dramatically. At the same time a report published in Sweden showed that Swedish prison doctors prescribed enormous quantities of benzodiazepines, in some cases up to 150 DDD (Defined Daily Dose) per 100 inmates every day. The result of this report was that a pharmaceutical committee was set up at the National Prison and Probation Authority in 1981. This committee was reorganised in 1995 as the Committee for Prison Medicine with a broader brief, which resulted in a quality manual for prison medicine. The aim of the committee has been to help prison doctors to prescribe drugs in a suitable manner. In full consensus with the Utah study, the Committee recommended from the very start strict restrictiveness in the prescription of benzodiazepines to prisoners. These drugs, which decrease feelings of anxiety, are soporific, muscle-relaxing and antispasmodic, but also addictive and clearly inappropriate for addicts except in difficult cases of detoxification. The book Basic Pharmacotherapy in the Prison and Probation Service provides recommendations for the choice of drugs that are suitable for prison patients. By feeding back the prescription statistics to all units in the prison services, every doctor is also given the possibility twice a year to review his own prescription practise of antibiotics, pain-killers, soporifics, tranquilizers and antidepressants.

Particular attention is paid to the prescription of benzodiazepines, and in recent years especially of Rohypnol or Flunitrazepam. Great differences in the prescription of benzodiazepines have occurred among doctors and in different regions in Sweden. Differences of up to 20 times in the prescription of benzodiazepines have been noted. Various explanations may be discerned but the committee's assessment is that the most important reason for the differences is the doctors' varying views on indications for benzodiazepines and the different therapy traditions that have developed in different parts of Sweden. For a long time western Sweden has had a higher level of prescriptions of benzodiazepines in prisons and in the public health services. Prescriptions of benzodiazepines in prisons have in recent years levelled out very considerably with continuous reductions, but after almost 30 years of active work on reducing the use of these substances for medically indicated detoxification there are still units that maintain a relatively high prescription of benzodiazepines. Doctors who prescribe large quantities of benzodiazepines seem to also prescribe larger quantities of other drugs. Parallel to the reduced prescription of these drugs there has been a considerable increase in the prescription of antidepressants.

Inmates in remand prisons and prisons often ask for analgesics, benzodiazepines and nowadays drugs that stimulate the central nervous system. It is a tricky task to meet this demand in a way that both creates trust and is reconciled with good health care based on science and evidence; furthermore, appropriate treatment should be based on actual needs and not on the patients' demands.

20.5.6   Issues in the Treatment of Prisoner Patients with Addictions

Prison has been called the "total institution" by the Swedish social psychologist Bertil Sundin where people are deprived of their freedom and where gangs, hierarchies, violence, riots and drug abuse are characteristic features as well as multi-relations between doctors, nurses and other persons. The internal socio-psychological climate is therefore both specific and dynamic. In prison medicine, as in forensic psychiatry and public medical services, it is the doctor's duty to represent the individual patient, but this self-evident focus on the patient has to be balanced in prison medicine against the duty also to represent all the other patients in the prison, that is, the group, and sensitive medical decisions must also, after mature consideration, be taken with regard for the needs of fellow prisoners, relatives, staff and the public.

Special attention has to be paid to the fact that three types of withdrawal symptoms occur: acute, protracted and conditioned. Acute withdrawal symptoms are brief (days-weeks), varying according to the substance, but are often characterised by anxiety, worry, sleeplessness and physical symptoms such as palpitations, a rise in blood pressure, fever, vomiting and cramps. Protracted withdrawal symptoms last for months and are characterised by depression, apathy and tiredness as well as changes in autonomous reactivity (stomach-bowels-heart) and in the levels of certain hormones. This is the grey reality for many drug abusers, contributing to their seeking again a 'chemical' lift to their mood. In a protracted abstinence phase – in prison, a clinic or the like – episodes of conditioned abstinence can easily occur. Conditioned withdrawal symptoms are experiences and behaviours that normally occur during acute withdrawal periods, but will, through associative learning, be triggered, much later, by conditioned stimuli such as a drug-related environment. During both protracted withdrawal symptoms and conditioned withdrawal symptoms the addict experiences an intense craving for drugs. A fellow patient or inmate who is under the influence of drugs will trigger a craving for drugs in addicts, for whom he/she represents a conditioned stimulus.

These conditioned withdrawal symptoms among other inmates are a further example of the socio-psychological complexity that a prison doctor faces.

20.5.7   ADHD

As a step towards improving the treatment of drug addicts suffering from personality disorders, a research project tested and approved by ethical committees is in progress in which inmates diagnosed with ADHD are offered treatment with methylphenidate. However, before the project was approved, there were ethical reservations: "It must be considered unethical that all individuals that meet the ADHD criteria and choose to take part in the study are after a short time given an amphetamine-like substance regardless of its effect. This approach could be seen as the offer of an amphetamine-like substance and lead to increased recruitment to the study, especially by individuals who have previously used amphetamine. At the same time, the scientific evaluation of the effect of the substance is negatively affected." (Regional Ethical Committee in Stockholm).

Treating amphetamine abusers suffering from ADHD-like personality disorders with the drug methylphenidate can of course be seen as 'doing good' and in the short term prove to be effective. But doing good for a vulnerable person should also of course be judged in the longer term, i.e. what this potent treatment means in the longer term for the individual, for society, for public health and for the potential to create new addicts.

The fact that up to now Swedish society has been permeated by negative attitudes towards both drug use and drug abuse of various types of narcotics probably explains why Sweden, compared with other European countries, has relatively few young drug addicts. This naturally also means that very many lives have been saved! Introducing treatment with narcotics-classed drugs in prisons means that the present negative attitude in society may change, involving a possible risk for public health.

20.5.8   Gun Laws

Swedish law concerning weapons (1996:67) aims at counteracting the use of guns in violent crime or their abuse in any other way; it also regulates a doctor's obligation to report to the police that a patient who is undergoing treatment for mental disorder is judged to be unsuitable to possess a gun. According to the National Swedish Board of Health and Welfare, a doctor should in every case consider whether a patient undergoing treatment for mental disorder is unsuitable to possess a gun. This obligation comprises not only psychiatric doctors but also other health and care services including doctors who are responsible for the treatment of inmates in prisons or at a unit for forensic examination where patients are treated for a mental disorder.

Whether being a prison doctor is compatible with the obligation to submit a report is a question that has ethical dimensions. The work of a prison doctor requires the provision of skilled medical and psychiatric care in a complex environment where the patient's demands often do not agree with his/her needs and where the requirements of the authorities are not balanced against resources. The percentage of unsuitable gun owners due to mental health problems is over-estimated and a rigid application of the law on weapons by prison doctors would jeopardise the alliance with our patients. Instead, it could be considered reasonable that reports on unsuitability to possess a gun should be made before the person is placed in custody.

20.5.9 Autonomy Versus Compulsion

Hunger strikes sometimes, though very infrequently in Swedish prison medicine, lead to a classic ethical dilemma whereby respect for the prisoner's self-determination and integrity is set against the doctor's duty to protect the prisoner's health and life. The Swedish Society of Medicine has judged that forced feeding is permissible in Phase 2 when the prisoner, owing to lack of nutrition, is confused and with whom it is difficult to communicate. On the other hand, the Swedish Medical Association has judged that forced feeding should not be used even in this life-threatening phase, with reference to the 1982 UN resolution. The Declaration of Malta (WMA Declaration of Hunger Strikers) lays down that forced feeding is not ethically defensible if two independent doctors judge that the prisoner has a clear and rational understanding of the consequences of hunger striking. Thus these viewpoints are divergent – as they are among doctors – and there is no legislation that strictly regulates a doctor's obligations. During the past 30 years, to the best of our knowledge, there has never been a need to take a stand on this difficult point in Swedish prisons. All inmates in prisons that have started a hunger strike have ended it before any danger to life has arisen.

The absence of insight into mental illness and the refusal to take medicine or accept necessary treatment means that a person held in a remand prison or a prisoner can be moved to a public or forensic psychiatric unit where forced medication is allowed after a doctor's decision.

Security reasons give senior prison staff the right to decide on the use of physical restraints in accordance with the law. In such cases, a doctor must always be consulted to assess the existence of mental illness, which should then be treated in a hospital, or whether the patient is suffering from a somatic illness that contraindicates the use of physical restraints. If there is no medical reason for discontinuing the use of physical restraints, it is the prison staff that decide when it shall be discontinued.

20.5.10 Rehabilitation Versus Social Protection

It is often necessary to weigh up the interest of an inmate's good health and respect for his/her right to self-determination against society's need for protection. The following case represents the experience of a prisoner at a psychiatric out-patient unit before his imprisonment:

> I'm a 31-year-old guy who was given Iktorivil (Clonazepam) prescribed in March 2001. My daily dose was 2 mg in the morning and 2 mg in the evening. To begin with I felt a high that came slowly but was strong and lasted a long time. I often combined Iktorivil with alcohol – I could take a 2 week ration, 28.2 mg tablets, at one time along with small amounts of alcohol. This mixture made me feel unafraid, cold. Many crimes, like assaults on guards and pilfering, when I scared the living daylights out of the staff with my cold behaviour, are directly connected with my use of Iktorivil combined with alcohol.

This story illustrates the problems associated with the prescription of certain tranquilisers. The doctor's intention to offer his patient help and support and to reduce his feelings of anxiety was contradicted by an increased risk of serious criminality. It is well known that the use of benzodiazepines is limited because of the side- effects as dependency or disinhibitory reactions.

Doctors in Sweden attend special training courses which also deal with assessing the risk of relapses into violent crime. Such assessments place particularly high demands on the doctor since the methods used have both low validity and low reliability and are therefore not accurate. One error of judgement can damage not only the individual who is being assessed but also a third party – other members of society. Assessment of risk is always carried out in combination with an analysis of the possibilities, based on the individual's problems.

20.5.11 Confidentiality

There are different levels of confidentiality between the work done in prisons by the criminal justice system and the health and medical care professionals. In addition, professional confidentiality in public health care is stricter than professional confidentiality in prison health care. This means that information that is revealed in public health care cannot be freely handed over to prison health care. Such information may in principle only be handed over from the public health services if the inmate permits it. However, there is close cooperation between medical care and prison care concerning many medical problems in prison care, for example when there is a risk of self-mutilation, suicide and serious aggressiveness and in the supervision of narcotics swallowers. In such cases, medical information is released when it is important for all those involved in the care of a prisoner to know about it.

20.5.11.1 Body-Searching

Swedish law concerning prisons mandates that prison doctors must carry out body searches at the request of the authority. This law presumes that there is informed consent since forced treatment is not permitted, but it does illustrate the fact that prison doctors are faced with ethical dilemmas and double loyalties. In accordance with both the WMA's and the Council of Europe's ethical rules, health-care staff working in prisons should only carry out examinations and operations that have a medical purpose. Doctors and nurses working in prisons should therefore not carry out examinations and tests at the request of the prosecutor and the police, which means that a prison doctor may be forced to choose between breaking the law or breaking recognised ethical rules.

Refusing to allow oneself to be body-searched because of the risk of the discovery of, for example, drug smuggling may imply both worry and an ethical dilemma for the doctor. The treatment possibilities and the medical observation are not optimal in the prison and the patient cannot automatically be transferred to public health care. Medical training does not always provide adequate confidence for this kind of assessment and this typical medical dilemma is best dealt with by referring to specific knowledge. 'Body-packers' swallow large amounts of narcotics; as they plan this, the substances are usually well packaged. 'Body-stuffers' on the other hand, swallow narcotics intended for sale in an unplanned way or in panic. In this case, the quantities are considerable smaller but the packaging might be worse. Body-packers smuggle narcotics in their own body orifices, mainly heroin, cocaine and amphetamine. Medical complications are rare but for obvious reasons there are a large number of unknown cases. Deaths are extremely rare and only occur in cases of undiagnosed intoxication. Medical complications may occur either in the form of intoxication because the package bursts – but intoxication occurs approximately 30 min after the package has burst and it takes several hours for death to occur without treatment – or in the form of mechanical obstruction because of the size of the package.

Suspicion that narcotics have been swallowed may be based on information from customs or the police or the client. This can be verified by X-ray, computer tomography and/or drug analysis of urine (packages usually leak even if they do not burst and the urine test should be repeated to eliminate the client's own drug abuse). The treatment consists of observation and possibly the use of laxatives (the only recommended laxative is lactulose, 30 ml, one dose, to avoid provoking mechanical or chemical damage to the package). If symptoms of intoxication occur, naloxone is administered for opiate intoxication and diazepam for cocaine/amphetamine intoxication or an operation is carried out. Removal by gastroscopy is not recommended.

20.5.11.2   Obligation to Report

In accordance with the European prison regulations (1992), a doctor must be particularly observant if violence occurs. If the violence is serious, in accordance with the law concerning emergency situations there is no need for agreement before informing the prison authorities. Deciding whether violence in a prison is serious or not may be a dilemma.

20.5.11.3   Urine Testing

Supervised urine testing for drug analysis in prisons has been considered a 'non-medical issue'. This may seem self-evident for prison representatives, but all urine testing could be claimed to be a medical issue even though the reason for testing is not medical. After all, it is a matter of analysing body fluids with requirements for reliable analysis and so on. If a doctor requests a urine test on purely medical grounds – for example, suspicion that a person being prescribed medication is under the influence of drugs – he/she risks holding information that an inmate is a drug abuser, information which for reasons of professional confidentiality he/she is not allowed to pass on. If, on the other hand, the prison takes urine tests purely for reasons of security, the doctor risks treating persons with drugs without knowing about the possible positive results of tests that have been taken.

Thus the principles governing the use of drug analysis differ depending on the problem and the aim. Certain basic principles apply. Quality requirements must be met, which means that all patients must be clearly identified and all urine tests must be taken under supervision by experienced staff in a toilet where there is no possibility of manipulating the test. The urine test must be marked with name and personal identity number in the presence of the patient and kept without any risk of exchange before it is sent to the laboratory or dealt with in the unit. In normal cases, the analysis, which comprises screening and verification of a positive result, must take place in an accredited laboratory. In situations where there is no time to wait for a reply from the lab, other analyses may be used, for example with urine dip sticks, but only if the following is taken into consideration:

- Dip sticks have considerable less precision but may, with acceptable security, help to exclude current drug influence when there is a negative result concerning opiates, cannabis and amphetamine. As for benzodiazepines, it is important to know that dip sticks are not able to detect flunitrazepam (Rohypnol) with sufficient sensitivity. The reliability of dip sticks is less in cases of positive results. Screening with dip sticks gives approximately 5 % false positive results above all for amphetamine, cannabis and benzodiazepines. A common reason for false positive amphetamine analyses is treatment with certain more recent antidepressants (Venlafaxine).
- Analysis with dip sticks should be totally avoided in matters of legal consequence such as LVM, LVU and driving licences.
- When dip sticks are used, their use should be documented and quality-controlled like all laboratory analyses in collaboration with an accredited laboratory.

20.5.12   Need of Psychiatric Care

As for assessments concerning the question as to whether an inmate needs psychiatric care, the opinions expressed by prisons and public health services often differ. An inmate in a prison may exhibit behaviour that makes the staff believe that he is in need of psychiatric care. When the inmate leaves the prison and enters the hospital environment, however, his need of care may not seem so evident, so he is sent back to the prison, becoming a so-called revolving-door case. As with other citizens, however, it is the responsible health care authority or in practice the doctor at the hospital who in his professional role decides whether the inmate's need of care is so great and of such a nature that hospitalisation is necessary.

20.5.13   Isolation

In accordance with prison legislation, it is the doctor who is responsible for examining at least once a month inmates who for various judicial reasons have been placed in isolation. This duty always involves an ethical dilemma since the doctor's usual assessment – that the patient seems mentally and somatically unaffected – means in principle that isolation is allowed to continue.

20.5.14   Loyalty Towards One's Colleagues

The WMA Declaration of Geneva includes the pledge: "My colleagues will be my sisters and brothers", but it is not always easy to follow this ethical norm. Even in the public health services responsibility towards one's colleagues often involves ethical dilemmas. Both experience and theoretical and practical medical knowledge vary among doctors, as do the individual doctor's attitudes and degree of commitment. Hierarchical rules that are as well known as they are unwritten between both specialists and individual doctors who are at different points in their careers may upset inter-collegial respect. Both integrity and awareness of collegial responsibility and of the complex challenges of prison service are required if one is to have an ethically well thought-out attitude towards one's colleagues in prison medicine.

The very frequent movement of inmates between prisons results in the inmates meeting a number of different doctors, which quite often means that the patients' medical problems are assessed and treated differently. Both manipulative tendencies in a patient and his/her demands for treatment may result in something very different from accepted and scientifically tested therapy. A possible pitfall is to satisfy demands at the cost of the patient's actual needs, and the downgrading by the doctor of real needs may reinforce the patient's manipulative behaviour, lead to inferior treatment for the patient, increase the risk of threats and violence and involve a serious departure from the professional guidance.

References

Bertrand, D., and T. Harding. 1993. European guidelines on prison health. *Lancet* 342: 253–254.
CPT (European Committee for the Prevention of Torture and Inhuman or Degrading Treatment or Punishment, 2011): CPT Standards. Strasbourg, Secretariat of the CPT.
Holmberg, G., A. Forsman, M. Grann, L.E. Ingerloo, S. Skagerberg, and L. Somander. 1999. Psykiatrisk vård för fängelsedömda (Psychiatric care for persons sentenced to prisons). *Nordisk Tidsskrift för Kriminalvidenskab* 206–219.
Levander, S., H. Svalenius, and J. Jensen. 1997. Psykiska skador är vanliga bland interner. (Psychiatric disturbances are common among inmates). *Läkartidningen* 94: 46–50.
Sundin, B. 1970. *Individ, institution, ideologi: Anstaltens socialpsykologi.* Aldus/Bonnier Stockholm: Stockholm.

Westin, H. 1992. Behovet av psykiatriska insatser för kriminalvårdens klientel (Need of psychiatric care for inmates). Kriminalvårdsstyrelsen & socialstyrelsen.

WMA. 1949. International Code of Medical Ethics. World Medical Association. http://www.wma.net/en/30publications/10policies/c8/index.html. Downloaded 24 May 2013.

WMA. 1964. Declaration of Helsinki – Ethical principles for medical research involving human subjects. World Medical Association. http://www.wma.net/en/30publications/10policies/b3/index.html. Downloaded 24 May 2013.

WMA. 1975. WMA Declaration of Tokyo – Guidelines for physicians concerning torture and other cruel, inhuman or degrading treatment or punishment in relation to detention and imprisonment. World Medical Association. http://www.wma.net/en/30publications/10policies/c18/index.html. Downloaded 24 May 2013.

World Medical Association. 1993. WMA statement on body searches of prisoners. http://www.wma.net/en/30publications/10policies/b5/index.html. Downloaded 22 May 2013.

World Psychiatric Association. 1977. The Declaration of Hawaii. World Psychiatric Association. http://www.codex.uu.se/texts/hawaii.html. Downloaded 24 May 2013.

Chapter 21
Prison Psychiatry in Switzerland

21.1 Introduction

Switzerland has some distinctive sociodemographic and geographic features which influence prison psychiatric services: The Swiss resident population is about 7.7 millions of which about 1.7 millions are foreigners, mostly from southern Europe and the Balkan states. The four official languages are Swiss German (63.7 %), French (20.4 %), Italian (6.5 %) and Rhaeto-Romanic (0.5 %). Switzerland is slightly smaller than the Netherlands; the population lives rather scattered in the 50 % of land which is habitable, forming 5 cities with more than 100,000 habitants, the largest agglomeration being Zürich with 1.1 million. A small fraction of the whole Swiss population live in remote alpine valleys, some of touristic interest, with 'Juf' at 2,126 m above sea level being the highest all-year inhabited commune of the Alps. Although Switzerland has probably one of the best public transportation services worldwide, a journey from west to east takes more than 8 h due to the complicated alpine geography. These geographic characteristics, with a location not only in the centre of the Alps but also in the centre of Europe with some of the most important transport hubs from south to north and vice versa passing through, contributed historically to the characteristics of the Swiss state: Since Roman times many different principalities fought for their independence against each other and the large surrounding empires. In 1291 the first small federation was chartered in the centre of the later Switzerland as a military alliance against Austria-Hungary. Other so called 'cantons' joined in until Napoleon finally not only defined Switzerland's frontiers in the Vienna congress in 1814/15 but also figured as godfather for the first Swiss constitution with its grounding in the principles of the French revolution. Switzerland then survived almost unharmed the heavy turmoils of the two World Wars

M. Graf (✉)
Forensic Psychiatric Hospital, Psychiatric Hospital of the University of Basel,
Basel, Switzerland
e-mail: marc.graf@upkbs.ch

N. Konrad et al. (eds.), *Ethical Issues in Prison Psychiatry*, International Library
of Ethics, Law, and the New Medicine 46, DOI 10.1007/978-94-007-0086-4_21,
© Springer Science+Business Media Dordrecht 2013

and even emerged in a strong position leading to wealth and a high degree of social security. The Red Cross became probably the most iconic symbol reflecting Switzerland's early efforts to promote human rights from a politically neutral position, a position that continues today.

Politically Switzerland consists in 26 cantons and half-cantons with a higher degree of autonomy than, for example, the German federal states. Switzerland has one federal Penal Code (SPC) but up to 026 different codes of criminal procedures which will fortunately be converted in a single federal one in the next years. However, the cantons will retain responsibility for the enforcement of sentences. They have affirmed three concordats for this duty to share institutions for the execution of penal sentences and court ordered treatment as well the so called "concordat commissions for the assessment of offenders dangerous to the public", whose role and functioning will be described in more detail later: The Swiss-German speaking part of Switzerland consists of two of those concordats whereas Latin Switzerland (Italian and French speaking cantons) form a third one. The health services are organised in a similar manner: In principle a duty of the communities, they delegate this to the cantons which provide services. Health insurance is mandatory and paid for those who cannot afford it by social welfare. While outpatient treatment is at the expense of health insurance, inpatient treatment is paid in half by social insurance and in half by the cantons. From 2012 onwards the largest share of Swiss people with basic insurance have free choice of hospitals throughout Switzerland which will enhance competition between hospital and cantons. All these factors contribute to the unique characteristics of Swiss prison psychiatric services.

21.2   Organisation of Prison Psychiatric Services

Switzerland has a relatively low prison population rate of 79 per 100,000 (Finland 60, Sweden 78, Germany 88, France 96, England and Wales 154, Israel 325, USA 748) (King's College 2010) which itself consists of a relatively high share of prisoners on remand (30 %). Sentenced prisoners contribute 59 % to the prison population, detained asylum seekers 7 % and others 4 %. Switzerland has only one prison with more than 400 places (Zürich) and only a handful of institutions only with more than 200 places. This means that an important share of prisoners is placed in small to medium sized prisons, many of them having less than ten places and being managed by part-time staff.

Few cantons have prison medicine or prison psychiatric services, run either by the penal department, health departments or University departments. In the other cantons individual correctional institutions may have contracts with nearby hospitals, outpatient services or doctor surgeries. Most large prisons have specialized medical wards though none of them have 24/7 emergency medical services. Prisoners with somatic (and often also psychiatric) emergencies are therefore usually transferred to a special ward ("Bewachungsstation") at the University Hospital of Berne which is under responsibility and run by staff from the prison services of the canton of Berne and offers 16 beds. A similar ward for the Latin-Swiss is at the University Hospital of Geneva (L'unité cellulaire hospitalière -UCH) with another 10 beds. Both wards have an extremely high capacity utilisation. For pure psychiatric emergencies the canton of Zürich has three high-security wards in its Forensic Psychiatric Centre "Rheinau" with a total of 27 beds.

Due to these diversities of service provision, it is quite difficult to summarise the system of prison psychiatry and to represent all clinical staff involved and safeguard their often very specific interests and to develop minimal standards for the provision of health care. Those are the aims of the Swiss Conference of Prison Physicians: This association was founded in 2004 after several years of loose congregation. Further aims of the association include quality assurance, continued education as well as annual scientific and corporate meetings (statutes as well as other information available online at http://files.chuv.ch/pediatrie/dpc_home/dpc_infos/dpc_infos_organisation/dpc_smpp.htm/). Similarly, forensic psychiatrists founded the Swiss Society of Forensic Psychiatry (http://www.swissforensic.ch) with one section each for the Swiss German and the Swiss Latin part as well as one for juvenile forensic psychiatry in 2006. It focuses on forensic psychiatric assessment and treatment, runs postgraduate courses and issues the certificate "Forensic Psychiatrist (SSFP)" to successful graduates of the curriculum, which is similar to the one of the German Medical Association (DGPPN). It is highly respected by courts and currently about 50 members are certified. Appreciating its originality and the urgent need for minimal standards especially in courtroom testimony, most probably the Swiss Board of Physicians (FMH) will introduce the subtitle "Forensic Psychiatry and Psychotherapy" officially and adopt the SSFP's curriculum within the next few years. Both these two associations support prison psychiatrists as well as forensic psychiatrists in their duties, often complicated due to well-known challenges such as threats to confidentiality, blurry responsibilities, a lack of high-security inpatient treatment facilities and others.

21.3 Ethics and Guidelines

Switzerland ratified the European Convention on Human Rights 1974 (some amendments are still a matter of negotiations) and follows the Recommendation No. R (98) 7 of the Committee of Ministers concerning ethical and organisational aspects of health care in prison as well as the recommendation Rec(2006)2 on the European Prison Rules. Furthermore, the Swiss Academy of Medical Sciences published medical-ethical guidelines for medical activities with regard to detained persons in 2004 (Restellini et al. 2004). These show that Swiss prison psychiatrists struggle in their routine duties with similar ethical dilemmas as psychiatrists from other European countries (Elger Bernice 2008) such as the problem of confidentiality in their professional relation with prison staff, constrained therapeutic options or the use of coercive measures in cases of possible self-harm. One such example is discussed below.

Switzerland has a long tradition of recruiting urgently needed physicians from neighbouring countries to compensate its lack of doctors due to the strict entry criteria to medical schools. Therefore the apparently little attractive positions in prison medicine and forensic psychiatry are often held by French and German doctors and so the different cultures with different attitudes clash within those of Switzerland. This can be illustrated with an actual example which has gained a lot of media attention: In 2008 the now 57 years old farmer Rappaz from the "Valais", an alpine canton in the south-western part of French-speaking Switzerland, was sentenced to 5 years and 8 months in prison after several convictions for infractions of the narcotics law and a house search discovering 51 t of hemp. His sentence was interrupted after 2 month because of Rappaz being on hunger strike and he was allowed house arrest at his farm, only to be sent back to prison as he had recovered. Subsequently a kind of a cat-and-mouse game started between Rappaz and the respective Minister of Justice. The fact that people from alpine areas have a proud tradition to withstand authorities' rulings and that the deregulation of Swiss' strict narcotics law, which cannot be enforced by the police, is currently debated in public and politics controversially, did not simplify matters. When Rappaz again went on hunger strike, the Minister of Justice instructed the responsible doctors to force-feed him if his health was at risk. As they denied doing so because Rappaz was judged to be legally competent and had stated in a directive that he did not want any medical measures to save his live, authorities initially transferred him to the above mentioned special ward at the University Hospital of Berne. After another period of house arrest he was sent back to prison.

While the media, instructed by his lawyer, reported him weakening, the Swiss High Court rejected Rappaz' appeal against the Minister of Justice's denial of another house arrest (BGE 6B_959/2010). It stated that health care in prison is warranted, law enforcement can instruct the doctors to force-feed Rappaz and that such force feeding is permitted either by cantonal law or the sweeping clause (Act 17 of the Swiss Penal Code declares an act as legal if its intention is to avert danger in favour of another person and if it is proportionate). After a description of the current practice in other western countries it mentions in its substantiations that only two cantons, Bern and Neuchâtel (Brägger 2011), have regulated for cases of hunger strike in their penal laws (the respective authorities are allowed to order force-feeding to avert serious health problems and the death of a prisoner, but in Neuchâtel only if this is not against the prisoner's will), and the canton Zürich allows coercion to avoid harm to the prisoner, the other cantons having no respective laws. The Court further argues that the recommendations of the Swiss Academy of Medical Sciences regarding the treatment of detained persons (Restellini et al. 2004) do not have the power of law. It continues to claim that, in the case of divergence between a rule of the law on the one hand and medical ethics on the other hand, doctors rely on the latter to remove themselves from their judicial responsibilities. However, those ethical recommendations should not stand in the way of authorities executing judgements ordering force-feeding nor dispense doctors from this duty, if the judicial prerequisites are fulfilled. The High Court concludes that in such conditions, force-feeding is not disproportionate to the right to freedom of expression and personal freedom nor does it violate laws against inhuman and degrading treatment, if carried out with dignity and according to medical standards.

The doctors' fury was and probably still is high: The president of the Swiss Medical Association fears the fundamentals of our work shaken and sees it as a duty of the medical fraternity to remember the fundamental principles of our social community. An administrative agency or a court of justice should not request medicine just to serve for their purposes. This would lead to a mechanical executing of medicine without relationship to its patients. A physician acting in that way, carrying out force-feeding, would automatically be equated with the law enforcement system by the prisoner and the essential mutual trust would be destroyed. This mutual trust, however, is a prerequisite to clarify the prisoners' motivations for a hunger strike and his determination to die. Several authors in the field of prison medicine challenged the High Court's decision in a publication in the Journal of the Swiss Medical Association and demanded complete autonomy for health care in prison (Gravier et al. 2010).

Not surprisingly in the question of whether or not to force-feed Rappaz (or other prisoners in general) the above mentioned differences in attitudes between the German and the Latin Switzerland become apparent: Whereas in the Latin part personal freedom and the right to of a capable person to make their own decisions are the most important arguments *against* force feeding; in the German part the duty of the prison services and therefore the prison physicians' duty to save the life of the prisoner is an argument *for* force-feeding.

As a matter of fact, in this question not only professional attitudes but also basic principles of science clash (Sen et al. 2007): In judicial science most variables are necessarily of a categorical if not dichotomous nature: Guilty or not, sentence yes or no, and so on. In medical science, by contrast, and as we more and more learn from neurobiological findings, most variables are of a dimensional nature, which means they range from a certain minimum to a certain maximum, following different types of distribution. The judicial construct of a person's capability to act is most probably based on the interactions of many different physiological capabilities like apperception, consciousness, memory, motivation, cognition, behaviour control, emotion and many others, which are not all-or-nothing principles with dichotomous, time-independent outputs. We shouldn't therefore quickly blame the judges to invade our very principles of medical science and see ourselves as advocates of human virtue but probably rather try to explain again and again these important differences in our sciences and help to translate our findings into judicial principles, as law follows a social society's moral and ethics and not vice versa.

Finally, we as physicians, and prison psychiatrists in particular, are not free from conflicts in our relationship with patients: Many of us would probably break the obligation of confidentiality when a prisoner, not suffering from mental disorder and with full capacity, announces that he will hang himself in his cell because he cannot stand the fatal perspective of a long lasting or even lifelong sentence. Some of us would detain the 'patient' (against his will if needed) in a psychiatric ward or in a hospital; some would order video surveillance or other measures. Although there are differences to a hunger strike situation, these almost daily problems are not completely different at its core. We also should remind ourselves about the origins of some of our most fundamental principles. The mutual trust and the obligation of confidentiality are based on the oath of Hippocrates. They should of course protect the patient and the therapeutic relationship but also serve the public. The principle of confidentiality was probably introduced in ancient Greece with the intention that people suffering from venereal diseases would not hide but instead search out a physician, receive treatment and education about risky behaviour in order not to further transmit the disease – and therefore protect the public. So these very roots of our medical principles, at least partially, were introduced by utilitarian motives, rather than virtue.

To come back to the different attitudes in different language regions: It is probably the very nature and strength of these differences within a very small country which has made it essential for centuries not only to find compromises but also to respect minority interests in a manner that goes beyond arithmetic democracy. In Switzerland this idea is called the principle of concordance. It contributes strongly to social security and diminishes the risk of extremism in either direction. For example, the Swiss Society of Forensic Psychiatrists SSFP organises annual seminars where these different positions can be proposed and discussed and the SSFP as well as the Conference of Swiss Prison Physicians consider representatives from all language regions for their boards. So hopefully this tradition will survive and contribute to good solutions for all involved parties, especially the patients in the prisons.

21.4   Boards for the Assessment of Offenders Dangerous to the Public and Preventative Detention

The worst-case scenario hit Swiss penal authorities in 1993 when a convicted sexual murderer and rapist on an unattended weekend leave brutally killed a young woman. Public outcry was immense and the expert's boards to examine the case found several shortcomings in risk assessment, therapy, and decision making in high-risk offenders (Dittmann 2000). The term 'offender dangerous to the public' was introduced as well as interdisciplinary boards for the assessment of such offenders. They were constituted for the first time in 1996 and consisted of representatives from penal authorities, prosecution, victim agencies, forensic psychiatrists and a judge as chair. Their function was and still is to perform risk assessments of dangerous offenders, to decide whether they fulfil the rather diffuse criteria to be 'dangerous to the public' and to give advice to the responsible authorities. They only act after an offender has been convicted and upon request from the authorities, whom they only *advise*. These boards can therefore be seen as a very early introduction of the principles of a peer-reviewed process. In 2007 the whole process involving these boards was codified in the Swiss Penal Code, before they were regulated only in form of by-law. Since 2007 the boards have been constituted in the three concordats and have most strict rules for members in relation to conflict. They now only comprise of representatives from penal authorities, prosecution, prisons and forensic psychiatry.

Remarkably since these boards took up work, no severe reoffense of an offender assessed by the boards has happened. The backside of this medal is the rising number of offenders in preventative detention: They currently exceed 200 despite the sentence not being passed more often (it is not actually a sentence as its purpose is preventative and it follows the prison sentence, though most often in the same prison and under the same conditions). Instead, only few offenders have been released from preventative detention since 1996. This conservative approach is more pronounced in the Swiss' eastern region and less towards the centre and the west.

Parallel to the growing population of offenders detained in this way, prison and forensic psychiatrists' concerns have grown: Therapeutic programs in prisons are still scarce and forensic-psychiatric wards are full and have year-long waiting lists. Once labelled as 'dangerous to the public' the offenders have no alternative than to 'prove' their improvement in therapy, if ever they qualify for therapy. As a consequence the therapist's appraisals of the prisoner, the therapeutic process as well as progress, are most important for the forensic psychiatrist who conducts assessments for the authorities, for the attention of the boards for the assessment of offenders dangerous to the public (the latter do not, with rare exclusions, hear the offender). However, the greatest controversyamong therapists in Swiss prisons is whether they should report about the therapy at all (and therefore break the obligation of confidentiality), only report with consent of the patient (and therefore select information), give the authorities the information they need for their decisions (and therefore select information too) or whether forensic therapies should be completely transparent as a prerequisite (without consenting to such terms the offender will therefore not have access to therapy). This controversy, resulting in diametrically divergent handling of certain offenders in different regions, one can understand, is highly criticised by authorities and judges as well as the prisoners concerned and their legal representatives.

Still suspicious about the risk posed by high risk offenders, by mean of a people's initiative, a group of individuals, amongst them relatives of a victim of a sexual offence, in 2004 was successful to introduce 'life-long preventative detention' in the Swiss constitution and the Criminal Code (Art. 64 SPC). In Switzerland any group of interest may propose changes in the Federal Constitution or any Federal Law by means of collecting 100,000 signatures from people entitled to vote. A popular vote then has to decide whether to introduce these propositions or not. As most preventative detentions were in fact life-long before this initiative, the most important difference now is that cases of this new detention will not be reviewed on a regular basis as it was mandatory before (at least every 4 years) in accordance with European Law (any deprivation of liberty must be reassessed periodically). People distrusted the capability of authorities and felt that offenders released from detention were not always low risk. The federal office of justice struggled to find a wording for the code to fulfil on one hand the intention of the new law and on the other hand not to contradict European law. They introduced a section in the new Article 64 (Art. 64c SPC) whereupon the authorities have to consider whether new scientific evidence is available to suggest that the respective offender could be treated so that he no longer poses a danger to the public. The authorities shall rely for this decision on a still to be constituted federal board of experts' recommendation. If such a treatment is available, it will be offered to the offender, and if this treatment shows that the offender's dangerousness can be reduced to a degree that he no longer poses a danger to the public, he then can be released into a further therapeutic court ordered measure in a closed institution. Experts of law still argue that this life-long preventative detention is not in line with European law and up to date no court has imposed it yet. As the legislative body wanted to fulfil peoples' expectancies for a stricter law, the already existing preventative detention was defined in a more tightened manner, making it necessary that all about 200 existing cases were reassessed and reviewed by criminal courts to identify whether they still qualify for preventative detention. A *whole third* was released into court ordered inpatient treatments (where they might be released, treated as long as needed or sent back to detention if therapy is not successful). Actually we have the paradoxical situation in Switzerland that although people voted for stricter laws against dangerous offenders, these laws are even less often made use of by the courts, because the threshold has risen.

In contrast to these tendencies for stricter laws and life-long preventative detention, a cohort study from the University of Basel (Graf et al. 2008) proved that even high-risk offenders dangerous to the public may be safely released under certain circumstances: About half of all the 150 offenders labelled as dangerous to the public since 1996 from the canton of Bern during the process of treatment, forensic-psychiatric risk assessment and review by the boards could be in some way released and none had to be sent back to preventative detention (two cases of robbery were the most severe re-offenses and one offender escaped during a visit at his embassy).

21.5 Conclusions

Switzerland has a quite good standard in prison psychiatry. Direct comparisons with other European countries (Blaauw et al. 2000; Stöver et al. 2007) provide limited information because Switzerland is not member of the European Union. In 2007 the chair of criminal law at the University of Zürich held a conference about prison medicine in Switzerland and other European countries and the contributions were published in German (Tag and Hillenkamp 2008). The treatment of mentally ill prisoners, be it on the basis of a court ordered treatment to reduce the risk of criminal recidivism or during a prison sentence for an occurring or pre-existing disorder, is still somewhat dissatisfying and available guidelines (Weinstein et al. 2000) are not always applied. Too often the staff involved (psychiatrists, prison wardens, nurses, psychologists and social workers) fail to create a comprehensive and integrated effort needed for a therapeutic climate and attitude and therefore therapies are most probably not as effective as they could be. It is proposed that it is most often not obstacles from authorities or institutions which cannot be overcome, but rather disinterest or even disregard for the topic of mentally ill offenders, bickering over responsibilities and inability to communicate well in order to enable interprofessional and interdisciplinary work which are the true problems. Swiss federal structures may add to this often observed fragmentation. From several years teaching in the Swiss Prison Staff Training Centre, an extremely valuable institution which contributes not only to prison staff but also supports prison physicians, nurses and authorities with advice, continuing education and scientific meetings, the author knows the complaints from prison staff all too well: "Why should we learn about psychiatric diagnoses and principles of treatment, when we are not allowed to have any kind of such information? We just bring the prisoner to the medical ward or the psychologist and we see how angry or sad he is, when we collect him afterwards. If the prisoner then decompensates during the night, it's our business". We really need to find a way to apply the principles for successful therapy, known from general psychiatry, to prison settings, without compromising important values like mutual trust and confidentiality.

References

Blaauw, E., R. Roesch, and A. Kerkhof. 2000. Mental disorders in European prison systems. Arrangements for mentally disordered prisoners in the prison systems of 13 European countries. *International Journal of Law and Psychiatry* 23(5–6): 649–663.
Brägger, B.F. 2011. Gefängnismedizin in der Schweiz – Analyse des bestehenden rechtlichen Rahmens. *Jusletter* 11: 1–12.
Dittmann, V. 2000. Die schweizerische Fachkommission zur Beurteilung "gemeingefährlicher" Straftäter. In *Giessener kriminalwissenschaftliche Schriften*. Vol. 9. *Forensische Psychiatrie*, Godesberg: Forum Verlag.
Elger Bernice, S. 2008. Medical ethics in correctional healthcare: An international comparison of guidelines. *The Journal of Clinical Ethics* 19(3): 234–248.
Graf, M., N. Händel, and V. Dittmann. 2008. Risk assessment and management of high-risk sex offenders in Switzerland by interdisciplinary boards using the method of structured professional judgment. *Forensische Psychiatrie und Psychotherapie* 15(Suppl. 1): 1.
Gravier, B., H. Wolff, D. Sprumont, B. Ricou, C. Kind, A. Eztan, et al. 2010. Ein Hungerstreik ist eine Protestbehandlung. Zwangsernährung widerspricht dem ärztlichen Berufsethos – welche Aufgabe haben Ärzte und Pflegefachkräfte? *Schweizerische Ärztezeitung* 39: 5.
King's College, London. 2010. Prison brief – highest to lowest rates. http://www.kcl.ac.uk/depsta/law/research/icps/worldbrief/wbp_stats.pbhp?area=all&category=wb_poprate
Restellini, J.P., D. Berner-Chervet, P. Grutter, O. Guillod, J. Osterwalder, F. Ramseier, et al. 2004. The exercise of medical activities in respect to detained persons. Medical-ethical guidelines of the Swiss Academy of Medical Sciences. *Swiss Medical Weekly* 134(9–10): 136–139.
Sen, P., H. Gordon, G. Adshead, and A. Irons. 2007. Ethical dilemmas in forensic psychiatry: Two illustrative cases. *Journal of Medical Ethics* 33(6): 337–341.
Stöver, H.M., M. McDonald, and S. Atherton. 2007. *Harm reduction in European prisons. A compilation of models of best practice. European network on drugs and infections prevention in prison (ENDIPP)*. Oldenburg: Cranstoun Drug Services London.
Tag, B., and T. Hillenkamp. 2008. *Intramurale Medizin im internationalen Vergleich. Gesundheitsfürsorge zwischen Heilauftrag und Strafvollzug im Schweizerischen und internationalen Diskurs*. Berlin/Heidelberg: Springer.
Weinstein, H.C., K.A. Burns, C.F. Newkirk, J.S. Zil, J.A. Dvoskin, and H.J. Steadmen. 2000. *Psychiatric services in jails and prisons. A task force report of the American Psychiatric Association*. Washington, DC: American Psychiatric Association.

Chapter 22
Current Ethical Challenges in Prison Psychiatry in England and Wales

Adarsh Kaul and Birgit Völlm

22.1 Introduction

As has been reported for most European countries (Salize et al. 2007), the prison population in England and Wales has increased dramatically in the last decade and currently stands at 85,117 (Ministry of Justice 2010b). Consequently, the number of mentally disordered offenders (MDOs) incarcerated within the prison system has also risen. At the same time, we have seen enormous changes in both the legal and policy context and the organisation of prison health care. Changes in criminal law have demonstrated a shift from a retributive to a preventive detention model leading to an increase in longer and indeterminate sentences (Völlm 2009). Policy developments have placed more emphasis on the treatment and management of personality disordered offenders both in prison and in psychiatric settings (National Institute of Mental Health for England 2003). The organisation of prison health care has recently undergone a major transformation owing to the move of ministerial responsibility from the Home Office (now Ministry of Justice) to the Ministry of Health in 2006. These changes have added additional ethical challenges to those inherent in working in a prison environment. This chapter describes the legal context of psychiatric care for MDOs in England and Wales, the different settings in which such care is provided, the organisation of the prison system and of healthcare provision within prisons as well as the main ethical challenges mental health care practitioners working in prisons face. We will consider ethical challenges encountered through

A. Kaul (✉)
Offender Health, Nottinghamshire Healthcare NHS Trust,
The Wells Road, Nottingham

B. Völlm
Section of Forensic Psychiatry, Division of Psychiatry, University of Nottingham,
Triumph Rd, Nottingham NG7 2TU, UK

Rampton Hospital, Nottinghamshire Healthcare NHS Trust, Woodbeck
e-mail: birgit.vollm@nottingham.ac.uk

N. Konrad et al. (eds.), *Ethical Issues in Prison Psychiatry*, International Library
of Ethics, Law, and the New Medicine 46, DOI 10.1007/978-94-007-0086-4_22,
© Springer Science+Business Media Dordrecht 2013

recent legal and policy developments, those related to working in a custodial setting, challenges associated with providing healthcare to mentally disordered prisoners and specific ethical issues such as food refusal.

Unlike in other countries, English mental health legislation does not require an offender to be found not guilty by reason of insanity or of diminished responsibility in order to enter the hospital (as opposed to the prison) system (Salize et al. 2007). The concept of 'diminished responsibility' only applies to cases of murder; a positive finding reduces the charge to manslaughter but this does not have any direct implications for disposal (prison or hospital). According to the Mental Health Act 1983 (as amended in 2007), a Hospital Order can be given if "the offender is suffering from a mental disorder... of a nature or degree which makes it appropriate for him to be detained in a hospital for medical treatment and appropriate medical treatment is available". Thus emphasis is placed upon the need for treatment at the time of sentencing allowing for the diversion of MDOs to the healthcare system. Individuals on Hospital Orders are rehabilitated through forensic-psychiatric services; there is no transfer back to prison at a later stage and the courts are no longer involved in decisions regarding discharge or transfer to less secure settings. Continued detention within the hospital system is determined on the basis of risk posed and therefore the success or otherwise of any interventions offered to the MDO.

English mental health legislation also allows for the later transfer of MDOs from prison to hospital at any time of their sentence if the individual fulfills criteria for detention in hospital. This 'Prison Transfer' enables provision for mental health needs not identified at the sentencing stage or indeed developing during the course of imprisonment; however, it is also used for late transfers owing to considerations of risk to the public by offenders close to release, a practise that has attracted considerable criticism and legal challenges (Mental Health Act Commission 2009). Transfer orders are made on the recommendation of two psychiatrists without involvement of a court placing significant responsibility onto the medical profession. Individuals on prison transfer orders may be returned to prison during the course of their sentence but can, and usually are, detained in hospital beyond the term of their prison sentence.

The English model of hospital orders and prison transfer for MDOs has distinct advantages but also raises important ethical issues such as identification of the 'right' individuals for diversion to the hospital system, the balance between consideration of mental health needs of the offender and public protection, deprivation of liberty, etc. as will be discussed in more detail below.

Legislation relating to criminal law has seen significant changes recently. Of particular importance has been the new Criminal Justice Act 2003 which introduced far reaching changes in police and court procedures and in sentencing. Compulsory life sentences have been introduced for more than 150 offences. The Act also introduced a new sentence, 'imprisonment for public protection (IPP)'. IPPs are indeterminate sentences for offenders identified as 'dangerous' but who do not qualify for a compulsory life sentence. These offenders are given a minimum term they must serve in prison (the 'tariff') after which time they can be considered for parole by the Parole Board if they are able to demonstrate they no longer pose a risk to the public. Following release they remain on 'licence' for life allowing for recall to prison if licence conditions are breached. IPPs have been used by judges much more frequently than anticipated (Sainsbury Centre for Mental Health 2008) – 2,000 IPPs alone were passed in the first year following implementation of the legislation, resulting in a dramatic increase in prisoners serving sentences without a specified release date and further burdening already stretched resources. Compared to the previous year the number of prisoners serving indeterminate sentences (life sentences and IPPs) had increased by 8 % (up 930) to reach 13,000 in May 2010 (Ministry of Justice 2010b).

22.2   The Prison System in England and Wales

The prison system in England and Wales in its current form, i.e. managed by the central Government, came into being following the 1877 Prison Act. Before that the prisons were locally managed and were generally under the control of local Magistrates. However, following the 1877 Prison Act the Secretary of State took over all the powers of prison administration and a new body, the Prison Commission, was established to manage prisons on his/her behalf. The Prison Commission lasted until 1963 when the Prison Service was absorbed into the Home Office as a separate department. However, these measures had very little impact on how prisons were run in that prison Governors managed the prisons as they saw fit whilst observing the prison rules and standing orders. In the early 1990s following riots in some prisons and the subsequent report by Lord Justice Woolf, the prison service was redefined as an agency of the Home Office in 1993. This was an attempt to separate the policy making arm which was to remain in the main Home Office from the new agency which was to be responsible for the operational management of prisons and to be headed by the Director General of the prison service. In 2004, the National Offender Management Service (NOMS) was created along with 10 Regional Offender Managers (ROMS) with NOMS being designated as an overarching body covering prisons and probation. The Chief Executive of NOMS now runs public prisons and manages performance across the whole system through service level agreements and contracts with private prisons, probation boards, etc.

Prisons in England and Wales are organised based on security classification and function. The security classification is from Cat A to Cat D with the former being high security prisons and the latter open prisons (Home Office 1966). In terms of their function the prisons are divided into local prisons, training prisons and open/resettlement prisons. Local prisons are there to serve the Courts, are often based in the centre of towns and cities and have a mixture of remand and sentenced prisoners. The role of these local prisons for remand prisoners is that of assuring that they appear before the courts and once they are convicted and sentenced to allocate them to appropriate prisons depending on their length of sentence and sentence planning needs. Local prisons also house those who have been recalled to prison whilst being on licence in the community. More recently some local prisons have been moving in the direction of becoming 'community prisons' in order to enhance the rehabilitation and resettlement of prisoners who may either have been serving short sentences or for those serving long sentences to bring them back to these community prisons towards the end of their sentences. The training prisons provide a variety of opportunities for education, vocational training and a host of offending behaviour programmes that enable the prisoners to address their offending and reduce the risk of the re-offending. These short and long term training prisons are usually for prisoners of category B and C. Category A prisoners are mainly located within the high security estate until their risks are considered to be adequately reduced. Lower risk prisoners move onto open prisons, particularly those nearing release on licence from a life sentence. Whilst at these open prisons prisoners are able to spend a considerable period of time every day out of the prison engaged in various educational and vocational pursuits. In addition to these standard prisons there are also some prisons with very specific roles for instance prisons such as Grendon Underwood which is a therapeutic prison and Whatton which is exclusively for sex offenders.

The prisons have a fairly robust system of independent monitoring and inspection. An independent inspectorate was set up in 1981. The inspectorate is able to visit all parts of every prison either through a programme of announced visits but also through unannounced visits. Reports of these visits are published in their entirety and over the years have established a fairly high degree of credibility and authority. As a result, although the inspectorate has no powers to order implementation of their recommendations, the system takes serious note of these recommendations and their implementation. In addition to Her Majesty's Inspectorate of Prisons, under the provisions of the Prison Act 1898 boards of visitors were established which were renamed Independent Monitoring Boards (IMBs) in 2003. These IMBs deal with complaints from individual prisoners and work much more closely with individual prisons and their management in order to maintain a degree of transparency and openness which is required to counter the potential abuses in any closed system. In addition to these systems of inspection and monitoring prisons in England and Wales, in common with other member states of the Council of Europe, all places in which people are deprived of their liberty are subject to independent monitoring by the European Committee for the Prevention of Torture and Inhuman or Degrading Treatment or Punishment (CPT).

22.3 Psychiatric Services for Mentally Disordered Offenders

Health care for MDOs is provided in a number of settings. Some of this care is given in the community, either as diversion from custodial sentences or following release. MDOs who require hospital treatment may be admitted to a forensic-psychiatric unit. However, given the large number of prisoners and the high psychiatric morbidity within the prison population (Fazel and Danesh 2002), the bulk of mental health care for MDOs is provided within a prison setting.

22.3.1   Community Care

People with mental disorders in the community come into contact with the Criminal Justice System in a variety of ways. These may include at the point of arrest, whilst they are on bail facing criminal charges or whilst they are serving a community sentence with or without a requirement to undergo mental health or substance misuse treatment. Equally there are those who are released on licence who are liable to be recalled to prison if they do not keep up the conditions of their licence or if they re-offend.

The prevalence of mental disorder for those in the community who in some way or another have come in contact with the Criminal Justice System is high. For instance, 7–15 % of arrestees are identified by custody officers as having a mental disorder. Thirty-three percent of OASys (Offender Assessment System) assessments, which is a system of risk assessment, completed at presentence report or during supervision in the community, revealed a psychological or psychiatric diagnosis (Home Office 2006). Hatfield et al. (2004) undertook a cohort study of 467 individuals in Probation approved premises. Staff members reported that 25.1 % of offenders had a known psychiatric diagnosis, 34.3 % had drug misuse and 30.6 % had alcohol abuse problems. Similarly, Keen et al. (2003) identified that 13.6 % of the total probation population were in contact with the local Mental Health Trust. Finally, a study by Brooker C, Fox C, Barrett P, Syson – Nibbs L (2008, Assessment of offenders on probation caseloads in Nottinghamshire and Derbyshire. Report of a pilot study, unpublished) of two probation areas in England using a health needs assessment approach using a variety of structured assessment tools in a sample of offenders (N = 183) indicated that 15 % of the sample had contact with mental health services in the preceding 12 months and 27 % had been seen at some point in their lives by mental health services. The majority of diagnoses reported by offenders was depression and/or anxiety, 44 % were identified as being at risk of alcohol abuse or dependence and 39 % of the sample was identified as being at risk of substance abuse.

In principal mentally disordered offenders in the community have access to mental health services similar to the rest of the population. This arrangement is that of a tiered provision with General Practitioners providing treatment for common mental health problems, Secondary Mental Health Care Services providing treatment for enduring mental illness and complex personality disorders as well as substance abuse and inpatient services for those who require psychiatric hospitalisation. However there are two problems. Firstly, many of the mental disordered offenders have a complex mixture of social disadvantage as well as psychiatric problems and in common with other such socially and psychiatrically disadvantaged populations they either do not access available services or if they do so such access is intermittent and crisis driven such as them seeing a mental health professional at an accident and emergency department following an overdose or injuries received in a fight or at the police station following arrest when concerns are raised about presence of mental health problems. Even those who do access some services do not do so in a sustained manner and often dip in and out of treatment. For instance, Brooker C, Fox C, Barrett P, Syson – Nibbs L (2008, Assessment of offenders on probation caseloads in Nottinghamshire and Derbyshire. Report of a pilot study, unpublished) found that nearly 39 % of offenders had visited an accident and emergency department or an National Health Service (NHS) walk in centre at least once in the previous 12 months. Secondly, the mentally disordered offenders often have a range of sub-threshold pathologies which may not meet the service criteria for individual services. For instance, they may have had brief psychotic episodes which may or may not be related to use of illicit drugs but these are not considered to amount to an enduring mental illness and hence do not cross the threshold for acceptance by a Community Mental Health Team. Similarly, they may have borderline intelligence or mild learning disability and hence may not be considered to have severe enough problems to require treatment and support from a learning disability service. The same is the case for substance abuse in that they may be poly substance abusers but not dependant on opiates or not considered to meet the access threshold of substance misuse services. Hence, although combination of complex social problems and sub threshold psychiatric pathologies may result in a very poor psychosocial functioning, they are not accepted by diagnostically defined services or the motivation or resources required to engage such a difficult population are not forthcoming. Consequently, those mentally disordered offenders in the community who have a severe mental illness such as Schizophrenia, do indeed receive a reasonable package of treatment but those who fail to reach that threshold, despite overall very poor psychosocial functioning, do not do so. Whilst treatment for patients with personality disorder exists in the community, unfortunately due to their impulsivity, poor motivation and lack of overall stability offenders are often not considered suitable to receive such treatment. Hence, the ethical challenge is that of MDOs in the community being denied access to the appropriate service because they do not meet the criteria when marked against service provision that is by and large structured based on diagnosis rather than overall level of psychosocial dysfunction and disorder. There is also of course the question of how much of this acceptance/rejection by services is consciously or otherwise as a result of MDOs being considered to be 'not nice' and deserving and who would have been described by Herschel Prins as the unloved, unloving and unlovable.

22.3.2 Forensic-Psychiatric Care

Forensic-psychiatric care in England and Wales is provided in hospitals of different levels of security (Sainsbury Centre for Mental Health 2007). While it is possible for MDOs on a Hospital or Prison Transfer Order to be treated in a general psychiatric setting, most MDOs are admitted to high or medium secure settings. There are currently three high secure hospitals and in excess of 50 medium secure units. Service provision in secure hospitals has undergone numerous changes since the inception of medium secure services in the 1970s in terms of capacity, organisation, patient composition, length of stay, etc. While we have seen a decrease in capacity in high secure beds of about 20 % over the past 5 years, the overall number of MDOs detained in secure psychiatric settings has risen annually for more than a decade (Ministry of Justice 2010a). Between 1996 and 2006 the forensic patient population has increased by 45 % (Sainsbury Centre for Mental Health 2007). Length of stay has also risen with about a quarter of patients being detained for over 10 years. At the end of 2008 there were just under 4,000 patients detained, about 700 of those in high secure settings. A significant proportion of the expansion of medium secure beds can be attributed to the growth of private sector provision. Those service may be under particular pressures, e.g. in terms of bed occupancy, which may impact upon overall length of stay.

Of particular relevance for prison psychiatrists is the fact that transfers of sentenced prisoners have increased representing now over 60 % of annual admissions to secure forensic settings. Significant changes have also occurred in the provision of services for MDOs with personality disorders (PD). Three hundred places for treatment of individuals with so-called Dangerous and Severe Personality Disorders (DSPD) have been established in recent years, about half in prison and half in high secure hospitals (Völlm 2009) although the future to these services is currently uncertain. Nevertheless there is an increased expectation that psychiatrists provide care for those with PD while traditionally individuals with a primary diagnosis of PD have often been excluded from medium secure settings.

22.3.3 Prison Mental Health Care

Historically health services in prisons were provided by prison medical officers and nurses employed by prison services. Although they provided a reasonable degree of physical and mental healthcare to prisoners including a screening of all offenders coming to prison within 24 h by the prison doctor, they were nevertheless subjected to a fair degree of criticism. A number of problems were considered to be responsible for this including professional isolation, lack of clinical leadership, etc. Concerns about issues such as death in prisons led to the publication of a thematic report on healthcare in prisons, Patient or Prisoner? (HM Inspectorate of Prisons 1996). This report was clear in stating that healthcare in prisons was not being provided to the same standard as in the wider community and a joint working group was set up between the Department of Health and the Home Office resulting in The Future Organisation of Prison Healthcare paper (HM Prison Service, NHS Executive 1999). Following this report the commissioning responsibility for prison healthcare was transferred from prisons to Primary Care Trusts which then triggered a significant change in the commissioning and provision of healthcare in prisons. In 2001 Changing the Outlook, a Department of Health policy document, advocated a more specific policy for modernising of mental health services in prison. It recommended the establishment of multi disciplinary mental health in-reach teams to provide specialist services for prisoners in the same way as Community Mental Health Teams do in the wider community. These in-reach teams were to follow the principals of mental healthcare recommended in the National Service Framework (Department of Health 1999) and as such they by and large concentrated on prisoners suffering from enduring mental illness. Prison appointed mental health nurses and doctors provide the primary mental health care for common mental health problems such as anxiety and mild depression. Integrated drug treatment services and other voluntary sector as well as prison appointment professionals provide treatment for substance abuse. In addition there are some prisons such as Grendon Underwood, Dovegate, Frankland and Whitemore which provide psychological treatment, along therapeutic community and CBT lines for patients with Personality Disorder and treatment of offending behaviours. Some of the prisons have inpatient units which have 24 h supervision by nurses and/or healthcare officers. These healthcare centres often house patients who are severely disturbed either as a result of a psychotic illness or those who are at a very high risk of self harm, many of them awaiting transfer to National Health Service secure hospitals. Psychiatrists, other medical specialists and healthcare professionals often visit the prisons either to provide regular sessions or on request.

However, despite the above, challenges remain in mental health care provision for prisoners, and whilst progress has been made, the hope and expectation of equivalent care similar to the wider community has not been consistently achieved. This is for a variety of reasons which include lack of appropriate integration between primary and secondary mental healthcare and substance misuse services in prisons, poor resourcing of prison mental healthcare in comparison to the needs of this population and lack of high quality clinical leadership and management across the board.

22.4 Ethical Issues Related to the Legal Context

Here we will discuss ethical issues specific to the legal context in England and Wales considering mental health as well as criminal justice legislation.

As outlined above, admission to the hospital system under mental health legislation is determined on the basis of the individual's need for treatment at the time regardless of questions of culpability. Consequently, psychiatrists have an important role to play in such diversions and transfers. This might be seen as an advantage in cases of, for example, acutely unwell psychotic offenders for whom most would argue hospital treatment is necessary and appropriate and should be provided whenever this need arises during a person's sentence. More complex issues often arise with personality disordered offenders who are not infrequently transferred from prison to hospital at a time close to their expected release date due to concerns regarding their risk (Mental Health Act Commission 2009). They may have been relatively settled during their sentence with no input from mental health professionals. They may or may not have engaged in behavioural programmes – those with high psychopathy scores, e.g., are often excluded from such programmes. Offender managers responsible for community follow up may only highlight public protection concerns in the context of release planning and then put considerable pressure on psychiatrists to use mental health legislation to prolong detention in a psychiatric institution, a request sadly often granted. These ethical dilemmas have been amplified since the changes in mental health legislation in 2007 (Mental Health Act 2007), abolishing the so-called 'treatability clause'. This clause stipulated that personality disordered individuals could only be detained in hospital if treatment was "likely to alleviate or prevent a deterioration of their condition". Since the changes in the Mental Health Act it has merely been necessary that medical treatment is "available" regardless of whether or not the individual makes use of or benefits from it. In any case, given the often lengthy stay in forensic-psychiatric treatment settings, incarceration of MDOs with full criminal responsibility is potentially extended significantly without the involvement of a court. This raises issues of discrimination (differential length of incarceration compared to offenders without disorder) and potentially infringes an individual's right to have a sentence imposed by an independent court.

It is of note that provisions for involuntary treatment outlined in the Mental Health Act 1983 do not apply in prison settings. Consequently, treatment cannot be given without the prisoner's consent except for in emergency situations where common law applies. Therefore, acutely mentally ill prisoners may not receive the medical treatment they require which is of particular concern given the frequent delays in transfers from prison to a hospital setting where treatment can then be initiated. During the consultation period of the recent amendments to the Mental Health Act some have argued the scope to the Act should be extended to include custodial settings. However, others have expressed concerns that this may lead to even more mentally ill prisoners remaining in an inadequate environment before being transferred to hospital (All Parliamentary Group on Prison Health 2006). When amending the Mental Health Act, the government also gave consideration to the issue of capacity. Current mental health legislation does allow for compulsory treatment of patients with full capacity who do not wish to receive treatment (in hospital settings). Despite the introduction of legislation regulating issues of capacity, this does not apply to compulsory treatment of patients detained under the Mental Health Act although some aspects of the Mental Capacity Act 2005 may be relevant to issues of prison health care such as treatment for physical disorders or food refusal as discussed below.

The introduction of indeterminate sentences for public protection (IPPs) has raised considerable new ethical issues. Judges pass IPP sentences on the basis of risk assessments which may or may not include assessment by mental health professionals. The other source of risk assessments is the probation service where risk assessments are made almost entirely on an actuarial basis. The shift from a retributive to a preventative model of detention has resulted in an increased expectation that mental health professionals will contribute to predicting future risk either as part of the initial assessment of 'dangerousness' or during Parole Board reviews. Unlike other psychiatric assessments where recommendations regarding treatment might be sought, assessments of 'dangerousness' serve the sole purpose – in case of a positive finding – to subject individuals to indeterminate incarceration which is, we would argue, not compatible with the core role of medical professionals. On the other hand, it might be argued that the involvement of mental health professionals will provide a more accurate assessment of the offender's mental health and needs and might contribute to diversion into an appropriate setting or prevent an IPP being imposed. In contributing to the assessment and review process of IPP prisoners psychiatrists have to balance their duty of care with considerations of public protection.

Currently about 40 % of IPP prisoners are over their tariff; the often short tariffs suggest that this type of sentence is used for a range of offences not just the most serious violent and sexual crimes (Prison Reform Trust 2010). Only 94 IPP prisoners in total had been released by the end of 2009. This is partly due to significant difficulties of the prison system providing the necessary programmes IPP offenders would need to attend in order to demonstrate to the Parole Board that their risk has reduced, a matter that has been subject to a number of legal challenges. Furthermore, deniers are usually considered unsuitable for participation in offence focused (risk reducing) interventions and release even though there is no evidence to demonstrate that they have a higher risk of re-offending compared to individuals who do not deny their offending. A significant ethical issue also arises from the poor evidence base for interventions designed to reduce risk.

Individuals with mental health difficulties may be excluded from offending behaviour programmes (OBP) or be unable to participate. Some prisoners have chosen to not disclose mental health difficulties out of fear about the impact this would have on Parole Board reviews (Sainsbury Centre for Mental Health 2007). Often OBPs are not suitable to address the issues underlying offending in MDOs, the sole reliance of OBPs as risk reducing measure therefore seriously disadvantages MDOs. Furthermore, there is a reluctance of community psychiatrists to take on MDOs following release. However, without psychiatric follow-up, the proposed release plan is unlikely to be considered as robust by the Parole Board and release is likely to be rejected.

Research has shown (Sainsbury Centre for Mental Health 2007) that IPP prisoners suffer higher levels of mental health issues than the general prison population or life sentenced prisoners. About 20 % of the IPP population was found to have received psychiatric treatment before and 5 % had been an in-patient in a forensic-psychiatric setting. The IPP itself causes emotional distress by eroding a sense of hope and self-determination. For prison mental health services the introduction of IPPs has meant a huge increase in mental health related needs without appropriate resource allocation or coordinated planning on how to cater for these needs.

22.5 General Ethical Issues of Working in Prisons

Over the years doctors and other mental health professionals have been very ambivalent about working in prisons. On the one hand they can see that imprisonment causes mental distress and may be responsible for the deterioration in mental functioning of many prisoners and as such they do not wish to be part of a system that in their view does very little good and a great deal of harm. On the other hand they can also see that prisoners need psychiatric care as much as anybody else, in fact more so due to their multiple social disadvantages as well as psychiatric disorders. Hence, the thought that by refusing to work in prisons they are contributing to further worsening of effects of imprisonment does not sit easy with the fundamental basis of their professional training and practice which is that of helping people irrespective of their location, class, creed, etc. They can also see that by coming into prisons they can contribute to opening up and letting some light into a system that can be very closed and opaque with the historically recognised abuses of closed institutions.

Some uncertainty and dilemma has also been caused by the difference between assumptions and reality. For instance, many psychiatrists have been of the view that no mentally disordered person should be in prison as prisons almost by definition cause worsening of mental health. Hence, they have acted as 'rescue' psychiatrists who have tried to move people out of the prison system into the healthcare system outside prisons but they have been able to do so with a limited number of prisoners with mental disorders only. However, the reality is also that some prisoners with mental disorder do find prison to be less harrowing than the outside world with its responsibilities, stressors, etc. Such prisoners with anxious and dependant personality traits or those who have become progressively institutionalised find the prison a refuge where they have a structured routine, their basic needs are well met and they can have some degree of control over the nature and amount of interpersonal stress to which they allow themselves to be subjected. Before the massive reduction in psychiatric asylums such people would have been long stay patients in such asylums. As a result of this it is not rare to see some prisoners who very quickly after their release from prison engineer their way back into prison by committing another offence. Hence is it ethically correct to get them moved out of prisons based on the community care dogma when such patients, in the absence of psychiatric asylums, find prisons a better place – despite loss of liberty – than the outside world?

Working in a prison environment is often quite difficult and alien to healthcare professionals whose training and history is that of predominantly, if not exclusively, working in a healthcare environment where the priority is health and the whole basis of such provision is trust between the patient and the doctor. Having come from such background, healthcare professionals find themselves working in an environment where the priority is safety and security and the predominant mindset of the organisation and those working in it is that of not trusting those it holds and where the attribution for most behaviours is that of a malevolent intent. The challenge of operating in such an environment is that of healthcare professionals either finding themselves becoming assimilated in the punitive culture of mistrust or remaining so isolated and encapsulated that they do not have the influence or the credibility to make any impact on the toxic culture. They may indeed face resistance from the system to such an extent that their ability to work and carry out their duties becomes extremely impacted upon. Walking the tightrope between these two extremes is not easy. Working in such an environment sometimes feels as if everything is conspiring against providing appropriate healthcare such as delay in getting to see patients, limited time periods during which patients can be seen, total lock out if the prisoner count is not correct, etc. In such a work environment it can be sometimes difficult to retain the objectivity and patience required and not to either get into conflict with the system and thus become isolated and consequently ineffective or to displace the anger onto the prisoners. Prisoners, with their developmental and life experiences of rejection and alienation, are very good at sensing such feelings towards them which can lead to them rejecting healthcare professional's interest before the feared rejection towards themselves. The challenge of trying to help somebody who, because of their own defences against rejection, want help but simultaneously fights against it. This situation is made more difficult by the attitudes of the prison staff who often mistake an attempt to understand antisocial behaviour as an attempt to excuse. They often find it difficult to see that it is possible to provide treatment for antisocial behaviour and mental disorder without in any way suggesting that the prisoner does not have any responsibility for his offences. Having said this, the importance of not getting 'duped' into almost totally focussing on the personal traumatic histories of prisoners rather than emphasising personal responsibility and the associated attitudinal change cannot be underestimated. In fact some authors such as Morris (2010) draw attention to the disadvantages of treating antisocial personality disorder in hospitals under mental health legislation due to diminution of culpability and personal responsibility both by the patient and the healthcare professionals.

22.6   Ethical Issues Related to Prison Health Care

One of the key dilemmas faced by psychiatrists working in prisons is that of being settled in their own mind as to what their role is in prisons. Is it to treat mental illness, reduce distressing symptoms or change behaviour, particularly antisocial behaviour and attitudes? Or is their role much broader than that involved in the patient doctor dyad? Whilst many feel fairly confident and clear that treating mental illness and even helping prisoners during a period of emotional crisis and stress, which may or may not lead to behaviours such as self harm, is quite legitimate, they do not feel so confident when it comes to treatment of personality disorder and criminal behaviour. This, at times, maybe due to a lack of competence and confidence in doing so but by and large it is due to lack of resources and hence priority needing to be given to those who are severely mentally ill. However, they may also feel that through their understanding of offending along a biopsychosocial model they are very able to treat and/or manage antisocial and criminal behaviour through treatment of personality disorder and other mental health disorders. Unfortunately some feel reluctant to do so due to the climate where psychiatrists and mental health professionals often find themselves being so criticised for the behaviour of their patients that they do not wish to be judged against an outcome measure such as reduction in offending. Others, despite the evidence of efficacy of medication in conditions such as paraphillias, feel reluctant to prescribe such medication due to concerns of being criticised for medicalising social control. This is despite the argument that Adshead (2010) makes when she suggests that treatment of antisocial and unempathic attitudes, let alone mental disorder, can have impact on quality of life years saved along with the social benefits such as fewer victims, reduced future legal costs and pro-social behaviour making offenders happier in the future. Indeed Grubin (2010) suggests that preventing the choice of medication for paraphillias may condemn men to years of further imprisonment in the name of public protection. The dilemma of being accused of medicalising social control as opposed to offering offenders relief from the compulsive nature of sexual fantasies and reducing risk of offending is indeed one that is not easy.

Mental health professionals are increasingly expected in prisons to have a role in assisting in the organisational running of the prison and participating in prison processes that are predominantly disciplinary rather than therapeutic in nature. This can lead to conflict with the prison officers and prison managers as they may view the attitudes and behaviours of mental health professionals who are hesitant in participating in such procedures as being obstructive. Participation in disciplinary procedures such as adjudication for rule breaking, etc. in prison causes its own tensions. On the one hand any involvement whatsoever in such a process can be seen as involving ourselves in the process of punishment but on the other hand it is also possible that by such involvement there maybe prisoners who are being saved from being punished. For instance, by explaining to an adjudication process that a prisoner who has broken his television screen has probably done so because he at the time was hearing voices coming out of the television, is likely to prevent him from being sent into a close supervision unit where he would be effectively isolated with the consequent stressors and worsening of mental state. Hence through their involvement and by providing an explanation for a prisoner's behaviour psychiatrists may enable the prison management to see that what may appear to be antisocial behaviour may not necessarily be so and thus may avoid the prisoner from being punished.

Although a custodial environment is almost by definition incompatible with autonomy, nevertheless, as described above, prisoners cannot be treated against their consent in this setting. Wilson and Dhar (2010) suggest that psychiatrists need to adapt clinically and ethically to a regime that focuses primarily on discipline and order but where the clinician is legally bound to respect the patient's right to consent or to refuse treatment. In practice, apart from some very psychotic and insightless patient prisoners, by and large prisoners do not refuse to take treatment offered to them. However, Wilson and Dhar (2010) also caution regarding the validity of consent as the consent must be given in an "informed" state of mind and must be made "voluntarily", free of any coercion or duress. They have also raised the issue of whether somebody living in a coercive environment is able to give informed consent and not feel that somehow they have to agree to do what another person in authority, such as a clinician, is asking them to do. Towl (2010) makes much the same point whilst discussing psychological treatments in prisons when he says "An understanding and appreciation of the impact of power relationships are important in informing ethical practice in prisons." The Mental Health Act does not apply in prisons and hence treatment cannot be provided against the patient's consent. Whilst treatment can be provided in an emergency under common law this often is done for medical emergencies. However when faced with an acutely and severy psychotic patient it is not easy to decide whether psychotropics should or should not be given under common law. If such prisoners are so ill that they lack capacity, then theoretically treatment for mental disorders can be provided under the Mental Capacity Act (2005). Having said so, there is little evidence that this has actually ever been used for such a purpose.

22.7 Confidentiality and Disclosure

Demands and expectations of mental health professionals working in prisons are varied and they are really put to test when it comes to the issue of disclosure of information. Whilst on the one hand the prisoner patient may at times be reluctant to disclose anything to the mental health professional due to his/her concerns about them being part of the 'system' by and large, considering the circumstances that prevail, it is very surprising how trusting and free they can be with personal information that they are willing to give to the psychiatrist and other mental health professionals. However, the value of such confidence in the doctors is not often appreciated by a system that is increasingly pre-occupied with risk and its prevention which results in an attitude that we should not even bother with concepts such as confidentiality when it comes to offenders. The 1998 Crime and Disorder Act talks about expectations of disclosure from all statuary services which leads to a view amongst prison officers, probation officers, the police, etc. to expect that the demands of risk assessments/risk management are paramount irrespective of other considerations. Unfortunately, the guidelines of professional bodies such as the General Medical Council, the Nursing and Midwifery Council, etc. are not always consistent nor are they always consistent with various other guidelines and local agreements. In our current climate there is a belief, accentuated by numerous homicide and suicide inquiries, that disclosure of information per se would always prevent such events from happening.

Confidentiality is central to the trust between medical practitioners and patients and without assurance about this patients may be reluctant to give doctors the information they need in order to provide good care. This 'duty' has built up over time on the basis of common law rather than being imposed through a statute.

In certain circumstances disclosure of information provided by a patient to a medical professional may be disclosed without the consent of the patient. This is usually in compliance with other legal obligations such as a court order or where the wider public interest outweighs the duty of confidence to the patient. In addition to this, the Data Protection Act 1988 places obligations in respect of personal data such as medical information. Hence the legal position is that any disclosure without consent should be in the public interest and in accordance with the Data Protection Act (DPA). However, there may be scenarios where disclosure in the public interest may be in breach of the DPA and vice versa. The Department of Health document

Confidentially, NHS Code of Practice (Department of Health 2003) provides useful guidance to assist all health professionals, irrespective of their discipline in the application of the public interest test. The confidentiality guidance by the General Medical Council (2009) provides specific guidance to Doctors. The significant issues in relation to disclosure of information appear to be 'consent' and 'public interest'.

There are a number of different scenarios that present themselves for professionals working in prisons that pose a considerable ethical dilemma and challenge, especially, as noted above, when the system that they work in seems to feel that this is an issue that has been exaggerated by mental health professionals and that offenders irrespective of the nature of their offence or the seriousness of the risk that they are likely to pose, do not have a right to such niceties such as confidentiality. Whilst some of them may not openly say so such a tension is invariably present in meetings and discussions regarding prisoners. Some of the scenarios where such challenges arise are as follows:

1. The patient discloses information that would lead us to believe there is a risk of 'serious harm' to someone.
2. The patient discloses information suggesting that he has thoughts and fantasies about causing other people serious harm but there may not be any history of such harm being caused and hence it is difficult to know if such thoughts/fantasies are likely to lead to action.
3. The patient discloses information which leads the professionals to believe that there is a risk of threatened or actual minimal harm which does not meet the 'serious harm' threshold.
4. The patient discloses information that is relevant to the good order and discipline of the prison establishment and is considered to be of interest to prisons under the broad umbrella of 'security'. Examples of these may be for instance a patient disclosing that he has bought or sold illicit drugs or medication from other prisoners.

In these circumstances if the patient gives valid, specific and informed consent for the disclosure of such information then there should be no problem in disclosure. Unfortunately, there can be issues regarding such consent–for instance the practice maybe to take a blanket consent when the professional sees the prisoner with the assumption that such a consent covers all information that has been disclosed by the patient to the doctor. Such blanket consent cannot possibly be valid as the patient is unlikely to be able to consider and think through the implications of the consent in different situations. Wilson and Dhar (2010) comment that for such consent to be valid the consent must be given whilst fully 'informed' and must be made 'voluntarily', free of any coercion or duress. Whilst some have tried to argue that the requirement of voluntariness may make it impossible for a prisoner to give informed consent it has been held that being a prisoner, per se, does not negate giving valid consent (Freeman v. Home Office 1984). Adshead (2010) comments on the unease about the deception of prisoners by professionals regarding disclosure and the implications of their decisions not being adequately spelt out to the prisoners.

The concept of 'serious harm' and the definition of serious crime are not entirely clear. Offences such as manslaughter, rape, treason, kidnapping, and child abuse or other cases where individuals have suffered serious harm may all warrant breaching of confidentiality as may serious harm to the security of the state or to public order. In contrast, theft, fraud or damage to property or loss or damages that are less substantial would generally not warrant breach of confidence. When talking about 'serious harm', it is not just the physical damage but the psychological impact also needs to come into the equation. The dilemma is also that whilst the General Medical Council (2010) guideline on confidentiality are specific about the threshold being 'serious harm' other professional and local guidelines are not necessarily as specific and seem to indicate that risk of any level of harm justifies disclosure if the prisoner does not give consent.

There is also the issue of disclosure without the consent of the prisoner being counter productive to the whole aspiration of risk management. Kaul (2001) comments on the case of a patient who has committed homicide in response to sadistic fantasies. In prison some of the officers have become incorporated in his fantasies. Psychological treatment requires disclosure, assessment and monitoring of such fantasies. However, the prison system feels compelled to take action on such disclosure in the interest of managing the risk towards the officers and does so by segregating the prisoner which is understandably seen by the prisoner as punishment. As a result of this the prisoner is unwilling to engage in further treatment which then further enhances the dangerous nature of such fantasies as he finds himself in a position where he has no control over his own circumstances and such escalating fantasies serve the function of obtaining mastery and self – efficacy.

22.8   Other Specific Ethical Issues

22.8.1   Resource Allocation

Resource allocation is a major ethical dilemma. Whilst resources available for treatment of MDOs in the system as compared to their complexity and need, are inadequate there are also challenges of how this limited resource is utilised. This is not helped by prevalence data, such as Singleton et al. (1998), being over a decade old and the lack of consistency in professional attitudes and views of how these resources should be spent. Some psychiatrists feel all those in prisons with a psychotic illness, irrespective of whether the symptoms are active or not, should be in hospital rather than in prison whilst others use the same thresholds of hospitalisation as in the community which is that the patient no longer needs to be in hospital if the symptoms have settled down. Some may take into account issues of culpability, i.e. recommendation for hospitalisation is made if it is felt that the offence was related to mental illness but by doing so appear to take on the functions of the judge and jury. MDOs are also often retained in expensive hospitals for risk reasons rather than need of treatment. Decisions about hospitalisation of those with a personality disorder are often arbitrary and most complex and costly treatment is not necessarily given to the patients with most complex and severe disorders. These decisions may at times be determined by factors such as whether a privately commissioned report making such a recommendation for admission to a private secure hospital was submitted to the court.

Over the past decade or two most of the resources for treatment of MDOs have been concentrated on secure mental health care, with expansion of private sector secure hospitals, with relatively little being spent on prison mental healthcare and care of MDOs in the community, which is the gateway in and out of the prisons. For instance, in the East Midlands region, approximately £100 million is spent on secure mental healthcare at an average cost of approximately £200,000 per patient per year. In contrast, in the best resourced prison in the region, HMP Nottingham, the amount spent on an average on treatment of a prisoner under the care of the Secondary Mental Health Team is £8,000 per year. The investment in secure mental health care has proven to be inadequate as demand continues to outstrip supply and new ways of demand management, which may mean rationing and prioritisation, may well have to be seriously considered. This does not necessarily mean that such methods of managing the demand are necessarily going to lead to worse care. The difference in quality of prison care vs. hospital care may well be the consequence of the huge difference in resource rather than because equivalent level of care cannot be provided in prisons. The high expenditure in secure mental healthcare has been brought about by the influence that mental health professionals have been able to have on commissioners of healthcare and hence, whilst they should take credit for this, we need to accept that more and more secure beds is unlikely to be the total solution and consequently to think of different ways of managing demand is likely to be an ethical as well as a practical challenge. Having to make decisions to manage demand which may appear to be rationing does not sit easy with ethical values of doctors. However, lessons from mental healthcare in the community are likely to be helpful. For instance, Glover et al. (2006) found that the demand for inpatient beds in general psychiatric services was significantly reduced by the advent of Early Intervention and Crisis resolution Teams. In order to bring about such a significant change in attitudes and practice difficult decisions may need to be made. These may include disinvestment in secure mental healthcare in order to provide resources for investment into prison mental healthcare and community care of MDOs. Changes in commissioning arrangements also need to be made so that money saved from one part of the system can be invested into other parts of the system. It would also mean gate keepers of secure mental healthcare having to seriously consider the perverse incentives that sometimes determine the length of stay and hence the cost of secure mental healthcare. Having said this, there are also genuine concerns that result in patients transferred for inpatient secure care being very infrequently sent back to prisons as the profession does not feel confident about the quality of prison mental healthcare. Hopefully better investment in prison mental healthcare associated with better clinical leadership would ensure that such anxieties and consequent ethical dilemmas will become less of an issue.

22.8.2   Risk Assessment

Assessing risk is part of the core business of a forensic psychiatrist. Such assessment requires great skill and clinical experience as well as training in the use of risk assessment instruments. Psychiatrists have to be aware of the limitations of the instruments they routinely use, e.g. in terms of their applicability to their specific population. It is generally recommended that Clinical Structured Judgement based on an individualised formulation provides the most valid assessment (Department of Health 2007). With the large number of prisoners needing assessments of their future risk to obtain release there is a risk of relying on simple, check-list type assessments without consideration of the specific circumstances of the individual which may over- or underestimate risk. Furthermore, whether or not risk has reduced during the term in imprisonment can be difficult to evaluate as prisoners may not be exposed to situations in which their risk would manifest due to the very restrictive environment (e.g. access to alcohol). On the other hand, a reduction in risk has to be demonstrated before the prisoner can move on to a less secure establishment where such risky situations might be more prevalent.

There appears to be an assumption within criminal justice services that prisoners can only demonstrate a reduction in their risk by engaging in offending behaviour programmes (OBP). However, their effectiveness is moderate at best (Dowden et al. 2003) and they may not be suited for all individuals. There are a range of factors that contribute to successful rehabilitation. The National Offender Management Service strategy (Home Office 2004), e. g., outlines accommodation; education, training and employment; health; drugs and alcohol; finance, benefits and debt; children and families; attitudes, thinking and behaviour. It is therefore important to address all these areas and not solely rely on the cognitive-behavioural approach to changing offenders' attitudes that offender programmes provide. Instead of focusing on completion of programmes, offenders should maybe be given targets to achieve whether or not they do so by participating in specific programmes.

22.8.3   Children in Custody

The UK has the lowest age of criminal responsibility within Europe, 10 years, a fact that has been widely criticised including by international bodies such as the UN. There are over 3,000 children in custody in England and Wales of which around four fifths are detained in prisons with the remainder in secure training centres or children's homes. As in adults, rates of imprisonment and sentence length have risen in recent years. There are now more children detained in England and Wales than in any other Western European country, many on remand due to a lack of alternatives for placement. Unlike in other countries, life sentences and other forms of indeterminate sentences are available for children. UK's approach to youth justice has consequently been criticised for being punitive rather than focused on the child's welfare and as out of sync with other European countries (Howard League for Penal Reform 2008). Children in custody have high rates of mental health problems. A study by the Youth Justice Board found that 19 % of children in custody had suffered from depression, 8 % had self–harmed, 11 % had presented with anxiety states, 11 % with post-traumatic stress disorder, 5 % with psychotic-like symptoms, 6 % with hyperactivity and 17 % with substance misuse. Twenty-three percent of young offenders were found to have an IQ below 70 and 60 % had difficulties with speech, language and communication (Prison Reform Trust 2009). There are different service models for mental health care provision in secure settings for children and adolescents the appraisal of which is beyond the scope of this chapter (for a fuller description see e.g. Harrington and Bailey 2005). Similar to services for adults though service provision does not match need. Specialist forensic adolescent psychiatric input is in particularly short supply. This is of particular concern as early input might well prevent future offending and further deterioration of health (National Collaborating Centre for Mental Health 2009).

22.8.4 Food Refusal

There are a number of different reasons why prisoners might choose to refuse food which are important to differentiate in order to take the most appropriate course of action. Reasons may include symptoms of a mental illness such as paranoid beliefs about being poisoned or various forms of protest. The prison psychiatrist plays an important role in determining the mental state and capacity of the prisoner concerned. For those with mental illness the necessary treatment has to be initiated and a referral for hospital treatment is likely to be appropriate. Prisoners who do not suffer from a mental illness and choose to refuse food often present more difficult ethical dilemmas to the mental health professional (Gregory 2005). An assessment of the capacity of the prisoner concerned has to be conducted following principles set out in the Mental Capacity Act 2005. If the individual lacks capacity decisions can be made on their behalf taking into account their best interest. However, in the case of protest food refusal ('hunger strike'), the prisoner is likely to have capacity and often aims to achieve a specific goal with his action. Protest hunger strikes are often widely publicised which might be part of a political strategy of the prisoner. Authorities have an interest in ending the hunger strike as a death of a prisoner in custody is likely to have a negative impact on their reputation and this may put pressure on the doctors involved.

Several professional organisations have given advice on the role of doctors in hunger strikes. The World Medical Association states in its Declaration of Malta on Hunger Strikes 1991, last revised in 2006, that "Hunger strikers should not be forcibly given treatment they refuse. Forced feeding contrary to an informed and voluntary refusal is unjustifiable." This advice is supported by the BMA (British Medical Association 2007). Particular issues may arise when the prisoner's cognitive function declines and he or she loses capacity. In this case the same principles apply, i.e., a decision has to be made based on best interest considerations which will include any advance decisions made. Similar issues arise from refusal to take necessary medication, such as e.g. insulin. However, one should not only focus on legal issues but also on understanding the reasons for such refusals which are mostly related to lack of control and self-efficacy as this may reduce the risk of ongoing refusal and therefore death.

22.8.5 Research in Prisons

The participation of psychiatric patients, particularly those incarcerated, in clinical research poses significant ethical challenges due to their potential vulnerability. Unlike in other countries, there is no prohibition on research in prison settings in England and Wales. While issues of potential (perceived) coercion have to be taken seriously, the exclusion of prisoners from participation in research would represent further exclusion and discrimination. Prisoners often welcome the opportunity to participate in research which can be an interesting and enjoyable activity and allows the individual to get involved in something potentially meaningful.

The same rules apply for research in prison as for any other research following accepted guidelines such as the Declaration of Helsinki (World Medical Association 2008) and the European Prison Rules (Committee of Ministers 2006). All research has to be approved by the relevant Ethical Committees and all participants have to give full informed consent. To provide additional safeguards, prison research has to be approved by the governor of the prison, the area psychologist or a National Research Committee depending on how many different prisons the research is proposed to include.

References

Adshead, G. 2010. Inside-outside: Ethical dilemmas in prison psychiatry. In *Psychiatry in prisons*, ed. S. Wilson and I. Cumming, 253–260. London: Jessica Kingsley.

All-Party Parliamentary Group on Prison Health. 2006. *The mental health problem in UK HM prisons*. London: House of Commons.

BMA Medical Ethics Department. 2007. *Advance decisions and proxy decision-making in medical treatment and research*. London: BMA.

Committee of Ministers. 2006. *Recommendation Rec(2006)2 of the Committee of Ministers to member states on the European Prison Rules*. Strassbourg: Council of Europe.

Criminal Justice Act. 2003. Office of public sector information. http://www.opsi.gov.uk/acts/acts2003/ukpga_20030044_en_1. Accessed 24 July 2010.

Data Protection Act. 1998. Office of public sector information. http://www.legislation.gov.uk/ukpga/1998/29/contents. Accessed 7 Oct 2010.

Department of Health. 1999. *National service framework for mental health: Modern standards and service models*. London: Department of Health.

Department of Health. 2003. *The NHS confidentiality code of practice*. London: Department of Health.

Department of Health. 2007. *Best practice in managing risk*. London: Department of Health.

Dowden, C., D. Antonowicz, and D.A. Andrews. 2003. The effectiveness of relapse prevention with offenders: A meta-analysis. *International Journal of Offender Therapy and Comparative Criminology* 47: 516–528.

Fazel, S., and J. Danesh. 2002. Serious mental disorder in 23 000 prisoners: A systematic review of 62 surveys. *Lancet* 359: 545–550.

Freeman v Home Office. 1984. 1, OB524, Great Britain, England, Court of Appeal, Civil Division.

General Medical Council. 2009. *Confidentiality. Guidance for doctors*. London: General Medical Council.

General Medical Council. 2010. *Guidance on confidentiality*. London: General Medical Council.

Glover, G., G. Arts, and K.S. Babu. 2006. Crisis resolution/home treatment teams and psychiatric admission rates in England. *The British Journal of Psychiatry* 189: 441–445.

Gregory, B. 2005. Personal views. Hunger striking prisoners: The doctors' dilemma. *British Medical Journal* 331: 913.

Grubin, D. 2010. Chemical castration for sex offenders. *British Medical Journal* 340: 433–434.

Harrington, R., and S. Bailey. 2005. *Mental health needs and effectiveness of provision for young offenders in custody and in the community*. London: Youth Justice Board for England and Wales.

Hatfield, B., T. Ryan, L. Pickering, H. Burroughs, and R. Crofts. 2004. The mental health of residents of approved premises in the Greater Manchester probation area cohort study. *Probation Journal* 51: 101–115.

HM Inspectorate of Prisons. 1996. *Patient or prisoner? A new strategy for healthcare in prisons*. London: Home Office.

HM Prison Service, NHS Executive. 1999. *The Future Organisation of Prison Health Care. Report by the Joint Prison Service and National Health Service Executive Working Group*. London: Department of Health.

Home Office. 1966. *Report of the inquiry in to prison escapes and security*. London: HMSO, Cmnd 3175.

Home Office. 2004. *Reducing re-offending. National action plan*. London: Home Office.

Home Office. 2006. *Final report of the Strategic Policy Team Project on Mentally Disordered Offenders*. London: HMSO.

Howard League for Penal Reform. 2008. *Punishing children. A survey of criminal responsibility and approaches across Europe*. London: Howard League for Penal Reform.

Kaul, A. 2001. Confidentiality in dual responsibility settings. In *Confidentiality & mental health*, ed. C. Cordess, 95–107. London: Jessica Kingsley Publishers.

Keen, J., J. Janaceck, and D. Howell. 2003. Mental health patients in criminal justice populations: needs, treatment & criminal behaviour. *Criminal Behaviour and Mental Health* 13: 168–178.

Mental Capacity Act. 2005. Office of public sector information. http://www.opsi.gov.uk/acts/acts2005/ukpga_20050009_en_1. Accessed 24 July 2010.

Mental Health Act. 1983. Downloaded from the Care Quality Commission website. http://www.cqc.org.uk/_db/_documents/Mental_Health_Act_1983_201005272747.pdf. Accessed 24 July 2010.

Mental Health Act. 2007. Office of public sector information. http://www.opsi.gov.uk/acts/acts2007/ukpga_20070012_en_1. Accessed 24 July 2010.

Mental Health Act Commission. 2009. Coercion and consent, monitoring the Mentalh Health Act 2007–2009. *The Mental Health Act Commission Thirteenth Biennial Report 2007–2009*. London: The Stationery Office.

Ministry of Justice. 2010a. Statistics of mentally disordered offenders 2008 England and Wales. *Ministry of Justice Statistics Bulletin*. London: Ministry of Justice.

Ministry of Justice. 2010b. Population in custody monthly tables June 2010. England and Wales. *Ministry of Justice, Statistics Bulletin*. London: Ministry of Justice.

Morris, M. 2010. Prison therapeutic regimes. In *Psychiatry in prisons*, ed. S. Wilson and I. Cumming, 210–222. London: Jessica Kingsley Publishers.

National Collaborating Centre for Mental Health. 2009. *Antisocial personality disorder (ASPD). Antisocial personality disorder: Treatment, management and prevention*. London: National Institute for Health and Clinical Excellence.

National Institute of Mental Health for England. 2003. *Personality disorders no longer a diagnosis of exclusion.* London: Department of Health.

Prison Reform Trust. 2009. *Children: Innocent until proven guilty.* London: Prison Reform Trust.

Prison Reform Trust. 2010. *Unjust deserts: Imprisonment for public protection.* London: Prison Reform Trust.

Sainsbury Centre for Mental Health. 2007. *Forensic Mental Health Services. Facts and figures on current provision.* London: The Sainsbury Centre for Mental Health.

Sainsbury Centre for Mental Health. 2008. *In the dark. The mental health implications of imprisonment for public protection.* London: The Sainsbury Centre for Mental Health.

Salize, H.-J., H. Dreßing, and C. Kief. 2007. *Mentally disordered persons in European prison systems – needs, programmes and outcome (EUPRIS).* Brusells: The SANCO Directorate General, European Commission.

Singleton, N., H. Meltzer, and R. Gatward. 1998. *Psychiatric morbidity among prisoners in England & Wales (Office for National Statistics).* London: HMSO.

Towl, G. 2010. Psychology in prisons. In *Psychiatry in prisons,* ed. S. Wilson and I. Cumming, 203–209. London: Jessica Kingsley Publishers.

Völlm, B. 2009. Assessment and management of dangerous and severe personality disorders. *Current Opinion in Psychiatry* 22: 501–506.

Wilson, S., and R. Dhar. 2010. Consent to treatment, the Mental Health Act, and the Mental Capacity Act. In *Psychiatry in prisons,* ed. S. Wilson and I. Cumming, 144–154. London: Jessica Kingsley Publishers.

World Medical Association. 2006. Declaration of Malta on Hunger strikes 1991. http://www.wma.net/en/30publications/10policies/h31/index.html. Accessed 27 July 2010.

World Medical Association. 2008. *Declaration of Helsinki. Ethical principals for medical research involving human subjects.* Ferney-Voltaire: World Medical Association.

Chapter 23
Application of the AMA Code of Medical Ethics to Psychiatric Practice in Correctional Facilities and Access to Psychiatric Care in the U.S.A.

Alan R. Felthous

23.1 Introduction

23.1.1 Fundamental Professional Ethics Versus Correctional Realities

The psychiatrist who passes through the sally port of a U.S. jail or prison to provide professional services enters a realm that is strikingly different from a private group practice, a clinic or a hospital. Professional ethics in a healthcare setting can be both implicit and explicit, but as a rule they are concertedly supported which creates an ethically comfortable and harmonious working atmosphere for psychiatrists. Correctional facilities in contrast serve different purposes than provision of healthcare: Security is emphasized and the leadership, management and administration of correctional facilities is driven by presumptions, customs, traditions and regulations that stress order, routine, safety and especially control.

The correctional psychiatrist, indeed the health provider of any discipline in this setting, faces ethical situations and challenges that are quantitatively if not qualitatively different from those in healthcare settings. The psychiatrist must navigate a course between the Scylla of dysfunctional idealism and Charybdis of thoughtlessly yielding fundamental ethical principles to the prevalent practices and persuasions of the greater correctional ethos. A correctional psychiatrist risks neglect of his or her ethical lodestar and of losing his or her ethical identity. Therefore, more so than in a purely healthcare setting, it behooves the correctional psychiatrist to consider how

A.R. Felthous (✉)
Department of Neurology and Psychiatry, Forensic Psychiatry Division,
Saint Louis University, School of Medicine, 1438 South Grand Blvd,
St. Louis, Missouri 63104, USA
e-mail: felthous@slu.edu

N. Konrad et al. (eds.), *Ethical Issues in Prison Psychiatry*, International Library
of Ethics, Law, and the New Medicine 46, DOI 10.1007/978-94-007-0086-4_23,
© Springer Science+Business Media Dordrecht 2013

fundamental ethical principles apply to correctional settings. In doing so it becomes evident that promoting access to psychiatric care can be the single most widespread yet underappreciated ethical challenge in correctional psychiatry. Before addressing specific ethical principles, the organization of U.S. jails and prisons, the prevalence of mental disorders in U.S. jails and prisons, and the organization of mental health-care in U.S. jails and prisons will be briefly reviewed.

23.1.2 Organization of Jails and Prisons in the U.S.A.

In contrast to countries where inmates who are facing trial are housed together with sentenced prisoners, in the U.S.A. jails and prisons are two separate systems. In jails in the U.S.A., administered locally by municipalities and counties inmates are detained to await trial. Many more suspects are 'booked' at local jails than are actually admitted and the U.S. Constitution allows defendants to remain in the community if they provide bail, i.e. money presented as surety that the individual will return to court to face trial. In addition to inmates who are facing trial, jails also house inmates who have been found guilty of a misdemeanor and are sentenced to jail time, typically less than 1–2 years. Through trial or plea bargaining, a defendant can be placed on probation, which allows him to live in the community under the supervision of a probation officer who monitors and reports to the court on the offender's adherence to the conditions of probation which for mentally ill offenders can include requirements for ongoing treatment. If found guilty of a felony offense, i.e., an offense that warrants at least 2 years in prison, the offender is sentenced to prison, state or federal, depending upon which jurisdictional law was violated. If the offender is released before his maximum sentenced time has elapsed, he will be placed on parole for the balance of his time. Similar to probation, parole requires monitoring by a parole office to ensure that the offender complies with the conditions of parole.

23.1.3 Prevalence of Mental Disorders in U.S. Jails and Prisons

From the 1950s to the present, state mental hospital populations have dropped dramatically as jail and prison populations have increased just as strikingly. From 1985 to 2000 the U.S. jail population grew by 156 %, going from 221,815 to 567,079 (American Psychiatric Association-APA 2000). In just the 12 years from 1985 to 1997, the population of state and federal prisoners rose from 744,208 to 1,725,842, a 132 % increase (APA 2000). By the end of 2003 the total number of state and federal adult prisoners was 1,470,045 (Harrison and Beck 2004). By 2005 a record of seven million individuals were imprisoned or under supervision (U.S. Department of Justice 2005).

Of the nearly 1.5 million prisoners, about 16 % were estimated to have a mental illness, according to the Bureau of Justice Statistics (Ditton 1999). In 2005 nearly half of all jail and prison inmates had mental health problems (Bureau of Justice Statistics 2007). Variation in definitions of mental illness, diagnostic criteria and methods of data collection confound accurate estimates, but Temporini's review (2010) provides some ranges for categories of mental disorders among incarcerated males: Psychotic disorders, 1.3–11.5 % (Gunter et al. 2008; Guy et al. 1985, Powell et al. 1997; Teplin 1994; Trestman et al. 2007), substance abuse disorders, 29.1–74.6 % (Gunter et al. 2008; Lo 2004; Peters et al. 1998; Teplin 1994), affective disorders, 13.8–33.3 % (Gunter et al. 2008; Trestman et al. 2007), anxiety disorders, 11.62–36.4 % (Gunter et al. 2008; Teplin 1994), personality disorders, 37.1–49.21 % (Gunter et al. 2008; Powell et al. 1997; Teplin 1994; Trestman et al. 2007). Caution is warranted in interpreting and comparing studies of different facilities and jurisdictions, and over different study periods. Furthermore, most studies on prevalence of mental disorders in correctional settings do not give attention to malingering mental disorder, feigning mental symptoms or feigning mental health.

In one study 15–24 % of prisoners endorsed symptoms of psychotic disorder, 25–30 % major depressive disorder, and 50 % mania (James and Glaze 2006). The most recent national survey indicates that 15–20 % of jail and prison inmates have serious mental illness. U.S. jails and prisons now house more mentally ill persons than hospitals (Torrey et al. 2010). McDermott suggests inflated symptom endorsement can be due to self-report or to feigning, and malingering in correctional settings is known to mental health practitioners and investigators (McDermott and Sokolov 2009; Felthous 2009). Possibilities of dissimulation do not mean that the mental health needs are less because the numbers and percentages of the mentally ill in jails and prisons may have been inflated. Rather the demands on professional time are increased due to the greater complexity of psychiatric and psychological assessments. Even with the possibility of inflated numbers, it is clear that incarceration of the mentally ill in the U.S.A. has reverted to the situation that existed in the 1840s before the movement to begin to provide hospital treatment for the mentally ill (Torrey et al. 2010).

23.1.4 Structure of Mental Health Services in U.S. Jails and Prisons

The public mental health systems are separate from U.S. jails and prison systems which in turn are separate from one another. Long before community mental health centers were established to serve the needs of the mentally ill with the commencement of the de-hospitalization movement, what little there was in the way of 'community mental health' served the needs of the mentally ill in local jails. Nonetheless, the mental health services for inmates in jails were woefully inadequate and did not keep pace with the exploding jail populations, including the increasing numbers of mentally disordered inmates towards the end of the twentieth century. Small police lock-ups were and are especially risky places for inmates in crisis as their mental health services were and are essentially non-existent.

Today there is great variability in how jails are staffed and equipped to treat mentally disordered offenders. Some jails have only a jail nurse, others have a consulting psychiatrist, large city jails have an infirmary where psychotic and suicidal inmates can be placed and some have multi-disciplinary treatment teams with psychiatrists, psychologists, social workers, counselors, and nurses. Infirmaries are not staffed to the sufficiency of hospital wards, thus, for clinical, legal and administrative reasons involuntary medication of psychotic inmates may not be an option. Jails are reliant on local and state hospitals and the 'system' is not always responsive to the psychiatric hospitalization needs of severely disturbed inmates.

State and federal prison systems are also entirely separate from state mental health systems and are responsible for the medical and mental health needs of their prisoners. Like local jails, the internal resources of prisons to handle the mentally ill were long abjectly poor, until spurred towards improvement through class action lawsuits.

The enormous Institutional Division of the Texas Department of Criminal Justice has prison units scattered across the state typically in remote areas where recruitment of health providers is a challenge. The State of Texas has a unique medical and surgical security hospital located within the University of Texas Medical Branch (UTMB) in Galveston, Texas. The state's method of improving medical and mental health services while containing costs was to assign UTMB with the responsibility of providing health services for the Eastern half of the state and Texas Tech School of Medicine with managing healthcare in prisons in the Western part of the state. Other state prison systems and jails turned to private managed care companies. The Texas approach brought the added benefits that come from academic centers working hand in hand with public mental health services. Like other states, and the federal government, the Texas prison system has its own mental hospitals. Texas was a pioneer in applying telemedicine to improve the quality and efficiency of medical and mental health services to remotely located prison units.

23.2   Professional Ethical Practices in Correctional Facilities

23.2.1   Psychiatric Ethical Codes

Correctional psychiatrists can find ethical guidance from the codes of the American Academy of Psychiatry and the Law (AAPL) (1995, 2005), the American Psychiatric Association (2009) and the American Medical Association (AMA) (2010)[1]. Much commentary has flowed from AAPL's Ethical Guidelines (Weinstock et al. 2003)

---

[1]Note: The AMA principles of medical ethics, as stated in the 2010–2011 edition of the Code of Medical Ethics, are without change from those upon which the current APA ethics (2009) are based (American Medical Association 2010).

which is intended for the practice of forensic psychiatry but also pertains to some extent to correctional psychiatry. Because correctional psychiatry is concerned primarily with providing psychiatric treatment to mentally disordered inmates, not forensic consultations to attorneys and courts, the APA's ethical code is especially relevant. Here, however, for grounding in the ethical tradition of psychiatry's core discipline, medicine, and to avoid overemphasis of the more commonly discussed ethical themes in correctional psychiatry, each of the nine principles of the AMA medical ethics will be presented with commentary that takes into account the APA and AAPL codes as well as the unique ethical challenges to be encountered in jails and prisons. Deserving special attention in correctional facilities is the last principle, access to medical care.

23.2.1.1 Compassion and Respect

I. A physician shall be dedicated to providing competent medical care, with compassion and respect for human dignity and rights.

Commentary

Capital Punishment

The AMA and APA ethical codes explicitly prohibit physicians from participating in a legally authorized execution, which has been interpreted as prohibiting physicians from giving lethal injections (Weinstock et al. 2003). Much has been written on the controversial psychiatric roles of participating in death sentencing hearings (Felthous 1989a, 2001; Weinstock et al. 2010; Wolfson 2007), competency to be executed hearings and providing treatment that restores competence to be executed (Knoll and Beven 2010).

Psychiatrists can become involved in death sentencing in one of three ways: (1) by conducting a presentencing evaluation and possibly testifying at the sentencing hearing (2) by evaluating the condemned prisoner for competence to be executed and (3) by treating the prisoner who was sentenced to death but adjudicated mentally incompetent to be executed and restoring him to competence. All three services are highly controversial, and all are practiced by U.S. psychiatrists.

Death Sentencing

Psychiatric participation in sentencing is considered a potential amelioration. Without mitigating factors, the offender's crime is punishable by death. Absence of aggravating factors can be more mitigating than so-called mitigating factors, if they establish a higher threshold. An aggravating factor or 'special condition' in Texas law, for example, is 'whether there is a probability that the defendant would commit criminal acts of violence that would constitute a continuing threat to society (Texas Code Crim Proc 1988).' Through an amicus brief the American Psychiatric

Association declared in a landmark case that psychiatrists cannot accurately predict future dangerousness and it is unethical for psychiatrists to give a professional opinion without first having personally evaluated the individual. In *Barefoot v. Estelle* (1982) the United States Supreme Court ruled that psychiatrists may testify in predicting future violence and then may give hypothetical testimony, i.e., without conducting a forensic evaluation, in death penalty cases. Participation in death sentencing in the United States is constitutional. Whether it is ethical is a separate question about which psychiatric opinion is divided (Leong et al. 2000).

Respected psychiatric commentators are also divided on the proper role for psychiatrists in death sentencing. In contrast to participation in the execution itself which is prohibited by the AMA, APA, and AAPL ethical codes, no national professional code prohibits psychiatric participation in death sentencing. Some argue that psychiatrists can participate in death sentencing and in keeping with the ethic of striving for objectivity should be prepared to testify in support of either imposing or not imposing the death penalty (Dekleva 2001). For example, if a psychiatrist is prepared to testify that treatment and rehabilitation would eliminate the probability of violent recidivism, he should also be prepared to testify that the offender is not amenable to rehabilitation if that is his finding. Others argue that because capital punishment itself is immoral, psychiatrists should participate but only in the interest of sparing the offender, not in support of the death penalty (Weinstock et al. 2010). Death sentencing is then unlike other psycholegal issues wherein the examiner should attempt to hold their bias in check and be prepared at least in principle to produce findings for or against the defendant. Even though the death penalty is immoral, psychiatrists should involve themselves in favor of mitigation, it is argued, because without such involvement, unethical or imprudent forensic experts will testify in support of the death penalty and their testimony can be determinative if left unchallenged (Weinstock et al. 2010; Bonnie 1990a, b). For various reasons many forensic psychiatrists avoid participating in death sentencing altogether.

Although not controlled by a professional ethical code, the present author ascribes to noninvolvement for two reasons. First, death is different from other dispositions and psychiatrists should not collaborate with the State in determining whom the State will kill. Even if the forensic psychiatrist violates his ethical striving for objectivity and control of bias by participating only to support mitigation, any involvement helps the State decide who should be put to death. By analogy it made little difference if Nazi concentration camp physicians determined who was too feeble to be productive and therefore subject to gassing or who was healthy enough to be productive and therefore should be spared. In either case the physician who makes either a pro-life or pro-death determination helps the State decide who will be put to death, an ethically untenable position.

Second, because death sentencing procedures are flawed, unfair and misdirected, psychiatrists are 'incompetent' to participate (Felthous 2001). A truck driver may be competent to drive a truck under normal circumstances but not a truck with a broken axle, defective breaks, and that is headed downhill and off the run-away lane.

Correctional psychiatrists are unlikely to be called upon to participate in death sentencing, because jail psychiatrists treat detainees without becoming involved in adjudication of guilt and punishment and the offender will have already been sentenced before entering prison. In any case it would be a clear and totally unnecessary violation of the ethical principle of avoiding forensic involvement in an inmate whom the psychiatrist is treating.

Assessment for Execution Competence

The American Medical Association's Council on Ethical and Judicial Affairs (1992) made recommendations based upon its interpretation of what kind of involvement constitutes 'physician participation in capital punishment, for the purpose of ethical prohibition of physician participation.' The Council did not consider 'testifying as to medical aspects of aggravating or mitigating circumstances during the penalty phase of a capital phase' (American Medical Association 1992) as constituting ethically prohibited participation. From this author's perspective the decision to execute is more directly causative of death than the finding of execution competence. The Council found the latter to be more problematic. Although the physician 'may offer a medical opinion that the trier of fact can consider' when determining execution competence, the 'physician should not determine legal competence to be executed,' according to the Council. A physician who is treating an offender who is execution incompetent, should not re-evaluate the individual for competence, rather this should be done by an independent physician examiner (American Medical Association 1992). Commentators on the ethics of assessment for execution competence are divided with recommendations varying from abstention, to participation in favor of mitigation, to full participation.

Treatment for Restoration of Execution Competence

Ethical guidelines for treatment of the execution incompetent offender are disturbingly ambiguous. The Council recommended that physicians not treat such a prisoner 'for the purpose of restoring competence unless a commutation order is issued before treatment begins'. The commutation exception is a non-sequitur because once the death penalty is lifted treatment could no longer serve the purpose of restoring execution competence. The psychiatrist employed at a maximum security hospital which occasionally receives an offender for restoration of competence faces an untenable dilemma. Treatment that restores execution competence is unethical; yet is not deliberate withholding of treatment for a serious mental illness also inhumane and contrary to any rational medical ethics? Drawing on recommendations of the American Medical Association (1992), Bonnie (1990a, b), and Scott (2006), Knoll (2010) proposes the following ethical guidelines for psychiatrists who because of their employment are faced with the question of whether or not to treat an individual who is incompetent to be executed and remanded to a security hospital for treatment and restoration of execution competence:

- *Primum non nocere* – first do no harm
- Do not treat for the purpose of restoring competence to be executed
- Treat all death row inmates undergoing extreme suffering
- Allow the inmate to make a decision about further treatment after a rational mental capacity has been restored

- Ensure that re-evaluations of competence are performed by an independent, non-treating psychiatrist
- As a treating psychiatrist, never offer a forensic opinion on patient's competence to be executed
- Obtain consultation on difficult cases

Perhaps these guidelines are as good as any. The problem of defining and discerning 'extreme suffering' in psychotically disturbed individuals is not easily resolved. Ultimately there is no satisfactory ethical solution to the question of treating the execution incompetent prisoner.

Respect

Of less concern and controversy than the death penalty, but of pervasive relevance to jails and prisons is the matter of respecting inmates, who have lost favor with society and whose alleged criminal behaviors and/or boorish conduct behind bars more easily elicits contempt and ridicule than respect and compassion. Some humor makes correctional health work more enjoyable, but humor at the expense of inmates can lead to insensitivity, scapegoating and distraction from the serious work of treatment planning. Psychiatrists can and should give due attention to policy, procedures, safety measures and need for limit setting and firmness, without diminishing his or her basic respect for human dignity that should be shown to patients in any setting.

23.2.1.2   Professionalism and Honesty

II. A physician shall uphold the standards of professionalism, be honest in all professional interactions, and strive to report physicians deficient in character or competence, or engaging in fraud or deception, to appropriate entities.

Commentary

Professionalism

The APA code prohibits sexual relations with patients, exploitation of patients, and jeopardizing the welfare of patients by practicing while mentally ill. Psychiatrists should practice within the area of their expertise, intercede if a mentally ill psychiatrist is putting patients at risk and clarify terms of the contractual arrangement with patients.

Dress

Professionalism for correctional psychiatrists, it should be added, includes appropriate attire. Although not necessary in all settings, the value of wearing a white smock or jacket is that it identifies the role of a medical/psychiatric trainee who is not a permanent member of the correctional mental health team. In any case, psychiatrists should avoid attire that is revealing or sexually provocative, and they should not give inmates personal information such as contact information. Such ethical guidance represents good judgment that is protective of both inmates and providers. The expectations for professionalism and other aspects of ethical conduct should be shared with trainees who are under the correctional psychiatrist's supervision.

23.2.1.3   Follow and Improve the Law

III. A physician shall respect the law and also recognize a responsibility to seek changes in those requirements which are contrary to the best interests of the patient.

Commentary

Informed consent

It is incumbent upon correctional psychiatrists to familiarize themselves with the legal regulations that pertain to psychiatric services in correctional settings. Depending on the nature and circumstances of the practice, following all mental health regulatory law can be challenging. For example, the large volume of inmates to be treated within a short timeframe, concerns about treatment refusal when hospital transfer is not easily available, and push back from other professionals who oppose full informed consent out of fear of noncompliance, can frustrate efforts to obtain written informed consent for psychotropic medication. In some busy, understaffed jails the implementation of procedures to ensure full written consent may need to be achieved incrementally, but this must be the goal.

23.2.1.4   Confidentiality and Privacy

IV. A physician shall respect the rights of patients, colleagues, and other health professionals, and shall safeguard patient confidences and privacy within the constraints of the law.

Commentary

Confidentiality

The APA code further explains the importance of maintaining confidentiality of patient records and of protecting patient anonymity in professional education and publications. AAPL guidelines require that an explanation be given to the evaluee regarding the lack of confidentiality of the forensic examination.

Several considerations are of special relevance to correctional psychiatry. Some inmates are charged with or convicted of highly publicized criminal offenses and others are well known because of their celebrity. Thus, anonymity is not assured simply by omitting obviously identifying information. Trainees under the correctional psychiatrist's supervision should be informed of this and reminded of the primacy of confidentiality.

Medical Record Documentation

Medical and mental health records require all the confidentiality safeguards of clinical records in any setting. Gratuitous information that would be stigmatizing, incriminating or embarrassing does not belong in the record. Details about the inmate's index offense should generally be omitted. Nonetheless, such information is occasionally highly relevant to risk assessment, for example, an inmate who is charged with homicide after entering a homicide-suicide pact, and the psychiatrist must determine the inmate's current risk for suicide. Another example is where the inmate requires hospitalization and a requisite legal criterion is risk of harm to self or others. If the inmate has made no threats of harming self or others since incarceration, but is charged with a violent act which appears to have been a result of his mental disorder which continues untreated and unabated, the recent violent act may need to be referenced to support court ordered hospitalization and treatment.

HIPAA and Access to Care

Today HIPAA (Health Insurance Portability and Accountability Act, 45 CFR 164.500 et seq.) is cited more often than any professional code as legal authority that prohibits communication needed for continuity of treatment when an inmate is transferred from one treating facility to another or when some disclosure is needed to initiate procedures for transfer to a hospital setting. Where dangerousness is manifested by recent overt acts and threats and the cognizant authority is the probate court or court designated for civil commitments, there is no objection to the breach of confidentiality that is needed. Another scenario, however, involves the jail inmate who is psychotic, in need of hospital treatment, refusing recommended medication, but who makes no threats of harming self or others. Without proper treatment he continues to suffer from psychosis and he may be placed in administrative segregation because he is not expected to function well in the general jail population. Unlike in some countries where such an individual may be found unfit to remain in jail, this is unlikely to happen in the U.S.A. Such an individual will invariably be found incompetent to stand trial and remanded to a hospital for treatment, but this can take months or even years. In such a case, neither HIPAA nor professional ethical codes should prevent the psychiatrist from contacting the appropriate legal authorities to expedite the order for competence assessment. Unfortunately, this issue seems to present a serious ethical ambiguity for correctional psychiatrists who practice in jurisdictions where this problem has not been effectively resolved.

Reporting Risks of Danger and Violation of Rules

An important ethical consideration is under what circumstances a psychiatrist should violate the confidentiality of an inmate and disclose information revealed by the inmate to the psychiatrist. Familiar to psychiatrists are the legal duties to protect third persons from serious harm or homicide when such harm is reasonably foreseeable. For example, if an inmate convincingly vows to shoot and kill a reasonably identifiable person in the community upon his release from jail, the psychiatrist may have a duty to notify law enforcement authorities and/or the potential victims or to initiate hospitalization before the inmate's release from the jail to prevent such tragedy from occurring (Felthous 1989b, 2010a). One example is the inmate who repeatedly and passionately threatens to kill an individual in the community (Felthous 1989a, b). A second is the serial arsonist, apparently unknown as such to authorities, who deliberately sets fire to homes while the residents are inside and is determined not to change his ways upon release, and yet such conduct is not the result of a mental disorder for which involuntary hospitalization would be a solution (Felthous 1994). Disclosures to authorities and/or potential victims in the community are governed by jurisdictional law (Felthous and Kachigian 2001, 2003) with which the correctional psychiatrist should be familiar.

When inmates threaten to harm others within the correctional facility, safety can often be maintained by environmental manipulation (e.g., transfer to the infirmary) and/or treatment of the underlying disorder (e.g., use of indicated medication). Placement on a more secure, restrictive status, such as secure 'psych lock' or 'secure move' requiring handcuffs and leg irons, as well as other measures, can be protective in extreme cases. Sometimes, however, correctional authorities must be notified of a specific risk to prevent serious harm by keeping the inmate separated from the would-be victim.

The American Psychiatric Association Task Force on Jails and Prisons (1989, 2000) allows breach of confidentiality in correctional settings not only when an inmate presents a serious risk of harm to self or others, but also when an inmate presents a clear and present risk of escape or when the inmate is responsible for "the creation of disorder within the facility" (American Psychiatric Association Task Force on Jails and Prisons 2000). Any expectation that a correctional psychiatrist indiscriminately report rule violation, however, may lead to unethical breaches of confidentiality (Pinta 2009). Although some rule violations would fall under the APA exceptions to confidentiality, others would not. Reporting that an inmate has a gun would be consistent with the APA exceptions, reporting that an inmate is masturbating would not. For analysis of the variety of situations that fall within the grey area between these extremes, the reader is referred to Pinta (2009).

23.2.1.5 Knowledge and Education

V. A physician shall continue to study, apply, and advance scientific knowledge, maintain a commitment to medical education, make relevant information available to patients, colleagues, and the public, obtain consultation, and use the talents of other health professionals when indicated.

Commentary

Research

Research on inmates in the 1950s and 1960s was done with little or no oversight or informed consent (Hoffman 2000; Kalmback and Lyons 2003). Abuses of excess were exposed and by 1978 the U.S. government virtually prohibited research on prisoners (Wakai et al. 2009). Prisoners then became an overprotected group (Moser et al. 2004) and even research that could have led to increased quality of treatment for mentally disorders inmates was eschewed. Correctional psychiatrists, even if not engaged in research themselves, can support research that is needed to develop effective treatments for mentally disordered prisoners and at the same time respects and protects the autonomy and welfare of inmates (Wakai et al. 2009).

Education

Likewise, involving medical students, residents, fellows and trainees of other disciplines in the assessment and treatment of inmates diminishes the therapeutic and educational isolation of inmates and prepares future healthcare providers for effectively meeting the psychiatric and medical needs of this population.

Informing Patient Inmates

Informed consent is perhaps even more important for individuals who are locked up in cells and cannot always freely access healthcare providers and who may not be seen again by the psychiatrist for several weeks or longer. A medication side effect is more likely to be identified early, and before it becomes serious, if the inmate himself can recognize that he is experiencing a side effect and then bring it to medical attention.

23.2.1.6   Freedom of Practice

> VI. A physician shall, in the provision of appropriate patient care, except in emergencies, be free to choose whom to serve, with whom to associate, and the environment in which to provide medical care.

Commentary

Provider Selection

By choosing to serve a given correctional population, the correctional psychiatrist has in effect already chosen whom to serve, with whom to associate and his work environment. He then cannot arbitrarily choose which mentally disordered inmates he will serve and which he will not among those in need of psychiatric services.

Nonetheless, choices of whom the psychiatrist will treat can be predicated on rational grounds that correspond to the inmates' treatment needs. The psychiatrist should not practice outside the scope of his competence. He should not provide treatment on inmate demand but that is not clinically indicated. For a variety of clinically sound reasons, he can and should refer mentally disordered inmates to other available colleagues.

23.2.1.7   Public Health

VII. A physician shall recognize a responsibility to participate in activities contributing to the improvement of the community and the betterment of public health.

Commentary

Continuity of Care

Unfortunately in many correctional settings, the correctional psychiatrist will not have enough time to tend to all the service needs within the jail or prison, let alone the health needs of the greater community. He should be informed of the role of his correctional facility within the greater health care delivery system, the significant risks of morbidity and mortality during arrest and initial pre-jail custody (Bureau of Justice Statistics 2007; Karch and Stephens 1999; Mohandie and Meloy 2000), the mortality following release from incarceration (Binswanger et al. 2007; Pratt et al. 2006), and should support if not actively strive for measures that would increase continuity of mental health care and substance use rehabilitation upon release.

23.2.1.8   Primacy of Patient Welfare

VIII. A physician shall, while caring for a patient, regard responsibility to the patient as paramount.

Commentary

Security versus Therapy

A new section not yet commented on in the APA ethical code (American Psychiatric Association 2009), the primacy principle of the AMA, is of critical importance to correctional psychiatry. In a correctional setting where physical safety, control, and discipline are paramount, a correctional psychiatrist's concern for the humane care and proper treatment can become attenuated. The psychiatrist must respect and take into account correctional and disciplinary procedures but without losing sight of the mentally disordered inmates' treatment needs which must be met, sometimes under adverse circumstances.

23.2.1.9 Access to Medical Care

IX. A physician shall support access to medical care for all people.

Commentary

Like the primacy principle, the access principle is a new addition to the AMA ethical code and not yet commented on in the APA ethics code (American Psychiatric Association 2009). Although not a saliently discussed ethical topic in correctional psychiatry, the basic challenge of promoting easy and prompt access to psychiatric care of adequate quality is perhaps the most ubiquitous ethical challenge. This challenge in correctional psychiatry can be both overwhelming and neglected. Because of the importance, prevalence and relative neglect of this issue, it deserves greater attention. Treatment can be insufficient, excessive, or due to understaffing, high inmate volume, and rapid turnover in jails, poorly titrated to the mentally disordered inmate's specific and fluctuating therapeutic needs.

Continuity versus Appropriateness of Treatment

If upon booking, an individual reports taking a variety of psychotropic medications, the psychiatrist might understandably favor continuing the medications for continuity at least until the newly admitted inmate can be evaluated. Some initial psychiatric screening at booking, even if only by telephone, is useful, because rubberstamp renewal of all medications is not always the best practice. Some psychotropics that are widely used in the community, such as psychostimulants for adults (Appelbaum 2010), benzodiazepines (Appelbaum 2010) and quetiapine (Burns 2010; Eder 2008; Pinta 2007) are problematic in correctional settings where they should be prescribed very selectively if at all for mental disorders. As Kenneth Appelbaum observes, inmates can arrive at a correctional facility having accumulated a variety of prescribed as well as illegal drugs. Incarceration provides an opportunity to review the inmate's authentic treatment needs and to discontinue, taper off, or detoxify from unnecessary and potentially problematic medications (Appelbaum 2010).

Access to Appropriate Pharmacotherapy

Correctional facilities, or correctional managed care entities, have categorically excluded SSRIs, allowing only tricyclic antidepressants on the formulary, in order to contain cost. Cost containment is an important ethical as well as budgetary consideration, but absolute exclusion of a category of medication, widely accepted in non-correctional practice, of demonstrated effectiveness, and with fewer side effects, should be resisted by correctional psychiatrists. Likewise, screening and monitoring methods for safe pharmacotherapy, such as laboratory tests, should be utilized without undue restriction.

Access to appropriate pharmacotherapy does not mean ready access to all psychotropic agents or prescription on request. Already mentioned in the context of screening at booking, is the appropriateness of limiting medications that are subject to abuse such as quetiapine, psychostimulants, and benzodiazepines. Hypnotics in general also belong to the list of medications that are prone to be abused by inmates. Avoidance of excessive and inappropriate use of psychotropics is as important an ethical consideration as prescription of indicated medication for mental disorders. Selectivity of treatment is integral to proper access.

Communication Barriers

When an inmate does not speak English, an interpreter may be needed. When his only fluent language is an unusual one in the U.S.A., there can be a delay in obtaining a translator. Then it may be necessary to attempt some primitive communication using other methods, gestures and picture drawing for example, pending proper translation. The inmate's difficulty in communication with correctional officers, nurses and other inmates must be kept in mind. Similar concerns and measures apply to inmates who are mute due to defect.

Gender Equality in Treatment Access

In some jails women have not been allowed admission to the infirmary because the cells have bars instead of walls and doors, compromising privacy. Where maximum security hospitals are all male and a female inmate's behavior is just as violent and destructive as male counterparts, further inequalities exist. The correctional psychiatrist must strive for equal treatment but in the meantime may need to find some creative solution to ensure that female inmates are provided comparable treatment and management.

Access to Care in Lockdown

A more commonplace occurrence is the mentally disordered offender who is in disciplinary lockdown or administrative segregation, or who because he is on secure move is not brought to the psychiatric clinic. Also, while some inmates, who do not have serious mental illness, may refuse clinic visits, others refuse clinic visits because they are paranoid or disorganized. In such cases the psychiatrist may need to interview the inmate at cellfront.

Involuntary Medication

Today with the weakened economy and dwindling revenues for state and local budgets, mental health services for jailed mentally disordered individuals, who do not enjoy popular political support, are increasingly at risk. For most who are acutely suicidal or psychotically disturbed in the community a mental hospital is where the appropriate level of treatment can be provided. In general jails are expected to treat suicidal and psychotic inmates who voluntarily accept recommended treatment. Small jails and city lockups that lack appropriate resources can transfer the acutely disturbed detainee to a large county jail that serves the metroplex and has an infirmary. Some of the largest jails today are also the largest inpatient psychiatric facilities as a result of the transinstitutionalization of the mentally ill, but also from the willingness of policymakers to reduce hospital availability for mentally ill inmates as a cost reduction, budget balancing measure. When provided with sufficient resources, county jails, like state prison systems with their own security hospitals, can be remarkably effective at managing suicidal risk and controlling psychotic symptoms. Nonetheless, death from suicide (Felthous 2011) and other complications remain problematic, especially in jails.

The psychotically disturbed jail inmates who refuse antipsychotic medication raise the ethical challenge of providing access to care of the appropriate level for such jail inmates. Currently two models exist in the United States to treat such individuals: involuntary emergency hospitalization and treatment, and involuntary medication in jail. Involuntary emergency hospitalization and treatment corresponds with the community standard for involuntary treatment and is therefore ethically acceptable. Typically the same standard as for psychiatric emergencies in the community must be satisfied, namely, imminent risk of harm to self or others and refusal of recommended, appropriate medication. Whether locally or state administered, the hospital must provide the security needed for jail inmates. After transfer to the hospital, the treating psychiatrist will independently determine whether the inmate satisfies criteria for involuntary medication and if so proceed with the procedural steps required by law to medicate involuntarily. If more than a few days of involuntary hospitalization are needed to initiate treatment safely, a formal civil commitment hearing is held. Once the inmate's condition has improved and stabilized and he accepts medication voluntarily, he is returned to the jail where pharmacotherapy continues.

The second model, involuntary medication during jail detention, is already in practice in some of the nation's large pre-trial detention facilities. Under current budgetary crises, policymakers are considering adopting this model where the hospitalization model is being used, in order to reduce expenditures for the mentally ill, in this case involving the most seriously and acutely mentally ill individuals. The administration of involuntary medication in jail, rather than a hospital, raises several ethical questions (Felthous 2010b). First, the purpose of jails is to detain pre-trial detainees or punish miscreants, not to provide the highest level of treatment for severely disturbed inmates. Security, not therapy, is emphasized in the structure, staffing and programming of jails. The relationship between the jail and its inmates, who are involuntarily detained for non-therapeutic purposes, is inherently adversarial. The pre-trial timing of medication makes its involuntary administration questionable in a non-hospital setting, as the inmate's procedural due process rights must be protected (See e.g., *Riggins v. Nevada* 1992 and Justice Kennedy's concurring opinion that would require hospitalization for pretrial, involuntary medication).

The second ethical objection to involuntary treatment in a jail setting is that most jails, even large county jails are poor proxies for psychiatric hospitals (Felthous 2010b).

Even those jails with infirmaries are not staffed and programmed like psychiatric hospital wards. Most jails categorically do not provide constant observation for those at acute risk of harm to self or others. Most do not have 'psych tech' and the few jail nurses do not have time to try to persuade reluctant inmates to take medication voluntarily. Modern inpatient mental health treatment is much more than giving patients unwanted intramuscular injections, yet the staffing even in infirmaries is below that which would be needed for comprehensive diagnostic assessments and multimodal therapies.

Other differences between jails and hospitals can complicate the matter further. Even inmates in the infirmary can be locked up in single cells, double cells, or dormitory type cells, which together with the lower provider:inmate ratio can make it less likely that medication side effects will be noticed promptly. Unlike hospitals, jails and their infirmaries have no diversionary policies: Treaters must concern themselves with releasing inmates from the infirmary and making room for the continued inflow of inmates in crisis, sometimes distracting the treaters' attention from titrating medication for some inmates by the therapeutic exigencies of psychotically disturbed inmates. Other psychotically disturbed but not imminently dangerous inmates continue to go neglected and untreated, sometimes by necessity in settings of questionable appropriateness such as in the lockdown section of the jail. If the infirmary section becomes more hospital-like with a therapeutic milieu and programming in order to justify involuntary medicine in the jail, inmates without serious mental disorders have more incentive to feign symptoms or malinger a mental disorder in order to be transferred to the infirmary. With the two step process of assessment prior to infirmary transfer and then further assessment prior to hospital transfer, feigning and malingering should be disincentivized and rendered more detectable.

Much of the second objection to involuntary medication in jail – a jail infirmary is not a mental ward – can be overcome by staffing and programming the jail infirmary as though it were a psychiatric hospital unit. More complete staffing and programming seems like a worthy objective for the ethical correctional psychiatrist even for severely disordered inmates who are medication compliant. Such major improvements can be a hard sell for policymakers and administrators whose decisions are driven by the pressure to cut costs. And, as suggested, there are disadvantages to having a fully equipped, staffed and programmed 'mental ward' within the jail that must be taken into consideration.

If involuntary medication is to be given within the jail, the model for attempting to ensure the inmate's due process rights and qualified right to refuse medication will involve either court-ordered medication or administrative review within the jail and without court involvement. The arguments for and against each contrasting model, the first favoring the inmate's rights, the second favoring the inmate's treatment needs, are intensified in the jail setting and both models demand more staff time. Given this choice the administrative review model should function more efficiently and ensure that involuntary medication is administered promptly, but at the expense of autonomy rights which can be problematic in a jail setting. Either model, administrative or judicial review, would best be carried out in a secure hospital setting where the staffing and programming is geared to handle the legally requisite procedures.

Most discussions on involuntary medication in correctional settings (e.g., Burns 2010; Ruiz 2010; Scott 2010) cite the landmark legal case *Washington v. Harper* (1990) in which the United States Supreme Court found an administrative review model of administering involuntary medication to be constitutionally acceptable. To be emphasized is that this case concerned the legality of involuntary medication in a prison setting, or more specifically a prison mental health unit, not in a jail (Felthous 2010b). *Harper* and the discussions that followed concerned legal exceptions to the prisoner's right to refuse medication, not the ethics of providing access to adequate treatment. Discussions on the involuntary transfer of a prisoner to a psychiatric hospital for treatment (e.g., Scott 2010) invoke the Supreme Court's *Vitek v. Jones* (1980) decision, which concerned transfer from a prison, not a jail, and the prisoner's qualified right not to serve his sentence in a hospital, not access to the appropriate level of care for jail detainees.

Although neither a Supreme Court opinion nor a decision that focused on involuntary medication, *Ruiz v. Estelle* (1980), a prison health reform case, addressed the need for sufficient quality of mental health services. A federal court that found the mental health services in the Texas prison system to be deficient proclaimed that six guidelines must be satisfied for a prison mental health system to be constitutionally acceptable. Two of these guidelines can be critical challenges in many jail facilities. 'Treatment for a prisoner must entail more than just segregation and close supervision,' and 'A prisoner cannot be treated with a prescription for behavior altering medication in dangerous amounts, by dangerous methods, or without acceptable supervision and periodic evaluations.' (Scott 2010, citing *Ruiz*). In jails such guidelines become especially critical if psychotropic medication is to be administered by physical coercion. Even without a *Ruiz*-type class action decision pertaining to jail, the coupling of involuntary medication with hospital level quality of care is ethically prudent.

Regardless what model is settled upon, the ethical correctional psychiatrist should strive to ensure access to the appropriate level of psychiatric care for mentally disordered inmates, especially psychotically disordered inmates. This favors coerced treatment, when needed, in a secure hospital setting (Felthous 2010b), but the timeliness and responsiveness of treatment is as important as its quality and intensity. Acquiescence to cost-cutting measures that reduce quality and/or timeliness of emergency psychiatric treatment is no support for access to psychiatric care. This critical ethical principle must inform legislative, judicial and administrative policymakers whose most pressing objective can be to reduce or eliminate public expenditure on involuntary hospitalization and the medication of psychotically disturbed inmates.

Access to Hospital Care for Non-dangerous but Seriously Disturbed Inmates

As a rule severely mentally disturbed inmates, even those who are psychotic and dysfunctional, are not transferred for hospital treatment if they are not imminently and demonstrably dangerous to themselves or others. State and federal prison systems have security hospitals within their respective systems whereas jails do not, creating a potential barrier for jail inmates who require hospital care. Although useful for most emotional crises, management of acute suicidality and even effective treatment of acute psychosis, the jail mental health unit is not typically equivalent to a hospital unit and some severely disturbed inmates require the higher level of care that only a hospital can provide.

One type of inmate who falls into this category is the treatment compliant inmate who, despite the best efforts of infirmary nursing, medical and mental health staff, has a disorder, usually schizophrenia, that simply does not improve to the extent that he can be treated in the general jail population (Felthous 2010b). Because the number of cells or beds in the infirmary is limited and some must be kept free for the emergencies that continue to occur, he may have to be released into another part of the jail where his condition deteriorates even further and then he must return to the infirmary once space is available. For this inmate the jail, even the infirmary of the jail, is anti-therapeutic, but legal procedures that would result in hospital treatment, such as addressing and resolving the question of competence to stand trial can be delayed for months or even years.

The second type of inmate is similarly severely disturbed, psychotic and dysfunctional, but unlike the first type, refuses antipsychotic medication (Felthous 2010a). Because he is not imminently and demonstrably dangerous to self or others, he does not qualify for hospital transfer through court order. Even in those jails that medicate inmates involuntarily, this inmate goes untreated because the dangerous criterion is also needed for involuntary administration of medication. Often the best hope for appropriate treatment is through an incompetency determination with subsequent hospital transfer (Felthous 2010b). Housing this inmate anywhere in the jail is unsatisfactory because the limited cells in the infirmary must be reserved for emergencies not taken up indefinitely by someone who does not accept treatment. Because of his untreated mental disorder he does not adapt well to the general jail population and could deteriorate further in the relative isolation of special housing placements such as administrative segregation. His mental disorder also increases the risk of his being subjected to jail disciplinary procedures (Torrey et al. 2010) and the anti-therapeutic effect of punishment. With the treatment non-compliant inmate the possibility of either gaining treatment compliance through persuasion and reasoning or coerced medication based upon *Sell* (*Sell v. United States* 2003) criteria is increased in the forensic security hospital, but the existence of mental disorder, rather than accelerating resolution of the competence issue, can delay it for months or longer.

Because of the limited freedom for detainees and the emphasis on security in jails, the mentally disturbed detainee does not have the same opportunity to act violently as in other settings. If there is concern that an inmate could become disruptive, he may be subject to lockdown in an individual cell for 23 out of 24 h in the day, secure move where he must wear handcuffs and leg irons and be escorted by one or two officers whenever out of the cell, thus, even though possibly violent, the potential is contained and not manifest owing to circumstances of confinement.

    The legal purposes for competence to stand trial determinations are concerned
with the defendant's procedural rights (Ennis and Hansen 1976), not the humanitarian
concern for treatment of a disorder marked by severe suffering or disability. If a
defendant had a severe medical illness it would be treated responsively despite any
legal concern or lack therefore for competence determination. But where a severe
mental disorder exists, and may even be made worse by continued jail placement,
the legal system is not so consistently responsible in responding to the inmate's
considerable treatment needs.

    Although in neither the medical nor the general psychiatric ethical code, the
AAPL guidelines for forensic psychiatrists states under Guideline IV, Honesty and
Striving for Objectively, 'Treating psychiatrists should generally avoid agreeing to
be an expert witness or to perform evaluations of their patients for legal purposes
because a forensic evaluation usually requires that other people be interviewed
and testimony may adversely affect the therapeutic relationship' (AAPL Ethical
Guidelines 2005). Where an individual's mental condition is so severely disturbed
that hospital care is needed for appropriate treatment, prompt provision of proper
care should preempt any concerns about a professional relationship which, because
of disturbance, cannot be therapeutic. Whether through civil or criminal commitment,
facilitation of indicated hospital transfer should not constitute a violation of the
important ethical guideline for honesty and objectivity.

    A patient's right to refuse treatment does not relieve a psychiatrist from the
responsibility of treating every patient that refuses (Pinals and Hoge 2003). As with
civil commitment, the patient's right to confidentiality and privacy and the ethical
guideline to avoid both treatment and forensic consultation of a patient by the same
psychiatrist, should not be used to avoid initiation of hospitalization through competence to stand trial assessment. When an inmate's serious mental disorder would
likely benefit from hospital treatment and is made worse by continued incarceration
in a correctional facility, such qualified patient rights and forensic guidelines must
yield to the ethical principle of primacy of patient welfare.

    The contemporary situation in many U.S. jails, at least for those seriously men-
tally ill who are deprived of adequate treatment, is not unlike the situation in large
state mental hospitals before corrected through class action lawsuit. In *Wyatt v.
Stickney* (1972) for example, a federal court found that involuntary hospital confinement without proper treatment and care was unconstitutional. The court established
minimal standards including a 'humane psychological and physical environment,'
sufficient number of qualified staff to provide adequate treatment, and "individualized
treatment plans." A major difference between jails and prisons is that individuals are
involuntarily confined for other legal reasons under criminal law.

    The unnecessary delays in obtaining hospital treatment for the seriously mentally
ill inmate whose treatment needs are not met in jail have been overcome by expedited
competency assessments achieved by effective inter-agency cooperation (Finkle et al.
2009; Olley et al. 2009). As with civil commitment, initiation of competency assessment
with resultant hospitalization for competence restoration can be expedited if ethical
guidelines of confidentiality and avoidance of the dual roles of treating psychiatrist
and forensic psychiatrist yield just enough so as to enable hospitalization through

legal procedures that protect the inmate's constitutional rights, including the qualified right to refuse treatment (Pinals and Hoge 2003) and inappropriate hospitalization (*Vitek v. Jones* 1980). Whether via civil or criminal commitment, court ordered hospitalization further protects an inmate's autonomy rights before he is subject to involuntary medication.

23.3   Conclusions

As in any setting, psychiatrists who provide services in jails or prisons must endeavor to serve the inmate's treatment needs and avoid causing harm to the inmate. In the absence of an ethical code specifically for correctional psychiatry, U.S. correctional psychiatrists are on firm ethical ground if they follow the ethical codes of the American Medical Association, the American Psychiatric Association and the American Academy of Psychiatry and the Law. Above all, the ethical correctional psychiatrist respects the human dignity of every inmate whom he evaluates or treats and strives to provide quality treatment that takes into account the special circumstances of the correctional setting.

References

American Academy of Psychiatry and the Law: Ethics Guidelines for the Practice of Forensic Psychiatry. 1995, 2005. Author. http://aapl.org/ethics.htm. Accessed 13 July 2010.

American Medical Association. 1992. Council on Ethical and Judicial Affairs: Physicians participation in capital punishment. *Journal of the American Medical Association* 270: 365–368.

American Medical Association. 2010. *Code of medical ethics of the American Medical Association: Council on Ethical and Judicial Affairs: Current opinions with annotations*, 2010–2011th ed. Chicago: Author.

American Psychiatric Association. 2000. *Psychiatric services in jails and prisons: A task force report of the American Psychiatric Association*, 2nd ed, xix–xx. Washington, DC: Author.

American Psychiatric Association. 2009. *The principles of medical ethics with annotations especially applicable to psychiatry*. Arlington: Author.

American Psychiatric Association Task Force on Psychiatric Services in Corrections. 1989. Position Statement on psychiatric services in jails and prisons. *The American Journal of Psychiatry* 146: 1244–1244.

Appelbaum, K.L. 2010. The mental health professional in a correctional culture. In *Handbook of correctional mental health*, 2nd ed, ed. C.L. Scott, 91–118. Washington, DC: American Psychiatric Publishing, Inc.

Barefoot V. Estelle, 103 S.ct.3383,1983.

Binswanger, I.A., M.F. Stern, R.A. Deyo, P.J. Heagerty, et al. 2007. Release from prison – a high risk of death for former inmates. *The New England Journal of Medicine* 356(2): 157–166.

Bonnie, R. 1990a. Dilemmas in administering the death penalty: Conscientious abstention, professional ethics and the need of the legal system. *Laws and Human Behavior* 14: 67–90.

Bonnie, R. 1990b. Healing-killing conflicts: Medical ethics and the death penalty. *The Hastings Center Report* 20(3): 12–18.

Bureau of Justice Statistics. 2007. States reported more than 2,000 arrest-related death from 2003 through 2005. http://bjs.ojp.usdoj.gov/content/pub/press/ardus05pr.cfm. Accessed 18 Jan 2010.

Burns, K.A. 2010. Pharmacotherapy in correctional settings. In *Handbook of correctional mental health*, 2nd ed, ed. C.L. Scott, 321–344. London: American Psychiatric Publishing.

Dekleva, K.B. 2001. Psychiatric expertise in the sentencing phase of capital murder cases. *The Journal of the American Academy of Psychiatry and the Law* 29: 58–67.

Ditton, P.M. 1999. Mental health and treatment of inmates and probationers. Bureau of Justice Statistics Special Reports, NCJ 174463.

Eder, A. 2008. Abuse of Seroquel in prisons reported. The News Journal. Do Delaware http://www.delawareonline.com/apps/pbcs.dll/article?AID=/20080803/BUSINESS/308030. Accessed 28 Sept 2008.

Ennis, B.J., and C. Hansen. 1976. Memorandum of law: Competency to stand trial. *Journal of Psychiatry and Law* 4: 491–512.

Felthous, A.R. 1989a. The use of psychiatric evaluations in the determinations of sentencing. In *Critical issues in American psychiatry and the law, criminal court consultation*, ed. R. Rosner and R. Harmen, 189–208. New York: Plenum Publishing Co.

Felthous, A.R. 1989b. *The psychotherapist's duty to warn or protect*. Springfield: Charles C. Thomas.

Felthous, A.R. 1994. Die moralische Pflicht, leute von der Gewalttaen der psychiatrischen ambulanten Patientes zu schützen (The Moral Duty to Protect People from Violent Acts of psychiatric Outpatients. DGPPN Kongress 1994. Deutsche Gesellschaft für Psychiatrie, Psychotherapie und Nervenheilkunde (Annual Meeting of the German Psychiatric Society) Technische Hochschule Darmstadt, Darmstadt, Germany, 3–7 Sept 1994, Abstract V-24-2.

Felthous, A.R. 2001. Are psychiatrists competent to assess who the state should sentence to death? *Current Opinion in Psychiatry* 14(6): 537–539.

Felthous, A.R. 2009. Introduction to this issue: Correctional mental health care. *Behavioral Sciences & the Law* 27(5): 655–659.

Felthous, A.R. 2010a. Personal violence. In *Textbook of forensic psychiatry*, Secondth ed, ed. R.I. Simon and L.H. Gold, 529–561. Washington, D C: American Psychiatric Press, Inc.

Felthous, A.R. 2010b. "The least of my brethren": Treatment of the seriously mentally ill in Saint Louis Metroplex jails. *St. Louis Magazine* online, Oct 2010.

Felthous, A.R. 2011. Suicide behind bars: Trends, inconsistencies and pracical implications. *Journal of Forensic Sciences* 56(6): 1541–1555.

Felthous, A.R., and C. Kachigian. 2001. The Fin de Millénaire duty to warn or protect. *Journal of Forensic Sciences* 46(5): 1103–1112.

Felthous, A.R., and C. Kachigian. 2003. The duty to protect. In *Principles and practice of forensic psychiatry*, 2nd ed, ed. R. Rosner, 147–155. London: Arnold.

Finkle, M.J., R. Kurth, C. Cadle, and J. Mullan. 2009. Competency courts: A creative solution for restoring competency to the competency process. *Behavioral Sciences & the Law* 27(5): 767–786.

Gunter, T., S. Arndt, G. Wenman, et al. 2008. Frequency of mental and addictive disorders among 320 men and women entering the Iowa prison system: Use of the MINI-Plus. *The Journal of the American Academy of Psychiatry and the Law* 36: 27–34.

Guy, E., J.J. Platt, I. Zwerling, et al. 1985. Mental health status of prisoners in an urban jail. *Criminal Justice and Behavior* 12: 29–53.

Harrison, P.M., and A.J. Beck. 2004. Prisoners in 2003.Washington, D C: *Bureau of Justice Statistics Bulletin*. NCJ 205335.

Health Insurance Portability and Accountability Act 45 CFR Subtitle A (10-1-03 Edition). subpart E – privacy of individually identifiable health information sections 164.500–164.534.

Hoffman, S. 2000. Beneficial and unusual punishment: An argument in support of prisoner participation in clinical trials. *Indiana Law Review* 33: 475–515.

James, D.J., and L.E. Glaze. 2006. Mental health problems of prison and jail inmates. Bureau of Justice Statistics Special Report. September.

Kalmback, K.C., and P.M. Lyons. 2003. Ethical and legal standards for research in prisons. *Behavioral Sciences & the Law* 21: 671–686.

Karch, S.B., and B.G. Stephens. 1999. Drug abusers who die during arrest or in custody. *Journal of the Royal Society of Medicine* 92: 110–113.

Knoll IV, J.L. 2010. Ethics in forensic psychiatry. In *Handbook of correctional mental health*, 2nd ed, ed. C.L. Scott, 111–149. London: American Psychiatric Publishing, Inc.

Knoll IV, J.L., and G.E. Beven. 2010. Supermax units and death rows. In *Handbook of correctional mental health*, 2nd ed, ed. C.L. Scott, 435–475. London: American Psychiatric Publishing, Inc.

Leong, G.B., J.A. Silva, R. Weinstock, and L. Ganzini. 2000. Survey of Forensic psychiatrists on evaluation and treatment of prisoners on death row. *The Journal of the American Academy of Psychiatry and the Law* 28: 427–432.

Lo, C. 2004. Sociodemographic factors, drug abuse, and other crimes: How they vary among male and female arrestees. *Journal of Criminal Justice* 32: 399–409.

McDermott, B.E., and G. Sokolov. 2009. Malingering in a correctional setting: The use of structured interview of reported symptoms in a jail sample. *Behavioral Sciences & the Law* 27: 753–765.

Mohandie, K., and J.R. Meloy. 2000. Clinical and forensic indicators of "suicide by copy". *Journal of Forensic Sciences* 45(2): 384–389.

Moser, D.J., S. Arndt, J.E. Kanz, M.L. Benjamin, J.D. Bayless, R.L. Reese, et al. 2004. Coersion and informed consent in research involving prisoners. *Comprehensive Psychiatry* 45: 1–9.

Olley, M.C., T.L. Nicholls, and J. Brink. 2009. Mentally ill individuals in limbo: Obstacles and opportunities in providing psychiatric services to corrections inmates with mental illness. *Behavioral Sciences & the Law* 27(5): 811–831.

Peters, R., P. Greenbaum, J. Edens, et al. 1998. Prevalence of DSM-IV substance abuse and dependence disorders among inmates. *The American Journal of Drug and Alcohol Abuse* 24: 573–587.

Pinals, D.A., and S.K. Hoge. 2003. Treatment refusal in psychiatric practice. In *Principles and practice of forensic psychiatry*, 2nd ed, ed. R. Rosner, 129–136. London: Arnold.

Pinta, E.R. 2007. Quetiapine addiction? *American Journal of Psychiatry* 164:174. http://ajp.psychiatryonline.org/egi/content/full/164/174. Accessed 28 Sept 2008.

Pinta, E.G. 2009. Decisions to breech confidentiality when prisoners report violations of institutional rules. *The Journal of the American Academy of Psychiatry and the Law* 37(2): 150–154.

Powell, T., J. Holt, and K. Fondacaro. 1997. The prevalence of mental illness among inmates in a rural state. *Law and Human Behavior* 21: 427–438.

Pratt, D., M. Piper, L. Appleby, R. Webb, and J. Shaw. 2006. Suicide in recently released prisoners: A population-based cohort study. *The Lancet* 368: 119–123.

Riggins v. Nevada. 504 U.S. 127, 1992.

Ruiz, A. 2010. Continuous quality improvement and documentation. In *Handbook of correctional mental health*, 2nd ed, ed. C.L. Scott, 149–165. London: American Psychiatric Publishing, Inc.

Ruiz v. Estelle. 503 F. Supp. 1265, S.D. Tex 1980.

Scott, C.L. 2006. Psychiatry and the death penalty. *Psychiatric Clinics of North America* 29(3): 791–804.

Scott, C.L. 2010. Legal issues regarding the provision of care in a correctional setting. In *Handbook of correctional mental health*, 2nd ed, ed. C.L. Scott, 63–88. London: American Psychiatric Publishing, Inc.

Sell v. United States. 539 U.S. 166, 2003.

Temporini, H. 2010. Conducting mental health assessments in correctional settings. In *Handbook of correctional mental health*, 2nd ed, ed. C.L. Scott, 119–147. Washington, DC: American Psychiatric Publishing, Inc.

Teplin, L.A. 1994. Psychiatric and substance abuse disorders among male urban jail detainees. *American Journal of Public Health* 84: 290–293.

Texas Code Crim Proc Ann Art 37.01 (6)(2) (Vernon Supp. 1988).

Torrey, E.F., A.D. Kennard, D. Eslinger, R. Lamb, and J. Pavle. 2010. *More mentally ill persons are in jails and prisons than in hospitals: A survey of the states*. Arlington: Treatment Advocacy Center.

Trestman, R., J. Ford, W. Zhang, et al. 2007. Current and lifetime psychiatric illness among inmates not identified as acutely mentally ill at intake in Connecticut's jails. *The Journal of the American Academy of Psychiatry and the Law* 35: 490–500.

United States (U.S.) Department of Justice. 2005. Almost 7 million adults under correctional supervision behind bards or on probation or parole in the community. http://www.ojp.usdog.gov/bjs/pub/press/ppus04pr.htm.

Vitek v. Jones. 445 U.S. 480, 1980.

Wakai, S., D. Shelton, R.L. Trestman, and K. Kesten. 2009. Conducting research in corrections: Challenges and solutions. *Behavioral Sciences & the Law* 27(5): 743–752.

Washington v. Harper. 494 U.S. 210, 215–217, 1990.

Weinstock, R., G.B. Leong, and J.A. Silva. 2003. Ethical guidelines. In *Principles and practice of forensic psychiatry*, Secondth ed, ed. R. Rosner, 56–72. London: Arnold.

Weinstock, R., Leong, G.B., and J.A. Silva. 2010. Competence to be executed: An ethical analysis post *Panetti*. *Behavioral Sciences and the Law* 28(5): 690–706.

Wolfson, J.K. 2007. Psychopathy and the death penalty in the United States. In *International handbook of psychopathic disorders and the law*, vol. II, ed. A.R. Felthous and H. Saß, 329–342. Chichester: Wiley.

Wyatt v. Stickney. 1972. 344 F. Supp. 373.

Part III
Conclusion

Chapter 24
Conclusion

Norbert Konrad, Birgit Völlm, and David N. Weisstub

Deinstitutionalization, the closure of mental hospital beds and changes to commitment laws were highly touted initiatives that provided the backbone of mental health reform policies implemented in many countries in the second half of the last century. These initiatives, however, have often been given as reasons for the increasing demands for forensic psychiatric services and an increase in the number of mental patients in prison. The net result of these developments is that patients who receive a label of "forensic" enter into a mental health ghetto with little connectivity or integration with the general mental health system (Arboleda-Florez 2003).

It has been argued that prison – in this book defined as a confinement facility for housing individuals convicted of felonies and as a correctional facility that confines persons before (jail) or after their adjudication (prison) – is harmful for mentally disordered patients, that it deprives individuals of basic human rights and needs, bringing physical, mental and social harm to prisoners and rendering them powerless and institutionalised (e.g. Goffman 1968). Prison social environments have an important bearing on prisoner health, in terms of prison organisation, culture and

N. Konrad (✉)
Institute of Forensic Psychiatry, Charité, University Medicine Berlin,
Berlin, Germany
e-mail: norbert.konrad@charite.de

B. Völlm
Section of Forensic Psychiatry, Division of Psychiatry, University ofNottingham,
Triumph Rd, Nottingham NG7 2TU, UK

Rampton Hospital, Nottinghamshire Healthcare NHS Trust, Woodbeck
e-mail: birgit.vollm@nottingham.ac.uk

D.N. Weisstub
Philippe Pinel Professor of Legal Psychiatry and Biomedical Ethics,
International Academy of Law and Mental Health (IALMH),
Montreal, QC, Canada

Faculty of Medicine, University of Montreal, Montreal, QC, Canada
e-mail: admin@ialmh.org

N. Konrad et al. (eds.), *Ethical Issues in Prison Psychiatry*, International Library
of Ethics, Law, and the New Medicine 46, DOI 10.1007/978-94-007-0086-4_24,
© Springer Science+Business Media Dordrecht 2013

relationships inside and outside prison, loss of privacy, overcrowding, social isolation, restrictive and repetitive routine, low stimulation and the prisoner social hierarchy. Although today's prisons are not completely closed systems or 'total institutions' (De Viggiani 2006), the restrictions and deprivations imprisonment legitimately impose require a theory of legal punishment's justifying aims (Lippke 2007).

Diverting mentally ill offenders to forensic-psychiatric institutions does not prevent people from becoming mentally unwell when imprisoned, nor does the presence or history of mental disorder automatically result in the absence of criminal responsibility. The high prevalence of mental disorders in prisoners has been impressively demonstrated in a systematic review of 62 surveys from 12 different western countries including 22,790 prisoners (mean age 29 years, 81 % men): 3.7 % of the men had a psychotic illness, 10 % major depression, and 65 % a personality disorder, while 4 % of women had a psychotic illness, 12 % major depression, and 42 % a personality disorder (Fazel and Danesh 2002). The data presented in the preceding chapters confirm the ongoing impact of mental disorders within the prisoner population.

In comparison to the general population, prisoners have an increased risk of suffering from a mental disorder; this transcends countries and diagnoses. This situation is of particular concern as the double stigma these prisoners experience reduces their chances of successful reintegration into the community and increases their risk of re-offending. The increased consultation of forensic psychiatry experts in this area reflects the interest of the relevant agencies in reducing the risk mentally disordered offenders pose to others as well as in decreasing the suicide rate in prisons and jails. Some authors have suggested that the suicide rate among prisoners is a marker of the inadequate or even inhumane treatment in prisons (Konrad 2006).

24.1 The Dual Role Conflict

Health care providers offering care in the context of criminal punishment encounter apparent conflicts between the treatment interests of the individuals, the wider interests of these individuals, legally protected interests, and the public interest (Schopp 2009). Most contributors to this volume have explicitly recognised this tension in their countries. The professional- medical role of a psychiatrist and/or psychotherapist working in prison has inherent conflicts. On the one hand the doctor/therapist acts according to the requests and interests of his/her imprisoned patient and, following the Hippocratic oath, assigns the highest priority to the preservation and restoration of the patient's health; yet, on the other hand, he/she is an employee of that authority which, in carrying out the punishment required by the state, implements measures which may well damage the prisoner's health. Unlike a surgeon or physician working in prison, who treats illnesses which may be pre-existing or which may have occurred regardless of imprisonment, psychiatrists in prisons deal with individuals with "prison reactions", which have arisen directly as a consequence of imprisonment. In those cases, the function of the psychiatric and psychotherapeutic treatment provided can, to some extent, be seen as serving the purpose to keep the prisoner fit for imprisonment, thereby having a pacifying and mollifying function. Prison psychiatrists find themselves in ethically questionable territory if they carry out psychopharmacological or other medical interventions for which there is no primary medical indication, in order to allow judicial proceedings and the penal system to run smoothly (Konrad and Völlm 2010). Furthermore, the disorders psychiatrists treat are often directly related to the offenses committed by the patient and may also be linked to future risk. The psychiatrist therefore uses his skills – and is expected to do so – to reduce the risk of the mentally disordered individually, hence ultimately serving the public safety agenda.

Of particular concern are disciplinary measures which are coercive by nature. Mentally disordered prisoners are more likely to become the subject of disciplinary measures due to misbehaviour that may be caused by the disorder. It is well known that specific coercive measures (e.g. solitary confinement) are likely to aggravate mental disorders. Thus, it is crucial to assess the psychological state of a prisoner prior to implementing such measures in order to avoid any additional harm. There are European countries where all prisoners requiring punitive or disciplinary measures – or at least any prisoner known to suffer from a mental disorder – will be assessed for fitness to undergo disciplinary measures prior to their implementation. In other European countries, such an assessment is not stipulated (Salize et al. 2007). This participation of medical personnel in the administration of punishment raises considerable ethical problems: Discipline and punishment are security and not health issues, and therefore the physician, who should be available to attend to the medical needs of prisoner under any form of punishment, has no role in deciding upon the administration of such punishment, e.g. in certifying that a person is mentally fit to withstand such a punishment (WHO Europe 2008). However, others have argued that the perspective of a mental health professional, e.g. in explaining the behaviour of a mentally disordered offender, might protect the best interest of the patient and might, on occasion, prevent disciplinary measures from being implemented (Kaul and Völlm in this volume).

In cases of psychiatric reports on refugees facing deportation, which bear considerable diagnostic and prognostic difficulties, the psychiatrist can have a major impact on an individual's life with grave consequences including deterioration of existing mental disorders (Konrad and Völlm 2010).

The most severe role conflict for psychiatrists exists in countries with capital punishment where forensic experts are used to assess the "competency to be executed", which could be achieved by treating the mental illness. The ethical dilemma in this scenario is obvious and some have called upon psychiatrist to not participate in any way, including by assessing "competency to be executed", in the death penaly. However, others, e.g. Keane (2008), argue that physicians may be causing harm to co-victims especially murder victims' relatives when they delay, halt or advocate against an execution.

Ethical problems regarding the dual role of mental health professionals working in correctional settings also arise through the participation in assessments and decisions related broadly to the risk mentally disordered offenders may pose.

Again, this issue has been raised by most authors of the volume, giving examples such as acting as experts on issues of "dangerousness" and participation in boards deciding upon leave, amongst others. A number of authors have argued that prison psychiatrists should not, as a matter of principle, and in order to avoid a conflict of roles, provide expert opinions on their own patients (Konrad and Völlm 2010) although adherence to this standard is not always maintained in practice.

24.2 Psychiatric Need

As noted above, psychiatric morbidity in prisons is high. The majority of authors of this volume note the discrepancy between need and resources to respond to this need. The vast majority of prisoners have a plethora of needs; frequently they present with double or triple diagnoses. Those with a co-occuring psychiatric and substance use disorder exhibit a substantially higher risk of multiple incarcerations compared to inmates with a psychiatric disorder alone or substance use disorders alone (Baillergeon et al. 2010). This complexity of needs often amalgamates to include mental and physical illnesses, homelessness, unemployment, and drug and alcohol addiction (Rutherford and Duggan 2009). These issues are compounded by the increasing numbers of individuals incarcerated, again a trend observed in many countries, which may lead to overcrowding of prisons.

Psychiatric screening and assessment procedures at prison entry and during imprisonment differ substantially and do often not fulfill recognized quality standards. In many countries the appointment of inadequately trained staff to perform such screenings increases considerably the risk that mental disorders or psychiatric needs of the inmates remain undetected (Dressing and Salize 2009). However, on a positive note, a number of countries described in this volume have recognized the importance of screening and have recently introduced relevant procedures and policies, particularly for screening of suicidal risk (e.g. Israel, UK). Despite this, a number of countries (e.g. Brazil, Romania, Slovenia) report that there is no systematic data collection which would allow estimation of prevalence of mental disorders which is clearly of concern as such lack of data seriously impacts upon service planning.

24.3 Service Provision

Although the assessment of different types of service models for the provision of mental health care for mentally disordered prisoners is not the primary focus of this volume, some comments will be made. Not surprisingly, different concepts of service delivery exist; an important distinction, which also impacts upon ethical issues, is between the provision of health care within the prison system and models which aim to transfer individuals to specific treatment facilities outside the prison system. Organisational issues are also important to note, in particular whether or not mental health care staff are employed by the prison (or relevant Ministry) or whether they are under a separate authority, e.g. the Ministry of Health.

Some have argued that due to the different aims of imprisonment and therapeutic intervention, it is impossible to ethically offer treatment within the prison system. However, due to the large numbers of mentally disordered prisoners and the lack, in some countries, of any specific forensic-psychiatric services, in reality most treatment of prisoners is provided within the prison. Furthermore, given that forensic-psychiatric treatment might lead to longer incarceration compared to prison disposal, the question arises whether there is sufficient evidence to support such treatment. Several authors have highlighted difficulties in deciding which prisoners should remain in prison and which should be transferred to the scarce (and more expensive) forensic-psychiatric treatment facilities. Clearly, this needs to be an area of future research in order to make the best use of the facilities available. It was encouraging to see what can be achieved within the prison system in the example of Sweden where nearly 3,500 prisoners completed treatment programmes in prison in 2009 (where the total capacity of prison places was under 5,000).

Only few countries have achieved (relative) administrative independence of health care staff from prison management. Of those considered in the volume, the UK and Israel have specifically noted the clear separation of administration of health care and prison staff. While this poses organizational challenges, considerable advantages of this model have to be noted, e.g. in relation to recruitment, work force training, monitoring of standards, avoiding professional isolation, etc. Such a model might also facilitate access to after-care, an area highlighted as particularly problematic by a number of contributors.

Individuals diagnosed with personality disorders may pose particular challenges to service providers. Some consider them responsible for their own condition, which is often viewed as untreatable (Kendall et al. 2009). Concerns have been expressed particularly in relation to individuals with "psychopathy" following the publication of evidence suggesting that treatment might not only not help such individuals but actually make them worse (Rice et al. 1992). Even though these findings have been widely disputed by a number of authors (eg. D'Silva et al. 2004), individuals with "psychopathy" continue to be excluded from some prison programmes and in some countries also, at least partly, from forensic-psychiatric care.

Prisoners presenting psychotic symptoms may be prone to be denied needed mental health services if evidence of psychopathic traits is used to bolster presumptions of malingering, although findings fail to support the clinical intuition that individuals with higher levels of psychopathy are likely to be more adept at malingering (Drob et al. 2009).

Clinicians need to be mindful of the negative connotations of the term "psychopath". As such, clinicians should cautiously apply this term and carefully explain their measurement of psychopathy and how they interpret high scores on the PCL-R and other psychopathy measures in their reports (Saleh et al. 2010).

24.4   Equivalence of Care

If one accepts that mentally disordered prisoners are to be treated in penal institutions, possibly in a hospital wing/ward within the prison, then the principle of "equivalence" of care between the community and provision for incarcerated mentally disordered persons should prevail (e.g. Konrad et al. 2007). Types of mental health treatment in correctional settings should generally parallel those available in the general population. Levels of care include crisis intervention, hospitalization, "day treatment" programs, outpatient programs, and walk-in clinics. Psychotherapeutic and medico-social programmes developed in prisons should be closely linked to the approach used in the community as a whole with regard to drug-dependant people (drugs, alcohol, medication).

Most countries represented in this volume accept this principle and some have introduced measures specifically to work towards this aim. However, it is doubtful whether the majority of prisoners with mental disorders receive appropriate care such as that mandated by the European Convention on Human Rights and other international charters. Indeed, as Felthous notes in the volume, ".....it becomes evident that promoting access to psychiatric case can be the single most widespread yet underappreciated ethical challenge in correctional psychiatry."

This essential principle of equivalence should also be applied to medical treatment of addicted prisoners and of withdrawal symptoms in prison. However, again this does not appear to always be the case. For example, medication-assisted treatment, endorsed by international health and drug agencies as an integral part of HIV prevention and care strategies for opioid-dependent drug users, is unavailable for most prisoners even if it is available to the general public in a particular country (Bruce and Schleifer 2008). Psychotherapeutic and medico-social programmes developed in prisons should be closely linked to the approach used in the community as a whole with regard to drug-dependant individuals (drugs, alcohol, medication).

Existing regimes of medication and the autonomy to self-medicate established in the community are disrupted and curtailed by the dominant practices and prison routines for the taking of prescribed medication. The continuity of mental health care is undermined by the removal or alteration of existing prescribed medication which exacerbate prisoners' anxiety and sense of helplessness. Prisoners with a dual diagnosis are likely to be doubly vulnerable because of inconsistencies in substance withdrawal management (Bowen et al. 2009). Furthermore, unlike the general public in most countries, prisoners cannot choose their doctor.

Follow-up treatment for released inmates should be provided for by community specialised services. It is essential that the prison doctor has ample notice of the forthcoming release of his patient so that he may arrange an outside appointment with all relevant services very shortly after the prisoner's release or assists the inmate in arranging the appointment. It should be ensured that all necessary documentation is dispatched to the providers of such services with the full consent of the patient. Prescriptions or opportunity for renewal of medication evaluation have to be provided.

Opponents of equivalence of standards of care for mentally disordered prisoners argue that prisoners do not deserve it or should not have (even) better care than outside of prison, where they may not have used already existing services or were considered problem patients. Commitment in this area hardly promises politicians votes, but it should be pointed out that imprisonment, imposed by society via the courts, establishes a special social responsibility, especially for the health of prisoners, even if psychiatric intervention does not primarily or indirectly prevent crime.

24.5 Standards

There is a plethora of standards governing doctors, including psychiatrists and those providing care to prisoners. A number of guidance documents by the United Nations (esp. Standard minimum rules for the treatment of prisoners and UN Convention on the Rights of Persons with Disabilities), the Council of Europe (esp. Recommendation No R (98) 7 on the ethical and organizational aspects of health care in prison), the World Medical Association (esp. Declaration of Tokyo 1975/2005), the World Psychiatric Association (esp. Declaration of Hawaii 1977) as well as the Oath of Athens (International Council of Prison Medical Services 1979) touch upon prison psychiatry (Perlin and Dlugacz 2009) but lack more detailed guidelines for dealing with mentally disordered prisoners. Therefore the Section Forensic Psychiatry of the WPA developed some standards (Konrad et al. 2007):

> Treatment in prison has to address inmate-specific problems and circumstances, including post-release services. This has to be guided by the functional level of the patient and the severity of psychiatric symptoms. The high prevalence of mental disorders supports the use of routine application of standardized diagnostic screening instruments as a component of the admission procedure in prison. In accordance with the principle of equivalence, every prisoner suffering from a mental disorder should receive appropriate treatment equal to the care that such a patient would receive if he was not in prison. Prisoners suffering from serious mental disorders should be kept and cared for in a hospital facility which is adequately equipped and staffed with appropriately trained personal. Inpatient treatment should not be restricted to the distribution of medication to mentally disordered offenders otherwise locked up 23 h a day in their cell but infers the availability of a multidisciplinary team comprising psychiatrists, psychologists, psychotherapists, occupational therapists and counsellors. That means that the treatment standards within a prison hospital should not be worse than in a community setting.

In addition to these standards, general principles of ethical conduct apply. Some authors (Ward et al. 2009) argue that an overarching model of human rights can supplement the ethical code and thus offer an additional framework for the clinical work. It has been acknowledged (Reid 2008; Palermo 2009) that the complex ethical demands of the unique practice area which is the subject of this volume, has received little attention within mainstream bioethics (Austin et al. 2009).

Austin et al. (2009) argue that relational ethics with its core elements engaged interaction, mutual respect, embodied knowledge, uncertainty and vulnerability, and interdependent environment, is a fitting framework for forensic practice and, further, that forensic settings are the very place to test the validity of such an ethic.

Candilis (2009) stresses the usefulness of robust professionalism for settings in which most forensic psychiatrists practice. This model recognises the formative influence of personal values (a set of well-regarded personal principles that remain mainly stable over time and are coherent), the salience of personal identity in one's work (verbal expression of those values and principles), and the connection of personal and professional identities (consistency between what one says and what one does). Robust professionalism is put into practice through the behaviors that operationalise the theory which have been called the habits and skills of the ethical practitioner. The physician (including the psychiatrist) working in prison is obliged to overcome the moral revulsion at the crime attributed to the prisoner and proceed with an ethical approach to treatment despite, possibly, feelings to the contrary. A prerequisite to be able to do this is to control the counter-transference processes.

24.6   Consent to Treatment

Consent to treatment should be sought from all patients, including offenders suffering from a mental disorder, provided they have capacity to consent. Obtaining the patient's consent, especially in the case of psychiatric pathology, is not only a legal requirement for any medical interventions but also essential if a "therapeutic alliance" is to be formed which is likely to make the patient more committed to the treatment offered.

If mentally ill prisoners refuse to accept medication, having made an informed decision not to consent, the problem arises as to whether it can be administered against their wishes. In line with principles of medical ethics a competent person cannot be forced to undergo treatment unless there is a risk to self or others. It is of note, however, that not all mental health laws recognise this right for self-determination. Some laws, e.g. the Mental Health Act 1983 of England and Wales, provide procedures to override the informed consent of capacitous patients through a second opinion doctor (Konrad and Völlm 2010). For individuals lacking capacity to give or withhold informed consent, Abramowitz (2005) suggested that the courts will usually support treatment for these individuals as long as it is consistent with professional standards of care, however, without asserting a specific, inalienable right of the individual to receive treatment.

Every patient has a right to refuse treatment or to informed "non-consent" that has a full right to manifest. However, such a decision may sometimes result from a conflict relating to non-medical issues; this is particularly the case when a prisoner goes on hunger strike to protest against a judicial or administrative decision. In this type of situation the doctor has to assess the reasons for refusal, the mental state the person and the physical health as a result of non-consent. It is crucial to record in great detail in the patient's medical file that he/she is able to understand and has refused treatment after being given detailed information. The practice of force-feeding of mentally competent individuals on hunger strike is inconsistent with medical ethics (Rubenstein and Annas 2009). The need for medical care of prisoners who persistently refuse food in order to make a protest is rare but challenging. Knowledge about the hunger strike quickly spreads and gets into the political arena. Governments want to resist the demands, which often have political overtones, but also do not want prisoners to die because of fear of a backlash of public opinion. Pressure is therefore brought on the prison health care staff, including psychiatrists, to keep the prisoners alive, if necessary, by force feeding. However, a doctor must obtain consent from the patient before applying his skills to assist him (Konrad and Völlm 2010). This is a principle accepted in all countries providing contributions for this volume many of which mention the issue of food refusal. It is of concern to learn about a current case in Switzerland in which medical professionals were ordered to force-feed a competent prisoner refusing food in clear contravention of a number of medical-ethical guidelines. However, this case is ongoing.

There seems to be wide variation with regards to the threshold applied to "risk to self and others", criteria often used as justification for involuntary treatment. It is also of note that some countries do not allow compulsory treatment to take place in a prison setting; therefore prisoners in need of such intervention have to be transferred to a hospital setting.

The issue of consent to participation in research within prison settings has also been discussed in this volume. Different regulations apply in different countries, the most extreme position being one of a complete ban of such research. However, this does not seem justified, results in further exclusion of mentally disordered prisoners from processes available to other members of society and may jeopordise research of potential benefit to them (for a full discussion of this subject see Arboleda-Flórez & Weisstub in this volume).

24.7 Confidentiality

The basic principles of confidentiality apply to all doctors, including forensic psychiatrists, and most countries have laws and/or professional guidance to govern this complex area (e.g. General Medical Council 2004 for the UK). The doctor must therefore not disclose information about the patient to third parties without the patient's consent except in a limited number of clearly specified circumstances, usually to prevent serious harm to the patient or others. If such a situation arises the patient should be informed about the disclosure and the reasons for disclosure clearly documented. Although this has traditionally received less attention, principles of confidentiality also apply to other professions, eg. psychologists (Younggren and Harris 2008).

In practise, there may be limited understanding among correctional staff regarding principles of confidentiality. Some authors of this volume have noted that local guidance may contradict professional guidelines and expect doctors to disclose more readily than only in circumstances involving significant harm. For example, psychiatrists may be expected to report to authorities serious inmate rule violations and plans for escapes or disturbances (Appelbaum 2005). There would probably be different opinions among mental health professionals about where to draw the line for breaching confidentiality, e.g. the exact definition of a security-threatening emergency (Pinta 2009). Pinta (2009) suggests a special decision-making process with the following elements: establishment of ethics-based priorities, period of deliberation, making a decision and taking responsibility for the decision as the essence of any ethics-based decision.

Clarity of roles in prison psychiatry is crucial for practitioners. Cooperation between the different occupational groups in the penal system is certainly necessary and benefits the patients. If, however, confidentiality is not respected, the patient-physician relationship will be even more jeopardized than it is in the therapy-hostile prison environment. In case of unavoidable disclosure the patient should be informed about the disclosure and the reasons for it.

24.8 Country Differences

The way the different contributions of the volume are made (i.e. topics chosen by contributors rather than according to a set format of topics) precludes a systematic analysis of differences between countries. Similarly, comparisons between different types of countries, e.g. developing vs. "third world" countries or those with Roman law vs. common law systems, are difficult to make, partly due to the low number of countries in each of these categories. However, such enquiry is recommended for future research projects.

Some preliminary remarks are nevertheless worth making. There are many similarities between developed and developing countries. E.g., both categories of countries report an increasing number of mentally ill prisoners and a lack of capacity to deal with the related demand. However, the scale of the problem is strikingly different: While in developed countries the concern is about inadequate provision of care, in developing countries there may not be any care and, even worse, even basics such as food and physical safety may not be available. Staffing numbers in the developing countries including in this volume, Brazil and India, are completely inadequate for even basic levels of care and as a result one country reported that prisoners themselves are called upon to help in the nursing of their peers. The disregard of human rights, while of concern to all countries, is again on a different scale in developing countries such that until not too long ago in India it was possible to imprison individuals who have not even committed any crime, just on the basis of being homeless or mentally ill. Needless to say that in such dire circumstances concerns such as intensive treatment programmes to reduce risk, are not on the radar of professionals struggling to even keep their patients alive. It is expected though that with improving economic conditions in these countries the situation of mentally disordered prisoners will also improve. This will then provide an opportunity to learn from those countries with more developed health care systems, hopefully avoiding some of the mistakes made in their organization.

24.9   Concluding Remarks

It is clear from the contributions to this volume that significant ethical challenges prevail in the mental health care of prisoners. Some countries struggle to establish even the most basic healthcare for prisoners (and probably more generally for their mentally ill patients) while others seem to be further ahead and try to achieve real equivalence of care. It is of concern that most countries report rising numbers of prisoners and a culture focused on punishment and incapacitation rather than rehabilitation. Together with cost cuts, there is little reason to expect a swift improvement of the situation of those most marginalised individuals in our societies. Changes will be slow to implement and will depend on the commitment and compassion of individuals. The importance of training, breaking the isolation of staff working in prisons, as well as effective monitoring and inspection mechanisms in this process cannot be overstated.

References

Abramowitz, M.Z. 2005. Prisons and the human rights of persons with mental disorders. *Current Opinion in Psychiatry* 18: 525–529.

Appelbaum, K.L. 2005. Practicing psychiatry in a correctional culture. In *Handbook of correctional mental health*, ed. C.L. Scott and J.B. Gerbasi. Washington: American Psychiatric Publishing.

Arboleda-Florez, J. 2003. Integration initiatives for forensic services. *World Psychiatry* 2: 179–183.

Austin, W., E. Goble, and J. Kelecevic. 2009. The ethics of forensic psychiatry: Moving beyond principles to a relational ethics approach. *The Journal of Forensic Psychiatry & Psychology* 20: 835–850.

Baillargeon, J., J.V. Penn, K. Knight, A.J. Harzke, G. Baillargeon, and E.A. Becker. 2010. Risk of reincarceration among prisoners with co-occuring severe mental illness and substance use disorders. *Administration and Policy in Mental Health* 37: 367–374.

Bowen, R.A., A. Rogers, and J. Shaw. 2009. Medication management and practices in prison for people with mental health problems: A qualitative study. *International Journal of Mental Health Systems* 3: 24.

Bruce, R.D., and R.A. Schleifer. 2008. Ethical and human rights to ensure medication-assisted treatment for opioid dependence in prisons and pre-trial detention. *The International Journal on Drug Policy* 19: 17–23.

Candilis, P.J. 2009. The revolution in forensic ethics: Narrative, compassion, and a robust professionalism. *The Psychiatric Clinics of North America* 32(2): 423–435. Review. PubMed PMID: 19486823.

De Viggiani, N. 2006. Surviving prison: Exploring prison social life as a determinant of health. *International Journal of Prisoner Health* 2(2): 71–89.

Dressing, H., and H.J. Salize. 2009. Pathways to psychiatric care in European prison systems. *Behavioral Sciences & the Law* 27: 801–810.

Drob, S.L., K.B. Meehan, and S.E. Waxman. 2009. Clinical and conceptual problems in the attribution of malingering in forensic evaluations. *The Journal of the American Academy of Psychiatry and the Law* 37(1): 98–106. Review. PubMed PMID: 19297641.

D'Silva, K., C. Duggan, and L. McCarthy. 2004. Does treatment really make psychopaths worse? A review of the evidence. *Journal of Personality Disorders* 18: 163–177.

Fazel, S., and J. Danesh. 2002. Serious mental disorder in 23000 prisoners: A systematic review of 62 surveys. *Lancet* 349: 545–550.

General Medical Council. 2004. *Confidentiality: Protecting and providing information*. London: General Medical Council.

Goffman, E. 1968. *Asylums: Essays on the social situation of mental patientsand other inmates*. Harmondsworth: Penguin Books Ltd.

International Council of Prison Medical Services. 1979. Oath of Athens. Adopted by the World Medical Assembly, Athens.

Keane, M. 2008. The ethical "elephant" in the death penalty "room". *The American Journal of Bioethics* 8(10): 45–50.

Kendall, T., S. Pilling, P. Tyrer, C. Duggan, R. Burbeck, N. Meader, C. Taylor, and Guideline Development Groups. 2009. Borderline and antisocial personality disorders: Summary of NICE guidance. *BMJ* 338: b93. doi:10.1136/bmj.b93. PubMed PMID: 19176682.

Konrad, N. 2006. Managing the mentally ill in the prisons of Berlin. *International Journal of Prisoner Health* 1: 39–47.

Konrad, N., and B. Völlm. 2010. Forensic psychiatry. In *Ethics in psychiatry*, ed. H. Helmchen and N. Sarorius. Heidelberg: Springer.

Konrad, N., J. Arboleda-Florez, A.D. Jager, K. Naudts, J. Taborda, and N. Tataru. 2007. Consensus paper: Prison psychiatry. *International Journal of Prisoner Health* 3: 111–113.

Lippke, R.L. 2007. *Rethinking imprisonment*. Oxford: University press.

Palermo, G.B. 2009. Psychologists and offenders: Rights versus duties. *International Journal of Offender Therapy and Comparative Criminology* 53(2): 123–125.

Perlin, M.L., and H.A. Dlugacz. 2009. "It's doom alone that counts": Can international human rights law be an effective source of rights in correctional condition litigation? *Behavioral Sciences & the Law* 27: 675–694.

Pinta, E.R. 2009. Decisions to breach confidentiality when prisoners report violations of institutional rules. *The Journal of the American Academy of Psychiatry and the Law* 37(2): 150–154.

Reid, W.H. 2008. The treatment-forensic interface. *Journal of Psychiatric Practice* 14(2): 122–125. PubMed PMID: 18360199.

Rice, M.E., G.T. Harris, and C. Cormier. 1992. An evaluation of a maximum security therapeutic community for psychopaths and other mentally disordered offenders. *Law and Human Behavior* 16: 399–412.

Rubenstein, L.S., and G.J. Annas. 2009. Medical ethics at Guantanamo Bay detention centre and in the US military: A time for reform. *Lancet* 374(9686): 353–355. Review. PubMed PMID: 19632495.

Rutherford, M., and S. Duggan. 2009. Meeting complex health needs in prisons. Public health. *Public Health* 123(6): 415–418. Epub 2009 May 30. PubMed PMID: 19482321.

Saleh, F.M., H.M. Malin, A.J. Grudzinskas, and M.J. Vitacco. 2010. Paraphilias with co-morbid psychopathy: The clinical and legal significance to sex offender assessments. *Behavioral Sciences & the Law* 28: 211–223.

Salize, H.J., H. Dreßing, and C. Kief. 2007. *Mentally disordered persons in European Prison Systems – Needs, Programmes and Outcomes (EUPRIS). Final Report*. Mannheim: Cenrtal Institute of Mental Health.

Schopp, R.F. 2009. Treating criminal offenders in correctional contexts: Identifying interests and distributing responsibilities. *Behavioral Sciences & the Law* 27: 833–855.

Ward, T., T. Gannon, and J. Vess. 2009. Human rights, ethical principles, and standards in forensic psychology. *International Journal of Offender Therapy and Comparative Criminology* 53(2): 126–144. Epub 2008 Feb 11. PubMed PMID: 18268080.

WHO Europe. 2008. Trencin statement on prisons and mental health. Copenhagen: WHO Europe. http://www.euro.who.int./Document/E914202.pdf. Retrieved 1 Mar 2010

World Medical Association. 2005. Declaration of Tokyo. Guidelines for medical physicians concerning torture and other cruel, inhuman or degrading treatment or punishment in relation to detention and imprisonment. Adopted by the World Medical Assembly, Tokyo in October 1975 and editorially revised Divonee-les-Bains in May 2005. http://www.wma.net/e/policy/c18.htm. Accessed Dec 2010.

World Psychiatric Association. 1977. Declaration of Hawaii. http://www.wpanet.org/content/ethics-hawaii.shtml. Accessed Dec 2010.

Younggren, J.N., and E.A. Harris. 2008. Can you keep a secret? Confidentiality in psychotherapy. *Journal of Clinical Psychology* 64: 589–600.

Index

Index

CPSIA information can be obtained at www.ICGtesting.com
Printed in the USA
LVOW07*0111290813

350120LV00009B/151/P